Trinidad
and Tobago

THE ROUGH GUIDE

D0645314

There are more than one hundred Rough Guide titles
covering destinations from Amsterdam to Zimbabwe

Forthcoming titles include
Bangkok • Central America • Chile • Japan

Rough Guide Reference Series
Classical Music • European Football • The Internet • Jazz
Opera • Reggae • Rock Music • World Music

Rough Guide Phrasebooks
Czech • Egyptian Arabic • French • German • Greek • Hindi & Urdu
Hungarian • Indoncsian • Italian • Japanese • Mandarin Chinese
Mexican Spanish • Polish • Portuguese • Russian • Spanish
Swahili • Thai • Turkish • Vietnamese

Rough Guides on the Internet
www.roughguides.com

Rough Guide Credits

Text Editor:	Chris Schüler
Series Editor:	Mark Ellingham
Editorial:	Martin Dunford, Jonathan Buckley, Samantha Cook, Jo Mead, Kate Berens, Amanda Tomlin, Ann-Marie Shaw, Paul Gray, Helena Smith, Kieran Falconer, Judith Bamber, Olivia Eccleshall, Orla Duane, Ruth Blackmore, Sophie Martin (UK); Andrew Rosenberg, Andrew Taber (US)
Online Editors:	Alan Spicer, Kate Hands (UK); Geronimo Madrid (US)
Production:	Susanne Hillen, Andy Hilliard, Link Hall, Helen Ostick, James Morris, Julia Bovis, Michelle Draycott
Picture Research:	Eleanor Hill
Cartography:	Melissa Flack, Maxine Burke, Nichola Goodliffe
Finance:	John Fisher, Celia Crowley, Neeta Mistry
Marketing & Publicity:	Richard Trillo, Simon Carloss, Niki Smith (UK); Jean-Marie Kelly, SoRelle Braun (US)
Administration:	Tania Hummel, Alexander Mark Rogers

Acknowledgements

The authors would like to thank those at TIDCO, particularly Tony Poyer, and all the people of T&T who patiently answered endless queries. Thanks also to those at the Rough Guides: Chris Schüler for sympathetic and constructive editing, Sam Cook for her supportive guidance of the project, James Morris for typesetting, Russell Walton for proofreading, and the Map Studio, Romsey, Hants, for the cartography.

Dominique: thanks to all the wonderful Kewley family: Stanton senior for perceptive political commentary and excellent driving, Molly for delicious food, Lisa for the books and sympathetic ear and last but certainly not least, Stanton Mark, for the endless love, support and understanding; to the Phillips family, especially Leon, Joan and Natalie for the borrowed books and informative titbits; to the Callaloo company for a deeper understanding of Carnival; and to English family and friends for encouragement and a shoulder to lean on. Most importantly, thanks to Jah, the creator, for guidance, inspiration and strength.

Polly: heartfelt thanks to all who gave assistance and taught me how to lime, particularly Dominique. As always, support beyond the call of duty came from Celia and Matt; respect and love to you and the extended west London family. In Tobago, thanks to Angelo, Josie, Nick, Natasha and Sasha Dagnino, Andrea Carrington, Gary, Suzanne Ramrattan, Mark and Zena Puddy, Stephen Dolly, Cynthia and Alan Clovis, Sheldon Roachford, Eon Rodriguez, Harris McMillan, Harris McDonald, Chris Morgan, Larry and Ingrid Bridglal, Claudia and Nigel, Davy Eastman, Jude and Janice. In Trinidad, to Gunda Busch-Harewood and family, Kevin, Vero, Lara and Briony Baden-Semper, Simon Marriot, Andy Rennie, Courtenay Rooks, Christo Adonis, Ishmael Angelo, Jan and Michelle Fricke, Laurence "Snakeman" Pierre, Philip Lee Wah, Steven Broadbridge, Pierro and all at Mount Plaisir Estate, Chance, Nigel and Anthony from Grande Riviere, Fred Zollna, Stanton Kewley senior and driving partner Christian Newton.

This first edition published October 1998 by Rough Guides Ltd, 62–70 Shorts Gardens, London WC2H 9AB.

Distributed by the Penguin Group:
Penguin Books Ltd, 27 Wrights Lane, London W8 5TZ.
Penguin Books USA Inc, 375 Hudson Street, New York 10014, USA.
Penguin Books Australia Ltd, 487 Maroondah Highway, PO Box 257, Ringwood, Victoria 3134, Australia.
Penguin Books Canada Ltd, 10 Alcorn Avenue, Toronto, Ontario, Canada M4V 1E4.
Penguin Books (NZ) Ltd, 182–190 Wairau Road, Auckland 10, New Zealand.

Printed in England by Clays Ltd, St Ives PLC
Typography and original design by Jonathan Dear and The Crowd Roars.
Illustrations throughout by Edward Briant.

ISBN 1-85828-379-5

Trinidad
and Tobago

Written and researched by
Dominique De-Light and Polly Thomas

THE ROUGH GUIDES

Help us update

We've gone to a lot of trouble to ensure that this first edition of the *Rough Guide to Trinidad and Tobago* is as up-to-date and accurate as possible. However, things inevitably change, and if you feel we've got it wrong or left something out, we'd like to know. All suggestions, comments and corrections are much appreciated, and we'll send a copy of the next edition (or any other *Rough Guide* if you prefer) for the best letters.

Please mark all letters "Rough Guide to Trinidad and Tobago Update" and send to:
Rough Guides, 62–70 Shorts Gardens, London WC2H 9AB or
Rough Guides, 375 Hudson St, 3rd floor, New York, NY 10014, USA.

Email should be sent to:
mail@roughguides.co.uk

Online updates about *Rough Guide* titles can be found on our Web site at *www.roughguides.com*

The authors

Dominique De-Light is a Carnival artist, photographer and freelance writer who regularly travels back and forth between England and Trinidad. It was her love of Carnival – inspired by creating costumes for Notting Hill – which first brought her to Trinidad, but the island's many qualities have ensured that her love affair with the country continues.

Polly Thomas is a freelance travel writer who is also co-author of the *Rough Guide to Jamaica* and is currently perfecting the art of feting.

Rough Guides

Travel Guides • Phrasebooks • Music and Reference Guides

We set out to do something different when the first Rough Guide was published in 1982. Mark Ellingham, just out of University, was travelling in Greece. He brought along the popular guides of the day, but found they were all lacking in some way. They were either strong on ruins and museums but went on for pages without mentioning a beach or taverna. Or they were so conscious of the need to save money that they lost sight of Greece's cultural and historical significance. Also, none of the books told him anything about Greece's contemporary life – its politics, its culture, its people, and how they lived.

So with no job in prospect, Mark decided to write his own guidebook, one which aimed to provide practical information that was second to none, detailing the best beaches and the hottest clubs and restaurants, while also giving hard-hitting accounts of every sight, both famous and obscure, and providing up-to-the-minute information on contemporary culture. It was a guide that encouraged independent travellers to find the best of Greece, and was a great success, getting shortlisted for the Thomas Cook travel guide award, and encouraging Mark, along with three friends, to expand the series.

The Rough Guide list grew rapidly and the letters flooded in, indicating a much broader readership than had been anticipated, but one which uniformly appreciated the Rough Guides' mix of practical detail and humour, irreverence and enthusiasm. Things haven't changed. The same four friends who began the series are still the caretakers of the Rough Guide mission today: to provide the most reliable, up-to-date and entertaining information to independent-minded travellers of all ages, on all budgets.

We now publish 100 titles and have offices in London and New York. The travel guides are written and researched by a dedicated team of more than 100 authors, based in Britain, Europe, the USA and Australia. We have also created a unique series of phrasebooks to accompany the travel series, along with the acclaimed series of music guides, and a best-selling pocket guide to the Internet and World Wide Web. We also publish comprehensive travel information on our Web site: *www.roughguides.com*

Contents

List of Maps

MAP SYMBOLS

══ Road	● Cave	🐢 Turtle nesting site
----- Path	∿∿ Mountains	🏊 Swimming area
– – – Ferry route	⚐ Viewpoint	Beach with facilities
—— Waterway	Swamp	Beach without facilities
––– Chapter division boundary	⚑ Waterfall	☼ Lighthouse
♦ Places of Interest	✈ Airport	*i* Information office
☨ Church	P Parking	⊠ Post office
Mosque	Petrol station	Building
♣ Hindu Temple	Bank	Cemetery
♛ Castle	Market	Park
◉ Accommodation	⊞ Hospital	Beach
▣ Restaurant	Golf course	

Introduction

Nudging the South American mainland they were once attached to, **Trinidad and Tobago** (usually shortened to T&T) form the southernmost islands of the Lesser Antilles chain and the most influential republic in the Eastern Caribbean. They are the most exciting, unexplored and uncontrived of Caribbean islands, rich in indigenous culture. A cultural pacemaker best known as the home and heart of West Indian **Carnival**, the nation can boast the most diverse and absorbing society in the region.

Trinidad and Tobago remain relatively inexpensive, and are well-geared to independent travellers without being fully fledged tourist resorts. Natural reserves of gas and oil twinned with a strong manufacturing industry have ensured economic independence, and you'll find the islands refreshingly unfettered by the pretensions of the tourist trade. Visitors are not corralled in all-inclusives or holed up on private beaches, and – though you could easily spend two weeks exploring seashores, which range from palm-lined white sand fringed by translucent waters to secluded, wave-whipped outcrops – you'll find there's far more to T&T than suntans and snorkelling.

These are among the richest destinations for **eco-tourism** in the Caribbean, combining the characteristic flora and fauna of the region with the wilder aspect of the South American mainland. You'd be hard pressed to come up with anywhere that offers such a variety of habitats in such a compact land area (Trinidad covers no more than 4830 square kilometres, Tobago just 300). In **Trinidad**, you can hike through undisturbed tropical **rainforest** where towering canopies of mahogany, teak and balata bedecked with lianas and epiphytic plants shelter opossums, red howler monkeys and ocelots. The wetlands and **mangrove swamps** harbour all manner of exotic wildlife, including the endangered West Indian manatee and the giant anaconda, while leatherback turtles lay eggs on remote and rugged beaches. Huge blue emperor butterflies flit around the cool water of innumerable inland rivers and waterfalls, and the **birdwatching** – with more than 430 brilliantly hued species – is among the world's best. Though

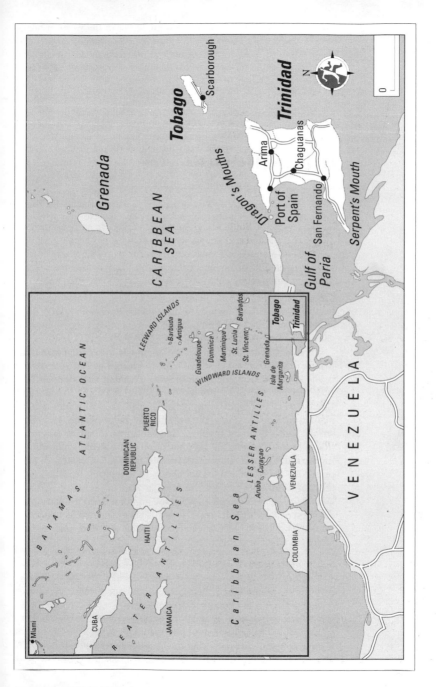

Scarborough

Tobago

Grenada

Trinidad

N

CARIBBEAN SEA

Dragon's Mouths

Arima

Chaguanas

Port of Spain

San Fernando

Serpent's Mouth

Gulf of Paria

VENEZUELA

0

ATLANTIC OCEAN

BAHAMAS

GREATER ANTILLES

Miami

CUBA

HAITI

DOMINICAN REPUBLIC

PUERTO RICO

JAMAICA

Caribbean Sea

LEEWARD ISLANDS

Barbuda

Antigua

Guadeloupe

Dominica

Martinique

St. Lucia

St. Vincent

Barbados

Grenada

WINDWARD ISLANDS

Isla de Margarita

LESSER ANTILLES

Aruba

Curaçao

VENEZUELA

COLOMBIA

VENEZUELA

Tobago

Trinidad

Tobago boasts the oldest protected rainforest in the western hemisphere, the smaller island is better known for its stunning coral reefs, declared third best in the Caribbean by Jacques Cousteau and favoured by graceful seven-metre manta rays and shoals of technicolour tropical fish.

Vital, crowded and dynamic, T&T's **towns and cities** are equally absorbing, unique showcases for the architectural, religious and cultural traditions of their cosmopolitan populations. Fretworked townhouses, Georgian-style mansions and barrack-house complexes built for plantation workers sit side by side with temples, mosques, Catholic cathedrals and Anglican churches. The varied ethnic groups brought to labour in the islands after the slaves were freed in 1834 have given rise to an unimaginably varied populace, hailing from India, China, Portugal and Syria as well as Africa, England, France and Spain. Though racial tensions are inevitably present, Trinbagonians (as they're collectively known) generally coexist with good-humour, and are proud of the multiculturalism that has so enriched the life of the nation. Nowhere is this more visible than in a lively **music scene** that rivals even that of Jamaica. The steel drum was invented in the Port of Spain suburb of Laventille, while calypso, first developed in African communities, evolved into contemporary soca. That in turn has spawned the Indian-influenced chutney soca and the danceable beats and politically conscious lyrics of rapso, the nation's newest musical creation.

Trinbagonians have a less harrowing past to contend with than many of their Caribbean neighbours. Neglected by the Spanish for most of their three centuries of rule, Trinidad experienced full-scale slavery for only fifty years, while the Dutch, French and English were too busy fighting over Tobago to turn it into a giant plantation. Consequently, the national psyche is characterized by a strong sense of identity and a laid-back enjoyment of the good things in life. This ethos is best displayed in the local propensity for **liming**, taking time out to meet friends, talk, and sink a Carib beer or a rum. Thirteen public holidays and numerous local festivals are mere limbering up for the republic's most famous party, the annual pre-Lenten **Carnival**, when the no-holds-barred small-hours abandon of Jouvert is followed by two days of pure joy as five-thousand-strong bands of intricately costumed revellers take to the streets in a celebration of life.

Where to go

As different as chalk and cheese but welded together for the convenience of the British empire, Trinidad and Tobago share little more than their status as a republic. Known chiefly as an island of oil refineries and metropolitan verve, **Trinidad** offers culture, ethnic diversity, music, great food and a wealth of gorgeous beaches. A more conventional holiday destination, **Tobago** boasts archetypal

Caribbean beaches thronged by hotels of every budget, water sports, "international" restaurants and a rapidly developing resort ethic. It's impossible to get a full picture of all the republic has to offer without visiting both Trinidad and Tobago, but a regular plane and ferry service make it possible to see the best of both even during a short stay.

A visit to Trinidad will inevitably begin in **Port of Spain**, the brash, bustling capital and centre of Carnival. With its museums, art galleries and restaurants, the best of local music and art, and most of the island's accommodation, this urbane metropolis is a natural base from which to explore the rest of the country. **Chaguaramas** to the west is the capital's playground, a national park with a string of upmarket open-air clubs providing lively, sophisticated nightlife. For the ultimate escape, however, it's not far to the rocky, wooded islands of the Bocas.

A sweeping curve of powdery sand and powerful waves, **Maracas Bay** is the first of many gorgeous beaches that make the north coast the most popular region with Trinidadians in search of rest and recreation. Between **Blanchisseuse** and **Matelot** runs a long stretch of completely undeveloped coastline – thirty kilometres of footprint-free sand and total seclusion – while the coastline further east is spectacularly rugged. Dominated by the densely forested peaks of the Northern Range, the northern **interior** offers excellent hiking along hunters' trails. The bird-watching is superb; even the lazy can see up to forty unusual species in a morning from the verandah of the **Asa Wright Nature Centre**. South of the hills, the traffic-choked Eastern Main Road links the capital with the sizeable town of **Arima** – home to the island's last remaining Caribs – and provides access to swimmable rivers, caves, and the oldest Benedictine monastery in the Caribbean, from which you get an awesome view of the unravelling plains below.

Dominated by flat agricultural plains with a population of primarily Indian descent, **central Trinidad** provides a fascinating contrast to the north. From the ethereal **Waterloo Temple** to the busy commercial centre of **Chaguanas**, Indian culture predominates. Just forty minutes from Port of Spain lies one of the island's richest natural attractions, the mangrove labyrinth of **Caroni Swamp**, home of the striking national bird, the scarlet ibis. On the **east coast**, the protected wetlands at **Nariva** are the habitat of manatee and anacondas, while four kilometres of fine brown sand lined by groves of coconut palms make **Manzanilla** a favourite spot to recover from the rigours of Carnival.

The burgeoning commercial city of **San Fernando** is a friendly base from which to explore Trinidad's "deep south", an area largely unvisited by tourists. Modern oil towns such as **Fyzabad** contrast with the picturesque fishing villages and calm, deserted beaches of **Cedros** and **Erin**, and **Mayaro Bay** on the southeast coast – a stunning, palm-fringed stretch of powdery sand. Just behind the coast, the rolling Southern Range provides an impressive location for the **Trinity Hills Wildlife Reserve**, home to strange bats and a huge mud lake.

Most people travelling to **Tobago** head for the translucent waters, coral reefs and excellent facilities of the island's low-lying western tip, staying in one of the hundreds of hotels slung along the coastline and playing golf on the island's lone, palm-studded green. The island's vibrant capital, **Scarborough** offers a more genuine picture of local life with its market and historic fort, while the rugged windward or Atlantic coast is best known for the waterfall at **Argyll** and the island's best scuba diving at **Speyside**. Heavily visited by day-trippers, the leeward or Caribbean coast is lined by a precipitous snake of tarmac that passes unspoilt fishing villages and gorgeous beaches at **Castara** and **Englishman's Bay**, while **Charlotteville** in the northwest is the perfect retreat, a picturesque fishing centre that tumbles down a hillside to a couple of pretty horseshoe beaches.

When to go

Most people visit T&T between January and March, when **Carnival** explodes into life, the trees are in blossom and the **climate** is at its most forgiving: the sun shines, rain is rare and the nights are cool. By May, however, the lack of rain has parched the formerly lush landscape: greens turn to yellow, dust clouds put the views into soft focus and bush fires rage through the hills. The only relief from the aridity takes the form of brief, sudden tropical rainstorms. At the end of May, the **rainy season** sets in, and it's not unknown for the skies to open with dramatic deluges that can last weeks. The rainy season often continues into December, but there's usually a respite from the downpours in September, a period of hot sunshine and blue skies known as the **petit carem**. It's an excellent time to visit, with flights at low season rates, though you'll find the resorts a little quiet. Officially, the **high season** (Dec 15–April 15) should mean hiked hotel rates in both islands, but in reality, only Tobago hoteliers bother with two rates, and many smaller hotels charge the same all year round in both islands. Many hotels in and around Port of Spain, however, put up their rates during Carnival week.

	Average daily temperature (°C)		Average daily temperature (°F)		Average monthly rainfall	
	max	min	max	min	mm	in
January	31	21	87	69	69	2.7
February	31	20	88	68	41	1.6
March	32	20	89	68	46	1.8
April	32	21	90	69	53	2.1
May	32	22	90	71	94	3.7
June	32	22	89	71	193	7.6
July	31	22	88	71	218	8.6
August	31	22	88	71	246	9.7
September	32	22	89	71	193	7.6
October	32	22	89	71	170	6.7
November	32	22	89	71	183	7.2
December	31	21	88	69	125	4.9

Part 1

The Basics

Getting there from Britain and Ireland

The vast majority of British and Irish residents visiting Trinidad and Tobago are on some form of package tour which includes a charter flight direct to Tobago. This is certainly the simplest way of going about things, and even if you plan to travel independently, a seat on a charter is normally the cheapest way to get out there. But charters do have their drawbacks, especially if your plans don't exactly fit into their usual two-week straitjacket.

When it comes to direct flights, however, you have a very limited choice. Only two airlines fly direct to Tobago from the UK – British Airways and Caledonian Airways, both departing from

---

Airlines

British Airways ☎ 0181/759 5511

BWIA ticket reservation ☎ 0171/745 1100

Caledonian Airways ☎ 01293/536321, *only sell tickets through the Golden Lion agency*, ☎ 01293/56800.

Discount travel agents

Budget Travel, 134 Lower Baggot St, Dublin 2 ☎ 01/661 1403.

Campus Travel, 52 Grosvenor Gardens, London SW1W 0AG (☎ 0171/730 8111) and offices nationwide.

Caribbean Travel, 367 Portobello Rd, London W10 5SG ☎ 0181/969 6230.

Council Travel, 28a Poland St, London W1V 3DB ☎ 0171/437 7767.

Flightbookers, 177–178 Tottenham Court Rd, London W1P 0LX ☎ 0171/757 2080.

Imbel Travel, 22 West Green Rd, Tottenham, London N15 ☎ 0181/809 5522.

Joe Walsh Tours, 34 Grafton St, Dublin 2 (☎ 01/671 8751); 117 Patrick St, Cork (☎ 021/277959).

London Flight Centre, 131 Earl's Court Rd, London SW5 9RH ☎ 0171/244 6411) and other branches across London.

New Look Travel, 111 High St, Harlesden, London NW10 4TR ☎ 0181/965 8212.

Newmont Travel, 85 Balls Pond Rd, London N1 ☎ 0171/254 6546.

North South Travel, Moulsham Mill Centre, Parkway, Chelmsford, Essex ☎ 01245/492882.

Redfern Travel, 1/3 Piece Hall Yard, Bradford BD1 1PL ☎ 01274/733551

STA Travel, 86 Old Brompton Rd, London SW7 3LH (☎ 0171/361 6262) and offices nationwide.

Stratford Travel, 41 Broadway, London E15 ☎ 0181/519 4921.

Thomas Cook Flights Direct, ☎ 0990/101520.

Trailfinders, 42–50 Earl's Court Rd, London W8 6FT (☎ 0171/938 3366); 4–5 Dawson St, Dublin 2 (☎ 01/677 7888), and offices nationwide.

The Travel Bug, 125a Gloucester Rd, London SW7 4SF (☎ 0171/835 2000); 597 Cheetham Hill Rd, Manchester M8 5EJ (☎ 0161/721 4000).

USIT, Fountain Centre, College St, Belfast BT1 6ET (☎ 01232/324073); Aston Quay, Dublin 2 (01/602 1600) and offices across the Republic.

Specialist package and tour operators

Airwaves, 10 Bective Place, London SW15, ☎0181/875 1188, email *xv105@dial.pipex.com*. *Flights and hotels in Trinidad and Tobago as well as meet and greet and car rental.*

Birding, Finches House, Hiham Green, Winchelsea TN36 4HB, ☎01797/223223. *Once-a-year birding holidays to Asa Wright in Trinidad and Blue Waters Inn in Tobago with daily guided bird-watching tours, including a trip to the seldom-visited St Giles islands off Tobago.*

Caribbean Connection, 93 Newman St, W1, ☎0171/344 3000. *Flights and hotel packages in all price ranges including a Carnival trip.*

Caribbean Journeys, 243 Euston Rd, London NW1 2BU, ☎0171/388 9292. *Tailor-made hotel and villa holidays in Tobago only, concentrating on more upmarket properties with a few guesthouses on the books.*

Caribtours, 161 Fulham Rd, London SW3 6SN, ☎0171/581 3517. *Reliable group offering luxurious packages to Tobago.*

Hammock Travel, Wickham House, 10 Cleveland Way, London E1 4TR, ☎0171/423 9400. *Reliable specialist in event holidays; Carnival, Easter in Tobago etc.*

Hayes and Jarvis, Hayes House, 152 King St, London W6 0QU, ☎0181/748 5050. *Large operator with good flight and hotel deals to Tobago.*

Kuoni Worldwide, Kuoni House, Dorking, Surrey RH5 4AZ, ☎01306/742222. *Flexible package holidays and good family deals.*

Ornitholidays, 1–3 Victoria Drive, Bognor Regis, West Sussex PO21 2PY, ☎01243/821230. *Oldest established birding operator; excellent Trinidad and Tobago packages with daily guided tours.*

Owner's Syndicate, 6 Port House, Plantation Wharf, Battersea, London SW11 3TY, ☎0171/801 9801, email *ownerssyndicate@compuserve. com*. *Good value for villa holidays in Tobago, with a few small properties on the books as well.*

Trips Worldwide, 9 Byron Place, Clifton, Bristol ☎0117/987 2626, fax 0117/987 2627 email *post@trips.demon.co.uk* . *Eco-tours and tailor-made holidays to T&T, in collaboration with Trinidad's Wildways tour company. Knowledgeable staff organize flights, accommodation, transport and tour guides for holidays costing £800 to £2000.*

Thomas Cook, 45 Berkeley Square, London W1X 5AE and high streets across the UK (nationwide ☎0990/666222); 11 Donegal Place, Belfast (☎01232/242341); 118 Grafton St, Dublin 2 (☎01/677 1721). *Package holidays, charter and schedule flights.*

Tropical Places, Freshfield House, Lewes Rd, Forest Row, East Sussex RH11 5ES, ☎01342/825123. *One of the best options for Tobago with small, medium and large properties and good rates for flight and accommodation packages.*

Villa Connections, 27 Park Lane, Poynton, Cheshire SK12 1RD, ☎01625/828428. *Tailor-made villa and small hotel holidays in Tobago, excursions to Trinidad, Carnival packages and flights and car rental arrangements.*

Wildlife Worldwide, 170 Selsdon Rd, South Croydon, Surrey CR2 6PJ, ☎0181/667 9158. *Tailor-made nature-oriented holidays to Trinidad (Asa Wright base with tours) and birding or diving in Tobago.*

Wildwings, International House, Bank Rd, Kingswood, Bristol BS15 2LX ☎0117/984 8040. *Birding tours to Pax guest house in Trinidad and Blue Waters Inn in Tobago; botanical tours to Trinidad as well.*

Worldwide Fishing Safaris, 55 English Drove, Thorney, Peterborough PE6 0TJ, ☎01733/849244. *Deep-sea fishing holidays to Tobago with flights and accommodation.*

London, Gatwick – and only one, BWIA, to Trinidad (from Heathrow). There are no direct flights from Ireland, but good connections via London or, on Aer Lingus or Delta, via New York or Miami.

Fares and flights

The price of your plane ticket depends very much on when you go. **Tobago**'s high season is during the summer holidays, at Christmas and at Carnival time. The situation in **Trinidad** is more complicated, however, as every school holiday and local festival pushes up the price – BWIA has no less than six different price categories. Basically it is less expensive to go during the wet season (August to December). It is worth remembering that both Trinidad and Tobago experience an Indian summer known as the "petite careme" in September. This break in the rainy season offers two weeks to a month of hot, dry weather at a time when air fares are usually a steal.

Tickets sold by **travel agents** work out far cheaper than those bought from the airlines direct – it is worth ringing round, as some agents make special deals with the airlines. The cheapest tickets can be found at **discount operators** – look for last minute deals on the Internet, Teletext or in Caribbean-oriented newspapers such as the *Voice*, the *Gleaner* and the *Caribbean Times*. If you're under 26 you can get excellent **discounts** from student operators; these can reduce the normal fare by as much as half.

Caledonian Airways is the cheapest option to T&T, with charter flights ranging from one to six weeks' validity. They fly twice a week, on Mondays and Saturdays, and prices range from £330 in November to £600 in mid-August. Carnival airfares in 1998 were £400. These prices are variable depending on availability, and you may get a ticket for as little as £200 if you're lucky. The air ticket between Trinidad and Tobago costs £40 return, so it is often worth travelling via Tobago when visiting Trinidad.

British Airways has only just resumed flying to Tobago, once a week on a Saturday. Its official prices range between £500 and £1000, though the airline has been offering a few good deals to promote the service. Once again, shop around – it's possible to get these figures greatly reduced by last-minute dealing and by buying advance purchase flights.

BWIA is Trinidad's own airline. Although its pricing classification is very complicated, the general price range is similar to BA's. There are daily flights from London Heathrow to Piarco, Trinidad; transfers to Tobago on BWIA flights that go twice a week on Mondays and Fridays can be arranged, and are included in the fare. Fares start at £450 for the end of April or end of September, but rocket up to £960 for the twelve days before Christmas. Carnival prices are around £750. These tickets are for scheduled flights, though, and are valid up to six months.

If you fancy flying around more than one Caribbean island, various Caribbean airlines offer 30-day air passes; see p.27 for details.

Packages and tours

If you're planning to spend your whole holiday in Tobago where you can see the island from a single base, booking a **package holiday** might be your best option. There are legions of specialist companies who can arrange flights, airport transfers and accommodation, often at a significantly lower rate than you'd get independently. You can book all grades of villas and hotels, as well as meal plans, all inclusive deals (where all meals are included in the room rate) or self-catering apartments. As Trinidad is less geared toward tourists, packages are thin on the ground beyond the bird-watching trips or Carnival packages; Tobago-oriented companies often offer a few days in Trinidad in conjunction with a Tobago trip, however. Alternatively, the companies listed under "Conventional Tours" (see p.44) as well as Accommodation and Adventures Unlimited, 33 Luis St, Woodbrook, Port of Spain ☎628 3731, fax 627 3737, email *owl@opus.co.tt* can arrange meet and greet services, airport transfers, car rental and accommodation booking. Lists of more tour operators serving the islands are available from the T&T tourist board in the UK (see p.13).

Getting there from North America

Cheap flights to Trinidad and Tobago are scarce, although flights from the east coast are considerably less expensive than from the west. With little competition, the few airlines that service the islands don't have much incentive to offer special youth rates or air passes and the Caribbean doesn't fit too well into a round-the-world (RTW) itinerary.

Barring special offers, the cheapest of the airlines' published fares is usually an advance purchase excursion, or **APEX** ticket, although this will carry certain restrictions: you have to book – and pay – at least 21 days before departure, spend at least seven days abroad (maximum stay three months), and you tend to get penalized if you change your schedule.

You can normally cut costs further by going through a **specialist flight agent** – either a con-

North American tour operators
Although phone numbers are given here, you're better off making tour reservations through your local travel agent. An agent will make all the phone calls, sort out the snafus and arrange flights, insurance and the like – all at no extra cost to you.

American Airlines Vacations
☎1-800/321-2121

Alken Tours
☎1-800/221-6686 or 718/856-7711

BWIA Vacations
☎1-800/780-5501 or 718/520-8100

Island Resort Tours ☎1-800/251-1755

Safaricenter ☎1-800/223-6046

Tour Host International
☎1-800/THE HOST or 212/953-7910

TourScan Inc ☎1-800/962 2080 or 203/655 8091; *www.tourscan.com*

Travel Impressions ☎1-800/284-0044

solidator, who buys up blocks of tickets from the airlines and sells them at a discount, or a **discount agent**, who in addition to dealing with discounted flights may also offer a range of other travel-related services such as travel insurance, car rentals, tours and the like. Some agents specialize in **charter flights**, although they are generally not available to Trinidad and Tobago from the western parts of the US or Canada. With all reduced-rate operations, departure dates are fixed and withdrawal penalties are high (check the refund policy).

Regardless of where you purchase your ticket, fares will generally be US$50–60 more during **high season**. There are two high seasons for T&T flights: between mid-June and mid-September, and between mid-December and mid-April. Note also that flying on weekends ordinarily adds roughly US$50 to the round-trip fare, and that during Carnival in late February flights can be scarce. The Easter holiday is another popular time to visit, so plan accordingly.

The following are typical high/low season APEX **fares** from US/Canadian cities to Piarco International Airport in Port of Spain, Trinidad: Boston (US$554/506); Chicago (US$718/666); Los Angeles (US$860/812); Miami (US$486/436); New York (US$554/506); San Francisco (US$860/812); Toronto (CAN$875/802); Vancouver

(CAN$1100/1032). Flights to Crown Point Airport in Tobago cost roughly the same amount, although direct flights are not available; you will most likely have to change planes in San Juan, Barbados, or Trinidad.

American Airlines flies most frequently to the islands from North America, with daily flights from most US and Canadian cities connecting through Miami to Trinidad and through San Juan to Tobago. **Air Canada** flies direct to Trinidad daily from Toronto at 7.55pm. You can also buy an Air Canada ticket from Toronto to Tobago, but you'll have to switch to a LIAT plane in Barbados (weekends only).

The Trinidadian airline **BWIA International** offers flights at competitive prices from New York and Miami in addition to a 30-day air pass, valid for travel around the Caribbean and available in the US. See p.27 for details.

By sea

The archetypal luxury vacation – a **Caribbean cruise** – is relatively accessible in North America. Prices on a luxury liner can scale the heights of silliness, although if you're willing to bunk in the "lower-class" rooms you can usually cut the price somewhat. Of the scores of shipping companies that peddle all-inclusive cruises, however, only a few include Trinidad and Tobago on their itineraries, and each line routes only a couple of ships per year through Trinidad and Tobago, so be prepared for inflexible travel dates. Another down-

North American cruise operators
The fares quoted are for single person/double occupancy "inside" (no ocean views) cabins, and are exclusive of port charges, which add an extra US$100 to US$150.

Carnival Cruise Lines ☎ 1-800/327-9501 or 305/599-2600; *www.Carnival.com*. *11-day cruises from Miami, Florida from $850.*

Cunard Lines ☎ 1-800/528-6273. *Cruises leave from Barbados and stop in Scarborough at highly variable prices.*

Holland America ☎ 1-800/426-0327 or 206/281-3535; *www.hollandamerica.com*. *10-day cruises from Fort Lauderdale, Florida from $1500.*

WindJammer ☎ 1-800/327-2601. *13-day cruise leaving from Freeport, Bahamas, for $1225.*

side of choosing a cruise is that you only get to see the tourist ports, and for just a few hours at that; the ocean liners listed on the previous page stop only in Port of Spain.

Packages and tours

If you're willing to trade flexibility for convenience, all-inclusive vacation **packages** are a tempting option. As might be expected, most of the packaged trips that are available are geared toward the big resorts in Tobago, with the main goal being a week or two spent relaxing on the beach or at the pool. Prices start at around $1050 for packages that include flights, airport taxes, transfers and seven nights accommodation. A few specialist operators offer more thematically designed **tours**, with itineraries centred around special interests or activities such as snorkelling, trekking or bird-watching. For these, however, you're usually better off waiting until you arrive and signing on directly with a local operator (see pp.44–45 for more information).

Getting there from Australia and New Zealand

The Caribbean is no bargain destination from Australasia. There are no direct flights from Australia or New Zealand to the islands of Trinidad and Tobago, so you'll have to take a flight to one of the main US gateway airports, and pick up onward connections from there.

The least expensive and most straightforward route is via **New York**, from where there are regular flights to Port of Spain and Scarborough, or via **Miami**, which has frequent flights to Port of Spain (see p.6 for full details of routes from North America). If you're planning to see Trinidad and Tobago as part of a longer trip, **Round-the-World** (RTW) tickets are worth considering, and are gen-

erally better value than a simple return flight. Whatever kind of ticket you're after, first call should be one of the **specialist travel agents** listed in the box opposite, which can fill you in on all the latest fares and any special offers. If you're a **student** or **under 26**, you may be able to undercut some of the prices given here; STA is a good place to start.

Fares and air passes

All the fares quoted below are for travel during **low season**, and exclude airport taxes; flying at peak times (primarily Dec to mid-Jan) can add substantially to these prices.

The best **fares** you're likely to find are the Air New Zealand, United and Qantas regular services to Los Angeles, with connecting flights to New York or Miami flying American Airlines or United: return fares to Miami cost around A$2259 from the eastern states, rising to A$2699 from Western Australia. From Miami to Port of Spain, return flights with American Airlines cost A$375, giving a total return fare in the region of A$2635–3075. **From New Zealand**, Air New Zealand, Qantas and United fly to Los Angeles, with connections on to Miami or New York. Through fares to New York start at NZ$2799; and the return to Port of Spain or Crown Point will add another NZ$460 or so.

If you plan to indulge in some **island-hopping** around the Caribbean, BWIA **air passes** can be worthwhile; available for purchase in conjunction with any international carrier, these allow unlimited stopovers within a thirty-day period, and prices start from A$555/NZ$600. Passes are valid only within the Caribbean region.

RTW Tickets

Given these fares and routings, **round the world tickets** that take in **New York or Miami** are worth considering, especially if you have the time to make the most of a few stopovers; see "Getting There from North America", p.6, for more on your options for getting to Trinidad and Tobago from the United States.

Ultimately, your choice of route will depend on where else you want to visit besides Trinidad and Tobago, but a couple of sample itineraries might whet your appetite: starting from either **Melbourne, Sydney or Brisbane**, you could fly to Bangkok, continuing on to Paris, Nice, New York, Los Angeles and then back to Melbourne, Sydney or Brisbane (from A$1999); or, starting from **Perth**, you could fly to Los Angeles, then on to New York, Paris and Nairobi before heading back to Perth (from A$2299).

Packages and tours

Package holidays from Australia and New Zealand to Trinidad and Tobago are few and far between, and many specialists simply act as

---

Specialist agents and tour operators

Caribbean Destinations, 4/115 Pitt St, Sydney; 38/525 Collins St, Melbourne, ☎1800/816717. *Comprehensive range of tailor-made Caribbean holidays, including a range of accommodation packages.*

Contours, 466 Victoria St, North Melbourne, ☎03/9329 5211. *Choice of accommodation-and-airfare package deals to Trinidad and Tobago, as well as other Caribbean destinations.*

Creative Tours, 3/55 Grafton St, Woollahra, Sydney, ☎02/9836 2111. *Caribbean cruise agents.*

Wiltrans, 10/189 Kent St, Sydney, ☎02/9255 0899. *Agents for a range of Caribbean cruise operators.*

---

agents for US-based operators, tagging a return flight from Australasia onto the total cost. **Cruises**, most of which depart from Miami, account for the largest sector. Prices are based on US dollars, and therefore fluctuate with the exchange rate, but all-inclusive 3-day cruises start from A$690, while 7-day cruises cost upwards of A$1000.

The luxury end of the market is also catered for by Caribbean Destinations and Contours, both of

---

Airlines

Air New Zealand Sydney ☎13/2476; Auckland ☎09/357 3000.

American Airlines Sydney ☎02/9299 3600, toll-free ☎1800/227101; no NZ office.

BWIA International Airways Sydney ☎02/9223 7004; no NZ office.

Qantas Sydney ☎13/1211; Auckland ☎09/357 8900, toll-free 0800/808767.

United Airlines Sydney ☎13/1777; Auckland ☎09/379 3800.

Travel agents

Anywhere Travel Sydney ☎02/9663 0411.

Brisbane Discount Travel ☎07/3229 9211.

Budget Travel Auckland ☎09/366 0061, toll-free 0800/808040.

Destinations Unlimited Auckland ☎09/373 4033.

Flight Centres in Sydney ☎13/1600; Auckland ☎09/309 6171.

Northern Gateway Darwin ☎08/8941 1394.

STA Travel in Sydney ☎13/1776; fastfare telesales ☎1300/360 960; Auckland ☎09/309 0458; fastfare telesales ☎09/366 6673; email: *traveller@statravelaus.com.au* Web site: *www.statravelaus.com.au*

Thomas Cook Sydney and Melbourne, local branch ☎13/1771, direct telesales ☎1800/063 913; Auckland ☎09/379 3920.

Tymtro Travel Sydney ☎02/9223 2211 or 1300/652 969.

which offer **resort-** and **villa-based holidays** as well as cruises, with a choice of accommodation on Trinidad and a limited range on Tobago. Prices start at around A$3500 for 14 days (based on twin-share accommodation and low-season airfares from Australia), but really the sky's the limit.

None of the adventure-tour operators ventures to Trinidad and Tobago; for independent travellers, the cheapest way to visit the Caribbean is as part of a round-the-world or American holiday, making creative use of airpasses – see overleaf.

Red tape and visas

Citizens from most western European countries do not require a visa for stays of less than three months, US citizens may stay up to two months without a visa. Nationals of Australia, New Zealand and South Africa all require visas

before entering the country; your travel agent should be able to advise you and obtain visas on your behalf. On arrival, you will have to provide an address where you will be staying, proof that you have adequate finances for the length of your stay, and a return or ongoing ticket. Your passport must be valid for the time of your trip.

Visa extensions, from an extra three months to one year, cost TT$100, but if you want one you must be prepared for some tortuously slow bureaucracy. Despite Trinidad and Tobago's relaxed lifestyle, the country's immigration department is proud to be as strict as those of Britain or the US. Prepare yourself thoroughly and take an unlimited stock of patience; you will be asked for endless proof of income, reasons for your visa extension, and letters from Trinidadian or Tobagonian individuals and organizations. It is best to speak on the phone to someone at the **Immigration Office** first (67

Trinidad and Tobago embassies, high commissions and honorary consuls abroad

UK
High Commission, 42 Belgrave Square, London SW1X 8NT, ☎0171/245 9351, fax 823 1065, email *trintogov@tthc.demon.co.uk*

US
Embassy, 1708 Massachusetts Ave. NW. Washington, DC 20036-1975, ☎202/467 6490, 6491, 6492 or 6493, fax 785 3130, email *embttobago@gslink.com*

Consulate General, Suite 800, 1000 Brickell Ave, Miami, Florida 33131-3047, ☎305/374 2199, fax 374 3199.

Canada
High Commission, Suite 508, 75 Albert St, Ottawa, Ontario K1P 5E7, ☎613/232 2418 or 2419, fax 232 4349, email *tthcotta@travel-net.com*

Consulate General, Suite 303, 2005 Sheppard Ave East, Willowdale, Ontario M2J 5B4, ☎495 9442, 9443, 7342 or 7847, fax 495 6934. email *ttcontor@idirect.com*

Australia
Honorary Consul Michael G. Agostini, PO Box 109, Rose Bay, NSW 2029, ☎337 4391, fax 437 4564.
Trinidad and Tobago does not maintain any diplomatic mission in New Zealand.

Frederick St, Port of Spain; ☎868/625-3571) to try and find out what you need. The policy regarding visa extension is not clear cut – your success may depend on the individual officer you get to see on the day.

Applications for **work permits**, which are required for certain types of paid and unpaid employment, are available at the **Ministry of National Security**, 18 Knox St, Port of Spain, ☎868/623 2441.

Money, banks and costs

Trinidad and Tobago is undoubtedly one of the cheapest Caribbean destinations due to its low profile on the tourist market. If you live like a local, it is possible to survive on £15–20/$US35 a day – if you're prepared to take the least expensive accommodation, eat at low-cost cafés and street stalls, and limit your travel to public transport. If, however, you stay at tourist accommodation and eat at restaurants, you will need at least £50/$US85 a day. Obviously if you rent a car this will be an added expense – around £20–30/$US40–50 per day.

During **Carnival season** all accommodation rates in Port of Spain are increased – a rise of ten to one hundred percent depending on the hotel. Carnival season often sees other price rises, such as entrance fees to clubs, drinks and taxi fares. Therefore if you intend to enjoy yourself during Carnival season, budget on £100 a day and up.

Costs vary around T&T – food and drink is less expensive in the country than the cities. Tobago is more costly than Trinidad as a result of its greater tourist trade. In Trinidad, accommodation is cheaper outside Port of Spain and the Crown

Point area. **Restaurants** vary greatly in price: fine dining establishments, recognizable by their plush decor, charge TT$100 plus per meal; the more basic restaurants, with plastic tables and buffet-style service, offer huge meals for less than TT$25.

Some independent travellers tend to be penny-pinching, especially when it comes to **taxi fares**. But although bargaining is sometimes expected when negotiating fares to off-route destinations, most prices are fixed. Many Trinbagonians assume that all foreigners are rich, and since their average wage is between TT$200–400 per week, a dollar is certainly worth more to them than it is to you. Under the circumstances, a few extra dollars on a taxi fare should not be begrudged.

Currency

The local currency is the **Trinidad and Tobago dollar**. This is usually abbreviated to **TT$**, and is divided into one hundred cents. Coins start at 1 cent and range up through 5, 10 and 25 cents. Notes start at 1 dollar and are in denominations of 5, 10, 20, 100. It is best to keep some of your cash in small denominations. Supermarkets and bars can usually exchange TT$100 but taxis and street vendors can not and should be paid with TT$20 or less.

Travellers' cheques and credit cards

Take along a mixture of **cash**, **credit cards** and **travellers' cheques** to cover all eventualities. Travellers' cheques and credit cards are accepted in most restaurants, malls, high-class shops and hotels. In smaller establishments and rural areas they are unlikely to take anything but local currency. **Personal cheques** are not usually accepted in hotels, and if you stay in a host home you may find they do not have the facilities for payment by credit card.

Changing money

It is best to buy only a small amount of TT$ abroad, as the exchange rate is much more favourable in the country – you may gain as much as five to ten percent on the transaction. The exchange rate at the time of publication is around TT$6 to US$1 and TT$10 to £1. **Piarco Airport Exchange Bureau** (6am–10pm) has a reasonable rate of exchange, although it is not as competitive as those of the banks in Port of Spain. Travellers flying in to Tobago can change money at the Republic Bank (Mon–Thurs 8–11am & noon–2pm, Fri 8am–noon & 3–5pm) in **Crown Point Airport**.

T&T **banks** will exchange most major currencies and travellers' cheques. Commission varies; some banks charge nothing for Amex cheques, while others impose a mandatory charge of around TT$5. You'll always receive a lower rate for cash than for travellers' cheques. There is usually no separate exchange counter, so avoid going during lunch hour (noon–2pm) or be pre-

pared for a long wait – early morning is the best time to catch the queues at their shortest. In **Trinidad** there are banks in most towns and all cities, as well as at the airport. In **Tobago** there is only one bank outside Scarborough, in Crown Point Airport, so bear this in mind when you head off to remoter regions. Both Piarco and Crown Point airports have 24-hour cash machines, which will provide cash advances on credit cards.

Banking hours vary slightly depending on the bank, but usually they are open between Monday and Thursday from 8am to 2pm. Opening hours on Fridays are 8am to noon, and 3pm to 5pm. Most banks in Trinidad's larger malls open and close later (9am–6pm) with no break. It is also possible to get local currency by using international cards at cash machines, which can be found at the airports and in larger towns.

Outside banking hours money can be exchanged in the larger hotels and in some shops in Port of Spain, though at a less advantageous rate. Most shops and vendors will accept **American dollars** for purchases – pay in small denominations and be prepared to receive your change in local currency.

Information and maps

Local and foreign offices and representatives of the T&T tourist board, TIDCO (Tourism and Industrial Development Company of Trinidad and Tobago), send out standard information packs on request, which include useful accommodation and "Calendar of Events" booklets, as well as some glossy promotional bumph and sometimes a road map.

Though they're few and far between, it's worth visiting the **local tourist board offices** once you've arrived; they dole out advice on hotels, transport and activities as well as free attraction/road maps and flyers. The main office is in Port of Spain, but the information booths at Crown Point and Piarco airports are more accessible and better geared up to dealing with the public (see opposite).

Tourist offices in Trinidad and Tobago

Trinidad

Information Office, Piarco Airport, ☎ 664 5196.

TIDCO, PO Box 222, 10–14 Phipps St, Port of Spain, ☎ 623 1923 or 1924, fax 623 8124, email *tourism-info@tidco.co.tt*.

Tobago

Information Office, Crown Point Airport, ☎ 639 0509.

TIDCO, Unit 12, IDC Mall, Sangster's Hill, Scarborough, ☎ 639 4333, fax 639 4514.

Tobago House of Assembly Division of Tourism, Level 3, NIB Mall, Scarborough, Tobago, ☎ 639 2125 or 4636, fax 639 3566.

TIDCO offices and representatives abroad

UK

Morris Kevan International Ltd, International House, 47 Chase Side, Enfield, Middlesex EN2 6NB, ☎ 0181 367 3752, fax 0181/367 9949.

USA

Sales, Marketing and Reservations Tourism Service, 7000 Boulevard East, Guttenberg, New Jersey 07093 ☎ 201/662 3403, 201 869 7628.

Canada

The RMR Group Inc, Taurus House, 512 Duplex Ave, Toronto MR4 3E3 ☎ 416/485 8724, fax 485 8256.

There are no TIDCO offices in Australia or New Zealand.

Trinidad and Tobago on the Net

There are literally hundreds of T&T-oriented **Web sites**, ranging from the puerile "Trini Guide to Phone Sex" to the genuinely informative, and the number of sites grows all the time. Hotels are lining up to market properties on the Web, and it's a convenient, hassle-free way to book your holiday. The yahoo browser (*msn.yahoo.com/regional/countries/Trinidad _and_Tobago*) is a great access point for many interesting sites.

www.visittnt.com
Maintained by TIDCO, this is the best all-rounder with country details, attraction listings, flight details and feature pages on Carnival, soca and calypso, with links to lots of other pertinent sites.

www.tidco.co.tt
The main tourist board Web site is worth a browse for up-to-date information on tourism and trade initiatives.

www.callaloo.co.tt
The site for Trini artist Peter Minshall's Callaloo Carnival company, with information on past projects and pages on in-house band Three Canal.

www.trinibase.com
Informative site with plenty of local statistics and links to lots of pages concerning all things Carnival.

www.anansi.mit.edu/tnt
Plenty of T&T links, including the *Trinidad Guardian* home page with all the latest news and pertinent features.

www.hartsCarnival.com
The home page for the prestigious Harts Carnival camp, with past projects and updated on yearly designs.

www.discover-tt.net
Marketing-based site with details of many hotels on the islands as well as flight information, and material on diving, sailing, sport and the media.

Carnival.ncc.com
Home page of the National Carnival Committee; plenty of rather outdated but still useful Carnival information including summaries of previous years.

www.travel-library.com
Select the Caribbean section for plenty of pages set up by Trinis abroad and lots of chat and gossip.

Other sources of local information are the **radio** and **national press** (see p.29), which carry advertisements for up-and-coming events, and three free tourist-oriented publications, *Discover Trinidad and Tobago*, *Tobago Today* and *Time Out Trinidad and Tobago*. Written by local people and updated yearly, glossy, fact-filled *Discover* includes features on subjects such as Carnival and eco-tourism, suggested touring schedules, and hotel, restaurant and tour operator listings, while the monthly *Tobago Today* newspaper (available in Tobago only) carries Tobago listings and topical features such as goat racing for the Easter issue as well as Tobagonian recipes and hints on etiquette. First published in March 1998, *Time Out* (not linked to the UK-based magazine) is a quarterly mini-listings title with sections on music, tours, shopping, dining and yachting. All are available at hotels and tourist offices.

Map and travel book suppliers

UK

Daunt Books, 83 Marylebone High St, London W1, ☎ 0171/224 2295.

National Map Centre, 22–24 Caxton St, London SW1, ☎0171/222 4945.

Stanfords, 12–14 Long Acre, London WC2, ☎0171/836 1321; 52 Grosvenor Gardens, London SW1W 0AG; 156 Regent St, London W1R 5TA.

The Travel Bookshop, 13–15 Blenheim Crescent, London W11 2EE, ☎0171/229 5260.

John Smith and Sons, 57–61 St Vincent St, Glasgow G2 5TB, ☎0141/221 7472.

Maps are available by **mail or phone order** from Stanfords; ☎0171/836 1321.

US

Adventurous Traveler Bookstore, PO Box 1468, Williston, VT 05495, ☎1-800/282-3963; *www.AdventurousTraveler.com*.

Book Passage, 51 Tamal Vista Blvd, Corte Madera, CA 94925, ☎415/927-0960.

The Complete Traveler Bookstore, 199 Madison Ave, New York, NY 10016, ☎212/685-9007.

Get Lost Travel Books, Maps & Gear, 1825 Market St, San Francisco, CA 94103, ☎415/437-0529.

Map Link, 30 S La Petera Lane, Unit #5, Santa Barbara, CA 93117, ☎805/692-6777.

The Map Store Inc., 1636 1st St, Washington, DC 20006, ☎202/628 2608.

Phileas Fogg's Books & Maps, #87 Stanford Shopping Center, Palo Alto, CA 94304, ☎1-800/533-FOGG.

Rand McNally, 444 N Michigan Ave, Chicago, IL 60611, ☎312/321-1751; 150 E 52nd St, New York, NY 10022, ☎212/758-7488; 595 Market St, San Francisco, CA 94105, ☎415/777-3131; call ☎1-800/333-0136 ext 2111 for other locations, or for maps by mail order.

Sierra Club Bookstore, 6014 College Ave, Oakland, CA 94618, ☎510/658-7470.

Travel Books & Language Center, 4931 Cordell Ave, Bethesda, MD 20814, ☎1-800/220-2665.

Traveler's Bookstore, 22 W 52nd St, New York, NY 10019, ☎212/664-0995.

CANADA

Open Air Books and Maps, 25 Toronto St, Toronto, ON M5R 2C1, ☎416/363-0719.

Ulysses Travel Bookshop, 4176 St-Denis, Montréal, ☎514/843-9447.

World Wide Books and Maps, 736 Granville St, Vancouver, BC V6Z 1E4, ☎604/687-3320.

AUSTRALIA AND NEW ZEALAND

Bowyangs, 372 Little Bourke St, Melbourne, ☎03/9670 4383.

The Map Shop, 16a Peel St, Adelaide ☎08/8231 2033.

Perth Map Centre, 891 Hay St, Perth ☎08/9322 5733.

Specialty Maps, 58 Albert St, Auckland (☎09/307 2217).

Travel Bookshop, Shop 3, 175 Liverpool St, Sydney, ☎02/9261 8200.

Worldwide Maps and Guides, 187 George St, Brisbane, ☎07/3221 4330.

Maps

The tourist board hand out free **maps** of both Trinidad and Tobago, showing main roads, beaches and tourist attractions, but detail is scant on some editions. The best alternative is the manageable 1:150,000 **road map** issued by the Land and Survey Department; though the print quality of the photos on the reverse is appalling and the last update was in 1990, it's the most detailed and useful source available. The *Historic Tobago* map, sold by gift shops and the tourist board on the island, has a comprehensive listing of local attractions and their historical background on the reverse.

Insurance

Trinidad and Tobago has only the most basic public health system; consequently if you fall ill while visiting the country it is advisable to go to a private doctor or hospital (see overleaf). Medical treatment is expensive; it is therefore essential that you take out travel insurance before entering the country.

This will also cover you against **loss or theft** of belongings and money. Flights paid for with a major credit or charge card offer some automatic cover, but usually only while travelling to and from your destination. Some package tours and specialist travel agents include insurance though usually it is an optional extra. Always examine the fine print of a policy and check it has a **24-hour medical emergency contact number**. Make sure that you are covered for all the things you intend to do; activities such as diving are usually excluded but can be added for a supplement.

If you need to make a **claim**, you must have a police report in case of theft or loss. Claims for medical expenses require supporting evidence in the form of bills, though with some policies, doctors and hospitals will be able to bill your insurers direct. Keep photocopies of everything you send to the insurer and don't allow months to elapse before informing them – most insurance policies require that you inform them of a loss within a specific time.

Travel Insurance Companies

UK AND IRELAND

Campus Travel ☎0171/730 8111.

Columbus Travel Insurance ☎0171/375 0011.

Endsleigh Insurance ☎0171/436 4451.

Frizzell Insurance ☎01202/292333.

STA Travel ☎0171/361 6262.

USIT Belfast ☎01232/324073; Dublin ☎01/679 8833.

NORTH AMERICA

Access America ☎1-800/284-8300.

Carefree Travel Insurance ☎1-800/323-3149

Desjardins Travel Insurance ☎1-800/463-7830. *Canada only.*

STA Travel Insurance ☎1-800/781-4040; *www.sta-travel.com*

Travel Assistance International ☎1-800/821-2828; *www.europeassistance.com*

Travel Guard ☎1-800/826-1300; *www.noelgroup.com*

Travel Insurance Services ☎1-800/937-1387.

AUSTRALIA AND NEW ZEALAND

Cover More ☎02/9202 8000 or 1800/251 881.

Ready Plan Melbourne ☎03/9791 5077 or 1800/337 462; Auckland ☎09/379 3208.

Health

Travelling around Trinidad and Tobago carries little risk to your health: the islands are non-malarial, and there are no mandatory immunizations, though some are recommended (see below), and the chlorinated tap water is safe to drink. The most likely hazards are over-exposure to the sun, too much rum and the inevitable minor stomach upsets that come with unfamiliar food and water. If you do find yourself in need of minor medical attention, remember that most insurance policies require you to pay up initially and retain the receipts in order to make a claim once you get home.

The main **hospitals** in **Trinidad** are Port of Spain General and the Mount Hope complex in St Augustine; there are also small, poorly equipped regional hospitals in all the main towns. **Tobago's** sole public hospital is in Scarborough, next to the Fort complex,. You won't have to pay for treatment at these public hospitals, but will be asked for a fee at Mount Hope and all others listed; however, the long waits and severely stretched facilities make it more sensible to plump for a private option straight away, particularly as your insurance should eventually cover costs in any case.

Though we have recommended reliable doctors and medical centres throughout the guide, it's also wise to enquire at your hotel if you need attention. Many have a resident nurse or can recommend someone who'll get there quickly. In Trinidad, you can call a Red Cross ambulance; ☎627 8215 in office hours, 627 8214 in the evening. In Tobago, call ☎639 2222.

If you prefer **alternative medicine**, Trinidad's best **homeopath** is Harry Ramnarine, an ex-surgeon turned alternative practitioner. His practice is at 403 Rodney Road, Chaguanas (☎665 8041).

Before you go

Though you should ensure that you're up to date with polio and tetanus vaccines, no **jabs** are needed to enter Trinidad and Tobago unless you're travelling from a country where smallpox vaccines are required. However, typhoid, yellow fever and hepatitis A immunizations are worth considering if you think you'll be spending a lot of time off the beaten track. Take precautions to ensure that you're as healthy as possible before you travel; have a **dental check-up** and bring supplies of any **prescription medicines** that you use regularly, as well as the generic name of the product in case you need any more once you've arrived.

Staying healthy in the heat

Heat and **humidity** make cuts and grazes slower to heal and more open to infection than in more temperate climates; clean all wounds scrupulously, apply iodine or antiseptic spray or powder (cream just keeps a cut wet and slows down healing) and try to keep the wound dry. You can use rum to clean wounds if nothing else is to hand. Sea water is said to help a cut heal fast, but as most of the ocean carries plenty of bacteria alongside the salt, you may be risking infection.

Regional hospitals

Trinidad

Arima District Hospital, Queen Mary Ave, Arima, ☎667 3503.

Community Hospital, Western Main Rd, Cocorite, Port of Spain, ☎622 1191 or 628 8330.

Mount Hope Hospital, Eastern Main Rd, St Augustine, ☎662 3552 or 4673.

Port of Spain General Hospital, 169 Charlotte St, Port of Spain, ☎623 2951 or 2952.

San Fernando General Hospital, Independence Ave, San Fernando ☎ 652 3581 or 3580.

St Clair Medical Centre, 18 Elizabeth St, St Clair, Port of Spain, ☎628 1451 or 8615.

Tobago

Tobago County Hospital, Calder Hall Rd, Scarborough, ☎639 2551 or 2552).

Travel medical kit

Listed below are items that always come in handy; though you can buy most of them while in T&T, it's cheaper to buy at home and much more convenient to have them with you when you need them.

Plasters

Scissors

Bandages and sterile gauze

Antiseptic spray or iodine liquid

Antiseptic wipes

Painkillers/aspirin

Diarrhoea remedy

Calamine lotion or any bite-soothing remedy

Medicated talcum powder

Thrush and cystitis remedies

Anti-fungal cream

The benign but unsightly fungal skin disease **pityriasis** – known locally as *lota* – is common; it appears on white skin as circular crispy patches and as lighter patches of discoloration on black skin. It's passed on through contact, and can be hard to avoid if you're susceptible. Though there are a thousand "bush remedies", the best treatment is to apply an anti-fungal cream, sulphur-based lotions or anti-dandruff shampoo. Failing to dry your feet properly and constantly wearing trainers or boots provide the perfect conditions for the **athlete's foot** fungus to flourish – treat it with anti-fungal cream such as

---

Aloe vera

The thick, spiky stems of aloe vera grow profusely throughout T&T, and in Tobago it's common for hustlers to hawk them on the beaches. A staple of local healing and skin care, the plant is a veritable cure-all, drunk as a purgative, juiced as a hair rinse and applied to cuts, grazes and burns to draw out infection. It's an excellent remedy for sunburn, heat rash and insect bites, and is even distilled into aloes wine.

To extract fresh aloe gel from the stem, cut off a section and pare away the spiky edges. Slice in half and wipe the vaguely mauve gel onto the affected areas, scratching the surface to release more jelly as needed and being careful not to get it on clothing – it leaves a stubborn purple stain.

Canesten, stick to open sandals as much as possible and wear flip-flops in communal showers and around the pool.

Be stringent about personal hygiene. If you live in a cool climate, your skin will need to adjust to the heat; sweat ducts take a little while to open sufficiently, and blocked ducts can cause itchy **prickly heat** rash. To treat or avoid it, wear loose cotton clothes, take frequent cold showers without soap and dust with medicated talcum powder. Avoid sunscreen or moisturizer on affected areas and try to spend some time in an air-conditioned room if it gets really bad.

With sweet fizzy drinks often the only available refreshment, **dehydration**, heat exhaustion and sunstroke can also be a problem – symptoms are light-headedness, headache, tiredness and nausea. If affected, rest in a cool place, drink lots of water (especially coconut) and take regular doses of a rehydration solution (see Stomach problems, below). Avoid **sunburn** by basking for no more than half an hour per day to begin with, getting some shade between 11am and 2pm, and always using a good quality, high factor cream – remember that sunscreen loses its effectiveness over time, so make sure your supply is relatively new. Bear in mind that you will be especially vulnerable to sunburn on boat trips, and that UV rays can penetrate even on cloudy days. If you do get burnt, liberally apply fresh aloe vera, after-sun cream or a weak vinegar solution. Hawaiian Tropic sunscreen and after-sun are widely available in T&T.

Stomach problems

Though serious dysentery-type **stomach bugs** are very rare, taking common-sense precautions lessens the chances of a bout of "travellers tummy". If you buy fresh fruit and vegetables, wash and peel them yourself. Stick to obviously popular food vendors and restaurants (all licensed, government-inspected vendors display a badge), and try to wash your hands well before you eat. If you do fall victim to **diarrhoea**, try to rest and drink plenty of fluid: water, herb tea, fruit juice, clear soup and especially nutritious, vitamin-packed coconut water, rather than fizzy drinks or beer. After every motion and once an hour, drink a rehydration solution consisting of a glass of water mixed with a teaspoon of sugar and half a teaspoon of salt to make up for lost minerals, and eat small quantities of bland foods like rice or bread; avoid fruit, fatty foods and dairy products and see a doctor (we've listed these in the Guide) if symptoms persist for more than three days. Though you may be tempted to take a commercial anti-diarrhoea remedy, this will merely prevent the body from flushing out whatever is troubling the system; use these only if you cannot get to a toilet, or before a long journey. Though it's generally heavily chlorinated and safe (if a bit unpalatable) **tap water** can sometimes become slightly contaminated after heavy rain, particularly in rural areas. It's probably best to stick to cheap and widely available mineral water during short stays unless you've got the constitution of an ox.

Animal and plant hazards

Though there are no poisonous **snakes** in Tobago, Trinidad's forests harbour four venomous varieties; the fer-de-lance and the bushmaster or pit viper (both known as mapepire, pronounced "mah-pee-pee"), and two species of brightly-coloured coral snake (for more detailed information on T&T's snakes, see Fauna and flora, p.305). As snakes shy away from contact with humans, bites are very rare, but it's best to wear long trousers, shoes or boots and socks when walking in the bush, and to refrain from investigating rock crevices with your bare hands. If you do encounter a snake – blocking a hiking trail etc – simply move it gently out of the way with as long a stick as you can find, and if you're unlucky enough to be bitten, keep calm; death from a snake bite is almost unheard of, and your worst enemy is panic since violent activity causes the venom to spread more rapidly through the system. If someone else is bitten, reassure the victim and keep them immobilized. Bandage the affected area tightly (if the bite is on a limb, tie a tourniquet above it), note down all that you can about what the snake looks like (but on no account try to capture it), and seek medical help immediately; all local hospitals have stocks of the relevant antidote.

A rather melodramatic point to note is the recent increase of **rabies** among cattle, cats and dogs, spread by the feeding activities of **vampire bats**. While it's highly unlikely that you wouldn't notice a bat nibbling on your ankle, it's probably best not to disturb sleeping bats and avoid petting stray animals; many have mange in any case. If you see a cat or dog behaving strangely,

report it to the police. If you are bitten, seek medical attention immediately.

Insect and arachnid bites

Insect bites can be a real nuisance, particularly if you visit during the wet season (Dec–May). **Mosquitoes** and **sand flies** (the latter deliver a small but incredibly itchy and long-lasting bite) are usually at their most aggressive at sundown, especially around standing water such as swamps or ponds. Cover your arms and legs at dusk and bring plenty of strong insect repellent; a spray, roll-on and a cream are useful. If you dislike using chemical repellents, try citronella or lavender oils. Once you've been bitten (and no matter how thorough your precautions, you will be), do not scratch the bites at any cost. Even touching them will make the itching last a lot longer, and breaking the skin with dirty nails almost always results in infection and scars. Applying soothing creams or sprays may help – homeopathic pyrethrum is particularly good – but one of the best remedies is a coating of fresh aloe vera gel (see box, p.17).

Though there is no malaria in Trinidad and Tobago, the *Aedes aegypti* mosquito can transmit **dengue fever**, a flu-like disease distinguished by headaches, dizziness, rashes on the torso, severe muscle pain and aching limbs, nausea and vomiting. It is only life-threatening if you are very young, old or infirm and succumb to the more serious **dengue haemorragic fever**, and as the periodic outbreaks are dealt with by the government through aerial spraying and warnings to get rid of collected water on private land, this isn't something to panic about. As there is no vaccination, the best way to avoid dengue is to avoid mosquitoes – if you arrive during an outbreak, choose a hotel room with anti-insect gauze on the windows.

Large, hornet-like **wasps** (known as jackspaniards) are common throughout both islands and deliver a nasty sting; keep well away, especially if they seem to be building a nest – alert staff if it's in the corner of your hotel room. **African bees** – distinguishable by their brown-black head and thorax and black-tipped orange abdomen – made the journey from Venezuela in the late 70s and are now common throughout Trinidad. They are extremely aggressive if disturbed, so keep out of their way; do not wear strong perfume in the bush and avoid brushing leaves and branches where hives are often hidden, particularly during the dry season when the majority of honey is produced. If you disturb a nest and the bees swarm, stand still, and don't plunge into water. Never kill a bee if you've been stung, as this will cause it to emit a pheromone which attracts even more bees. And don't panic – remember that despite the "killer bee" scare stories, it would take more than 300 of these painful stings to lead to the demise of a healthy adult.

There are a number of creepy-crawlies to watch out for in forested areas. **Scorpions**, found on both islands, are particularly fond of dead wood. Though their sting is painful, it is not usually serious; the severity of the effect varies with individual susceptibility, but you should consult a doctor if worried; you might want to avoid the local remedy of eating the offender. Some **centipedes** can also deliver a painful bite. To minimize chances of a nip or sting from either, step over rotting wood while walking in the bush rather than treading on it, and if your surroundings are rustic, shake shoes before putting them on. The bite of **tarantulas** is about as severe as a wasp sting, and though it will inevitably be unsettling, you need only seek medical attention if you feel seriously unwell. The large black or red-brown **leaf-cutting ants** (*bachac*) that you'll see everywhere also deliver an extremely painful nip – they are easy to spot, so avoid them.

Marine animals

Given the local predilection for consuming **shark**, you could be forgiven for believing that the waters of Trinidad and Tobago are swarming with voracious great whites; however, this is far from the truth. Death-by-jaws is unheard of and you are only likely to encounter a shark (usually of the rather benign nurse variety) if you go snorkelling or scuba diving around their reef feeding-grounds or dive into very deep offshore water. Endowed with sharp teeth and a bit of an attitude if cornered, **barracuda** are best admired from a distance, as are moray eels. Don't stick your hand into rock crevices when diving or snorkelling, and never touch **coral**; quite apart from killing the organism with a caress, you'll probably come away with an unattractive, slow healing rash, particularly if you touch fire coral. A far more likely encounter is with one of the many spiny black **sea urchins** that inhabit reefs and

bays; if you tread on one, remove as much of the spine as possible, douse the area in vinegar (or even urine) and see a doctor; washing with vinegar is also the best way to treat **jellyfish** stings. Most common are the globular, 4–5cm "wasp" variety which occasionally swarm onto beaches – their sting is no worse than a bee sting, but take care to avoid the long trailing tendrils of the purple Portuguese Man O'War, seek medical help if you think you've been stung by one of these.

Take care to avoid the poisonous **manchineel trees**. They are not difficult to identify; they grow to around 12 metres, with a wide, spreading crown of small, dark green leaves on long stalks and innocuous-looking green flowers. The milky sap, however, causes severe skin blisters. Do not touch any part of the tree, and don't even shelter under the boughs when it's raining. Although manchineels have been removed from many popular beaches and warning signs put up where they've been allowed to remain, some still grow unnoticed in wilder coastal areas, and the round, green and incredibly poisonous fruit occasionally wash up on other stretches of sand, so take care if you're beachcombing.

Sexual health

As cases of **sexually transmitted diseases** such as gonorrhoea and even syphilis – not to mention HIV – are on the increase, casual sex is a pretty reckless pastime. Though the government reports 2613 cases of fullblown AIDS and the WHO estimates that there are around 6000 HIV-positive people in Trinidad and Tobago, the popularly quoted layman's figure is that one in ten local people carry the HIV virus. Bringing **condoms** – and using them – makes sense. Following strenuous government health campaigns, safe sex awareness is fairly good, and condoms are widely available – the most popular local brands are Rough Riders (ribbed) and Panther – but you might feel more secure if you use a familiar brand name. If you use the **contraceptive pill**, take more supplies than necessary, as vomiting or diarrhoea may lessen its effectiveness.

For advice on HIV/AIDS, call the **National Aids Hotline;** ☎ 625 2437. For **Alcoholics Anonymous** call ☎ 665 1251, and advice on drug related issues is available on ☎ 627 0337.

Women's health

It's a sad inevitability that time in the tropics creates the perfect conditions for a bout of **thrush** – bring bifidum acidophilus capsules with you, and take them daily to balance yeasts. Bring plenty of Canesten cream or pessaries, keep heavily perfumed products and soap away from the vagina and always wear cotton underwear if you know you're susceptible. Dehydration and the stress of travel can encourage **cystitis**; to avoid it, drink copious amounts of water and be rigorous about vaginal hygiene. If you suffer regularly, bring sachets of acidifying remedies which contain potassium citrate. You should bring more than enough sanitary protection, as your favourite brand will be more expensive, and bear in mind that flushing towels or tampons down the toilet is often a straight route to the sea.

Accommodation

Though Trinidad and Tobago are not the most tourist-oriented islands in the Caribbean, this doesn't mean that there's any shortage of places to stay. In Trinidad, due mostly to the annual Carnival invasion and the flow of visitors from other Caribbean islands, there are plenty of options in Port of Spain and the larger towns. Tourist-oriented Tobago has every category of room in the lowlands area, and plenty of options throughout the island.

Though it's always reassuring to have pre-arranged somewhere to stay for the first couple of nights, you should have no problem finding suitable accommodation once you've arrived. The staff at the tourist board desks at Piarco and Crown Point airports can direct you to a place that suits your plans and budget. Many hotels, particularly in Tobago, also offer airport pick-ups as an extra incentive.

Though accommodation in T&T is cheaper than you might expect for a Caribbean destination – ranging from as little as US$10 per night for a basic room in Port of Spain to US$35–50 for a standard air-conditioned, balconied unit throughout the islands – it's still likely to be your major **expense**. Most hotels and guesthouses in Trinidad use year-round rates which change only at Carnival time, but in tourist-oriented Tobago, properties tend to have two rates; one for the summer **low season** (mid April–mid Dec) and another for the winter **high season** (mid Dec–mid April). However, many local hoteliers are perfectly open to a bit of **haggling**, particularly in summer. You may also get a discount if you arrange to stay for more than a couple of weeks. Don't be surprised if the Trini in front of you gets the same room at a lower rate; this is normal practice, and ensures that local people get as much from their resorts as the tourists.

There are a couple of hidden extras to watch out for: **room tax** (10–15 percent) and **service charge** (10 percent) are added to quoted room rates. Throughout the Guide, we have taken the tax and service charge into account when giving price codes, but it's worth checking whether these charges have been included each time you rent a room.

There is one time of year when you simply cannot count on getting a room in Trinidad: three weeks or so before and after **Carnival**. This is the biggest event in the local calendar, and rooms must be booked months in advance – even the grottiest of box-cupboards are in demand, and Carnival regulars don't leave Trinidad without

ACCOMMODATION PRICE CODES

All accommodation listed in this guide has been graded according to the following **price categories**:

① under US$10   ② US$10–20   ③ US$20–35

④ US$35–50   ⑤ US$50–70   ⑥ US$70–100

⑦ US$100–150   ⑧ US$150–200   ⑨ US$200 and above

Rates are for the cheapest double or twin rooms, including 10 percent tax and 10 percent service charge where applicable. In Tobago, rates quoted are those used during the high season, normally mid December–mid April. During low season (mid April–mid December) rates are liable to fall by up to 25 percent. There are no high and low seasons in Trinidad, but rates may rise by up to 70 percent during Carnival. Many hotels give rates in US dollars – we have followed suit. Payment can be made in either US or TT currency.

reserving a room for the following year. Most hotels, bed and breakfasts and host homes (see below) offer special Carnival packages for the Friday before Carnival to Ash Wednesday; expect to pay between US$70–90 per night for even a basic room. If you're around a month or so in advance, it's worth checking newspaper classified columns or asking around to see if any locals have a spare room to rent – many people open up their homes to make a little cash at this time of year and you'll probably pay less than at an established hotel or guesthouse.

Whatever level of accommodation you choose, you can pretty much guarantee that it will be **clean**; West Indian hygiene standards tend to be high, and even the most basic of rooms will usually be spotless.

Hotels and guesthouses

Most of T&T's **resort-type hotels** cluster around the better beaches of Tobago; here you'll find everything from expansive, landscaped enclaves with hundreds of rooms, high walls, private beaches and possibly a golf course to "eco" hotels and holistic havens. In between these are no-nonsense concrete monoliths dedicated to the needs of the package tourist, and legions of eight-to-twelve room properties with pastel decor, loud bedspreads and a pool. The **all-inclusive** trend that's swept through the rest of the Caribbean has not yet caught on here. At many resorts, however, you may be offered the option of a "meal plan" – the most common are CP (Continental; room and breakfast), MAP (Modified American; room, breakfast and dinner) or FAP (Full American; room and all meals including snacks and tea etc).

In Trinidad, large-scale hotels meet with international standards; air-conditioning, TV (usually satellite or cable), telephone, private bathroom with hot water and maybe a balcony as well as restaurants, bar and a pool on site. However, most of the smartest hotels cater largely to business travellers, so you won't find much in the way of organized entertainment or a holiday atmosphere.

It's difficult to define local interpretations of exactly what a **guesthouse** is; it can be a couple of rooms tacked on to a private home or a smoothly run nine-room establishment. Whatever form it takes, you won't necessarily pay any less than you would at a hotel. Generally, though, a guest house is a small-scale property with less in the way of facilities than you would expect at a hotel; a pool is not guaranteed and you're more likely to get a fan than an a-c system. You may also be offered cold water or a shared bathroom.

A final point to note for independent or budget-minded travellers – a disproportionately high number of T&T hotel and guesthouse rooms have a **kitchen** or kitchenette (the latter usually consists of a hot plate and fridge), which doesn't necessarily mean a hugely hiked rate. Most provide utensils; make sure that an inventory is taken in your presence to ensure that you are not held liable for breakages that occurred before you arrived. Lastly, though **camping** is a popular activity for Trinidadian families during holiday weekends – most of whom make do with a tarpaulin spread over bamboo rather than a tent – it's not recommended in either island unless you are with a local group or can be sure that someone will stay awake to provide security.

Host homes and bed and breakfast

Private **host homes** or **bed and breakfasts** are excellent and inexpensive accommodation options; neither attract room tax or VAT, and you may get a little more insight into local lifestyles and attitudes than you'd experience in a regular hotel or guesthouse. Monitored and inspected by the tourist board, host homes consist of little more than a spare room in someone's house. They normally rent at around US$20–35 per person, though owners are often open to a bit of bargaining, especially if you plan an extended stay. Bed and breakfast – basically the same deal as a host home but with your morning meal included in the room rate – is best arranged through the **Bed and Breakfast Associations** that oversee this kind of accommodation. In Trinidad, write to the Trinidad and Tobago Bed and Breakfast Co-Operative, PO Box 532b, Port of Spain, ☎ & fax 663 4413, email *la-belle@trinidad.net*. In Tobago contact Ms Miriam Edwards, c/o Federal Villa, 1–3 Crooks River, Scarborough, ☎639 3926.

What you get for your money varies enormously in both host homes and B&Bs; from a-c and a private bathroom with hot water to a bed, a fan and a shower at the end of the corridor. Whatever the facilities, most hosts tend to be incredibly hospitable and great sources of local information.

Villas, beach houses and long-term rentals

Most **holiday villas** rented to tourists are in Tobago; most have full staff and ample facilities such as a kitchen and pool. Though you might expect a villa to break the bank, they can actually be quite cost effective if you're travelling in a group; plan on paying US$150 per week for the most basic villa to as much as US$4000 for something in the lap of luxury. Most are privately owned, but represented by **agencies**; in Tobago, contact the Tobago Villas Agency on Shirvan Road, PO Box 301, Scarborough, ☎ & fax 639 8737, or Island Investments, 30 Shirvan Rd, ☎639 0929, fax 639 9050, email *islreal@tstt.net.tt*. In the UK, try The Owners' Syndicate, 6 Port House, Plantation Wharf, Battersea, London SW11 3TY, ☎0171/801 9801, fax 801 9800, email *ownerssyndicate@compuserve.com*.

In Trinidad, there are **beach houses** in many "resort" areas; Manzanilla, Mayaro and the Toco coast are particularly well served. Beach houses are generally geared up to locals on a break, and you can get some real bargains by scanning the local papers. Bear in mind though, that there are often two rates; one for Trinidadians and another (more expensive) for foreigners; rental periods start from a weekend.

If you are planning to stay in Trinidad for a month or more, it's well worth considering a **furnished apartment**. The best place to start looking is the newspaper classified pages, particularly in the *Guardian*. One-bedroom apartments in and around Port of Spain rent at around TT$800–1500 per month, though good deals can be hard to find and you'll probably see loads of rooms before you find one to suit you. Ads for "tourist" or "vacation" accommodation often mean higher rates, though you might get a more palatial apartment for the extra money and you'll probably pay less than in a hotel.

Getting around

Travelling around Trinidad and Tobago takes ingenuity and patience. Public transport is minimal and erratic, and an unofficial, private system of route taxis and maxi taxis has developed to fill the gaps.

There are four types of transport available: **buses**, **maxi taxis**, **route taxis** and **private taxis**. If you wish to see more than the urban areas, however, it is advisable to **rent a car**. It is also useful if you're planning to go out late at night; public transport runs all night – albeit infrequently – in Port of Spain and San Fernando, but elsewhere it peters out after midnight. Whatever form of transport you are using, avoid travelling at **peak hours** (6–8am, 3–6pm), when the roads are clogged and maxis and taxis heave with people.

Buses

There is a small network of **public buses**; in Trinidad they travel between the towns and cities, in Tobago they run from Scarborough to Crown Point and Plymouth. Along Trinidad's east coast, the former course of the railway – running parallel to Eastern Main Road – has been designated a **Priority Bus Route**, reserved for buses and maxis. The service is somewhat flexible in its interpretation of the timetables, so patience is essential. Despite its drawbacks, this is the least expensive and quickest form of transport in Trinidad.

There are two types of buses, the **blue transit** – known as "Super Express" – and the red, white and black **ECS bus**. Despite its name, the transit is the slower option, and has no air conditioning or music. You can sit or stand on these – during rush hour they become very sweaty and crowd-

ed. ECS buses are quicker and more frequent, running every twenty to twenty-five minutes from 5am–9pm (7pm on weekends). They are also air-conditioned, play music and allow only seated passengers.

All buses in Trinidad leave and terminate at **Citygate** in Port of Spain. This is the main transport hub of Trinidad, sometimes referred to as **South Quay** in official literature. It is also the main terminus for maxi taxis that travel across the country. In Tobago, they leave from the bus terminal in Greenside Street in Scarborough. **Bus stops** are recognizable by the small concrete shelters on the side of the road; sometimes there is a sign attached to a nearby telegraph pole.

ECS **fares** work out at around TT$3 from Port of Spain to Arima or Chaguanas, TT$6 for a longer haul – to San Fernando, for example. The blue transit costs around 50 cents less. **Tickets** must be bought in advance, either from the main terminus in Port of Spain, the Scarborough bus terminal, or from small general stores around the country. Weekly and monthly tickets are available from the main bus stations.

Information on bus services can be obtained from the security office next to the ticket booth in Citygate, or by ringing ☎623 2341, 2342, 2343, 2344 or 2345.

Maxi taxis

Maxi taxis are minibuses containing ten to twenty people – privately owned but formed into associations with set routes and standardized fares. In the past they were famed for their loud music, which made the maxi a travelling disco, but a controversial new law – passed to assuage worries that schoolchildren were grooving aboard their favourite "party maxi" when they should have been doing their homework – now requires drivers to pay a fee if they wish to play music in their vehicles.

A ride in a maxi is still an entertaining experience, however. The internal decor reflects the taste and inclinations of the owner, and may declare anything from religious faith to a devotion to love, money and good times. More ornate maxis have padded ceilings, photographs of favourite personalities and hand-painted interiors. Many have a recognizable slogan across their front windshield: the nickname of the driver, perhaps, or their personal motto: "Mister Painter", "Young Adult" or "Black Man Redemption".

The maxis are organized by region and have **colour coded** stripes relating to the area in which they work. Each area has a main meeting point for maxis in the nearest large town. In Trinidad, **yellow striped** vehicles work from Port of Spain to the Western Tip; **red stripes** in the east; **green stripes** in the centre and south of the island; **black stripes** in and around Princes Town; and **brown stripes** from San Fernando to the southwest peninsula. **Blue striped** maxis operate in Tobago; there is only one set route, from Scarborough to Charlotteville, and the rest are used mainly to ferry schoolchildren or as private charters for tourists.

As the vehicles are privately owned they are a law unto themselves, with **no set timetable**. There are more of them around during busy periods (every five minutes between 6–10am and 3–8pm). The later it gets, the fewer there are; after 8pm you can expect a ten- to twenty-minute wait. During the night, maxis run intermittently, serving areas with fetes and concerts, and commuting between the major towns. You will always manage to get home eventually, though sometimes you will have walked half the distance before you get transport.

Maxi **routes** radiate out from the main centres, which means that to get from one small town to another you may have to travel twice the distance. They can be hailed anywhere along their route – just stick out your hand and if they have space they will pick you up – but it is often quicker to go to the main stand; since maxis wait until they are full before leaving, they may not have free seats until they reach their destination. Once you are aboard, the maxis will let you off at any point; press the buzzers by the windows, just above head height, to stop the bus.

Fares are fixed, and go up only when price of petrol does. The rates are not displayed as it is presumed that everyone knows their fare. Where possible these prices have been listed in the guide. Usually these range between TT$2 and TT$5; from Port of Spain, for example, it costs TT$3 to Chaguanas, TT$4 to Arima and TT$5 to San Fernando. Long distances to out of the way places work out more expensive as you will probably have to take more than one maxi. If

you're unsure of the fare, it is best to give TT$10 and wait for the change.

It takes a while to get used to the maxi system in T&T as there are many variables: drivers sometimes make detours to pick up more passengers, or take a faster route if the vehicle is full. **Off route drops** may also be made, though this depends on the driver's good will and the destination requested.

Route taxis and private taxis

Route taxis follow similar rules to maxis, but they rarely have a main meeting point; the stands for their various destinations are scattered around the towns and cities. They can take a maximum of **five passengers** and are usually slightly more expensive than maxis. Taxis will not leave their stand until they are full, which means you may have to wait while the driver cries out "one to go". They are usually quicker than maxis as they have fewer passengers and therefore stop less, but they are more cramped as everyone squeezes in with shopping bags and personal belongings. They are every bit as entertaining as maxis, as passengers will often strike up conversations about current affairs and controversial topics.

To stop a taxi en route, hail it with your hand. There is a widely accepted code of **hand signals**; point left or right to indicate which direction you want to take at the next major turn-off. When entering the car it is normal to greet the other passengers with a "good morning" or a "good afternoon". To stop the taxi tell your driver as you are approaching your destination – in Trini speak, "nex corner drive."

Private taxis take you direct to your destination, with you as the only passenger. They are **unmetered**, so a price must be agreed beforehand, and they can work out just as expensive as a cab in Britain or the US. If you want to be taken door to door, they are the only official option, although it is often possible – and more economical – to bargain with a route taxi driver to drop you where you want.

The only way to distinguish between private cars and vehicles for hire is the **number plate**: private cars have **P** at the front, route taxis (and maxis, though these are easily recognizable by their stripes; see above) have **H** for hire. Some P licensed cars also operate as taxis. These are actually illegal, but have become an accepted part of the transport system. They usually operate late at night or on small distances restricted to a few roads, and their main raison d'etre seems to be to transport people with large bags of shopping up steep hills – although many look as though they wouldn't be able to drive five metres.

Driving

Driving in T&T requires **patience** and constant **awareness**; you simply cannot take your eyes off the road for one moment, and the packed streets of Port of Spain with their complicated one-way systems can be a nightmare at first. Throughout the islands, drivers will habitually stop at short notice, turn without indicating and happily block the traffic to stop and chat with a friend for a minute. The best thing is to accept it; beeping your horn out of irritation will just get you withering stares, though horns are widely used as a thank-you gesture and as an indication of an intention to overtake.

Often you will feel that Trinbago drivers must have a sixth sense that enables them to judge when taxis and maxis will brake sharply in front of them or when cars might overtake (often on corners) despite oncoming traffic; you probably don't, so stay aware of the position of taxis and maxis, expecting them to brake at any moment, and always drive **defensively**. Trinbagonian drivers are generally courteous, especially when confronted with a rental car, often stopping to allow you to pull out or shouting advice whether you need it or not. Some, however, take to the road at night with only one head or tail light, and being dazzled by full-beam headlights soon becomes the norm. Flash once to alert the other driver; if they don't dip, reduce speed and keep your eyes to the left verge of the road. Another puzzling practice is the use of **hand signals**, an art which route taxi drivers have perfected and one which is often appropriated by those gesturing in the middle of a heated in-car debate. In general, an up-and down movement indicates that the driver in front is about to stop, though it can be an instruction to stop due to a hazard ahead. Whatever the motivation, slow down if faced with a hand signal.

Though the wide lanes and fast flow are actually less of a problem than traffic and pedestrian-choked city streets, driving on **highways** can feel initially hair-raising – a favourite Trinbago habit is a high speed weaving technique which looks as

though it ought to cause a multiple pile-up, but rarely does. Unless you are used to such antics take extra care, especially behind taxis and in the **tropical rains**. Storms often seem to come out of nowhere, catching drivers unawares and causing plenty of accidents as visibility is reduced and the wet and oily road surfaces turn into the equivalent of black ice; slow down and put on your headlights if necessary.

Local **traffic lights** can be confusing. There are usually three, each relating to the relevant lanes; left for left-hand turn-offs, middle for straight on, right for right-hand turns. In Tobago, you'll see drivers apparently breaking red lights to make a left hand turn; this is entirely legal so long as you come to a full stop at the line and check that the coast is clear before moving off. In Trinidad, you'll see flashing red or yellow lights at major road junctions; both mean "proceed with caution"; yellow means it's primarily your right of way, red that it's someone else's.

A widespread disrespect for authority, and the idea that "we don't drive fast enough to have an accident", mean that many traffic regulations are cheerfully ignored. The wearing of **seat belts**, is compulsory, but seldom practised. **Drinking and driving** is also illegal, though it is not unknown to see a taxi driver with a beer in his hand, and many people will go to the beach at the weekend, have a few drinks and drive home. The law also demands that drivers be properly attired; it's possible to be charged for "driving bareback", so always keep a T-shirt handy.

You'll find **Tobago's** roads much quieter than those in Trinidad; the main hazards are blind corners on tiny roads (sound your horn if you can't see), the occasional monumental pothole, and cows put out to graze by the road. Both Tobagonians and their animals tend to take their time when moving out of the way or crossing the road; drive slowly, particularly of you have to cross an animal's tethering rope.

The **roads** in T&T are much better than those on many other Caribbean islands due to the country's relative prosperity and natural access to the finest asphalt in the world from the Pitch Lake (see pp.194–195). Despite these advantages, and the government's best efforts, you will still find bumpy roads; the country straddles geological fault lines which break up the surface with annoying frequency. In some areas, such as southwest Trinidad, the roads have to be repaired every few months.

Vehicle rental firms in Trinidad and Tobago

Trinidad

Autocentre, 8a Ariapita Ave, Port of Spain, ☎628 8800.

Auto Rentals, Piarco Airport, ☎669 2277; eight other branches in Trinidad.

Econo Cars, 191–193 Western Main Rd, Cocorite; ☎622 8072; Piarco Airport ☎669 2342. *The cheapest in the capital.*

Kalloo's Car Rental, 32 Ariapita Ave, Port of Spain, ☎622 9073. *Friendly and efficient.*

Greene's General Cycle Ltd, cor. Dickson and Eastern Main Rd, Arouca, ☎646 2453 or 646 7433. *Trinidad's only motorcycle/scooter rental service.*

Tobago

All the firms listed are located within walking distance of the airport complex.

Autocentre, Crown Point, ☎639 4400.

Auto Rentals, Crown Point, ☎639 0644.

Econo Cars, Crown Point, ☎639 0610.

Baird's, Crown Point, ☎639 2528.

Rattan's, Crown Point ☎639 8271.

Rollocks, Crown Point, ☎639 0328.

Thrifty, Crown Point and *Turtle Beach* hotel, ☎639 8507 or 8111.

Motorbikes

Baird's, Crown Point, ☎639 2528.

Island Bikes ☎639 8587.

Bicycles

First Class, Crown Point, pager ☎662 3377, ID1973.

Glorious Rides, Pigeon Point junction, ☎639 7124.

Road signs are based on the **English system** (although distances and speed limits are in kilometres), and you must drive on the left. The speed limit is **80kph** on highways and **55kph** on main roads in built-up areas.

Petrol stations are scarce outside urban areas – in Tobago, those in Scarborough stay open until 11pm–midnight, but others shut up shop by 8pm (see p.280 for details). It is therefore wise to keep the tank full, especially if you're planning to make long journeys.

A valid international **driving license** or one issued in the US, Canada or the UK is required for driving both cars and motorcycles for up to 90 days. Apply to the Licensing Division on Wrightson Road, Port of Spain (☎625 1031) if you intend to stay longer.

Car rental

Of the major **international chains**, only Thrifty has locations on Trinidad and Tobago, although there are many local firms (see box above). All companies require that you are 25 and over and must have held a driving licence for a minimum of two years; and most firms request a deposit, usually a credit card imprint. All request that you carefully check the car before you take it away. You may be offered a **collision damage waiver** at an extra fee (usually US$3–5 per day); without one, you may be liable for damage. If your car is stolen and you don't have the keys, you will have to pay replacement costs, so never leave keys in a parked car. **Prices** vary according to the time of year and the availability of special promotional

---

Car rental agencies overseas

UK

Avis ☎0181/848 8733.

Budget ☎0800/181181.

Holiday Autos ☎0990/300400.

North America

Budget ☎1-800/527-0700; *www.budgetrentacar.com*

Dollar ☎ 1-800/421-6868; 1-800/800-6000; *www.dollarcar.com*

Kemwel Holiday Autos ☎1-800/422-7737; *www.kemwel.com*

Thrifty ☎1-800/367-2277; *www.thrifty.com*

Australia

Thrifty ☎1800/652 008.

New Zealand

Thrifty ☎0800/737 070.

---

rates or frequent-flyer discounts, so shop around; they tend to start at around US$30 per day in Trinidad and US$45 in Tobago for the smallest vehicle, inclusive of third-party insurance and unlimited kilometres. Larger companies can usually rent you **baby car-seats** on request.

Travelling between Trinidad and Tobago

There are two options available if you wish to travel between the islands – the **ferry**, slow but inexpensive, and the **plane**, quick but pricier. It is far easier to go by air, though if you have spare time the boat crossing can be a romantic starlit experience.

Travelling from Trinidad to Tobago, boats leave daily (except Sat) from the Government Shipping Service Passenger Service opposite Twin Towers on Wrightson Road, Port of Spain, usually at 2pm. This journey takes five to six hours and can be rough – take **sea sickness tablets**, as strong currents in the Bocas make even the staunchest stomach queasy. The crossing from Tobago to Trinidad is usually calmer; the boat leaves daily at 11pm from the Scarborough docks on Carrington Street.

Tickets cost TT$50–60 return, a cabin for two is TT$160. **Tickets** should be bought in advance, unless you're prepared to join the queue at least three hours before the boat leaves. The ticket office at the Government Shipping Service in Port of Spain opens from Mon–Fri, 7am–3pm. In Scarborough, you can buy tickets at the ferry terminal in Carrington Street. For further information call ☎625 4906 or 3055 in Port of Spain and ☎639 2417 in Tobago.

Air Caribbean (☎623 2500) has eight **flights** daily between Trinidad and Tobago. They leave Trinidad's Piarco Airport roughly every two hours from 6.40am until 9pm. The journey takes twenty minutes. Planes leave from Tobago's Crown Point between 6am and 8pm. You are supposed to check in two hours before departure, but most people cut this down to an hour. Even when flights are fully booked it is often possible to get a standby ticket, as all seats still unclaimed half an hour before departure are resold. A recent hike has raised prices considerably if you're a foreign national; local people or foreigners holding residency or work permits pay TT$150 one way

Flights to other Caribbean islands

There are three airlines that fly between Trinidad and Tobago and other Caribbean islands. BWIA (☎627 2942) flies from Trinidad to Barbados (one to three flights per day), Antigua (one per day), Jamaica (one per day), Grenada (once a week on Saturdays), and St Maarten (twice a week). Air Caribbean (☎623 2500) flies once daily, excluding Saturdays, from Trinidad to Barbados and Grenada. LIAT (☎624-8211) flies from Trinidad (5 daily) and Tobago (1 daily) to all islands in the eastern Caribbean, linking up with various connecting flights. BWIA and LIAT both sell Caribbean air passes that allow for multiple trips around the Caribbean on their airline only. LIAT's is the best value at US$80, allowing you to stop off at any of their destinations in a 21-day period. You can take as many flights as you want, as long as each country is only visited once. The pass can only be bought outside the Caribbean in conjunction with a long-distance air ticket. BWIA's 30-day air pass costs US$399, and covers fewer islands. You may visit each country once, but your route is restricted.

As with everything in the Caribbean, airlines are more informal than their European and American competitors. Flights are cancelled at the last minute and planes do not necessarily leave on time. Always ring ahead to check your departure time, and be prepared to alter your plans.

or TT$300 return, but foreigners pay TT$336 one way and TT$472.50 return (2–12 year-olds pay half fare, under twos pay 10 percent). They are best bought in T&T, as outside operators have been known to double the price.

BWIA (☎627 2942) also fly from Trinidad to Tobago on Mondays and Fridays at 6.10am and 8.40pm, returning on the same days at 7am and 9.30pm. The fare is TT$150 single, TT$300 return, and there's no extra charge for foreign passport holders. For general enquiries on flight arrivals and departures ring Piarco Airport ☎669 8048 or Crown Point International Airport ☎639 8547.

Communications, post and phones

There is no need to be out of touch when you are in Trinidad and Tobago. There are public payphones – most of which can be used to make international calls – all over the country, while the postal service is trustworthy, if somewhat slow.

Mail

Plans for privatization of the Post Office may result in a faster service in future years, but at present, while outgoing **post** travels reasonably quickly (one to two weeks to Europe and the US, three to Australia), receiving mail can take an eternity. The closer you are to the capital, the sooner you will get your letters. The local post office may receive your mail days after it was sent, but then take another two weeks to deliver it. **Parcels** tend to take longer to arrive, and if they were sent around Christmas or Easter, expect to wait weeks or even months.

If your post is a matter of urgency, it is best to arrange a **private box** at the general post office in the capital; you can then have your letters sent poste restante to any post office in T&T. They will keep your mail for up to two weeks – to collect you must bring ID such as a passport or a driving license. If items are valuable it is better to have them sent by registered mail.

Most towns and villages have a **post office**; these are open from Monday to Friday from 8am to 4.15pm. **Post boxes** on the street are small, red, rare, and easily missed; many still bear the insignia of the British postal service, a survival of the colonial era. **Stamps** are sold at post offices. Letters and postcards to Europe cost TT$3 and to America TT$2.50. Beautiful aerogrammes, decorated with scarlet ibises, can be sent worldwide for TT$1 from any post office.

Phones

Using the **telephone** in T&T is simple. Most public phones use a phonecard system, though a few still take twenty-five cent coins. **Phonecards** come in denominations of TT$20, TT$60 and TT$100, and are sold in many local shops and the Telecommunication Service of T&T (TSTT) offices.

If your phonecard has enough credit, **international calls** can be made from all public payphones in Trinidad, and a limited number in Tobago (see Chapter Five, p.281), but it is not possible to call the international operator or make collect calls. Hotels and guesthouses offer a telephone service but the rates are usually higher than using a payphone. International calls are less expensive between 11pm and 7am. Numbers that are toll-free in the US can be called from T&T by dialling 880 rather than 800 – you will be charged TT$6 per minute.

Useful numbers

Area code for Trinidad and Tobago 868
Local and international operator 0
Directory enquiries 6411

Phoning abroad from Trinidad and Tobago
To the UK dial 011, then 44 then the area code (without the first zero) and number. Cost TT$5.50 per min.

To the US and Canada dial 1, then the area code and number. Cost TT$5–8 per min.

To Australia dial 011, then 61, then area code and number. Cost TT$6.85 per min.

The media

Dipping into the local media is an excellent way to acclimatize yourself to the nation's cultural and political life. From the outspoken columnists and scurrilous headlines of the daily papers to the many locally produced slots on TV, the media offers an unadorned picture of Trini society – especially during Carnival, when TV shows preview costumes, road march songs and fetes, and the papers hotly debate the merits of the year's calypsos.

Newspapers

Trinidad's main **daily newspaper** is the *Trinidad Guardian*, a stately broadsheet with a somewhat conservative attitude that led a group of its reporters to break away and align themselves with the more forthright *Independent*. The other well-established dailies are the tabloid *Express* and *Newsday*, picture-dominated with plenty of space for their sometimes outspoken **columnists** – look out for Donna Yawching, Kevin Baldeosingh and Keith Smith, as well as the excellent mini travel guide pieces by Heather Dawn Herrera, which appear in the *Guardian* on Mondays and describe local sites of natural beauty or specific interest in detail. Lesser-read evening papers are the *Sun* and the *Evening News*, and the *Mirror* appears each Friday and Sunday. All the dailies have fat weekend editions with extended music, lifestyle and kiddies' features, but the selection of salacious weekend scandal rags – *Bomb*, *Blast*, *Heat* and particularly *Sunday Punch* – are incredibly popular; *Blast* claims to be the most widely read title in T&T. All carry hysterical headlines and plenty of bikini-clad women, as well as some wicked political satire and thinly-disguised attacks on public figures. **Tobago** boasts only one paper, *Tobago News*, which is published on Fridays and concentrates on local events. Sold at Piarco and Crown Point airports, supermarkets and book stores, **foreign** magazines – *Time*, *Newsweek*, *Cosmopolitan* etc – are easy to get, but newspapers – bar *USA Today* – are practically non-existent; try the airports. Of local glossies, lifestyle and culture mag *Ibis* and women's magazine *Esse* are worth a look, and Carnival souvenir magazines from previous years provide a good insight

into T&T's biggest festival. Local newspapers are sold at petrol stations, supermarkets, pharmacies and by vendors who trade at busy corners; dailies range from 50 cents to TT$1.50; weekend papers range from TT$2–3

TV and radio

Trinidad and Tobago have three **terrestrial TV** stations. CCN TV broadcasts on channels six and eighteen, AVM on channels four and sixteen and government-owned TTT on channels two, nine, thirteen and fourteen. All show American soaps and game shows – *The Bold and the Beautiful* maintains as strong a grip on the local imagination as it does in most other Caribbean islands – alongside some more locally focused programming.

On CCN, the *Rhythm and Grooves* music programme and *Caribbean Style* are interesting introductions to local culture, while TTT's all-night-long *Sun TV* slot is unmissable; terrible production and home-video style wobbly camera angles betray the tiny budget, but the coverage of local music, arts and events by enthusiastic and deliciously amateurish local presenters is brilliant. Local news (plus the main international stories) is shown on CCN at 8am, 5pm, 6pm and a main slot at 7pm, while TTT has news at 3.30pm, 6pm, 9pm and 11.30pm. Though a staple in Trinidad, **cable TV** has only recently become available in Tobago; many hotels also have **satellite** links picking up US channels such as Discovery, HBO and CNN.

Radio is hugely popular in Trinidad and Tobago. It's a good source of information on up-and-coming events and parties. Talk shows give an excellent insight into local culture and attitudes, while music programming reflects Trinidad's kaleidoscopic musical styles (see p.298). From November until Ash Wednesday, most stations are entirely devoted to soca and calypso, but after Carnival, the mood switches abruptly and you'll hear reggae, R&B, hip-hop, rock and the inevitable "slow jams". The favourite stations among the youth are YES FM (98.9), POWER 102 and Caribbean Tempo (105), but WEFM (With Energy For Music) is particularly popular, the main draw being a regular slot from the nation's most popular DJ stables, **Chinese Laundry** and **Matsimela** (see overleaf).

Radio stations and frequencies

Central Radio, 90.5 FM. Religious programming and light music.

Radio ICN, 91 FM. Music and talk.

Gem, 93 FM. Magazine programmes, light music

Radio Superior, 94.1 FM. "Alternative" music.

Rhythm Radio, 95.1 FM. Non-stop music for the more mature listener.

WEFM, 96.1 FM. Music-based, with Chinese Laundry DJs each afternoon (4–7pm) and a topical Sunday chat show (11am).

Radio 97, 97 FM. Dated music with the emphasis on smoochy stuff.

YES, 98.9 FM. Lively and firmly music-based, with soca and reggae.

100 FM. News and music.

Power 102, 102 FM. Soca and reggae, interspersed with lighthearted chat.

103 FM. Music and talk with an Indian flavour.

Caribbean Tempo, 105 FM. Caribbean news, sports reports, soca and reggae.

Sangeet Radio, 106.1 FM. Indian film music and chutney.

Radio Trinidad, 730 AM. Magazine programmes, government info slots and music.

Trouble, harassment and drugs

Visiting Trinidad and Tobago poses relatively few security risks. The islanders are generally more interested in going about their business and perfecting the art of feting than in harassing you or one another. Though downtown Port of Spain can feel a bit hairy at night, it's hardly a den of iniquity with a criminal on every corner.

If you use your common sense and take the **precautions** you would in any strange environment, you should find the prospect of trouble is minimal. Avoid walking alone or in small groups late at night, keep flashy jewellery to a minimum, and think twice before accepting lifts from strangers and don't go telling everyone where you're staying – or letting new acquaintances into your hotel room. Carry only as much cash as you need, get small bills when changing money so that you don't have to pull out wads of hundreds and never leave belongings unattended on a beach or in a car. Have your valuables locked in a hotel safe or use the security deposit box if you have one. In **rural areas** of both islands, you have little to fear – many Tobagonian doors are still sometimes left unlocked – but as a foreigner you may be a target. If you do get something stolen or an offence is committed against you, report the incident immediately, as you'll need a police report to make any insurance claim. Local officers are generally pleasant and happy to help, though things may take a little longer than you're used to.

> To call the police in an emergency, dial
> ☎ 999; for emergency services (fire and
> ambulance), it's ☎ 990.

Trinidadians are far more likely to avoid tourists than hassle them; even in the more heavily tourist-oriented Tobago, **harassment** hasn't reached anything like the proportions that it has in more established destinations. Many locals make their living from foreign visitors, you will be approached on the beach by itinerant vendors selling crafts or aloe vera, but most are extremely polite and rarely pushy. If you do feel that someone is hassling you, letting other people know will probably embarrass the offender into checking his or her behaviour. Remember, though, that you are in someone else's country where personal space may not be as important as it is at home, and try not to get worked up over trivialities.

Drugs

It's common for visitors to the Caribbean to assume that all West Indians move around in a permanent haze of marijuana smoke. Though many people do of course indulge, this is hardly the reality. **Cannabis** (also weed, herb, ganja) is illegal to grow, sell or possess in Trinidad and Tobago, and penalties are severe. Tourists caught in possession are highly likely to be deported without a moment's notice, and jail sentences and fines are frequently imposed; the excuse that "it's OK at home to carry a little marijuana for personal

use" is not acceptable. Local people who choose to smoke do so with extreme caution, shutting windows and doors and lighting plenty of incense. You probably will be offered weed (sometimes sold ready-rolled), particularly in Tobago. If you don't want it, refuse politely and firmly; if you do, be extremely careful about who you buy from, and equally cautious when smoking. Don't light up in the street, bars, nightclubs and popular beaches, and never leave the associated paraphernalia lying around your hotel room.

Marijuana is not the only illegal drug with a local following; **crack cocaine** is becoming increasingly common in T&T. Geographically well-placed as a convenient trans-shipment point from South America, both Trinidad and Tobago have been badly affected; narcotics police regularly patrol stretches of the coastline, and there are "crack blocks" in every large town. However, you are more likely to be offered the drug in Tobago, where some visitors' taste for cocaine has provided a lucrative market. The same rules apply as with marijuana; if you are offered it, refuse calmly and politely. Also remember that where there is crack, there is also **crack-related crime**, including robberies and muggings; be wary walking late at night, check the security of your hotel room and beware of putting too much trust in new-found friends. Finally, do not consider taking drugs out of the country under any circumstances; customs officers have seen all the methods of concealment before and it is highly likely that you will be caught; a few years in a T&T jail is not a happy prospect.

Women travellers

Like other Caribbean countries, T&T has a predominantly macho culture. Trinbago women usually go out in groups or with their partners, so be prepared to meet surprised reactions if you're a woman travelling on your own. Remember that most Trinbagonians don't leave home till their late twenties and then usually to get married.

Independent travellers are still a novelty in the country. Women travelling solo will experience a greater degree of **harassment** than they would get in Europe, the US or Australia. However, this usually consists of verbal comments and is rarely threatening. It is normal in T&T to be friendly to strangers, acknowledge people passing in the street and even make small talk with them – as a woman it is expected that you will be flattered by the attention, and the comments are often very humorous. It is nevertheless important that you follow all the normal safety precautions and listen to your instincts, but you are more likely to find people warning you to be careful than actually to experience any trouble.

Foreign women, whether white or black, will usually get more of this attention, as they are regarded as being on holiday, and out to have a good time with money to spend; rightly so in some cases, as many women appear to visit with the idea of a Caribbean lover in mind. Some such "romances" have blossomed, sometimes spanning years of holiday time. In Tobago, the situation has become so entrenched that some men will openly introduce themselves as "beach bums", and the terms "rent-a-dread" and "rastitute" are becoming part of the vocabulary. If sex is not on your agenda, say no and mean it; giggling, blushing or presenting the boyfriend-back-home excuse will be read as a come-on. If you feel that someone has a sexual interest in you, trust your instincts; they probably do.

On the whole it is best to watch the Trinbago women and learn. They are confident and assertive and will respond to comments politely but firmly, often with a joke. T&T is still a traditional society; most women wear long, baggy clothes, saving their shorts and tight tops for the fetes and parties. To reduce attention from undesirable males it is best to follow their example. Swimsuits and bikinis should be restricted to the beach or the river – many local women bathe with a t-shirt and shorts over their swimwear, and nude or topless sunbathing is definitely not acceptable on T&T's beaches.

Feminism has made few inroads here, though women make up 38 percent of the workforce, and 39 percent of all families list women as the head of the household – the main breadwinner or single parent. Yet despite women's economic power, **sexism** remains an accepted part of Trini life. Women are a favourite topic for Trinbagonian men, who usually refer to them as 'tings'. They will declare their unending passion for the female

---

Women's organizations

There are lots of international organizations based in T&T with their own section dedicated to women, often with both local and foreign women members. **Network** (☎ 627 5192 or 3394) is an umbrella organization of NGOs relating to women, who can put you in touch with the relevant group. The **Women's Affairs Division** (☎ 625 7425 ext 265) is a government department that oversees NGO activities, and includes the **Domestic Violence** and **Rape Crisis Units**; the latter can also be reached on ☎ 622 7273 or 1079, or 657 5366.

sex, and a multitude of calypsos have been written about womankind.

Trini men are known for their smooth "lyrics", as chat-up lines are known locally. These are often imaginative and highly flattering, but usually very crude. An unending topic of debate in male Trinbago culture is women's bottoms. Recent highly popular calypsos on this topic include "Wine up to the Big Truck" by Machel Montano (the road march song for 1996) and the controversial hit by Iwer George in 1997, "Bottom in the Road". The larger and more wiggly the backside the better – many Trini women have cultivated this art form, causing their bottoms to "roll" as they walk. Wining with the woman in front and the man behind, emphasizes this skill, providing a little sexual excitement in this morally conservative country.

Food and drink

One of the highlights of time spent in Trinidad and Tobago is the chance to sample the cuisine, a unique and addictive blend of African, Indian, Chinese, European and Latin American influences. It's hard to overemphasise the centrality of food to Trinbagonian culture; a true Trini would never lime without a full stomach, and many leisure activities – river or beach limes – revolve around the preparation of food. It's rare to visit a private home without being offered something to eat, and you may be regarded rude if you refuse, but as the local cuisine is so good, it's rare to find yourself without hunger pangs.

Trinbagonian cuisine

Although you may be offered insipid tourist-oriented fare in Tobago's resorts, **local cooking** still reigns supreme for the most part. "Local" can mean anything from **Indian curry** and **roti** to **Creole coocoo** and **oil down**, or Spanish and **South American** style **pastelles** and **arepas** (Christmas cornflour patties filled with ground meat, olives and raisins and cooked wrapped in a banana leaf).

Local cooks have a far lighter hand with the **hot pepper** than you might expect, preferring to allow the delicate flavours of fresh herbs such as the ubiquitous coriander-like **chadon beni** to come through. Heat is added later at the table, in liberal dashes of fiery **hot pepper sauce** made with scotch bonnet or Congo peppers. This can be shop-bought, but is home-made by serious cooks, most of whom also add a dash of their own secret-recipe marinade to everything they cook. If you don't like things too hot, remember to say so when eating out, or your meal may be automatically smothered with pepper sauce and a gloopy conglomerate of tomato ketchup and mustard.

Creole cooking

In culinary terms, **Creole** refers to African-style cooking which has picked up many other influences along the way. Usually served with a slice of **zaboca** (avocado), **pelau** is classically Creole, utilizing the "browning down" tradition of caramelizing meat in nearly-burnt brown sugar. The layer of semi-burnt food at the bottom of the pan is regarded by some as the best part of the dish. Pelau centres on chicken, to which rice, pigeon peas, garlic, onions and vegetables are added and cooked in coconut milk; its poor cousin is the self-explanatory and well-seasoned **vegetable rice**.

Caramelizing is also used to make the traditional Sunday **baked chicken**, accompanied by cheesy macaroni pie and potato or green fig salad. Another Creole staple is **callaloo**; chopped dasheen leaves cooked with ochroe, coconut milk and occasionally crab meat into a glutinous mixture that's sometimes pureed into a soup. It's often served with **coocoo**, a kind of cornmeal polenta flavoured with ochroe. Almost always backed up by a hearty rearguard of ground provisions (see Fruit and vegetables, below), other Creole main meals include spicy **oxtail** (cow's tails stewed with vegetables and butter beans or split peas), and **curry goat**, tender goat (and sometimes mutton) cooked in a curry sauce. Two dishes not for the squeamish are **black pudding**, a highly-spiced pigs' blood sausage, and **souse**; pigs' feet marinated in lime juice and peppers, served cold. A classic accompaniment to main meals is **oil-down**; vegetables (particularly breadfruit) stewed in coconut milk.

Though increasingly rare these days, **"bush meat"** (see Fauna and flora, p.304) such as agouti, lappe, manicou, tattoo, quenk and even iguana end up in the pot where available; these days, the best place to taste wild meat is in rural communities; wild meat is also a staple of Tobago's harvest festivals.

Creole **soups** include **san coche**, a lentil soup cooked with pig's tail for flavouring, and **cowheel soup**, thick with split peas and slowly cooked meat which should fall off the bone. Many feature seafood; **fish tea** is a watery and delicious fortifying broth padded out with boiled green bananas and dumplings, while **pacro water** is similar but substitutes pacro (a small mollusc known as **chip-chip** in Trinidad) for fish. Reputed to be a strong aphrodisiac, it's sometimes called "Man Water".

Seafood in general is extremely popular; you'll be offered thick steaks of meaty kingfish, shark, grouper, cavalli, carite, barracuda and dolphin (not the mammal), as well as smaller fillets of "red fish", moonshine, snapper, parrotfish, flying fish and fresh water tilapia. Creole-style fish is usually fried or stewed in a peppery tomato-based marinade of onion, sweet and hot peppers and garlic, while **curry crab and dumplin'** (crab cooked in its shell with a coconut curry sauce served with bland boiled dumplings) is a

marvellous Tobago speciality. Though you'll mostly see it on Tobago menus, local **lobster** is doused in the classic butter of lemon, garlic or herbs and sometimes curried, while the slightly chewy and extremely nutritious **conch** (lambie) is made into chowder, curried or steamed.

Indian cooking

Though the obvious staple of Trinidadian Indian cooking is **curry**, the T&T version is somewhat different to that served in India, using fresh hot peppers rather than chilli paste and a blend of curry powder that's peculiar to the islands. One of the most popular curry dishes is **duck**, which forms the centrepiece of a "curry duck lime". The unofficial national dish, **roti**, is made by everyone and eaten as a convenient lunch or evening snack. A stretchy flat bread (called a skin) is used to wrap curried meat, vegetables or fish, a style of preparation that originated in Trinidad. There are several variations of roti skin including **dhalpourri** (with seasoned, ground split peas layered into the dough) and **buss-up-shut**, a thin, moreish shredded skin that resembles a torn cloth shirt and is usually used to spoon up mouthfuls of curry. Fillings range from curried chicken and beef to conch, shark and shrimp or channa (chickpeas), aloo (potato), pumpkin, bodi beans and bhaji greens (spinach), and in a restaurant, you may be offered a bowl of thin and peppery lentil dahl as an accompaniment. Many vendors include meat on the bone in their roti – if you don't fancy following locals in sucking out the marrow, ask for no bones, and if you have problems consuming a roti without dribbling channa down your front, try keeping the greaseproof paper wrapping on and peeling it down as you eat.

The other mainstay of Trinidadian Indian cookery is the vast array of **chutneys** and **relishes**, ranging from super-sweet to tart or pepper hot. The recipes are too numerous to list, but look out for sweetly curried mango on the seed, peppery **anchar** and **kucheela**, a hot mango pickle that's universally plopped into rotis, doubles and aloo pies.

Fruit and vegetables

Local **fruit and veg** is plentiful and relatively cheap, particularly if you buy from large markets. You'll see some unfamiliar fruits alongside the more recognizable items; super-sweet and extremely popular, the **sapodilla** is grey and globular with gritty, sweet pulp, while **chenets** are cherry-sized with smooth green skin and a large seed surrounded by a thin covering of sweet, slightly acidic flesh. The knobbly green and brown skin of the **soursop** surrounds a milky white pulp that is often made into ice cream or drinks; its smaller cousin the **sweetsop** is less common. The round **pomme cythere** (called pomsitae) is sweet and yellow when ripe, but is often eaten green with salt and pepper as "chow", as is the star-shaped **carambola** (five finger) and unripe mango. Round with a purple or green skin, **kymets** are quite rare and completely delicious with a gloopy, off-white pulp inside; equally sought-after, **balata** fruit are similar to chenets, with a stone in the middle surrounded by glutinous, perfumed goo; take care when eating both, though, as they leave a sticky chewing-gum-like substance on the lips. Though the grey-green skin is smooth, **mamee apples** are the same size as an orange, with dense apricot flesh that tastes faintly of peach. If you arrive during the main June to August season, don't miss out on the perfumed white flesh of the crimson-skinned, pear-shaped **pommerac**.

Green-skinned with a soft, aromatic, orange flesh, **pawpaw** (papaya) is a staple of hotel fruit plates, as are bananas (usually called **figs** – look out for the exceptionally tasty tiny finger variety or young green bananas boiled and eaten as a savoury), **watermelon** and **pineapples**, though the latter are a relatively new addition; the local fruits are powerfully perfumed and very sweet. **Passion fruit** (granadilla) and **guava** are often blended into drinks. **Citrus fruit** is ever-popular; you'll see lemons, limes, oranges and grapefruit (both sweeter than in cooler climates), while **portugals** are easy-peel, thick-skinned mandarins with lots of pips and juice.

The king of the island fruits, though, are the many varieties of **mango** which grow so profusely in rural areas that whole communities are perfumed with the distinctive aroma of rotting fruit during the season. The most popular (and most expensive) strain is the rosy, medium-sized julie, while the long stringy mango is best avoided unless you have dental floss handy. Bright orange West Indian **cherries** are too sour to eat raw, but are juiced and sugared to make a refreshing drink.

The most frequent **vegetables** seen on the Creole dinner plate are the Caribbean staples known locally as **blue food** or **ground provisions**; boiled root vegetables such as the many varieties of **yam** which range from the delectable powdery yellow type to the more dense white tubers as well as chewy, purple-tinted **dasheen**, **eddoe** and **tannia**, **cassava**, orange or white **sweet potato** and regular potatoes. Dasheen leaves are also hugely popular, cooked up with **ochroe** (okra or ladies' fingers) to make callaloo (see opposite). You'll also see aubergine (locally called **melongene**), **christophenes** – pear-shaped and light green with a bland, watery taste similar to marrow – as well as pumpkin, green **bodi** string beans and **breadfruit** (pembois), green and thick-skinned with clothy white flesh that can be baked, boiled or fried. Definitely an acquired taste, **caraili** is long and thin with knobbly green skin and tastes bitter enough for its acclaimed properties as a blood cleanser to seem plausible, while **pak choy** arrived with Chinese immigrants and is widely used as a green vegetable. Popular accompaniments to most meals are slices of avocado (**zaboca**) and fried or boiled **plantain**, a larger, denser but still sweet member of the banana family.

Thanks to the Indian influence, **pulses** (called peas) are widely used; you'll see red lentils cooked into dahl, green lentils cooked with veg in a coconut oil-down sauce, chickpeas curried into channa, and pigeon or gungo peas and black eye peas cooked with rice, seasoning and coconut milk to make the Caribbean classic of rice and peas.

Eating out

In **Trinidad**, where the tourism industry is just beginning to develop and most people prefer to eat at home, a serious **restaurant culture** is only just beginning to develop. There are some splendid and stylish places to eat Indian, Creole, Chinese and international cuisine in and around Port of Spain, where you'll also find a huge lunchtime variety in the shopping mall food courts, but the majority of eateries are no-nonsense type places where decor and ambience come second to the food, which is invariably inexpensive and delicious; curries, roti, Chinese staples, macaroni pie and lentils, potato or green fig salad, Creole-style fish and chicken or the ubiquitous pelau.

When Trinidadians do eat out, it's usually to fill up on the marvellous array of **street food**. Almost every city corner is an impromptu trading post for some kind of food, particularly brown paper bags of salted (or "ital") freshly roasted peanuts. Western Main Road in the St James district of Port of Spain offers particularly rich pickings, with food available throughout the night. All vendors are subject to stringent regular hygiene checks; a clean bill provides an official badge, so eating on the hop rarely constitutes a health risk.

In **Tobago**, you'll see more variety in the restaurants, many of which are decidedly upscale and aimed at the tourist market, with prices to match. Local seafood, curries, Creole sauces and roti do feature, but you'll encounter plenty of imported US steak or fish and chips as well. With fewer office workers and late-night revellers to fuel the trade, street food is far less widely available, and the best place to sample typical Tobagonian dishes such as **crab and dumplin** is probably the *Blue Crab* restaurant in Scarborough or the tiny cookshops serving up for the market traders.

In both islands, **breakfast** is traditionally a hearty meal, ideally taken with a steaming mug of **chocolate tea**; hot chocolate made with fresh cocoa rolled into an oily ball with nutmeg, cinnamon and sugar, which is grated and mixed with hot milk or water. Designed to stand you in good stead for a hard day's work, a good local breakfast may consist of smoked mackerel or herring cooked up with onions and hot peppers, fried fish or the classic semi-salad **buljol**, a blend of soaked, boiled and flaked saltfish, fresh onions, tomatoes, lime juice and hot peppers, usually eaten with avocado and a couple of light and airy rolls called **hops**. Other popular breakfast breads include banana bread or fried **bakes**, non-yeast rolls of variable shape that are sometimes sweetened or flavoured with grated coconut to make the classic **coconut bake**. If you don't fancy eating heavily in the morning, most hotels offer a "continental" option of toast, juice, fruit and coffee or tea.

One important point to note is the addition of a **tax** (up to 15 percent) and a **service charge** (usually 10 percent) to your bill; these extras are not usually included in prices given for individual dishes, and can make what seems a moderately priced meal considerably more expensive. If the service charge is included, you don't need to leave a tip.

Fast food and street food

Though the international **fast-food** chains – *Pizza Hut, Kentucky Fried Chicken* and *McDonald's* – are now a part of the scenery, local outlets still manage to draw the crowds; best for chicken is *Royal Castle*, which uses a tasty blend of spices and herbs in the batter as well as serving flying fish-sandwiches and veggie burgers. *Mario's* or *Pizza Boys* are other good options for burgers and pizza, and many branches deliver, while the chain of *Donut Boys* do a nice line in fancy cakes, filled croissants and doughnuts.

However, Trinidad's **street food** is by far the best option if you're after a bite to eat on the go, with everything from halal meat or fish sandwiches to fried chicken and, of course, **roti**. Everybody has their favourite roti shop or stall, and you're guaranteed to find something tasty if you head for the vendors along Western Main Road in St James, Port of Spain. Other good shops include *Patraj* in Tragarete Road, *The Hott Shoppe* on Mucurapo or Maraval roads, the *Home Cooking Restaurant* in St James and Arima and *Ali's* on Back Chain Street, San Juan.

The other popular Indian snack is **doubles**, two pieces of soft, fried **bara** bread sandwiching a runny channa (chickpea) curry and spiced up with pepper sauce and kucheela mango chutney. Curried potato wrapped in *bara* bread and fried **aloo pies** are another popular snack, as are pastry-based cheese, beef or fish pies sold by "pie men", from large wicker baskets or hole-in-the-wall shops; there's usually more pastry than filling, though. A little less substantial are the selection of seasoned breads such as **pholouri** (split pea fritters) or **sahina**, a ground channa and dasheen leaf fritter.

Port of Spain's Savannah and most junctions along the Eastern Main Road are flanked by the flaming flambeaux of vendors selling small local **oysters** harvested from mangrove swamps. Said to revive flagging libidos, they're served with a peppery, vinegary tomato sauce and slurped from a cup. However, fears of contamination by industrial pollution and the threat of cholera have led to periodic government bans; buy only from vendors who have a queue.

Creole street delicacies include the staple **corn soup**, a thick and satisfying split-pea broth with vegetables, chunks of young sweetcorn on the cob and mini dumplings – a favourite hangover cure. *Errol's* outside *Smokey and Bunty's* in St James, is one of the best vendors. Boiled in a thin, flavoured broth or roasted on coals, **corn on the cob** itself is also popular, though it can be a little tougher than you may be used to. **Accra**, a peppery salt fish fritter, hails from the African population, while the ubiquitous **bake and shark** is best consumed on the sand at Maracas beach, where vendors compete to produce the tastiest version of this sandwich of fried bread and a slab of shark meat. At Maracas, you'll also be offered a choice of chadon beni sauce, garlic sauce, avocado, salad and coleslaw as an accompaniment. Elsewhere, you may be unlucky enough to encounter stale bake and cold fish; check when it was cooked before buying.

In recent years, Trinidadian Rastafarians have popularized **ital** cooking, which strictly speaking refers to fresh vegetables, fruits and pulses prepared with no salt or additives. However, though Trini ital food stalls haven't managed to relinquish salt, the cooking remains some of the most wholesome you'll find, with beautifully seasoned soya mince, black-eye peas, split-peas, rice, macaroni pie and mixed veg served in a carton as "food" or in a roti skin; check the truck near to *KFC* in Independence Square, Port of Spain (Weds–Sat), or *Chinkies*, opposite *Smokey and Bunty's* in St James or at the croisee in San Juan. Note that the Jamaican-style jerk chicken sold at street stalls isn't a patch on the real thing.

Desserts and sweets

With so much locally grown cane sugar and raw cocoa, it's not surprising that there's plenty on both islands for the sweet tooth. **Desserts** like the moist and moreish **paimie**, a coconut, cornmeal and pumpkin pudding boiled in a banana leaf (or clingfilm these days) and **pone**, a wet cake made with cassava and sometimes sweet potato spiced with nutmeg, or the classic **black cake** – a ridiculously rich, rum-soaked Christmas speciality – are sublime, and there are a thousand variations of chocolate cake. Sold everywhere from street stalls, home-made fruit **ice cream** is particularly good, as is the Guinness-flavoured variety. Pastries include stodgy and delicious **currant rolls**, **rock cakes**, **bread pudding** and **sweetbread**, a spicy, fruity loaf.

Sweets come in numerous varieties. In Tobago, look out for **benet**, a tooth-crunching ball of sesame seeds and sugar, and **coconut cake**, a slab of shredded coconut boiled in sugar syrup and pink food colouring. **Tamarind balls** take a little getting used to, combining the tart taste of tamarind with sugar and salt, as do **salt prunes** (seasoned, sweet-and-sour prunes rolled in a dusty red colouring, often dropped into white

rum for flavour) and **red mango**, which is green mango, well-seasoned with spices and sugar and doused in bright red colouring. Other candies include **toolum**, a sticky ball of grated coconut, molasses and ginger, **pawpaw** balls, shredded green papaya boiled in sweet syrup and rolled in sugar, and an amazingly sugary **fudge**, while the often sickly-sugared and fried **Indian sweets** come in hundreds of varieties. Among them, **kurma** (sweet fried dough balls) is probably the most popular, sold everywhere in plastic bags, but **sawain** (noodles, raisins and nuts simmered in condensed milk and spiced with cardamom and cinnamon) is less common.

Drinking

Given the remarkable local capacity for consuming huge amounts of **beer**, it's hardly surprising that the national brews go down extremely smoothly. The market leader, **Carib**, is a light, golden lager while its close competitor, **Stag**, is a little sweeter; marketed as "a man's beer", it tends to be popular with the more macho. Both taste better drunk out of the bottle. **Guinness** is brewed in Trinidad but, though bitter and refreshing, it bears little similarity to the draught or bottled versions produced elsewhere. The sweeter **Royal Extra** or **Mackeson** stouts are excellent local alternatives.

Both dark (called "red") and white **rum** are downed with equal enthusiasm, the white rum tending to be less abrasively strong than the overproof brands of other islands; T&T regular rums stick to 43 percent volume. **Angostura**, the islands' largest distiller, produce the most popular brands, **Old Oak** and **Vat 19** white and gold rums. **Royal Oak** and **Angostura Premium White** are a little higher in quality, and the paint-stripping **puncheon** should be consumed with caution. Though it's illegal to produce and possess, home-produced cane spirit – called **bush rum**, **babash** or **mountain dew** – is eternally popular, with a strangely pleasant taste and a wicked kick (it's rumoured to be strong enough to make ice sink to the bottom of the glass), but take care to ensure that it's been distilled cleanly. Many drink their rum straight or with water, but Coke, tonic and coconut water are all excellent mixers, often with a splash of **Angostura bitters** (see box overleaf). Trinidadian **rum punch** is delicious, using blended fruits, syrup, bitters and a generous topping of ground nutmeg. Sweet and strong home-made **wines** – cashew, banana, aloes, hibiscus etc – are also excellent if you can get your hands on them; imported wine is widely available, though it's usually fairly expensive. Brand-name **spirits** are expensive and much sought after, but various local alternatives (**Angos Dry** gin, **Molotoff** vodka) are more than acceptable. Imported Jamaican coconut rum is a favourite tipple, and locally produced **Mokatika** coffee liqueur is a worthy after-dinner drink.

Of the available **soft drinks** beyond Coca-Cola and Sprite, energy-boosting **Ginseng-Up** is best

in lemon-and-lime or apple flavours but comes in pineapple and bitter "original" as well, while **Bentley** is a refreshing bitter lemon type soda. **Shandy Carib**, in sorrel and ginger varieties, is a delicious thirst-quencher, but the best thing to drink in the heat is vitamin and mineral-packed fresh **coconut water**, sold in water or jelly varieties; the contents of one nut will keep you going for ages. Grouped around Port of Spain's Savannah and busy junctions, vendors will expertly chop off the outer husk with a machete to expose a drinking hole (ask for a straw as the

---

The Angostura saga

Being producer of T&T's favourite rum is honour enough, but having cricket supremo Brian Lara as figurehead and years as a main sponsor for the steelpan competition Panorama ensures that **Angostura** enjoys the highest profile of any Trinbago company. Trinbagonians stick by Angostura with nationalistic zeal, declaring its rum the best in the world and adding a dash of its **aromatic bitters** to everything from drinks to marinades, soups and puddings, as well as swearing by the mixture as a cure-all for almost any ailment.

The company was founded by **J.G.B. Siegert**, a German surgeon who left his homeland to join Simon Bolivar in the fight for Venezuelan independence from Spain. Alarmed at the debilitating stomach ailments which plagued Bolivar's troops, Siegert began experimenting with South American herbs and spices to concoct a remedy. In 1824, he succeeded, creating the secret blend of botanicals that still make up the bitters today. He named his tonic after the Venezuelan town where Bolivar's movement was based.

Popularized by sailors who brought wind of its curative powers to England, the mixture was first exported six years later, and demand increased rapidly. Production was shifted to the more economically and politically stable Trinidad, and the George Street plant dominated the small town of Port of Spain. Siegert died in 1870, his company's affairs taken over by his sons. The founder's great grandson Robert Siegert, who took the helm in 1928, steered Angostura to ever-greater heights, establishing the Caribbean's most modern distillery in 1949 and exporting Trinidad's best-known branded product all over the world.

As the company became more valuable, so foreign investors began to make ever-more generous takeover bids. By now, however, Angostura had become so central to the psyche (and the economy) of Trinidad that the government stepped in, taking control of the company in the mid-1950s, and returning it to Siegert Holdings, who offered cut-price shares to employees and affirmed Angostura as the "people's distiller".

Despite its bitters being voted the world's worst displayed product by the British Advertising Council in 1995 (the packaging has changed little since 1824), Angostura has gone from strength to strength, buying out other local distillers, establishing a shiny new factory on the outskirts of Laventille and winning hundreds of awards; no less than seven monarchs, including Britain's Queen Elizabeth, have given bitters the royal stamp.

The company continues to take its traditions seriously, and the **secret recipe** for bitters remains cloaked in mystery. None of the five people who have memorized a section of the recipe are allowed to enter the blending room (or even travel) together. After mixing the ingredients, each sends their part of the blend down a chute to the same percolating container that's been used since the company began trading in Trinidad, where the herbs and spices are "shampooed" in alcohol for twenty hours before fermentation and bottling.

Tours of the Laventille factory take place on Wednesdays and Thursdays (US$5; $12 with lunch) and cover the history of the company as well as a look around the distilling areas and a chance to sample some of the products; contact Glenn Davis, ☎623 1841 ext 170.

juice and husk stains clothing), and then chop the nut in two so you can scoop out the jelly using a portion of the husk as a spoon.

Made from boiled tree bark and aniseed, reddish-brown (and sometimes yellow) **mauby** is deliciously bitter and refreshing, but a bit of an acquired taste; it is said to be a tonic as well as a great way to cool off; Mauby Fizz is a commercially produced soda variation. Other unusual drinks include tart, bright pink **sorrel**, made from the petals of a hibiscus relative and usually enjoyed at Christmas, as is the strong **poncha crema**, an eggnog boosted with plenty of rum. **Sea moss**, a white and glutinous preparation made from sea moss and milk, is widely believed

to enhance sexual performance; other stamina-inducing potions are the **bomb**, a blended concoction of Guinness, nutmeg and condensed milk or a carton of Supligen energy drink. Cinnamon and nutmeg infused **carrot juice** and **peanut punch**, blended with condensed and fresh milk, are a meal in themselves, sold from stalls all over the island; vendors will add glucose or granola for an extra energy burst. The best place for delicious blended juice drinks is *Mother Nature* on the corner of Frederick Street and St Vincent Street, Port of Spain; aside from wonderful fig, pineapple or beetroot and cane juice blends, they also sell channa, ochroe and male or female "sex" punches.

Festivals and public holidays

Trinbagonians have a well-deserved reputation for partying. With thirteen public holidays there are plenty of occasions to celebrate, and no religious event passes without some festivity. Banks and workplaces are closed and many take the opportunity to enjoy the country's beaches. Concerts are organized, shops have holiday sales and the newspapers are full of events and articles relating to the celebrations.

Public holidays embody T&T's cultural and ethnic diversity: there are holidays acknowledging Hindus, Muslims, Baptists, Roman Catholics, Trade Unions, and those of African and Indian descent. Every year there is a debate whether the Chinese should also be given a day for Chinese

New Year. There is frequent debate, too, as to whether the country has too many days off, but each festival is avidly defended by its own lobbying group, and no politician can risk offending a sector of the community.

There are other celebrations that, for all intents and purposes, are public holidays though they are not officially recognized as such. The most famous is **Carnival**, held on the Monday and Tuesday before Easter. In Trinidad, especially in Port of Spain, everything shuts down for these two days, and often for Ash Wednesday as well, as people recover from the celebrations.

Most celebrations are local events based on African and Indian traditions, which entail audience participation. **Street festivals** feature local artists, good street stall food and lots of music. Makeshift bands with instruments ranging from a bottle and spoon to the steel drum drive around on the back of pick-up trucks entertaining spectators.

Many **religious days** are also celebrated in small ways, even by those who are not followers of the religion – many will light a *deya* for **Diwali** (a Hindu festival), then the next week light a candle for the Roman Catholic celebration of **All Souls** night (Nov 2). Contact TIDCO (☎868/623 1932) for the latest information on festival events.

Festival Calendar

January

New Year's Day A quiet day, usually spent recovering from the celebrations of 'Old Year's Night' as New Year's Eve is known in T&T. This public holiday signals the opening of Port of Spain's calypso tents, where calypsonians compete with each other in a battle of wit and satire in the run-up to February's **Calypso Monarch Competition**.

February

Carnival Monday and Tuesday The country's most famous festival, celebrated nationwide with costumed street processions and lots of music. Carnival will fall on February 15–16, 1999; March 6–7, 2000; February 26–27, 2001; February 11–12, 2002; and March 3–4, 2003 (for a detailed description of Carnival events, see pp.94–95).

Eid-ul-Fitr has no fixed date as it signals the beginning of the Islamic New Year and is determined by the position of the moon. A relatively private and subdued affair, the festival marks the end of Ramadan and a month of fasting for Muslims with ritual songs in mosques around the country. Donations are given to the poor and gifts exchanged.

The **Crate Race** used to take place in August in central Trinidad, but due to its popularity it has now been moved to Chaguaramas in Trinidad's Northwest Tip, and takes place three to four times a year, in February, March, August and October. The participants build makeshift sailing craft – no motors or real boats are allowed. Many spectators come to see the all-women teams decked out in bikinis rather than the ingenuity of the craft.

March

The **Phagwah** festival, celebrated nationwide, is best seen in Central Trinidad. It's not a public holiday, but many Trinis of all backgrounds participate. Based on the Indian tradition – known as Holi – of the celebration of the arrival of spring, it has grown in popularity over the years to become the Hindu equivalent of Carnival. (See p.163 for more on this festival).

Good Friday and **Easter Monday** are public holidays in T&T. People make huge meals, visit relatives and go to the beach. On the Tuesday after Easter in Buccoo on Tobago, **crab and goat races** are held. These bizarre spectacles are entertaining to watch – though for those betting on their

favourite they're no laughing matter. Tobago also hosts the **Carib International Fishing Tournament** at Pigeon Point at this time of year. **Shouter Baptist Liberation Day**, held on March 30, is a new public holiday in recognition of the African based religion that suffered persecution in colonial Trinidad (for more information on Shouter Baptists see p.294). The day has not yet become an established tradition and therefore the celebrations are somewhat subdued.

Crate Race (see February).

April

The festival of **La Divina Pastora** is held on the third Sunday after Easter in Siparia in southern Trinidad. The Black Virgin statue is carried in procession through the streets of the town, while locals, decked out in their new clothes, celebrate the event with general feasting and merrymaking (see p.191).

May

Rapso Month is a recent addition to the musical calendar, featuring new and old Rapso artists (for more on Rapso see p.303). The annual "Breaking New Ground" concert in Port of Spain features up-and-coming young artists and is usually of a high standard.

Pan Ramajay is a steel band festival held all over T&T. Small-pan ensembles play a wide range of music including classical and jazz, with a large dose of improvisation.

Corpus Christi is a Roman Catholic public holiday on May 29. Some small villages celebrate it with processions but in urban areas it tends to be a quiet day.

Indian Arrival Day on May 30 commemorates the arrival in 1845 of the first indentured Indian labourers in Trinidad (for more on the background to this holiday, see p.286).

Yachties from all over the Caribbean come to compete in the **Angostura Yachting Week Regatta**. Most of the events are held around Pigeon Point, Mount Irvine and Stone Haven Bays in Tobago.

June

The Islamic festival of **Hosay** changes date every year, moving between May and June. Originally a procession of mourning commemorating the martyrdom of Hussein and his brother Hassan, grandsons of the prophet Mohammed, in

Trinidad the event has become carnivalesque, with a spectacular procession of handmade tombs and excellent tassa drumming. The best place to see the festival is in St James, a suburb of Port of Spain, though it is also celebrated in Curepe, Tunapuna, Couva and Cedros. (For more on this festival see p.83).

Labour Day on June 19 is a public holiday in recognition of the trade unions and workers in T&T. It is most publicly celebrated in Fyzabad in southern Trinidad, the town at the centre of the establishment of the powerful Oil Workers' Union (see p.192 for more information).

St Peter's Day on June 29 (or the nearest weekend) is celebrated in fishing communities throughout T&T with huge fishermen's fetes on the beaches, where pots of fish broth sustain dancing to the strains of pumping sound systems.

July

The **Charlotteville Fisherman's Fete**, held on Man O' War Bay beach, Tobago, in the middle of the month, is one of the largest fetes in Tobago – a wild beach party that goes on all night.

The **Tobago Heritage Festival** is held in the last two weeks of July all over the island. Festivities include a traditional calypso competition, an "old-time" Tobago wedding ceremony and sports events. Villages from all over the island contribute to the festival with local delicacies and examples of art and craft.

August

Emancipation Day on August 1 commemorates the abolition of slavery in 1834 with a procession through Port of Spain. During the week leading up to it you will see many people dressed in traditional African clothes in affirmation of their heritage. Talks, workshops and performances are held in the grandstands at the Queen's Park Savannah, where an "Emancipation village" features local arts and crafts and African goods.

Tobago celebrates Emancipation Day with the **Great Race**. Speedboats navigate the dangerous currents of the Dragon's Mouth in a race from Trinidad to Tobago. It starts from Chaguaramas in the morning, but the festivities take place at the finishing line at Store Bay in Tobago.

Columbus' Discovery Day was replaced by Emancipation Day in 1985, but diehards of the older festival still celebrate it in Moruga in southern Trinidad (see p.202).

Independence Day on August 31 celebrates the independence of T&T from Britain in 1962. Flags and bunting decorate all public buildings, banks and large institutions, while fetes and street parties feature performances by local soca and dub artists.

The last week in August also sees the **Santa Rosa Festival** in Arima in north central Trinidad. Celebrating the culture and tradition of the first Trinbago people, the Amerindians, it features musical and acrobatic performances as well as the obligatory feasting and street parties.

Crate Race (see February).

October

Mid-October sees the start of the **Best Village Competition**, a nationwide event where villages send their best dancing troupes, musicians, actors, playwrights, handicrafts and cooks to contests in Port of Spain. The competition lasts until November when the Prime Minister announces the winner.

Towards the end of the month there is the **World Steel Band Festival**, also known as "Pan is Beautiful". Concerts hosted in venues around Trinidad feature the best steel bands displaying their skills by playing classical and calypso music plus a specially composed test piece.

During Tobago's annual **Cycling Festival**, cars make way for the hordes of cyclists that take up the roads in a fury of competition.

At the end of October, the festival of **Diwali** celebrates Mother Lakshmi, the Hindu goddess of light and spiritual wealth. Many households light up their yards with *deyas* (tiny flickering oil lamps in clay bowls), irrespective of their religion, while Hindus prepare large amounts of food and invite their friends for a Diwali meal. The **National Council of Indian Culture** (NCIC) celebrates Diwali with nine days of shows, stalls and events (for more information see p.164).

Crate Race (see February).

November

Trinidad's **Pan Jazz Festival** is an international event celebrating the diversity of the steel drum with open-air concerts featuring pan ensembles from around the world. These events can be expensive, but there is usually a free night of entertainment down on Brian Lara Promenade in Port of Spain. The festival usually occurs every year, though lack of finances have led to cancellations in recent years.

December

December is the **parang** season – a tradition of singing nativity songs in Spanish with a mix of French patois dating from colonial days. Parang groups perform in many bars and nightclubs; local groups go from door to door, filling the streets with the rich, haunting music. Hearing these songs you could be forgiven for thinking you were in South America – until you detect the deep Trinbago accents of the singers. (For more on parang, see p.298).

Christmas Day, December 25, is celebrated in typical Trinbago fashion with large social gatherings and plenty of food and drink. People visit friends and relatives during the day and eat the obligatory Christmas fare at each house. In the evening the celebrations continue in the bars, clubs, fetes and parties.

Boxing Day on December 26 is the public holiday that marks the start of the Carnival season. Radio stations start to play continuous soca and calypso music, and fetes and parties are advertised with increasing frequency.

Outdoor activities and adventure tours

A far cry from your average sun-sand-and-sea Caribbean destination, T&T offers plenty to do beyond the beach, and its rich natural environment affords plenty of opportunity for outdoor activities such as bird-watching and hiking, while offshore pursuits include a wide range of watersports.

Bird-watching

Bird-watching is a popular pastime among tourists and locals alike; Trinidad and Tobago rank among the world's top ten countries in terms of bird species per square kilometre, boasting a species diversity unmatched in the Caribbean; more than **430 recorded species** and around 250 known to breed. Migrant species from South America are most common between May and September, while birds from North America visit between October and March. The dry months (January to March or April) are traditionally the most popular time for birders to visit; during the wet season, however, birds tend to grab whatever chance they can to feed between the showers, so you'll still see a lot of activity.

The best place to start in Trinidad is the acclaimed **Asa Wright Nature Centre** (☎667 4655; see pp.133–4) in the middle of the Northern Range; workers assert that you can see as many as 150 species even on a relatively short visit, and it is certainly the only place where you can see the nocturnal, cave dwelling **oilbird** without a strenuous hike. Other essential stops include the **Caroni Bird Sanctuary** (see pp.160–1), south of Port of Spain, where you can take an afternoon boat tour to see the startling flocks of **scarlet ibis**, the national bird and most arresting of the 156 species that live in this swampland. The **Point-a-Pierre Wild Fowl Trust** (☎637 5145 or 662 4040; see pp.167–168) is an important conservation centre for endangered species of waterfowl nestling amid an industrial wasteland.

The best **book** to bring is Richard ffrench's encyclopedic *Guide to the Birds of Trinidad and Tobago*, which describes calls as well as plumage, habitats and behaviour etc. There are plenty of tour companies and individual guides that specialize in **birding tours** of the island (see p.45 for details). Other highlights of any birding itinerary include the **Arena Forest** and **Dam**, just south of Arima, the **Heights of Aripo** and the **Aripo Savannah**, off the Valencia Road (see p.148), **Hollis Reservoir**, **Mount St Benedict** (pp.141–2), the Northern Range along the **Arima–Blanchisseuse Road** (p.132–4), the **Piarco Water Treatment Plant** near the airport, the **Port of**

Spain Sewage Plant, Nariva Swamp on the east coat (pp.175–6) and **Oropuche Lagoon** in the southwest (p.190).

In Tobago, head for **Little Tobago** or **Bird of Paradise Island** on the windward coast (see pp.267–9) to see seabirds in a natural environment; the **Bon Accord Lagoon**, **Arnos Vale Estate**, **Hillsborough Dam** and the **Grafton Caledonia Bird Sanctuary** (see p.230, p.247, p.261 and p.244 respectively) are also fine bird-watching sites. At the protected **Tobago Forest Reserve** (see pp.278–9), there are plenty of well-trained guides to accompany you.

All of the above sites are particularly rich in bird life, but you need a permit from WASA to enter Arena dam, Hollis and Hillsborough reservoirs and the sewage and water treatment plants, and the Wildlife Division to go to Nariva (see p.170 and p.176).

Hiking

Trinidad and Tobago are ideal for **hiking**, though you'll have to be pretty hardy if you plan to attempt long walks in the searing sun – the best plan is to start early and cover plenty of distance before the midday heat sets in. You don't have to be supremely fit to go hiking if you stick to easy trails, nor do you need any special equipment. There is excellent hiking to be had in the forests of the Northern Range and the Chaguaramas hills; other areas offer less public land and are poorly geared up for walkers.

It's a terrible idea to hike alone as there is no one to provide assistance or raise the alarm if you run into problems; experienced local hikers travel in groups of five or more. There are plenty of tour companies that provide hiking trips (see box overleaf). Another option is to join one of the excellent local groups on their regular jaunts into rural areas. The best bet are the **Sacketteers Hiking Club**, c/o Garth Assing, Allied Sewing Supply Co, 49 Saddle Rd, San Juan, ☎675 1742 fax 675 1230, or Ricardo Rambally, ☎623 5070 or 674 8969. Immensely popular among local hikers, some trips attract up to 100 walkers. Hikes take place almost every Sunday; you assemble at 7am at the meeting point, pay your TT$20 and set off. You must provide your own transport, food and water, though the group can usually get you there if you call ahead. Call for details of up and coming walks. Established for more than 100 years, the **Trinidad and Tobago Field Naturalists' Club**

Things to bring on a hike

Shoes

A pair of stout shoes with good grip suffice if you don't have hiking boots – trainers are inadvisable as they have less hold and don't allow feet to breathe. Clip your toenails short before a long or steep walk to prevent rubbing, and always wear socks to protect against blisters.

Clothes

Wear cotton trousers or leggings to protect against nettles, razor grass and insects with a long-sleeved shirt over a vest in case you need to cool off; a hat is good protection against sun and rain and you should carry a light waterproof mac in rainy season. Bring a swimsuit if a dip might be on the agenda.

Food

Bring a sandwich lunch as well as concentrated high energy food such as chocolate, dried fruit or nuts; a bag of cut sugar cane is great for maintaining energy and quenching thirst. A good quality water bottle is a necessity and you'll appreciate the worth of one that keeps your liquids cool.

Sundries

Insect repellent, sunscreen, a good torch and spare batteries, toilet paper, rope, matches, plasters.

(c/o Selwyn Gomes, ☎624 8017, postal address 1 Errol Park Rd, St Ann's, Port of Spain) is another, slightly less visitor-friendly group that hike on the last Sunday of each month. Their definitive *Trail Guide* (see Books, p.320) makes essential reading if you can get hold of it, describing nearly fifty walks in minute detail. The **Forestry Division** (Long Circular Rd, Port of Spain; ☎622 4521 or 7476) are also well worth contacting; they can advise you on access and conditions and might be able to arrange for a forest ranger to accompany you on a hike.

Abiding by **hiking etiquette** will ensure that the trails you walk stay beautiful. Starting a bushfire is to be avoided at all costs; do not discard matches or cigarettes carelessly and make sure that cooking fires are completely extinguished. Stick to paths and trails wherever possible; carelessly placed feet destroy plants and crops and may lead to soil erosion, as well as drastically

Tour operators in Trinidad and Tobago

Local tour companies offerings range enormously from eco-oriented **hiking** excursions, **birdwatching** trips and **kayaking** to more conventional **driving tours** of the islands' "highlights": Caroni Swamp, markets in Chaguanas, Ajoupa pottery, the Pitch Lake, the islands off the Chaguaramas coast and Gasparee caves, the Northern Range with birding at Asa Wright and the north coast beaches. Both extremes (and some in the middle) are listed below, as are recommended individual guides. Note that you'll often get a reduced rate if you book in groups of four or more; some operators will not set out with less than four in any case.

Conventional tours

These companies use cars and maxis to visit the most popular sights, and prices vary little; expect to pay between US$30–60 depending upon group size and destination.

A's Travel Service, 177 Tragarete Rd, Port of Spain, ☎622 5502, fax 628 6808.

Blue Bird Tours, 114–116 Saddle Rd, Maraval, ☎622 3297, fax 622 3232.

Sightseeing Tours, 12 Western Main Rd, St James, Port of Spain, ☎628 1051, fax 622 9205.

Travel Centre, Uptown Mall, Edward St, Port of Spain, ☎623 5096, fax 623 5101, email *trvlcentre@wow.net*.

"Eco", birding and adventure tours

Avifauna, c/o Roger Neckles, 17 Morne Haven Condominiums, Jilkes St, Morne Coco Rd, Diego Martin, ☎633 5614, fax 633 2580. *Trini-English Neckles is one of the island's most respected bird photographers, and his tours are excellent for serious ornithologists and amateur birders alike. Prices from around US$40 per person depending upon group size and destination.*

Caribbean Discovery Tours, c/o Stephen Broadbridge, 9b, Fondes Amandes Rd, St Ann's, Port of Spain, ☎624 7281, fax 622 7062, homepage *tradepoint.tidco.co.tt/cdt. Ecological, cultural and historical walking and driving tours which can be custom designed: birdwatching/wildlife tours, waterfalls, and a kayaking trip along the undeveloped section of the north coast, camping in a deserted bay. From US$50 per person.*

Chaguaramas Development Authority, Airways Rd, Chaguaramas, PO Box 3162, Carenage, ☎634 4364 or 4349, fax 625 2465. *Waterfall and walking tours around the Chaguaramas peninsula as well as trips "down de islands" from US$25 per person (see p.107).*

---

increasing your chances of getting lost. Leaving **litter** is a criminal offence; bring rubbish – including cigarette butts – home with you, and bury or burn used toilet paper. Finally, don't collect plant or wildlife specimens, and try to keep noise to a minimum so as not to disturb wildlife.

Watersports

Snorkelling and **scuba diving** are extremely popular; both are far better in **Tobago**, where the water is clearer due to the island's relative distance from the sediment-heavy Guyana currents. The best dive spots are centred around Speyside on the windward coast, where you can see pristine reef and a host of fish, including deep water manta rays and the odd shark. Other top spots are offshore Charlotteville and the Sister's Rocks on the leeward side, as well as the Shallows or Flying Reef at Crown Point; Buccoo Reef remains the most popular, as the disintegrating coral sadly reveals. Everywhere, you'll see a dazzling variety of fish, from larger barracuda and grouper to angel, parrot, damsel and butterfly fish as well as spiny sea urchins and lobster nestled among the coral. Throughout the Guide, we have listed reputable dive operators (most of whom also rent snorkelling gear for around US$10 per day) in relevant sections; expect to pay around US$30 for one to three dives, US$45 for one-day resort courses, US$300 for five day open water certification courses, US$200 for advanced open water and US$35 for a skin dive.

If you prefer to stick to **swimming**, bear in mind that undertows and strong currents make many of Trinidad's (and some of Tobago's) beaches downright risky. However, most of these are

Calypso Inn, Calypso Rd, Manzanilla Beach, Trinidad, ☎ 668 5113 or 680 0965, fax 668 5116. *A good option for east coast excursions. Trips include a boat tour up the Le Branch River looking for caiman, snakes and porcupine. Inclusive of food, drink and transport, tours cost US$35–65 per person.*

Kayak Centre, c/o Merryl See Tai, 27 Moka Estate, Maraval, Trinidad, ☎ 629 2680, email *kayak@wow.net. All-inclusive kayaking excursions to Nariva Swamp, the Ortoire River, and along the undisturbed coast between Blanchisseuse and Matelot. US$80 per person for groups of four; $100 per person for two.*

South East Eco Tours, Fuentes St, Rio Claro, ☎ 644 1072. *Walks and hikes to destinations inlcuding Nariva, Ortoire River and Trinity Hills Reserve. US$35–80.*

Wildways, 10 Idlewild Rd, Knightsbridge, Cascade, Port of Spain, ☎ and fax 623 7332, email *wildways@trinidad.net. Trinidad hikes to Arena forest, Tamana bat caves, Marianne, Paria and Salybia waterfalls, Mount El Tucuche and the rainforest around Grande Riviere; Tobago hikes include the forest reserve. Kayaking and cycling tours in both islands are also available. US$50–100 per person depending upon group size and destination.*

Independent guides

Ishmael Angelo, ☎ 628 1753. *One of the foremost birding experts in Trinidad, Ishmael has an encyclopedic knowledge of bird calls and makes a pleasant and informative guide to all the major sites in both islands. Tours start from TT$400 per day; if you use your own vehicle, prices start at TT$200 per day.*

Gunda Busch-Harewood, 11 East Hill, Cascade, Port of Spain, ☎ 625 2410, fax 623 8560. *Lively, informative German- and English-speaking driving tour – Caroni, Chaguanas markets, Gasparee caves and north coast beaches. From US$30 per person.*

Lawrence Pierre, Pierre Felix Drive, Diego Martin, Trinidad, ☎ 632 4204 or 634 4284. *Adventurous hikes around less accessible parts of Trinidad; Paria, Rincon, Madamas and Sobo waterfalls, Guanapo Gorge, Tamana caves, Heights of Aripo and bush camping. From US$20–75 per person depending upon group size.*

Courtenay Rooks, 44 La Seiva Rd, Maraval, Trinidad, ☎ 622 8826, fax 628 1525, email *rooks@pariasprings.com. Hiking trips to Madamas and Paria waterfalls, Guanapo gorge, Nariva Swamp and climbs to the peaks of El Tucuche and El Cerro del Aripo. Bird-watching is also a speciality, with overnight packages available. US$30–60 depending upon destination and group size.*

marked with red flags, with yellow and red flags marking safe areas; in their absence, don't swim until you've checked with somebody local. The regular Sunday crowds, hordes of food vendors, excellent facilities and a swathe of fine yellow sand and cool, clear green water make Maracas Trinidad's most popular beach; a few miles down the road at Las Cuevas and Blanchisseuse lie several more stunning places to swim, though all are sometimes subject to rough seas and undertows. Elsewhere, the Toco surrounds of the other end of the north coast offer sublime swimming, as does Mayaro in the east, the longest (and probably the widest) stretch of sand on the island. Away from the oil refineries, many parts of the south coast offer fabulous swimming as well.

Most agree, though, that T&T's best beaches are in Tobago, where the water is cleaner and

calmer and the tourist infrastructure more developed. The epitome of a Caribbean seashore, Pigeon Point with its crystal water, white sand and pretty palm-thatched gazebos is the queen of them all, though its overt commerciality rather mars the spot. Nearby Store Bay and Mount Irvine are also lovely, but the undeveloped allure of Castara, Parlatuvier, Englishman's Bay and Pirate's Bay on the leeward side are far more stunning. Beyond the ocean, both islands offer marvellous possibilities for **freshwater swimming**, though you should beware of the caiman that inhabit Hillsborough Reservoir in Tobago and many of Trinidad's central rivers. Some of the most stunning waterfalls are Argyll in Tobago and Blue Basin, Paria, Maracas and La Laja in Trinidad; though these are just a few of the many beautiful cascades.

Most of the larger Tobago hotels have all you need in the way of non-motorized **watersports** – kayaks, small sailboats, windsurfing etc. In Trinidad, Chaguaramas is the main watersports area, where you can take a guided kayak tour (see p.45) or go windsurfing. Thankfully, jet-skis have yet to make an impact in T&T, and environmentalists are already pushing for a total ban. If you're serious about **windsurfing** or want to watch one of the many local competitions, contact the **Windsurfing Association of Trinidad and Tobago** (☎637 3567).

During the winter, big breakers – especially around Mount Irvine in Tobago and Toco in Trinidad – make ideal conditions for **surfing**. You can rent boards in Tobago, but in Trinidad you'll probably need to bring your own; check with the **Surfing Association of Trinidad and Tobago** (☎637 0763) for details of events and further contacts.

T&T also boasts excellent sport **fishing**, though at around US$250 for a half day and $400 for a full day, it doesn't come cheap. However, as many boats accommodate up to six , and rods, tackle and bait are included, it makes sense to share the cost. For your money, you're pretty much guaranteed some excitement; main catches include marlin, sailfish, tuna and dolphin. Boats available for charter are listed in relevant sections throughout the Guide, and if you want more information about sport fishing, contact the **Trinidad and Tobago Game Fishing Association**, 91 Cascade Rd, Port of Spain (☎624 5304).

The main **yachting** centre is Chaguaramas. A calm natural harbour outside the hurricane belt, this strip of marinas is a haven for yachties sheltering from rough weather in other parts of the Caribbean and taking advantage of the insurance benefits such protection affords. Chaguaramas is also the base for boat trips "down de islands", normally rum-soaked party cruises to the series of islands off the north west coast (see pp.111–114). For more information on yachting services, contact the **Trinidad and Tobago Yachting Association** at the Sailing Centre in Chaguaramas (☎634 4519 or 4376), the **Yacht Services Association** at Power Boats in Chaguaramas (☎634 4938), or the Bayshore, Point Cumana **Trinidad and Tobago Yacht Club** (☎637 7945). You can also consult the **Boaters' Directory**, available from the tourist board's Marine Industry Section (☎623 1932).

Competitive sports

Trinidad and Tobago offers a wide variety of competitive sports for both spectators and participants. Sport is as much a national pastime as liming, and local people are justifiably proud of their country's sporting prowess; Trini born cricket supremo Brian Lara is exalted as nothing short of a hero and Ato Bolden's gold medal at the 1997 Olympics electrified Trinidad and, particularly, Tobago, where he was born.

Cricket and other team sports

A Caribbean obsession, **cricket** remains extremely popular in T&T, and is the source of much national debate. Main matches take place during March and April at the Queen's Park Oval in Port of Spain and on the main Queen's Park Savannah itself, and are great fun even if you're not a cricket fan; soca blares in the intervals, plenty of cold Carib gets downed, and fans are vocal in their support or derision, blowing conch shells, beating drums and shouting raucous comments. Tickets for Test matches cost from TT$40 to TT$200 for an all-inclusive pass to the Trini Posse stand, where flowing drinks and a party atmosphere make it a day's lime rather than an afternoon watching a spectator sport; they are available from the **Queen's Park Cricket Club** (94 Tragarete Rd, Port of Spain; ☎622 2295 or 6050). Other major games take place in the south at Guaracara Park, Point-a-Pierre. Details of forthcoming play schedules are available from the club as well as being heavily advertised in the

The rules of cricket

The **rules of cricket** are so complex that the official rule book runs to twenty pages. The basics, however, are by no means as Byzantine as the game's detractors make out. There are two teams of eleven players. A team wins by scoring more **runs** than the other team and dismissing the opposition – in other words, a team could score many runs more than the opposition, but still not win if the last enemy **batsman** doggedly stays "in" (hence ensuring a draw). The match is divided into innings, when one team **bats** and the other team **fields**. The number of innings varies depending on the type of competition; one-day matches have one per team, Test matches have two.

The aim of the fielding side is to limit the runs scored and get the batsman "out". Two players from the batting side are on the pitch at any one time. The bowling side has a **bowler**, a **wicketkeeper** and nine **fielders**. Two umpires, one standing behind the stumps at the bowler's end and one square on to the play, are responsible for adjudicating if a batsman is out. Each innings is divided into overs, consisting of six deliveries, after which the wicketkeeper changes ends, the bowler is changed and the fielders move positions.

The batsmen score runs either by running up and down from wicket to wicket (one length = one run), or by hitting the ball over the boundary rope, scoring four runs if it crosses the boundary having touched the ground, and six runs if it flies over. The main ways a batsman can be dismissed are: by being "clean bowled", where the bowler dislodges the bails of the **wicket** (the horizontal pieces of wood resting on the stumps); by being "run out", which is when one of the fielding side dislodges the bails with the ball while the batsman is running between the wickets; by being caught, which is when any of the fielding side catches the ball after the batsman has hit it and before it touches the ground; or "LBW" (leg before wicket), where the batsman blocks with his leg a delivery that would otherwise have hit the stumps.

These are the bare rudiments of a game whose beauty lies in the subtlety of its skills and tactics. The captain, for example, chooses which bowler to play and where to position his fielders to counter the strengths of the batsman, the condition of the pitch and a dozen other variables. Cricket also has a beauty in its esoteric language, used to describe such things as fielding positions ("silly mid-off", "cover point", etc) and the various types of bowling delivery ("googly", "yorker", etc).

---

media; for further information on the local game, contact the **Trinidad and Tobago Cricket Board of Control** at Isaac Junction, Couva (☎636 1577). Alternatively, check out any of the thousands of informal amateur games that take place on Port of Spain's Savannah and any spare scrap of land every weekend; most towns and villages have a thriving local team.

Football

Football (soccer) is also extremely popular; major matches take place at the National Stadium on Wrightson Road, Port of Spain (☎623 0304 or 0305); for more information, contact the Trinidad and Tobago Football Association, Skinner Park, San Fernando (☎652 1172).

Golf

While it's not the greatest **golfing** destination in the Caribbean, T&T does boast some lovely courses, most of which have clubs and carts for rent as well as in-house caddies. In Trinidad, the best is probably St Andrew's in Moka, Maraval (☎629 2314). The only public course is the nine-hole Chaguaramas Golf Course, Bellerand Rd, Chaguaramas (☎634 4227 or 4364). There's only one course in Tobago, eighteen palm-dotted holes attached to the *Mount Irvine Hotel* (☎639 8871); St Andrews and Mount Irvine also host various professional and amateur tournaments (for details see Calendar of Events, p.39–42). For more information on the local golfing scene, contact the Trinidad and Tobago Golf Association (c/o Derek Poon Tip; ☎622 2909).

Other sports

Basketball is also catching on fast; some games are held at the National Stadium – for more details, contact the National Basketball Federation, Abercromby St, Port of Spain (☎623 8802). Other popular sports include **hashing**, a kind of cross-country race with lots of beer and rum drinking. The *Pelican Inn* in Port of Spain is a good place to make contacts if you want to have a go, and **cycling** (contact the Trinidad and Tobago Cycling Federation; ☎636 2547). Though Port of Spain's Savannah is no longer a venue for galloping gee-gees, **horse racing** remains a popular sport. Major meets take place at the Santa Rosa Race Track, Arima, ☎646 7223 or 2450. A recent addition to the local sporting scene is **drag racing**; regular, well-attended meets take place at the Wallerfield Race Track on the Arima outskirts; for more information, contact Autosport Promotions (☎671 6112).

Fitness freaks will find Trinidad well-equipped with **gyms**, which tend to get packed in the run-up to Carnival, when everyone wants to look their best in a skimpy costume. For a reliable establishment, contact the **Trinidad and Tobago Aerobic and Fitness Association**, 48a Pembroke Street, Port of Spain (☎627 0370). If you want to keep up your game, you'll find **tennis** courts at the *Hilton* and *Holiday Inn* hotels in Port of Spain and the *Mount Irvine*, *Turtle Beach*, *Crown Point Beach* and *Grafton* hotels in Tobago; the latter also has air-conditioned **squash** courts, as does the *Pelican Inn* in Port of Spain and *Valley Vue* hotel in St Ann's, Port of Spain.

Shopping

Trinidad and Tobago offers a wide variety of souvenirs and products to suit every budget. You can buy everything from woven palm hats on the beach to the most expensive jewellery in Frederick Street in Port of Spain. Local artists produce fine woodcarvings, shell and bead jewellery, paintings and beaten copper pieces. T&T has an excellent reputation for producing good music and talented writers – purchasing a few books and CDs will enable you to carry a little of the country's culture back home.

The widest variety of shops is in Port of Spain in Trinidad and Scarborough in Tobago. **Opening hours** are Monday to Friday from 8am to 5.30pm, and on Saturdays from 8am to 2pm. Malls are open for longer, Monday to Saturday from 9am to 8 or 9pm. As with everything in T&T, these times are changeable – opening hours depend on the shop and the mood of the individual shopkeeper.

T&T's rich **musical culture** (see p.298) has spawned an astonishing variety of styles – steel drum, calypso, soca, rapso, chutney, dub and parang – and produced many marvellous songs with strong lyrics and powerful rhythms. Local labels to look out for are Rituals, Mad Bull, Jo-Go, Engine Room and Kiskedee Records. The best places to buy music are Crosby's, 54 Western Main Rd, St James, Port of Spain, and Rhyner's, 54

Prince St, Port of Spain, but there are shops in most malls and main streets.

Local **bookshops** are usually full of US titles and schoolbooks. The chain Trinidad Book World (R.I.K. Services) and the Metropolitan Book Suppliers in Port of Spain sell the widest range of books by local authors. Many Trinbagonian authors are published by foreign companies, however, so – if you want to get a taste of T&T's culture – it may be best to buy their work before you come (see p.316).

A wide selection of inexpensive **fabric** can be found in shops in Port of Spain on and around Queen Street. Imported from all over the world, the cloth on offer far exceeds any choice provided by shops in New York or London. Locally designed **clothes** range from the most elegant evening-wear to beautiful batiks to model on the beach. Well-executed painted T-shirts, featuring everything from Bob Marley to the T&T wildlife, are sold in malls and shops, streetside and from beach stalls.

Local crafts such as carved calabashes, woven palm grasshoppers, shell jewellery and carved driftwood are usually sold on or near the more popular beaches and in souvenir shops. Ornate carvings are also sold in art galleries and at individual stalls that occasionally appear on country roads. You'll often see Rastafarians selling handmade leather sandals from market stalls or on the street.

T&T has some of the highest quality **coffee** and **cocoa** in the world, unavailable outside the country, where the high grades are mixed with lower grades by multinationals. Local coffee in a variety of delicious flavours, such as coconut and rum, can be bought in souvenir shops. The rich, creamy cocoa can be bought in small shops and from street vendors – ask for cocoa sticks. These are solid blocks of cocoa that have to be melted, and then mixed with milk and sugar.

They say the reason the island's White Oak **rum** is not well-known worldwide is because the locals keep it to themselves and consume the total production. Trinidad's famous **Angostura Brewery** produces a wide range of excellent rum as well as their ever-popular bitters. These are readily available in many local shops. Starting at TT$35 for a litre of white rum, they are excellent value and make a popular souvenir.

Prices

Prices are generally higher in Tobago than in Trinidad, and prices of most purpose-made souvenirs are hiked up as a result of the tourist trade. Paintings and woodcarvings may seem expensive in comparison with other local produce, but these works of art are unique and the prices are far lower than can be found in an art gallery back home.

If you are looking for **bargains**, check out the streetside vendors and small backstreet shops. Souvenir shops, boutiques and the malls have higher prices, though they usually have a wider variety of products on offer. Bargaining is conducted to a certain extent with street and beach vendors but not in shops. Vendors may lower the price a little but do not push for too much; this is their livelihood, after all.

Directory

Addresses and directions Street signs and house numbers can be confusing in T&T, as some roads have none and most houses are unlabelled. Consequently addresses often include "Corner of" (abbreviated to "cor.") followed by the names of two cross streets. When someone is giving directions, they will often describe the route by landmarks, and the colour and shape of the building; people often know a street but not its name, so be aware of such visual clues.

Cigarettes The most accessible international brand of cigarettes is T&T's locally-made Benson and Hedges, which also come in the "lights" and menthol varieties. There are also various local brands – du Maurier (strong, also available in menthol), Mt Dor (strong) and 555 (similar to B&H). Other foreign brands can be found in large supermarket chains and malls. Imported cigarettes cost TT$8 and local brands TT$7. **Bidis** (Indian cigarettes) are also available. Known locally as hemp, they are actually made from low-grade tobacco wrapped in a eucalyptus leaf tied with cotton – no filter, plenty of tar. The cheapest smoke at TT$5 a pack, they can be bought from street vendors and some local shops in Trinidad's northwest corridor.

Children As most local people are fond of children and used to accommodating their needs, you'll find that travelling with youngsters is rarely a problem, and can often help to break the ice and

forge friendships. Almost all local hotels are happy to accept families, and many provide baby-sitting services; alternatively, you can usually find someone reputable by asking around. As many of the beaches in Trinidad (and some in Tobago) can be risky for swimming, it's best to keep a close eye on small children when in the sea; even Maracas has a strong undertow; Tobago's Store Bay and Pigeon Point are the calmest you'll find, but Macqueripe in Trinidad can be quite benign too (see pp.225–6, 227–9 and 109). Check with locals; if there's a chance of risk, stick to paddling.

Departure tax On leaving the country by air or boat you must pay TT$100 in local currency after you have checked in and passed through security. Ensure you have the right amount as changing TT$ outside the country is difficult and uneconomical. It is possible to avoid the queues at the departure tax desk by paying the tax through a cash machine in the airport's Bureau de Change; the machine takes the amount off your card and gives you a departure tax form.

Disabled travellers There is little infrastructure in place for those with disabilities. If you want to make local contacts, try Disabled Peoples' International or Disabled Woman Network, both based at 13a Wrightson Rd, Port of Spain (☎625 6658 or 627 0203).

Electricity Currents run on 110 or 220 volts, 60 cycles, so you'll need an adapter plug to use foreign appliances. The current is often sluggish around peak times, particularly in Tobago, making everything run a little less efficiently than at home.

Embassies and consulates Foreign diplomatic missions and honorary consuls are all based in Trinidad, most of them in or near Port of Spain, and are listed on p.97.

Etiquette T&T is a conservative and friendly society. As a foreigner you will be treated politely and it is expected you will do the same. Outside the cities, it is polite to acknowledge people passing on the street with a nod of the head (upwards), "good day", or just "alright". Before starting any conversation, whether buying something in a shop or asking for directions, it is expected that you will say "good morning" or "good afternoon".

Everything is slowed down in T&T; people take a little longer to interact, converse and to serve you. If you arrange to meet someone, be prepared to wait – being on time in T&T means being 30–45 minutes after the time originally

arranged, and no apologies will be given. Don't get frustrated; be flexible and tolerant and you will save yourself a lot of stress.

Religion still holds strong in T&T, especially in Tobago. Though you may see overtly sexual dancing and hear lewd lyrics, the people are still morally quite conservative. Couples in T&T tend to be very undemonstrative in public, although at fetes and parties you may see highly erotic dancing between friends and lovers. If you dance this way with a stranger you will be considered a "sketel" (an immoral person, usually in reference to a woman). Beachwear should be restricted to the beach; nude and topless bathing is not allowed. Obscene language is illegal and though the law is not often enforced, it is important to be aware of it.

Gay and lesbian Officially it is still illegal to be gay in Trinidad and Tobago but there is a creeping acceptance of the gay community and the government is under pressure to change the law. The legislation is rarely enforced but it does mean that there are no openly advertised gay clubs or bars – the scene is very underground and all events are publicized by word of mouth. Gay and lesbian travellers are unlikely to suffer any direct prejudice – the typical attitude you'll meet is "I don't agree but it's not my business". Even so, be aware of your surroundings and be discreet in your behaviour if you do not want to attract any negative attention. There are a few bars and clubs in urban areas that are gay friendly, such as the *Pelican Inn*, *Smokey and Bunty's* and *Just Friends* in Port of Spain.

Laundry There are plenty of laundries in T&T that do dry-cleaning; some will also do "wet" cleaning, though this is expensive. Hotels and guesthouses usually have facilities to do washing, whether it is a laundry service or a concrete washing sink out back. Some people earn a living from handwashing; ask your host for the local washer.

Photography Print film is less expensive in T&T than in Europe, but getting it developed can cost 25 percent more. In Port of Spain many shops develop within the hour; there are no budget rates for a longer waiting time. Slide film is very expensive and difficult to get outside the capital; there are no development facilities apart from those offered by a few professional photographers. As a result of these high prices, photography is not as common as it is in Europe or the US. Consequently people are less used to having their photograph taken, and you will be conspic-uous if you walk the streets with a camera round your neck. Be discreet and ask for permission when taking pictures of locals.

Time Trinidad and Tobago is four hours behind Greenwich Mean Time (five during the summer months), and one hour ahead of Eastern Standard Time.

Tipping Most taxi drivers in Trinidad don't expect a tip, but in Tobago, where many make their living from foreign visitors, a 10 percent tip is usual if you are the only passenger. Never tip in a route taxi or a maxi. Restaurants often add a service charge into the bill; if this is the case, a tip is not necessary – if it's not included, 10–15 percent is the norm. If you're staying in a hotel, you might consider leaving some dollars for your hotel chambermaid.

Working It is illegal to take paid employment while staying in T&T on a tourist visa. Some cultural exchanges can be arranged to teach languages and specific skills, but these should be worked out before you arrive.

The Guide

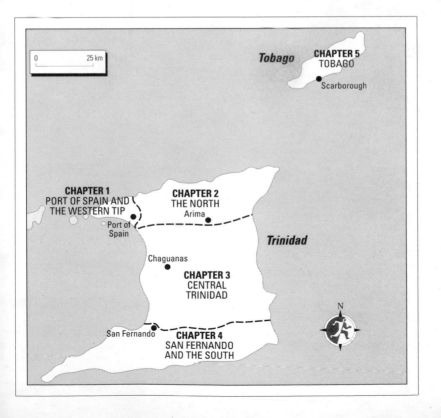

Chapter 1

Port of Spain and the Western Tip

Trinidad's **Western Tip** – a peninsula extending between the Gulf of Paria and the Caribbean towards Venezuela – encompasses both the most urbanized and the least developed parts of the island. Along its southern curve, between the rainforested mountains of the Northern Range and the gulf, sprawls Port of Spain, the country's capital and the commercial and cultural centre of the island. Nearly a third of Trinidad's population lives within its boundaries. For years it has enticed people from the rural areas with its employment prospects, metropolitan verve and late night entertainment; no matter where you go in Trinidad, locals will speak of visiting the capital as "goin' to town". Port of Spain's thriving economy has also attracted many immigrants from other islands, making it the hub of the southern Caribbean.

Beyond the western residential districts of Port of Spain, the landscape becomes increasingly rural. The **Chaguaramas** area, much of which is still covered by ancient rainforest, has been sensitively developed, with new clubs and restaurants unobtrusively incorporated into the landscape. Large areas of national park are etched with a network of forest trails, while the area's largely undeveloped sandy beaches and sheltered coves offer many opportunities for swimming and watersports.

The further west you go, the more wild and undeveloped the terrain becomes. Beyond Chaguaramas, the Western Tip crumbles into a series of rocky islands separated by rough, swirling channels known as the **Bocas del Dragon** – the Dragon's Mouths. Though the islands – the largest of which are **Gaspar Grande** and **Chacachacare** – lie just a short distance offshore, they are completely free of motorized traffic. In the eighteenth century, they were a refuge for whalers, smugglers and pirates; today, they are the preserve of yachting enthusiasts, fishermen, and anyone in search of tranquillity.

Port of Spain and its suburbs have a wide range of **accommodation** to suit all budgets. Whether you are visiting the city for Carnival

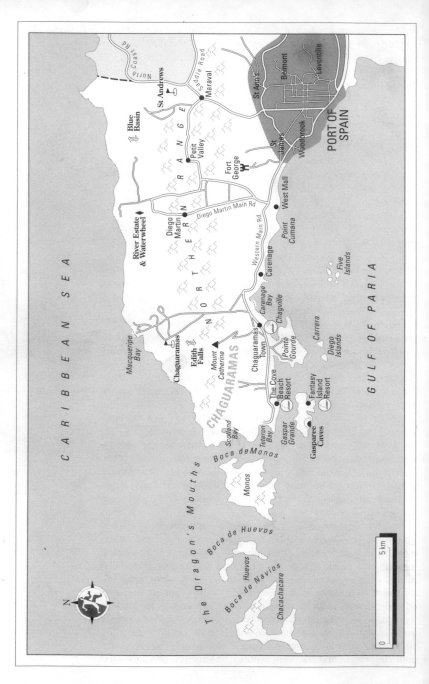

or plan to explore the rest of Trinidad, you will almost certainly end up staying here at some point. Beyond the city, accommodation is sparse in the Western Tip; fortunately, the whole of the area – and the rest of Trinidad, can be reached within a day's travel, whether by public transport or rented car.

Port of Spain

PORT OF SPAIN occupies a crucial place in Trinidad's national psyche. The government and media are concentrated here, keeping the city in the public eye. It is the hub of Trinidad's booming economy, and the main port of arrival for many immigrants from other Caribbean islands. It is also the crucible of Trinidad's rich **cultural life**, with countless mas camps, art galleries, panyards and theatres; it was here that Carnival was first established in Trinidad, and – in the suburb of Laventille – the steel drum was invented.

It's a busy metropolis, proud of its cosmopolitanism and style. Some 51,000 people jostle for space in its compact centre; the latest soca tunes blare from every shop, car and pavement stall, while locals lime on street corners. Yet beneath the hectic urban rhythms, you can still feel the quieter pulse of rural Trinidad. The green crumpled folds of the Northern Range provide a constant backdrop, hand-painted advertisements coexist with sleek new shopping malls, and street traders sell tree bark flavourings alongside disposable lighters. Port of Spain is a friendly place where everyone seems to know everyone else, and at times its atmosphere can seem almost village-like.

The mish-mash of architectural styles can at first sight seem rather ugly, especially **downtown**, with its traffic-choked streets, grimy docks and frenzied commercial activity. On exploring the city, however, you will come across many fine nineteenth-century buildings: dignified churches and state offices, the grandiose mansions of colonial planters, and quaint "gingerbread" houses with their intricate fretted woodwork. Many of these older buildings are located **uptown**, a gracious district created by enlightened town planning in the early nineteenth century around the large open space of the **Queen's Park Savannah**.

The city's suburbs – such as **Woodbrook, Belmont, St James** and **Laventille**, previously old plantation estates, stretch along the flat coastal plains and creep up the hills of the Northern Range. These districts pulsate with multicultural vitality: Muslim processions and African drumming can be heard on their streets, Hindu temples rub shoulders with panyards. It is here that many **mas camps** are located and, in the months preceding Carnival, the costumes are made.

And **Carnival** – the Monday and Tuesday before Ash Wednesday – is of course the very best time to be in Port of Spain, as the city's volatile mix of style, hedonism, creativity and joie de vivre explodes onto the streets and bands of fantastically arrayed revellers wind their way through the city to be judged in the grandstands on Queen's Park Savannah.

Some history

Port of Spain became Trinidad's capital almost by accident. In 1757, the new Spanish governor, Don Pedro de la Moneda, discovered the governor's residence in the then capital St Joseph to be uninhabitable, and established his base in Port of Spain instead. At that time, the town consisted of no more than two streets with a few hundred residents. Though built on swampy ground with a tendency to flooding, it did have the great advantage of a fine natural harbour, and quickly became estabished as the permanent capital.

As French Catholics flooded into Trinidad in the 1780s, the capital's economy boomed and the city spread. Land was reclaimed from the sea, and streets were built over the surrounding mangrove swamps and woods. The last Spanish governor, Don Maria José Chacon, greatly facilitated this expansion when, in 1787, he diverted the Rio Santa Ana (now St Ann's River) to the outskirts of the town, along the foot of Laventille Hill, alleviating the floods that had often troubled the city.

Chacon was less effective, however, when it came to defending the city against **human attack**, and in 1797 the British met little resistance when they invaded and took over the island. A devastating fire in 1808 led the British governor, Sir Ralph Woodford, to make a number of improvements to the city, establishing the Queen's Park Savannah and developing Woodford Square. Learning from Spanish mistakes, the British also improved the city's defences by building Fort George and Fort Picton.

After **emancipation** in 1834, freed slaves left plantations to find work in the capital, squatting the hills to the east of the city, where they established the suburbs of Laventille and Belmont. With an increasing population of workers, traders and entrepreneurs, the city sprawled outwards into the old plantations of Maraval and St Ann's. Indian immigrants, brought to Trinidad under indentured labour schemes, settled in St James. In addition, immigrants from China, Portugal, Venezuela and Syria all came to Trinidad to try their luck in the island. Descendants of these groups, and those of the French, Spanish, African and Indian communities, ensure that Port of Spain retains its cosmopolitan mix of peoples and cultures.

As the nation's capital, Port of Spain has naturally been the focus for both the **political turmoil** and the **growing prosperity** of the twentieth century. From the water riots of 1903, through the independence movement of the 1950s down to the bloody coup attempt of 1990, **Woodford Square** has been an arena of political strife (see pp.72–73). The dredging of the city's **deepwater harbour** in the 1930s made Port of Spain the leading port the southern Caribbean, while the discovery of offshore oil in the 1970s left the city with a sleek **financial district**, dominated by the imposing twin towers of the Central Bank. And although a slump in oil prices in the 1980s put a dent in the nation's newfound economic confidence, the 1990s have seen a wave of buoyant consumerism, with new air-conditioned malls springing up monthly, while a government-sponsored beautification programme is brightening up many of the city's public spaces.

Arrival

Port of Spain is about 20km northwest of **Piarco International Airport**, where a small **tourist information office** (daily 8am–midnight; ☎669 5196), located between customs and the main arrival hall, can provide you with **maps** and **information** on the capital and the island as a whole. Official **airport taxis**, which wait outside the main entrance, will take you into the town centre for US$20 (30min, 1hr during rush hours, 6–8am and 4–6pm). Prices to all destinations, quoted in US$, are listed in the domestic arrival hall. If you are arriving from Tobago, the taxi drivers will also accept local currency.

Alternatively, you can walk out of the airport onto the main road (behind the wire fencing), and take a shared **route taxi** to Arouca Junction on the Eastern Main Road (TT$2). From there, you can catch an eastbound **red band maxi taxi** to **Citygate**, the main transport terminus downtown (TT$3.50). **Route taxis** to Arouca Junction from the airport are also open to negotiation to take you direct to Port of Spain, and at TT$60–80 are a cheaper option than the official airport taxis.

There's a route taxi map on pp.62–63.

A **bus** runs into town twice a day from the main exit (Mon–Fri 8am & 4pm; TT$6). You pay at the end of the journey, when you reach the main bus terminus.

By sea

All ships arriving in Port of Spain dock at one part or another of the **King's Wharf:** boats from **Tobago** at the **Government Shipping Service Passenger Service** opposite Twin Towers on Wrightson Road, and ships from **Venezuela** at the **Cruise Ship Complex** on Wrightson Road. Private taxis tout for passengers at both places; the route- and maxi taxis that run along the Wrightson Road are much cheaper, but since the Tobago boat docks at 4–5am, you may opt for convenience over economy.

Orientation and information

Port of Spain has a compact city centre based on a grid system. The **downtown area** is bordered by the **docks** on the Gulf of Paria and Wrightson Road. **Brian Lara Promenade/Independence Square** runs parallel with the docks and spans the width of the city centre. **Citygate**, the main transport terminal, and many route taxi ranks are located in this area. Most of the sights are within walking distance of each other,

There's a map of Port of Spain on p.56.

The tourist office is open Mon–Fri 8am–4.30pm; ☎ 623-1932.

but bear in mind that the hot sun drains your energy. The **uptown** area is ranged around the large expanse of the **Queen's Park Savannah.**

As many of the inner suburban districts become increasingly commercialized, it is getting hard to tell where the **suburbs** begin and the city centre ends. There are four main roads out of the centre. **Wrightson Road** from downtown joins the Audrey Jeffers Highway, which takes you to Diego Martin, West Mall and the west. **Tragarete Road** runs from uptown Park Street through Woodbrook before joining the Western Main Road into St James. **Saddle Road** leads from the northwest corner of the Queen's Park Savannah to Maraval and eventually Maracas Beach. From the northeast corner of the Savannah, **St Ann's Road** takes you to St Ann's and Cascade.

TIDCO, 12–14 Phillip St, can provide **tourist information** including details on accommodation and tour operators, and maps of Trinidad and the major towns. They also produce monthly and yearly calendars of festivals, sports and Carnival events.

City transport

There are four types of **transport** to get around Port of Spain and its environs; the **yellow band maxi taxis**, **route taxis** and **private taxis. Buses** run to Diego Martin and down to the Western Tip, but it is usually easier to catch a **route taxi.**There are plenty of these around during the day, especially at peak hours. After midnight, however, especially from Monday to Wednesday, it is difficult to find transport except on the most popular routes – when setting out at night, check with the taxi driver how easy it will be to return to your accommodation, and if necessary ask them to collect you at an appointed time.

Buses

While **PTSC buses** provide a fast, cool and clean means of travelling longer distances between towns, they are not the best means of getting around the capital; they are irregular and infrequent, and tickets for specific routes must be purchased in advance. It is usually easier, therefore, to catch a route taxi or maxi taxi. All buses start from **Citygate**; for bus information contact ☎ 623 2341. The three routes serving Port of Spain and its environs are:

Diego Martin: Wrightson Rd, Ariapita Ave, Mucurapo Rd, Audrey Jeffers Highway, Diego Martin. TT$2, hourly, 6am–8pm.

Chaguaramas: same as Diego Martin route, but once on Audrey Jeffers Highway the bus continues onto the Western Main Rd; passing West Mall, West Moorings, Glencoe, Carenage and Chaguaramas, ending at The Cove. TT$2, Mon–Fri, every 30min (5am–9pm), Sat & Sun hourly (5am–7pm).

Central Port of Spain (Citygate special): Citygate, Abercromby St, New St, Frederick St. TT$1.50, every 30min (5.30am–5.30pm).

Maxi taxis

Maxi taxis operating in Port of Spain and the west have yellow stripes painted on them. Routes are set (see map overleaf) although some drivers may be willing to make off-route drops, and if the maxi is empty, the driver may vary the route in the hope of picking up some passengers.

There are three main places to catch maxi taxis for travelling around Port of Spain. For **Diego Martin/Petit Valley**, the maxi rank is at the junction of South Quay and St Vincent St. Maxis bound for **Maraval** (and sometimes **Diego Martin**) via **St James** start at the corner of Charlotte and Oxford Streets. Maxis for **Carenage** and **Chaguaramas** via **Ariapita Avenue, Woodbrook**, start at Green Corner (corner of St Vincent and Park Street).

To Diego Martin: TT$3; short drops on route, eg St James, TT$2; off-route drops add TT$3 to the fare. Route ends at Diego Martin waterwheel.

To Maraval: TT$2; off-route drops add TT$2 to the fare. Route ends at Maraval village/Paramin.

To Petit Valley: TT$3; short drops on route, TT$2; off-route drops add TT$3 to the fare. Route ends at Mount Coco Road.

To Woodbrook: TT$2; no off-route drops. Route continues to The Cove or Carenage.

Route taxis

Route taxis hold four to five people in addition to the driver, and apart from the H numberplate they are indistinguishable from private cars (which have P numberplates). They come in various states of repair: though some are brand new and air-conditioned, the majority are old but functional cars. If you're unlucky you may get a wreck with no windows, rusty paintwork and rattling doors. The same rules apply to route taxis as to maxi taxis; all off-route drops depend on the driver's goodwill. Starting points for the routes are dotted around Port of Spain (see map overleaf). From 7pm until 5am, many taxi stands relocate to Independence Square/Brian Lara Promenade.

To Belmont: cor. Charlotte and Queen St. TT$2 flat fee; off-route drops add TT$1 to the fare.

To Diego Martin: cor. Abercromby St and Brian Lara Promenade South. TT$3.50 to the route end at Diego Martin waterwheel; short drops within Diego Martin TT$2, except from West Mall to Diego Martin, TT$3.50; off-route drops add TT$3.50 to the fare. The route goes through Four Roads and down Diego Martin Main Rd. After 6pm Diego Martin taxis can be found near the Arthur Cipriani statue on Brian Lara Promenade.

To Laventille: cor. Nelson and Prince streets. TT$2.50 to route end at Red Hill; TT$2 to Our Lady of Laventille Shrine; off-route drops add TT$1 to the fare.

To Maraval/Paramin: cor. Charlotte and Duke St. TT$2 flat fee; off-route drops add TT$2 to the fare. Route ends at Maraval village/beginning of Paramin. Jeeps at end of route charge TT$2.50 into Paramin.

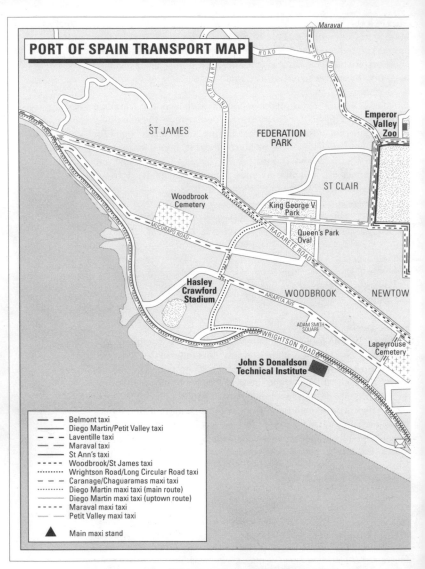

PORT OF SPAIN TRANSPORT MAP

Maraval

ROAD

ST JAMES

FEDERATION PARK

Emperor Valley Zoo

ST CLAIR

Woodbrook Cemetery

King George V Park

Queen's Park Oval

MUCURAPO ROAD

TRAGARETE ROAD

Hasley Crawford Stadium

WOODBROOK

NEWTOW

ARIAPITA AVE

ADAM SMITH SQUARE

WRIGHTSON ROAD

Lapeyrouse Cemetery

John S Donaldson Technical Institute

- – – Belmont taxi
- ——— Diego Martin/Petit Valley taxi
- – – – Laventille taxi
- — — Maraval taxi
- ——— St Ann's taxi
- - - - - Woodbrook/St James taxi
- ·········· Wrightson Road/Long Circular Road taxi
- – – – Caranage/Chaguaramas maxi taxi
- ·········· Diego Martin maxi taxi (main route)
- ·········· Diego Martin maxi taxi (uptown route)
- - - - - Maraval maxi taxi
- — — Petit Valley maxi taxi

▲ Main maxi stand

To Petit Valley: cor. Abercromby St and Brian Lara Promenade South; after 6pm near the Arthur Cipriani statue on the promenade. TT$3.50 to Petit Valley; short drops TT$2; off-route drops add TT$3.50 to the fare. Route ends at Mount Coco Rd at the Capaldeo Flats.

To St Ann's: Hart St, same side as the Trinity Anglican Cathedral. TT$2 to St Ann's hospital; TT$3.50 to Valley Vue Hotel; TT$4.50 to end of Ariapita Rd; off-route drops add TT$2 to the fare, except those to the *Trinidad Hilton* (usually around TT$10). Route ends at Ariapita Rd.

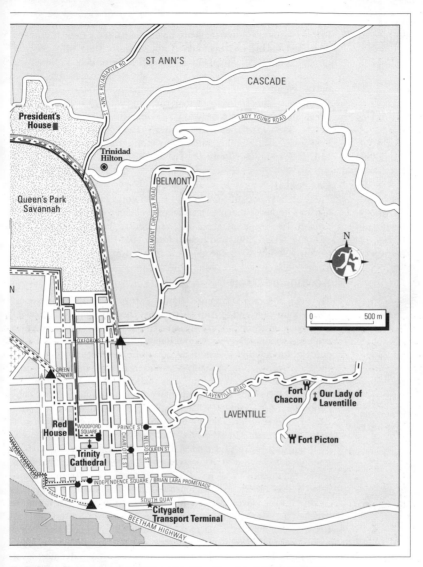

To St James/Tragarete Rd: Hart St, on the side adjacent to Woodford Square, from 7pm–5am cor. Independence Square and Henry St. TT$2 flat fee; off-route drops add TT$2 to the fare; no off-route drops into Woodbrook.

To Wrightson Rd/Long Circular Rd: cor. Chacon St and Brian Lara Promenade South (next to *McDonald's*); after 6pm near the Arthur Cipriani statue. TT$2 up to Jean Pierre Complex, TT$2.50 for rest of route; off-route drops add TT$3 to the fare. Route ends at *Ambassador Hotel* on Long Circular Rd.

Private taxis

Privately-run non-route taxis are distinguishable by their H number plate and clean, well maintained appearance. They will take you direct to your destination, but are as expensive as cabs in New York or London. They are not hailed on the street, but ordered by phone or by going to their ranks at Independence Square/Brian Lara Promenade, the *Holiday Inn* or the *Trinidad Hilton*. Reputable firms include: **Ice House Taxi Service**, Brian Lara Promenade, ☎627 6984; **Independence Square Taxi Service**, Brian Lara Promenade, ☎625 3032; and **St Christopher's Taxi Co-Op Society Ltd,** ☎624-3560 (*Hilton Hotel*) or ☎625 4531 (*Holiday Inn*).

Car rental

*For advice
on driving
conditions in
Trinidad and
Tobago, see
p.25.*

There are a variety of **car rental firms** in Port of Spain. Most usually ask for a deposit or an imprint of your credit card. Prices vary so look around. Two reputable firms are **Autocentre**, 8a Ariapita Ave, Port of Spain ☎628 8800 and **Econo Cars,** 191–193 Western Main Rd, Cocorite ☎622 8072, the cheapest firm in town.

Accommodation

The main areas for accommodation in Port of Spain are the city centre, **Woodbrook** and **St Ann's-Cascade**. The **city centre** is obviously convenient, though you may have to put up with some noise and cramped rooms. The big international hotels are located here, and some of the smaller places in the area offer excellent rates outside the Carnival season, especially if you are prepared to accept rooms with shared bathrooms and fans instead of air conditioning. Woodbrook has the most inexpensive accommodation with a concentration of **guesthouses**. These are more basic than hotels – with less likelihood of air conditioning, though it is increasingly difficult to tell them apart. Guesthouses usually offer fewer services, homelier decor and more of a personal touch. Transport to this area is good, and if you stay at the eastern end of the suburb the city centre is only ten minutes' walk away. This area is also ideal for those interested in mas camps, as the majority of them are based here.

*For more on
guesthouses
see pp.20–22.*

The St Ann's-Cascade area at the base of the Northern Range is greener, breezier and less urbanized than Woodbrook or the city centre. It is also more difficult to get to on public transport than other areas, especially after 8pm, and its accommodation tends to be more upmarket. **Newton**, which shares many of the advantages of Woodbrook, also has a few slightly more expensive guesthouses. Though it lies outside the city limits to the north, **Maraval** is easily accessible and also has a good range of accommodation (see p.99).

The busiest time of year for accommodation is **Carnival**, and if you intend to stay during this time it's essential to book well in advance. Regular carnivalgoers book their accommodation on Ash Wednesday for the following year, and most hotels require as much as six

ACCOMMODATION PRICE CODES

All accommodation listed in this guide has been graded according to the following
price categories:

① under US$10	② US$10–20	③ US$20–35
④ US$35–50	⑤ US$50–70	⑥ US$70–100
⑦ US$100–150	⑧ US$150–200	⑨ US$200 and above

Rates are for the cheapest double or twin rooms, including 10 percent tax and 10 percent service charge where applicable. In Tobago, rates quoted are those used during
the high season, normally mid December–mid April. During low season (mid
April–mid December) rates are liable to fall by up to 25 percent. There are no high
and low seasons in Trinidad, but rates may rise by up to 70 percent during Carnival.
Many hotels give rates in US dollars – we have followed suit. Payment can be made in
either US or TT currency.

months' notice. It is still possible to find rooms nearer the time, provided you don't expect to get your first choice. If booking within a
month of Carnival, settle for anything you can get.

Carnival prices, which can be up to 50 percent higher than normal high season rates, apply from the Friday preceding Carnival
through to Carnival Tuesday. The majority of hotels require you to
pay for the full five days, even if your stay is shorter. In the list below,
where Carnival rates apply, the normal rate is listed first, followed by
the Carnival rate.

Hotels

Abercromby Inn, 101 Abercromby St, ☎623 5259, fax 627 6658. Rooms are
on the small side, but well equipped with cable TV, telephone, a-c and en-suite
bathrooms. Communal sun deck, good central location and breakfast included.
④/⑥

Ambassador Hotel, 99A Long Circular Rd, St James, ☎628 9000 or 628
7607. Very plush new hotel opposite the US ambassador's residence. Large,
luxurious rooms; all have a-c, cable TV and en-suite bathrooms, and balconies
with excellent views over either Port of Spain or the Northern Range.
Restaurant, cocktail lounge, swimming pool, ballroom and nightclub on the
premises. Breakfast included in the Carnival rate. ⑦/⑨

Copper Kettle, 66–68 Edward St, ☎625 4381. Basic rooms, some with a-c
and some with fans; all have en-suite bathrooms. Slightly run-down despite
recent redecoration, but inexpensive for its central location. ③/⑤

Halconia Inn, 7 First Ave, Cascade, ☎623 0008. Old colonial mansion converted into a basic, functional dormitory-style hostel for groups of four people
and up. Kitchen facilities and canteen dining room. Negotiable rates for large
groups. ②/③

Holiday Inn, Wrightson Rd, ☎625 3366, fax 625 4166. Typical corporate
hotel with all mod cons. All rooms have excellent views over the Gulf of Paria
and Port of Spain. Good downtown location, breakfast included in the normal
rate. 24-hour check in. ⑧/⑨

Kapok Hotel, 16–18 Cotton Hill, St Clair, ☎622 6441, fax 622 9677, email
kapok@trinidad.net. Elegant hotel decorated with rattan furniture and batik.
All rooms are spacious with a-c, satellite TV, radio, clock, phone and en-suite

bathroom. Swimming pool, gym and sun deck. Breakfast included in Carnival rate. ⑥/⑧

Normandie, 10 Nook Ave, St Ann's, ☎624 1811, email *normandie@ wow.net*. Well-equipped hotel with natural pine furnishings. All rooms have a-c, cable TV, phone with voice mail and en-suite bathroom. Excellent facilities include a theatre, art gallery, craft shops, swimming pool, sun lounge and a hairdressing salon. Two restaurants on site feature live entertainment. Quiet location on a cul de sac five minutes' drive from the Queen's Park Savannah. Breakfast included in the room rate. ⑥/⑧

Trinidad Hilton, Lady Young Rd, St Ann's, ☎624 3211, fax 624 4485. "Upside down" hotel built down the side of a hill with the reception area at the top and the floors numbered downwards from 1 to 11. Each room has a balcony with excellent views over Port of Spain and the hotel's landscaped garden, plus all the usual Hilton luxuries. Breakfast included. ⑨

YWCA, 8a Cipriani Blvd, Newton, ☎627 6388. Basic but adequate women-only lodging house. One overpriced room is available for short rental only; the other rooms are available only on a monthly basis, and you must be prepared to share. Rates for the latter are negotiable. Cooking and laundry facilities. Good location, breakfast included for short term rental. ⑤/⑥

Guesthouses

Alicia's House, 7 Coblentz Gardens, St Ann's, ☎623 2802, fax 623 8560. All rooms have wicker decoration, a-c, en-suite bathroom, phone, fridge and cable TV, and there's a swimming pool and sun deck. Located on a quiet road close to the Queen's Park Savannah. Breakfast included in Carnival rate. ⑤/⑧

Fabienne's, 15 Belle Smythe St, Woodbrook, ☎622 2753. Friendly atmosphere and comfortable rooms, with en-suite bathrooms and fans, and some a-c. There's also a swimming pool and laundry facilities. Excellent value. ④/⑥

Five Star, 7 French St, Woodbrook, ☎623 4006. Homely guesthouse with large rooms, some with a-c and bathrooms. There's a sun deck and a large communal verandah. ④/⑥

Johnson's, 16 Buller St, Woodbrook, ☎628 7553. The hosts are friendly and helpful, the rooms, all with fans, well maintained. Excellent value just ten minutes from town centre. ③/⑥

La Mansion Rustique, 16 Rust St, St Clair, ☎622 1512. Converted colonial house. Rooms at front are airy and spacious, those at the back dark and cramped – and overpriced. Some rooms are en-suite, but only one has a-c. A small self-catering cottage in the back yard, with separate doorbell, is also available to rent. ⑥/⑨

La Calypso, 46 French St, Woodbrook, ☎622 4077. Functional but lacking atmosphere, with spartan decor. Facilities vary from room to room – some have a-c, kitchenette and bathroom. There's also a jacuzzi. ④/⑥

Mauges, 15 Gordon St, ☎624 5402, fax 625 2335. Pleasant and modern, though rooms are cramped. All have fans, TV and VCR, but only half of them have en-suite bathrooms. Good central location. Price includes breakfast. ④/⑦

Par-May-La's Inn, 53 Picton St, Newton, ☎628 2008, fax 628-4707. Large a-c rooms with phone, en suite bathroom, and TV. On quiet street, with helpful hosts and chirping parrakeets on the communal verandah. Breakfast included. ⑤/⑦

Pearls, 3–4 Victoria Square East, ☎625 2158. A large old colonial mansion with a verandah overlooking picturesque Victoria Square. The basic rooms have sinks and 1960s furniture but no fans or a-c. Friendly hosts, excellent value. ②

Pelican Inn, 2–4 Coblentz Ave, Cascade, ☎627 6271 fax 624 7486. Old colonial house with veranda overlooking busy Coblentz Ave, next to a popular pub/disco. Functional rooms with ceiling fans, a-c and en-suite bathrooms. Breakfast included in Carnival rate. ④/⑦

Schultzi's, 35 Fitt St, Woodbrook, ☎622 7521. Most rooms have TV, fridge, bathroom en suite and fans. Fancy wood-panelled bar and a large aquarium with tropical fish in the back yard. Helpful host, good value for money. Breakfast included in Carnival rate. Minimum stay during Carnival week is 7 nights. ④/⑦

Sundeck Suites, 42–44 Picton St, Newton, 622 9560 or 9561. Brand new self-catering apartments with kitchenette, ceiling fans, fridge, en suite bathroom and TV; half of them also have a small balcony. There's a sun deck on the roof, and facilities for the disabled. ⑤/⑦

Ville de French, 5 French St, Woodbrook, ☎625 4776. Large rooms in an old, well-located colonial house, all with fans and sinks. The friendly hosts will arrange tours for you. Excellent value. Breakfast included in the Carnival rate. Minimum stay during Carnival week is 7 nights. ③/⑥

Williams Villa, 69 Luis St, Woodbrook, ☎628 0824. Comfortable, homely atmosphere if you don't mind the religious stickers everywhere. Spacious rooms with a-c, cable TV, fridge and en-suite bathroom. Breakfast included. Jacuzzi in back yard. ⑤/⑦

Downtown

Dating back to the 1780s, Port of Spain's **downtown** area is the oldest part of the city. Despite its run-down appearance, this is the **shopping** and **finance centre** of the capital, constantly reinventing itself in a frenzy of modernization. Within the compact grid of streets surrounding broad **Brian Lara Promenade** and bustling **Frederick Street**, the latest shops jostle for space with old Spanish warehouses, coffee exporters' offices, finance houses and the paraphernalia of the docks, while the thoroughfares are jammed with traffic, pedestrians and pavement vendors.

Around the docks

Port of Spain scarcely presents its most picturesque face to the visitor on arrival; whether you've come from the airport, disembarked from a boat, or travelled by bus from another part of the island, your first sight of the capital will probably be the gritty industrial area **around the docks** at the southernmost edge of the city. This is the nexus of the city's transport system, the location of the **King's Wharf** docks and the **Citygate** bus station. Within its tangle of congested roads and transport terminals, however, are a couple of curious relics of the colonial cra.

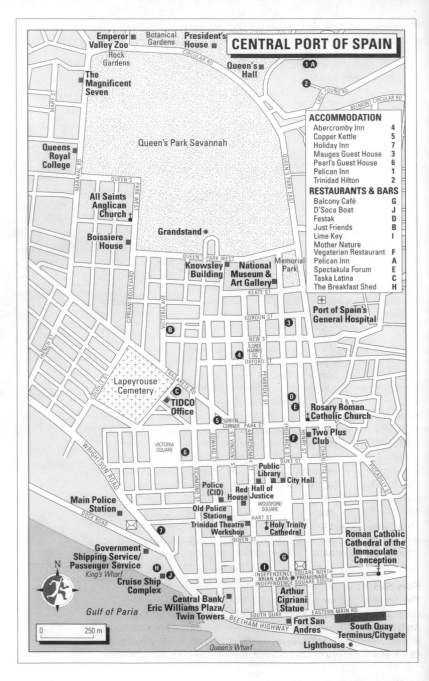

CENTRAL PORT OF SPAIN

Emperor Valley Zoo
Botanical Gardens
President's House
Rock Gardens
Queen's Hall
The Magnificent Seven

Queen's Park Savannah

Queens Royal College

All Saints Anglican Church †

Boissiere House

Grandstand •

ACCOMMODATION
Abercromby Inn   4
Copper Kettle   5
Holiday Inn   7
Mauges Guest House   3
Pearl's Guest House 6
Pelican Inn   1
Trinidad Hilton   2

RESTAURANTS & BARS
Balcony Café   G
D'Soca Boat   J
Festak   D
Just Friends   B
Lime Key   I
Mother Nature
Vegaterian Restaurant   F
Pelican Inn   A
Spectakula Forum   E
Taska Latina   C
The Breakfast Shed   H

Knowsley Building
National Museum & Art Gallery
Memorial Park

Port of Spain's General Hospital

Lapeyrouse Cemetery

TIDCO Office

Rosary Roman Catholic Church †

Two Plus Club

Victoria Square

Public Library

Police (CID)
Red House
Hall of Justice
City Hall

Main Police Station

Old Police Station
Trinidad Theatre Workshop
Holy Trinity Cathedral

Government Shipping Service/Passenger Service
King's Wharf

Cruise Ship Complex

Roman Catholic Cathedral of the Immaculate Conception

N

Central Bank/Eric Williams Plaza/Twin Towers

Arthur Cipriani Statue

Gulf of Paria

0   250 m

Independence Square North
Brian Lara Promenade
Independence Square South

South Quay

Fort San Andres

South Quay Terminus/Citygate

Lighthouse •

Queen's Wharf

King's Wharf and the Cruise Ship Complex

With its busy docks, vast warehouses and jagged skyline of cranes and gantries, King's Wharf is the hub of Trinidad's booming import-export trade. Everything from imported cars to green bananas passes through this hectic port, as dockers heave cargoes onto pick-up trucks, administrators scuttle about with sheaves of paperwork, and entrepreneurs fume while customs clearance grinds its slow and painstaking course. Most of the action takes place in the early hours, when it's still relatively cool; activity gradually slows as the temperature rises.

The deep-water harbour, dredged in the 1930s, allowed Port of Spain to accommodate deep-draught ships, boosting Trinidad's economy and consolidating the city's position as the most important port in the southern Caribbean. It is also the **arrival** and **departure point** for boats to other Caribbean islands, and to **Venezuela**. The **Cruise Ship Complex** on King's Wharf caters for cruise passengers in their few hours on dry land. When a ship is docked it comes alive in a frenetic burst of activity, with shops selling souvenirs and duty free goods, and an overpriced craft market outside. When the ship leaves, most of the shops close and the complex becomes a ghost town.

South Quay Bus Terminus/Citygate

Commonly referred to as **Citygate**, the grand Victorian stone building on South Quay, just to the east of the docks, was originally Port of Spain's **train station**. The railway, established in 1876 with a line to Arima, was shut down in the 1960s and is now remembered with nostalgia as Trinidad's roads become increasingly traffic-clogged. Citygate remains the hub of Trinidad's transport system, however, and is now the terminus for PTSC buses and maxi taxis running to all parts of the country.

Port of Spain's **lighthouse**, built to warn fishermen away from the rocky coastline, has since been marooned inland by reclamation. It now stands, looking somewhat bewildered and out of place, in the middle of a traffic island on Wrightson Road behind Citygate. The heavy traffic that thunders past has turned the lighthouse into a Trinidadian leaning tower of Pisa, skewing it 5° from the vertical. It is not open to the public, and its only function today is to serve as an advertisement hoarding for a local paint company.

Fort San Andres

The unassuming terracotta-painted building that stands between Citygate and the maxi taxi terminus on Broadway is **Fort San Andres**, the best example of a wooden Spanish fort in Trinidad. Built in 1787, it was Port of Spain's main defence when the British invaded ten years later. Recently restored, the fort has been earmarked as

---

Port of
Spain

*Global Steam
Ship Company
(☎ 625 2547)
boats sail from
Port of Spain
to Marguerita
(12hr, TT$587)
and Guiria
(4hr, TT$486)
in Venezuela
every Tuesday;
also weekly to
St Vincent,
Barbados and
St Lucia.*

*See pp.60–61
for details of
buses from
Citygate.*

a future museum, but the plans seem dogged by uncertainty and the building remains closed to the public. When the fort was built, the sea would have lapped against its southern stone rampart; now the cannons, which once confronted arriving ships, overlook a car park, and the nearest shoreline is occupied by the busy docks. An old steam engine, a forlorn relic of Trinidad's long-vanished railway, stands at the edge of the fort.

Brian Lara Promenade/Independence Square

The wide boulevard that runs the width of the city centre just north of the docks is **Brian Lara Promenade/Independence Square**. It consists of two parallel streets, divided by a paved area, that have recently been refurbished with benches and chess tables, making it a popular after-work hang-out where locals lime on the benches, stalls are set up against closed offices and street food vendors do a brisk trade. During the festival season, the promenade hosts **free concerts** and performances, advertised in the local press and radio.

The cumbersome moniker is a result of frequent name changes in recent decades. Until independence in 1962, the thoroughfare was called Marine Square (the land had been reclaimed from the sea in 1816); there's still a sign bearing this name at the centre of the promenade. Rechristened Independence Square in 1962, it was recently renamed again in honour of Trinidad's most famous cricketer. Most locals still call it Independence Square, while media and tourist publications use both names. This has resulted in an official compromise: the two parallel streets are named Independence Square north and south, while the paved area between them is known as the promenade.

The western end of the promenade is dominated by the twin towers of the **Central Bank of Trinidad and Tobago**. Opened in 1985, the two 22-storey buildings are the highest in Trinidad. The heart of Port of Spain's **financial district**, the complex houses the Central Bank, the Prime Minister's offices and the Central Bank Auditorium. Halfway down, at the junction with Frederick Street, is the **Arthur Cipriani statue**. A white French Creole who had served in the British West Indian Regiment during World War I, Cipriani campaigned energetically for compulsory education and self-government for the island. As president of the Trinidad Workingman's Association (later the Trinidad Labour Party) and mayor of the city in the 1920s, he was the only legislator of his day to defend workers' rights, though by the following decade his increasingly reformist stance had disillusioned many former supporters. He died in 1945 and is buried in the Lapeyrouse Cemetery in Woodbrook (see p.80).

*The UCW
Drag Brothers
Mall is open
10am–5pm.*

Just east of the statue, opposite the *Royal Castle* fast-food outlet, is the **UCW Drag Brothers Mall**. Locally known as the **"Drag Mall"**, the ten small shops specialize in handmade leather

sandals, local arts and crafts and Rastafarian souvenirs. If none of
the sandals take your fancy, you can order a pair to be made to your
own design.

As you continue east down the promenade, you come to the
imposing **Roman Catholic Cathedral of the Immaculate
Conception**, another legacy of Governor Woodford's post-fire
reconstruction. Catholicism, the religion of the Spanish-French
Creole establishment, had come to play a major role in the political
and cultural life of Trinidad, and Woodford, though himself an
Anglican, realized a building appropriate to state occasions was
required.The twin-towered Gothic cathedral took sixteen years to
build, and was finally completed in 1836. The ironwork frame was
shipped from England, while the blue metal stone came from the
local Laventille quarries; for the high altar, **Florentine** marble was
imported from Italy. Period drawings on display in the National
Museum show that when the church was completed, on newly
reclaimed land, the sea lapped against its eastern wall. In 1984, the
cathedral underwent extensive renovations, including the addition
of sixteen new **stained glass windows**, made to order in Ireland,
which depict the many ethnic groups which have contributed to the
population of Trinidad and Tobago. The church is open to all, and
has services every evening and on Sundays. All Catholic holidays
are celebrated; special masses are held at Christmas, Easter and on
Ash Wednesday.

The promenade comes to an end just east of the cathedral at
Columbus Square. Despite its brightly painted statue of the explorer, the square is very run-down, with beggars hanging out on the
street corner.

Frederick Street and around

Frederick Street is Port of Spain's main shopping drag, a narrow
street crammed with shops and malls selling clothes, shoes, materials and souvenirs; its pavements are thronged with street vendors
selling homemade jewellery, belts, and arts and crafts. Like much
of the downtown area, it's in the throes of modernization, with new
malls and expensive international-style shops opening every
month. At the **People's Mall** on the corner of Frederick and Queen
streets, small stalls and tiny shops sell clothes and shoes imported
straight from New York, alongside hand-painted T-shirts, incense
and Rasta craft.

Woodford Square

Halfway up Frederick Street, the pretty, tree-shaded **Woodford
Square** is named after the British governor who created it in the
early nineteenth century. Its western side is dominated by the grand
Edwardian facade of the **Red House**, seat of Trinidad and Tobago's
parliament. On the south side stands the city's **Anglican Cathedral**,

*The Chee
Mooke Bakery
on the north
side of
Columbus
Square sells
the most deli-
cious bread in
town. Open
Mon–Sat
6am–6pm.*

while in the square itself are a picturesque colonial bandstand and an elegant, if not always functional, cast-iron fountain supported by mermaids and mermen, which dates back to 1866.

Woodford Square is best known, however, as a centre of **political activism**. As early as 1903 it was the scene of a protest meeting against the introduction of new water rates; the demonstration got rapidly out of hand, and in the ensuing riots the original Red House was burned to the ground. It was in 1956, however, that the square's reputation as a political cockpit really got going with the establishment of the "University of Woodford Square". This was the brainchild of **Eric Williams**, historian, father of the national independence movement and first prime minister of the country, who would deliver weekly public lectures in the square on the issues of the day. In the 1970s, the square became a focal point for the Black Power movement, who renamed it the "people's parliament". It held the largest funeral ever seen in Port of Spain, that of Basil Davis, a young Black Power member shot by the police.

Debates from Woodford Square are broadcast on Power Radio, 102FM, on Wednesdays at 7.30pm.

To the present day, Woodford Square remains a lively political forum where issues are fiercely debated. In the southeast corner, a blackboard lists the topic for discussion each day. Predominantly middle-aged men argue passionately about contemporary issues, from local affairs to international events. Anyone can join in, if they can get a word in edgeways; it's not a platform for the faint-hearted or softly-spoken.

Members of the public can view the parliament in session on Fridays at 1.30pm; use the entrance on Knox St.

The Red House

Beneath its massive green copper cupola, the imposing neo-Renaissance **Red House** is actually more a faded terracotta. The seat of Trinidad and Tobago's parliament inherited its popular name from an earlier building on the site, which was painted bright red to celebrate Queen Victoria's diamond jubilee in 1897. The present structure, completed four years after its predecessor was burnt down in the 1903 water riots, was itself attacked in the coup (see box opposite), and bullet holes still scar the stonework. Outside the front entrance, facing Woodfood Square, an eternal flame commemorates government and security personnel who died in the 1990 coup.

The Public Library, Hall of Justice and City Hall

On the northwest side of Woodford Square stands the **Trinidad Public Library**, built in 1901. Newspapers are pasted up daily outside the main entrance of this large cream stone building, incongruously sandwiched between two brutally functional modern slabs of glass and concrete. To its left is the **Hall of Justice**; built in 1979, it houses the Supreme Court of Trinidad and Tobago. To the right of the library is the 1961 **City Hall**, home to Port of Spain's city council and the mayor's office.

The 1990 coup

At 6.30pm on the evening of July 27, 1990, **Abu Bakr,** leader of the fun-
damentalist revolutionary group **Jamaat-al-Muslimeen,** announced on
television that he had overthrown the government of Trinidad and Tobago.
Thirty minutes earlier, members of the group had stormed the Red House
and taken several government ministers, including Prime Minister **Arthur
Robinson,** as hostages. The police headquarters round the corner on
Sackville Street was firebombed and practically destroyed (see overleaf).
Looting took the capital by storm, and a **state of emergency** was
enforced, requiring all citizens to remain indoors after dark.

The Jamaat-al-Muslimeen had already had many run-ins with the authorities over a land dispute and the killing of one of its members by the police.
Relying on the army to support the revolt, they also hoped to capitalize on
public discontent with the government's harsh fiscal policies, satirized by
the calypsonian Sparrow in his song "Capitalism Gone Mad". Yet however
little love they may have had for the government, few Trinidadians were
willing to support its violent overthrow by an armed group of religious
extremists. With little public support, and surrounded by loyal government
troops, the rebels surrendered after a six-day siege. Abu Bakr and his colleagues were tried and sentenced to death, but the judgement was overturned on appeal, and the coup leaders are at liberty today.

Many Trinidadians found it hard to believe that such events could take
place in stable, democratic, fun loving Trinidad. With characteristic
humour, the crisis was soon turned into a fund of amusing stories. Ask any
Trinidadian about the coup and you will hear tales of wild **"curfew parties"** and imaginative explanations given to the police of the five TVs found
in a neighbour's house.

Holy Trinity Cathedral

The Anglican **Holy Trinity Cathedral** on the south side of Woodford
Square was another of the governor's many initiatives to improve the
public spaces of Port of Spain. The original idea was to build it in the
middle of the square itself, and work was already under way when
Woodford bowed to popular protest and moved it to its present site.
This elegant stone church was built in 1818 on traditional Gothic
lines, with a large clock tower. The cool, shady interior is relatively
unadorned, its outstanding feature the mahogany hammer-beam
roof, made in England and modelled on a medieval original in
London's Westminster Hall. A life-size **effigy of Governor Woodford**
lies on his tomb by the south wall; the plaques nearby commemorate
various other colonial dignitaries.

Trinidad Theatre Workshop

The dilapidated stone building opposite the Holy Trinity Cathedral,
on the corner of Hart and Abercromby streets, is the home of the
Trinidad Theatre Workshop (TTW). Founded in 1959 by poet and
playwright Derek Walcott, it established a theatrical tradition in
Trinidad, made acting a recognized profession and launched the

careers of many of the Caribbean's most famous actors. Errol Jones, Stanley Marshal and Albert Labeau were all influential in the development of the TTW, and among the many actors to cut their teeth here was Helen Camp, who went on to establish the internationally successful Trinidad Tent Theatre.

Although the TTW enjoyed its heyday in the 1960s and 1970s, Walcott's 1992 Nobel Prize for literature inspired a regeneration of the centre, giving rise to a new generation of talented Trinidadian actors. Many who were influenced by the TTW – including Roger Roberts, Wendell Manwarren and Cecilia Salazar – were in turn instrumental in the establishment of prestigious local theatre groups such as the Bagasse Company. The TTW holds workshops in acting, dance and deportment, as well as staging plays in a small theatre in the building. Walcott's plays are still the main focus of its productions, though it also stages work by other Caribbean playwrights, and English classics with a local twist.

The Trinidad Theatre Workshop is open to the public while courses and lessons are running, and anyone can participate in these for a small fee. Courses range from one-day workshops to week- and month-long events. For a current programme, ring ☎624 4681.

The Old Police Station

Contrary to appearances, the ruined building just west of Woodford Square at the corner of Sackville and Vincent streets is not an ancient monument, but wreckage of the **Old Police Station** that was firebombed in the 1990 coup. While some maintain that it's an eyesore that ought to be demolished, others would prefer it to remain as a warning to any who might think of following in the Jamaat-al-Muslimeen's footsteps. The police still occupy a small part of the building, although a new headquarters has been built on the other side of the road.

The emblem of Trinidad and Tobago's police force displayed on all police vehicles and police stations consists of a hummingbird and a police badge inside a Star of David. The hummingbird is the national symbol which replaced the crown after independence, while the star is a colonial leftover that has given rise to much confusion. Contrary to popular belief, it is not the Jewish Star of David but the symbol of Governor Picton's patron saint, St David.

Rosary Church

At the corner of Henry and Park streets stands the **Rosary Church**. Built between 1892 and 1910, this dignified Gothic Revival church is if anything more impressive than either of the city's cathedrals, though its imposing towers and ornate stonework are hemmed in by buildings on all sides. You're in luck if you find it open, for the spacious interior is an oasis of peace in the hectic city, and the old **stained glass**, with its finely detailed Biblical scenes, is the most beautiful in Port of Spain. Unfortunately the effect is somewhat spoilt by the neon lighting, peeling paint and general dilapidation; the church is currently fundraising for repair work.

Uptown

Ranged around the broad, grassy expanse of the **Queen's Park Savannah** and framed by the foothills of the Northern Range, Port of Spain's uptown district oozes prosperity. Along the wide boulevards that ring the Savannah, the palatial mansions of the colonial plantocracy compete with the *Trinidad Hilton*, the residences of the republic's president and prime minister, and the glitzy modern headquarters of insurance companies. Away from this circuit of roads, which forms Port of Spain's busiest one-way system, the streets exude the sober opulence of embassy quarters the world over, untouched by the urban razzmatazz of downtown Port of Spain.

Queen's Park Savannah

The **Queen's Park Savannah** is Port of Spain's largest open space. Within the 3.7-kilometre circuit of its perimeter roads, its grassy expanse is crisscrossed by paths and shaded by the spreading branches of old samaan trees. Originally part of the St Ann's sugarcane estate, the Savannah was bought by Governor Woodford in 1817 to be developed into a city park. Subsequent attempts to build on parts of it were seen off by vigorous public protest, and the park has remained its original size.

Often deserted during the hot daylight hours, the Savannah comes to life after 4pm, with football games, joggers and couples and families taking an early evening stroll. It is particularly busy between 4pm and 8pm, when temporary food stalls, serving tasty local snacks such as roasted corn, bake and shark and rotis are set up. People take their daily constitutional, sit and chat on the benches lining the circumference of the park, or play football and cricket; and in the windy months of March and April, the Savannah is full of children flying kites.

The **Trinidad Turf Club** at the southern end of the park was once Trinidad's premier horse racing track. The races have now moved to Arima (see p.145), but all the Carnival competitions, including **Panorama, Dimanche Gras, Parade of the Bands** and **Champs in Concert**, are held in the grandstands. Many other events take place here, including performances by visiting international artists. Though the seats are numbingly hard, the setting is incomparably atmospheric, with performances taking place against a backdrop of the mountains and the starry Caribbean sky.

Right in the middle of the Savannah, in total contrast to the public conviviality taking place all round, is an eerie enclave of silence. From behind its high stone wall, the **Peschier family cemetery** – burial ground of the owners of the St Ann's estate – exudes an air of mystery. The graveyard is closed to the public, and all that can be seen over the wall is an ancient and towering palm tree.

See the Carnival calendar of events on pp.94–95 for detailed descriptions of the various Carnival competitions.

Queen's Park West

Travelling clockwise around the Savannah on **Queen's Park West**, you
will come across numerous examples of "gingerbread" architecture
built by the Glaswegian architect George Brown, who had the distinctive fretted woodwork mass-produced and used it extensively on all his
buildings. Built in 1904, the ornately decorated **Knowsley Building** on
the corner of Chancery Lane resembles a child's fantasy doll's house;
it's odd to think that it now houses government offices. The **George
Brown House** at the corner of Stanmore Avenue is somewhat plainer,
though still graced by a great deal of refined fretwork. **Boissiere
House** on the corner of Cipriani Boulevard is fondly called the
"Gingerbread House" by locals, and you'd be hard pushed to find a
better example of the style. It's a splendidly whimsical concoction of
fretted wooden finials and bargeboards, with stained glass depicting
meandering strawberry vines and a small pagoda-like roof over one
room. None of these buildings is open to the public, which is a pity,
since their interiors are reputed to be just as graceful and imaginative.

National Museum and Art Gallery

*The National
Museum and
Art Gallery is
open Tues–Sat
10am–6pm;
free. Leave
bags at the
door with the
security
guard.*
☎ *623 5941
or 624 6477*

*There is now
a sign*

The large white gabled building at the corner of Frederick and Keate
streets is the **National Museum and Art Gallery**, although there's no
sign to announce the fact; it still has the legend **Royal Victoria
Institute** inscribed over its door, recalling the fact that it was built in
1892 as part of the preparations for Queen Victoria's jubilee.

The collection is an extensive one, however, covering everything
from early **Amerindian history** to the technology of the **oil industry**.
Unfortunately, many of the artefacts are unlabelled, and where information is provided, it is poorly displayed. One of the more interesting displays charts the development of the **steel drum** as a musical
instrument (see p.302). A slightly dusty collection of old **Carnival
costumes** does scant justice to the art form, though it does give some
idea of the detailed work involved, and the photographs of previous
Carnival kings and queens provides a glimpse of the skill of
Trinidad's mas makers and designers.

The upper floor is occupied by a permanent exhibition of
Trinidadian art, ranging from lithographs of the old Port of Spain by
Michel Cazabon to the work of internationally known contemporary
artists such as **Carlisle Chang, Leroy Clarke, Vera and Ralph
Baney, Nina Squires** and **Dermot Lousion**. Many of the works draw
on Trinidadian folklore, with depictions of Papa Bois, a friendly spirit who saves animals from hunters; the Soucouyant, a woman who
turns into a ball of fire to suck human blood; and La Diablesse, who
leads drunken men astray and then throws them into thorn bushes.

The "Magnificent Seven"

North of Queen's Park West on Maraval Road stands a bizarre group
of mansions affectionately known as the **Magnificent Seven**. A

magical-realist parade of European architectural styles with a tropical slant, these remarkable buildings are the result of the competing egos of rival plantation owners, each of whom tried to outdo his neighbour in grandeur. All the mansions were constructed in 1904, except for Hayes Court, which was built in 1910. Although none of the buildings is open to the public, their exteriors are easily visible from the road.

The first of the seven is **Queen's Royal College**, Trinidad's most prestigious school, whose former pupils include the authors VS and Shiva Naipaul, and the country's first prime minister, Eric Williams. It is built in German Renaissance style, with arcaded balconies and cream and ochre stucco offsetting the blue limestone cornerstones; the tall clock tower can be seen from many parts of Port of Spain.

Hayes Court, home to the Anglican bishop of Trinidad, is next, a grand mansion displaying a mix of French and British architectural influences. **Mille Fleurs** is an elaborate gingerbread house, with intricate wooden fretwork. Now the office of the National Security Council, it was originally built for Dr Henrique Prada, a successful doctor who went on to become the city's most distinguished mayor between 1914 and 1917.

Roomor, a florid exercise in the French Baroque style, was commissioned by the estate owner Lucien Ambard. The fabric of the building includes marble imported from Italy and tiles from France, while its columns, galleries, towers and pinnacles are decorated with elaborate ironwork. The **Archbishop's House**, official residence of the Roman Catholic Archbishop of Port of Spain, is a weighty neo-Romanesque pile of Irish marble and red granite, capped by a copper roof.

The next house along is **Whitehall**, a Venetian-style palazzo whose gleaming white paintwork gives it the air of a newly iced birthday cake. Originally the home of a cocoa estate owner called Agostini, the building has subsequently had a somewhat chequered career. During World War II it was commandeered by the US military, after which it became a cultural centre, a library and then a broadcasting unit. In 1954 it was sold to the Trinidadian government and now houses some of its departments.

The most outlandish structure of the seven, **Killarney**, stands at the northern end of Maraval Road just before it turns east into Circular Road. A fairytale castle of brick and limestone, bristling with turrets and spires, it was built for a German plantation owner called Stollmeyer by the Scottish architect Robert Giles, who modelled it on Queen Victoria's residence at Balmoral. The delicious absurdity of this fantasy has been perfectly captured by the architectural historian John Newel Lewis: "A German built a bit of an untypical Scottish castle in Trinidad and called it by an Irish name. He must have been by that time a Trinidadian, because only Trinidadians do these things." The Stollmeyer family sold the castle to the Trinidadian government in 1979, and it now houses government offices.

*The Emperor
Valley Zoo is
open daily
9.30am–6pm,
last tickets sold
5.30pm. Adults
TT$4, children
(3–12) TT$2.*

*The Botanic
Gardens are
open daily
6am–6pm;
free.*

Emperor Valley Zoo and Botanic Gardens

On the northern side of the Savannah is the **Emperor Valley Zoo**. Opened in 1952, its collection of local and foreign animals – though small by international standards – is reputedly the most extensive in the Caribbean, and includes many species of deer, a large selection of monkeys, snakes, parrots, ocelots and the odd crocodile.

Next door, the exquisite **Botanic Gardens**, established in 1820 by Governor Woodford and the botanist David Lockhart, contain the oldest collection of exotic plants and trees in the western hemisphere. There is no official guide, though some knowledgeable Trinidadians frequent the garden, and may offer to show you round for a small fee. The plants are labelled with their botanical names, though many of the more unusual trees have acquired nicknames such as the "Hat Stand", "Raw Beef" and "Napoleon's Hat". A small cemetery, partly fenced off from the rest of the gardens, contains the crumbling gravestones of Lockhart and many of the island's governors, including Solomon Hochoy. Beneath the Palmiste palms, a plaque marks another burial, that of an Australian wallaby, a pet of the Prince of Wales which died during his visit to the island.

Behind the Botanic Gardens, in well manicured gardens, stands the **President's House**. This austere, stately villa was built in 1876 as the residence of the island's British governors, and continued to fulfil that function until independence in 1962. A good view of the building can be gained from the Botanic Gardens, but the grounds are not open to the public. The **Prime Minister's Residence** is hidden from view behind the President's House, and closed to the public.

The western suburbs

Crammed between the Gulf of Paria to the south and the uphill incline of the Northern Range, the **western suburbs** of Port of Spain are the cultural centre of the capital. For most of the year, the area looks purely residential, but as **Carnival** draws near, many of the houses are converted into mas camps, where the bands who organize the parades have their bases. The creative energy of **Carnival production** is concentrated in **Woodbrook**, while the streets of **St James** are alive with partying revellers every night of the week. The prosperous residential area of **St Clair** is far more sedate and aloof, while the thriving commercial centre of **Newton** has become the base for much of Trinidad's media.

Woodbrook

The elegant old district of **WOODBROOK** stretches for about a kilometre across the flat expanse between **Tragarete Road**, **Phillip Street** and the **Maraval River**. The area was originally a sugar cane estate owned by the Siegert family, creators of Trinidad's famous Angostura Bitters (see p.38), and many local streets – such as Carlos,

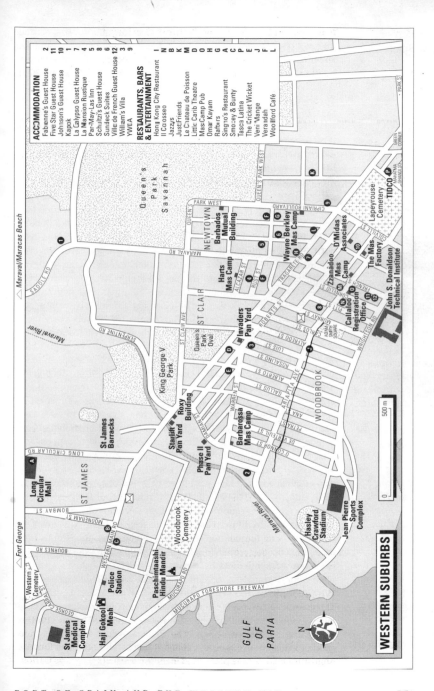

ACCOMMODATION

Fabenne's Guest House	2
Five Star Guest House	11
Johnson's Guest House	10
Kapok	1
La Calypso Guest House	7
La Mansion Rustique	4
Par–May–Las Inn	5
Schultz's Guest House	8
Sundeck Suites	6
Ville de French Guest House	12
William's Villa	3
YWCA	9

RESTAURANTS, BARS & ENTERTAINMENT

Hong Kong City Restaurant	I
Il Crosseo	N
JazzyS	B
JustFriends	K
Le Chateau de Poisson	M
Little Carib Theatre	D
MasCamp Pub	O
Omar Kayam	H
Rafters	G
Singno's Restaurant	A
Smockey & Bunty	C
Tasca Latina	P
The Cricket Wicket	E
Veni Mange	J
Veradah	F
Woolford Café	L

Queen's Park Savannah

Maraval/Maracas Beach

Fort George

NEWTOWN

Barbados Mutual Building

Harts Mas Camp

Wayne Berkley Mas Camp

D'Midas Associates

Zzanadoo Mas Camp

The Mas Factory

Callaloo Registration Office

John S. Donaldson Technical Institute

Lapeyrouse Cemetery

TIDCO

Invaders Pan Yard

Queen's Park Oval

King George V Park

Starlift Pan Yard

Roxy Building

Barbarossa Mas Camp

Phase II Pan Yard

ST CLAIR

WOODBROOK

St James Barracks

ST JAMES

Long Circular Mall

Woodbrook Cemetery

Paschimtaashi Hindu Mandir

Police Station

Haji Gokool Meah

St James Medical Complex

Western Cemetery

Hasley Crawford Stadium

Jean Pierre Sports Complex

Maraval River

Mucurapo Foreshore Freeway

GULF OF PARIA

500 m

N

Port of Spain

Luis and Siegert streets – bear their names. The suburb, first settled in 1911, was traditionally a middle-class residential area, and its streets are still graced by old houses with wonderful fretwork barge-boards, delicate balustrades and finials. Though it has become increasingly commercialized in recent decades, it is a safe and pleasantly nightspots.

Lapeyrouse Cemetery is open daily 6am–6pm.

At the edge of Woodbrook, on Phillip Street, is the entrance to the **Lapeyrouse Cemetery**, a walled burial ground dating back to 1813. Victorian tombs adorned with Gothic spires, angels and ornate fretwork are eerily framed against the lush, tropical backdrop; long strands of ivy trail over the unkempt graves, while gravediggers, shaded by makeshift tents, dig spaces for new residents. The Siegert family is buried here, as are the Trinidadian labour leader Arthur Cipriani, the Calysponian Melody, and Charlie King, the policeman killed in the Butler Riots in the 1930s (see p.193). The names on the gravestones bear witness to the diverse origins – Chinese, Spanish, African, Indian and European – of Port of Spain's inhabitants, and the inscriptions reflect its varied religious affiliations: Catholics, Anglicans, Baptists and many other faiths are represented here. The cemetery's newest residents, the vagrants who sleep in the more dilapidated tombs, have become a talking point in recent years, provoking press articles about the problem of homelessness.

The Queen's Park Oval is open 8am–4pm; ask the security guard on the gate to let you in. Seats cost TT$ 55 in the stands, TT$100/ 150 in the covered area. For information call ☎ 622 2295 or 3787.

At the western end of **Tragarete Road** – a mix of shops, restaurants and offices – stands the **Queen's Park Oval**. Originally built in 1896, this is Trinidad's premier **cricket ground**, hosting national and international matches in season (Feb–April), as well as other sporting events and exhibitions. Cricket fans should try to see a Test Match here; it's a unique experience. The game is a national obsession in Trinidad, and matches are followed with passion, especially if local hero Brian Lara is playing. The atmosphere is rowdy but good natured, with music blaring from a sound system after every over and wicket, while vendors sell cold beer, nuts and roti round the stands. All events are advertised in the local media.

The Callaloo registration office is open Nov–Feb; ☎ 634 4491 for current information.

The streets of Woodbrook are home to numerous **mas camps**, which burst into life during Carnival season, from November to February. Now famous for its calypso nights, the **Mas Camp Pub** (see p.93) on the corner of Ariapita Avenue and French Street was once the workshop and headquarters of Peter Minshall's Callaloo mas camp, which subsequently relocated to Chaguaramas (see p.107). The **Callaloo registration office**, where Minshall's Carnival designs are displayed, is still located next door. You can register here to play with the Callaloo band – usually around 3000 masqueraders, all wearing costumes designed by Peter Minshall. Like other mas camps, Callaloo displays the designs from which you can choose your costume – prices start from TT$800.

The **Zzanadoo** mas camp, diagonally opposite the *Mas Camp Pub*, is a relative newcomer to the scene and rapidly establishing an enviable reputation. The long-established **Mas Factory**, run by Albert Bailey one block away on Buller Street, is famous for its portrayal of traditional characters and skilful wire bending. They'll let you watch the Carnival costumes being made if you ring in advance (☎628 7600). Round the corner at 15–17 Kitchener St, **D'Midas Associates** also provide good examples of traditional Carnival design with lots of feathers, sequins and beading – all the painstaking, handmade work which is gradually being cut out by more

---

Mas camps

Mas camps – the headquarters of the Carnival bands – are usually established in old gingerbread family homes. During the Carnival months furniture is stored away and the largest room turns into a workshop full of feathers, sequins and sewing machines. Some of the long-established camps have now become year-round mas factories. The camps provide a focus for the whole Trinidadian art community; many a famous Trinidadian artist, actor, dancer or writer will be found at a mas camp during the Carnival season.

All the bands display some ten to twenty designs, representing the different sections of the band, at their camp in the run-up to Carnival. Anyone can choose a costume from the designs, and watch as it is made. In recent years costumes have increasingly catered to the masqueraders' desire to wear as little as possible in the tropical heat, though Minshall and a few others still make more elaborate, artistic creations.

The list below represents a selection of the best mas camps in Port of Spain: for a full list of bands, contact TIDCO, ☎627 5912. Near Carnival time, the bands are often listed in the newspapers.

Barbarossa
26 Taylor St, Woodbrook,
☎ 628 6008
(Richard Affong)

Big Mike, Ian & Friends
88 Roberts St, Woodbrook,
☎ 622 7466
(Mike Antoine/Ian McKenzie)

Callaloo Company
Western Main Rd, Chaguaramas,
☎ 634 4491
(Peter Minshall)

D'Midas Associates
15–17 Kitchener St, Woodbrook,
☎ 622 8233
(Stephen Derek)

Harts Ltd
5 Alcazar St, St Clair,
☎ 622 8038
(Thais & Gerald Hart)

Mas Factory
15 Buller St, Woodbrook,
☎ 628 7600
(Albert Bailey)

Masquerade
49–51 Cipriani Blvd, Newton
☎ 625 7257
(Wayne Berkeley)

Old Fashioned Sailors
51 Pelham St, Belmont,
☎ 624 3692
(Jason Griffith)

Poison
1 Harrowden Place, Petit Valley,
☎ 632 3986
(Michael Headley)

Zzanadoo
Ariapita Ave, Woodbrook
(Winston Rajah)

For more on Trinidad's Carnival, see p.291.

The
Barbarossa
mas camp is
open 24 hours
during
Carnival
season.

modern, profit-oriented bands. Again, you can see the costumes being made if you ring in advance (☎622 8233). As with all mas camps the opening times are variable, usually opening at 9am and working till at least 10pm.

At the eastern end of Woodbrook, at 26 Taylor St, is the **Barbarossa mas camp**. This popular band attracts the young and beautiful of Port of Spain, and during Carnival season its bikini mas designs are displayed on the porch. Visitors are welcome to view production.

St James

It was in **ST JAMES** that the British landed in 1797. Legend has it that they fortified themselves with rum punch they found here, giving themselves the courage to go on and capture Port of Spain. Once the Peru sugar cane estate, the area was settled by Indian indentured labourers after emancipation. The names they gave to their streets – Calcutta Street, Delhi Street and Madras Street – bear witness to their homesickness.

Today, St James is one of the capital's most cosmopolitan districts, with residents from all the country's ethnic groups. The streets are lined with modern houses with Indianesque capitals on concrete columns and colourful clusters of puja flags in the garden; the upper storeys often remain unfinished, an empty frame of reinforced concrete stilts waiting for the next generation to build upwards. It's a bustling place, especially at night when it becomes the prime liming spot in Port of Spain. Music blasts from cars, bars and clubs, locals dressed in clubbing gear lime alongside old men in jeans and T-shirts, and street stalls sell roti, oysters and corn soup.

The approach to St James from Woodbrook at the start of the Western Main Road is dominated by the imposing **Roxy Building**. It was built as a cinema, but its ritzy classical-moderne colonnade now houses a branch of *Pizza Hut*. On the other side of the road is a statue in tribute to the grandmaster of calypso, **Lord Kitchener** – still alive and performing at fetes and concerts today (see p.300). The entrance to St James itself is marked by the bridge over the Maraval River, on which an ornate green and pink oriental-style **gateway** was built in 1997 to raise visitors' awareness of the suburb and heighten local pride – though whether it has done so is a matter of controversy.

Western Main Road, which runs through the centre of St James is a broad thoroughfare lined with shops, bars and takeaways. Street vendors sell vegetables, incense and crochet work on corners during the day, while at night there is a food stall every couple of metres along the street. Halfway down the road, **St James Market** fills the air with the smell of fresh fish and meat in the early mornings. There are some old gingerbread houses, mostly turned over to commercial use – look out for the lottery outlet with the red, gold and green surrounding wall. Towards the western end of the road, the **Haji Gokool Meah Mosque** is one of the oldest in Trinidad. Built in 1927, this tiny white and green minareted building is characteristic of the Muslim places of worship found throughout the island; it is not open to the public.

Western Main Road is most notable, however, as the scene of the annual Muslim **Hosay** processions, which take place over four days in May or June (see box below). In the weeks running up to Hosay, it is possible to watch the craftsmen building the ornate minareted tombs made from bamboo and coloured paper (**tadjahs**) that are carried in procession; the houses where they work have large flags planted in their yards.

There are just five families who build the structures each year. Four are based in St James and one in Cocorite. They have to be approved by a local committee, and strict rules apply – they must be the direct descendants of Indian immigrants with an ancestral tradition of *tadjah* building. The task involves great financial, physical and spiritual sacrifice; the materials can cost up to TT$30,000, and the builders have to fast during daylight hours and refrain from alcohol and sexual activity for the duration. Understandably, perhaps, not many of the younger generation find the prospect appealing, and as the years pass fewer and fewer *tadjahs* are being built.

Hosay

The Islamic festival of **Hosay**, commemorating the martyrdom of Mohammed's grandsons Hussein and Hassan during the *jihad* (Holy War) in Persia, has been celebrated in Trinidad ever since the first Indian Muslims arrived in 1845. Its exposure to the island's other cultures turned it into something carnivalesque, with lewd dancing and loud music, but local Shi'a Muslims have recently taken great pains to restore the occasion's solemnity.

Hosay is also celebrated in Curepe, Tunapuna, Couva and Cedros (see p.140, 142, 166 and 196–8 respectively), although the best place to see it is undoubtedly in St James. Trinis of all religions come here to view the festivities, which take place over four days in either May or June. All the parades take place at 11pm at night and continue to the early hours of the morning.

The first procession is **flag night**, when hundreds of devotees walk through the streets with multicoloured flags representing the beginning of the battle of Kerbela, in which the brothers lost their lives.

On the **second night**, two small *tadjahs* are carried slowly through the streets to the throbbing beat of tassa drums.

The **third night** is the most spectacular. Large *tadjahs* more than two metres high are paraded through the streets, while dancers carry two large sickle moons representing the two brothers. At midnight there is the ritual "kissing of the moons", as the dancers symbolize a brotherly embrace.

On the **fourth night** the exquisite *tadjahs* are thrown into the sea, a sacrifice to ensure that prayers for recovery from sickness and adversity will be answered.

Port of Spain

The *tadjah* families also resent the lack of sponsorship from the bars of St James, who make a mint on Hosay night – especially as the festival is supposed to be non-alcoholic. There is talk of reducing the onlookers' alcohol consumption by moving the procession away from the bar-lined Western Main Road to Mucurapo Road and the coastal highway; this would also bring the event closer to the sea where the *tadjahs* are finally disposed of. Watch the press for future developments, and the exact date of the festivities.

The southern edge of St James is bounded by Mucurapo Road and the **Woodbrook Cemetery**, also known as Mucurapo Cemetery. The tombs – few of which date back earlier than the 1920s – are nowhere near as ornate or picturesque as those of Lapeyrouse Cemetery (see p.80), although the grounds are much better tended. The Trinidadian sportsman and aviator Mikey Cipriani is buried here, as are calypsonian Natty Myers and the musician Sel Duncan.

The best time to visit the Paschimtaashi Hindu Mandir Temple is after 2pm, when the pundit is free to show you around; call first to make an appointment (☎ 622 4949).

Off Mucurapo Road at 2b Ethel St is the spectacular **Paschimtaashi Hindu Mandir Temple**. A gleaming white modern interpretation of traditional Hindu religious architecture, the temple has tall round towers and latticed windows enabling you to view the ornate statues of Hindu gods inside. These **murtis** (religious images worshipped by Hindus), brought from India, represent the ten major incarnations of **Lord Vishnu**; at the back of the temple is a shrine to the goddess **Kali**. The temple's pundit, Mr Persaud, is an approachable man who will happily explain the significance of the temple and its sculptures; his approach, informed by comparative religion, is very accessible, and he will refer to the philosophers of all the major religions in his explanation of Hindu beliefs.

Fort George is open 10am–6pm, admission free. Private taxis leave from Bourne's Road corner on Western Main Rd; the fare is around TT$10.

To gain one of the most spectacular views of Port of Spain, it is well worth taking a taxi up to **Fort George**, a popular family picnic spot at weekends, just ten minutes' drive from the Western Main Road. If you're feeling energetic, it's a one-hour walk; after a steep climb on St James Terrace, the incline becomes gentler and it's a relaxing stroll to the top. Built in 1804, the fort defended the island against the French Caribbean fleet during the Napoleonic Wars; you can see the original cannons and cannonballs, and a replica of the dungeon. Stone defensive walls, surviving to a height of one to two metres, surround the wooden signal station designed by the exiled West African Ashanti Prince Kofi Nti. During the nineteenth century, Fort George contained the largest contingent of British troops in the Caribbean. At some point, these soldiers mutinied, although the details, suppressed at the time, are still buried in the depths of British military records.

To the northeast of St James is the residential area of **Federation Park**. Its name, and those of the streets in the area – St Lucia Street, Antigua Drive, St Vincent Avenue and so on – commemorate the idealism of the short-lived West Indies Federation, which lasted from just 1958 to 1962 and collapsed when its two largest members, Jamaica and Trinidad, withdrew (see p.289). During the two world wars this area, along with King George V Park in St James, housed internment facilities for Germans residing on the island. Federation Park is now the home of well-to-do Trinidadians and government officials.

Newton and St Clair

Amid the unlikely surroundings of **NEWTON**, a quiet, predominantly residential suburb, is the mas camp of the band **Masquerade**, run by **Wayne Berkley**. Winner of the prestigious band of the year award eight times in the last 25 years, Berkley designs for Port of Spain, St Vincent, St Martin and Notting Hill carnivals every year. He is famous for strong colours, professional construction and some of the best "bikini mas" designs (see p.292). Visitors are welcome to view production, which takes place from August to mid-January.

The Wayne Berkley Camp, 49–51 Cipriani Blvd, ☎ 625 7257, is open daily 9am–5pm.

Berkley's only serious rival is Peter Minshall, leader of the band Callaloo. An example of his work can be seen up the road at the **Barbados Mutual Building** at 16 Queen Park West, where the lobby is dominated by his 15-metre **mural** made of thousands of sequins tagged to plastic netting, colourfully depicting the flowers and hummingbirds of Trinidad.

ST CLAIR is more upmarket, an enclave of well-to-do Trinidadians whose lavish houses shelter behind high walls, ferocious dogs and sophisticated security systems. It is also home to the long-established **Hart's Mas Camp**, run by the same family since 1959. Famous for their designs of abstract colours and revealing, erotic costumes, the Harts are at the forefront of the development of "bikini mas".

The Hart's Mas Camp, 5 Alcazar St, ☎ 622 8038, is open daily Sept–Jan 8am–4pm.

The eastern suburbs

Port of Spain's **eastern suburbs**, which nestle on the lower slopes of the **Northern Range**, are its oldest. In **Belmont**, original wooden houses survive from the days of its first settlers, while the ramshackle wooden houses of **Laventille** – the city's poorest area, and the birthplace of the steel drum – seem to tumble over one another down the Laventille Hill. The many panyards located in its winding lanes make it an essential stop for the pan enthusiast.

Belmont

BELMONT's maze of narrow winding lanes is one of the most densely populated areas of Port of Spain. The city's first suburb, it was settled in the first half of the nineteenth century by Africans who had escaped slavery on other Caribbean islands. The names of these early residents are commemorated in streets such as Zampty Lane. After emancipation, they were joined by freed slaves from Trinidad and a number of peoples from West Africa. In 1868, the tribal chieftain of the **Rada community** – a religious group from the French protectorate of Dahomey – bought land in the area to establish a settle-

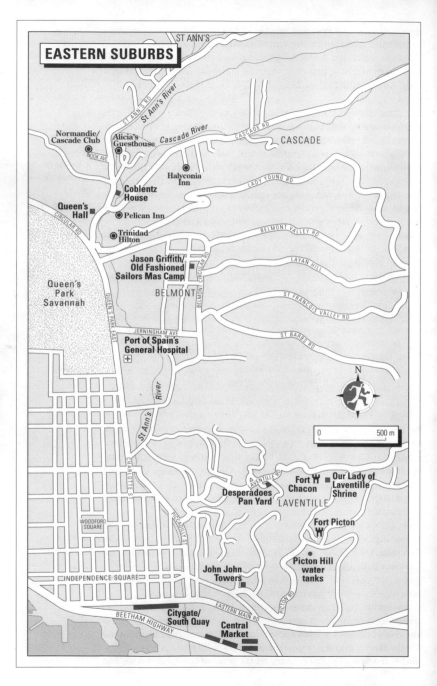

EASTERN SUBURBS

ST ANN'S

ST ANN'S RD
St Ann's River
Cascade River
CASCADE RD
CASCADE

Normandie/
Cascade Club

Alicia's
Guesthouse

NOOK AVE

Halyconia
Inn

LADY YOUNG RD

Coblentz
House

Queen's
Hall

CIRCULAR RD

Pelican Inn

Trinidad
Hilton

BELMONT VALLEY RD

LAYAN HILL

Jason Griffith/
Old Fashioned
Sailors Mas Camp

BELMONT CIRCULAR RD

Queen's
Park
Savannah

QUEEN'S PARK EAST

BELMONT

ST FRANCOIS VALLEY RD

ST BARBS RD

JERNINGHAM AVE

Port of Spain's
General Hospital

N

St Ann's River

0   500 m

CHARLOTTE ST

LAVENTILLE RD

Fort
Chacon

Our Lady of
Laventille
Shrine

Desperadoes
Pan Yard

LAVENTILLE

WOODFORD
SQUARE

Fort Picton

PICCADILLY ST

Picton Hill
water
tanks

INDEPENDENCE SQUARE

John John
Towers

PICTON RD

EASTERN MAIN RD

Citygate/
South Quay

BEETHAM HIGHWAY

Central
Market

ment. Representatives from the Mandingo, Ibo, Yoruba and Krumen tribes also came to live here, and Belmont became an established African settlement. The community was well-organized and close-knit, ensuring the survival of African traditions such as the Orisha religion (see p.295), whose feasts and festivities are still practised in the area.

Port of
Spain

Today, Belmont is home to the mas camp of Jason Griffith's **Old Fashioned Sailors** band. The nautical costume has appeared in Carnival since the nineteenth century, when revellers would impersonate British sailors – a tradition that took on a new satirical edge with the arrival of the US Navy on the island in 1941. Though everyone in the band is dressed as a sailor, each decorates their own costume, so every outfit is unique. Griffith, who has been bringing out his band since 1968, retains a loyal following; his is one of the few bands to remain faithful to traditional themes and production techniques at a time when many bands are abandoning them in the pursuit of profit.

*The Old
Fashioned
Sailors Mas
Camp is open
Dec–Feb daily
2–10pm
☎ 624 3692.*

Laventille

Between the steep and winding streets and alleys of **LAVENTILLE**, ramshackle houses made from salvaged boards and galvanized roofing perch on the hillside in defiance of gravity. The place hums with life as people bustle about their business, washing at standpipes in the road and exchanging intrigue on street corners. The suburb was established in the 1840s when freed slaves squatted the area, right "on the eyebrow of the enemy", as the Trinidadian novelist Earl Lovelace put it.

Laventille has often been dismissed as a slum, and many visitors are put off by scare stories involving bandits and street crime. Much of this is exaggerated, however, and provided you take the usual precautions you should be no more at risk than in downtown Port of Spain. Laventille has an undeniable confidence and verve, perhaps born of the fact that within its winding streets **the steel pan**, Trinidad's most famous instrument, was born (see p.302). The area has spawned many a great pan player and calypsonian, and was celebrated by the Nobel laureate **Derek Walcott** in his poem "The Hills of Laventille".

A brand new cultural centre, its walls strikingly decorated with pan illustrations, has been built on Laventille Road to house the **Desperadoes Panyard**. Established by Rudolph Charles, the Desperadoes are the longest-running steel band in Trinidad, with many first places at Panorama to their credit (see p.302). Visitors are welcome to watch them rehearse during Carnival season.

Laventille Hill is crowned by **Our Lady of Laventille Shrine**, an imposing landmark that can be seen from all over Port of Spain. Atop the 16-metre belfry of this white stone church stands a statue of the Virgin Mary, received from France in 1876. Pilgrims journey to the shrine from all over the country on the feast of the Assumption, and

Panyards

The best way to hear pan is live, in the open air. There is nothing as roman-tic as hearing the rich chiming harmonies drifting on the wind on a warm starry night. Throughout the year Port of Spain hosts events in which pan figures prominently, but for free entertainment you can go to the open-air panyards and listen while the musicians practice. The informal setting pro-vides a greater insight into the music, as the players repeat melodies and phrases time and time again. If you're lucky, you may hear the band's full repertoire, including excellent renditions of jazz and classical numbers, as well as the usual calypso, or even get a quick lesson after the rehearsal. The best panyards to visit in Port of Spain are the Desperadoes, Amoco Renegades and the Petrotrin Invaders and Phase II.

Amoco Renegades
Workshop: 17A Oxford St,
Port of Spain.

Pan Theatre:
71 Charlotte St, Port of Spain.
Rehearsals Fri 9pm–1am.

Blue Diamonds
George St, Port of Spain.

Desperadoes
Laventille Community Centre,
Laventille.

Humming Birds Pan Groove
Fort George Rd, St James.

Kool
25–27 Baneres Rd, St James.

Laventille Sound Specialists
Eastern Quarry, Laventille.

Neal and Massy All Stars
Duke St, Port of Spain.

North Stars
63 Bombay St, St James.

Pan Vibes
St Francois Balley Rd,
Port of Spain.

Pandemonium
3 Norfolk St, Belmont.

Petrotrin Invaders
Tragarete Rd, opposite the Oval,
Woodbrook.

Phase II Pan Grove
13 Hamilton Holder, Woodbrook.

Starlift
187 Tragarete Rd, Woodbrook.

T&Tec Power Stars
14 Western Main Rd, St James.

the devotions are popular with several of the island's many other reli-gious denominations.

The crumbling remains of **Fort Chacon,** just opposite the shrine, takes its name from the last Spanish governor of the island, who built it in 1770 to deter British attacks. His choice of location proved a poor one, however, as the fort did little to prevent the British from overrunning the island in 1797. Its current ruinous state seems to reflect its sad past, and there's little to be seen apart from a dilapi-dated stone wall. The fenced-off remains, currently used as a police wireless station, are closed to the public.

To the west of the shrine is **Observatory Street**, on the site where the Spanish navigator and astronomer **Don Cosmos Damien Churruca** made history in 1792 by establishing the first accurate meridian of longitude in the New World.

Downhill from the shrine on Picton Road is **Fort Picton**, built by the notorious British governor of that name (see p.286) in the late

1790s. The circular stone building, with thick walls and small loop-hole windows, was intended to protect Port of Spain from counterattack by the recently defeated Spanish. A tunnel is believed to have linked the fort to King's Wharf. The construction of this bolthole – known as **"Picton's Folly"** – suggests that the British were still far from confident about their ability to retain the island.

In recent years, Laventille has become something of a political football, with successive governments outlining new plans to improve the area. The postmodern apartment blocks at the base of the hills are the **John John Towers**, the controversial result of an initiative to create much-needed housing. Unfortunately the apartments were far too expensive for the majority of Laventille residents, and the towers remain empty while the government searches for a way to make them more affordable to local residents.

Meanwhile, a government-led "beautification" process is underway to encourage tourists to visit the suburb. Its most impressive result to date is the painted **scarlet ibises** on the large water tanks on Picton Hill. Dominating the Laventille Hills when viewed from the Eastern Main Road, the bright red birds bring a spark of nature to this very urban environment.

Eating

Even in the capital, Trinidadians are far more likely to eat at home than visit a restaurant, and consequently most **restaurants** and **cafés** are small fast-food outlets with a few plastic tables for people with nowhere better to go. Though there are branches of *KFC* and *Pizza Boy*, **Chinese**, **Indian** and **Creole** food dominate the menus, and all the shopping malls have food courts serving huge, satisfying meals for less than TT$20. There are a few **"fine dining"** establishments – in Trini speak, this means you should dress smartly, though not necessarily formally – frequented by rich Trinidadians, businesspeople and their clients or those celebrating a special occasion. Aimed largely at the European palate, these places tend to serve blander food than the local Trini fare, and you'll usually need to reserve a table.

We've listed phone numbers only for restaurants where you might need to book a table.

Some **bars** – such as *Martin's* – also serve lunch and dinner, and all the big **hotels** have smart restaurants serving international food at expensive prices – open to anyone who can afford them.

Balcony Café, Second Level, Colsort Mall, Frederick St. Small pleasant café overlooking Frederick Street. Serves a variety of teas, including herbal, and coffees, simple sandwiches, snacks and home-made cakes at reasonable prices.

The Breakfast Shed, Wrightson Rd. Next to the Cruise Ship Complex. Established in 1936 to provide workers' meals, this large shed serves excellent local food. Eat at long trestle tables with dock workers while watching the women prepare the food in the kitchen areas around the room. Delicious traditional breakfast of bake and shark and cocoa for TT$15. Daily 6.30am–4.30pm.

Port of Spain

Café Trinidad, Normandie Market, 10 Nook Ave, St Ann's. European-style café overlooking the *Normandie Hotel* swimming pool. Serves sandwiches and salads at inflated prices. Average meal TT$40. Daily10am–6pm.

Festak, 106 Frederick St. Intimate West African restaurant decorated with Ghanaian artefacts. Tasty, filling food cooked by the knowledgeable and informative Mr and Mrs Senah, who have spent many years in Ghana. Extremely good value. Average TT$40. Mon–Sat 11am–11pm.

Hong Kong City Restaurant, 86A Tragarete Rd, Newton, ☎622 3949. Large portions of standard Chinese fare in a very plush upstairs restaurant. Daily 11am–11pm. Average meal TT$35.

Il Colosseo, 47 Ariapita Ave, Woodbrook, ☎623 3654. Fancy Italian restaurant serving authentic food, cooked by a genuine Italian chef, in grand Renaissance-style surroundings with plaster cherubs and engraved glass. English afternoon tea, Tues & Thurs 3–5.30pm. Mon–Fri 11am–2.30pm, 6–10.30pm, Sat 6–10.30pm. Average meal TT$150.

La Boucan, *Trinidad Hilton*, Lady Young Rd, St Ann's, ☎624 3211. Large restaurant serving appetizing international food with a good view over the Queen's Park Savannah. Open for buffet lunch noon–2.30pm. Live entertainment over afternoon tea, Wed–Fri 4–6pm. Dinner 7–10.30pm. Average dinner TT$200.

La Fantasie, *Normandie Hotel*, 10 Nook Ave, St Ann's, ☎624 1181. Creole nouvelle cuisine – less spicy than street food, and smaller portions, but satisfying none the less. There are good paintings on display by local artists, though the green, pink and yellow walls could put you off your food. Daily 6.45–11pm. Average meal TT$75.

La Ronde, *Holiday Inn*, Wrightson Rd, ☎625 3366. Typical, expensive international cuisine served in a revolving restaurant that gives a 360° view of Port of Spain; the Thursday night lobster buffet is delicious. Daily noon–2.30pm, 7–10.30pm. Average meal TT$250.

Le Chateau de Poisson, 38 Ariapita Ave and Cornelio St, Woodbrook, ☎622 6087. Upmarket fish restaurant in an exquisitely maintained colonial gingerbread house. Delicious fresh fish, lobster and mussels. Attentive and friendly service. Mon–Sat 11.30am–2.30pm, 6.30–11pm. Average meal TT$150.

Mother Nature Vegetarian Restaurant, 84 Frederick St. Excellent vegetarian meals in a buffet style café. Wonderfully filling fruit punches made from everything from beetroot to papaya. Mon–Fri 6am–6pm, Sat 6am–2pm. Average meal TT$20.

Omar Kayam, 9 Warner St, Newton. Small and intimate restaurant, serving local spicy Indian food in a comfortable atmosphere. Mon–Sat 11am–10pm. Average meal TT$45.

Rafters, 6A Warner St, Newton, ☎628 9258. Colonial stone building with an American style bar for buffet lunches and an elegant dining room serving à la carte international food for dinner. Good food, with something for everyone. Mon–Sat 11am–11pm. Lunch TT$75, dinner TT$150.

Singho's Restaurant, Level 3, Long Circular Mall, St James. Large restaurant serving excellent Chinese food in typical red and gold decor. Daily 11am–11pm. Average meal TT$75.

Solimar, 6 Nook Ave, St Ann's, ☎624 6267. Creole, European, Latin American, Oriental and African dishes served in rustic taverna decor. Holds food festivals celebrating everything from the Scottish Burns Night to curries of India. Highly qualified and experienced chef. March–Nov Tues–Sat, Dec–Feb Mon–Sat 6.30pm–2am. Average meal TT$150.

Tiki Village, *Kapok Hotel*, 16–18 Cotton Hill, St Clair, ☎622 6441. Excellent Chinese/Polynesian cuisine in restaurant overlooking Port of Spain. Elegantly decorated with bubbling spring, and rattan furniture providing a relaxing ambience. Widely regarded as the best upmarket restaurant in town. Reservations recommended. Daily 6.30am–10.15pm. Average meal TT$150+.

Veni Mange, 67 Ariapita Ave, Woodbrook, ☎622 7533. Delicious international cuisine with a Caribbean flavour and tasty vegetarian options in a bistro type setting. It's a favourite spot for Trinidadian celebrities, with a friendly atmosphere and lively party scene on Fridays. Mon–Thurs 11.30am–3pm, Wed also 7.30pm–midnight, Fri 11.30am–11.30pm. Reservations recommended. Average meal TT$75.

The Verandah, 13 Rust St, St Clair, ☎622 6287. Exclusive restaurant in a nicely converted suburban house decorated with local art. Excellent local/international food in a quiet and peaceful setting. Reservations recommended. Mon–Fri 11.30am–2.45pm, Thurs also 7–10.45pm. Average meal TT$80–100.

Woodford Café, 62 Tragarete Rd, Woodbrook. Tasty and filling traditional Creole cuisine in a pleasant café; very popular at lunchtimes with office workers. Mon–Sat 11am–11pm.

Drinking, nightlife and entertainment

Trinidadians seem to live to party, celebrating anything from a public holiday to the end of a working day, and Port of Spain has a wide variety of places to let your hair down. There are few **nightclubs** in the European/American sense, and most of those that do exist are well outside the city centre. Most people do their dancing at parties known as **fetes**, usually held out of doors in community centres and sports complexes. These lively events, usually featuring live bands, draw large crowds. Watch the local press and listen to radio stations (see p.30) for information on these.

Most bars and clubs come alive after 10pm and are busiest from Thursday to Sunday. Many state that they are open "till", which means that they close when the last customers leave, usually around 2 or 3am, though some, such as *Smokey and Bunty*, keep going all night. If a place advertises its opening hours as "anytime, anyday", it means that the owners have a 24-hour license and open and close when they feel like it.

The capital also boasts a number of good **theatre** companies, including the **Trinidad Theatre Workshop**, the **Bagasse Company**, **Ragoo Productions** and **Raymond Choo Kong Productions**. The TTW (see p.73) puts on world-class drama, specializing in the work of Derek Walcott, while most of the other companies focus on light-hearted comedies. All productions have a Trinidadian flavour, since even foreign comedies are given a local twist.

*For more on
the history of
Carnival,
see p.291*

Carnival

Port of Spain is the centre of Trinidad's annual **Carnival**, one of the world's great pre-Lenten bacchanals, which equals – if not surpasses – those of Rio de Janeiro and New Orleans for exuberance, inventiveness and style. Brought to Trinidad by French Catholics in the eighteenth century, who celebrated it with masked balls at private houses and a sedate street procession. Carnival was taken up by freed slaves after emancipation. They introduced the percussion instruments, satirical costumes and spooky characters such as the devil (known as "jab jab") and the stilt-walking moko jumby, that make Carnival such an exhilarating occasion today.

Unlike in many other international Carnivals, in Trinidad anyone can **play mas**, as being a masquerader is called. Organizations known as Carnival bands – ranging in size from 500 to 9000 members – provide costumes and music; to become a member all you have to do is go to the band's **mas camp** (see p.81), where the costumes are made, choose from the designs on display, and buy one. Prices range from around TT$800–1000 for anything from a skimpy bikini outfit ("bikini mas") to a grander costume with backpack and cape; the purchase of a costume will allow you to join in the band's parade.

Though the climax of Carnival is the Monday and Tuesday preceding Ash Wednesday, the build-up is enormous. People save all year to afford a costume, and as soon as Christmas is over, the parties and outdoor concerts known as **fetes** begin, growing in intensity and frequency as the big event approaches.

The festivities begin on Monday morning with **Jouvert**, when revellers wear home-made costumes satirizing public figures and people covered in mud and paint dance through the streets of Port of Spain in wild abandon; if you wear white, they will deliberately embrace you. In the afternoon of **Carnival Monday**, an enormous street party takes place as the bands preview their costumes – usually simpler versions of the outfits worn the following day. **Carnival Tuesday** is an amazing mix of colour, music and partying revellers dancing down the street behind large sound trucks playing soca music. When the bands pass the judging points, the masquers fall into sections, each section wearing one particular design; most bands have ten to twenty sections. The band making the greatest visual impact and showing the most energy and spirit wins the prestigious **band of the year** prize. The highlight of the procession is the final judging point at the Queen's Park Savannah, where people summon up their last ounce of energy to perform their best moves for the judges and the TV cameras. The soca song most frequently played by the bands when crossing the judging points is declared the "**road march**" – you'll have heard it hundreds of times by the end of the day.

The following day, **Ash Wednesday**, the citizens of Port of Spain desert the city in droves to chill out on Maracas beach (see pp.121–123), serenaded by soca artists and calypsonians. The weekend after Carnival, the competition winners strut their stuff at **Champs in Concert** in the Queen's Park Savannah and, at a later date, in Shaw Park in Tobago (see p.232).

Bars

There are **rum shops** on practically every corner in Port of Spain. These tend to be small, basic shacks frequented by middle-aged men.

Bars (especially "sports bars") are usually a little more upmarket, with pumping music. It is often difficult to differentiate between **bars** and nightclubs, as many bars have dancing areas.

The Cricket Wicket, 149 Tragarete Rd, Woodbrook, ☎628 6766. This small bar overlooking the busy Tragarete Road opposite the Queen's Park Oval is mostly frequented by office workers and sports enthusiasts. Mon–Sat 11am–2.30am.

Just Friends, Lobby of Bretton Hall, 10 Victoria Ave, Newton, ☎624 4414. This intimate bar-cum-disco attracts a mature crowd. Thursday is the very popular karaoke night. Gay parties monthly TT$30. Sun–Wed 4pm–midnight, Thur & Fri 4pm-3am Sat 6pm–1am. Entrance Thur & Fri TT$20 in exchange for TT$20 a drink chit. Prices vary on other nights.

Martin's, 13 Cipriani Blvd, Newton, ☎623 7632. Pleasant and intimate bar with attractive patio seating area. Also serves lunch and dinner – international food with a Creole flavour. Open Mon–Sat 11.30am–midnight. Sun 6pm–midnight.

Mas Camp Pub, Ariapita Ave, Woodbrook, ☎623 3745. Popular with the older, local crowd. Nightly events include local calypsonian talent shows. Mon–Fri 11am–1/2am Sat–Sun 11am–4am. Entrance TT$20.

Pelican Inn, 2–4 Coblentz Ave, ☎624 7486. A Caribbean version of an English pub. Popular with tourists, it's quiet during the day, but comes to life at the weekend with a young crowd, packed dance floor and resident DJ. Daily 11am–2am. Small cover charge at weekends.

Smokey and Bunty, cor. Dengue St at 97 Western Main Rd, St James; no phone. Named after the owners' nicknames, this is a popular late liming spot with a very mixed crowd – young, old, arty, gay and straight. The clientele spills onto the pavement, loud music dominates and a funky atmosphere prevails. Open Mon–Thurs 10pm–3am Fri–Sun 10pm–7am.

Soca Boat, Cruise Ship Complex. Bar and restaurant run by the Calypsonian Organization of Trinidad. It features Calypso nights (Fri & Sat) that attract an older crowd and tourists.

Tasca Latina, 16 Phillips St, ☎625 3497. Intimate bar and restaurant with dance floor in Spanish taverna style. Live entertainment, popular and lively at weekends, attracts mature crowd. Entrance TT$30 Mon–Fri 11am–2am Sat 4pm–2am, Sun 11am–midnight.

Nightclubs

Cascade Club, 10 Nook Ave, St Ann's, ☎624 1181. The blend of music, in which country and western and calypso feature prominently, attracts an older crowd, mostly 30 plus. DJ Fri 5pm–3am, entrance free; live entertainment Sat 5pm–3am, entrance TT$15.

Club Coconuts, *Valley View Hotel*, Ariapita Rd, St Ann's, ☎623 6887. Late twenties crowd. Thurs reggae night, other nights calypso, dancehall and soca music. Wed–Sat 9.30pm–4.30am. Wed TT$60, free drinks all night; Thurs student ID gets you free entry; Fri TT$50; Sat TT$20/25.

Jazzys, 48 Western Main Rd, St James, ☎628 6355. A true Trini clubbing dive – dark, hot and seedy, always full and pumping at the weekends. Mon–Thurs 11am–1/2am, Fri–Sun 11am–3/4am. Entrance (weekends only) TT$10.

Lime Key, 68 Independence Square, ☎623 2346. Three a-c floors, including buffet style restaurant, bar and disco. Decorated with a mural of a Trinidadian village, it features popular local DJs and hosts Carnival events. Mon & Tues 10am–8pm, Wed–Fri 10am till late.

Port of Spain

Carnival calendar

January

Opening of Calypso Tents: calypsonians battle it out in the "tents" – these days regular buildings – for a place in the finals. The best known venues are: Spektakula Forum, 111–117 Henry St (☎623 2870); Kaiso House, Deluxe Cinema, Keate St (c/o TIDCO ☎627 5912); Calypso Revue, SWWTU Hall, 1d Wrightson Rd (☎625 1351); and Kaiso Karavan Naipaul Building, cor. Queen and Sanchez streets, Arima (☎667 2262).

Stickplay Competition: an exciting and skilful traditional sport based on the stick fighting of the 1880s, an art thought to have originated in the practice of using bamboo sticks to fight fires in the cane field.

Panorama Competition: steel drum bands display their skill in all types of music as they compete for the prestigious first prize. The finals are held in February.

Junior Calypso Competition: children compose and sing hard-hitting calypsos, full of satire, humour and social commentary.

National Chutney Soca Monarch Competition: hear the best of Trinidad's popular music as local artists compete to win this title. The finals are held in February.

International Soca Monarch Competition: international soca stars sing for the prestigious Trinidad Soca Monarch title. The finals are held in February.

Talk Tent: Similar to the calypso tent, but featuring cabaret and comedy artists. Performances go on throughout the Carnival season.

February

Calypso Fiesta: calypsonians engage in a battle of wit and satire – go with a Trinidadian who can explain the political references.

Kiddies' Carnival: the children's costumes and characters rival those of the adults. There are three **parades:** at the **Red Cross Children's Carnival** ten days before Carnival; at **St James Kiddies' Carnival** the week before Carnival; and at the **Junior Parade of the Bands** in the Savannah on the Saturday before Ash Wednesday.

Panorama Finals: a day-long marathon pan competition, fuelled by adrenalin and free-flowing rum.

Poolside Fiesta, *Trinidad Hilton,* Lady Young Rd, St Ann's, ☎624 3211. A tacky and overpriced tourist attraction featuring steel band, calypso, limbo and a buffet with rather bland local food. Mon 7pm. Entrance TT$135.

Spektakula Forum, 111–117 Henry St, ☎623 2870 or 0125. Large building next to Ministry of Planning department. One of the great calypso tents, established for twenty years. Many of the past and present grandmasters of the art form and calypso monarchs have performed here. Events, featuring both local and international artists, are advertised in the press. Entrance TT$30–40.

Two Plus Cultural and Recreation Club, 94–96 Henry St, ☎627 8224. Near the junction with Park Street, this club hidden upstairs is a popular venue for ballroom dancing fanatics. From Monday to Thursday a teacher holds lessons from 7–9pm, then the music – ranging from old calypsos to the latest soca – continues to the early hours. No entrance fee except for special events.

Queen's Park Savannah's rowdy North Stand is the place to be if you want to party, while the grandstand is for those who want a more sedate view of the proceedings. Though seats in the stands are inexpensive (TT$30–50), those on a budget or wishing to move around should go on "the tracks", the road leading towards the stage where the bands practice. Panorama takes place on Saturday before Ash Wednesday.

Calypso Monarch Finals: after weeks of build-up in calypso tent competitions, the best calypsonians sing their hearts out for the prize of Calypso Monarch. At the Queen's Park Savannah grandstands, in the week before Carnival.

Dimanche Gras (Carnival Sunday): the finals for the King and Queen of Carnival. The sheer size of the costumes, and the skill and sequins expended, are amazing, though every year the entrants are getting to look more and more like sculptures on wheels. At the Queen's Park Savannah grandstands.

Jouvert (pronounced *Joovay*, from **"Jour Ouvert"**, the break of day): marking the beginning of the festivities, Jouvert is "dirty mas", raw, earthy and energetic. Wear as little as possible and no jewellery. Starts 2am Monday before Ash Wednesday and continues till dawn.

Carnival Monday Parade of the Bands: bands parade their costumes through the streets of Port of Spain; individual bands follow set routes, but there is no set route for the whole parade. From 1pm.

Carnival Tuesday Parade of the Bands: the full display of all the costumes. The route is the same as Carnival Monday; the best place to view the costumes in their full effect is from the stands at the Queen's Park Savannah or at the bleachers set up at the various judging points around the town. Starts 8am.

Ash Wednesday: International soca artists and calypsonians entertain a huge post-Carnival crowd on Maracas Beach (see pp.121–123). This party is getting busier each year; if you're driving, leave early or be prepared for a slow journey home.

Champs in Concert: A parade of the winning bands, held in the Queen's Park Savannah grandstands the weekend after Carnival.

Theatres

The Trinidad **theatre season** is from March to the end of November. After this Trinidadians become preoccupied with Christmas events, such as Parang concerts (see p.298) and the continuous live entertainment of the Carnival season. Tickets, which cost from TT$20 for smaller amateur productions to TT$50+ for the well known companies, are excellent value compared to international prices.

Central Bank Auditorium, Twin Towers financial complex, Brian Lara Promenade, ☎ 625 4835 or 5028. Entrance through Eric Williams Plaza. The most comfortable and high tech theatre in Port of Spain, features productions by well known Trinidad theatre companies – usually comedies. Wear long sleeves to counteract the overenthusiastic a-c.

Little Carib, cor. White & Roberts streets, Woodbrook, ☎622 4644. Opened in 1948, this intimate and historic theatre concentrates on plays and shows highlighting local talent and culture.

The **Queen's Hall**, 1–3 St Ann's Rd, St Ann's, ☎624 1284. Opposite the *Trinidad Hilton*. The largest arts venue in Trinidad, featuring drama, dance, music and fashion shows. Tickets from TT$25–60.

Trinidad Theatre Workshop, 3 Hart St, ☎624 4681. A small hall-type theatre on the upper level of the building opposite the Trinity Cathedral. Specializes in Derek Walcott's work.

Under the Trees, *The Normandie*, 10 Nook Ave, St Ann's, ☎624 1181. Atmospheric evening performances featuring local artists – doing everything from solo comedy performances to local plays – under the stars, in grounds of the *Normandie* hotel.

Shopping

*Port of Spain's
shopping malls
are open
9am–6pm.*

Port of Spain's **main shopping area** is based around **Frederick Street** and the few outlying malls such as **West Mall**, **West Moorings**, **Ellerslie Plaza**, **Maraval** and **Long Circular Mall**, St James. Foreign **imported goods** can be bought all over town, especially in the large malls.

Since most Trinidadians have their clothes made to measure, there is an abundance of **textile** shops. Concentrated on Queen Street, these offer a greater variety of materials than you'd find in New York or London at very reasonable prices. Between 1984 and 1991, Trinidad banned the import of **clothes**, spurring the country's fashion industry to great heights and bringing forward a wave of first-rate designers. Look out for **Radical Designs** (Excellent City Centre Mall, Frederick St, ☎627 4425), featuring elegant, classic clothes by Diane Hunt; the **Z Meiling** store (Excellent City Centre Mall, Frederick St, ☎623 9573), selling classic cuts and stylish underwear by Meiling, Trinidad's top designer; **The Cloth** (Normandie Market, 100 Nook Ave, St Ann's, ☎624 1181 ext 4348), for Robert Young's brightly coloured abstract designs on loose cotton; and **Jamoo** (contact Mrs Rihama, ☎656 0593) for unique flowing cotton clothes with nature-inspired designs by Avianne Blackman. **Zoom** (Excellent City Centre Mall, Frederick St, ☎624 7873) sells the best T-shirts in the city, while **Ontic Designs** (cor. Ariapita Ave and French St, ☎627 7549) have a beautiful range of batiks.

Local music is sold by street vendors touting the latest soca cassettes, though these are poor quality pirate copies, and none of the money goes to the original artists. For CDs and original cassettes, try any of the music stores on Frederick Street. **Crosby's** (54 Western Main Rd, St James, ☎622 7622) has a wide selection, and also sell tickets for all the big fetes and parties. If Trinidad has inspired you to become a pan player, **steel drums** can be bought from **Lincoln Enterprises** (68 Ariapita Ave, ☎628 7267) though be warned, they're very expensive.

Local crafts can be found on street stalls and at inflated prices in the malls. For the best selection of handmade leather sandals and

Rastafarian goods, visit the shops at the **United Craft Workers Drag Brothers Co-Op**, (southern end of Piccadilly Street and Brian Lara Promenade). There's a large selection of wickerwork on sale at the **T&T Blind Welfare League** (118 Duke St, ☎624 1613). **Susan Dayal's** beautiful handcrafted wire decorations can be found in the Normandie Market (10 Nook Ave, St Ann's, ☎625 3197). **African Trophies** (39 Tragarete Rd/12 Roberts St, ☎622 9476) specializes in fine African carvings, furniture, clothes and jewellery. If you're looking for **Indian crafts** and **ornate filigree jewellery**, however, the best place to shop is in Chaguanas (p.161–163).

Bookshops in Port of Spain are usually disappointing, full of school textbooks and cookery books, and stocking little work by local authors. There are a couple of exceptions in Port of Spain: **Trinidad Book World** (87 Queen St, ☎623 4316) has a wide selection, and is particularly strong on Trinidadian writers, while **Metropolitan Book Suppliers** (upstairs at Colsort Mall, Frederick St, ☎623 3462) is the best bookshop in Trinidad for books on the history and culture of the island.

African Trophies functions as a cultural centre as well as a shop, with a library and space to view videos on African culture.

Listings-

Airlines BWIA, 30 Edward St, ☎627 2942; Air Caribbean, 90 Independence Square, ☎623 2500 fax 627 3040; American, 63–65 Independence Square, ☎669 4661, fax 669 0261; LIAT, 30 Edward St, ☎624 8211; Air Canada, Piarco Airport, ☎669 4065.

Airport 24hr information line: ☎669 8047 or 8048 or 8049 ext 204 or 247.

Art Galleries Art Creators, Flat 402, Aldegonda Park, 7 St Ann's Rd, St Ann's, ☎624 4369. Exhibits prominent Trinbago artists such as Leroy Clarke and Neal Massy. Open Mon–Fri 10am–5.30pm, Sat 10am–2.30pm. 101 Art Gallery, 101 Tragarete Rd, Woodbrook, ☎628 4081. Gallery 1,2,3,4, *The Normandie*, 10 Nook Ave, St Ann's, ☎625 5502: small gallery with four rooms, featuring local well-known artists in all media. Daily 9.30am–5pm. On Location, Long Circular Mall, St James, ☎628 3404 fax 622 5616.

Banks Bank of Commerce, 72 Independence Square, ☎627 9325; Citibank, 12 Queen's Park East, ☎625 1040; First Citizen, 50 St Vincent St, ☎623 2576; Republic Bank, 11–17 Park St, ☎ 625 4411; Royal Bank, 19–21 Park St, ☎623 1322; Scotiabank, 1 Frederick St, ☎623 1253; Western Union, 44–58 Edward St, ☎623 6000.

Cinemas Excellent value for money and entertaining as much for the audience participation as the films, an outing to the cinema will cost between TT$10–15 for a double bill, usually featuring American action movies and international blockbusters. You are still allowed to smoke in Trinidad's cinemas plus alcohol and other refreshments are on sale. Deluxe, 9–11 Keate St, ☎623 6532; Globe, cor. St Vincent and Park st, ☎623 1063. See press for details.

Embassies and high commissions British High Commission 19 St Clair Ave, St Clair, ☎622 2748, fax 622 4555. Mon–Thurs 7.30am–noon & 1–4pm, Fri 7.30am–12.30pm. Canada High Commission 3–3a Sweet Briar Rd, St Clair, ☎622 6232, fax 628 2619. Mon–Thurs 7.30am–4pm, Fri 7.30am–1pm. **US Embassy** 15 Queen's Park West, ☎622 6371, fax 628 5462. Mon–Fri 7.30–11am.

Port of Spain

Hospital Port of Spain General is at 169 Charlotte St, ☎623 2951/5, 625 3622, 623 7715, though you may have to wait a few hours to be seen if you turn up at casualty. Two other options if you're in a hurry and have good medical insurance are the private Community Hospital, Western Main Rd, Cocorite, ☎622 1191, 628 8330 and St Clair Medical Centre, 18 Elizabeth St, St Clair, ☎628 1451 or 1452 or 8615.

Laundry Self-service launderettes are very rare in Trinidad, though there are three Ashleigh Phillip's Coin Laundries, all based in or around Port of Spain. They can be found at: 10 Western Main Rd, St James, ☎628 2268; 44 Diego Martin Main Rd, Diego Martin, ☎622 9026; and 12 Sierra Leone Rd, Diego Martin, ☎632 7444. Open Mon–Sat 9am–9pm, Sun 9am–2pm. Costs TT$20 for wash and dry. Dry clean laundries usually do "wet" cleaning as well, but at expensive rates. Most people do their own or have someone who does their handwashing for them. Ask around for the local clothes washer.

Pharmacies Bhaggan's, Independence Square, ☎627 5541, is open until 11pm; Alchemists, 57 Duke St, ☎623 2718, until 1am; Crichlow's Pharmacy, 100 Western Main Rd, St James, ☎622 5095, until 9.30–10pm.

Police Main Police Station, Wrightson Rd, ☎625 2684; general crime can also be reported to the CID, in the white building cor. of St Vincent and Knox St, ☎627 4145. In emergency dial 999.

Sports The **Hasley Crawford Stadium**, cor. Ariapita Ave and Wrightson Rd, ☎623 0304, contains an athletics track and football field, and hosts both local and international events. The Jean Pierre Sports Complex next door has facilities for lawn tennis, netball, basketball, table tennis, gymnastics, badminton and a gym. Events are advertised in local media.

Swimming pool YMCA, Benbow Rd, off Wrightson Rd, ☎625 9622. Daily noon–3.45pm, TT$6 for a 45min session.

Post office, Wrightson Rd, opposite *Holiday Inn*, ☎625 2121. Open Mon–Fri 7am–5pm. Poste Restante, at the enquiry window is open 8am–4pm. Post office also at southern end of Frederick St.

Travel agents Courtesy, 68–70 Sackville St, ☎625 1455, fax 627 6412; Eastern Credit, 22 Park St, ☎624 5059; Alstons Travel, 69 Independence Square, ☎625 2201, fax 625 3682.

Tour operators T&T Sightseeing Tours, upstairs at Galleria Centre, 12 Western Main Rd, St James, ☎628 1051, fax 622 9205; A's Travel Service, 177 Tragarete Rd, ☎622 5502, fax 628 6808; Caribbean Discovery Tours, Fondes Amandes Rd, St Ann's, ☎624 7281, fax 627 3526; Classic Tours and Travel, 102b Woodford St, ☎628, 5714 fax 628 7053.

Visa extensions Immigration Division, 67 Frederick St, ☎625 3571. Ring before you go to get advice as to exactly what you need for your extension, and be prepared for a long wait and for more than one visit.

Maraval and Paramin

Some five kilometres north of central Port of Spain, **MARAVAL** lies at the base of the Northern Range, surrounded by lush green hills. Originally a small village on the outskirts of the capital, it is rapidly becoming an upmarket residential suburb, with a concentration of hotels and guesthouses aimed at middle- and upper-income visitors.

Dominating the hillside at the centre of Maraval is the cream and
maroon neo-Romanesque **Maraval-Paramin Roman Catholic
Church**, originally built in 1879 and enlarged in 1934.

Beyond the village of Maraval and the expansive, well-kept St
Andrew's golf course, the road takes a scenic route over the Northern
Range, providing good views of the forested slopes of the Maraval valley and eventually arriving – after many steep inclines and hairpin
bends – at Maracas Beach on the north coast (see pp.121–123).

Immediately west of Maraval, up the slopes of the Northern Range,
is the quiet, community-oriented neighbourhood **of PARAMIN**, the
"herb basket of Trinidad". The local cottage industry produces
"Paramin seasoning", whose ingredients include French and Spanish
thyme, peppermint and onions. The local population is of Spanish
ancestry, the descendants not of colonial Spaniards but of
Venezuelans who came here in the nineteenth century to plant cocoa.
This close-knit community maintains many of its Venezuelan traditions, most famously its **Parang** singers, who travel from house to
house during the Christmas season, singing nativity songs in a mix of
French and Spanish. The Monday before Christmas, Paramin hosts a
Parang festival at its unofficial community centre, The Basement. On
Carnival Monday Paramin is overtaken with blue devils – traditional
Carnival characters that enable people to express their wilder side –
feting in the streets. Harvest Sunday, the second in November, is celebrated with games, music and traditional feasts of wild meat.

Practicalities

Though it is officially outside the boundaries of the capital, **Maraval**
is increasingly thought of as a suburb of the city, and many people
stay here because of its proximity to central Port of Spain; regular
maxi- and **route-taxis** do the 10-minute run up the Saddle Road from
the northwest corner of the Queen's Park Savannah. After 8pm during the week, it gets harder to find taxis into the area, and if you
intend to be in town after 10pm, be sure to prearrange your return
journey. To negotiate the steep hill up to Paramin, you need to catch
a **jeep** from Maraval village junction for (TT$2.50).

*See p.61 for
details on
where in Port
of Spain to
catch taxis to
Maraval.*

Accommodation

Most of the **hotels** and **guesthouses** are located on Saddle Road,
which runs through the centre of Maraval. Many of them are new and
fairly upmarket; their high standards and wide range of facilities –
restaurants, swimming pools and jacuzzis – are, unsurprisingly,
reflected in the prices.

Hotels

Chaconia Inn, 106 Saddle Rd, ☎628 8603, fax 628 3214. Well-maintained
and pleasant hotel. All rooms are large with TV, fridge, a-c, phone and en-suite
bathroom. Atmospheric rooftop restaurant overlooks the swimming pool. ⑥/⑦

Maraval and Paramin

Royal Palm Suite Hotel, 7 Saddle Rd, ☎628 6042. Impersonal, standard hotel, all rooms with a-c, en-suite bathroom and cable TV. Facilities include swimming pool, 24 hour taxi service, on site shops, restaurants, bars and laundry service. Breakfast included in Carnival rate. ⑥/⑧

Suites Elysees, 123A Long Circular Rd, ☎622 4111. Spacious two-bedroom self-catering apartments. Excellent value. Cream and grey building, no sign or number. Carnival rates last from January to April. ④/⑤

Tropical Hotel, 6 Rookery Nook, ☎622 5815, fax 628 3174. An old plantation estate house. All rooms have a-c, phones and en-suite bathrooms. Well maintained with a swimming pool, thatched palm pool bar and in-house steak restaurant. Behind *KFC*. ⑥/⑧

Villa Maria, 48A Perseverance Rd, Haleland Park, ☎629 8023 fax 629 8641. Quiet, well kept hotel with a restaurant and cocktail bar overlooking the swimming pool. All rooms have cable TV, a-c and en-suite bathrooms. Breakfast included in normal rate. Opposite the St Andrew's golf course at top end of Maraval. ⑤/⑦

Guesthouses

For details of the accommodation price codes used in these listings, see pp.20–22

Carnetta's House, 99 Saddle Rd, ☎628 2732, fax 628 7717, email *carnetta@ trinidad.net*. Well-laid out rooms in two Maraval sites. All with a-c, phone, cable TV – some have kitchenette. Owners are extremely hospitable and great for local information. Breakfast included in Carnival rate. ⑤/⑦

Jireh's Guesthouse, 109 Long Circular Rd, ☎628 2337. Colonial house, all rooms with a-c and bathrooms, some with kitchenette. Laundry facilities, homely atmosphere. ⑤/⑥

Monique's Guesthouse, 114–116 Saddle Rd, ☎628 3334, fax 622 3232. Long-established and friendly, with a variety of plush rooms; all have a-c, phone, cable TV – some have kitchenette, balcony and disabled access. Good restaurant and bar. ⑤/⑦

Zollna House, 12 Ramlogan Terrace, ☎628 3731, fax 628 3737. Comfortable and homely guesthouse with friendly and knowledgeable hosts, if a little overpriced considering the location (difficult to get to without a car). Rooms with fans. Breezy communal balcony overlooks the Maraval Valley. Breakfast included. Off La Seiva Rd off Saddle Rd. ⑤/⑦

Eating and entertainment

Maraval's **restaurants** tend to be upmarket, and serve food geared to international tastes; though good, it can be bland in comparison with the local Creole food and expensive compared with equally tasty meals offered at downtown restaurants or street stalls. After dark, most people go into Port of Spain for amusement, and Maraval stays quiet. There are the usual small rum shops, while *Flags* restaurant, has a bar-cum-disco that plays American-English easy listening.

Restaurants

Ali Baba, Royal Palm Plaza, 7 Saddle Rd, ☎622 5557. Excellent Middle Eastern cuisine in a pleasant atmosphere. Reservations recommended. Mon–Sat 11.30am–10.30pm. Average meal TT$150.

Flags, 141 Long Circular Rd, ☎628 3000. Typical international cuisine. Flags of the world decorate the wooden furniture and fittings. The sports bar downstairs features live music. Daily 11am–11pm. Average meal TT$100.

Gourmet Club, upstairs at Ellerslie Plaza, ☎628 5113. An exclusive "fine dining" establishment serving very good quality Italian dishes. Mon–Sat 6–11pm. Average meal TT$250.

Pavio's Shoppes of Maraval, Saddle Rd, ☎622 7026. Posh Italian restaurant serving tasty fare, reservations recommended. Mon–Sat 6–11pm. Average meal TT$175.

Nightlife

The Attic, Shoppes of Maraval, ☎622 8123. Latin nightclub that attracts mature crowd; the liveliest nights are Tues and Thurs. Daily 4pm–4am. Entrance TT$10/20.

Outer Limits, Royal Palm Plaza, 7 Saddle Road,☎622 0100. Sports bar with pool tables, one reserved for women only. They organize a party bus on the weekends; TT$40 buys you unlimited drinks as you travel around Port of Spain at night to pumping clubs. Free tequila for women customers on Sundays between 3pm and 4pm. Daily 11am–2am.

West to Chaguaramas

From Port of Spain, the Western Main Road winds its way along the coast, past the turn-off to the newer residential areas of **Diego Martin** and **Petit Valley**. The WMR is lined with ribbon development: high rise apartments, the ever-expanding **West Mall**, and exclusive suburbs such as **West Moorings** and **Goodwood Park**. After upmarket **Glencoe**, the landscape becomes more rural, the villages smaller. Rickety wooden stalls line the road, selling brightly coloured fruit and vegetables and fresh fish weighed out on old-fashioned scales. Faded wooden rum shops and general stores carry advertisements for "Stag – the man's beer" and hand-painted signs request "no urine here". People dressed in everything from suits to boxer shorts conduct their business and lime by the roadside. The sea sways in and out of view, providing breathtaking glimpses of calm blue waters and the rocky, forested protrusions of the islands in the Bocas (see p.111).

The **Chaguaramas** area is distinguished by wide expanses of grassland and miles of untouched forested hills, much of which have been set aside to form the Chaguaramas National Park. Beyond the cluster of former military buildings that makes up **Chaguaramas town**, a plethora of yachting facilities brings sunburnt American and European yachties to the area. You'll spot them a mile off; with their cutoff shorts and small tops, both men and women sporting ponytails, they frequently find themselves the butt of the witty Trinidadian *picong*.

Diego Martin and Petit Valley

The residential districts of **DIEGO MARTIN** and **PETIT VALLEY** are built on land once owned by the River Estate cocoa plantation. Bought by the government in 1897, the area has undergone massive development in the last hundred years. There are few specific sights, apart from the odd historic building and a scenic waterfall. Amid the suburban development of the Diego Martin Main Road, watch out for "Rainorama", a large modern corner house that is the home of the calypsonian Lord Kitchener, and was named after his 1973 calypso about that year's washed out Carnival.

Diego Martin Estate

At the top end of Diego Martin Main Road (at the end of the Diego Martin maxi route) is the **Diego Martin Estate**, an enclave of lush greenery that forms a surprising contrast with the sprawling, suburban environment just a couple of minutes away. The old estate house – a wooden building of elegant simplicity – has recently been renovated, though the small museum inside offers little more than a fairly uninspiring pictorial display devoted to cocoa production on the estate, which was owned by Cadbury's from the mid-nineteenth to the mid-twentieth century. Across the road, the large **water wheel** dates back to 1845, when the estate produced sugar. An aqueduct once ran from the Diego Martin River to power the wheel, which in turn drove the rollers that crushed sugar cane for the production of molasses.

Opposite the museum, the original **coach shed** of the estate is now used as storage space for the local panyard. Behind this are some original **barrack houses**, among the few surviving examples of the galvanized-roofed wooden shacks where the indentured plantation workers had to live. Each building consisted of four rooms, each of which was occupied by a family. The appalling conditions have been described by Trinidadian writers such as Alfred Mendes (see pp.316–7). Few barrack houses are left, thanks to government efforts to improve living conditions.

Blue Basin Waterfall

To get to the Blue Basin Waterfall from Port of Spain, take a Diego Martin maxi to the end of its route, then a route taxi to the base of the waterfall (TT$2–3).

One of the most accessible falls in Trinidad, **Blue Basin** is also one of the smallest. Like so many others in Trinidad, the 6-metre fall has sadly been affected by the general reduction in water levels, and no longer gushes with its full force. The setting, with rainforest on all sides, is still beautiful, however, and you may catch the odd glimpse of blue emperor butterflies and exotic birds fluttering through the undergrowth. The small circular pool at the base of the fall is good for bathing, and while it gets busy at weekends and after school, you will often find it deserted on weekdays.

The waterfall is considered sacred by some religious groups, and you may come across Baptists or Rastafarians conducting their rituals by the waters. A small statue of the Virgin Mary sits in an alcove at the base of the falls, and along the track Baptist flags fly from tall bamboo poles. The area around the waterfall is rumoured to be a favourite haunt of "bandits" out to relieve you of your wallet, so it's wise to go in a group, if possible with a Trinidadian. Downriver from the waterfall are various good bathing pools; at weekends they are filled with children "takin' in the springs". To reach the waterfall, keep on the main road past the water wheel, then turn right onto Blue Basin Road. Go up the steep hill till you reach a sign pointing to a track for the waterfall, and follow this on foot for five minutes.

West Mall, West Moorings and Glencoe

The area stretching from Diego Martin to Carenage, now known as West Mall, West Moorings and Glencoe, was a swamp until it was reclaimed in the 1940s. Now it is dominated by luxury houses defended by high walls and ferocious-looking dogs. Postmodernist apartment blocks by Stephen Mendez (one of Trinidad's foremost architects) dominate the skyline, while West Mall provides the latest in upmarket American-style shopping. **Glencoe** is the home of the Trinidad and Tobago Yacht Club.

Carenage

The first clearly defined settlement on the WMR, **CARENAGE** sprawls far into the hills, its winding lanes flanked by modern concrete homes, dilapidated huts and general stores covered in posters and hand-painted adverts. There is little to see in Carenage, apart from the crumbling wooden **St Peter's Chapel** at the water's edge, next to the petrol station on the main road. On St Peter's Day (the last Sunday in June), the clergy bless fleets of fishermen's boats here.

The town owes its name to the fact that it was to its harbour that the Spaniards brought their ships to be careened (scraped clean of barnacles). After the Spanish departed in 1797, Carenage sank into torpor as a sleepy fishing village, but its character changed drastically with the arrival of the Americans in 1941. When Chaguaramas was turned into a US military base (see p.105), all the residents of the peninsula were relocated here. The town soon acquired a seedy reputation as a place where American soldiers went to have fun and find local women.

Chaguaramas

Beyond Carenage, the WMR winds through the mountainous, forested peninsula of **CHAGUARAMAS** (pronounced Shag-ger-rarm-ms). The greater part of the area has remained virtually untouched, with shallow beaches and miles of virgin rainforest in its interior, and is now a national park. Leisure development has, for the most part, been sensitive and unobtrusive. The strip of flatlands along the south coast shelter a scattering of restaurants and nightclubs, and the only built-up area, **Chaguaramas town**, universally – if confusingly – known as Chaguaramas. There is a string of **beaches** along the south coast, though the sea can be dirty and polluted here, especially in the wet season, and signs warn that bathing is not recommended. Better swimming can be had on the north coast, particularly at **Macqueripe**

West to
Chaguar-
amas

The Trinidad and Tobago Yacht Club provides yachting facilities and offers deep sea fishing trips. US$275 for four hours, US$350 for six hours, US$425 for 8 hours; contact Mr Sagomes ☎ 637 8771 or Mr Da la Rosa ☎ 637 7389.

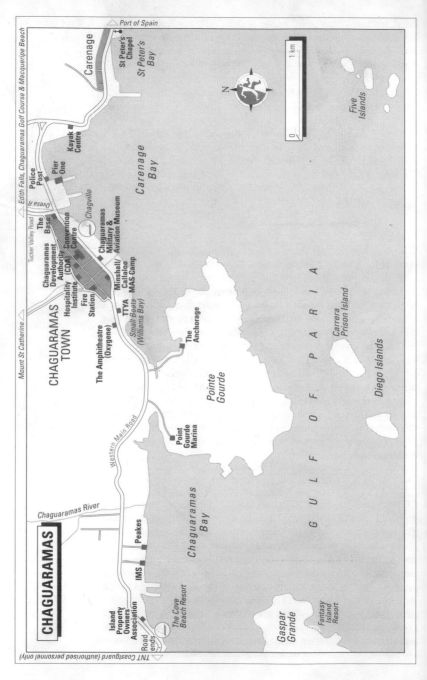

CHAGUARAMAS

Port of Spain

St Peter's Chapel
St Peter's Bay

Carenage

Edith Falls, Chaguaramas Golf Course & Macqueripe Beach

Mount St Catherine

Tucker Valley Road

Dyesa R

Kayak Centre

Pier One

Police Post

The Base

Chaguaramas Development Authority (CDA)

Chagville

Convention Centre

Chaguaramas Military & Aviation Museum

Minshall/ Callaloo MAS Camp

CHAGUARAMAS TOWN

Hospitality Institute

Fire Station

TTYA

Small Boats (Williams Bay)

The Amphitheatre (Oxygene)

The Anchorage

Pointe Gourde

Western Main Road

Point Gourde Marina

Chaguaramas River

Peakes

Chaguaramas Bay

IMS

Island Property Owners Association

The Cove Beach Resort

Road ends

TNT Coastguard (authorised personnel only)

Gaspar Grande

Fantasy Island Resort

Carenage Bay

Five Islands

N

1 km

0

Carrera Prison Island

Diego Islands

G U L F   O F   P A R I A

Beach, a delightful cove that's easily accessible by road from Chaguaramas town.

Go down to Chaguaramas on a weekend and you'll see people liming on the beaches, taking a "seabath", fighting the currents in kayaks and hiking in the forests; while at night, a more glamorous crowd comes in from Port of Spain to frequent the open-air nightclubs.

Some history

The name Chaguaramas, derived from the Amerindian word for the palms which once lined this coast, is the only remnant of the area's indigenous population. The region's natural harbour provided the **Spanish** with a hiding place for their ships when the **British** invaded, though when it became clear that defeat was obvious, the ships were scuttled. The harbour was also the reason the **US military** wanted the area as its Caribbean base during World War II, leasing it from the British in 1940 in return for fifty used destroyers. The area was then closed to the general public, the population relocated to Carenage (see p.103), and the military base which now forms Chaguaramas town constructed.

The US soldiers, initially greeted with a warm welcome, quickly became unpopular. Many Trinidadians resented the US occupation of the best beaches and countryside within easy reach of the capital, as well as the social effect of so many young American men living in the region. The GIs outnumbered the local men, who could not compete with their ostentatious wealth, and the resentment this generated was immortalized by Lord Invader in his famous calypso "Working for the Yankee Dollar":

"Rum and Coca-Cola, Go down to Point Cumana,
Both mother and daughter, Working for the Yankee Dollar."

The situation was not improved by the Americans' attitude towards race. A 1945 edition of *Life* magazine reported that "US soldiers confused by the mix of color lines would keep a brown paper bag at the doorway into their parties. Anyone whose skin was lighter than the bag was considered 'white' (and allowed entry)."

With the growth of the **independence movement**, Chaguaramas became a focus of conflict between the British colonial government and the local population. In April 1960 thousands of local residents marched through the rain to campaign for the return of Chaguaramas. Their goal was achieved the following February, when the area was returned to Trinidad and the Americans departed.

Chaguaramas has long been a recreational area for Trinidadians, and with this in mind the government declared the region a **national park** in 1961. The town – with its many buildings abandoned by the Americans – was promoted as the seat of the future Caribbean parliament, but these plans were thwarted by the collapse of the West Indian Federation in 1962. Subsequently the **Chaguaramas Development Authority** was established, to maintain the nature reserve and encourage businesses concerned with leisure into the area.

West to Chaguaramas

Maxis for Chaguaramas leave from Green Corner in Port of Spain and run to Chagville Beach (TT$4) and The Cove (TT$6).

Accommodation

Despite all the leisure facilities in Chaguaramas, there is relatively little accommodation in the area; most visitors stay in the capital, just
twenty minutes' drive away.

The Bight, Peakes Marina, Western Main Rd, Chaguaramas, ☎634 4839, fax
634 4387. Smart small hotel and restaurant in Peakes boatyard overlooking
the marina, used mainly by visiting yachties. All rooms are tastefully furnished
and have a-c and en-suite bathrooms. ⑤/⑥

The Cove, Western Main Rd, Chaguaramas, ☎634 4319, fax 634 4278.
Spacious, peaceful and well-maintained self-catering apartments sleeping two
to six. Most have TV, fridge, hot and cold water. Daily maid and laundry service. Avaliable for short and long term rental. Use of The Cove beach resort is
free for occupants. ⑦

*For details of
the accommo-
dation price
codes used in
these listings,
see pp.20–22.*

Wellington's House, 47a Gairloch Rd, Glencoe, ☎632 4472. A comfortable
and homely B&B in a 1940s house in a quiet suburban street. All rooms have
fans and a sink. ④/⑤

Chaguaramas town

Situated on the WMR facing Chaguaramas Bay on the southern coast is
the region's only built-up area, **Chaguaramas town**. Known to locals
simply as Chaguaramas, this odd collection of fifty or so buildings
scarcely merits the description "town" – no one lives here, and there are
no shops or churches. The place was constructed in three months in
1940 by the US military and local labour, and turned over to civilian use
in 1961. Today it consists mostly of aircraft hangars, warehouses and
official buildings that have been converted for use by businesses or government departments. It's an ugly place, littered with old ammunition
bunkers, some abandoned, others now used as storage facilities.

*Chaguaramas
Golf Course,
Bellerazand
Road, is open
daily 7am–
6pm.*

The "town" is clustered around two main roads, the coastal WMR,
and a curved road that slopes gently uphill, known locally simply as
"the back road". There's little to see except for a few **beaches**, a **military museum**, and Peter Minshall's **Callaloo mas camp**. It also
boasts the only public golf course in Trinidad – set in lush rainforest
surroundings – and the **Chaguaramas Development Authority**,
which offers excellent wildlife and nature tours.

Chaguaramas Military History and Aviation Museum

*The Military
History
Museum,
☎634 4391,
is open 9am–
6pm daily.
Adults TT$10*

Located on the Western Main Road, the **Chaguaramas Military
History and Aviation Museum** is hard to miss – there's a large sign
out front and a collection of military hardware on the forecourt.
Chronicling the military history of Trinidad and Tobago from 1498
to the present day, the museum has a series of photos highlighting
the role of local soldiers in international warfare; while pictures and
text deal with famous pirates, the history of the Trinidadian police,
and local battles, with detailed drawings of the battle of Scarborough
Bay in Tobago and the British takeover of Trinidad. Newspaper photographs from the 1990 coup give you a glimpse of the turmoil
Trinidad suffered during the six-day siege (see p.73).

During July and August, the museum runs two-week-long **summer camps** for children, including model building, first aid, self defence lessons and field trips into the forest (TT$300 per child).

West to Chaguaramas

Callaloo mas camp

The **Callaloo mas camp**, in a large warehouse-type building surrounded by a wire fence opposite the old heliport, is the workshop of Trinidad's most famous mas company, led by designer **Peter Minshall**. Known for innovative techniques, high quality and immensely detailed costumes, Minshall and his crew use everything from leaves to bottle tops to manufacture the amazing costumes that have so often won them the title of **Band of the Year**. While most mas camps are based in Port of Spain, Callaloo has been leased this building as a reward for its contribution to Trinidad Carnival.

Open all year, the camp is busiest in the run-up to Carnival, when the crew work 24 hours a day in a whirl of fabric, sequins and natural materials. Known to those who work there as "the factory", the building includes a sewing room, a workshop, a large production space, kitchen and office area. Parts of old costumes decorate the camp: collars produced for the opening ceremony of the Barcelona Olympics are used as lampshades; a giant puppet made for the band **Odyssey** stares through its one eye onto the production floor; costumes from last year's Carnival hang from the ceiling; **burroquite costumes** – 3D structures worn around the waist, usually by children – depicting flying elephants, mice and birds are suspended from the walls. Outside at the back, in the shade of a mango tree, are a series of large stone blocks. These blocks, now used as convenient seats, are in fact a broken **British coat of arms**.

Outside Carnival season, costumes and puppets are made for international events such as the **Olympic Games** and **World Cup** ceremonies and **Jean Michel Jarre** concerts. The camp also makes and restores furniture. Visitors are welcome, though bear in mind that during Carnival season production is at its most hectic; look around as quickly and quietly as possible, to avoid disrupting production or incurring the wrath of exhausted crew members.

The Minshall-Callaloo mas camp is open Mon–Sat 10am–6pm. For more information ☎ 634 4491.

For more on Trinidad's Carnival, see pp.92, 94 & 291.

Chaguaramas Development Authority (CDA) ✩

On the back road on Chaguaramas town is the **Chaguaramas Development Authority**, set up to promote the region. Their **information centre** contains little more than a display of the odd live snake, turtle, and a few specimen jars containing dead reptiles and baby sharks. The CDA's activities are rather more inspiring. During the summer, it runs a **nature camp** for children (aged 7–13) which includes hiking, bird-watching and outdoor survival (TT$200 for two weeks). They also run **tours**, with experienced and knowledgeable guides, to the **Bocas** (see p.111) and eco-educational tours in the **Chaguaramas National Park**. These include a 7-kilometre hike through lush vegetation and cultivated forest of the **Tucker Estate**, the first citrus plantation in the

West to
Chaguar-
amas

If you ask any Trinidadian about their opinion of **Peter Minshall**, be prepared for a long reply. In a country where Carnival is of the utmost importance, Minshall is the most talked about, most controversial and most
admired of all Carnival designers, and his unique combination of traditional Carnival characters with innovative new techniques is presented
with a strong sense of theatre.

Minshall was born in Guyana and raised in Trinidad. He studied theatre
design at the Central School of Art and Design in London, becoming a mas
designer almost by accident after his mother asked him to make a costume
for his adopted sister. The design, called "Flight of the Hummingbird",
won Junior Carnival Queen and Individual of the Year, and made such an
impression on Trinidad it was even featured on postage stamps.

Minshall returned to England, where he designed his first Carnival band
for the Notting Hill Carnival in 1975, and embarked on a career as a theatre designer. Returning to Trinidad soon afterwards, he designed
Paradise Lost, the first of many nationally acclaimed bands he has contributed to the nation's Carnival. His Callaloo Company, formed in 1991,
includes many of Trinidad's top actors, dancers and artists. Callaloo is a
production company, construction factory and performance group. This
close-knit and loyal crew takes its name from Trinidad's national dish,
whose various ingredients reflect the country's ethnic mix; "all ah we is
one" is the company's philosophy.

Unlike many Carnival costumes, which are thrown away on Ash
Wednesday, Minshall's decorate houses throughout the land. While most
contemporary mas tends to concentrate on escapist, fantasy themes with
minimal costumes, Minshall's lavish and detailed works deal with spiritual
and political issues – the environment, the interconnectedness of humani-
ty and the transience of life. Many of his pieces are more like kinetic sculptures than costumes in the traditional sense – huge puppets with moving
limbs, and butterflies with enormous fluttering wings. In emphasizing the
aspect of Carnival that allows people to escape their own identity in playing a role, Minshall is continuing the tradition of Carnival as theatre for all:
"In most countries," he has often remarked, "people pay to see others perform, however in Trinidad people pay *to* perform."

*The
Chaguaramas
Development
Authority is
open Mon–Fri
8am–3.45pm.
Tours cost
US$25 plus.
Call* ☎
*625 1503 or
634 4364 or
634 4349.*

island. The **Covigne River** tour entails a hike upriver through a twisting
gorge, and up a waterfall to an emerald bathing pool. Tours up Mount
Catherine are good for bird-watching, and the trail affords some excellent views over the rainforests of the area. The CDA also provides
guides for the **Edith Falls** trail (see opposite).

It is possible to rent a tent from the CDA (TT$40–80 per day) and
camp in the forest. The facilities are very primitive, with no facilities
except for drinkable water from the nearby stream, but the environment is awe-inspiring as you pitch tent in virgin rainforest, surrounded by parrots, monkeys and bubbling brooks.

Chagville Beach and Small Boats

Immediately beyond the police post on the WMR as you come into
Chaguaramas, **Chagville Beach** is an unremarkable pebbly strip,

fringed by grass and almond trees. The sea can sometimes get quite rough, though it is calmer in the mornings. Despite the fact that swimming is not recommended during the wet season due to downstream pollution, the water still gets packed with bathers at weekends and public holidays. Facilities are limited – basically toilets that are sometimes open, a car park, a bar and a snack parlour, *Checkies* – but there are plenty of restaurants within five minutes' drive in either direction.

A calmer – though not necessarily any cleaner – spot for bathing is a couple of minutes' drive down the road at Williams Bay, adjacent to the Trinidad and Tobago Yachting Association. Known locally as **Small Boats**, this is a popular place for a swim at any time of day or night, despite the fact that the narrow, pebbly beach is often polluted by refuse washed up from the sea. There are no facilities, though refreshments can be bought at the fashionable *Anchorage* restaurant and bar nearby.

Edith Falls

North of Chaguaramas town on the Tucker Valley Road is a well-signposted left turn to the **Edith Falls**. This will take you onto Bellerazand Road, but you'll have to keep an eye out from here as the beginning of the small trail to the falls – on the left of the road just before the practice range of the Chaguaramas Golf Course – is not clearly marked. Once found, however, it's an easy 30-minute walk (1.5km) through the rainforest, which is rich in **exotic flora**: bamboo stools, halconia flowers, fishtail palms, and rubber trees seeping their black squidgy sap. **Red howler monkeys** roar like sea lions; yellowtails and bluejays glide around, and large **blue emperor butterflies** brush past, unperturbed by your presence. At the end of the trail, you must scramble up a few boulders to reach the waterfall. Water seeps through the steep craggy rockface, sending showers tumbling 180 metres into the shallow pool below.

Macqueripe Beach

The small cove of **Macqueripe Beach** lies on the north coast, at the far end of the Tucker Valley Road. A curve of coarse brown sand sheltering beneath a steep wooded hillside, it's an idyllic spot with stunning sunsets and – on a clear day – a distant view of the mountains of Venezuela. The sea on this side of the peninsula is unpolluted and perfect for swimming, and though the beach can get crowded at weekends, you'll often find it deserted the rest of the time.

In the 1930s and 40s, Macqueripe was a fashionable resort, the haunt of movie stars such as Errol Flynn. There is no longer any accommodation on the bay, however, and the beach can only be reached by private transport. The car park barrier is the entrance to the beach; a series of steps takes you down to the sea. There are basic facilities; toilets in the car park and a shower on the beach, though you will need to bring your own refreshments – the nearest food outlet is *Checkies* in Chaguaramas town.

The T&T Yachting Association offers sailing lessons to adults and children. A two-week course for children age seven upwards costs TT$500. Call ☎ 634 4519 or 4210.

Macqueripe Beach is open 6am–6pm.

The marinas: Crews Inn, Peakes and Industrial Marine Services (IMS)

The **marinas** along Western Main Road have been developed in recent years to serve the radidly growing yachting fraternity, which docks in Trinidad to avoid the hurricane season in the rest of the Caribbean. **Peakes** (☎634 4420) has a supermarket, ABM, a fast food outlet and a well-stocked boat shop. Deluxe **Crews Inn Marina**, the newest of the three, has a doctor's service, an attractive restaurant and a series of smart shops selling everything from marine equipment to books. The **Industrial Marine Services** provides technical and maintenance support for yachties and their craft. TIDCO produces an excellent *Boaters' Directory* that includes all boat services, information, tide tables and Trini titbits.

The Cove

The Cove is open daily 7.30am–6.30pm. TT$5 adults, TT$2 children. ☎634 4319.

The Cove, at the end of the Western Main Road, is a narrow beach of coarse brown sand with the most developed, best maintained facilities along this stretch of coast. The sea is calm and, though the water is the cleanest on the south coast, it is still quite polluted, and cannot really be recommended for bathing. The entrance charge means that the beach is usually quiet. There's a lifeguard on duty during the day, and there are changing cubicles, showers, toilets and a swimming pool. There is also a bar serving refreshments and light meals (6.30am–2am).

Beyond The Cove, the land belongs to the Trinidad and Tobago coastguard, and is closed to the public.

Eating and entertainment

Chaguaramas has several excellent **restaurants**, **bars** and **nightspots**. The only problem is the lack of public transport after dusk – if you do not have a car it is best to arrange a return taxi in advance.

The Anchorage, Point Gourde Rd, Chaguaramas, ☎634 4334. Continental food with a local flavour served in an open-air restaurant overlooking the rainforest and harbour – one of the most romantic views in Trinidad during the day, though you can't see much at night. Elegant casual dress is required. Average meal TT$100. The restaurant is also a fashionable nightclub at weekends, mostly attracting people of 25 and over. Dance to a variety of music and watch the catfish swirl about the pier. Opening hours vary. Entrance fee varies, starting at TT$50.

The Base, cor. Airways and Macqueripe Rd, Chaguaramas, ☎634 4004. Attracting a young, well-to-do crowd, this club has been the subject of press allegations that it operates a racist door policy. Plays dancehall, calypso and alternative music. Smart casual dress. Fri & Sat 9pm–4.30am. Entrance TT$30–50.

Baya's On the Beach, Western Main Rd, Carenage, ☎637 2222. Restaurant and pub built out into the sea. International and Creole food, disco and calypso music. Attracts mature office worker clientele. Open Tues–Sun 4pm–midnight. Average meal TT$150.

The Bight, Peakes Marina, Western Main Rd, Chaguaramas, ☎634 4839. Small a-c restaurant and bar, with a verandah overlooking the marina – an excellent place to meet yachties. Serves international food – sandwiches to steaks – at international prices. Daily 7.30am–midnight. Average meal TT$50–100.

Buccoo Rouge, Upper Level, West Mall, West Moorings, ☎632 4601. New upmarket French seafood restaurant. Exquisite lobster bisque and delicious desserts from the chef who previously cooked for Francois Mitterand and the QE2. The oyster bar is open all day. Open Mon–Sat 11am–11pm. Average meal TT$200 plus.

Club Millennium, The Cove, Western Main Rd, ☎634 4166 or 637 6535. The least expensive nightclub in the area. Playing a wide selection of music from disco to reggae to jazz. Busy at weekends; during the week people chill out playing pool, cards and dominoes. Very mixed crowd – all ages from 19 to 65. Open Mon–Thurs 6.30pm–2am, Fri & Sat 9pm–5am. Entrance fee between TT$20 and TT$40.

The Lighthouse, Crews Inn Marina, Point Gourde, Chaguaramas, ☎634 4384. Attractive open-air restaurant and bar overlooking yacht marina, underneath red and white striped lighthouse. Serves international food with Creole specialities aimed at mainly yachtie clientele. Daily 7.30am–10pm. Bar open till 11pm. Average meal TT$60–100.

Moon Over Bourbon Street, West Mall, West Moorings, ☎637 3448. Café-bar with large balcony and expensive drinks. A good pre-clubbing spot, it attracts an arty crowd; occasional live entertainment including pan, jazz and alternative rock. Open Sun–Thurs 5pm–midnight, Fri–Sat 5pm–2am.

O2 (Oxygene), The Amphitheatre, Welcome Bay, Chaguaramas, no phone. Open-air auditorium overlooking Small Boats beach. Concerts advertised in the press. Entrance fee varies.

Pier One, Western Main Rd, Chagville, ☎634 4472 or 4426, fax 634 4556. Open-air nightclub overlooking the sea. Attracts yuppie crowd. Live acts publicized in press. Open Wed (Latin night) & Fri 7pm–3am, Sat (1980s music) 8.30pm–1am. Entrance fee varies.

Upper Level Club, Second Level, West Mall, West Moorings, ☎637 1753. Small glitzy nightclub attracting all ages from 20-somethings up. Thurs (dub/soca), Fri & Sat (dancehall/soft rock) 10pm–4am. Entrance TT$20.

The Bocas

When you hear Trinidadians refer to the **BOCAS**, they talk of "down de islands" in tones of wistful longing. These rocky islets are separated from the mainland, and from one another, by the the **Bocas del Dragon (Dragon's Mouths)**, a series of channels connecting the Gulf of Paria with the Caribbean. The name is appropriate, for the coastlines here are jagged and rocky, and the sea hides lethal currents and undertows that can make even the short journey to the nearest island, **Gaspar Grande**, a rough ride.

The islands had a thriving **whaling industry** in the eighteenth century, with whaling stations on Gaspar Grande, **Monos** and **Chacachacare**. Today they are sparsely inhabited, their interiors covered with dense forest, uncrossed by any roads. Scattered around

The Bocas

the coasts are a few holiday homes, accessible only by boat. The islands have always been the Trinidadians' escape from the mainland, but apart from the *Fantasy Island* resort on Gaspar Grande, there are no hotels, guesthouses, restaurants or bars; visitors must bring their own food. Once there, for the most part, you will be alone with the birdsong and the sound of the sea. The atmosphere is so still it can verge on the uncanny, especially on deserted Chacachacare, with its abandoned leper colony and tales of ghosts.

Getting to the islands

The **Island Property Owners' Association** (on Western Main Road, just before The Cove) has boats (known locally as a **pirogues**) that go to the islands. Prices are for up to six people, so it is cheapest to go in a group or share a boat with mainlanders who service the islands' holiday homes going to and from work at the beginning and end of the day. Fares (one way) are TT$50 to Gaspar Grande (unless you're staying at the resort; see opposite), TT$60 to Monos and TT$400 to Chacachacare; for more information, call ☎634 4331. Members of the **Trinidad Yacht Club** (☎637 4260) can also arrange transport to and from the islands. If you want to **tour the Bocas** for the day, you can also rent a boat (and driver) for TT$600. Before disembarking, arrange a pick-up time to ensure you are not stranded on the islands.

Both the **Chaguaramas Development Authority** (☎634 4364) and **Dreamtime Tours** (☎637 5694, email *xavier01@trinidad .net*) run a variety of day trips to the Gasparee Caves and Chacachacare. A standard trip costs US$100 for up to eight people. They also offer diving trips around the area as well as **fishing** tours. The islands are renowned for their **fishing**, and it is possible to go out with local fishermen in Gasparee Bay; a 90-minute trip costs TT$150; contact *Fantasy Island* resort (☎678 9001) for information.

Gaspar Grande

The Gasparee Caves are open daily 9am–3pm.

Just fifteen minutes by boat from the mainland, **GASPAR GRANDE** (also known as **Gasparee** and **Fantasy Island**) is the most accessible of the islands. The eerie **Gasparee Caves** (TT$10 adults) at Point Baliene – "Whale Point" – were once used by pirates, and though you may not find any buried treasure, they are full of brightly coloured stalactites and stalagmites. It's also an excellent place to observe the **fruit bats** which live in the caves and the many local species of bird which congregate outside them.

The one cave open to the public is the largest; follow the concrete path from the jetty to the white and mustard wooden house, where you'll find a **CDA tour guide** to show you around. It's a mysterious and weirdly beautiful place, some 35 metres deep. Reflected sunlight causes calcium crystals in the rocks to sparkle, and a deep, clear pool reflects the extravagant colours and strange shapes of the stalactites and stalagmites, which the locals have given names such as "the

Lovers", "Buddha" and the "Virgin Mary". Apart from the chirping fruit bats and dripping water, the cave is totally silent.

Incidentally, the small rocky island you'll see to the east on your way to Gaspar Grande is **Carrera**, Trinidad's equivalent of Alcatraz. Its only building is the prison, established in 1876, where convicts still do hard labour. No one has ever escaped – the strong current makes the short swim to the mainland a death-defying venture.

The Bocas

Fantasy Island Resort

On the other side of Gaspar Grande from the caves, the **Fantasy Island Resort** (postal address 67 Mucurapo Rd, St James, ☎678 9001or 622 4588; ⑤) consists of a restaurant, café, beach with facilities, swimming pool, hotel and self-catering apartments. The small beach, with shaded palm huts, a sun deck, and a **waterslide** into the sea, is very popular with locals at the weekend. The resort provides pleasant rooms with a-c, phone, en-suite bathroom and fridge; some have a sea view. Fully furnished **apartments** can be rented for the same price per person. The *Lobster House* restaurant (7.30am–3am daily), built to resemble a steamboat, has a lovely view over the sea to the mainland. It serves excellent fresh fish; the average meal costs around TT$70.

To get to the resort, take the Fantasy Island boat from the Island Property Owners' Association at The Cove (see opposite). Shuttle service every hour on the half hour, 8am–6.30pm. TT$2.

Scotland Bay, Monos and Huevos

Though actually part of the mainland, **Scotland Bay** is always considered as being "down de islands", since it can only be reached by boat. A favourite with Trinidadian weekenders, this idyllic small cove at the westernmost end of the Western Tip is blessed with soft sand and calm waters. Yachts are often moored in its shelter, although the beach has no facilities. It was from nearby **Staubles Bay** that the government shelled the Northern Range during the Black Power uprising in the 1970s (see p.289).

Scotland Bay looks out across the swirling waters of the Boca de Monos to the island of **Monos**, uninhabited bar a few holiday homes belonging to rich Trinidadians. The densely wooded interior supports a large colony of red howler monkeys – the island's name is Spanish for apes. Beyond the sheer western ramparts of Monos and another fierce *boca* lies the privately owned and seldom visited island of **Huevos**.

Chacachacare

Chacachacare is the largest island of the Bocas and, an hour's journey from the mainland, also the farthest-flung. It is utterly peaceful, and its idyllic coves, with their excellent **fishing** and **swimming, are** ideal for those who want to get away from it all. There are none of the well-to-do holiday homes found on the other islands, and the mountainous interior is covered in dense forest. There is just one usable road, leading from the jetty to the lighthouse; the others, which once serviced the **abandoned leper colony**, have long been overgrown, and only tracks remain.

The island's name may derive from *chac-chac*, the Amerindian word for cotton, which grows profusely on the island, or might have something to do with the chattering of the monkeys once found here. Amerindian remains, dating from around 100–400 AD, have been discovered on the island. Under Spanish rule it became a cotton plantation, and subsequently a whaling station was established. It developed into a popular health and holiday resort with Trinis from the mainland until, to their consternation, a leper colony was established in 1887. The Dominican nuns ran the colony like a prison, and conditions provoked strikes among the patients to gain such rights as male-female fraternization. The last 30 patients left in 1984, and all that remains is the decaying wooden houses, the nuns' quarters and the church. The island is now uninhabited except for the two men who work the small, white **lighthouse**, built in 1885, although the leper colony is said to be haunted by the ghost of a nun who committed suicide after becoming pregnant by a local fisherman.

On the southeast of the island is **La Tinta Bay**; the name, meaning ink, alludes to the black sand of its beaches. Once a favourite place for smugglers, today this coarse-grained beach is deserted save for the refuse washed up by the tide, and the odd iguana and scavenging hawk. Nearby is the **Salt Pond,** a sulphurous lake. The chemical promotes the growth of unusual trees such as the campecho, known locally as the **bread and cheese tree** on account of its textured fruit and cheesy taste. The odd **manchineel** tree also grows on the island's beaches. Its beautiful yellow flowers hide the fact that it produces a sinister fruit, used by the Amerindians to make poisoned arrows. Avoid contact with any part of this tree: its sap causes painful blisters (see pp.124 & 244).

Chapter 2

The North

Stretching 80-odd kilometres from the Saddle Road which climbs out of Port of Spain in the west to Galera Point in the east, the north of Trinidad is dominated by the rainforested mountains of the Northern Range, which form a rugged east–west spine through the centre of the region, and boast the island's highest peaks, El Cerro del Aripo and El Tucuche. Trinidad's most splendid beaches line the coast to the north of the range, with the enduringly popular Maracas Bay and Las Cuevas playing host to what often seems like the entire population of Port of Spain come the weekends. Beyond Las Cuevas lies the glorious seashore of Blanchisseuse, where the North Coast Road dissolves into kilometres of undeveloped coastline. The Arima–Blanchisseuse Road then swings inland through the forest, providing an opportunity to see most of the island's prolific bird life at the Asa Wright Nature Centre.

Away from the uninhabited, jungle-smothered hills is some of Trinidad's most **densely populated** landscape outside of Port of Spain, home to the majority of the island's **African** population. Though you'll see the odd temple, mosque and prayer flag, Indian culture is far less visible than in the south; Creole cooking reigns supreme and the soundtrack that blares from shops, bars and maxis is **soca** and Jamaican **dancehall** rather than chutney. To the south of the mountains, a string of busy communities crowd along the traffic-choked **Eastern Main Road** (EMR) and the faster flowing **Churchill Roosevelt Highway** which runs parallel to it; both end abruptly just east of Arima, replaced by the winding minor roads that span the weatherbeaten northeast coast. Inland of the EMR, river valleys cut into the Northern Range, providing access (and public transportation) to the naturally abundant interior.

The main transport artery of the **East–West Corridor**, the EMR is the route to a host of interior attractions; there are **waterfalls** and **river swimming** at **Maracas Valley, Caura** and the **Hollis Reservoir**. The **Heights of Guanapo Road** boasts two of the island's most spectacular cascades, **La Laja** and **Sombasson**, as well as the challenging **Guanapo Gorge**, a spectacular water channel that's not for the fainthearted. Many of the towns along the EMR are equally absorbing,

The North

particularly **St Joseph**, the island's first Spanish capital, with its historic church and barracks. The largest town in the region, **Arima** is great for window shopping, and the town's **Carib** community go on parade in late August at the **Feast of Santa Rosa**.

Past Arima, the road continues to the **Northeast Tip.** This wild and rugged peninsula, jutting some 20km into the Atlantic Ocean, is Trinidad's best-kept secret. The populace is overwhelmingly friendly, and along the **Toco coast** on its northern side, **leatherback turtles** clamber up the wave-battered sandy beaches to lay their eggs.

The 1998 issue of TIDCO's road map has a blow-up of the Northern Range; all the major attractions are marked and there's a lot of detail.

Though parts of the north are well-served by **public transport** – buses, taxis and maxis serve every village and town along the East–West Corridor – a **car** is useful to visit the more remote north coast, where long waits often ensue if you don't have your own vehicle. Surprisingly, there is not a huge amount of **accommodation** in the region; though there are lovely guesthouses at Blanchisseuse and Grande Riviere, it's often easier to explore from Port of Spain as you can see all the sights during day trips. However, reached after a minimum of three hour's driving from town, the remote northeast is the only place where you might be better off renting a room.

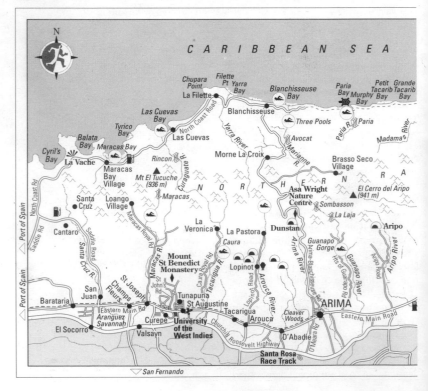

The Saddle to the North Coast Road

Saddle Road (usually called "the Saddle") makes one of the region's
best scenic journeys, climbing the western flank of the range dividing Maraval valley from Port of Spain, squeezing through a narrow
mountain pass and descending on the other side into lush **Santa
Cruz** valley. However, most drive straight past the Saddle turn-off
and continue upwards, navigating the coastal fringes of the Northern
Range along the **North Coast Road**, smooth and spectacularly
enhanced by borders of glittering Caribbean sea and cliff sides
smothered with tangled jungle that becomes quite crowded at the
weekends when crowds descend from nearby Port of Spain heading
for **Maracas Bay** and some of the finest **beaches** on the island.
Though it's Trinidad's major concession to sun, sand and sea,
Maracas is not a "tourist beach", and like the other seashores in the
region, you'll find more local than foreign devotees soaking up the
sun. Nonetheless, the Maracas coast does represent the island's most
tourist-oriented region, a ravishing coastline sprinkled with rest
stops selling crafts and cold drinks, designated "scenic areas" to stop

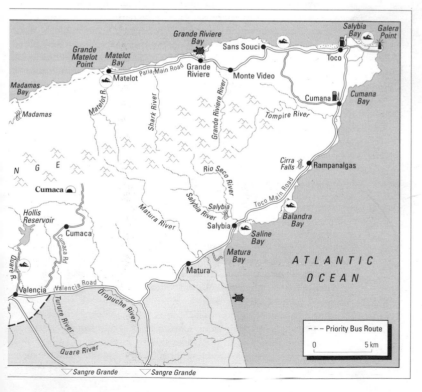

ACCOMMODATION PRICE CODES

All accommodation listed in this guide has been graded according to the following **price categories**:

① under US$10   ② US$10–20   ③ US$20–35
④ US$35–50   ⑤ US$50–70   ⑥ US$70–100
⑦ US$100–150   ⑧ US$150–200   ⑨ US$200 and above

Rates are for the cheapest double or twin rooms, including 10 percent tax and 10 percent service charge where applicable. In Tobago, rates quoted are those used during the high season, normally mid December–mid April. During low season (mid April–mid December) rates are liable to fall by up to 25 percent. There are no high and low seasons in Trinidad, but rates may rise by up to 70 percent during Carnival. Many hotels give rates in US dollars – we have followed suit. Payment can be made in either US or TT currency.

and admire the view and miles of sandy beaches with well-maintained facilities. You can whisk past the whole lot in a couple of hours of driving, but the area hasn't yet compromised its local character or succumbed to leisure development; most villages still rely on **fishing** or **farming**, and hotels are few and far between.

Beyond Maracas and shimmering **Las Cuevas**, a stunning sandy cove riddled with underwater **caves**, the north coast remains quiet, maintaining equanimity in the face of seemingly inevitable development. Gorgeous **Yarra beach** is customarily deserted and slow-paced village life at hamlets such as **La Filette** make interesting distraction from the sea. At **Blanchisseuse**, you can choose between a host of small-scale **guesthouses** and countless rugged beaches; beyond here, the coast road ends, replaced by miles of **undeveloped coastline**. Perfect coconut-littered beaches and a series of **waterfalls** – **Paria** is particularly beautiful – make this prime **hiking** territory, and you can even stay in the area; **Petit Tacarib** Bay houses the island's most remote guesthouse.

The Saddle to Santa Cruz

Gliding by St Andrew's Golf Course and the last of Maraval's grand residences (see pp.98–101), Saddle Road begins its serpentine ascent into the Northern Range. The roadside buildings gradually give way to abundant rainforest, and after a succession of hairpin bends, two 3-metre high stone pillars make a rather unexpected border to the tarmac and mark a **junction**. To the left is the **North Coast Road**; to the right, **Saddle Road** squeezes through a narrow gorge of solid rock (if driving, beep your horn and approach with caution) before meandering downhill through pastoral **Santa Cruz valley**, a half-hour scenic jaunt along a single main road through cattle pastures and farmland to the urban bedlam of San Juan (see p.136). Neat cocoa groves, crumbling tapia houses and dilapidated gingerbread palaces are punctuated by towering samaan trees and impressive clumps of bamboo, mango, sapodilla and banana, while a thriving **quarrying** concern has gouged messy yellow scars into the hillsides. Cricket supremo **Brian Lara** spent his childhood in **Cantaro Village**, the valley's largest community. The place has a friendly, suburban feel, its main focus the lively main street, lined with shops and rum bars, which swings off from Saddle Road. Past the village, the Saddle cuts through the countryside for several pleasant kilometres before the roadside houses of the San Juan suburbs block the views.

A serene Port of Spain satellite cut off from the city and the coast by mountains rather than distance, the valley is the starting point for a hilly but popular **hike** to Maracas Bay along the **La Sagesse trail** – less often attempted are treks to Las Cuevas or the Maracas-St Joseph valley, though an experienced guide is essential to prevent you from getting lost. As the La Sagesse–Maracas Bay route is so heavily travelled, it's pretty easy to follow on your own; however, reports of robberies make it sensible to travel with a group, and preferably with a local guide; see Basics (p.45) for a list of options. It's a pleasant 8-kilometre, 2- to 3-hour up-and-down hill walk through secondary forest with good views of the northern coastline on the descent; to get to the start, turn off the Saddle at Gasparillo Road (marked by a signpost for a quarry) and carry straight on, passing the quarry on the right. The hike begins where the houses end; ask for directions to the first stretch of path.

The North
Coast Road
to Maracas

If you're hungry, try the roti shop cum general store on the main road near the petrol station on the outskirts of Cantaro; alternatively, there are plenty of small local restaurants in the village.

The North Coast Road to Maracas

Taking the left turn at the Saddle-North Coast Road pillars sets you off on one of Trinidad's most dramatic drives, teetering along 300-metre cliffs and tunnelling past precipices of teeming rainforest with the occasional view of faraway peaks swinging into sight. Bois cano trees drop claw-like leaves onto the tarmac and mineral springs pour down into roadside gullies; the water is chilled, delicious and safe to drink, and in places has been channelled through bamboo pipes at which people stop to fill bottles. Despite its spiralling course, this is also one of the smoothest roads on the island, built by US Army engineers in 1944 as a recompense for the American occupation of the Chaguaramas peninsula (see p.105), which deprived the citizens of Port of Spain of sea bathing at Macqueripe and other western bays. This route to Maracas Bay was offered as the alternative, and it's still sometimes called the "American Road".

The first of many panoramas stretches over the Maraval valley and across the hills to the tiny spice and parang centre Paramin (see p.99) and right down into the outskirts of Port of Spain, with the sea just visible over the National Stadium and compacted buildings of Woodbrook and Mucurapo. Cliffs and jungle close in beyond here (though you get a few glimpses of Santa Cruz to the right), but a few kilometres further on, the vegetation dissolves to reveal a marvellous coastal prospect, the ocean far below dotted with rocky islets. The

*"P" and "H"
registration
jeeps run the
45min Port of
Spain–
Maracas route,
from the cor-
ner of Prince
and George
streets or
Queen and
George streets.
Services can
be sporadic;
fares are TT$6
to Maracas
and TT$7 to
Las Cuevas.*

largest is 100,000 square metre **Saut D'eau**, a breeding colony for brown pelicans and home to the chestnut-collared swift and the rufous-necked wood rail. Getting down to the sea isn't easy here, though; the cliffs are steep and most bays are only reachable by boat. However, a secluded dip is the reward for a stiff 20-minute walk down to **Cyril's Bay**, a pebble beach just before the La Vache look-out point (see below); to make the descent, look for a cream painted board house. Just past the house, a road sign says "slow, sharp bend"; beyond this and a couple more hairpin bends is the overgrown mouth of the path, next to a grassy lay-by where you can park. The agreeably strenuous 20-minute walk weaves down through balata-dominated evergreen forest humming with bird and animal life. As the path nears the sea, you pass a stone house; if at home, owner Frank welcomes visitors to his menagerie of ducks, geese, dogs and squirrels. You must also pass through his land to get to a 3-metre **waterfall** which he has harnessed and dammed – as it's his drinking water, swimming is discouraged. He also guides trips to nearby islands and caves aboard his pirogue; one nearby cavern supports a colony of **oilbirds** (see p.307). Swimming is pretty safe – the murki-ness of the water is the result of sediment from the River Orinoco rather than pollution, and there's a couple of offshore rocks that you can dive from.

La Vache Scenic Area

Past Cyril's Bay, the road continues its stomach-lurching circumnav-igation of the cliffs. The brightly painted *Hot Bamboo Hut* is a friendly place to stop for soft drinks and coconut candies; cool breezes and sea views add to its allure. Tourist trinkets and coconut shell or crystal jewellery are on sale; their chess pieces are fashioned from shark bones. If you stop by between 4 and 6pm, ask the owner to call the flock of **toucans** that inhabit the forest above, and watch them swoop impressively down to their cliff-side roosts. The air cools noticeably as you climb to **La Vache Scenic Area**, a viewpoint overlooking the sea laid at the highest point on the North Coast Road; the coastal views are marvellous. At weekends, vendors sell fruits and cold drinks to the hordes on their way to Maracas beach, and likely-looking targets are serenaded by the resident **busker**, who improvises calypsos; he'll expect a few dollars if he makes you laugh.

Below La Vache, a precipitous tarmac road leads 280m down the cliff to **Timberline**, an former cocoa estate house on a secluded bluff, now transformed into a restaurant and guesthouse (☎638 2263; ⑤). The constant sea breeze, magnificent views of Balata Bay to the right and Cyril's to the left, and occasional glimpses of Venezuela, make this an alluring place to stop. Iron tables on the grass are perfect for a quiet cocktail or creole **lunch** (around TT$70); if you fancy a romantic dinner from the excellent seafood menu (from TT$75), you'll need to call in advance. If dining or drink-

The magnetic road to Maracas Bay

A small stretch of apparently ordinary tarmac between La Vache and
Maracas Bay has a unique claim to fame; according to local folklore, this is
the "**magnetic road**", where vehicles roll up the incline in defiance of gravity. Though it cannot be rationally explained, it's easily experienced. Stop
just before the North Coast Road begins its descent to Maracas Bay. As the
cliffs to the right recede, revealing the Northern Range, the road ahead
appears to have a definite upward incline. On stopping your vehicle,
putting the gears in neutral and releasing the handbrake, you'd assume that
the car would obey the rules of gravity and roll backwards; however, you
move in what you would imagine to be completely the wrong direction.
Although the more level-headed conclude that this apparent marvel is nothing more than an optical illusion, more romantic locals insist that the contrary movement is the work of God, Obeah or a bizarre magnetic field.

ing you can also make the 25-minute downhill scramble to a **beach**
so seldom-used it might as well be private. This is also the only
accommodation option between Maraval and Maracas; two basic
rooms in the old estate manager's home (quaintly called Sunlight and
Moonlight) have hot and cold water and huge windows; rates include
breakfast and dinner.

   Timberline is also the point from which to explore **Balata Bay**, a
pretty shingle and coarse sand beach with two small rivers running
into the ocean; take the concrete path that leads off to the right just
before the guesthouse, and ask permission from the caretaker who
lives on the estate surrounding the bay – the staff at *Timberline* usually know where to find him. They can also point you in the direction
of a bench trail which runs westward along the coast to Cyril's Bay.

Maracas Bay

The smell of burning brake linings fills the air as the road plunges
toward **MARACAS BAY**, three-quarters of an hour's drive from Port
of Spain. The most popular stretch of shore on the island, this is
more than a beach – it's an institution. Hundreds make the traditional Sunday pilgrimage from Port of Spain to show off their newest
swimwear, frolic in the water and promenade around *the* place to
swim, sunbathe, network – and be seen by everyone else to be doing
it in style. Deck chairs, umbrellas, coolers packed with beer or rum
and hampers of cooked food are de rigueur, while boogie boards
flash through the surf, muscle-men play beach tennis and local lads
put on the occasional acrobatics display – if they can find space
between the beach accoutrements. It's also the island's main Ash
Wednesday chill-out spot, where revellers come to relax after the
mayhem of Carnival, and sound systems keep the prostrated bodies
twitching to the beat.

   At the eastern end of the bay, *Uncle Sam and Son*'s bar pumps
reggae and soca over the sand, while the bake and shark vendors do

Maracas Bay

a roaring trade. Unusually for a Caribbean beach, Maracas is whole-heartedly dedicated to local people rather than tourists, and you'll find yourself sharing the sand with everyone from Port of Spain's fashionable elite to extended families enjoying a day in the sun. On weekdays it's a much quieter place – the sand is almost empty and the extensive facilities built by the tourist board look a bit out of place.

Maracas deserves all this attention; it's a gorgeous beach, a generous 1850-metre curve of fine off-white sand bordered by groves of skinny-stemmed palm trees. To the west of the bay, a river divides the bathing area from **Maracas Bay Village**, a fishing hamlet whose catch is in demand throughout the north; super-fresh carite, cavalli, shark and "small fry" are sold here once the boats return in the afternoon. Here you'll find a couple of snack parlour-cum-rum bars, a loose arrangement of houses, lots of beached pirogues and drying nets, a profusion of scavenging dogs and fewer people bathing; most stick to the main beach and avoid the odd fishy entrail. Wherever you swim out to sea, you'll get a sublime view of the beach and its backdrop; cloud-tipped peaks rise up in a majestic swell of deep green, while the forested bluffs funnel breezes on even the hottest of days. Licked into a fury by passing currents and the wind tunnel effect of the surrounding headlands, the waves often reach a metre high and make for an exhilarating swim; the water is usually clear and emerald green. It's never a good idea to go out too far, however, as the tides and undercurrents are often dangerously strong; stick to the areas between red and yellow flags. Lifeguards stand by (daily 10am–6pm), whistling furiously if anyone goes too far.

Practicalities

Built by the tourist board in the mid-1990s, Maracas' **facilities** have transformed the beach and somewhat obscured its beauty; concrete huts interspersed with palm-thatched shade covers are scattered all over the main stretch of sand. The huge car park (TT$10 per entry; you'll get a ticket if you park elsewhere at weekends) has a block of showers, changing rooms and toilets (daily 10am–6pm; TT$1). **Watersports** are somewhat limited: there are surf bikes for rent (TT$30 for half an hour) some weekends, and kayaks are occasionally chugged in from Chaguaramas – call ☎633 7871 for details.

The only **accommodation** option is the imaginatively-named *Maracas Bay Hotel* (☎669 1914 or 1643, fax 623 1444; ④), a bland if serviceable dollop of concrete at the west end of the bay. Rooms are plain but well equipped, with tile floors, a-c and balcony. You may also be able to rent a room in the village (ask for Uncle Sonny), though many Trinis simply spread a tarpaulin and camp during holiday weekends.

When it comes to **eating**, bake and shark is the obvious choice; if you don't fancy shark, some shacks serve kingfish instead. Alternatively, you can also find aloo and fish pies or roti. The *Maracas Bay* hotel (see above) is a good option for a sit-down meal of fish or local fare. The *Bay View* restaurant, on the headland west of the bay, has great views, though its fish meals are mediocre – best to stick to the cold beers. On the beach, alcohol is sold at *Uncle Sam*'s bar and from a couple of shacks on the sand; all of the bake and shark vendors sell soft drinks or freshly squeezed orange juice.

Tyrico Bay

Hidden from Maracas by a steep headland, **TYRICO BAY** is about 1 kilometre east. Inexplicably popular with the Indian community, who flock here for weekend picnics, family beach cricket tournaments and camp-outs, the bay is roughly half the size of Maracas with slightly less in the way of wave action, making it a better choice if you are travelling with children. Luxuriant fine yellow sand and a gentle shelve add to the feeling of calm, and as there are no food and drink vendors, Tyrico is quieter and more unspoiled than its neighbour. The only buildings are the lifeguard towers (guards are on duty daily 10am–6pm) and portable toilets, and you can drive right down to the sand.

Las Cuevas Bay and around

After an inland curve that provides impressive views of the jagged double apex of Mount El Tucuche, Trinidad's second highest mountain (see p.139), the North Coast Road turns back to the sea at **Las Cuevas Bay**, the north coast's second most popular strip of sand, with a fishing village spreading uphill to the east of the beach. That bit further from Port of Spain, Las Cuevas is less of a fashion parade at the weekends than Maracas, and during the week, it's often deserted. It's hard to imagine why, as this deliciously unadorned swathe of whitish sand is wide and clean, fringed by impossibly tall, windbent coconut palms and inviting green sea. Headlands enclose the cove in a tight horseshoe, affording protection from the wind and a relatively gentle surf. Named by the Spanish after the caves that riddle the rocks to the west end of the bay as well as the seabed, Las Cuevas is a great place for beachcombing especially along the seldom-visited western reaches, littered with shells and stones. The only drawback is the legendary **sandfly** population, a particular problem in the late afternoon or after rain – take repellent and try to cover up as the day wears on.

Though there's no development on the beach itself, there is a car park above the bay (free), as well as changing rooms, showers and toilets (10am–6pm; TT$1). Lifeguards patrol and put out yellow and red flags to advise on safe bathing spots. Vendors sell water coconuts, and if you're **hungry**, try *McLean's* bar at the western edge of the car park, a favourite with local fishermen, serving Creole breakfast and lunch alongside the Carib and rum; even wild meat – manicou, iguana or agouti – is on offer if you ask in advance. The *Las Cuevas Rec Club*, right on the road before the bay, is a low-key **drinking** spot; they also sell pholouri and aloo pies. Sadly, there's nowhere to **stay** in Las Cuevas at present, unless you want to camp out on the beach.

Las Cuevas Bay

The petrol station on the eastern edge of Maracas Bay is the last on this section of coast, so it's wise to fill up if you haven't already done so.

North Coast Road maxis and taxis from Port of Spain (see p.61) usually stop at Las Cuevas; unless you're lucky enough to meet one for Blanchisseuse, you'll have to thumb a lift to go any further.

One Thousand Steps Beach

On the eastern outskirts of Las Cuevas, secluded **One Thousand Steps Beach** is so called because of the seemingly endless concrete steps which wind down the cliffs to the sand. Easily missed and ideal for a secluded swim, this curve of soft greyish sand is backed by almond trees – one growing horizontally over the sand – and a few **manchineels**, which should be treated with caution (see pp.124 & 244). At the eastern end, the sea has pounded a lookout hole through the rocks, and you can climb over boulders at the western corner to another deserted bay. Though the water is often glassily smooth, you should be careful when swimming here, keeping to a depth you can stand in – the tides can be strong even on apparently calm days, and there's no one to help if you encounter problems. To find the beach, turn down Mitchell's Trace, a dirt track opposite the larger Rincon Trace, which strikes inland from the North Coast Road a kilometre or so east of Las Cuevas. The latter is also the route to spectacular **Rincon Waterfall** and pools, a two-and-a-half-hour uphill walk through the bush. You'll need a guide to find this and nearby **Angel Falls**, though the latter is often dry or filled in by small landslides. Laurence Pierre (☎632 4204 or 634 4284) makes a good guide as he knows the area intimately.

La Filette and Yarra

The wide, clear road surrounding Las Cuevas narrows as it enters the fishing village of **LA FILETTE**, an improbably pretty cluster of neat houses and blooming front gardens straddled over two hillocks. A parlour in the centre of town (opposite a phonecard booth) sells groceries and snacks, while a sparkling new rum bar on the western outskirts is good for watching the world go by with a "beastly" cold beer or gossiping with the fishermen about the rumoured **contraband** landing spots on this part of coast.

Beyond the village, after a long, straight stretch of road, all vehicles must slow down to cross a rickety plank bridge over one of the **Yarra River's** many strands. There are four smaller board bridges to cross before the road passes a young teak plantation and enters **YARRA**, a rather deserted hamlet made up of grand beach houses. Look out for a grassy turn-off toward the sea, the only one not leading to a house; this goes to **Yarra Beach**, another perfect, deserted seashore. Wide and sweeping, with white sand fine enough to remain on the limbs long after a shower, Yarra has two main bays which shift in size and shape according to the season. Offshore is a rock painted with the legend "Yaradise Bay", and as you're likely to have the whole place to yourself, it's not difficult to imagine that you really are in Eden. Another Yarra River tributary runs down to the sea, sometimes deep enough for a white-water body surf right into the ocean, where the water is pleasantly active and clear. As always on this coast, take care while swimming and be sensible if you feel strong tides. About

30m past the entrance to the beach, look out for another offshore
rock on which the word "**hollyweed**" has been painted in foot-high
letters – an allusion to the bales of marijuana which are said to be
imported and exported from these beaches.

Blanchisseuse

Five minutes' drive along the narrow, jungle-lined road from Yarra
brings you back to the coast and into **BLANCHISSEUSE** (pronounced "blaan-she-shers"), the last village before the road tails off
into the bush. With a population of around 3000, Blanchisseuse isn't
exactly a hamlet, and the clutch of flashy holiday homes on the western outskirts – some garish, some tasteful – are testament to its
growing popularity as a retreat. At present, though, things are still
pretty quiet; the atmosphere is relaxed and supremely friendly, and
there are as many local holidaymakers as there are foreign. Tourists
divide their time between the succession of marvellous sandy **beaches**, or hiring a local guide and hiking through the rainforest for river
swimming in the unpolluted waters of nearby **Three Pools**, **Paria
Beach** and **waterfall**, or the **Avocat Waterfall** on the
Arima/Blanchisseuse Road (see pp.128, 130 and 132).

Accommodation

Blanchisseuse has the greatest number of **rooms** along this part of
the coast. It's wise to book ahead if visiting on weekends or national
holidays when Trinidadians come down for a bit of rest and relax-
ation. All the guesthouses are small scale; tucked away at the very
end of the road, *Laguna Mar* is the largest and most professional,
with twelve rooms. The rest of the guesthouses are strung along the
North Coast Road, with the majority in the more lively surrounds of
the upper village. If you've got a tent – or a piece of tarpaulin, the
local material of choice – you can **camp** on the beach at the
Marianne Beach Resort for TT$30 per tent; this includes the use of
toilets, showers and rather lax security protection.

Almond Brook, ☎678 0822. By far the most atmospheric place in the upper
village, with wood-panelled rooms decorated with shells and plants; all have
mosquito nets, private bathroom and queen-size bed; one has a full kitchen,
the others fridges. Breakfast is included in the rates, and the extremely genial
owner also rents a two-bedroom beach house in its own garden with a verandah and full amenities. ④

Laguna Mar, c/o Zollna House, 12 Ramlogan Development, La Seiva, Maraval,
☎628 3731, fax 628 3737. The most established hotel in Blanchisseuse, this
takes pride of place at the end of the road with its own access to Marianne
beach. Rooms are on the inland side of the road, housed in blocks of six with
a lovely communal balcony; each has two double beds, fans and private bathroom. The German/Trinidadian owners are well-known local figures and great
hosts. ⑤

Northern Sea View Villa, ☎637 7619 or 4619. The least expensive option in
town, these two stark and basic apartments offer little in the way of luxury, but

Blanchi-
sseuse

*Another
accommoda-
tion option is
the secluded
nature resort
at Petit
Tacarib, a
half-hour boat
journey (or
four hour
walk) from
Blanchisseuse
(see p.131);
owner Gordon
De La Costa
(☎ 624 1774)
organizes the
vessel.*

*There are a
couple of small
groceries dot-
ted around
town, as well
as a post office
in the lower
village.*

the location opposite Marianne beach is great and the owners are extremely
friendly. Both have two bedrooms with a fan, a kitchen, verandah and living
room. Excellent if in a group or on a budget. ②

North Star Villa, ☎ 637 7619 or 4619. Owned by the same family as *Northern
Sea View*, this spacious yellow villa on the hill before the road descends to
Marianne beach has clean, basic rooms with a shared bathroom or a self-contained studio apartment with wooden floors, double bed, kitchenette with
microwave and a constant sea breeze from the balcony. ④/⑤

Surf's Country Inn, ☎ 662 2554, fax 669 2475. Precipitously placed above the
surfers' beach, the three rooms are great value, attractive and fully mosquito-
screened ,with terracotta floor tiles, fridge, fan, nice bathroom and verandah or
terrace. The on-site restaurant is excellent; rates include breakfast. ④

Vista Del Mar, ☎ 662 7534, fax 663 1454. A coolly attractive blue and white
building overlooking the surfer's beach; two self-contained apartments have
rattan furnishings, full kitchens, living room and a verandah with great sea
views, while bedrooms and bathrooms are suitably luxurious. There's a sun
deck, hammock-dotted gazebo and barbecue pit on the lawn below – meals are
available on request and breakfast is included in the rates. ⑤

Windrush, ☎ 669 5111, fax 623 1634, email *delisle@carib-link.net*. A well-
maintained private home tucked away on the corner of Paradise Hill Road in
the upper village, offering bed and breakfast. You're living pretty much with
the family, but the double room is pleasant, spotless and comfortable with a
private bathroom. A cottage opposite Marianne beach is also available; the two
bedrooms have a single and a double bed, full kitchen, living room, patio and
private garden. ④

The village
Lower Blanchisseuse to the west is the older portion of the village,
an attractive assortment of weather-beaten board houses and crumbling tapias wreathed by rambling bougainvillea and neat croton
hedges. Steep cliffs plunge down to the ocean and breaks in the
palms or almond trees reveal the white-tipped waves of the intensely
blue sea below. The villagey atmosphere is sealed by a couple of rum
bars, a fishermen's co-operative building, a post office and a boxy,
single-spired Catholic **church** overlooking the sea, complete with
three bells housed in an outdoor tower. Young men stare as a vehicle
passes by, octogenarians while away the hours in front of the bars
and chickens pick for scraps in the middle of the tarmac.

    Upper Blanchisseuse begins after the road descends downhill and
loops inland to meet the Arima–Blanchisseuse Road. This is the main
residential section, dominated by the attractive arched windows and
cream porticoes of the Georgian-style **police station**. General stores
(including the wonderfully-named *Fattah Foods*) and more pastel-
painted homes cluster by the roadside, while residential streets trail
uphill into the bush. Behind the police station is the community centre and a playing field which sees some serious football in the late
afternoon; more or less opposite is the roadside shack housing
Lloyd's Leather Craft – the work is well-executed and inexpensive,
and Lloyd is something of a character.

Past Lloyd's shop, buildings start to thin out, and another downhill stretch brings the coast road to sea level, running parallel to Marianne beach, the town's largest (see pp.127–128). The last building is the *Cocos Hut* restaurant; beyond here, the road runs parallel to the Marianne River lagoon, ending at the **Silver Suspension Bridge** which straddles the water and is a popular swimming spot with bridge diving possibilities. Over the bridge, the tarmac ends, replaced by a rutted dirt road. You can drive on for a kilometre or two (not recommended in the rainy season), but otherwise, the only means of progressing east to Paria and beyond is on foot (see pp.129–130).

Blanchisseuse beaches
Like most in this section of coastline, **Blanchisseuse beaches** are ruggedly beautiful. However, while it's unlikely that you'll be swept away during your first dip, they do have a reputation for rough and **treacherous waters**, particularly between November and February when mighty breakers crash onto the sand and the surfers come into their element. Whatever the time of year, it's wise to ask local advice before taking the plunge, and keep to a depth you can stand in.

The first of the three main beaches can be reached via the concrete steps opposite *Surf's Country Inn* (see opposite) before you enter the lower village. Popular with crowds of sun-bronzed surfers, the beach has been locally renamed in their honour as **surfer's beach**; its true name – **L'Anse Martin** – is seldom used. The seashore here is wide and open with an almost imperceptible shelve that makes for excellent waves. Craggy rocks border each end and the forest drips down from the cliffs onto the sand. It's also popular for a spot of late afternoon **fishing**, with anglers casting lines from the water's edge.

Another easy path to the sea starts next to the fishermen's co-operative in the lower village. This fishermen's beach is a place to lime and admire the view rather than to swim, since the measly pebble shore is littered with dead boats and straddled by a half-built wooden jetty; the concrete foundations of the unbuilt portion are gradually being eroded by the surf. Just 50m further down the road, though, down some steps marked by a broken sign atop a green pole, is a marvellous **bathing beach**, with around 200m of soft grey sand and a feeling of complete seclusion. Headlands provide protection and gentle waves, while almonds and sea grapes tangle down the cliffs. Watch out for a few offshore rocks while swimming.

Marianne is the main – and the longest – beach in Blanchisseuse, stretching around 2km from the busiest portion of the upper village, where concrete steps lead down to the sand, right to the *Cocos Hut* restaurant (see p.129) and the river lagoon at the end of the North Coast Road. It's a completely breathtaking seashore, wide and straight with both coarse and fine yellow sand battered by crashing

A reputable guide to local attractions is jovial Eric Blackman, owner of Northern Sea View Villa (see p.125), where he's usually available to arrange excursions; his fees are reasonable.

waves and awe-inspiring views of the uninhabited coast beyond –the perfect place to watch the moon rising over the headlands from the east. At the eastern end is a huge, vegetation-smothered boulder; past this, the clear river water is partially dammed by the sand into a lagoon – an inviting place to swim, particularly if the sea looks rough. Locals tend to congregate here for an after-work bathe, and fishermen paddle rough canoes in search of freshwater salmon.

Following a track over the forested headland at the eastern corner of Marianne takes you to another seldom-used beach, but most choose to swim right opposite the lagoon. The owners of *Laguna Mar* resort (see p.125) have cut a path through the swampland which divides the eastern portion of the beach from the road, and put in a couple of picnic tables and benches. You can use the showers and toilets at a sandy car park grandly named the *Marianne Beach Resort* (TT$5), 100m or so west of the *Laguna Mar* entrance.

Marianne River and Three Pools

Spanned by the **Silver Suspension Bridge** – graceful and still solid despite its hundred years – the **Marianne River** is the source of much local recreation, as well as the village's name: dating from French Creole times, "Blanchisseuse" refers to the laundresses who washed clothing in the river. Regular buses of **bird-watchers** park up at a lay-by to the side of the bridge to see the green woodpeckers, yellow orioles and silvered antbird.

The Marianne itself is a typical Northern Range watercourse, originating at Brasso Seco (see p.133) and tumbling downhill, carving deep swimming pools and waterfalls along the way. You can take a watery trek along the riverbed to **Three Pools**, an hour or so from the mouth of the Marianne. Most people hire a guide in the village to lead the way and draw attention to the abundant plant, bird and animal life, but it's a fairly straightforward route that you can follow independently. Following the riverbed is the fastest way to get there, a combination of splashing through calf- (and sometimes waist) deep water and swimming (sticking to the banks takes a lot longer), so don't carry anything that can't get wet. To reach the pools, take the path into the woods to the right of the road just before the bridge (the "No Entry" sign is universally ignored); you meet the water after five minutes. Overhung by vines, ferns and huge buttress-rooted trees, it's a gorgeous and easy wade, bar the odd overhanging bank. Though the water deepens to form several enticing swimming pools along the way, the stunning Three Pools easily surpass any of the other swimming spots. At around 12m across, the first is the least impressive, though it does have a **water-slide** of sorts, formed by the current coursing through a narrow rock channel. Over this, the smooth grey rock which characterizes the pools begins; huge boulders rise up from water so deep it's hard to touch the bottom, and a second gushing channel creates a **natural jacuzzi**. Though it's the smallest, the

last pool is the most impressive, overhung by tall cliffs. The water
here has worn a deep channel, carving the rock into bizarre folds and
small caves; you can swim right in and climb a little to see the waterfall above. To go beyond this point to Avocat Falls (see p.132), you'll
need a guide; almost everyone in the village knows the way, or you
can go with Eric Blackman of *Northern Sea View Villa* (see p.125).

Eating and drinking

Blanchisseuse has a good but limited selection of low-key **restaurants**, though you should give advance notice for dinner as many
kitchens cook to order or close early. Prices are moderate – expect to
pay around TT$90 for dinner. Grandest are the hotel restaurants; by
far the most popular is *Cocos Hut* (☎628 3731), a converted cocoa
drying house across the road from *Laguna Mar*. The Germanic decor
and music policy may be more evocative of the Rhine than the
Caribbean, but once soca replaces the marching bands and owner
Frank Zollna turns on the charm, this intimate eatery with indoor and
outdoor seating is great for a sit-down meal. Dinners consist of tasty,
local-style fish, chicken, beef or pork, though vegetarians are catered
for – ask in advance. Breakfast (eggs, bacon, toast and fruit etc) and
lunch (hot meals or salads and sandwiches) are served daily. The bar
is nice for an evening drink, its end-of-the-road location and regular
clientele providing a sense of cosy isolation. Another option for semi-
upmarket dining is the open-air restaurant at *Surf's Country Inn*
(☎669 2554), beautifully located on a boardwalk overlooking the sea
and shaded by silk cotton boughs. The seafood-based menu stretches
to innovative preparation of vegetables; they also do breakfast and
lunch. In the upper village, try *Gilbert's*, perched on the cliff by a
bend in the road with a couple of tables overlooking the sea.
Breakfasts of bake and scrambled egg, bacon or cheese sandwiches
and lunch or dinner of stew or jerk chicken, peas, veg and potatoes
with onions are tasty and inexpensive.

Blanchisseuse tends to quieten down early, but as the locals still
need to lime and unwind at the end of a day's work, the **rum shops** are
fairly lively after dark, particularly on a weekend. In the lower village,
Casbah is a classic Trinidadian drinking hole with a pool table, dim
lights, a verandah for catching the breeze and "no bareback, spitting
on the floor or obscene language" notices painted on to the walls. The
Butterfly Rec Club, behind the playing field in the upper village, is
more or less the same, bedecked with coloured fairy lights. Another
large bar-cum-parlour in the lower village tends to close early.

The north coast bench trail

Beyond Blanchisseuse, the North Coast Road gives way to the only
remaining piece of **undeveloped coastline** in Trinidad. The next
piece of tarmac is some 30km away in Matelot (see p.154); in
between, you'll find some of Trinidad's most impressive hiking

The north coast bench trail

along a **bench trail**; the local name for the old donkey tracks cut in the late nineteenth century for transporting goods and produce between the villages and servicing the then-thriving cocoa estates. Well-trodden, the trail dips and climbs through the remnants of abandoned estates and secondary forest, with the sea swinging spectacularly in and out of view.

There are periodic government suggestions for the construction of a **road** along this stretch of the coast; environmental groups and landowners (most of the coast is in private hands) have successfully lobbied against the idea, though most agree that it's only a matter of time before tarmac is laid through the forest. At present, though, the area remains a sanctuary for bird and animal life, and many of the beaches are prime laying spots for the **leatherback turtle** (see p.305).

Though few attempt it, you can hike the bench trail all the way from Blanchisseuse to Matelot, but only the fittest could hope to complete the journey in a day. Most make the trip in two stages, making camp along the way. Though the trail is easy to follow, it is not a good idea to walk in this area alone; it's remote enough to make getting help difficult if you run into trouble, and reports of drug landings at deserted bays suggest that you may feel safer if accompanied by a guide (and his/her cutlass). If you prefer a solitary hike, walk during the week; Saturdays, Sundays and public holidays are prime times for local hiking groups or individual ramblers to take to the bush.

Blanchisseuse to Paria Bay

Though you should start the Paria hike with a full bottle, don't worry about conserving water; the trail passes streams from which it is safe to drink.

From Blanchisseuse, the most often-attempted hike is the moderately challenging round-trip trek to **Paria Bay** and its inland **waterfall**, a moderately challenging trek that you can do in a couple of hours at a good pace, though most stop to admire the scenery and make a day of it. Past the suspension bridge, the track passes beach houses for the first couple of kilometres; an uphill fork make an attractive if unnecessary detour, bringing you back to the main trail after a few minutes. Logging vehicles have widened the bench trail in some parts, and as a result it can get muddy in the rainy season, but little can detract from the marvellous forest around; look out for massive bachac nests and a splendid specimen of the weird **cannonball tree**, with its heavily perfumed, rotund pink flowers and dangling, twisted branches which sprout 5-centimetre wide brown "cannonballs" from the base of the trunk to the main boughs. Birdsong is a constant accompaniment, the soothing calls often shattered by the raucous shriek of passing parrots.

Depending upon your pace, you'll reach Paria Bay in two to three hours. The **beach** is an idyllic 1km of fine, coconut-littered golden sand backed in true treasure island style by jungle and groves of palms. Other than a couple of ramshackle fisherman's shelters, it's

Making Carnival costumes

Playing the steel pan

Kiddies' Carnival

Relaxing after work, Port of Spain

Central Port of Spain

Boissiere House, Port of Spain

Football on the beach at Las Cuevas

Manzanilla.coconut groves

Baptist prayer flags at Toco

The Waterloo Temple

Ice cream stall on Manzanilla Beach

Grande Riviere beach

Hand-painted sign in central Trinidad

Coconut grove on Manzanilla beach

completely undisturbed, with craggy grey rocks out to sea and a river at the eastern end; the high headland above is **Paria Point**. A cliff at the western corner has been eroded at the base to form an arch. Swimming is safe and the waves are usually moderate. If you want to press on to the **waterfall**, walk two-thirds of the way up the beach and head inland at a "no trespassing" notice which everyone ignores. The path meets the Paria River, which brings you to the waterfall in about fifteen minutes. Crystal clear and freezing cold spring water crashes down the 5-metre cascade into a deep swimming pool around 10 metres across.

Paria Bay to Matelot

Past Paria Bay, the bench trail is less well-travelled and a little more overgrown. After ten minutes' walk, you come to another attractive beach, **Murphy Bay**. You can carry on up the coast from here to **Petit** and **Grande Tacarib bays**; the walk to Petit Tacarib will take around an hour and a half. Both have marvellous sandy beaches, separated by half an hour's walk and the inexplicably-named **Trou Bouilli-Riz Point**; from here, it's a six hour walk to civilization at Matelot.

Another hour and a half from Grande Tacarib along the bench trail through less well-travelled jungle, you come to **Madamas Bay**, another curve of deserted off-white sand which rivals Paria in the beauty stakes. Half an hour inland from the beach is another gorgeous cataract, **Madamas waterfall**, though you'll need a guide to find it. However, if you want to see the area without straining your muscles, you can now arrange to **stay** at **Petit Tacarib**, but as preparing for guests is time-consuming, the resort only takes groups of four or more, preferably for more than four days. Almost single-handedly, local landowner Gordon De La Costa has built three cedar-framed bamboo cabanas and a cooking shed right above the bay; the whole ensemble is simply called *Petit Tacaribe* (c/o 5 Moore Ave, St Ann's, Port of Spain; ☎624 1774, *email tacaribe@wow.net*; ④). Most people get there via boat from Blanchisseuse (organized by the *Tacaribe* owners), which costs TT$200 each way and takes about half an hour; six people and their baggage can cram in, but you can always hike if feeling hardy. Rates cover food and drinks, though you should buy any extras – beer, rum, chocolate etc – yourself. Undoubtedly the most unusual resort in Trinidad, *Petit Tacaribe* is a magical place, completely secluded and drenched in natural beauty. Leatherbacks lay eggs on the sand during the March–June season, and as the surrounding bush is well-stocked with agouti, armadillo, manicou and quenk, you may get wild meat for dinner as well as freshly caught fish or chicken brought up from Blanchisseuse. Days are spent lazing on the beach or in the hammocks, hiking to Madamas, hunting in the bush or bird-watching, and if you like the natural life, this is a chance in a million.

There's an alternative route to Paria Bay and Waterfall from Brasso Seco (see p.133), but you'll need a guide; try Carl Fitz-James Jnr (☎667 5968), who lives in Brasso Seco.

The Arima–Blanchisseuse Road

Inland from Blanchisseuse, the **Arima–Blanchisseuse Road** cuts south through the middle of the steamy Northern Range forest, climbing high into misty, breeze cooled peaks and descending to the **Asa Wright Nature Centre**, one of the Caribbean's finest bird-watching sites. Small villages like **Morne La Croix** and **Brasso Seco** seem contentedly stuck in a time warp, and make excellent starting points for exploring the **waterfalls** that course through the mountains. Light filtering through the overhanging canopies of mahogany, teak, poui, cedar and immortelle colours the tunnel-like road green, and every available surface is smothered in plant life; mosses, ferns and lichens cover rocks and tree trunks already laden with massive wild pine bromeliads; vines and monkey's ladder lianas trail down to the tarmac and the manic calls of crested oropendolas and bearded bellbirds echo across the peaks.

Wet and humid, the first portion of road from Blanchisseuse is carpeted by composting leaves. A succession of hairpin bends set a slow pace as the road begins a gentle climb, each quarter mile marked by a post at the roadside put in during English control of the island. Just before the twenty-and-a-quarter marker, look out for a neat grove of pommerac trees to the left; here, a track leads past a few modest dwellings and provision grounds to the **Avocat Falls**. After a ten-minute walk, you reach a river (a tributary of the Marianne); turn left and walk along the banks or the riverbed for twenty minutes until you reach a watery junction. Wade over the river and grab hold of one of the roots that wreathe the steep bank. Haul yourself up, and straight in front of you is a pretty 12-metre cascade with a deep pool below; there are even some vines for swinging on.

Morne la Croix

*For a glossary
of Trini
English terms,
see p.312.*

Past Avocat, the Arima–Blanchisseuse Road climbs a steep hill before entering the tiny hamlet of **MORNE LA CROIX**, a pretty village where most of the inhabitants still speak French Creole as well as Trini English. Development comes slow in the middle of the Northern Range; when government planned to install electricity poles in 1996, there was much debate over whether the villagers wanted a current at all – to date, only a few houses and the general store are hooked up. Just beyond the town, look for a hedge of purple-flowered vervain, a favourite haunt of yellow-breasted ruby-topaz **hummingbirds** and the distinctive red crest of the tufted coquette. There are some stunning views of the mountains below here, too, and you're more or less guaranteed to see **bird life** wherever you stop; the spectacular metre-long, teardrop-shaped nests of the crested oropendola are commonplace. As the road climbs ever higher, you pass a lookout point adjacent to a dirt road called Andrew's Trace. A break in the forest and an elevation of just over 600m provides chilly breezes and sweeping views across the valleys, with the sea just visible if the mists haven't set in; ornate hawk-eagles and black or grey hawks coast on the thermal updraughts as they scan the bush for food.

Brasso Seco

The only sizeable village past La Croix, **BRASSO SECO** is tucked away at the end of a signposted turn-off from the Arima–Blanchisseuse road. A ten-minute drive past converted cocoa houses and still-occupied tapia houses brings you into the village's main street, where there's a rum shop-parlour, a church, a school and an overwhelmingly languorous atmosphere; kids play cricket in the middle of the road, young men lime outside the rec club and everyone has time to greet each other with an exchange or a wave.

There are some lovely walks in the area; naturalist Courtenay Rooks guides **nature hikes** and **bird-watching trips** from his base at Paria Springs, a ten-minute drive from the centre of the village. He can also introduce you to local families with a spare **room** if you want to stay in Brasso Seco (see p.45 for more details of his tours). Paria Springs is soon to be an eco resort built in Amerindian style, with canopy walkways and a research station, but none of the cabanas have gone up as yet, and at the moment, the resort consists of an old cocoa house serving as office and caretakers' lodge. Brasso Seco resident Carl Fitz-James Jnr (☎667 5968) is another good guide for exploring the may local waterfalls; he lives in the village – ask anyone to direct you to his home.

Asa Wright Nature Centre

A bird-watcher's paradise contained in the 800,000 square metre Spring Hill estate, the **Asa Wright Nature Centre** (PO Box 4710, Arima, Trinidad; ☎667 4655, fax 667 4540; in US via Caligo Ventures, ☎1-800/426 7781, fax 914/273 6370; ⑥) was originally a coffee, citrus and cocoa plantation. In 1947 it was bought by one Dr Newcome Wright and his Icelandic wife, Asa. Both were keen amateur naturalists and bird-watchers, so when the New York Zoological Society set up the Simla Tropical Research Station on neighbouring land, the couple began to accommodate visiting researchers. After her husband died, Mrs Wright sold the land on condition it remained a **conservation area**; a non-profit-making trust was set up in 1967, which established a nature centre to accommodate naturalists and birdwatchers, a first in the Caribbean. Simla closed in 1970, but donated its land and the research station to the centre – botanists and ornithologists still study here today. Twenty years later, Asa Wright is Trinidad's most popular birding retreat, and commitment to conservation remains; a further square kilometre of land recently acquired from the government will be left in a natural state, and an interpretative centre is under construction to raise environmental awareness among local kids.

The centre revolves around the **great house**, a 90 year-old maze of polished mahogany floors and stately heirlooms with a **verandah** overlooking the spectacular Arima valley. At 360m above sea level, the views of the rainforest are incredible, and since Mrs Wright began feeding them in the 1950s, the verandah has attracted a huge variety of **birds**; you can see up to forty species per day. Face-level feeders attract dazzling-hued, thumb-sized hummingbirds, and trays of fruit below are gorged by green and red-legged honeycreepers, blue-grey tanagers and white-bearded or golden-headed manakins as well the ever-present quota of precocious bananaquits and a host of more sporadic visitors. Matte lizards and agoutis clear up the scraps, and the surrounding trees glitter with the brightly coloured feathers of nesting and roosting birds; rufous-tailed jacamars, toucans, mot-mots, woodpeckers, trogons, yellow orioles and the yellow-tailed crested oropendola, which nests in a bois cano tree to the left of the verandah. This multitude of bird-life attracts daily crowds, the low murmur of voices broken by the excited squeals of an unusual sighting, or by the whirr and click of paparazzi-standard zoom lenses. A network of well-marked **trails** for walks ranging from ten minutes to two hours threads through the grounds; you can walk them alone or join the expertly conducted **guided tours** (daily 10.30am & 1.30pm; free). Residents of more than three nights get a tour of **Dunston Cave**, which houses the world's most accessible colony of **oilbirds**.

For more on oilbirds, see p.307

The centre is open to the public (daily 10am–5pm; US$6); entrance fee includes a tour and access to the verandah and you can have an excellent buffet lunch for TT$40; sandwiches and drinks are available on the verandah if you don't want a cooked meal. Resident guests tend to be middle-aged American bird fanatics toting state-of-the-art binoculars or camera equipment, and checklists of a day's sightings are enthusiastically compiled over sunset rum punches. **Accommodation** is quite luxurious, with large screened verandahs, en-suite bathroom and two double beds; rates include three meals a day and afternoon tea. Informed field trips to Trinidad's premier birding sites are also on offer to resident guests.

Beyond Asa Wright, the road dips downhill, rounding spectacular corners and passing hillsides cleared for christophene cultivation, the vines supported by a rough trellis network. As you near Arima (see p.144), the jungle thins out and a few sporadic buildings – including a bar – appear at the roadside. Look out for the tiny do-it-yourself Hindu temples to the left of the road just before the right turn to Calvary Hill; locals refer to the area as "**temple village**".

The East–West Corridor

Running along the southern flank of the Northern Range, the **East–West Corridor** is the main route between the east and west coasts of the island. It is traversed by the **Eastern Main Road**, a dri-

ver's nightmare for the unfamiliar, ruled as it is by capricious local
driving practices. If they're not avoiding the rush by taking the
Priority Bus Route, a fast track commuter thoroughfare built where
the now-obsolete **train tracks** were in service, the back-to-back
maxis and route taxis that shuttle between each community seem to
delight in stopping abruptly with insouciant abandon that's terrifying
if you're behind the wheel but extremely convenient if you're relying
on **public transport**. Hot and dusty as it is, the slow pace does at
least allow you to absorb the commercial chaos; lined by a constant
parade of shops, stalls, restaurants, bars and offices, the EMR buzzes
with life – dodging delivery trucks, shoppers throng the pavements
and vendors fill the air with the sweet aromas of street food. The mer-
cantile aspect doesn't let up until you've passed **Arima**, the corridor's largest town and home to what's left of Trinidad's **Carib** community. In between, some interesting towns are slung along the road;
bustling **San Juan** with its frenetic crossroads and the old Spanish
capital of **St Joseph**, where elegant colonial edifices sit incongruously with this century's rash of concrete, are both interesting to
explore, but most of the communities are so close together, it's hard
to tell where one district tails off and another begins.

However, as the EMR skirts the foothills of the Northern Range
and a host of attractions, there's good reason to navigate this often
fraught route, if not to stay here; all of the sights can be seen in day-
trips from Port of Spain. Inland of St Joseph, the **Maracas Valley
waterfall** crashes magnificently down 90m of sheer rock to a decent
bathing pool; the area is a holy spot for followers of the Hindu, Orisa
and Spiritual Baptist faiths. East of the falls, **Caura** and **Lopinot** have
plenty of possibilities for **picnicking**, **hiking** and **river swimming**;
the latter also has a network of **caves** to explore. At 240m above sea
level, the **Mount St Benedict monastery** dominates the hillside, providing a panoramic view of the Caroni plains and a restive spot for
afternoon tea. Beyond Arima, the buildings let up and almost-
impenetrable rainforest rises sharply from the road, but a few country lanes lead to some marvellous natural attractions; **La Laja** and
Sombasson waterfalls are two of the most impressive on the island,
while **Guanapo Gorge**, a 400m water channel overhung by towering
grey rock, is completely breathtaking. At **Aripo**, you can hike
through undisturbed forest to the island's largest cave network and
see a colony of squawking **oilbirds**; the forests are also richly populated by the full quota of Trinidad's **mammals**, and hunters make
regular forays after agouti, armadillo, wild pig and manicou; if you're
really lucky, you might catch sight of one of the ocelots that live on
the flanks of **El Cerro del Aripo**, the island's highest mountain.
Inland of quiescent **Valencia**, the **Hollis Reservoir** rises like a sea in
the middle of the forest, a host of birdlife twittering in the trees.

The EMR is paralleled by the snaking **Churchill Roosevelt
Highway**, which doubles up as an impromptu market place; fruit and

veg stalls or trucks filled with "fresh Maracas fish" line the hard shoulder while itinerant vendors hawking everything from Portugal oranges to Congo peppers, steering wheel covers, toys and newspapers lie in wait at the traffic lights, while road signs tacked to the bridges – locally called "walkovers" – exhort you to "relax and enjoy the drive". The highway comes to an abrupt **end** after Arima, replaced by a smaller dual carriageway which takes you on to the Eastern Main Road and Valencia.

San Juan

The easternmost of a succession of communities that sprawl along the length of the Eastern Main Road, brash, commercial **SAN JUAN** (pronounced sah-wah) avoids being a Port of Spain satellite by the skin of its teeth. The town's focal point is the **"croisee"** (pronounced *kwaysay*), a bustling junction marked by the Scotiabank clock tower, which was named when French Creole was the main local vernacular – "croisee" translates as "crossroads". It's a scene of agreeable, organized pandemonium; doubles vendors, fruit and veg stalls and racks of sportswear line the streets while gangs of limers compete for the pavement with perusing buyers, and fleets of taxis honk endlessly. The croisee is equally lively after dark, when the flambeaux of oyster salesmen throw up whiffs of pitch oil and "power punch" milkshake vendors provide party-goers with sustenance.

South of the croisee, between the EMR and the highway, is **El Socorro** district, a community dominated by the **Aranguez Savannah**, a main venue for the annual **Phagwa** celebrations in March (see p.163). If you're **hungry**, forgo the host of eateries on the EMR and head for Back Chain Street, adjacent to the Savannah, where *Ali's* serve up particularly delicious roti.

St Joseph

Past the vast West Indian Tobacco Company and Carib beer factories at **Champs Fleurs** on the outskirts of San Juan, a major junction of the EMR leads to the Uriah Butler Highway, the route to the "deep south" (see p.188); left of the highway is the smart Eric Williams Medical Science Complex at Mount Hope, Trinidad's best-equipped hospital. After the junction, the EMR's commercial trappings temporarily thin out; once you pass the Water and Sewerage Authority (WASA) offices, a venue for one of the larger **carnival fetes**, you're in **ST JOSEPH**, Trinidad's oldest European town and first official capital. The streets of St Joseph still reek of history, with genteel colonial French and Spanish architecture jostling with newer concrete structures, market stalls and swarms of children attending one of the many schools, and it's one of the better places along the EMR to get a flavour of the East–West Corridor.

Some history

In 1592, acting on behalf of Spanish Governor Don Antonio de Berrio y Oruna, Lieutenant Domingo de Vera founded a town on the site of an Amerindian settlement. Christening it **San José de Oruna**, de Vera built a church, a prison-cum-police barracks, Governor's residence and a *cabildo* (town hall). In 1595, **Sir Walter Raleigh** attacked San José, burning down the church and the barracks; by 1606, both were rebuilt, only to be destroyed by the **Dutch** in 1637 and ransacked by **Caribs** in 1640. In 1687, Capuchin missionaries arrived from Spain, settling in a monastery adjacent to the church, and San José struggled along for the next eighty years. Neglected by Spain, which dismissed Trinidad as little more than a convenient stop-off during journeys to South America, the 500-odd residents scratched a living through small-scale farming.

During the eighteenth century, San José began to prosper as a **plantation town**, but in 1766 it was hit by a devastating **earthquake**. It never really recovered from this blow, and eighteen years later, Don José Maria Chacon relocated the capital to Port of Spain. San José's troubles weren't over yet, however; in 1837, a detachment of the West Indian Regiment stationed at the police station **mutinied**. Led by a Yoruba ex-slave known as Daaga, they were protesting against the apprenticeship system that kept freed Africans in a state of semi-slavery for four to six years after so-called emancipation. They set fire to the barracks, seized ammunition and fought for several days before being overwhelmed. In the aftermath, forty Africans lay dead; a firing squad **executed** Daaga and two of his comrades in front of the police station. Since then, the town has grown ever-larger, becoming a bustling commercial centre with residential districts expanding to the north into what was once Maracas Valley and has now become Maracas-St Joseph Valley.

The town

Old meets new as you cross the bridge into town; on the left is the old **police station** and **barracks**, the graceful curves and porticoes smothered by a coating of blue paint; Trinidad's first **telegraph** arrived here in 1870. Directly opposite is the imposing and elaborate **Mohammed Al Jinnah Memorial Mosque**, resplendent with a crescent and star-topped main dome flanked by two minarets; there's not much to see inside, but if you want to take a look, check at the caretaker's house, left of the Moslem school behind the mosque.

Opposite Al Jinnah, **Abercromby Street** strikes uphill into the mountains. A couple of hundred metres up, **St Joseph's Catholic Church** has undergone many changes since it was first consecrated in 1593. Its three previous incarnations were sacked along with the rest of the town, and today's Gothic-style stone and red-brick structure dates back to 1815. Impressed by the religious devotion of the townspeople who clubbed together to fund the first stages of con-

St Joseph

struction, British Governor Sir Ralph Woodford, though a Protestant himself, donated £2000 towards construction and laid the foundation stone. Inside, beautiful **stained-glass** windows depict the holy family, St John and St Andrew; the ornate Italian marble **high altar** was imported from Dublin in 1912. The graveyard behind contains headstones with inscriptions in French, English and Spanish; the oldest tombstone in the island, a weathered slab known as the **tombstone of the pirates**, is marked with a skull and crossbones and the date 1682, but no one knows the identity of the buccaneer below. Further up Abercromby Street and framed by elegantly fretworked colonial houses, **George Earl Park** was the old Spanish town square, used for evening promenades, military parades and as a burial ground; the single remaining stone, dated 1802, commemorates one Mr Thomas.

Accommodation

There's no **accommodation** in St Joseph itself, but there are two good options nearby. Tucked away on the upper reaches of Upper Quarry Drive in Champs Fleurs (follow the signs), the excellent value *Mountain View Guesthouse* (☎645 0700 or 662 6547; ②) has apartments with sitting room, full kitchen, TV, a-c; they can accommodate four people (US$30; $50 at Carnival time). Route taxis, which run all day from the junction of Quarry Drive and the EMR, can take you to your door for about TT$3. Slightly further away at 108 Valley View Drive in the Maracas-St Joseph Valley (see below), *La Belle Maison* (☎663 4413, email *la-belle@trinidad.net*; ④), is a beautifully designed private home. Owner Merle Lynch is current secretary of the Bed and Breakfast Co-Operative and a mine of local information, and *La Belle* is an excellent, friendly base for exploring the area. The three rooms have lovely valley views and private or shared bathrooms; breakfast is included and tours are available.

The Maracas-St Joseph Valley

Turning inland opposite the mosque, Abercromby Street becomes **Maracas Royal Road** less than a kilometre from the EMR, crossing the grand First River Bridge and winding north into the lush **Maracas-St Joseph Valley**, overlooked all the way by the peaks of **El Tucuche**, the island's second highest mountain. **Maracas** itself is a tiny place, all but swallowed by the suburbs of St Joseph; once you've passed its postal agency and steepled church of St Michael, the houses thin out, separated by clumps of fluffy bamboo and neat provision grounds. Some 10km from the EMR, the road ends at **Loango Village**, where there's a bar and a parlour. The bumpy tarmac of San Pedro Road, which makes a T-junction with the end of the Maracas Royal Road, provides easy access to the **bathing pools** along this section of the Maracas River, though the deepest are usually filled with swimmers from the village. The riverbed is scattered with the sparkling bronze sedimentary rocks which fed rumours of local **gold** deposits in the first years of the twentieth century.

From here, you can **hike** over the mountains to Maracas Bay, a stiff two-hour trek along an old fisherman's trail that's been more or less unused since the construction of the North Coast Road. Another possibility – if you've got stamina and don't mind heights – is to climb the 936-metre El Tucuche (variously pronounced *tuh-cutchee* or *too-koosh*). It's an eight-hour round trip, and some of the trail is bordered by a terrifying 300-metre cliff, but you'll be rewarded by spectacular epiphyte-laden **montane** forest as well as high-altitude, mist-drenched **elfin** forest. If you're lucky, you'll see **red howler monkeys** and the **golden tree frog**, Trinidad's only endemic animal, which lives in the waterlogged leaves of wild pine bromeliads. If you want to tackle Tucuche, a **guide** is essential – see p.45 for a list of options, but Laurence Pierre and Courtenay Rooks are particularly recommended.

Maracas Waterfall

Most people head to the valley for **Maracas Waterfall**, one of Trinidad's highest; to get there, turn right from the Maracas Royal Road onto the signposted Waterfall Road; the turn is about 8km from the EMR. After five minutes, the road starts to climb; here, you'll probably be met by Trevor Raymond, a local hunter and unofficial guide to the falls who rushes out of his house at each passing car. He's pleasant, knowledgeable and used to the bush, and recent reports of robberies suggest it might be wise to hire him if he's not already taking someone else up; you negotiate the fee. It's safest to park at the bottom of the hill, where there are people around, but you can drive up for another five minutes and park by an abandoned building. After fifteen minutes of uphill walking along a wide rocky track lined by groves of tall balata trees, a path strikes off to the right. This leads to the **first cascade**, three tiers of mini-waterfalls with two swimmable, ice-cold **pools**; the main waterfall is another twenty minutes' walk. Signs warning "no candles" posted on tree trunks are puzzling until you near the falls; here you'll see clusters of black and red candles or pools of wax on the rocks, left by followers of the Hindu, Spiritual Baptist and Orisa religions, who regard the waterfall as a sacred place, marking it with tall coloured flags among the trees. Rumours that some of the rituals performed here are not altogether wholesome give the place a somewhat eerie feel, but little can detract from the awesome beauty of the waterfall. Falling some 90m down a sheer rock face, the water splashes on to a rocky basin, the sunlight shimmering rainbow prisms through the droplets of spray. Water levels are low during the dry season, but you can almost always take a shower. Trevor Raymond can also guide you to **Three Steps**, a series of pools at the top of the falls where he's constructed a cooking hut and a place to camp.

Maracas Waterfall

Route taxis run from Curepe to Maracas Valley between 7am and 6pm; the fare is around TT$4; you'll pay more if you go off-route along Waterfall Road.

Curepe and St Augustine campus

Loosely arranged around the Eastern Main Road, CUREPE is another of the EMR's busy transport hubs. The Priority Bus Route runs
parallel to the road here, and maxis and taxis trickle off to park up
outside the bus terminus – a converted train station – and hawk for
trade. Cars heading for the Southern Main Road or Churchill
Roosevelt Highway create a constant traffic jam, and there's little to
stimulate the imagination.

Just past the junction, the Priority Bus Route mounts an attractive
cut-stone flyover, and a tunnel cuts underneath it to the island's academic powerhouse, the **University of the West Indies St Augustine
Campus**. Usually referred to by its acronym, UWI (yoo-wee) also has
branches in Jamaica and Barbados. The spacious campus was formerly a sugar plantation, and the great house now serves as the principal's home. The students are a cosmopolitan Caribbean mix who
descend on Port of Spain en masse for special club nights, and the
campus is the annual venue for Trinidad's priciest **all-inclusive
Carnival fete**, a massive party which usually boasts every single soca
performer of note.

Practicalities

If you want to explore the Northern Range from here, route taxis and
maxis run east and west along the EMR and inland along all the major
roads, though the more remote your destination (Lopinot, for example), the longer you'll wait. Most inland taxis leave from the EMR by
the appropriate junction, ask locals where to catch one. Out of the few
accommodation options *Naden's Court*, 52, St Augustine Circular
Rd (☎645 2937 or 662 1341, fax 645 2358; ②) is by far the best
choice, a supremely friendly, attractive place close to UWI – take a left
opposite the campus entrance. Rooms are not fancy, but functional
and very clean with shared or private shower; some have a-c. There's
an area for washing clothes and meals are available. *Scarlet Ibis*
(☎662 2251 or 663 1914; ③) is a down-at-heel 1970s tower on the
EMR just past the university turn-off, with run-down rooms – each has
bathroom, fan and an ancient a-c unit – a restaurant, pool and exces-
sive rates; you might want to haggle. Christians can try the rather
overpriced *Hosanna Hotel*, Santa Margarita Circular Road, St
Augustine (☎662 5449, fax 662 5451; ⑤); signs warning "no smoking, no unmarried couples, no arms and ammunition, no alcohol" are
pasted up in reception. Rooms are quite nice, with a-c and TV, and
there's a restaurant and intermittently-filled pool.

For **food** and **drink**, you'll find the usual selection of local restaurants and darkened rum shops along the EMR; there are late night roti
and doubles vendors at Curepe junction, while *KFC* and *Pizza Hut*
share a building on the highway. If you're in the mood to **party**, try the
Flamingo Penthouse (☎662 2251), on the EMR between St
Augustine and Tunapuna or the excellent Sunday School dance

*[handwritten: Carribean Lodge
662 3000
32 St Augustine]*

(10pm–4am; TT$10) run by Rastafarian sect Twelve Tribes. It's held right on the EMR; look for red, gold and green Rasta flags draped over the entrance. Kay Donna drive-in **cinema** is on the corner of Churchill Roosevelt Highway and the Southern Main Road; turn right at Curepe junction, and check daily newspapers for programme details.

Mount St Benedict

Just past the main body of Curepe, the **Exodus panyard** occupies the corner of the EMR and St John's Road, its pans stacked neatly in the practice space. Until 1998, when Arima's Nutones steelband scooped the coveted **National Panorama** title, Exodus – guided by long-time arranger Pelham Goddard – were one of only two bands from the East Zone to clinch the annual pan tournament, and they regularly take the regional title.

*See p.302 for
more on steel
pan music.*

Crucifix-lined St John's Road climbs uphill through St John's village to the **Mount St Benedict Monastery**, still a place of pilgrimage. A network of eye-catching white-walled, red-roofed buildings dominating the hillside, the monastery was established in 1912 by Benedictine monks fleeing religious persecution in Brazil. The first of its kind in the Caribbean, it initially consisted of nothing more than a mud-walled, thatch-roofed ajoupa at the peak of Mount Tabor, which was eventually abandoned in favour of this more accessible site. Additional buildings were added over the years, including a gorgeous burnt orange central tapia house in 1918, now crumbling slowly. With a boxy steeple tower forming the tallest portion of the complex, the imposing **church** was consecrated as an **abbey** in 1947. With a motto of *ora et labora* (prayers and work), though, the 25-odd resident monks are a vibrant, active community, maintaining an apiary and producing delicious yoghurt and honey for commercial sale. Mount St Benedict houses the Caribbean's main regional training college for priests, the **St John Vianney and the Uganda Martyrs Seminary**, which is also UWI's theology faculty. The nearby **St Bede's Vocational School** is run by the monks, who teach local youngsters practical skills such as machining, welding, plumbing and carpentry.

At 243m above sea level, even the monastery's car park commands spectacular views across the Caroni plains to the Trinity Hills and Mount Tamana, and the complex is a traditional spot for **afternoon tea** (daily 3–6pm), a feast of home-made breads, cakes and pastries taken at the tea garden or a terrace facing the hills. Hospitality to strangers is a Benedictine tradition, and they offer **accommodation** in the *Pax Guesthouse* (☎ and fax 662 4084, email *pax-g-h @trinidad.net*; ⑥) adjacent to the monastery. Catering mainly for birders and nature lovers, *Pax* has varnished wood floors, antique furniture – including an ancient phonograph – and an atmosphere of complete peace. Rooms lead from an impeccably clean, school dorm-like corridor; recently modernized and fitted with solid furniture made by the monks or taken from plantation homes, some have a private

Leading local ornithologist Ishmael Angelo (☎ 628 1753) is the main tour guide at Pax, and is an excellent choice for trips to other birding sites in the area; see p.45 for prices.

bathroom, others share. Numbers 1–7 have clear views over the central plains while the others face the monastery. Rates include breakfast and an excellent three-course evening meal; the dinner gong echoes through the corridors at 7.30pm.

Pax's manager Gerard Ramsawak organizes **birding tours** through the two square kilometres of surrounding land, home to a huge array of birds; the elevation means that raptors – hawks, vultures, kites and falcons – are particularly common, as are woodpeckers, parrots and hummingbirds. Five **trails**, ranging from half an hour to two hour's walking wreathe through jungle and secondary forest of Caribbean pine; a beautifully illustrated trail guide is available from the guesthouse. For a panoramic view of Trinidad that surpasses even the vistas at the monastery, take the Alben Ride trail and climb the **fire tower**, built to give warning of blazes in the cane fields below; the views are completely awe-inspiring, particularly at dusk when the sun disappears behind faraway Port of Spain and the lights twinkle in the distance.

Caura Valley

Curepe merges imperceptibly into **Tunapuna**, yet another nondescript collection of shopfronts and residential roads which uses the EMR as its main street. Just east of here, the Caura Royal Road turns off into the **Caura Valley** to the north – one of the most popular **picnic spots** in the East–West Corridor. Carved by the multi-tributaried, serpentine Tacarigua River, the valley was nearly turned into a reservoir in the 1940s, but though the inhabitants were relocated to Lopinot (see opposite), the proposed **dam** was never built, thwarted by the sandy soil.

The Royal Road passes Caura waterworks about a kilometre from the EMR; 5km further north is a right turn to the first popular swimming spot; a graffiti-smothered abandoned building here is the last vestige of the abandoned dam project. Picnic tables line the bamboo-fringed riverbanks, and at the weekends, cooking fires smoulder and the water is crowded with families enjoying a dip. From here, there are several walkable dirt tracks of varying length into the **Tacarigua Forest Reserve**, an attractive patchwork of abandoned plantations and lower montane woodlands. Hikes range from ten-minute jaunts to whole-day treks to the peak of El Tucuche. There's another equally popular swimming site a little further up the Royal Road, with a larger, rutted car park that usually accommodates enormous buses. Both places offer passable **river swimming**, but as the surrounding countryside is predominantly farmed, there could be some risk of pesticide pollution, and the shallow water often looks murky in the dry season.

If you need extra snacks or cold drinks for your picnic, there's a bar and a parlour on the road before the Caura picnic spots.

Past the picnic spots, high walls of bamboo form an intermittent tunnel over the road, opening up occasionally to reveal the small-scale farmlands and homes of **La Veronica** hamlet. As the Royal Road emerges onto the riverbanks again, the water deepens a little and picnicking is more secluded. The road is eventually terminated by a tributary of the Tacarigua. The drive back to the EMR affords some spectacular views of the central plains that are easily missed on the way up.

Lopinot

Uninspiring and easily missed if you're not scanning a map, **Arouca** is notable only as the point where you turn off the EMR for snaking Lopinot Road, which shoots north through gorgeous, undulating countryside of richly fruited vales and hillsides of jungle and Caribbean pine. Eight kilometres from the EMR, **LOPINOT** is a pretty hamlet clustered around a sports field and the neat flower beds of the **Lopinot complex**, a former cocoa estate that has been transformed into a beautiful, secluded picnic spot (daily 6am–6pm; free).

The valley was first settled by one Charles Josef, **Compte de Lopinot**, a planter who fled Haiti following Toussaint L'Ouverture's 1791 revolution. After a spell in Jamaica, he arrived in 1800 with his wife and 100 "faithful" (so the on-site board assures us) slaves. It's not difficult to see why he chose to settle in this absurdly abundant alluvial valley surrounded by high, protective mountains, and the cocoa thrived. He built a *tapia* estate house, a prison and slave quarters and amassed a small fortune before his death in 1819. The Compte is buried alongside his wife by the Arouca River, which runs through the valley, and local legend has it that on stormy full moon nights his ghost rides through the estate on a white horse.

The modest **great house** has been carefully restored, with a glassed-over section showing the original mud walls behind the newly-rendered exterior. Meticulously maintained, the surrounding gardens are linked to the road by a quaint wooden bridge, its roof smothered with ferns and wild pine bromeliads, while picnic tables are shaded by several enormous samaan trees with branches laden down by epiphytic plants. Inside the great house, a small **museum** is dedicated to the culture of local residents. The community, relocated here when the Caura dam was proposed (see opposite), is of Spanish, African and Amerindian descent; it has spawned some of Trinidad's finest parang players, inspiring villagers to call Lopinot the "**home of parang**". The village is one of the few places where each Christmas, a band of roving players still serenade each household. Site caretaker Martin Gomez is a parang master who delights in treating visitors to a song, accompanying himself on the cuatro. The museum displays photographs of local parang elders as well as a couple of dusty Amerindian artefacts and the dried-out husks of large grasshoppers and tarantulas, presumably on show to scare the tourists.

The boxy, cut stone **La Veronique RC church**, by the roadside on the other side of the playing field, was originally built in Caura in 1897, but was taken piece by piece from the neighbouring valley during the Caura evacuation and reassembled here. Past the church and the primary school, lichen-smothered cocoa trees line the road, and

Lopinot's annual harvest – a festival of parang fuelled by excesses of food and drink – usually takes place on May 17, though a shift to July has been known.

For more on the parang tradition, see p.298.

Arima and around

The route taxi fare from Arouca to Lopinot is TT$3; cars are fairly frequent (Mon–Sat 5am–6pm), but the service is reduced on Sundays.

a downhill turn-off leads to the **La Pastora** chapel and shrine, one of many on the island to share the title. This dedication to the Virgin of Shepherds stems from Capuchin monks who established several missions during the late seventeenth century, instilling devotion to La Pastora in their Amerindian converts. Carved in the 1940s, the plain white shrine inside depicts the Virgin Mary, and is said to have been chipped directly from the mountain.

After passing several small, friendly villages, the road eventually forks; a left down San Francisco Road brings you to a series of deep, swimmable **pools** on the river. There is good **hiking** in the surrounding mountains; Martin Gomez can arrange a guide who'll take you to nearby bat-filled **caves** – Mr Gomez discovered one of them himself, and it bears his name.

Arima and around

Past Lopinot, the EMR takes on a distinctly more rural aspect, with the shops and offices interspersed with the odd cattle pasture or overgrown empty lot. At the diminutive village of **D'Abadie**, the EMR wreathes through the pines and cocorite palms of **Cleaver Woods**. On Cleaver Trace, there's a gravel car park and the entrance to an **Amerindian museum** (daily 7am–6pm; free). Though the museum, housed in a thatch-roof ajoupa hut, is a bit neglected, the displays are interesting: including pottery, hunting traps, bows and arrows and equipment used to process cassava, which was farmed by Amerindians and formed a major part of their diet. The surrounding forest has a few short **trails** and picnic tables, but it's wise to explore only the trails on the northern side of the road – the museum caretakers warn of robberies on the other.

Named "Naparima" by the Amerindians who were the first to settle in the area, **ARIMA** is situated smack in the middle of the East–West Corridor. The largest town in the area, it's also one of the easiest places to get lost, as the EMR departs from its normally ruler-straight path and gets swiftly swallowed up in the urban clamour of endless shops, banks and wandering pedestrians.

The town has a far deeper history than its commercial facade would suggest, however, being home to what's left of Trinidad's **Carib** community, most of whom live around the crucifix-strewn **Calvary Hill**, a precipitous thoroughfare that overlooks the town and connects to the Arima–Blanchisseuse Road. You can still see remnants of Indian features in these distant relatives of the Carinepogoto tribe who once inhabited the Northern Range, but links are becoming ever-more tenuous as intermarriage slowly erodes the physical aspect of the **Karina nation**, as they like to be known – Carib is regarded as a European corruption of their correct title. However, Carib culture still has a stronghold here, and the **Santa Rosa Carib Community Association** was formed in 1974 to look after the interests of the dwindling tribe. Their headquarters on Paul Mitchell Street, behind the cemetery, sells good quality traditional Amerindian craft such as woven baskets or carved calabashes, as well as giving information about local Carib culture. The only remaining **ajoupa** – the traditional Carib thatched building – on Calvary Hill sits in the front yard of Christo Adonis, the local Carib shaman and vociferous defender of his people; if you can catch him at home, he's a mine of information on Amerindian medicine and all things pertaining to the Karinas.

Exploring Arima is best done on foot, as a recently introduced one-way system is confusing even to those who know the town well. You should be able to find the main landmark, the **Arima Dial**, pretty easily, however – it now forms a traffic roundabout. Don't set your watch by it, though – presented to the townspeople in 1898 by their Mayor, John Wallen, this elaborate timepiece is somewhat temperamental. On **Hollis Road**, market stalls detract attention from a statue of venerated calypsonian **Lord Kitchener** pretty easily. The open-air **market** here is liveliest on Fridays. On the town end of **O'Meara Road**, the route from central Arima to the highway, a semi-permanent **children's fun park** known as Coney Island (daily, no set hours; free) has a ferris wheel, merry-go-rounds and some more adult-oriented fairground rides, while the **Santa Rosa Race Track** (☎646 2360), off the highway, holds occasional **horse racing** meets. Leaving town along the Eastern Main Road, you pass **Nutones panyard** on the right, whose dedicated beaters brought unexpected glory to Arima in 1998 when they won the **National Panorama** title with their arrangement of David Rudder's "High Mas".

There's no good reason to stay in Arima, and no hotels or guesthouses, but if you're **hungry**, you'll be spoilt for choice by the profusion of small **restaurants** and **fast food** joints along the main streets, as well as the usual quota of rum shops.

The Feast of Santa Rosa

During the last weekend of August, Arima's Carib community celebrate the **Feast of Santa Rosa de Lima**, the only place in Trinidad where the first canonized Roman Catholic Saint of the "New World" is honoured. Following a morning of church services, a Carib King and Queen are crowned, and a white-swathed statue of Santa Rosa is paraded through the streets, the procession bedecked with white, yellow, pink and red roses. An all-day party ensues; rum flows, and traditional Amerindian foods such as pastelles and cassava bread are eaten. The origins of the festival are somewhat skewed, but in fairytale style, Carib elders relate that three hunters chanced upon a young girl lying in the woods, and brought her back to Calvary Hill. She disappeared three times, only to be returned to the community. A local priest told the Caribs that this was no normal child, but the spirit of Santa Rosa, and that they should make an image of her while she was still with them, for if she vanished again, her physical body would never again be seen. They made the statue, and Santa Rosa duly disappeared, leaving only a crown of roses at the spot where she had first been discovered. Ever since, Santa Rosa has been the patron saint of the Carib community.

Heights of Guanapo Road

On the eastern outskirts of Arima, the EMR switches abruptly from commercial thoroughfare to rural road, dominated by farmlands and cattle pastures rather than shopfronts and honking traffic. Just after the Arima Bypass meets the EMR, a turn-off at the WASA Guanapo Waterworks sign brings you to the **Heights of Guanapo Road**. Striking through thick forest, this is a hikers' paradise, but it's not a place to explore without the help of a knowledgeable **guide**; Laurence Pierre is recommended (see p.45). To get to good walking territory, drive past the waterworks along a country lane that's recently been partially wrecked by the huge wheels of logging vehicles; expect a lot of mud if you arrive in rainy season, when it's best to have a four-wheel drive. Though you can drive further uphill to **La Laja Heights**, which gives lovely views over the Guanapo Valley, it's a good idea to park in the large clearing where logging workers have built a hut as from here onwards, the road becomes pretty treacherous; there's also a nice swimming spot in the Guanapo River, next to a concrete bridge. The main attractions of the area are the breathtaking **Guanapo Gorge**, and the **La Laja** and **Sombasson waterfalls**. With effort, you can see both the falls and the gorge in a day, but you'll need to be pretty fit.

Guanapo Gorge

A little nearer to the EMR than the waterfalls, **Guanapo Gorge** is a narrow channel whose vine-wreathed walls of smooth grey rock rise 15 to 30m above the water. Dark and cool even on a hot sunny day, the gorge runs for some 400m; exploring it – wading and swimming all the way – can be quite hard work. Though you can start the trek from the southern (downstream) end, a far more exciting option is to begin upstream, where a large boulder blocking the river has created a small waterfall. From here, you enter the gorge by jumping from the boulder into a deep pool and swimming for a few yards before your feet meet the riverbed. Water levels vary according to the time of year, but you should have to swim for no further than 25m at any point, and travelling from one end to the other is quite simply one of Trinidad's most thrilling journeys. The tiny **Tumbason River** threads through rocks to meet the Guanapo at the southern end of the gorge; if you walk up for about 45 minutes, you'll come to a small **waterfall** with a deep **pool**.

The La Laja and Sombasson waterfalls

The **La Laja and Sombasson waterfalls** are hidden deep in the folds of the Northern Range. Getting to them necessitates a longer and more difficult hike, passing through abandoned cocoa plantations and forests of bois cano, sandbuck, nutmeg, balata and silk cotton. The trail dips and climbs constantly, but frequent use by hunters, who come here for the rich stocks of wild meat, have kept the majority of the trails fairly free of bush, though you may need to blaze a trail in the last stages of the walk, marking your path by slashing the undergrowth or leaving other easily-recognizable marks. The first of the falls, **La Laja** is the smaller at about 20m high, with a couple of good pools below; the water is kept icy cold by the overhanging cliffs and dense foliage. Above La Laja, you're in virgin forest, and the trek to Sombasson falls is harder, but the three-tiered 50-metre cascade with deep pools is worth the effort.

Reputable hiking guides are listed in Basics, p.45

Aripo Caves

Yet more lonely fields line the EMR east of Guanapo, where the non-descript-looking **Aripo Road** runs north into the mountains following a valley cut by the Aripo River. A pretty, meandering uphill route leads deep into the bush for some 14km. Its end marks the start of a hike to Trinidad's largest system of caverns, **Aripo Caves**, which support one of the island's few **oilbird colonies**. It's also a main starting point for the climb to Trinidad's highest mountain, **El Cerro del Aripo**. At 941m, the peak is covered with prehistoric-looking elfin forest; short, scrubby and smothered with lichen, mosses and epiphytic growth. It's a tough full-day hike, but as the temperature at the peak is some ten degrees lower than in the lowlands, overheating is one thing you don't have to worry about. As the Aripo Road is rough and periodically potholed, you'll need a car with high clearance if you're driving; in the wet season, a four-wheel drive is a good idea. It's a pretty route, tracing the valley and passing through some quiet rural communities; artist **Leroy Clarke** has a home up here. If you're in the mood for a **river swim**, look out for a metal arch with the inscription "Jai Guru Data" soldered from iron rods; take the steps down the hill to a deep **pool**.

You can still make out the forestry department signs along Aripo Road – though they're weather-beaten and battered – which point the way to the caves; follow them past **Aripo**, the last village, where you should be able to hire a guide if you haven't travelled up with someone who knows the way. After a cocoa grove sporting fruits that turn purple when ripe rather than the usual orange, there's a final cave sign by a grassy clearing where you can park. The signs end here, and as parts of the original trail have been obscured by large, messily cut logging tracks, an experienced guide is essential to get to the caves. The fairly taxing two- to three-hour trek, with plenty of hills and gullies to navigate, is best undertaken in the dry season (Jan–March), when the three rivers that cross the path usually slow to a trickle; if it's been raining, you'll have to wade them. In the rainy season, you'll also have to get wet to enter the caves, as a river courses straight into the mouth; take care, as the going can be slippery.

The forest is thick, but if you squint through the leaves you can get the occasional view of the Central Plains below. On nearing the main entrance of the caves, you'll start to hear the unearthly rasping shriek of the **oilbirds** inside. The **mouth** is large and dramatic, with a musty mist rising constantly from the depths. Water drips from the limestone roof, and every surface is covered with fruit stones dropped by oilbirds returning from night-time feeding forays as well as a thin film of guano. With a good torch, you can navigate the rocks and go fairly deep inside, but doing so increases the oilbirds' cries to an ear-splitting pitch; it's not difficult to imagine why the Amerindians named them "Guacharo", meaning "the one who wails and mourns". If you want to go any further into the cave, you'll need rope, a compass and some spelunking experience.

For more on oilbirds, see p.307.

The Northeast Tip

Stretching from **Matura** in the east to **Matelot** in the north, the wild and rugged coastline of Trinidad's **Northeast Tip** has a far more remote feeling than anywhere else in the region; it takes a minimum of three hours to drive from Port of Spain to Matelot, where the paved road ends. Cut off by a break in the coast road and by the rainforests of the Northern Range, the region seems suspended in a time warp; people and houses are few and far between and an air of hypnotic quiet pervades. The villages strung along the coast are close-knit and spirited communities, with proud residents clipping verges and planting flowers in voluntary beautification projects and making their own entertainment at the **rum shops**, country parties and fishermen's fetes. **Farming** and **fishing** are the mainstays of the economy, and you'll lose count of the signs advertising shark oil, salt fish and sea moss for sale, while tiny roadside stalls offer fresh fruit and vegetables at knock-down prices.

The narrow Matura Road loops through neat farmlands and stark, untamed bush, with unreachable rocky coves enticing you to scramble down the cliffs. At wind-whipped **Matura**, **leatherback turtles** lumber up the sand to lay eggs, while the eastern headlands provide plenty of sheltered spots for a dip in the foaming Atlantic. At weekends, sublime stretches of yellow sand such as **Saline** and **Balandra bays** become popular retreats for seclusion-seekers, as does the reef-fringed seashore adjacent to **Galera Point**, where a lighthouse guides ships through the treacherous waters between Trinidad and Tobago. Inland, **Salybia Waterfall** is one of the island's best, and you'll usually have it all to yourself. The largest town in the area, **Toco**, is relatively tiny, but has lent its name to the surrounding region, with its awe-inspiring untamed coastline of weather-beaten cliffs and crashing sea. **Surfers** ride the breakers at **Sans Souci**, and the **rivers** and **waterfalls** inland from **Grande Riviere** and Matelot make jungle hiking a rewarding adventure.

As most people see the coast in a day trip, there aren't a lot of **accommodation** options. The fabulous hotel on the beach at Grande Riviere is one of Trinidad's best, however, and there are plenty of beach houses advertised for rent in the classified pages of the national newspapers. To visit the Northeast Tip you need your own car; maxis and taxis do run all the way to Matelot, but the service is sporadic, and you'll have to change vehicles several times. If you're driving from Port of Spain, it's quicker to avoid the car-choked EMR and take the Churchill Roosevelt Highway; turn left at the end of the highway, and then right onto the quiet portion of the EMR to Valencia, from where the Valencia Road swings north to the Toco coast.

Matura

Straight and smooth, the **Valencia Road** swings through mile upon mile of open country; other than the odd home or small provision field, signs of human habitation are few and far between and it's rare to pass another car. Though there's a sign, the sharp left-hand **turn** for the **Toco Main Road** is easy to miss; carrying on takes you straight to Sangre Grande (see p.173). Don't be distracted by road signs that insist, at several different places, that the next village, Matura, is 1 kilometre away.

A one-street town, **MATURA** consists of little more than a police station, a school, a health centre and a few modest houses slung along the tarmac. Other than stopping for a drink at the rum shop, the only reason to spend any time in the area is the **beach**, a windswept, 4-kilometre stretch of fine yellow sand strewn with coconut husks, chip-chip shells, driftwood and the odd bit of flotsam and jetsam washed up by the fearsome waves. Though local people often take a dip, it's not a place for the uninitiated to swim, as the currents are extremely powerful. The real attraction is the **leatherback turtles** which haul themselves on to the sand to lay eggs. The beach is a prohibited area during the laying season (March 1–Aug 31), and you need a permit to enter (see p.176). If you visit at the right time of year and want to see the turtles, check the offices of **Nature Seekers Incorporated** on the main road; they have trained guides who take you on to the beach to watch the amazing process (for more on turtles, see p.304). There are two entrances to the beach, both marked by Forestry Division signs. The first is in the centre of Matura; follow a rutted dirt road to the right. The other end of the shore, reached from the far side of town, is known as **Rincon Beach**.

Salybia Falls

Past Matura, the Toco Road meets the east coast for the first time. The view is often obscured by a thick cover of bush, though you do get some stunning views of small, wave-battered coves. The first safe place to swim is a beach just past the tiny village of **Salybia**, which consists of little other than a government school and *Freddy's Rest* bar. Just past the buildings, a large concrete bridge crosses the Rio Seco, flanked by a couple of huts selling crafts and soft drinks. A turn-off to the right leads down to **Saline Beach**, a popular chill-out spot during the weekend when families come to bathe and picnic.

Opposite the beach is the route to one of the area's more spectacular **waterfalls**, beautifully placed in the **Matura Forest Reserve**; to get there, take the unmarked inland track (not Knaggs Trace). You can drive up for about 10 to 15 minutes if there's been no recent rain, but if the ground is wet, it's best to leave your car at the beach and tackle the rocky, uneven road on foot. It's a pleasant walk up a gentle incline enclosed by thick forest. Look out for a tall royal palm just before the pink house; on the tree are several of the teardrop-shaped **nests** of the black and yellow **crested oropendola**.

Past the house, the road has been churned into a muddy, rutted track by the wheels of forestry department vehicles. After 10 minutes, you should pass a wooden house on a hill to the left; carry straight on, skirting a small field of dasheen and sweetcorn and passing signs warning "Take only pictures, leave only footprints" and "Stay on the trail". After 10 minutes' walk through the forest, the trail splits; left heads to the river and an attractive, fairly deep swimming pool, while the right-hand, uphill track leads to the falls. A mossy picnic table and chairs carved out of felled trees and some rather incongruously placed signs punctuate the path; for no discernible reason, one of them declares the place a "nature habitat". You cross a river tributary and climb another hillock before descending to the falls – it's possible to follow the river all the way up to the main waterfall, passing some small cascades. The last stretch, bordered by rickety rails, is steep, but you get a good prospect of the waterfall below. Usually known as **Salybia Waterfall** but marked on some maps as Rio Seco Falls, this is a stunning place to bathe. The trunk of a huge silk cotton forms a bridge over the riverbed rocks and into a blue-green pool, 7m deep and 12m wide. The waterfall itself tumbles some 8m down the rocks, with plenty of handholds for an easy climb up and a dive from the top. Emerald light filters through the surrounding canopy, while a break in the cover above the water provides some direct sunlight. From the road, the walk should take about an hour, and the falls make a great picnic spot.

Balandra Bay

After cutting inland across some wild and undeveloped bush, the Toco Road rejoins the coast at **BALANDRA**, a pretty fishing village with a popular beach. Before the town, you pass a large sign for *Balandra Beach Resort*, now closed; a shame, as the location on a bluff overlooking the beach provides some marvellous coastal views. You can still drive straight through the property to the eastern corner of the beach, where a small river runs onto the sand. The main entrance to the **beach** is at the western end, and is marked by a small sign; you should be able to find a space in the car park unless you visit at a weekend, when cars line the path to the road.

Backed by the fishing village and fringed by palm trees and Indian almonds, the beach is wide and inviting, with clean yellow sand and moderate waves. Most of the weekend crowds swim by the sheltered walled area past the car park, though swimming is safe along the whole length of the beach. A small shack by the car park sells soft drinks, pies and pholouri.

Rampanalgas and Cumana

The next settlement along the coast, the sizeable village of **RAM-PANALGAS** clings to the landward side of the road. It's a friendly sort of place – the local hot-spot is *Arthur's Grocery* on the outskirts of town, boasting a lively bar with a pool table, a grocery that sells cakes and snacks, and a postal agency. From a backroad which strikes off the Toco Road just past the village name-sign, a trail leads to the **Cirra Falls**. The path crosses a stream and winds uphill, passing a rather grand board house on the right; after a 10-minute walk you'll come to a river, where crazy paving put in by the villagers leads to the cascade. The waterfall is small but attractive, with a deep, greenery-wreathed pool and a tree stump which forms a diving board for local kids. You can climb up the bank to the top of the falls, where there's another, smaller cascade.

The next village along the Toco Road, **CUMANA**, manages the dizzy heights of a **petrol station**, several noisy **bars** where rum-drinking patrons tend to be incredibly friendly, and a good **roti shop**, *Rose's*, on the western outskirts. A turning by an unattractively stone-clad Catholic church leads to a scrappy fisherman's beach, but it's not a place for swimming; vultures wait patiently for fish innards and there's a distinctly briny aroma.

Toco and Galera Point

The largest community along this stretch of coast, **TOCO** is an attractive, quiet fishing village which retains a distinctly antiquated air. Most of the buildings are dilapidated gingerbreads, and weather-beaten wood reigns supreme. Though most residents make their money from fishing or farming, many have recently begun to sell off family land to prospective developers, tempted by the high real estate prices brought about by the often-mooted suggestions to build a **ferry terminal** here, forming a second sea bridge to Tobago, a mere 20km away and easily visible on clear days. Most of the route taxis from Sangre Grande turn around at Toco; if you're heading further west, you may have to wait here for quite a while, or hitch a lift. Unless you want to spend time in the town or see Galera Point, its a good idea to try and find a ride to Matelot in "Grande" (see p.173).

As you enter the town, **Galera Road** strikes off to the right, passing a good **beach** along the way. A gorgeous double horseshoe of yel-

Toco's tiny petrol station is the last place to fill up before Matelot, but opening hours are sporadic and it tends to close early.

low sand scattered with white fragments of finger coral, the beach is busy on weekends, when it's a popular spot for a cook-out, and fried fish, soft drinks and local sweets are sold from a thatch-roofed stall. Surfers skim along beyond the reef, but the water close to the shore is translucent and pretty calm.

Past the beach, the road meanders to **Galera Point**, the island's extreme eastern tip and site of the Galera **lighthouse**. A stocky tower built in 1897, the lighthouse flashes its red beacon over a notoriously treacherous stretch of sea known to fishermen as the "graveyard". If the keeper is in a good mood, he'll let you climb all 83 rickety steps to the top for a fantastic view over inland coconut estates and down the coast to Matelot. Below the lighthouse is a windblown, rocky bluff pounded by crashing waves that send up mists of salty spray; several currents swirl in the shallows, a blowhole under the rock gives off occasional moans, and the point where the royal blue Caribbean sea meets the murky, pastel-blue Atlantic Ocean is easily visible far out to sea. It's a strange, wild spot, filled with an uneasy energy; the lighthouse keeper maintains that the point is haunted, relating tales of car doors slamming when there is no car, and ghostly wails in the still of the night. He might be right; during a 1699 **rebellion** at a Spanish encomienda in San Rafael, Amerindians killed three Capuchin monks. Incensed, Spanish forces pursued the culprits to Galera, where they leapt off the cliffs to their deaths rather than be killed by their slave-masters.

Sans Souci and around

Past Toco, the road becomes **Paria Main Road** as it rounds the end of the peninsula onto the north coast, running perilously close to the cliffs. Shattering all illusions of what a Caribbean seashore should look like, huge waves crash onto the wild and rugged coast, and jagged rocks poke out of a surging ocean in which only the suicidal would swim. There are several relatively safe beaches, however, around the next village, **SANS SOUCI**, all boasting waves large enough to make this the island's **surfing** capital and a regular venue for competitions. The largest is known simply as **Big Bay**; here, the waves are a little smaller and there's a nice place to **stay**. Still waiting for a phone to be installed, *Talk of the Town* (②) is incredibly good value; the basic but clean apartments have two or three bedrooms and a kitchenette, and meals are available. The bar below has a sweeping view over the bay, and it's a nice place to relax for a while; there's even a pool table, and the owner makes corn soup and barbecued chicken at the weekends. Past the bay, Paria Main Road winds inland through impossibly lush jungle which lets up only at the tiny **Monte Video** village, notable mostly for the cold beers on sale at the lone bar.

Grande Riviere

One of the most appealing villages of the Toco coast, **GRANDE RIV-IERE** is also the only place with any kind of tourist infrastructure. A beautiful **hotel** right on the beach has spurred a host of local residents to open up **guesthouses**, but the remote location has kept development low-key, and the town remains one of the most unspoilt, idyllic places you'll find anywhere on the island. Interaction between visitors and local people has none of the money-oriented duplicity of other resorts, and local people tend to be incredibly welcoming, often throwing parties when a set of guests leave.

Named after the wide, fast-flowing river which originates deep in the Northern Range and runs down to the sea at the eastern end of town, Grande Riviere also boasts a superlative **beach**, a wide, gentle curve of coarse yellow sand with a few unobtrusive buildings blending seamlessly into otherwise unbroken jungle. Tall forested headlands border the sand to the east, where the river gives a nice opportunity for a freshwater bathe, while a good kilometre away, the western end is sealed from the rest of the coast by rocky outcrops. Strong waves provide passable surfing, an invigorating swim, and give **leatherback turtles** the extra push they need to haul themselves up the sand at laying time. This is one of the best places to see turtles, and at the peak of the season, it's common for ten or more to lay simultaneously. As in Matura, the beach is a prohibited area between March 1 and August 31, and you need a permit to enter between dawn and dusk. Local residents have formed a voluntary patrol to guard against poachers; they also make knowledgeable guides, scouting the beach for turtles or hatchlings and escorting visitors; you pay a fee of TT$12.

*For more on
leatherback
turtles, see
p.305.*

The liveliest part of the beach centres around the *Mount Plaisir Estate* hotel (see overleaf), where the **bar** is everyone's favourite liming spot, and most people who stay in town divide their time between the beach and the interior, where there are hosts of **waterfalls** and **river walks** as well as excellent **bird-watching** – the rare **piping guan**, a kind of wild turkey that has died out in more developed areas, is quite common in the area; ask at the hotel for Cyril James, who guides most of the trips. He can also organize a night's **camping** in the bush, building a tree house at the end of a day's hike. Local character Jakatan, the originator of the "**Earth People**", a loose family group who live the natural life deep in the bush according to their own set of customs, also takes groups to "Jakatan Falls", a waterfall that he "discovered" and which has been locally named in his honour. Jakatan makes an excellent source of information on local folklore and is working on a campsite in the hills. Most tours cost around TT$100 per person. Another option is a **snorkelling** trip to nearby Langosta Cove or **boat trips** to remote beaches; ask at the hotel.

Practicalities

By far the best place to **stay** is right on the beach at *Mount Plaisir Estate* (☎670 8381 or 680 4553, fax 680 4553; ⑤). Overflowing with easy style, the rooms are fitted with solid, locally made furniture, while beautiful paintings hang on the walls and surfaces are decorated with driftwood oddities. Most rooms sleep four people, some six; try and get one with a stable door overlooking the beach. The hotel is also the best – and more or less the only – place for a sit-down meal, and the food could easily hold its own in the swankiest of Port of Spain's eateries: home-made bread, local-style meat or chicken and imaginative vegetarian options. Breakfast and lunch are available, and three course dinners cost around TT$75. Across the track which leads to the beach is *Le Grande Almandier* (c/o *Mount Plaisir*; ④), owned by Cyril James. Rooms are almost as nice as at *Mount Plaisir* and a little cheaper; most can sleep four. The bar downstairs is a good place for an evening drink, and chips or hot dogs are available. In the village, you can stay at the dingy but economical apartment above *Guy's Rec Club* (☎670 0048; ②); there's two bedrooms, a living room and a kitchen. The bar downstairs is a lively liming spot, with music (turned down if guests request it) and a pool table. You'll need to ask around to find the other options; check at the hotel. Opposite the community centre and playing field, Miss Freda (③) has several simple double rooms above her home; bathroom and kitchen are shared. Two houses are available for rent, Matthew Charles (③) has a four bedroom unit with full kitchen and one bathroom, while Mr Roseman's pink two-bedroom house on a hill overlooking town has two bedrooms, a kitchen, outside shower and toilet and a verandah with a gorgeous view; the rent is TT$200 per week.

You'll have to make your own **entertainment** here; apart from the strains of Roots and Branches, Grande Riviere's local band, whose nightly sessions echo over the village from the rehearsal hall on top of a hill above *Guy's*, things are quiet in the evening. *Jamesy's Stone Wall Bar* on the main road is a friendly spot, though, as is the *First and Last Bar*. You can buy **snacks** and **food** from *Guy's* or the *Crystal Fountain Grocery*.

Matelot and around

Of the many plank-lined bridges that pepper the Paria Main Road past Grande Riviere, the one crossing **Shark River** is the largest. The river is a popular swimming spot, with a couple of deep **pools** just before the water meets the sea and plenty more upstream; during holiday weekends, campers pitch tent along its banks. Walking upriver makes a great excursion, though you have to clamber over some mighty rocks to reach the best pools, and you'll need a guide to negotiate several tributaries and the occasional swing off into the bush.

Beyond the river, it's another ten minutes' scenic coastal drive before you reach the fishing hamlet of **MATELOT**, the last settlement on the Paria Main Road. The village square is flanked by a plain Catholic church and a couple of rum shops; from here, a track leads down to the fishermen's beach. Houses, some of them quite grand, meander up the hillsides. The best recreation round here is swimming in the **Matelot River**; take the uphill road to the left and bear right. There's a wooden bridge from which brave souls can take a dive, and the water runs crystal clear down to the sandy **beach**. A sparse thatched hut provides an outdoor cooking space. If you want to **stay** in town, you should be able to find someone willing to put you up in their home; there are no hotels or guesthouses.

Past here, the road ends; there's nothing but a bench trail along the wild and undeveloped coast to Blanchisseuse, 19km to the west (see p.125). Local fishermen can usually be persuaded to take you along the undeveloped coast from Matelot Paria, Madamas or Blanchisseuse; a round trip will take about four hours depending upon conditions (about TT$500 for the whole stretch). The forest inland of Matelot is riddled with hunters' trails, including a half-day trek to the 3-metre **Matelot Waterfall**, with its wide, deep pool. Guides are available at a house on the way to the river – look for the "nature tours" sign.

Chapter 3

Central Trinidad

Spanning a compact area of no more than 350 square kilometres, **central Trinidad** encompasses an astonishing variety of landscape and settlement. The **west coast** is gritty and industrialized, punctuated by brash commercial towns such as **Chaguanas**, but even here you can find the **Caroni Swamp** – home of the scarlet ibis – and the **Pointe-a-Pierre Wildfowl Trust**. Inland, the agricultural **Central Plains**, dotted with somnolent villages, rise gently to the wooded **Montserrat Hills** in the south; to the north and south of these hills are the two largest dams and reservoirs in the country, **Arena** and **Navet**. In the **East Coast** region, there's only one town of any size, the busy market centre of **Sande Grande**; south of here, there's just the stunning **Manzanilla Beach** with its seemingly endless avenues of palms, and the weird mangrove scenery of the protected **Nariva Swamp**.

The population is mostly descended from Indian indentured labourers who came here in the 1840s to replace the freed slaves. You'll see Hindu shrines in every other yard; Indian delicacies are sold in shacks along the street and Indian music blasts out of roadside cafés and bars. In places such as the **Waterloo Temple**, on the west coast, and the odd isolated village, it is easily possible to imagine that you are in India and not thousands of miles away in the southern Caribbean.

Away from the west coast and the country's only airport at **Piarco** to the north, much of central Trinidad remains deeply traditional or, as Trinis put it, "countrified". On the Central Plains, wide, flat expanses of sugar cane and coconut estates stretch as far as the eye can see, while in the heart of the island around the Montserrat Hills, huge reserves of awe-inspiring **rainforest** shelter countless species of flora and fauna. **Wildlife**, including scarlet ibis, manatees (seacows), red howler monkeys and caymans, can easily be seen by visiting the swamps, reserves and reservoirs, and with many of the island's 420 species nesting in the protected areas, the region is excellent for **bird-watching**.

Some people still subsist by hunting manicou (a large rat-like animal), agouti (similar to a rabbit) or iguana, and by growing bread-

fruit, potatoes and dasheen bush, though things are changing. The
forests are protected reserves, and hunting is no longer permitted
outside of season. An increase in the number of bandits (the local
name for thieves and muggers) means that the forest is no longer the
safe place it once was, and children are warned not to venture too far
into the "bush". In the last fifteen years, the majority of the traditional mud *tapia* houses built by the indentured Indians have been
replaced by concrete homes constructed on stilts as a protection
against flooding, which is frequent during the wet season.
Mechanical harvesters now reap the fields in place of labourers with
machetes, and the sight of a man leading his buffalo cart is less common now that much of the produce is taken to the market or factory
in trucks. And while country Christmases are still celebrated with
wild meat, home-made wines and lively parang music, even this tradition is declining in popularity.

Transport is no problem along the west coast; its towns are easily accessible from the **Uriah Butler-Solomon Hochoy Highway**,
which runs from port of Spain to San Fernando in the south, though
some of the signs are faded or have disappeared altogether.
Reaching the rural areas inland can be a problem, however. **Maxis**
and **taxis** take long circular routes to the villages, and the absence of
road signs can make driving confusing. In many places, asking for
directions is often the only way to find the right road, although country directions are often frustratingly vague – "just round the corner"
could mean anything from a hundred metres to five kilometres.

Accommodation in this little-touristed region is minimal. What
hotels there are cater for industry personnel, or are the motel type rented by the hour by Trini couples trying to get some privacy. There are a
few **host homes**, which can be contacted through the Bed and
Breakfast Co-Operative Society (☎ and fax 663 4413) or
Accommodations Unlimited (☎ 628 3731, fax 628 3737). It is not necessary, however, to stay in central Trinidad to visit it; even the remotest
areas can be reached from Port of Spain in less than two and half hours.
For those who wish to get away from the bustle of the capital, there are

---

ACCOMMODATION PRICE CODES

All accommodation listed in this guide has been graded according to the following
price categories:

① under US$10	② US$10–20	③ US$20–35
④ US$35–50	⑤ US$50–70	⑥ US$70–100
⑦ US$100–150	⑧ US$150–200	⑨ US$200 and above

Rates are for the cheapest double or twin rooms, including 10 percent tax and 10 percent service charge where applicable. In Tobago, rates quoted are those used during
the high season, normally mid December–mid April. During low season (mid
April–mid December) rates are liable to fall by up to 25 percent. There are no high
and low seasons in Trinidad, but rates may rise by up to 70 percent during Carnival.
Many hotels give rates in US dollars – we have followed suit. Payment can be made in
either US or TT currency.

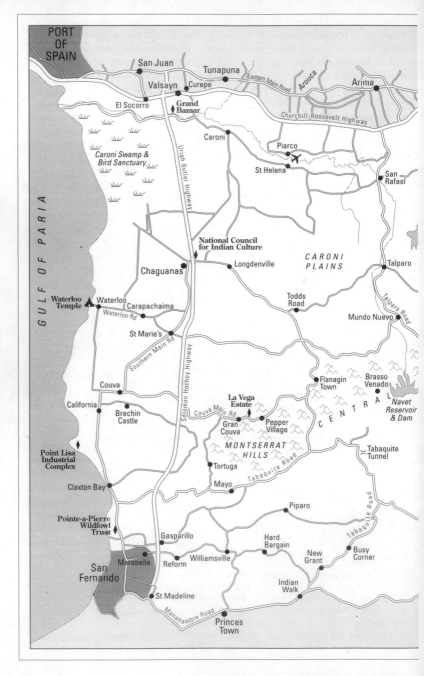

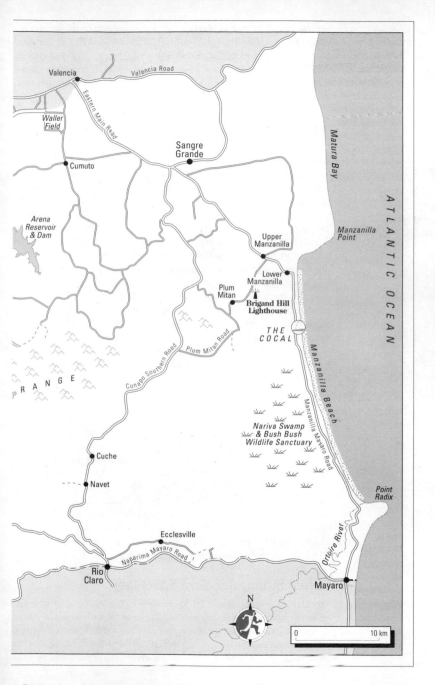

various places to stay in Mayaro and San Fernando in the south (see Chapter 4, pp.204–206 & 179–188) that are also convenient for visiting central Trinidad. **Restaurants** and **nightlife** are very limited, though there are plenty of **fast food** places serving cheap, filling meals, especially Indian and Chinese food, while the many small **bars** and **rum shops** provide friendly conversation and a good night out.

The west coast

The **west coast** is an uneasy mix of nature and industry. Oil refineries and cement factories compete with workers' dormitory suburbs along the Uriah Butler-Solomon Hochoy Highway, which runs down the coast from Port of Spain through the rapidly developing commercial town of **Chaguanas** and the industrial zone of **Point Lisas**. Yet despite its inauspicious appearance, the coast harbours a couple of rich habitats for birds and other fauna: the **Caroni Swamp** in the north, and the **Pointe-a-Pierre Wildfowl Trust** to the south. The predominance of Indian culture is immediately noticeable from the highway, as the 12-metre statue of Swami Vivekananda that presides over the **National Council of Indian Culture** complex looms into view on the eastern side of the road; while the **Waterloo Temple**, picturesquely built out over the sea, is one of the country's most well-known places of Hindu devotion.

A few high-class, fine dining **restaurants** have recently been established at the postmodern oriental-style **Grand Bazaar Mall**, at the junction of Uriah Butler-Solomon Hochoy and Churchill Roosevelt highways, about 10km east of Port of Spain. The *Imperial Garden*, ☎662 6970 (Mon–Thurs 11am–10pm, Fri & Sat 11am–11pm) is a swish Chinese restaurant where the average meal costs TT$130. *Botticelli's*, ☎645 8733 (Mon–Sat 11am–11pm), decorated in ostentatious Italian style with Roman columns and a fountain outside, serves a wide variety of Italian dishes, some given a Creole twist by the use of local fish and vegetables – their average meal costs TT$200. *Apasara*, ☎662 1013 or 645 5450 (Mon–Sat 11am–11pm) is a magnificently furnished North Indian restaurant serving excellent food. It is very exclusive, and has no sign to advertise its presence except for a doorman in traditional Indian dress – it is diagonally opposite the *Imperial Garden*. The average meal costs TT$170 and reservations are recommended.

Caroni Swamp and Bird Sanctuary

The **Caroni Swamp** and **Bird Sanctuary** is Trinidad's most promoted environmental attraction and the only roosting place in the island of the spectacular **scarlet ibis** – the national bird. These 60 square kilometres of swamp bordering the Gulf of Paria between the mouths of the Caroni and Madame Espagnole rivers are home to more than

150 species of birds, including white flamingos, egrets and blue herons, while caymans, snakes and anteaters can be observed in the water and the surrounding mangroves. It's a quiet, mysterious place, and the mangrove trees themselves are weirdly reminiscent of something out of a science fiction film: some have long aerial roots growing downwards into the water, while others have roots that grow upwards, emerging from the murky depths like stalactites.

People have been visiting the swamp to view the scarlet ibis since the 1930s; to do so today you must take a boat – usually a fifteen-seater wooden pirogue – with either James or Nanan tours. The boatmen know the swamp and its wildlife well, pointing out birds, plants and animals of interest as they lead you through a maze of waterways to the mangrove islands where the scarlet ibis roost at dusk. The boat engines shudder to a halt, and a spectacular scene unfolds: as the birds flock in, an area of green mangrove gradually turns a vibrant red. It is not possible to get close to the birds' roosting spot without disturbing them, so bring binoculars or a powerful zoom lens, or you'll see little more than red specks against the dark green foliage.

Tours of the Caroni Swamp (TT$60) take place daily at 4–4.30pm and last two and half hours; advance booking is advisable. Tour operators: Nanan ☎ 645 1305; James ☎ 662 7356

The ibis's intense red plumage derives its pigment, carotene, from the birds' main prey, the **tree-climbing crabs** which inhabit the swamp in their millions; in captivity the birds become a faded pink. During the day the scarlet ibis fly to Venezuela to feed, returning at dusk to roost in the upper branches of the mangrove islands. Since the 1960s, the scarlet ibis has failed to breed in the swamp, possibly because pollution has killed certain food essential to its diet. Experts disagree as to whether breeding has restarted, and whether the bird is at risk; its habit of commuting daily between South America and Trinidad makes it hard to judge.

Driving to the swamp from Port of Spain, you'll need to leave at 3pm to catch a 4pm tour. The exit off the Uriah Butler-Solomon Hochoy Highway is well signposted. **Maxis** and **taxis** run from Port of Spain to Chaguanas; ask them to drop you at the Caroni Swamp exit, from where it is a five-minute walk. Facilities at the swamp are limited: there are toilets, and some drinks are sold from a cooler in the boat, but you should bring your own water.

Chaguanas and around

CHAGUANAS, halfway down the Uriah Butler-Solomon Hochoy Highway, is one of Trinidad's oldest settlements, its third largest town, and the **shopping centre** of the country, with a couple of glitzy new shopping malls alongside its rambling old market. It is also one of Trinidad's great centres of **Indian culture**: just outside town lie two of the country's most important religious sites, the **National Council of Indian Culture** and the **Waterloo Temple**, and a group of **potteries** working in the traditional Indian style; while the elegantly crumbling **Lion House** on Main Street is the birthplace of the acclaimed Indo-Trinidadian novelist V.S. Naipaul.

Some history

The town's name is derived from that of an Amerindian tribe, the Chaguanes, which once lived in the region. The place really took off after Indian indentured labourers came to work on the sugar and cocoa estates in the area in the 1840s, and by the 1880s it had become the most important market town in central Trinidad, with good transport connections that included both train and steamer to Port of Spain. As the sugar industry declined in the early decades of the twentieth century, many Indians moved into professions such as journalism and the law, creating the middle-class intelligentsia from which V.S. Naipaul emerged and which forms the milieu for some of his early novels. Though the trains and the steamer are long gone, the construction of the Uriah Butler-Solomon Hochoy Highway in the late 1940s ensured that the town remained easily accessible. The oil boom of the 1970s brought a new lease of life to Chaguanas; conveniently located near the oil-rich south, it has developed rapidly into a shopping centre for those who prefer not to travel all the way into Port of Spain.

Arrival, information and accommodation

There is no **accommodation** to speak of in Chaguanas, though the town is easily accessible from the capital. **Maxis** from Citygate, Port of Spain take you to the maxi stand next to Mid Centre Mall in Chaguanas for TT$3. **Route taxis** from Broadway, Port of Spain, will drop you on Chaguanas Main Road by *KFC* for TT$5. Maxis and taxis to the rest of the West Coast can be taken from here. **Buses** leave Citygate, Port of Spain for Chaguanas every 20–25 minutes and cost TT$2–3. The **post office** is located on Railway Road, opposite the **police station**. There are several **banks** in the town centre, including First Citizens, Market Street, ☎665 4125; Republic, City Centre Mall, ☎665 3386; and Royal, Medford Plaza, ☎665 2313.

The town

The centre of town, ranged around the junction of Chaguanas Main Road and the old Southern Main Road, is a busy amalgam of new shops, hand-painted signs and street-side clothes stalls. It is dominated by two large malls: the **Mid Centre Mall** and **Centre Point Mall** (also known as Ramsarran Plaza), both great places to find bargains in shoes and clothes imported direct from New York and India. The big old-fashioned **market** on the southern side of Main Road offers a complete contrast – narrow alleys wind their way through covered sheds and open yards, lined by hundreds of wooden stalls selling fruit, vegetables, ornaments and fashion accessories. Old women sit behind stalls groaning under the weight of plantain, dasheen, chillies and ground provisions. Plastic hair slides, necklaces and earrings are displayed in their hundreds, and you can buy anything from locally made leather sandals to the latest Nike trainers.

Phagwa

A lighthearted, joyous celebration of the new year and the arrival of spring, the Hindu Holi festival – known in Trinidad as Phagwa (pronounced "pag-wah") – is held around the first full moon in March to mark the end of the Hindu calendar's twelfth month (Phaglun). Upbeat and carnivalesque, Phagwa celebrations are massive outdoor parties that represent a symbolic triumph of light over darkness and happiness over suffering. In Indian religious mythology, the festival commemorates the death of Holika, the sister of an evil king who repeatedly tried to murder his son Prahalad, because of his insistence on worshipping Vishnu as the only God. Immune to flames, Holika was persuaded to do the deed by carrying Prahalad into a fire, but the gods ensured that she burned to death; her brother was later slain by Vishnu. Holika's conflagration is re-enacted the night before the main festivities, when sins amassed in the previous year are ceremonially consumed by the flames of large bonfires.

The main festivities revolve around traditions such as the singing of devotional folk songs called **chowtals**, composed specifically for Phagwa and accompanied by goatskin *dholak* drums and brass cymbals called *ghanj*. Local businesses sponsor *chowtal* competitions in the weeks preceding Phagwa, and the winners perform on the main day. The main focus of the festival, though, is an intense fuschia pink dye known as **abir**, which is strewn about as powder or mixed with water and squirted from a plastic bottle renamed a *pichakaaree*; participants wear white to make the most of the ensuing glorious mess. Accompanying the *abir* squirting are **pichakaaree songs**; topical ditties sung in a mix of English and Hindi which relate current issues to religious concepts, while classical Indian dancers display their movements and chutney soca fuels the more risqué dancing. Games add to the fun; adults participate in **makhan chor**, where teams form a human pyramid in order to grab a suspended flag, while roti eating contests are the source of much hilarity; skins are stringed through the middle and tied in a line for children to eat; no hands are allowed.

Chaguanas hosts one of the largest celebrations in Trinidad, the Kendra Phagwa Festival, in an open space off Longdenville Old Road. There are other gatherings at Aranguez Savannah in San Juan and at Couva, but none is widely publicized – to find the exact date, you'll have to scan the community events listings in the newspapers, or call TIDCO (☎ 623 6022).

The very imposing, white-painted **Lion House**, a few hundred metres further down Chaguanas Main Road from the market, was the birthplace and childhood home of Trinidad's most famous writer, V.S. Naipaul (see p.317). It's a fine, albeit deteriorating, example of North Indian architecture which takes its name from the lions that adorn the stout columns supporting its grand arcade. Built in 1926 by the Pundit Capildeo, it became the residence of the Naipaul family when the writer's father Seepersad married Capildeo's daughter Droapatie. In his 1961 novel *A House for Mr Biswas*, Naipaul describes his experience of growing up in this house, surrounded by his mother's wealthy, religious and domineering family. Still a private residence, the Lion House is not open to the public, although the exterior can easily be viewed from the road.

For an explanation of the
religious
significance
of Diwali
see p.41.

National Council of Indian Culture

The large complex of the **National Council of Indian Culture** (also known as the **Diwali Nagar** site) on the Uriah Butler-Solomon Hochoy Highway at the Endeavor flyover, just north of Chaguanas, is dominated by a 12-metre **statue of Swami Vivekananda**, a nineteenth-century Calcutta-based thinker held in high regard in Trinidad for his insistence that Indians should find freedom through education, technology and physical fitness.

The complex was set up as a venue for traditional Indian festivals. In itself, the place consists of little more than the statue, a large fenced off area, a portakabin office and a concrete structure where stalls can be set up. But during the the many festivals that punctuate the Indian year – all of which are attended by many of the country's top dignitaries – the place is utterly transformed. The highlight of the year is **Diwali** (the festival of lights), nine days and nights of celebration at the end of October. All aspects of Indian culture in Trinidad are represented: the complex is decorated with paintings and statues of Hindu gods; every type of music, from Indian classical to chutney (the Indian version of soca) is played; and there are performances of Indian folk theatre and modern dramas. The stalls – more than sixty of them – provide a fascinating mix of culture and commerce: at the Hindu Credit Union a man in a Lakers basketball hat gives free palm readings, while stalls selling burglar alarms and furniture do a roaring trade alongside those packed with people trying to find their Diwali souvenir trinket.

Call
☎ 671 6242
for exact dates
of festivals at
the National
Council of
Indian
Culture.
Admission
during festivals is TT$7.

Christian and Muslim Indians also have their own festivities at the site for Christmas and Eid (see p.40), while **Indian Arrival Day** (May 30) re-enacts the docking of the *Fatel Rozack*, which carried the first 225 Indian immigrants to Trinidad in 1845. Displays reveal the way of life and working conditions of the indentured labourers.

Chaguanas potteries

Five kilometres south of Chaguanas on the Southern Main Road, a number of stalls line the road. These are the famous **Chaguanas potteries**, the oldest and most famous of which is Benny's Pottery Works, at the back of Radika's Pottery Shop. The thousands of *deyas* (pottery lamps produced for Diwali), windchimes, wall plaques, pots and ornaments on sale in the shop are all produced here by traditional Indian methods passed down from the present owner Sylvan Benny's grandfather, who learnt his craft in India.

Benny's
Pottery Works
is open daily
7am–6pm;
☎ 671 1763.

It's a fascinating process to watch. The clay, dug from the nearby Carlsen Field, is soaked, and kneaded by foot to remove all stones and lumps. It is then hand rolled or shaped on a wheel before being fired in the large open kiln that dominates the centre of the workshop. Fuelled by wood, the kiln has no temperature gauge – the process relies entirely on the potter's experience and judgement. There is something for every budget in the shop, and if you can't see what you want, Sylvan Benny will make it for you.

Friendship Hall

A little further down the SMR on the eastern side, halfway between
the name sign for Chase Village (now virtually a suburb of
Chaguanas) and the turning to Waterloo Village, is the grandiose
Friendship Hall. With its elaborate balconies, steep gables, corner
turret and fanciful roofscape clad in rusting galvanized iron, it's a
fine, if rather dilapidated, example of the estate houses that were
common throughout Trinidad in the mid-nineteenth century. It was
built by a Scotsman, Hugh MacLeod, in 1864. On his deathbed he
bequeathed it to his estate agent, whose family still live there today.
The house is not open to the public, though the splendid exterior is
easily visible from the road.

Waterloo Temple

About a kilometre south of Chase Village, the Orange Field Road cuts
west off the SMR through the **Orange Valley Estate** to join the
Waterloo Road down to the sea. This is prime sugar territory: fields
of cane stretch out on either side, and tall palms line the road as they
have done since the early plantation days. Passing through a cluster
of neat bungalows built in the 1920s for estate managers, you come
to sleepy **Waterloo Village**, where Hindu prayer flags flutter in the
gardens next to trees with blue plastic bottles hanging from their
branches – an old Trinidadian superstition to ward off bad luck.

This superb drive culminates half a kilometre down the road
where, as you emerge at the sea, you'll be greeted by an astonishing
scene. Opposite an old Anglican cemetery where buffalo graze
between the headstones, the gleaming white, onion-domed **Waterloo
Temple** stands on a pier surrounded by fishing boats bobbing in the
waters of the Gulf of Paria. The flatlands, the funeral pyres at the
water's edge, and the flags (*jhandes*) – representing prayers and
offerings – flapping in the breeze, all contribute to the impression
that you are standing by the River Ganges rather than on a Caribbean
island.

At the landward end of the pier leading to the temple is a life-
sized statue of **Seedas Sadhu**, an Indian labourer to whose zeal
and persistence the place owes its existence. Sadhu built the original temple on the seashore in 1947, but since the land was the
property of the state sugar monopoly Caroni, the government bull-
dozed the structure in 1952 and sent him to jail for 14 days. Sadhu
then decided to resite his temple in the sea, where no permission
was required. A lonely, determined figure, he struggled single-
handedly for the next 25 years to build the shrine, using a bicycle
to carry the foundation rocks out into the water; at low tide he
placed barrels on the sea floor and filled them with concrete. No
sooner had he constructed one part of the building than the sea
would erode his previous work, ensuring that the shrine was never
completely finished.

*The Waterloo
Temple is open
on Saturday
and Sunday
from 7am to
7pm. The
grounds are
open daily
between 7am
to 7pm.*

Help finally came in 1994, when the 150th anniversary of the arrival of Indians in Trinidad inspired the government to declare the temple an Unemployment Relief Project (URP). With labourers paid by the state to rebuild the structure, the temple was swiftly completed. The octagonal shrine covers an area of more than 100 square metres, with coloured glass windows that enable you to see the brightly painted stone and marble gods inside. The pier – planted with hibiscus and bougainvillea – allows visitors to walk to the temple at all times (it was previously only accessible at low tide). The local Hindu community uses the temple for weddings and puja ceremonies in which fruit and flowers are offered to the gods. Anyone can enter the temple, providing they remove their shoes first.

To get to the temple by **public transport**, take a route taxi from Chaguanas to the start of Orange Field Road (TT$2–3), where you pick up another taxi (TT$3) to the temple.

Eating and entertainment

There is no shortage of **fast food** outlets in Chaguanas: along with *KFC* on Main Road, there is a plethora of roti stalls, doubles shacks and Chinese food vendors on the two main streets. For something slightly more upmarket, there are also two **restaurants**: *Eagles*, 44 Eleanor St, Chaguanas (Mon–Thurs 10am–10pm, Fri & Sat 10am–11pm), a dark Chinese eatery serving standard fare at around TT$30 a meal; and *Bougainvillea*, 85 Rivulet Rd, Brechin Castle (Mon–Sat 11am–10pm), an intimate, comfy restaurant serving Chinese dishes, steaks and seafood at around TT$50 a meal. The adjoining **bar** can get quite lively at the weekends.

Chaguanas also has central Trinidad's only **nightclub**. The *Tunnel*, Ramsaran St, ☎671 4819 (Mon–Thurs noon–midnight, Fri & Sat 10pm–4am), is a sports bar with facilities to play pool and darts during the week. At the weekend it becomes a lively club playing dancehall, calypso and hip hop to a young, mixed crowd. The typical entrance fee is TT$20.

Couva

Of the smoggy, industrial towns that line the west coast below Chaguanas, the liveliest is **COUVA**, with its beautiful old gingerbread houses gradually deteriorating on the main road. The **Holy Faith Convent**, on the northern side of the road beyond the police station, occupies a fine old colonial house originally built for a plantation overseer. As in many other parts of Trinidad, however, the old buildings are being torn down in favour of cheap, concrete structures: the old Anglican church at Couva junction, for example, is currently marked for demolition to make space for a new housing development, and there are plans afoot to build an 800-room hotel in the area.

The only **restaurant** in town is *Bal Tar Zzar*, on the corner of Edgar Street and Southern Main Road, ☎636 2786 (Mon–Thurs

11am–10pm, Fri & Sat 11am–midnight) which serves standard Chinese fare; an average meal costs around TT$50.

Point Lisas

Just south of Couva, you hit **California**, a drab residential suburb of the massive **Point Lisas Industrial Complex**, whose belching chimneys are already visible from the SMR. The complex was built as a flagship for the Trinidadian economy during the oil boom years of the 1970s. No expense was spared to create the factories, which produce liquefied natural gas, steel and fertilizers. Industrial it may be, but Point Lisas still has its wildlife. Every year between December and June, thousands of **blue crabs** make the hazardous journey from the swampland next to the complex across the highway to lay their eggs in the sea. During these months, the only noise you hear as you drive past Point Lisas is the crunch of crabs under car wheels.

Maxis run from San Fernando (main stand opposite the hospital) to Couva. You can also take a Port of Spain–San Fernando **bus**, **maxi** or **taxi** and get them to drop you at the relevant exit on the Uriah Butler-Solomon Hochoy Highway, and then hail a route taxi and persuade the driver to take you to your destination.

Pointe-a-Pierre Wildfowl Trust

Past **Claxton Bay**, an industrial suburb cloaked in dust from the nearby cement factory, you come upon a stunning oasis of nature, unexpectedly located in the grounds of the Petrotrin Oil Refinery at Pointe-a-Pierre. The only nature reserve in the Caribbean maintained by the oil industry, the **Pointe-a-Pierre Wildfowl Trust** came into being in 1966, when a hunter who worked at the refinery realized that wildfowl stocks were diminishing, and set aside an area within the complex to breed the birds. In time the area became an established reserve, funded and supported by the refinery.

The Wildfowl Trust consists of 250,000 square metres of attractively landscaped grounds around two lakes filled with waterlilies and lotus flowers. Many rare species of bird can be found here, including the wild **Muscovy duck**, the **red-billed whistling duck** and **white-cheeked pintail**. Some of the rarer birds, including **scarlet ibis**, are caged to allow breeding programmes to continue. The well-maintained information centre at the entrance has good photographic displays of flora and fauna found on the reserve, and a small collection of Amerindian artefacts, with a very good account of the culture and belief systems of Trinidad's original inhabitants. The guides are vastly knowledgeable not only about the bird life, but also about the **medicinal qualities** of the indigenous plants: a chemical in the white periwinkle for example, is used to fight leukemia, while certain mango leaves are used to reduce nervous tension.

*The Pointe-a-
Pierre Wildlife
Trust is open
Mon–Fri
8am–5pm,
Sat & Sun
10am–4pm;
contact Molly
Gaskin (☎ 637
5145) 48hr in
advance for an
appointment.
Admission,
including
guided tour,
is TT$5.*

The Trust may be viewed **by appointment** only, to ensure that the birds are not scared away by overvisiting. To **drive** to the Trust from Port of Spain or San Fernando, leave the Uriah Butler-Solomon Hochoy Highway at the Gasparillo exit and follow the signs to the Petrotrin Oil Refinery. If travelling by **public transport**, take a Port of Spain–San Fernando maxi, taxi or bus, and get out at the Gasparillo exit, from where the refinery is a two-minute walk. Once inside, it's another fifteen-minute walk to the Trust. The best time to visit is before 11am or after 3pm, as the animals hide in shade during the hottest part of the day.

The few **hotels** around Pointe-a-Pierre cater mainly for oil workers and businessmen. For the widest choice of accommodation, your best bet is to stay in San Fernando (see pp.179–188), just a ten-minute journey away. If you're stuck, however, the *Farrel House*, St Margaret Rd, Point-a-Pierre Rd, Claxton Bay (☎659 2271; ⑤), is a smart, quiet hotel overlooking the sea, with swimming pool and restaurant. Convenient for the Wildfowl Trust, the quiet, excellent value *Mikanne*, 15 Railway Ave, Plaisance Village, Pointe-a-Pierre (☎ & fax 659 2584; ④), has TV, a-c and en-suite bathrooms in all rooms, a small swimming pool, sun lounge and an inexpensive restaurant.

The Central Plains

The **Central Plains**, just one to two hours from Port of Spain, are an ideal place in which to enjoy Trinidad's countryside and escape from the city. Most of the country's sugar cane is produced here, and apart from **Piarco International Airport** and its immediate environs, the area is deeply rural. The plains are bounded to the south by the low, rolling **Montserrat Hills** (part of the Central Range), which shelter huge cocoa estates; on and around the hills, kilometres of protected rainforest enfold the grandeur of the **Arena** and **Navet Dams** and **reservoirs**. There is little in the way of tourist infrastructure, but that's part of the charm: the area is perfect for peaceful afternoons, picnicking and watching wildlife.

Public transport is slow and difficult, and the only **accommodation** is located around the airport. The *Bel Air International* (☎ & fax 669 4771; ⑤), a 1940s hotel with 1970s decor 200 metres from the airport exit, is mostly frequented by in-transit passengers, businessmen and honeymooners. All rooms have a-c, phone and en-suite bathroom; there's a swimming pool and restaurant/bar with live entertainment on Fridays. During Carnival season breakfast is included. The *Airport View Guesthouse*, in the small village of St Helena (☎669 4186; ④), provides free transport to and from the airport (a ten-minute drive). Basic but functional, all rooms have a-c, TV and en-suite bathroom, and there's a 10 percent discount for stays longer than a week.

Entertainment revolves around village rum shops, and if you are not taking a picnic, **food** can be bought at the numerous fast-food outlets at the airport in Piarco or at snack parlours along the roadside. Alternatively, street vendors in the villages sell roasted corn, aloo pies, snow cones, and doubles.

The Piarco area

Although best known for its airport, the **Piarco area** in the northwest of the Central Plains is an overwhelmingly rural area of winding country roads and small villages. Piarco itself consists of very little except for the airport and a few small houses, the homes of the airport workers. Established in 1931, **Piarco International Airport** is the base of British West Indian Airlines (BWIA), fondly referred to as "Bee wee" by locals. The company was set up during World War II to provide a transport route that avoided the German submarines that infested the Caribbean. The small airport has duty-free shopping, a currency exchange, and a plethora of booths serving a variety of Chinese, Indian and Creole food.

The village of **St Helena**, 1km south of the airport, consists of little more than a smallish cluster of houses, but is expanding as a result of airport trade. On the outskirts by the airport you'll pass a few traditional whitewashed *tapia* houses, built of mud on a bamboo frame, though most of these have now given way to new concrete buildings. **San Rafael**, 9km to the east through a flat landscape of cane fields and citrus groves, is scarcely larger – a church, a school, and a few old board houses. Its peaceful aspect hides a violent past, however. In 1699, the local Amerindians, angered by Spanish missionaries' attempts to force them to convert to Christianity and use them as slave labour in the construction of churches, rebelled. They killed the priests, dumping their bodies into the foundations of the church, and then laid an ambush for the Spanish governor, José de León y Echales, and his party, whom they successfully captured and killed. In retaliation, the Spanish massacred the region's entire Amerindian population. Today, a statue of St Raphael, the healer of all wounds, presides ironically over the village's main junction in front of the church.

Waller Field, 9km to the northeast, recalls more recent conflicts. When it was occupied by the Americans during World War II, this was the largest airbase in the world, but the hangars, barrack blocks and control rooms are long gone, and what's left of the airstrip is used for weekly drag racing. Further on, the plains are dotted with small villages. **Cumuto** is typical: a quiet place with the odd bar and shop, it has declined from its early twentieth-century heyday when it was the centre of the region's large-scale cocoa cultivation. In the 1940s the community was given a new lease of life by its proximity to the US base at Waller Field, but like Carenage (see p.103) suffered a loss of reputation as the village became the playground for lonely

*For informa-
tion on flights
to and from
Piarco
International
Airport see
Basics, pp.4–9.*

Route taxis to
St Helena and
Piarco (TT$2)
leave from
Arouca
Junction on
the Eastern
Main Road.

young soldiers, and rumours of wild parties and immoral behaviour
ran rife. Not all Trinidadians regard the US occupation as entirely
negative, however; it is said that the money earned from the
Americans during these years funded new housing developments in
the region in the 1970s.

The Arena Dam and Reservoir

From San Rafael, Tumpuna Road runs south through serene rainforest where you will rarely meet another car. This is the beginning of
the area designated as the **Central Range Wildlife Sanctuary**,
though you'd scarcely notice the first low foothills beneath the luxuriant vegetation, as bamboo thickets jostle with papaya, mango,
banana, cashew and breadfruit trees. The blooms of the golden poui
dominate the woodlands in April, while from December to March the
magnificent immortelle trees blaze a fiery red. In the seventeenth
century, the forests sheltered Amerindians fleeing Spanish persecution – many of the Amerindian artefacts in the National Museum in
Port of Spain (see p.76) were found here.

The Arena
Dam is open
daily
9am–2pm.
Tickets
(TT$5.75)
must be pur-
chased in
advance from
WASA, Farm
Rd, St Joseph
(☎ 662 2302)
or at Kew
Place, Port of
Spain (☎ 625
7812).

Within the sanctuary, the **Arena Dam** and **Reservoir** lie 9km west
of Cumuto and 3.5km south of San Rafael on the Arena Road. They
are well signposted by the Water and Sewerage Authority of Trinidad
and Tobago (WASA), but the road is bumpy and, in local parlance,
"mash up" – after heavy rains it is often impassable, so check with
WASA before starting out. Built in 1975, the dam is an awesome 760
metres long, the largest in Trinidad; the 7 square kilometre reservoir
it created provides 75 percent of the nation's water. It's a favourite
weekend spot for families, with picnic tables, swings and climbing
frames, but swimming is not allowed in the reservoir. The wildlife is
astounding: **parrots**, **hawks**, **corbeaux** and **white egrets** fly around
the dam; **blue emperor butterflies** flutter among the bamboo and
settle on the reeds by the water's edge; **caymans** lurk in the swamps
that border the reservoir, while **red howler** and **capuchin monkeys**,
toucans and **tree porcupines** inhabit the surrounding forest.

There is no **public transport** to the Arena Dam; you can either
book a **taxi** for the day from Arima or Port of Spain (around
TT$150), or **rent a car** (see pp.26 & 64).

The Montserrat Hills

South of the Arena Dam, the Central Range becomes more noticeable
as you ascend through the forests into the rolling **Montserrat Hills**.
The Talparo Road peters out after the village of Mundo Nuevo, where
you have to detour westwards to skirt the highlands. This is real
backwoods country, full of winding roads with rickety wooden
bridges, small villages and run-down banana, cocoa and coffee plantations. The scenery is wonderful: the nineteenth-century English
novelist Charles Kingsley, who visited the region in 1870, described

"the panorama from the top of Montserrat" as "the most vast and most lovely which I have ever seen."

Most of the villages have little specific to recommend them apart from the odd picturesque colonial house, a few faded board houses, and a great deal of rural charm. Life focuses around the football field and the rum shop. Quiet during the day, these little places liven up in the evening, when people return from work and drink rum with their neighbours on street corners. The history of **Flanagin Town** is characteristic. In the early years of the twentieth century, when it was surrounded by highly productive cocoa estates, the place bustled with labourers and traders who poured into its train station. But most of the estates have long since returned to the forest, their location marked only by the red blaze of the immortelles planted to shade the cocoa trees; the trains are long gone; and many of the youth have moved to the capital or down south to the oilfields. All that remains of Flanagin Town's prosperous past is the old stationmaster's house behind the community centre.

La Vega Estate

An experimental commercial nursery dedicated to cultivating exotic plants, the **La Vega Estate** lies about 7 kilometres west of Flanagin Town on the Couva Main Road, between Pepper Village and Gran Couva. The on-site nursery has the largest variety of ornamental plants in Trinidad, including 30 different species of **bougainvillea**, rambutan trees from Malaysia, which have spiky fruit, and caryota plants with their amazing mop-like tendrils. The whole estate covers about a square kilometre, of which nearly a quarter consists of exquisitely **landscaped gardens** devoted to public recreation. Guided tours and nature trails highlight the work of the estate and the variety of flora, and provide an opportunity to spot local animals such as **manicou**, **agouti** and **wild deer**. There are large ponds for **canoeing** and **fishing**, a childrens' play area, public toilets, a meditation garden and picnic tables in sheltered bamboo groves.

The La Vega Estate is open daily 9am–5pm. Charges range from TT$5 to TT$30 according to the facilities used.

Route taxis set out for La Vega Estate from KK Plaza at Couva (TT$4); they're rather infrequent, however. To get there by **car**, take the Gran Couva exit from Uriah Butler-Solomon Hochoy Highway and follow the road past Gran Couva for about ten minutes.

Tortuga

TORTUGA, which sprawls up the slope of the Montserrat Hills just fifteen minutes from the busy Uriah Butler-Solomon Hochoy Highway, is another village of old board houses with the odd rum shop. At the top of the village stands the Catholic **Church of Our Lady of Montserrat**, a grand, green-painted wooden gingerbread built in 1872 with a big gable and a graceful arcade. Inside are many old plaster statues, carved wooden Stations of the Cross and, to the left of the altar, a shrine with a **Black Virgin**. The small statue, half

*Route taxis for
Flanagin
Town, Tortuga
and around
leave from
Chaguanas.*

*The Navet
Dam is open
daily
9am–2pm.
Tickets
(TT$5.75)
must be bought
in advance
from the
WASA offices at
Farm Road,
St Joseph
(☎ 662 2302)
or at
Kew Place,
Port of Spain
(☎ 625 7812).*

a metre high and swathed in an oversized white dress, was brought to the island by the early Capuchin missionaries. From the church, you get an excellent view over the rolling plains of central Trinidad, with the distinctive, half-flattened San Fernando Hill in the distance (see p.184).

Navet Dam and Reservoir

South of Tortuga you hit the Tabaquite Road, which runs eastwards along the southern slopes of the Montserrat Hills. Sugar cane, cocoa and coffee estates border the road, while the rolling slopes are clad in seemingly endless tropical rainforest. Past the tiny village of Tabaquite, you come to an abandoned **railway tunnel**; an attempt in the early 1990s to turn it into a recreation centre was defeated by vandalism and neglect. A few kilometres further on, the road edges up a valley towards the towering **Navet Dam**. Constructed in the early 1960s, the dam is 320 metres long, while the **reservoir** behind it forms an intricate pattern of inlets and coves, some 2km in length and 3km across at its widest points. With only the minuscule hamlet of Brasso Venado nearby, it's an isolated place, excellent for quiet picnics and bird-watching – many species of wildfowl frequent the reservoir in the early mornings and late afternoons.

The public facilities are not as good as those at the Arena Dam, however: just one picnic table and some toilets. Nor is there any **public transport** – your options are to make friends with a car-owning Trini, rent a car or book a taxi for around TT$150 a day.

The east coast

South of **Sangre Grande**, the largest town on this side of the island and a transport hub of considerable commercial vigour, central Trinidad's **east coast** is dominated by **The Cocal**, four spectacular kilometres of unbroken sand lined by grove upon grove of coconut palms that begins at **Manzanilla** and stretches south as far as Mayaro (see Chapter Four, pp.204–206). The lure of the seashore and a slow but steady increase in tourism has ensured a couple of places to stay around Manzanilla Village, but otherwise, the area is totally devoid of human development. The Manzanilla–Mayaro Road runs the length of the beach, fringed inland by the pristine rainforest and mangrove-smothered wetlands of **Nariva Swamp**, a primary breeding ground and habitat for all manner of rare and exotic animals and birds.

This east coast is also the origin of most of the coconuts sold in Trinidad. The coconut estates add to the breathtaking environment, with their deserted beaches and waving palms reminiscent of exotic film backdrops and high-class fashion magazines. Sadly, it is unlikely to stay this way for long as a result of the increased tourist trade, though it will probably suffer less than Mayaro Bay. Hopefully the owners of the Central Trinidad's East Coast coconut estates will not sell out to hotel developers, and the beach and protected swamp will retain their idyllic seclusion.

The east coast

Sangre Grande

A thriving market town slung along the Eastern Main Road, **SANGRE GRANDE** – pronounced "sandy grandy" but usually just called "grandy" – is the largest town in the east, a bustling transport depot and the only place in the region where you can get to a bank. Residents of surrounding villages crowd the pavements every Friday, descending to deposit their wage cheques, shop at the **market** stalls or take a fast food fix at the conglomeration of neon-flashing takeaway chains. Friday evenings see Grande at its liveliest, as wages are spent at the rum bars and roadside food stalls do a roaring trade in doubles, jerk chicken or roti.

Most people pass through Grande to change taxis and maxis, and aside from the shopping, there's no real reason to spend much time here unless you need to stock up on food, fill your gas tank or exchange money. Most **taxis** and **maxis** leave from the square behind Royal Castle in the middle of the main drag; ask around to find the correct queue. The banks and petrol stations (one opens until midnight) are also nearby.

Maxis and route taxis from Sangre Grande to Manzanilla Beach cost about TT$8.

The Cocal

Eight kilometres of newly laid tarmac link Sangre Grande with **The Cocal**, the collective name for the large coconut estates that line the Manzanilla–Mayaro Road. This is an awe-inspiring drive – 24 kilometres of graceful leaning coconut trees dancing in the wind, unspoilt beach and preserved rainforest. If you're lucky you may see an experienced coconut picker shinning up and down a tree in the flash of an eye. The docile long-horned animals grazing between the coconuts at the edge of the road are **buffalypso,** bred for their meat and milk. The result of selective breeding of water buffalo, they are highly profitable; a farmer can raise four of them for the same cost as one cow, and each will command a higher price than a cow at market.

Nearing Mayaro, the road runs past a small grove of huge palm trees, their nuts processed at a plant recognizable by the huge mounds of coconut husks that surround it. After miles of bendy, leaning coconut trees, these tall upright palms stand out in firm resolution against the sea breeze. Between 5.30pm and 6pm every night the air is raucous with the calls of the **red-chested macaws** that come to roost in the trees, while the surrounding swampland is a popular spot for southern lapwing and the rare red-breasted tanager. The ponds in this area are full of cascadura (also known as cascadoo), a small brown freshwater fish, similar to catfish, with a tough skeletal covering. They can be spotted by circles appearing on the

> **Coconuts**
>
> Grown on estates throughout eastern Trinidad, coconuts are in constant demand on account of their sheer versatility. Depending on when they are harvested, they can be a source of drink, food, flavouring, oil, soap and animal feed, while their fibrous husk makes an alternative to peat for potting plants. Green young nuts are full of sweet water, a popular drink sold fresh from the fruit from many an old Bedford van around the country. As the nut matures, much of the liquid is replaced by an edible white jelly. A few weeks later, the jelly solidifies into firm white flesh, which can be grated, dried and roasted in cooking. Later still, a bread-like substance grows in the centre of the fruit; if caught at the right time, it makes a tasty snack. Soon afterwards, it develops into a sprout, from which a new tree will grow. Depending on the type, a tree will take five to ten years to mature; it will live for many years, and produce nuts all year round.

pond surface, and are caught on a line or by using nets. It's said that if you eat their chewy brown, tuna-like meat (invariably served as a curry), you will be sure to return to end your days in Trinidad.

There are no hotels or restaurants anywhere along the road between Manzanilla and Mayaro, but there are a few stalls selling the shellfish known as chip-chip, while young boys and men sell freshly caught crabs and fish by the roadside.

Manzanilla

A quiet and attractive village strewn with gingerbread houses at the northern end of The Cocal, **MANZANILLA** is divided into Upper and Lower sections, interspersed with lush swathes of coconuts, banana and mango trees. The section of **beach** near to the village is the most popular part of the whole four-kilometre stretch; if you're after a swim, go through Upper Manzanilla along the Eastern Main Road and turn left opposite Plum Mitan Road. After passing a handful of small groceries and rum shops, you'll find yourself on the seashore, at the beginning of the Manzanilla–Mayaro Road. Behind the first stretch of beach is an ugly, desolate tract of ploughed-up land that's been cleared for development by the owners of *Calypso Inn* (see opposite); Manzanilla is fast growing in popularity, and the hotel will probably be followed by others hoping to cash in on the beach's awesome, unspoilt beauty.

South of the building site, the **Manzanilla Beach** runs the whole length of the east coast, with only the odd decrepit building interrupting palm groves that line the wide, expansive stretch of fine, brownish-grey sand littered with flotsam and chip-chip shells. Windswept and exposed, Manzanilla is deserted during the week, but becomes a popular swimming spot at the weekends. The water is often quite bracing, and you should take care while swimming as the undercurrents can be dangerous. The beach has experienced something of a renaissance in recent years; TIDCO have put in spanking new changing and showering facilities at the northern end (daily

10am–6pm; TT$1) as well as a car park that rivals Maracas in capacity. Manzanilla is also fast overtaking Maracas as the island's most popular Ash Wednesday chill-out spot, the wide sand providing more space for the crowds of recovering revellers to sunbathe or dance to the sound systems that set up in the northern section. Beyond the northern section, there are no facilities at all.

If you want to **stay** near Manzanilla Beach, there are a couple of options. *Calypso Inn* is closest to the sand (☎678 2315 or 668 5113, fax 668 5116; ④), stuck at the end of a newly cut dirt track that cuts through a building site cleared by the owners. Brand new (an annexe is still to be added) and beautifully located on a stretch of beach protected by the headland separating Manzanilla from Matura Beach (see p.149), the hotel has smart double rooms with a balcony overlooking the sea, TV and a-c. There's a bar and restaurant with outdoor and indoor eating and drinking areas, and hammocks slung between the seashore palm trees. A less expensive possibility is *Dougies* (☎668 1504; ②), a large block of rooms adjacent to a popular rum bar and grocery set five minutes walk from the beach in Lower Manzanilla. Basic rooms have fan and private bathroom, but self-contained two-bedroom apartments with full facilities are also on offer; the place is friendly and the rum shop is a lively liming spot after dark.

Brigand Hill Lighthouse

Built in 1958, the stubby white **Brigand Hill Lighthouse** is one of only three in Trinidad. It's not possible to enter the lantern itself, though if you climb the twenty-odd iron stairs that run up the outside, you can get a magnificent view from Toco in the north to Galeota Point in the south, taking in the local rainforest, Nariva Swamp and the odd glimpse of wild monkeys – if you have your binoculars with you. To reach the lighthouse from Manzanilla, take the Plum Mitan Road off the Eastern Main Road after Upper Manzanilla. It's a steep climb; a hard thirty-minute walk or a five-minute drive in an unloaded car. A word with the security guard will gain you entry at the gate.

Nariva Swamp

One of Trinidad's best-kept secrets, the internationally recognized wetland of **Nariva Swamp** covers 15 square kilometres behind the coconut estates along the east coast to the south of Manzanilla. The area is made up of reed-fringed marshes, eerie mangroves and, deep in the swamp, the 15 square kilometre **Bush Bush Sanctuary**, an island bordered by moriche palms and covered in hardwood forest and silk cotton trees. Unexploited by tour companies, it is not an easy area to get to, but its unique freshwater ecosystem offers large concentrations of rare **wildlife**, with over 58 species of mammals and 171 species of birds. The swamp also harbours 92 species of mosquito, so remember to bring your insect repellent.

*Brigand Hill
Lighthouse
is open
8am–5pm,
entrance free.
Large groups
and those with
young children
need first to
gain permission from the
Ministry of
Works
Maritime
Services,
☎625-3858.*

The 1996 Ramsar Convention – to which Trinidad and Tobago is a signatory – designated the swamp a wetland of international importance, placing a legal obligation on the government to ensure the area is protected and maintained. In an area of low employment, however, it is not always easy to reconcile human economic needs with the demands of conservation. Many people turn to hunting as a means of subsistence, and large-scale illegal rice farming has destroyed some of the habitat. (The government eventually expelled the rice farmers after pressure from environmentalists). In addition, bush fires have ravaged almost half the territory in recent years.

Nariva is also the only place in Trinidad to see the cute but threatened **manatee** or sea cow, a peculiar elephantine mammal that once fuelled rumours of mermaids lurking in the brackish depths. These shy, bizarre creatures can grow up to three metres in length and weigh over 900 kg, and live in freshwater ponds, where they feed off water hyacinth, moss and waterlilies. They are currently in danger of extinction: in the 1970s hundreds inhabited the swampland, but now their numbers are down to double figures.

The swamp is also an excellent place to view **caimans**, **red howler monkeys** and a wide variety of birds including **orange-winged parrots** and the **yellow-capped Amazon parrot**. Its most alarming inhabitants, however, must be the **anacondas**, reputedly washed **here** from South America on the current of the Orinoco River. These terrifyingly large greenish-brown, black-spotted snakes grow up to 9 metres long; they're the heaviest reptiles in the world, and the largest in the Americas.

Those wishing to visit the sanctuary must first obtain a free permit from the **Wildlife Division** of the **Forestry Department** in St Joseph; the division will advise you which guides to contact. Alternatively you can ring the guides directly; they will get the passes for you and organize your trip. For those with a more amateur environmental interest, a limited budget and desire to gain some knowledge about the human residents of the area as well as the wildlife, South East Eco Tours (☎644 1072) offers excellent, well-rounded day trips involving hikes into the swamp, boat rides up the nearby Ortoire River, lunch with local residents and trained guides from the local community. Tours cost between TT$35 and TT$80. Caribbean Discovery Tours (☎624 7281) also works with South East Eco Tours local guides and offers kayak trips into the swamp for slightly higher rates. Wildways (☎623 7332) specialize in wildlife and adventure tours and take you into the swamp by kayak for TT$100 per person. Those who want an expert ornithologist to guide them should call William Nanan (☎645 1305).

Permits for the Nariva Swamp are available from the Wildlife Division, Forestry Department, Farm Road, St Joseph. Mon-Fri 8am–4pm ☎662 5114.

Chapter 4

San Fernando and the south

Geographically, Trinidad's **south** presents a mirror image of the north: a long littoral of land extending beyond the main body of the island, with the low ridge of the forested Southern Range as its spine. In the curve of the Gulf of Paria, where the south-west peninsula crooks a finger towards the Venezuelan mainland, Trinidad's second city, **San Fernando**, sits at the base of its oddly-shaped hill.

That's as far as the comparison goes, however; San Fernando is a serious, booming business town, but beyond its city limits the region is the most sparsely populated in Trinidad. Although many inhabitants still earn a living from agriculture – mainly sugar and rice – and from fishing, the economy is dominated by **oil**. This, ironically, is what has left the region so unspoilt; with its well-paid jobs, the industry means that the local population do not have to pander to the tourist dollar – a refreshing experience for holidaymakers in the Caribbean. In addition, the petroleum business leases large expanses of forest from the government; these remain largely undeveloped apart from a few discreet oil pumps.

Most of the land is covered with untouched rainforest – an environmentalist's dream. In the deep **southeast,** the protected rainforest of the **Trinity Hills Wildlife Reserve** shelters countless species of bird and exotic mammals such as the ocelot, while the **Oropuche Lagoon** on the southwest coast is a wildlife-rich mangrove swamp seldom visited by tourists. The architecture, like elsewhere in Trinidad is changing rapidly – brand new out-of-town malls are springing up all over the place – but many old colonial gingerbread buildings remain, their state of gradual deterioration only adding to their air of enchantment.

Tourists rarely venture this far south – those that do visit the **Pitch Lake**, in the least attractive part of the peninsula. Few make it as far as the picturesque areas of **Cedros** and **Erin**, or the remote and eerie fishing village of **Moruga** on the south coast. **Mayaro**, a gorgeous

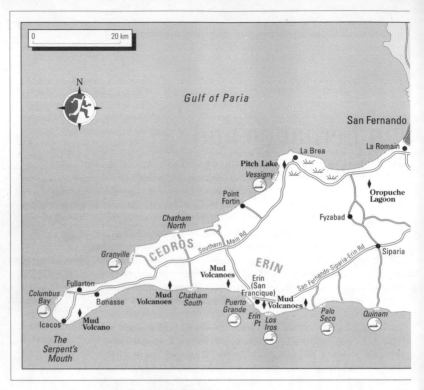

swathe of sand on the southeast coast, has long been a popular holiday resort with Trinidadians, but remains almost entirely undiscovered by foreign visitors.

The lack of tourism is, of course, a mixed blessing, as there are few facilities for visitors in the region. **Transport** is tortuous, especially to the south coast. Rent a car, if you can afford to; if not, you'll need a

---

ACCOMMODATION PRICE CODES

All accommodation listed in this guide has been graded according to the following **price categories**:

① under US$10	② US$10–20	③ US$20–35
④ US$35–50	⑤ US$50–70	⑥ US$70–100
⑦ US$100–150	⑧ US$150–200	⑨ US$200 and above

Rates are for the cheapest double or twin rooms, including 10 percent tax and 10 percent service charge where applicable. In Tobago, rates quoted are those used during the high season, normally mid December–mid April. During low season (mid April–mid December) rates are liable to fall by up to 25 percent. There are no high and low seasons in Trinidad, but rates may rise by up to 70 percent during Carnival. Many hotels give rates in US dollars – we have followed suit. Payment can be made in either US or TT currency.

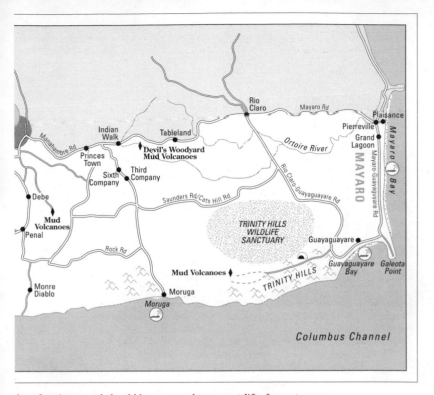

lot of patience and should be prepared to accept lifts from strangers. **Accommodation** is minimal and in the extreme south pretty much non-existent, despite the area's many gorgeous beaches; find a comfortable base in San Fernando, Point-a-Pierre or Mayaro and be prepared to travel. TIDCO (☎623 1932) has a small list of host homes in the area – it's worth contacting them before you set out.

San Fernando

Nestled against the base of the bizarrely-shaped **San Fernando Hill**, the city of **SAN FERNANDO** is the most striking in Trinidad. Usually referred to as the industrial capital of Trinidad and Tobago, it has an old-fashioned charm that comes as some surprise. Its steep streets and sea views are reminiscent of a miniature, low-key San Francisco, while a warren of old winding lanes are studded with charming gingerbread buildings that have survived the city's rapid development in recent years.

San Fernando – usually referred to as "**Sando**" by Trinis – is far quieter than Port of Spain; life moves at a slower pace, there are

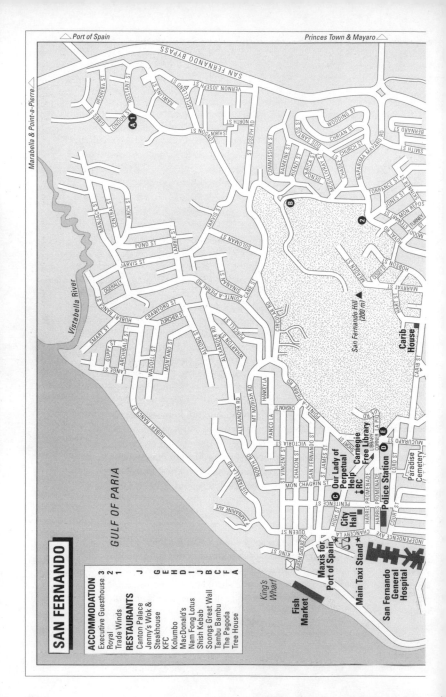

SAN FERNANDO

ACCOMMODATION

Executive Guesthouse	3
Royal	2
Trade Winds	1

RESTAURANTS

Canton Palace	J
Jenny's Wok &	
Steakhouse	G
KFC	E
Kolumbo	H
MacDonald's	D
Nam Fong Lotus	I
Shish Kebab	J
Soongs Great Wall	B
Tambu Bambu	C
The Pagoda	F
Tree House	A

GULF OF PARIA

Vistabella River

Port of Spain

Princes Town & Mayaro

SAN FERNANDO BYPASS

Marabella & Point-a-Pierre

VERNON JOSEPH ST

HERRERA ST

LONDON ST

ROSTANT ST

RAWLIN'S ST

MCKELLINO ST

NORTH ST

GORDON ST

NORTH ST

COMMISSION ST

RAMKIN ST

RIENZI ST

WOODING ST

CHRIAN ST

DOS SANTOS ST

SERICA ST

CHURCH ST

CHARLES ST

NAPARIMA MAYARO RD

BERNARD ST

SMITH ST

TORRANCE ST

JONES ST

LAS MON REPOS

STEWART ST

ROYAL RD

HOBSON ST

MARRAVAT ST

HART ST

San Fernando Hill (200 m)

Carib House

CARIB ST

MUCURAPO

Paradise Cemetery

LORD ST

MANJACK ST

CENTRAL ST

ARCH ST

POND ST

JARVIS ST

HUBERT RANCE ST

POINTE-A-PIERRE RD

SOLOMAN ST

CAVE ST

SINANAN ST

CIRCULAR RD

AMBIS ST

UGERALLY

CRANFORD ST

ZURCHER ST

SMART ST

ARCHIBALD ST

WADDELL ST

MONTANO ST

ALEXANDER RD

WHARTON ST

PURCELL ST

MT MORIAH RD

PANGO LA

CHISHOLM ST

LANGE ST

GUPPY ST

HANKEY LA

HANKEY LA

ALEXANDER RD

NORTH BR

VISTABELLA RD

TAMARINE AVE

VICTORIA ST

ST VINCENT ST

CHACON ST

SAN FERNANDO ST

ST JAMES ST

MON CHAGRIN ST

PENITENCE ST

HIGH ST

LIBRARY LA

LORD ST

Carnegie Free Library

Our Lady of Perpetual Help RC

City Hall

HARRIS PROMENADE

HARRIS PROMENADE

CHANCERY LA

COURT ST

Police Station

San Fernando General Hospital

INDEPENDENCE AVE

QUEEN ST

KING ST

QUEEN'S WHARF RD

Maxis for Port of Spain

Main Taxi Stand

King's Wharf

Fish Market

THE GUIDE: CHAPTER 4

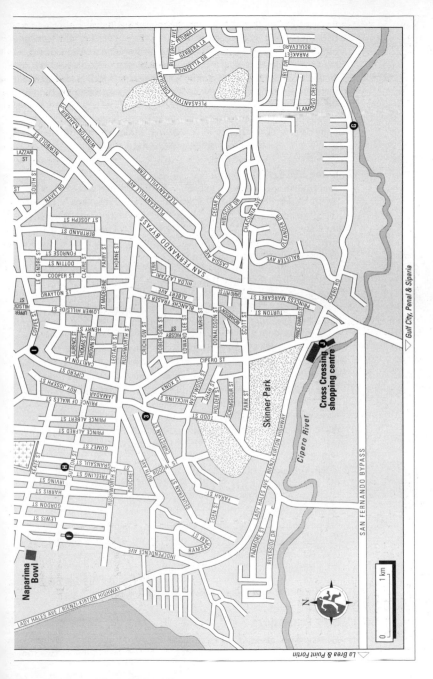

Naparima
Bowl

Cross Crossing
shopping centre

Skinner Park

Cipero River

◁ *Gulf City, Penal & Siparia*

◁ *La Brea & Point Fortin*

1 km

N

fewer people on the streets, and the interaction between them is far friendlier. Long ignored or belittled by the capital for which it, in turn, has scant regard, San Fernando has always maintained an independent spirit. It is scarcely promoted as a tourist destination; a commercial city first and foremost, it gets many business visitors but few sightseers. You will be overwhelmed by local attention, although there is no need to feel intimidated; it is entirely well meant.

San Fernando has plenty of **restaurants**, **shops**, and the odd **nightclub**. It is the hub of the region's **transport** system, just one hour's drive from the superb beaches of the south coast.

Some history

Amerindian legends, dating back to 8000 BC, emphasize the sacred nature of San Fernando Hill. It was the final resting place of **Haburi the Hero** and his mother, who were fleeing from the **Frog Woman** in the Orinoco Delta in Venezuela. They reached Trinidad safely, only to be turned into **"Anaparima"**, the original Amerindian name for the mount. Amerindian tribes from the South American mainland made an annual pilgrimage to the site from 6500 BC to the early 1900s.

The settlement's first European contact was the arrival of **Sir Walter Raleigh** in 1595 – he was unimpressed and sailed on. Nearly a hundred years later in 1687, **Capuchin priests** established a mission here. However, it was between the years of 1784 and 1792 that the settlement finally began to flourish. French plantation owners attracted by the *cedula* of 1783 (see p.285) were allocated land in the area and established the first estates. In 1784, José Maria Chacon, the last Spanish governor of Trinidad, renamed the town San Fernando de Naparima in honour of King Carlos III's new son. By 1797, when the British captured the island, San Fernando had more than a thousand inhabitants, twenty sugar mills and eight rum distilleries. Surrounded by fertile agricultural land, the town continued to grow, and by 1811 the population had trebled. In 1846 "Sando" was officially recognized as a town.

San Fernando became the **hub of the south**, a busy trading centre for successful planters, with a regular coastal steamer to Port of Spain – the overland route took three days of rough riding through forests, and swamps. The arrival of the railway in 1882 led to another population increase, and by the late 1880s San Fernando had been thoroughly modernized. Suburbs grew as the plantations disappeared – the result of falling sugar prices in the 1920s – and the town became dominated by the burgeoning oil industry. The municipality continued to grow throughout this century with little planning or design, until it was finally designated a city in 1988.

City transport

There are no buses or maxis in San Fernando. **Route taxis** charge a flat fare of TT$2 for most journeys, with an added dollar or two for off-route drops. **"Round the road"** taxis follow a loop around the city centre, circling San Fernando Hill. They have no stand; you can hail one on any main street. Taxis for the town's main shopping malls, **Cross Crossing** and **Gulf City**, can be caught adjacent to *KFC* on **Library Corner** (junction of Harris Promenade, Mucurapo Street, La Pique Road and High Street) – these also cost TT$2. Two local **private taxi** firms are Mattadeen's Taxicab Service (☎658 4973) and St Anthony's Taxicab Co-Operative (☎648 3941).

Accommodation

Of the few **hotels** in San Fernando, only two cater for the foreign market – and these mainly for oil industry personnel. More accommodation can be found in Point-a-Pierre (see p.168) and Point Fortin (see p.196), ten to twenty minutes' drive away from the city centre. There are a few other hotels designed for Trinidadian couples seeking some privacy from living with their extended families. With motel-style chalets, very basic facilities and non-stop music in all rooms, they usually charge by the hour.

Executive Guesthouse, 11 Todd St; no phone. Small basic rooms with painted concrete floors, double bed, fan, toilet and shower. Guests must arrive between 9am and 10pm. ③

Royal Hotel, 46–54 Royal Rd, ☎652 4881, fax 652 3924. The most expensive accommodation in town, comfortable but overpriced; all its rooms are a-c, with cable TV, phone, fridge and en-suite bathrooms. They also have spacious self-catering apartments. ⑥

TJ's By the Sea, Southern Main Rd, La Romain, ☎657 9278, fax 657 1423. Despite its rooms overlooking the sea 2km south of San Fernando, this is not as enticing as it sounds – the hotel is sited on a busy road, and the sea is impossible to swim in at this point. All rooms have a-c, cable TV, en-suite bathrooms, phones and nice rattan furniture. There is a **restaurant** serving international fare, a swimming pool, and a collection of caged animals optimistially called a nature park. ⑥

Tradewinds Hotel, 38 London St, ☎652 9463, fax 653 8733. This friendly, reasonably priced hotel is located on a breezy hill in the quiet suburb of St Joseph. All the rooms have a-c, cable TV, fridge, mini bar, kettle and en-suite bathrooms. There is a 5 percent price rise during July and August. ⑤

The city

San Fernando's compact centre is bordered by the Gulf of Paria on one side and the rocky, wooded outcrop of **San Fernando Hill** on the other. Most of the historical sights, shops and transport stands are located on and around the **Harris Promenade**, a broad, elegant boulevard running west from the foot of the hill. The wider urban area is defined by two main roads, **Lady Hales Avenue** (also known as Rienzi-Kirton Highway), which skirts the coast, and the **San Fernando Bypass** inland. The environs, such as the well-to-do suburb of **St Joseph Village**, sprawl up the slopes of San Fernando Hill,

San Fernando

For information on long distance transport out of San Fernando, see p.188.

while more recent developments such as **Pleasantville** and the large
shopping malls are located on the outskirts, beyond the bypass.

San Fernando Hill

At 200 metres, **San Fernando Hill** dominates the town centre. For
many years the hill was quarried to provide gravel for the building of
the city's streets, giving it its strange profile – half the hill is flattened
with steep protruding points, while the other half maintains its natural outline. In 1980 it was declared a national park, providing a
pleasant recreation area with picnic tables, planted flowers, a playground, a fountain, public toilets and a viewing gallery. The road to
the summit lies between *Soong's Great Wall* restaurant and the
Love Boat pub on the Circular Road – it's clearly signposted. Though
you can drive a car to the top, it is only a twenty-minute walk, or ten
if you take the footpaths – popular with young couples and dog walkers – that provide a shortcut.

*San Fernando
Hill road is
open daily,
9am–6pm.*

Harris Promenade and around

The centre of civic life and the location of San Fernando's official
buildings is the **Harris Promenade**, named after the British governor
of Trinidad from 1846 to 1854, runs from the long 1950s facade of
San Fernando General Hospital to Library Corner in the east. It
consists of two parallel streets with a paved centre lined with benches and tables, the odd statue and an ornate Victorian bandstand. Like
the Brian Lara Promenade in Port of Spain (see pp.70–71), it has
recently been refurbished to provide a pleasant hang-out for the
city's residents. It is far more picturesque than its equivalent in the
capital, for it is lined with attractive colonial buildings.

On the south side of the promenade towards its western end
stands an old-fashioned, round-arched yellow stone building reminiscent of an English parish church or country mansion – the bright
blue postmodern extension behind it more accurately reflects the
building's function as the city's **police station**. Across the road, the
grand neoclassical **City Hall** was built in 1930, and dominates the
western end of the promenade – though it faces stiff competition
from the Catholic **Church of Our Lady of Perpetual Help** one block
to the east, a huge white modern building with a tall clock tower that
can be seen from most places in the city. The interior is unusually
stark for a Catholic place of worship.

At the centre of the promenade is the **Mahatma Gandhi Statue**,
brought to Trinidad in 1952 from India. On Gandhi's birthday
(October 2), the day of his death (January 30) and Diwali (see p.41),
the local Gandhi Seva Sang Organization holds a commemorative
service on the promenade below the statue. The aspirations of the
Afro-Caribbean population are acknowledged by a brightly painted
statue of **Marcus Garvey** at the eastern end of the promenade, typical of Trinidad's more modern monuments.

Here, the promenade's two roads converge, in front of the **Carnegie Free Library**, a large, ornate terracotta building built in 1919 and financed – like many others the world over – by the Scottish philanthropist Andrew Carnegie. In front of the libary, an old **steam locomotive** recalls the last run from Port of Spain to San Fernando in 1968. People packed the carriages, hanging out the windows to be part of this historic occasion, which was subsequently immortalized by Lord Kitchener's famous calypso "'The Last Train to San Fernando". Engine 11, which stands on the promenade today, is not the actual machine that pulled the last train, but one of the last engines in use from the sugar estates. The junction of seven roads just beyond the library is known as **Library Corner**. At its centre stands a modern four-faced clock, of which only one face is currently working. This spot is a popular rendezvous – "meet meh library corner" is a common refrain among the city's residents.

Walking down the **High Street** from Library Corner brings you into the busiest part of town. This is San Fernando's main shopping street, lined with clothes stores and shops selling household goods, while street vendors hawk plastic trinkets and leopardskin underwear on the pavement. At its southern end, as the High Street doglegs into Queen Street, the sea comes into view. The area, ironically known as **Happy Corner**, is the most run down in the city, but a few renovated colonial buildings give it some architectural interest, while the patrons of the local rum shop add a touch of raffish life. Happy Corner gives on to **King's Wharf**, a scruffy tarmac dock lined with dilapidated wood and galvanized iron huts overlooking a small harbour where fishing boats bob up and down on the swell. In the **fish market**, a plain whitewashed building that has changed little since it was built in 1924, the fishermen gut, clean and sell their catch – snapper, kingfish and shark, alongside the occasional deep-sea monster.

Carib Street and "The Coffee"

To the south of San Fernando Hill runs **Carib Street**, fringed by ramshackle old colonial houses. Though less picturesque than its wooden neighbours, the **Carib House** – on the corner of Upper Hillside Street and Carib Street – is the oldest in San Fernando, a plain, eighteenth century stuccoed Spanish colonial building. Despite its age, there is no plaque or sign indicating its history or date of construction.

Coffee Street, which turns off Carib Street towards the south, takes its name from the coffee plantations that once grew here. "The Coffee" – as the street is familiarly known – was the original home of many of the south's steel bands, including the highly acclaimed **Fonclaire**, led by Professor Philmore. A brightly painted statue of a pan player at the junction with Cipero Street celebrates the area's musical heritage. A little further down on the left is the **Skiffle Bunch panyard**. Behind a small empty patch of rough ground, a narrow decaying building houses the pans. The crumbling walls that flank

*The Skiffle
Bunch
panyard is
usually open
after 4pm
from
November
until Carnival
– ask a local
for the time of
the next
rehearsal.*

the open space are decorated with frescoes. Known as the **Dancing Walls**, these fading images were painted in 1994 by local artist Glen Steel. The animated figures – executed in spiky black outline – capture the energy and excitement of the steelband as they trace its development from the tamboo bamboo of the 1940s (see p.302) to the present day. Interwoven with the pan players are traditional Carnival characters such as Jab Molasses and the sailors (see p.291). The panyard itself, a big open space hung with bunting and strings of lights, is at the back, and doubles as the parking lot for the *Southern Food Basket* grocery across the road.

At the southern end of Coffee Street is a fine 1930s Art Deco **power station** – now disused and gradually deteriorating – its predecessor on this site provided San Fernando with its first electricity in 1923.

Eating

There are few **restaurants** in San Fernando, most of them serving reasonably priced international cuisine or ever-popular Chinese food.

Al Keyahm, Upper Level, Gulf City Shopping Complex, ☎653 5247. An intimate restaurant despite its location on a balcony overlooking the shopping mall. Tasty Middle Eastern cuisine served by friendly staff. Mon–Sat 10am–9pm. Average meal TT$60.

Canton Palace Restaurant, Cross Crossing Shopping Centre, Lady Hales Ave, ☎652 5993. Large Chinese restaurant with pleasant decor, recommended for its crab and pepper shrimp. Mon–Thurs 11am–10pm, Fri & Sat 11am–11pm. Average meal TT$35–50.

Jenny's Wok & Steakhouse, 175 Cipero Rd, ☎652 1807. Fine dining establishment serving Chinese food, steaks and seafood. Mon–Thurs 11am–10pm, Fri & Sat 11am–11pm. Average meal TT$100 plus.

Kolumbo Restaurant, 34 Sutton St, ☎653 7684. International cuisine with gourmet burgers and patés. Set in a restored colonial building, this stylish restaurant is very romantic at night, with live piano playing on the upper level. Also serves afternoon tea. Mon–Sat 11am–10pm. Average meal TT$60–80.

Nam Fong Lotus Restaurant, 91–93 Cipero St, ☎652 3356. Serves huge Chinese lunches and dinners at inexpensive prices. A relaxing, comfy and more upmarket atmosphere than the usual plastic tables. Mon–Sat 10am–10pm. Average meal TT$20.

Royal Hotel Restaurant, 46–54 Royal Rd, ☎652 4881. Small traditional style restaurant serving steak and fish, and sandwiches at lunch on a pleasant patio. Mon–Sun 6am–10pm. Average meal TT$80–100.

Shish Kebab, Top Floor, Cross Crossing Shopping Centre, Lady Hales Ave, ☎652 4069. Intimate restaurant decorated in cosy Mediterranean style, serving creative international cuisine from kebabs to steaks and seafood platters. Mon–Sat 11am–10pm. Average meal TT$200.

Soong's Great Wall, 91 Circular Rd, ☎652 9255. High quality Chinese food – as well as the obligatory steak dinners – served in an ornate pagoda-shaped building. Mon–Thurs & Sun 11am–10pm, Fri & Sat 11am–10.30pm. Average meal TT$50–80.

Tambu Bambu Restaurant, 778 High St, ☎657 2435. Huge, satisfying Creole buffet meals in dark eating area. Mon–Sat 9.30am–4pm. Average meal TT$15–25.

The Pagoda, 59 Independence Ave, ☎657 6375. Cosy restaurant serving usual Chinese fare; the steamed fish is recommended. Mon–Thurs 10.30am–10pm, Fri & Sat 10.30am–10.30pm. Average meal TT$30–40.

Tree House, 38 London St, ☎653 8733. Pleasant, friendly place, next to the *Tradewinds Hotel*, where you can dine on excellent international dishes on a balcony overlooking the city. Open early for breakfast; reservations are recommended for dinner. Mon–Thurs 4am–10pm, Fri–Sun 4am–2am. Average lunch TT$35, dinner TT$120.

Nightlife and entertainment

Clubs and nightspots are very limited in San Fernando, but there are plenty of **rum shops** to choose from, with loud music and lively conversations.

Club Celebs, Top Level, Gulf City Shopping Complex, ☎652 7641. The most popular nightspot in the city – a modern club and sports bar playing a wide variety of music to a young crowd. Entrance fee ranges between TT$25 and TT$50. Sun–Thurs 3.30–11pm, Fri & Sat 11am–4am.

Submarine Club, Southern Main Rd, La Romain, ☎653 2980. In the same building as *TJ's By the Sea* (see p.183), this club is decked out with comfy chairs, mirrorballs, pool tables and flashing lights. It plays a mixture of music – from disco to calypso – for a mature crowd. Mon–Thurs 4pm–midnight, Fri & Sat 4pm–2/3am.

The Naparima Bowl, 19 Paradise Pasture, ☎652 4704. Comfy theatre and outdoor amphitheatre hosting plays, which regularly come here after showing in Port of Spain, and big calypso and steelband events. Ticket prices range between TT$25 and TT$40.

Tree House (see above) The restaurant's friendly, intimate cocktail bar sometimes features live music from solo singers and small bands.

Shopping

The best place for shopping is the **Gulf City Shopping Complex** (Mon–Thurs 9am–8pm, Fri & Sat 9am–9pm), a typical international mall on the Link Road on the southern outskirts of the city. Another mall with fewer shops is the **Cross Crossing Shopping Centre** opposite Skinner Park on Lady Hales Avenue. For more local produce, the **Chancery Lane Market** at the end of the High Street features a number of stalls selling local arts and crafts made by Rastafarians, who make up a significant proportion of San Fernando's residents. Sandals, hats, jewellery, belts and straw goods can be found here for very reasonable prices; particularly good quality goods with friendly service can be found at the **Junior Roots** stall.

Listings

Banks Bank of Commerce, 1–3 Coffee St, ☎652 4519; Republic, 92–94 Cipero St, ☎652 4627; Royal, 11 High St, ☎652 2233.

Cinema Hobosco 2, 21–23 Mucurapo St, ☎652 4543; National Cinema, cor. Gomez and Keate streets, ☎652 2343; Metro, 41–43 Harris Promenade, ☎652 4107.

Hospital San Fernando General, Independence Ave, ☎ 652 3581.

Laundry Elegant Dry Cleaners, Cross Crossing Shopping Centre, ☎652 8993; Ng Pack Laundry, 4 Mucurapo St, ☎652 3276.

Police The main police station is at the western end of Harris Promenade, ☎652 2561.

Post office King St, ☎652 3431. Mon–Fri 8am–4pm.

Sports Skinner Park, Lady Hales Ave, ☎ 657 7168; hosts local football and basketball games and the odd concert. Entrance tickets range from TT$5–20.

Moving on from San Fernando

The **main transport stand** to take you out of the city to the rest of the south, and the arrival point for maxis and taxis from Port of Spain, is adjacent to the San Fernando General Hospital in Chancery Lane. **Maxis** go from here to La Brea (TT$4), Vessigny (TT$4), Penal (TT$3.50), Siparia (TT$4), Fyzabad (TT$3.50) and Point Fortin (TT$5). For Palo Seco, you will have to take a maxi to Siparia and then change. Route taxis from this stand run to: La Brea (TT$6), Vessigny (TT$6), Erin (TT$8), Siparia (TT$6), Palo Seco (TT$7), Fyzabad (TT$4), and Point Fortin (TT$8).

Other destinations have their stands located around the city centre. Maxis for **Port of Spain** (TT$5) leave from behind the Chancery Lane Market; for **Couva** (TT$3) and **Chaguanas** (TT$4) they depart from St James Street, and for **Princes Town** (TT$3) they go from Coffee Street. Route taxis to **Penal** (TT$5) leave from the High Street, those to **Princes Town** (TT$3) depart from the top of Harris Promenade, next to *McDonald's*. To go to **Granville** and **Icacos** you have to change at Point Fortin. To get to **Mayaro** you need to go via Princes Town or Sangre Grande in the northeast.

Bus ticket office: Mon-Fri 5am-8pm, Sat 6am-7pm, Sun noon-7pm. For information ring ☎652-3705.

The **bus depot** and **ticket office** are at the bottom of **Queen Street** by the fish market. Buses run from here to Port of Spain (ECS: 5am–8pm, 15min, TT$6. Transit 4am–9pm, 45min, TT$4), Chaguanas (ECS: 5am–8pm, 15min, TT$3. Transit; 4am–9pm, 45min, TT$2.50), Point Fortin (Transit; 2.30am–9pm, 1.5hr, TT$3) and La Brea (Point Fortin bus, TT$3).

The southwest peninsula

Trinidad's **southwest peninsula**, known locally as the "deep south", offers a mix of gritty oil towns and marvellous drives through sleepy backwaters, forested hills, and teak and coconut plantations down to beaches of soft brown sand backed by red earth cliffs and lapped by calm seas. The pace of life is very slow, so take time to enjoy the relaxed atmosphere and incomparable countryside.

Trinidad's oil industry

When oil was first discovered in Trinidad in 1819, in Guayaguayare in the
southeast, the samples were reported to be "of such fine quality that the
chemists regarded them as artificial". Exploration was begun in earnest
in 1857 by the Merrimac Company, and ten years later they drilled the
first oil well in the world in **La Brea**. The English novelist Charles
Kingsley - he of the Water Babies - visited the site in 1870 and was
appalled, denouncing the sputtering well as an interference with God's
work and declaring that "man should mind his own business". The success of the well was short-lived, however, and the industry didn't really
take off until 1893, when **Randolph Rust**, an entrepreneur of disputed
nationality, started prospecting. With Canadian funding he established a
well in 1902 on the banks of the Pilot River in Guayaguayare, and persuaded the British government – which was converting the Royal Navy to
oil-powered ships – to invest in the industry.

World War I boosted demand, and by the 1920s there were dozens of
oil companies in the island. By 1932 the black gold made up 50 percent of
the nation's exports, and by 1946, Trinidad accounted for 65 percent of all
the British Empire's oil production. The situation remained stable until the
1974 international oil crisis, when prices went through the roof. Prime
Minister Eric Williams declared that "money was no problem", and the
country went on a wild spree with the government spending millions on
lavish and ambitious projects. The most infamous was the proposed horse
racing complex – including air-conditioned stables – to be built on the
Caroni Plains. Escalating costs and the opposition's cry of "houses before
horses", saved Trinis the estimated TT$400 million it would have cost; but
not before substantial sums had been spent on negotiating contracts and
designing the facilities.

Trinidadians speak of these days with a mixture of disgust and nostalgia. Stories abound of people who went to work at 8am, returned at 10am
and were paid a full day's wage. Everyone seemed to have money and the
latest consumer goods, but the traditional Trinidadian collective values
were eroded by greed, individualism and corruption. Not all the money
was wasted though. The Point Lisas Industrial Complex was established on
the west coast (see p.167), improvements were made to the infrastructure
and educational grants were made available for T&T citizens. Trinidad's
good fortune did not last long, however; declining oil prices in the 1980s
forced people to realize that the easy life was over. Over-ambitious projects had drained public resources, unemployment rose and crime
increased. Harsh measures such as the devaluation of the dollar were
required to put the economy back on track.

Although the boom is over, oil has remained the mainstay of the economy, employing more than 16,000 people and providing 25 percent of the
nation's GDP. It has ensured that Trinidad remains one of the strongest
economies in the Caribbean. Ironically, this has helped to preserve the
island's natural environment – unlike other Caribbean nations, Trinidad
has not been obliged to develop an extensive tourist trade, leaving the
coastline free of multinational hotel chains and the rainforests to grow
unabated.

The
southwest
peninsula

*For details of
transport to
the southwest
from San
Fernando, see
p.188.*

*Caribbean
Discovery
Tours (☎ 624
7281) will take
you into the
Oropuche
Lagoon by
kayak;
Wildways
(☎ 623 7332)
arrange tours;
and William
Nanan (☎ 645
1305) offers
expert guid-
ance for seri-
ous environ-
mentalists.*

Despite its proximity to San Fernando, the mangrove swampland of the **Oropuche Lagoon** is a seldom visited wildlife haven teeming with birds. Indeed, few tourists venture further than the well-publicized **Pitch Lake** at **La Brea**, but it is worth travelling on south to the areas of **Cedros** and **Erin at** the tip of the peninsula. Small fishing hamlets line the coast, while the beaches are an escapist's dream – small sheltered coves, usually deserted apart from the odd fisherman or truanting child. The road down to **Icacos Point**, the extreme southwest tip, is one of the most spectacular drives in Trinidad, lined with coconut plantations where herds of buffalypso graze.

The larger towns, such as **Point Fortin** and the **Siparia-Fyzabad conurbation**, are dominated by the oil industry; they come to life after 4pm when people finish work. Though of little interest in themselves, they do provide the only **accommodation** and **restaurants** in the area.

Oropuche Lagoon

The **Oropuche Lagoon** – 56 square kilometres of tidal mangrove swamp alongside the Southern Main Road 6km south of San Fernando – features on the itineraries of very few tour companies. That's just how the government plans to keep it – an undisturbed haven for fish and endangered wildfowl bred in the Point-a-Pierre Wildfowl Trust (see p.167) and released into the wild here.

Oropuche's inaccessible location amid swampy marshland discourages hunters as well as visitors, and as a result it teems with animals and birdlife. It is an excellent place to view **butterflies**, while **birds** include egrets, black-bellied whistling duck, American bittern, ringed kingfish and a variety of herons. The waters of the swamp are inhabited by a variety of fish including tarpin and the catfish; and the area is also known for its shrimping grounds. Though it is less disturbed than the Caroni Swamp (see p.160), the lagoon is under threat from pollution due to oil leaks from pumping jacks – there are more than 1600 scattered around the south, many of them disused and left to rust away until they break, causing damaging oil spills.

The Siparia-Fyzabad conurbation

Some 10 to 13km south of San Fernando, surrounded by the rolling pastures and endless sugar cane fields of the **Philippines Estate**, is the **Siparia-Fyzabad conurbation**, powerhouse of the country's oil industry. The government has recently designated the magnificent untouched forest on either side of the road as the **Palmiste National Park**. The small agricultural town of **Penal**, which produces a large proportion of the country's rice, holds little of interest for the visitor, but it marks the beginning of the built-up area; from here it is easy to drive into the lively old Spanish town of **Siparia** without noticing where one starts and the other ends. To the north, the urban area also encompasses **Fyzabad**, a gritty place that played a crucial role in the development of Trinidadian trade unionism and political struggle. These hectic towns are excellent places to buy **Indian** sweets, pies and snacks that are sold on roadside stalls in little wooden glass cases known locally as "safes".

Siparia

Action in **SIPARIA** is focused on the main street, lined with attractive colonial houses interspersed with more modern constructions and fringed by rickety market stalls. It's a lively place full of shoppers and market vendors, though there are few specific sights, unless you are interested in the variety of vegetables, ground provisions and fruit on offer.

The town was originally settled in 1758 by Capuchin priests from Spain, who established a mission to convert the Amerindians in the area. The legacy of Catholicism is still very much in evidence in the feast day of **La Divina Pastora** (see box below) held in Siparia three weeks after Easter. The **Black Virgin**, a small statue of the Virgin Mary normally housed in the church at the top of the hill (follow the road that branches off the SMR opposite the Republic Bank), is carried through the streets to the beat of tassa drums and showered with offerings of gold bracelets. The festival is one big street party, with the whole town coming out to celebrate in their best clothes. Despite the festival's Catholic origin, Trinidadians of all denominations now participate – Hindus also worship the statue, calling her Soparee Kay Mai (Mother Kali), while local Baptists attribute the Black Virgin with mystical powers.

The Festival of La Divina Pastora

Held on the second Sunday after Easter in Siparia, the **Festival of La Divina Pastora** – the divine Shepherdess – was brought to Trinidad from Andalucia by way of Venezuela in the eighteenth century. Decked out in new clothes, the locals make offerings to the **Black Virgin** statue, carried in procession through the streets, and celebrate with general feasting and merrymaking. Some believe that the wooden statue was in fact the prow of the ship in which the priests travelled from the mainland, found in refuse from a shipwreck on Quinam Beach by passing Warwarrhoons Indians. Others claim it was brought to Siparia from Venezuela by a Spanish priest whose life it had saved. Whatever its origins, many miracles have been attributed to the statue. In the 1890s, Hindu indentured labourers saw the dark and supposedly Indian features of the statue, and concluded that the icon represented the goddess Kali, the destroyer of sorrow. Renaming the statue Soparee Kay Mai, the Hindus started their own form of worship – if Kali answered their prayers, Hindu women would offer the statue locks from their children's first haircut. The Catholic Church attempted to discourage this devotion in the 1920s, but the cult had already grown too strong, and even to this day there are Hindu devotees at the festival.

Quinam Beach

A well signposted, if rather bumpy, 7.5km drive down the Coora
Road/Penal Quinam Road, through teak plantations and forest inhabited by deer, takes you to **Quinam Beach** on the south coast of the
peninsula. The sands are fine and brown, though at high tide they
disappear beneath the waves; the waters are calm and good for
swimming; and Baptist flags flap in the breeze on the seashore –
followers of the faith believe the sea here has mystical qualities.

This is the most popular beach with locals on the south coast –
on weekends the small car park on the seafront is packed with
Trinis coming to take their "seabath". Families and friends chill out
under the palm huts, eating large picnic lunches, and the babble of
lively conversation and music from stereos fills the air. The
Quinam Bay Interpretive Centre (daily 9am–6pm) just by the
beach, displays pictures of the local flora and fauna, and also provides sheltered picnic facilities, firewood cooking stoves and a special praying area. You'll need to bring your own food and drink
unless you want to buy aloo pies, snow cones or soft drinks from
the beach vendors. There is no **transport** to the beach, but you can
persuade a Siparia taxi driver to take you there for an agreed fare
(around TT$10–20).

Fyzabad

The bustling town of **FYZABAD**, on Fyzabad Road 5km north of
Siparia, occupies a unique place in the history of trade unionism and
the struggle for equal rights in Trinidad. Established in the nineteenth century by CanadianPresbyterian missionaries, Fyzabad took
its name from the district in Uttar Pradesh, India, where most of its
settlers originated. After oil was discovered in the area in 1917, however, the town's character changed dramatically. Fyzabad quickly
developed into a busy industrial town, the centre of the emergent
labour movement, while the original Indo-Trinidadian presbyterian
community were soon outnumbered by migrants who came from
Grenada and St Vincent to work on the oilfields, and whose descendants still dominate the town.

The compact commercial centre, a blend of dilapidated colonial
buildings and modern concrete, clusters around Charlie King
Junction. **The Oil Workers' Trade Union Hall** and the painted statue of the workers' leader **Uriah Butler** (see box opposite) in his
black suit and bowler hat, dominate the junction, ironically named
after **Charlie King**, the policeman killed when he tried to arrest
Butler for political agitation. The junction is also the focus of the
Labour Day (June 19) celebrations organized by the OWTU every
year. The streets are blocked, a stage is erected and a street party,
with a political message, ensues – union leaders make fiery speech-
es, a wreath is laid on Butler's grave, and DJs entertain the crowd.

Uriah Butler

Tubal Uriah "Buzz" Butler – Trinidad's foremost trade union activist – was a Grenadian who came to work in Trinidad's oilfields in 1921. After an industrial accident in 1929 left Butler unfit for oil work, he joined the Moravian Baptist church and became a preacher, developing the fiery oratorical skills that characterized his political career. Disillusioned with Cipriani's Trinidad Labour Party (see p.288) after it failed to support an oilworkers' strike in 1935, he established the **British Empire Workers** to further the "heroic struggle for British justice for British Blacks in a British colony".

The BEW campaigned for better pay and working conditions in the oilfields, where many of the managers were white South Africans who had instituted an apartheid-type regime. Among the workers' many grievances were low wages, long working hours, and the frequency of industrial accidents, for which there was no compensation. Workers were liable to instant dismissal and, once sacked, a blackballing system made it impossible for them to find work elsewhere.

In June 1937 strikers started a **sit-in** at the **Forest Reserve oilfield**. The police broke up the protest, and in response two wells in the Apex oilfield were set on fire. When the police arrived at Fyzabad to arrest Butler on a charge of agitation, they found him addressing a large crowd. As they attempted to serve the warrant, a riot broke out. One plainclothes officer, the deeply unpopular **Charlie King,** fled into a nearby shop, found himself trapped, and jumped from an upstairs window, breaking his leg; the furious crowd burned him alive, and when his colleagues tried to retrieve his body, a British police officer was shot dead. A 1938 calypso caught the popular mood: "Everybody's rejoicing, How they burned Charlie King, Everybody was glad, Nobody was sad, When they beat him and they burned him, In Fyzabad."

Strikes spread like wildfire, and became increasingly violent, with a mounting death toll on both sides. Butler, in hiding after the riot, was soon discovered and sentenced to two years in prison. But the strikes won important concessions: public workers were granted an eight-hour day and a new minimum wage. The government recognized the trade unions, though the police continued to harass trade union officials. On his release in 1939, Butler was given a hero's welcome, but during his imprisonment the BEW had changed, adopting a more mainstream position. After Butler agitated for a strike in defiance of a Union Executive decision, he was expelled from the BEW. In September 1939 he was once again incarcerated for sedition, and remained behind bars till the end of World War II.

Butler continued to be politically active after his release in 1945, campaigning in the national elections; but though his party won the largest block of seats in 1950, he was outflanked by the rise of Eric Williams's nationalist politics (see p.288), and his star faded. In remembrance of his part in defending workers' rights, the Princess Margaret Highway linking north and south Trinidad was renamed in his honour in the 1960s. In 1971 the government awarded him with the Trinity Cross – the highest honour in the land, and June 19, the day of the riots, was declared a public holiday.

La Brea and around

Eighteen kilometres south of San Fernando on the SMR, a turn-off winds through rainforest and teak plantations to **LA BREA**. The village's name – Spanish for pitch – announces its main claim to fame: the nearby **Pitch Lake**. There's little else to see – the most memorable feature of the village itself is its excruciatingly bumpy roads – a car suspension's nightmare, caused by the underground volcanic eruptions that replenish the lake. La Brea's residents put up with it, finding compensation in the free pitch that bubbles up all over the place, used as paving for driveways and as an unusual garden weedkiller.

The Pitch Lake

Some of the finest quality asphalt in the world comes from the **Pitch Lake**, 1.5km south of La Brea on the SMR. Trinis may claim it as the eighth wonder of the world, but to the sightseer it bears a remarkable resemblance to a car park or the wrinkly hide of an elephant. It is a genuine curiosity, however – there are only three such lakes in the world, the other two being in Los Angeles (Rancho La Brea) and Venezuela (Guanaco).

Five to six million years ago, asphaltic oil flowed into a huge mud volcano, developing over time into the high quality asphalt that is now extracted from the lake and used to pave roads all over the world. The asphalt is continually churned up from an estimated depth of 80 metres – a measuring attempt in 1910 was foiled when the cast-iron measuring pipe was snapped by currents 50 metres down.

According to local **legend,** a Carib tribe who killed and ate the sacred hummingbird in celebration of a tribal victory angered the Great Spirit of the Amerindians. The spirit punished them by trapping them forever under the Pitch Lake – a story reinforced by the many Amerindian artefacts yielded up by the lake over the years, and now displayed on shelves in local homes as well as in glass cases in the Port of Spain museum.

Sir Walter Raleigh discovered the pitch lake in 1595, used the pitch to caulk his ships, and reported on its quality to Queen Elizabeth I. The lake was not commercially exploited until the 1860s, however, when it was developed by the British, who continued to control the excavation of pitch until 1978. The National Museum in Port of Spain (see p.76) has a collection of photographs of streets from London to Australia, India and Singapore, surfaced with Trinidadian pitch.

Covering more than 40,000 square metres, the lake is probably the largest deposit in the world. Bird of paradise flowers grow around its edge, competing with the unsightly factory that excavates 240 tonnes of pitch daily. If you visit between 8am to 4pm, you'll see the workers loading the substance onto trolleys and dragging their load across the surface to the factory. The "**mother of the lake**" – the soft centre where the pitch is replenished – is firm enough to walk on in most places, though not in high heeled shoes. The pitch is extracted from the "mother of the lake" by peeling off the hardened top layer. Cracks that form in the surface are often filled with sulphuric water reputed to be excellent for mosquito bites, rashes, skin conditions and cleaning jewellery. After working hours the lake fills with people taking their evening dip in the natural springs that appear at its centre during the wet season; locals will expound on the healing qualities of the sulphuric waters.

Despite many attempts to set up a formal system, the **guides** are still unorganized, touting persistently – and sometimes aggressively – for business at the entrance to the car park. Usually there will be a guide and a "demonstrator", who will show the lake's various textures and fluidity, posing for photographs with sticks covered in runny pitch. Both expect to get paid, so agree your price beforehand and stick to it; the going rate is around TT$30, and a generous tip – around TT$10–20 – is expected on top. Wear shoes with low heels and be careful not to let the pitch touch your clothes – it is a nightmare to clean off.

The Pitch Lake is open daily 10am–6.30pm. Admission TT$30/US$5.

Vessigny Beach

Three kilometres past the Pitch Lake, **Vessigny Beach** is a delightful little cove of brown sand lapped by calm seas. It's a popular spot with Trinis at the weekends, and the destination for evening excursions that turn into high-spirited beach parties. During the dry season (December to May) the sea is clean, though from June to November the water becomes brackish from river discharge. There are no lifeguards on duty, so be careful when swimming. This is the only developed seaside on the south coast; its well-maintained facilities include a snack bar (open at weekends and during school holidays), changing rooms and picnic tables. Trinidadians sometimes camp on the grass by the beach – it is not an official campsite, and there is no charge if you wish to do the same.

The facilities at Vessigny Beach are open 10am– 6pm. A small fee is charged.

Point Fortin

Five kilometres on from Vessigny beach, through forest, bamboo groves and small villages, is the oil town of **POINT FORTIN**. Evidence of the industry is everywhere: large storage tanks pop up in the suburbs, and the rhythmic motion of an oil pump will catch the corner of your eye from a side street. Shell, which once owned the refinery and tank farm, built extensive facilities for its expatriate management; scattered around town are tennis courts, a golf course and an old country club, while the suburbs are full of large houses with satellite dishes and barking dogs. In some roads, the old **workers' houses** can be seen – rough concrete boxes that are a far cry from the luxurious mansions of the managers.

The southwest pensinsula

There is little to see in Point Fortin unless you have a personal interest in the oil industry. The place only comes to life after 4pm, when the workers come out to lime in the bars and hang around the main junction. Locals go to swim at **Clifford Beach,** by the oil storage tanks. It must have been a nice spot once, but the bar has closed down, leaving only the tables with their thatched palm canopies as a reminder. The sea and sand are clean during the dry season, but from June to November they're polluted by brackish water and litter swept downstream.

There's not much in the way of **accommodation.** *Cinnamon House*, 118 Cinnamon Drive, Clifton Hill (☎648 2349, fax 648 1419; ⑤), is an attractively decorated small hotel with a-c and cable TV in all rooms, most of which are en suite. The comfortable **restaurant** serves good Creole/international food. The place is hard to find – ring first for directions. *Vanessa Cottage*, 71 Clifton Hill, Point Fortin (☎648 2468; ④/⑤), is a lovely, spacious, old house once owned by a Shell manager, whose daughter now runs a B&B with two comfortable a-c rooms.

Cedros and Erin

The areas of **Cedros** and **Erin**, occupying the extreme tip of the southwestern peninsula, are the most picturesque and untouched in Trinidad. The **environment** is stunning, as the teak plantations that line the Southern Trunk Road to the north are replaced by miles of palm and coconut trees. The best beaches in the country, lovely sheltered coves lapped by a calm sea, are located here and – unimaginably in the tourist-dominated Caribbean – you'll find them practically deserted. At the furthest tip of the southwest peninsula, **Icacos Point** looks out across the swirling waters of the **Serpent's Mouth** to the South American mainland just 11 kilometres away.

The residents earn their living by fishing, indifferent to the region's growing tourist trade – though even this is relatively low key, as few visitors make the three- to four-hour drive from Port of Spain. Charming **board houses** line the road, their inhabitants watching the occasional passer-by from their verandahs. Small groceries sell traditional snacks such as fruit preserved with salt, lime, pepper and herbs. Village life centres on the bar and the football field, where lively games take place in the cool light of dusk. In the evenings villagers catch the breeze on the seafront beneath the red, orange and green almond trees, while the snow cone man rides his bicycle cart along the promenade, ringing his bell to drum up business. At night the bumpy streets are quiet and often unlit. Animals rule here, not cars; the occasional **buffalypso** herd will wander across your path, or you may come head to head with an unruly goat.

Cedros

Cedros takes its name from the **giant cedar trees** that lined the bays in the early 1700s, though sadly none of these have survived. It was first settled by Spaniards, whose influence lingered longer in this isolated region than in the rest of the island; despite an influx of Indian indentured labourers, Spanish was still widely spoken until the 1880s, almost a century after the British had captured Trinidad. A hundred years ago, during the nineteenth-century heyday of the sugar estates, Cedros was a bustling place with a population twice as large as it is today. Famed for its rum, this small district boasted no less than seven distilleries.

Every bay in Cedros seems to have a picture postcard **beach**, usually a small sheltered cove with soft brown sand and calm waters. The idyllic settings more than compensate for the total lack of facilities. The beach at **Granville** is so far off the beaten track – 5.5km from the Southern Trunk Road through the well-kept village of the same name – that it's often completely deserted. Its fine sands are a very light brown and the waters are calm, though underwater currents that drag sand from the bottom give the water a somewhat murky aspect. Unless you fancy a brisk walk to the sea from the main road, you will have to negotiate a fare with a taxi driver from Point Fortin.

Though Cedros is actually the name of the whole area south of Granville, many people from outside the district use it to refer to **Bonasse, a** sleepy, charming village on **Cedros Bay**, a 10km beach used mainly by local fishermen. Two kilometres from neighbouring **Fullarton** is the lovely 3km beach on **Columbus Bay** – an excellent spot to find interesting pieces of driftwood. This is very quiet during the week and large enough to avoid bumping into people at the weekends. The view has changed little from the one that greeted Columbus when he visited these sands after his landing at Moruga in 1498.

From Columbus Bay the road winds on through a huge, spectacular coconut estate, down to the sleepy little village of Icacos *(Ih-car-cus)*; a little further on it comes to an end at **Icacos Point**, the southwesternmost point in Trinidad. There's nothing much to see at this faraway spot apart from the crumbling sea wall, the pelicans, the buffalypso herds, and the vague outline of the Venezuelan coast. The dividing channel is called the **Serpent's Mouth** – an apt description, for the bay forms the shape of an open mouth, while the three rocks jutting out at sea at the northern end resemble the serpent's fangs. The serpent fails to scare the drug smugglers who reportedly use these beaches to bring in crack cocaine from Colombia via Venezuela. Rumours abound that the area is awash with drug money now that the Caroni Swamp – the smuggler's previous entry point – is well patrolled by the T&T coastguard.

To reach Icacos by public transport, take a maxi from Point Fortin to Bonasse, a route taxi from Bonasse to Fullarton (TT$2) and then another route taxi to Icacos (TT$5).

Nine kilometres to the west, you can see the craggy silhouette of **Soldado Rock**. This small, 60-metre high island marks the division between Venezuela and Trinidad's territorial waters – its name means "the soldier". It is has been a wildlife sanctuary since 1934, as it is the only major seabird breeding site in Trinidad, home to frigate birds, grey-breasted martins and brown pelicans, and the nesting site of sooty and noddy terns. During nesting season – March to July – these birds lay over 5000 eggs on the rocky protrusion. Its varied and dramatic rock formations are of great interest to geologists, and even amateurs can spot the many fossil beds. Those interested in visiting the island should negotiate with one of the fishermen from Icacos. It is difficult to land on the rock, however, and you must be careful not to sail into Venezuelan waters unless you fancy a night in a South American jail.

Erin

Rounding the tip of the peninsula to **Erin Point,** you pass many quiet villages where the only noise comes from the school playground. **Erin** (**San Francique** on many maps) is one of the most picturesque, with old board houses set in flowering gardens and colourful fishing boats bobbing on the seashore. Little changes here – the population is roughly the same size as it was a hundred years ago, when it had the reputation of producing some of the finest cocoa in the world. These days it's Trinidad's most important fishing village, with the biggest catches in the country. During the Erin fishing season (June to December), the village is frenetically busy with fishermen landing their catch and buyers and sellers haggling on the shore. From January to May the community returns to a more peaceful existence, and the fishermen depart for Moruga where the catch is greater.

Erin's beach, known as **Puerto Grande,** is the centre of its fishing activities. Fishermen painstakingly mend their nets with huge needles, weigh fish on large old-fashioned scales and discuss prices in discreet tones. It is a busy working beach, but if you can put up with the fishy smell it's not a bad place for a swim, provided you keep to the ends of the sands to avoid boats bringing in the latest catch. It is the best place in the region to buy fresh fish; you can watch your purchase being pulled out of the water and you will pay half the price advertised in the supermarket in town. There are a few snack parlours and bars on the waterfront, catering to the fishermen.

If you want a more private bathing spot, try the pretty cove of **Los Iros** 2km east of Puerto Grande. The water is calm and clean, and though the beach is popular at weekends, you'll find it deserted during the week apart from the odd fishing boat. There is a small snack parlour and a bar nearby, but if you are planning to spend the whole day, follow the Trini example and bring your own food; at weekends it is common to see whole families with pots, containers and coolers, as they bring their large Sunday lunch down to the beach.

Los Iros cove boasts the only **accommodation** in Erin or Cedros. The *Beach Boys Guest House* (☎ 657 9826) consists of four basic but functional self-catering apartments 15m from the beach. Each has two bedrooms with double beds, a lounge with TV and fans. There is a kitchenette, but little running water. Book early, especially for the holiday weekends, and remember to bring your own

Trinidad's fishing industry

Fishing in Trinidad is big business. Over the last twenty years the industry has developed from local self-sufficiency to an organized business, becoming an excellent earner of foreign exchange. Its potential persuaded the government in 1977 to provide incentives to encourage people to become fishermen. The policy was highly successful: the industry now employs 9000 people, and the catch weighed 8.7 million kg in 1996. As well as providing for the domestic market – it is estimated that every Trinidadian eats 18kg of fish per year – Trinidad exports TT$70 million worth of fish annually, mostly red snapper, carite and kingfish.

This success story has brought its problems, however. T&T's fishing grounds are becoming seriously depleted, and disputes regularly arise when Trinidadians are caught in Venezuelan waters. Declining fish stocks are variously blamed on increasing pollution and the large foreign trawlers that haunt T&T's waters, though some point the finger at the use of "ghost" nets – transparent plastic netting that is banned in many other countries – by their own countrymen. The fishermen argue that they are obliged to use ghost nets to ensure a decent catch during the day, since increasing crime has prevented them from fishing at night, when larger catches can be hauled.

food and, if possible, water – otherwise you'll have to buy it from the visiting water truck.

Eight kilometres east of Erin is another marvellous **beach** at Palo Seco Bay. Turn onto **Beach Road** by the YKC & Son supermarket at Palo Seco village. This takes you past the Petrotrin beach club, where it is best to park, as beyond it the road degenerates into a steep dirt track. This leads to a 4km beach scattered with driftwood and lapped by the typical calm seas of the region. It is a fifteen-minute walk from the San Fernando–Siparia–Erin Road, the route of the maxis from Siparia or taxis from San Fernando.

The southern central region

The **southern central region** is one of the most impenetrable in Trinidad. The only transport artery, made up of the Manahambre, Naparima and Mayaro roads, runs from the west to the east coast, through rolling plains of sugar cane, linking the region's two main towns, **Princes Town** and **Rio Claro**. The road is dotted with Hindu temples, Muslim mosques, Christian churches and agricultural villages with little to interest the visitor beyond the well-publicized **Devil's Woodyard** with its over-hyped mud volcanoes, and a predeliction for bizarre place names.

South of the main road, much of the landscape is swathed in wild forest dotted with the occasional oil well. There are very few passable roads, signs are almost non-existent, and trying to follow a map is a lesson in frustration – what is marked as a road may turn out to be no more than a dirt track. If you need directions, it's best to ask how to get from

A to B – few locals know the official names of the roads. You may have problems finding anyone to ask, as the area is largely uninhabited – when you do stumble on someone, they will usually turn out to be oil workers mending leaks, or loggers working in the forest. If you don't know Trinidad well, it is best to stick to the main roads and not venture onto the dirt tracks – many are dead ends, or lead to no more than an oil pump. Just one decent road penetrates this wilderness, running down to the small fishing village of **Moruga** on the south coast – a strange, isolated place, undisturbed by visitors and steeped in ancestral African faiths that give the place an eerie and mystical atmosphere.

Maxis and taxis are frequent along the Manahambre Road from **Princes Town** to **Rio Claro** (TT$4/5). To go to **Devil's Woodyard** take a maxi from San Fernando to Princes Town (TT$3), change here and get a taxi to take you to Hindustan Road (TT$4). You will then have to change again or cajole your driver into taking you to the site for another TT$4. You can get a maxi or taxi to **Moruga** from Princes Town for TT$5.

Accommodation is extremely limited in this area, but the two nearest concentrations of hotels, in San Fernando and Mayaro are easily accessible. Restaurants in the American or European sense are non-existent, but there are many Chinese fast food parlours and the usual roadside stalls selling snacks, home-made pies and preserved fruit.

Princes Town and around

The unremarkable **PRINCES TOWN**, 7km east of San Fernando on the Manahambre Road, resembles a permanent traffic jam. En route you pass the **St Madeleine Sugar Factory** – during harvest season, the smell of burnt sugar fills the air along with ominous billows of smoke. Princes Town is developing faster than its infrastructure can cope with. New buildings are springing up in every imaginable style, competing with traditional places of worship such as the grand mosque with its copper dome and steel plated minarets on the east side of the town centre. The town's most curious feature, however, best glimpsed when driving in from the west, is Randy's Enterprises, a large electrical goods shop covered in murals and reliefs of Hindu gods and the Statue of Liberty. Around the corner on the left stands the Anglican **St Stephen's Church** – its two poui trees were planted by Prince Albert and Prince George in 1880. It was this visit by the future kings Edward VII and George V that led to the village, previously known as Mission, being renamed in their honour. The English novelist Charles Kingsley visited the town in 1870, and is commemorated in a street name.

The tiny villages of **First**, **Third**, **Fourth** and **Fifth Company** surrounding Princes Town are a legacy of the black American **soldiers** of the War of 1812. These former slaves had fought on the British side in return for promises of land, and after the British defeat they were allocated lots in Trinidad. There is no village called Second Company – this unit was lost at sea on the voyage to Trinidad.

The soldiers settled here in 1816, bringing with them the Baptist faith that still dominates village life. They cleared the land and established successful plantations in a place that had previously been uncharted jungle, earning themselves a reputation for the pioneer spirit. They complained bitterly to the then governor, Ralph Woodford, about the condition of the land they had been granted, but without success; he wanted to open up the interior, and also to keep the radical black soldiers far away from potentially rebellious slaves.

The small village of **Indian Walk**, 5km east of Princes Town, is of little interest except for its unusual name, which recalls the many Amerindian traders who travelled this route selling parrots, food and ornaments. Seven kilometres to the east, the small village of **Tableland** has what is claimed to be the second oldest Hindu temple in the western hemisphere (the oldest is in Martinique). Pundit Mahant Moose Bhagat Dass, an indentured labourer who had migrated from Bharat Desh in India, built the small temple on the northern side of the road in 1904. The pundit had removed some stones from a stream and placed them near his house. That night in a dream, the spirit Shiva Bhagwan asked him to build a temple, as his previous home in the stones had been disrupted by the pundit's action. To this day the stones remain in the temple, housed in the shrine of Shiva.

Devil's Woodyard

Devil's Woodyard, with its **mud volcano** is a highly publicized tourist attraction, but despite the intriguing name, the sight is disappointing. The route down Hindustan Road, 3km past Indian Walk, is well signposted; it's a pretty but very bumpy drive through rolling pastures, teak and citrus plantations. The name came about in 1852 when a large eruption shook the surrounding houses.

Mud volcanoes

The many **mud volcanoes** scattered around southern Trinidad are promoted as environmental curiosities by TIDCO, which highlights them on its maps. The majority are largely inaccessible – unless you like taking hikes through dense forest – and in most cases it's not worth the effort. The volcanoes are small mounds less than a metre high that seep and bubble grey sulphuric mud, which is believed to be good for skin conditions.

The volcanoes can appear anywhere: in the middle of the bush, in people's back gardens and by the road. They are usually ignored, though those who live near them do so at their peril, for they have a tendency to explode every few years. The most recent and damaging **explosion** was in Piparo in central Trinidad in 1997, where a road was completely destroyed; the villagers had to endure repeated tremors and the pungent smell of sulphuric gas, while the mud-filled gutters provided an excellent breeding ground for mosquitoes.

The local Amerindians believed the mud volcanoes were passages between this world and the one below, and that the explosions were the Devil coming out to shake the earth. The present reality is less dramatic – little more than a small mound of earth with grey mud bubbling lazily to the surface. If you are curious to see a mud volcano, though, this is the most accessible, and has the best facilities, including picnic tables and toilets (though the latter are often locked). Bear in mind, though, that like all natural phenomena, its level of activity can vary; most of the time the eruptions splutter harmlessly, though in some years the eruptions have been violent enough to shower the picnic tables with mud.

Moruga

MORUGA is a pretty, isolated village on the central south coast, 21km from Princes Town, by a sheltered cove lined with soft brown sand. The place seems to have changed little since it was first settled: the bright, contrasting colours of the old board houses have weathered to pastel shades; colourful wooden fishing boats lie on the seashore; and fishermen while away their spare hours liming outside the two shops on the main road.

For more information on obeah and other ancestral beliefs, see p.296.

The Catholic church on the seafront dominates both the surroundings and the life of the village. This is a place of strong – but heterodox – beliefs; villagers may avow allegiance to Catholicism, to the Baptist faith, or to obeah, but many will believe in aspects of all three. A religious, almost superstitious atmosphere pervades the village. Locals speak of **obeah spells**, and stories abound of **Papa Neiza,** an African herbal doctor, immortalized by the calypsonian Sparrow in his song "Melda", who could allegedly exorcise devils – and instill them in people. An obeah woman, **Madame Cornstick**, still lives in the village, though she is rarely seen nowadays. Her powers are reputed to be great, and many people still come to Moruga to consult her in the hope of solving their romantic or financial problems. Residents mumble that she does more harm than good, though no one speaks too loudly in case they fall victim to one of her curses.

The village's main event is its **Columbus Festival**, held on August 1 each year. Situated near the spot where Columbus landed in 1498 (see box opposite), Moruga is the only place left in Trinidad to celebrate **Discovery Day**, which has been replaced everywhere else by Emancipation Day (see p.41). The organizers hold the controversial view that without Columbus, the majority of Trinidadians would not have the benefit of living in the island, or of the Catholic faith. Besides, the yearly festival brings much-needed money, and provides the locals with a good party and street bazaar. The festivities take place on the beach, where three boats are decorated in fifteenth-century style and locals play the part of Columbus and the Amerindians who greet the explorer peacefully

Columbus in Trinidad

Christopher Columbus had nearly run out of drinking water when, on July 31, 1498, he sighted the three peaks of the Trinity Hills (see p.207), which apparently inspired him to name the island Trinidad. He landed near present-day Moruga, where he gathered fresh water from the river. The sailors reported seeing fishing implements that had clearly been abandoned in haste, and realized that they had arrived in a country that was already well populated. In fact, there were an estimated 35,000 **Amerindians**, from the Arawak, Shebaio, Nepoio, Carinepagoto and Yao peoples, then living on the island which they called "Ieri", the land of the hummingbird.

Columbus encountered the country's residents the next day when he was anchored off Icacos Point. Twenty-four Amerindians armed with bows and arrows went in a large canoe to investigate the foreign ship. Columbus ordered a drum to be played and the sailors to dance, believing the indigenous population would be entertained by this spectacle. However, the Amerindians thought it was a war dance and rained arrows on the Spaniards; as the latter returned fire, the Amerindians fled. That night, Columbus had little sleep as strong currents tossed the ship. Huge waves crashed against the boat, rocking it so violently the anchor broke. A bewildered and fearful Columbus named the passage the Serpent's Mouth, and quickly sailed away.

For more on the early history of Trinidad, see p.285.

and exchange gifts – hardly an accurate account, but it makes an entertaining spectacle.

Catholicism also inspires the two other celebrations in Moruga. On **St Peter's Day** (the last Sunday in June) the fishermen's boats are blessed, and there is also a street festival on the Sunday after **Easter**.

Rio Claro

Located on the Naparima–Mayaro Road 24km east of Princes Town, **RIO CLARO** is the administrative hub for the central and southeastern region. This makes it a busy place compared to its surroundings – but that's not saying much in this somnolent corner of the island. The town enjoyed something of a boom between 1914 and 1965, when it was connected to Trinidad's major cities by the railway, but once that closed down, the place went into decline as young people abandoned agricultural work for more profitable jobs in the oilfields and the bigger cities.

As you enter Rio Claro from the west, a grand wedding-cake-pink and ice-blue **Catholic church** and a resplendent white **Hindu temple** with a stepped dome and gold and blue trimmings face each other across the road. After this majestic entrance you come upon the main junction and town centre, with its lively stalls, maxi stand and four-armed signpost pointing to all the corners of Trinidad. A large mosque dominates the main road going out of town to the east, amid a cluster of businesses and banks. The town's Spanish heritage emerges towards Christmas, as Rio Claro's famous **parang** singers (see p.298) come out and entertain the clientele of the local bars and clubs.

The southeast

Trinidad's **southeast** is bounded on its Atlantic coast by **Mayaro Bay**, the longest beach in the country, an astonishing – and astonishingly undeveloped – 22.5km of palm-fringed sand running from Point Radix in the north down to **Galeota Point**, a small peninsula that marks the country's southwesternmost extremity. Just inland, the low Southern Range rises to the **Trinity Hills**, the trio of peaks that inspired Columbus to name the island Trinidad; swathed in dense rainforest, they are now part of a rugged, unspoilt and seldom-visited **wildlife reserve**. Despite the presence of the oil industry in and around Galeota Point and the nearby town of **Guayaguayare**, the southeast has a holiday ambience, and many Trinidadians take their vacations here. It is the ideal place to get away from it all, soak up the sun and, as the Trinis say, "just chill".

Accommodation consists mostly of beach houses and self-catering apartments on Mayaro Bay – as yet there is only one hotel in the area. **Public transport** to the region is tortuous and slow; travelling from Port of Spain can take three to four hours, as opposed to two by private car.

✓Mayaro Bay call fose first

Mayaro Bay's greatest attraction is its beach, a gentle, coconut tree-lined curve of clean, soft brown sand. The only settlement of any size is the holiday village of **Mayaro**, towards the northern end of the beach – though the upmarket resort of **Grand Lagoon**, 2km south on the Mayaro–Guayaguayare Road, is rapidly sprouting new beach houses in anticipation of the growth in the area's tourist trade. Continuing south, you will see, with increasing frequency, the large luxurious houses built by the oil companies for their managers and workers. Men sell fresh fish by the roadside, and small boys will tempt you with strings of crabs and conks; these delicacies, rarely served in restaurants, are well-kept local secrets. Despite its stunning setting and wonderful beach, Mayaro remains practically undiscovered by foreign visitors. Enjoy the peace and quiet while you can; the resort is already being developed in preparation for the opening of the new San Fernando–Mayaro Highway, scheduled for the year 2000.

Some history

Originally inhabited by the Amerindians, the bay was settled by French royalist planters fleeing the wars and rebellions that ravaged the West Indies in the 1790s. The place boomed in the nineteenth century on the strength of its cotton and coconut estates. With the opening of a train service in 1914, it began to flourish as a seaside resort, but after the railways were closed down in 1965, the village went into economic decline. Its fortunes revived during the oil boom of the late 1970s, when it once again became a popular holiday resort with Trinidadians, and hotels and beach houses lined the coast. After the boom went bust in the mid 1980s, many of these fell into disrepair, and the largest hotel was taken over by an oil company as a retreat for its workers. Mayaro's fortunes are set to change again. The new **highway** will halve the journey time – currently two hours – from San Fernando, no doubt bringing flocks of city folk at weekends, while new discoveries of oil and gas off the southeast coast are already attracting foreign investment and business visitors.

The

southeast

Arrival and accommodation

If you're **driving** to Mayaro from Port of Spain, the quickest route is via the Churchill Roosevelt Highway to Valencia, through Sangre Grande and down the east coast. This is also the quickest way if you are going by **public transport** – take a maxi to Arima, then one to Sangre Grande, and then one down to Mayaro. If you're coming from San Fernando and the west coast, drive east along the Manahambre, Naparima and Mayaro Roads. Maxis go from San Fernando to Princes Town; change here for a maxi to Mayaro.

There are a variety of **beach houses** to rent, from the most basic to the most luxurious – look out for the hand-painted advertisements along the main road. Advance booking isn't necessary unless you plan to visit during a public holiday. Most Trinidadians go on holiday in large groups, and the accommodation caters for this – plenty of spare mattresses are provided. *Westside House*, Beaumont Rd (☎652 8276; ③) is a three-bedroom house sleeping a maximum of twelve people, two minutes' walk from the beach. It's clean but basic, with no a-c or fans, and you'll have to bring your own dishes and linen. *Amar's Beach Resort* (☎663 4961; ⑤), well signposted on a dirt track off the main road in Mayaro and is built directly onto the beach. The clean, fully furnished house has three bedrooms that can sleep up to seventeen people, but again, you'll have to bring your own linen.

In Grand Lagoon, the *Atlantic Shores Resort*, Eccles Rd (☎630 9180) is a recently completed block of upmarket, one- and two-bedroom self-catering apartments right on the seafront – you'll only have to step out of your door to touch the sand with your toes. All are fully furnished, with a-c, TV, fridge, and stove, and have security and maid service. There is also a **restaurant**, casino and bar. *Azee's Guest House*, 31/2mm Guayaguayare Rd (☎630 4619; ⑤) is a small, friendly hotel just two minutes' walk from the beach. All rooms have a-c, cable TV, telephone, fridge and en-suite bathrooms, and there's a homely bar and a restaurant. *B's Host Home*, 4/5mm Guayaguayare Rd (☎630 8510; ④) – the third house after the fenced Amoco complex – is run by Beulah Parriag, a pillar of the local community and an informative and friendly host. Rooms are a-c with cable TV; an excellent breakfast is included.

For details of the accommodation price codes used in these listings, see p.178.

Mayaro village

MAYARO – 16.5km east of Rio Claro and 24km south of Manzanilla – has grown out of two old French villages, Pierreville and Plaisance, and is still marked as such on some maps. **Pierreville**, on the main Guayaguayare Road, is the business end of town, a small nexus of shops and local businesses. A side road cuts east to the seaside quarter, **Plaisance**, a lovely place with a thoroughly relaxing atmosphere. Residents and day-trippers eat and drink at the roadside cafés and bars, people wander on and off the beach, towels round their necks and a sprinkling of sand on their casual clothes, while music, lively conversation and the odd burst of raucous laughter drift on the air.

The beach here is one of the most popular bathing spots on Mayaro Bay. There are no changing facilities or toilets, but there is a lifeguard on duty from 10am to 5pm. The sea in this area has **strong currents,** so it is important to exercise caution.

Eating and drinking

There are not many places to eat in Mayaro – Trini holidaymakers tend to barbecue their own food on the beach – except for a few **fast-food outlets** and snack parlours. For more formal dining, the **restaurant** in *Azee's Guest House* (see overleaf) serves delicious Creole food. There's also a few lively **rum shops** if you feel like a drink and a lime.

Galeota Point and Guayaguayare

Galeota Point, the southeast tip of Trinidad, is dominated by American oil companies. The area is dotted with oil storage tanks, and many oil wells can be seen offshore. The point itself is owned by Amoco, who do not permit public access to the end of the peninsula.

Two kilometres past Galeota Point on the south coast is the small town of **GUAYAGUAYARE**. The sea has been eroding the coast here for centuries, but the growing population seems unconcerned; the inhabitants build their houses away from the seafront, and a sea wall has been erected. The brown sandy **beach** is 4km long, with good calm seas for swimming. In the dry season it attracts people on outings from all over Trinidad. During the rainy season (June to December) however, the water is full of brackish oily water washed down from the river.

Guayaguayare changed the fortunes of Trinidad, for it was here that oil was first discovered on the island in 1819 (see p.189), and the village blossomed in the early twentieth century when the petroleum industry really got going. Unless you are here in connection with the oil business, however, it's a quiet and uneventful place. Local residents still remember the big day a few years ago when a smuggler's ship, chased by the T&T coastguard, abandoned its cargo of cocaine. Large quantities of the drug were washed up on Guayaguayare beach, giving some of the locals an opportunity to make a quick killing before the law enforcers arrived.

The *Sea Wall Beach Resort* (☎630 9255; ②) on the Guayaguayare Main Road west of the village has three cheap and very basic rooms overlooking the sea. It is also a lively **bar** and nightspot, serving inexpensive **meals** of freshly caught fish. Three times a year at Easter, August and November they hold large **parties**, attracting heaving maxis full of people from all over the country. The owners also run The Eastern Diving Company (☎630 8572). Though this business is mainly directed at the oil industry, its internationally qualified (PADI) instructors can teach you to **scuba dive**; there are no spectacular reefs around here, but they do offer unusual trips under oil rigs, and will teach you **spear fishing** out on the open seas.

Trinity Hills Wildlife Sanctuary

The **Trinity Hills Wildlife Sanctuary and Reserve** encompasses 65 square kilometres of evergreen forest in the extreme southeast of Trinidad, running alongside the Rio Claro–Guayaguayare Road down to the sea. Situated in the highest part of the Southern Range, it includes the famous Trinity Hills – allegedly the inspiration for Columbus' naming of the island – and Mount Derrick, at 314 metres the tallest peak in the south. The hills form a watershed that's vital to the nation's water supply, ensuring that the area was declared a reserve as early as 1900; it received wildlife sanctuary status in 1934.

The many **rivers**, **streams** and **waterfalls** are excellent for bathing. The lush forests of **carat**, **redwood**, **cooperhoop** and **bois pois trees**, shelter wild animals such as lappe, agouti, quenk, tatoo and red howler monkeys, and you may even sight such rare beasts as ocelots, capuchin monkeys, buck deer, armadillos and opossums. The wide variety of birds includes the rare **mountain quail dove**, while deep in the hills, mysterious caves harbour many rare species of bats. A 45-minute hike from the road is a **mud volcano** and lake known as **Lagoon Bouffe**, at 100 metres in diameter possibly Trinidad's largest.

Information on the reserve is hard to find due to its remoteness and the paucity of visitors. A few tour companies do visit the area, however, and it is possible to visit independently, though you'll need to get a permit from Petrotrin, who have a pipeline running through the reserve. There are, it's alleged, marijuana fields in the hills, so it is wise to go with a local to avoid stumbling into dangerous areas. South East Eco Tours (☎644 1072) offer trips, ranging from easy to strenuous, guided by trained local people, for US$35–80; they need 48 hours (working days) notice to arrange the permit. Caribbean Discovery Tours (☎624 7281) will visit the area, and for serious hikers, Wildways (☎623 7332) does an "adventurous trail lasting four to five and a half hours along twelve-inch ridges with long sheer drops".

For a permit to visit Trinity Hills, ring Petrotrin, ☎649 5539, after 4pm Mon–Sat; on Sundays and public holidays call ☎649 5500 or 5501.

Chapter 5

Tobago

An elongated oval of just 41 by 14km, **TOBAGO** manages an astonishing richness within her craggy coastal fringes. Abounding with natural allure – deserted palm-lined beaches, pristine coral reefs and a wealth of lush rainforest – the island really is the last of the "unspoilt Caribbean", a tropical idyll unfettered by all-inclusive enclaves but suitably geared toward visitors nonetheless. Tourism has taken root with breathtaking speed – 40,000 people now visit the island each year – and the subsequent reliance upon foreign dollars has inevitably had negative effects, eating away at the very attributes which make the island so special. Huge resort developments are springing up along hitherto undisturbed seashores, and in the tourist strongholds, the traditional values held high in the otherwise deeply religious, close-knit communities are being replaced by a hustler mentality.

Tobago is hardly the typically jaded resort island, though. Local people and tourists co-exist in an easy equilibrium, and celebrations such as the Easter **goat races** are attended by more Tobagonians than tourists. Everyone frequents the same beaches, bars and nightclubs, and local culture is honoured at the annual **Heritage Festival** each August. The uniquely friendly and collective Tobagonian mentality can be seen at the **harvest festivals**, where entire villages open their doors to passing revellers, and the marvellous **fisherman's fetes**, usually held around St Peter's Day at the end of July, where huge vats of fish tea are cooked up on the beach and served to the strains of booming sound systems.

Nevertheless, tourism *is* changing Tobago: helping hands sharing the labour of pulling in seine fishing nets are still called by a resonant toot on a conch shell, but nowadays the fishermen often wait until they've captured an audience before hauling the catch onto the sand, and the African drumming that forms a major part of local **Orisa** and **Spiritual Baptist** ceremonies (see Religion, p.294) is now the soundtrack of many a hotel floorshow. However, Tobagonians take their culture – and their heritage – very seriously, and it's difficult to penetrate far beneath the surface of this clannish, almost insular small-island community.

Physically, Tobago is breathtaking; heavy industry is confined to Trinidad, so the beaches are clean and the landscape left largely to its own devices. The flat coral and limestone plateau of the southwest – **Lowlands** – is the island's most heavily developed region, comprising commercialized powder sand beaches such as **Pigeon Point** and **Store Bay**, where watersports, frothy drinks and sun-tanning are the order of the day, as well as quieter stretches of sand along the smart hotel coast of the south west, where glass bottom boats head for **Buccoo Reef**, palms sway over the **Mount Irvine** golf course, visitors puzzle over the "**Mystery Tombstone**" in residential **Plymouth** and hotels run night excursions to watch giant **turtles** laying eggs on the beach. Strong currents also provide some excellent **surfing** possibilities; rough seas between November and February (the height of the tourist season) provide massive breakers at bays like **Mount Irvine**. However, the tourist clamour is kept in check by the mercurial rush of the capital, **Scarborough**, a lively, picturesque port town tumbling down a lighthouse-topped hillside.

Pummelled by the dark green, wave whipped Atlantic, the island's rugged **windward** (south) **coast** is lined with appealing fishing villages; **Speyside** and **Charlotteville** in the remote eastern reaches have **coral reefs** as ornate and lively as you'll find anywhere in the Caribbean – Jacques Cousteau declared them the third finest in the region, and **scuba diving** is a burgeoning industry. Tobago is an excellent and inexpensive place to learn to dive, and there's plenty of challenging drift diving for the more experienced, while the many reefs within swimming distance of the beaches make for fantastic **snorkelling**. Coral sands and glassy Caribbean waters along the **leeward** (north) coast provide some of Tobago's finest beaches; some, like **Englishman's Bay**, are regularly deserted, while at **Castara**, **Parlatuvier** and **Bloody Bay**, you'll share the sand with local fishermen.

The landscape of the eastern interior rises steeply into the hillocks and rolling bluffs which make up the central **Main Ridge**. These mountains shelter the **Forest Reserve**, the oldest protected rainforest in the western hemisphere, an absurdly abundant tangle of mist-shrouded greenery dripping down to fabulous coastline with – in places – neither building nor road to interrupt the flow. Ornithologists and naturalists flock in for the **bird** and **animal** life that flourishes here; David Attenborough filmed parts of his celebrated *Trials of Life* series at **Little Tobago**, a solitary seabird sanctuary off the coast of Speyside, while **hiking** through the squawking, chirruping forest offers plenty of opportunities for bird-watching or a splash in the icy **waterfalls**.

Some history

Though treated with indifference by the Spanish, Tobago has been hotly contested by other nations over the centuries. The original **Carib** population fiercely defended their paradisical *Tavaco* (the

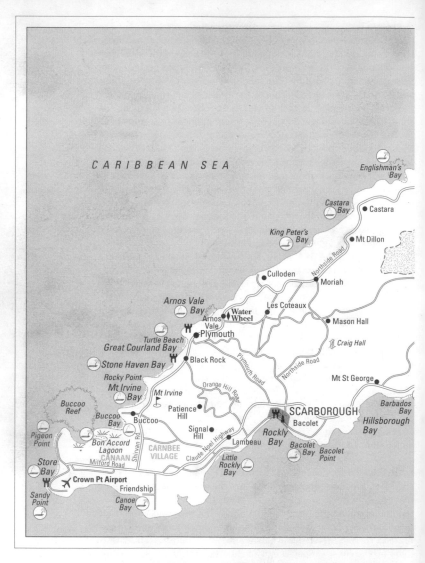

name is derived from the Indian word for tobacco) against other Amerindian tribes, and drove off several attempts by European colonists throughout the late 1500s and early 1600s. English sailors had staked Britain's claim in 1580, tacking a flag to a tree trunk during a water stop en route to Brazil, and in 1641, England's King Charles I presented Tobago to his godson James, the Duke of Courland (in modern Latvia). A group of **Latvians** arrived a year

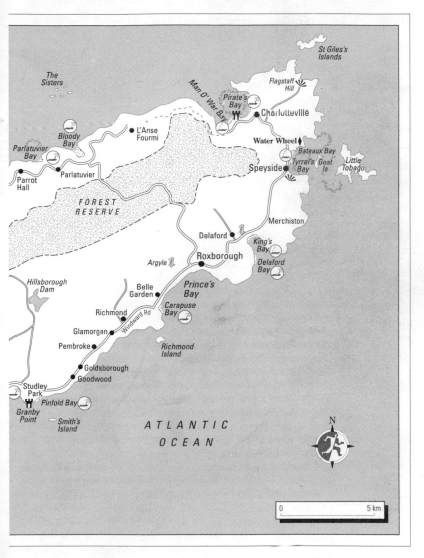

later, but their settlement at Plymouth underwent constant attacks from the Caribs, and in 1658 was finally taken by the Dutch, who called it "Nieuw Vlissingen". Twenty years later, the Courlanders left for good, but a group of their Latvian ancestors still make an annual pilgrimage to Plymouth. In the following years, most of the Caribs migrated to Amerindian colonies in St Vincent, and the Indian population slowly petered out, while the belligerent shenanigans of the

Tobago

For more on Tobagonian history, check out the small but excellent Tobago Museum, stunningly located at Scarborough's Fort King George (see p.254).

Dutch, English and French turned the coasts of Tobago into a war zone; the island changed hands 31 times before it was finally ceded to the British in 1814.

Forts sprang up at every vantage point, and Tobago descended into turmoil, plundered by **pirates** and officially declared a no man's land in 1684 under the treaty of Aix La Chapelle, which opened up the island to settlers from any nation. French, British and Dutch colonists lived fairly peaceably alongside free Africans, slaves and the remnants of the Caribs for the next eighty-odd years, but a French attempt to seize control in 1648 had shaken the neutral status and worried the British, who had no wish to allow the island to fall under Gallic rule. In 1672, Britain flexed her naval muscles and sent a powerful fleet to Tobago, taking possession of the island with swift precision. **Plantation culture** began in earnest, sustained by the promise of stability that came with British control. The crown appointed a **governor** a year later, and the island developed rapidly into a highly efficient sugar, cotton and indigo factory. Africans were imported to work the estates as slaves, and by 1772, 3000-odd Africans were sweating it out under less than 250 300 whites. The economy flourished, and by 1777, the island's eighty-odd estates had exported 160,000 gallons of rum, 1,500,000lbs of cotton, 5,000lbs of indigo and 24,000 hundred-weights of sugar. The numerical might of the slave population led to many bloody **uprisings**, with planters doling out amputations and death by burning and hanging to the dissenters.

In 1781, however, the **French** again prevailed, razing plantations and forcing the besieged British governor to surrender. The island remained French for another twelve years, but sugar production, shaken by rampant destruction of the estates during the take-over, fell into decline. English planters refused to honour old land debts, and the economy floundered. Following a bloody mutiny of French troops in 1790, British forces again invaded, taking Tobago in 1793 only to relinquish her back to their enemy less than ten years later. Following Britain's formal declaration of war against France in 1802, the island was finally ceded to the British under the 1814 Treaty of Paris, and another phase as a successful sugar plantation ensued.

Tobago prospered until the 1840s, her newly emancipated African population taking to the bush to plant small-scale farms, forming coastal fishing communities or continuing to work the estates as free men and women. **Moravian missions** began to provide them with education, and many converted to Christianity; today, the faith is incorporated with African belief systems to form the Spiritual Baptist sect (see p.294); today, Tobago boasts T&T's strongest concentration of the faith. When Britain removed its protective tariffs on sugar sales, however, Tobago's unmechanized industry was unable to compete with more efficient producers. A severe hurricane in 1847 twinned with the collapse of the West India Bank which underwrote the plantations marked the beginning of the end. In the aftermath of the **Belmanna**

Riots (see p.264), Tobago's Legislative Council relinquished its tenuous rule, and the island became a Crown Colony in 1879. Having reached a suitable level of industrialization via the riches of Caribbean sugar, England had little further need for troublesome, ailing Tobago and washed her hands of the island. In 1899, Tobago was made a **ward** of Trinidad, effectively becoming the bigger island's poor relation with little control over her own destiny. With the collapse of the sugar industry, the islanders fell back upon other crops, planting the acres of limes, coconuts and cocoa that still stand today; boosted by the arrival of **free Africans** in the mid 1800s, the black population clubbed together to farm the land, tending their food crops in the efficient **"Len-Hand" system** of shared labour that is still celebrated in the annual round of Harvest Festivals. By the early 1900s the island was even exporting fruit and vegetables to Trinidad, and in 1927, the island was granted a single seat on the legislative council.

In 1963, **Hurricane Flora** (see p.278) ravaged Tobago, razing whole villages and laying waste to most of the island's crops. In the restructuring programme that followed, attempts were made to diversify the economy and the first tentative steps towards developing a tourist industry began. By 1980, the island had her sovereignty partially restored when the **Tobago House Of Assembly** (THA) was reconvened, but it had authority only over the island's more mundane affairs while the main decisions were still made in Trinidad, though the lobbying of Tobagonian-born former Prime Minister **Arthur Robinson** gave Tobago a stronger profile in the republic's affairs. With agriculture on the decline and tourism slowly becoming the main earner, the island's economic future is still uncertain; in spring 1998, Tobago was officially declared an underdeveloped and low-income region in order to qualify for aid from the UN and EC. However, as Tobago and her people have so often demonstrated formidable strength in the face of adversity, the island seems set to prosper, though some worry that the island's unique culture and mentality will be sacrificed to development.

Arrival and information

Most people arrive via **Crown Point International Airport**, an airy, open plan affair that despite a recent expansion remains small enough to feel overwhelmed by the arrival of a single jet. Opposite is a row of shops; among them is a branch of the Republic Bank (Mon–Thurs 8–11am & noon–2pm, Fri 8am–noon & 3–5pm) for **currency exchange**, a gift shop and a small newsagent, while the cheerful and busy *Star Café* (daily 6am–10pm) serves hot meals, snacks, beers and ice cream. Local **phonecards** (TT$20, $50, $100 etc) are available from the shops opposite the airport.

For **information**, head to the tourist board office; the last shop to the left of the parade (daily 6am–10pm; ☎639 0509). Staff are always helpful and can advise on accommodation, transport and

All visitors must pay TT$85 departure tax, in local currency, at the smoked-glass window at the front of the airport complex (daily 6am–10pm).

Tobago

activities, and may even call hotels to book ahead. If you're heading anywhere further than Plymouth or Scarborough (eg Charlotteville or Speyside), this is well worth doing, as chartering a taxi is quite expensive and many hotels throw in free airport pick-ups as an incentive to choose them over the many alternatives. The tourist board also have copies of the free, tourist-oriented *Tobago Today* listings newspaper as well as the latest version of the more detailed *Discover Trinidad and Tobago* booklet.

Travel between Tobago and Trinidad

Air Caribbean (☎639 2500) operates daily **flights** between the two islands; flying time is twenty minutes. A recent hike has raised prices considerably if you're a foreign national; local people or foreigners holding residency or work permits pay TT$150 one way or TT$300 return, but foreigners pay TT$336 one way and TT$472.50 return (2–12 year-olds pay half fare, under twos pay 10 percent). Flights are permanently over-subscribed at weekends (particularly Sunday afternoons) and holidays, but if you can't get a confirmed booking, try the **standby** service; turn up at least one hour before your proposed flying time, buy a ticket, give your name in at the desk and if you're lucky, you'll be called half an hour before departure. Confirmed passengers must check in an hour before departure, as half an hour before the flight departs, all unclaimed seats are turned over to standby.

In the early months of 1998, **BWIA** introduced a limited service between Trinidad and Tobago, giving Air Caribbean their first competition in years and giving rise to plenty of contention between the companies. Currently, BWIA offer flights on Friday evenings and Monday mornings, but the pricing system is confused; though BWIA initially advertised as charging one price for locals and tourists (TT$150 one way and double for a return), you may be charged an increased fare if you hold a foreign passport; you'll need to call the airline to check prices and flights (in Trinidad ☎627 2942, in Tobago ☎639 0276). For details of flights between Trinidad and Tobago, see p.27.

If you need to leave Tobago fast or you want to do a little aerial sightseeing, you could consider **chartering a small plane** or helicopter from Briko in Crown Point (☎639 8446).

Getting around

Tobago's **public transport** system not as comprehensive as Trinidad's, and as in the sister island, **renting a car** is essential to see the island independently and avoid the hassles, confusion and long waits that inevitably ensue if you rely on route taxis or buses. Blue-banded **maxi taxis** (see Basics, pp.23–24) are rare, most operating private school runs or attempting to ferry tourists at inflated prices; the only regular route runs from Scarborough to Charlotteville (see

Organized tours

Several established tour companies offer rather sterile itineraries of Tobago's main sights, ranging from snorkelling on the Buccoo Reef and a barbecue at No Man's Land to Scarborough and Fort George, and trips to Speyside, Little Tobago, Argyll Waterfall, the Forest Reserve, Charlotteville, Plymouth or the mystery tombstone. These are great if you want a zero-hassle overview of the island, but at worst, you can feel completely distanced from what flashes by through the window. Full day tours almost always include lunch and cost US$40–55 per person; groups must be of four or more. Most people book through reps who visit the main hotels or trawl the beaches, but you can sign up individually as well. **Classic Tours** (☎639 9891-2 or 0618), and **Sun Fun Tours** (☎639 7461; *www.trinidad.net/sunfuntours*) are the best of the bunch.

For a more **alternative** angle, try Margaret Hinkson's thoughtful Educatours (☎ & fax 639 7422); they'll pick you up from your hotel, and excursions can be custom designed to suit your interests. Prices start from US$52 for a guided trek through the rainforest and on to Argyll Waterfall (6hr). Renowned naturalist David Rooks (☎639 4276, fax 639 5440) leads informed and professional tours to **Little Tobago** (Thurs, 8–9hr; US$65) and the Forest Reserve (Sat, 6hr; US$45), though you may have to share him with up to 15 others. Pioneer Journeys (☎660 4327 or 5175) offer more rugged jaunts including a hike along the **Louis D'Or River** to see crayfish, crab and wetland birds; prices start at US$30. Mark Puddy (☎639 4931) leads offbeat **hiking trips** to a deserted beach (6hr; US$35) or a seldom-visited waterfall (4hr; US$20); rates include transport to and from your hotel as well as drinks, snack lunch and a fabulous dinner. A good bet for **birding** is UK-trained ornithologist **Harris McMillan** (email *cattours@ trinidad.net*), who runs a full day all-inclusive rainforest, Argyll Falls and Buccoo Marsh tour (US$45) as well as tailor-made jaunts. Adolphus James (☎639 2231) is an excellent guide for serious birders. Escorted by the man himself, Peter Cox Island Tours offer the usual itineraries (from US$50), but groups are small, and Peter is excellent for birding; his 2hr Buccoo Marsh tour costs US$15. Part-time Store Bay lifeguard Harris McDonald (☎639 0513) does a lively, informative all-day Leeward coast, forest reserve and Little Tobago tour (US$50, plus US$10 for the boat to Little Tobago). **Jeep or dirt bike safaris** booked through Ricarda Solomon at *Coconut Inn* (☎639 8493, fax 639 0512) take you to less accessible parts of the island, along ancient trails through deserted plantations, stopping at beaches and waterfalls; you can ride pillion on request. Ten hour bike and jeep tours cost US$60; both include food and drink. Their Atlantic coast tour is also above average, including Argyll waterfall, lunch at Jemma's, Charlotteville and a boat to Pirates Bay, as is the rainforest trip; (both US$60). Tobago's only female taxi driver, Liz Lezama (☎639 2309) offers a nice Englishman's Bay barbecue and island tour for US$55 with plenty of stops at small rum shops and a good local perspective. Adventurous **sea safaris** aboard hobie cat mini-catamarans are available from Cool Runnings (☎639 8363, fax 639 1832 email *coolrun@ tstt.net.tt*). A No Man's Land picnic costs US$20, a trip to Castara is US$35, and an Englishman's Bay safari includes snorkelling, all meals and a night's camping on the beach; from US$115, depending upon group size. They also offer seven-night packages.

For more information on Forest Reserve tour guides, see p.45

Scarborough, pp.248–258). However, the **route taxi** network is extensive and convenient for short hops in the western portion of the island: taxis run along all the main roads, and travelling between Crown Point, Buccoo, Mount Irvine or Plymouth simply involves standing on the right side of the road for your destination, sticking out your hand and asking the driver where they're heading: note that in Tobago, not all route taxis have the usual "H" taxi registration plate; the best way to recognize one is to watch out for a car with multiple passengers and a driver clutching a wad of dollars. If you're heading further afield, say to Castara, Charlotteville or Speyside, you'll need to travel into Scarborough, where route taxis depart to the rest of the island; see p.256–257 for details.

Taxis

You can **walk** to most of the hotels in Crown Point, but if you're travelling further, such as Mount Irvine, Plymouth, Charlotteville or Speyside, check the taxi price list on the wall of the arrivals lounge. The rates are used by all the **licensed drivers** who meet each flight – they're high, but not wildly so. If you're on a budget, you can cross the street and haggle with the drivers who are not part of the authorized airport queuing system; they may reduce their rates (to the wrath of the licensed guys). For reputable operators on the phone (including a woman driver), see Listings, p.215.

Buses

Relying on the cumbersome, diesel-billowing Public Transport Service Company (PTSC) **buses** to get you around the island is certainly inexpensive, but it's also slow and often a complete hassle. Though the half-hourly shuttle service between Crown Point (there's a stop just outside the airport complex) and the main Scarborough **depot** on Greenside Street (see p.251) is convenient, relying on the buses to see the island is not a good idea. Most of the main communities are covered, but the handwritten timetables posted on the depot walls are confusing and often contradictory – your best bet is to turn up early in the morning and ask. From Scarborough, buses run along the windward coast to Mount St George, Studley Park, Glamorgan, Argyll Falls, Roxborough, Delaford, King's Bay,

---

Bus prices

Scarborough to:	
Castara: TT$5	Mount St George: TT$3
Charlotteville: TT$8	Parlatuvier: TT$6
Belle Garden: TT$5	Pembroke: TT$4
Delaford: TT$6	Roxborough: TT$5
Glamorgan: TT$4	Speyside: TT$8
Mason Hall: TT$2	Whim: TT$2

Speyside and Charlotteville (5 daily). The leeward coast route covers Les Coteaux, Moriah, Castara, Englishman's Bay, Parlatuvier and Bloody Bay (3 daily). Whim, Mason Hall, Mount Irvine, Black Rock and Plymouth are covered separately (4 daily). Services start as early as 5am, with most returning to Scarborough in the late afternoon. All tickets must be **pre-purchased** as drivers will not accept cash; they are available from the shops opposite the airport complex or from bars and mini-marts throughout the island.

Car and bike rental

Most of the international **car rental** firms and the local guys with two or three vehicles are clustered around the airport; prices for standard jeeps and manual/automatic cars can vary; stick-shift cars and jeeps are less expensive than automatics. Local operators tend to be cheaper, but the smaller the company, the less likely you are to be offered 24-hour assistance and adequate coverage in case of an accident; best among the internationals is the local franchise of Thrifty (☎639 8507) which offers a wide choice of vehicles and efficient service. Most companies ask for some kind of **deposit**, usually a credit card imprint; a notable exception is Auto Rentals (☎639 0644), which has one of the largest fleets in Tobago.

Shopping in Tobago

The widest variety of local crafts – carved calabashes, Rasta hats etc – are sold at the huts adjacent to Store Bay Beach, but you'll get better deals at the vendors' mall in Scarborough; good carvings are on offer from a lone vendor who sets up in A.P.T James Park. Also in town, Tobago Treasures on Carrington St sell a nice line in brightly painted fish, carvings etc. On the Arnos Vale Road, inland of Plymouth, keep a sharp eye out for a small, brightly painted shop selling drums and beautifully tailored African-style clothing, but real craft aficionados should call Mr and Mrs Cyrus (☎639 5172), whose leather Rasta hats, belts, silver jewellery and original paintings are of such good quality that they are never seen on the stalls.

Funky and distinctive **clothing** can be bought from Radical Designs on the corner of Main and Bacolet streets in Scarborough; their trade-mark T-shirts are far more chic than your average souvenir specimen – you'd actually want to wear them at home. Reflections, next to Hendrix Bar in Buccoo village sell a chic range of natural linen clothes alongside their cool selection of Tobago T-shirts. You can buy inexpensive **art** prints and pricier originals at The Art Gallery, just off Old Milford Road along Allfields Crown Trace, and the Fine Arts Centre at the Scarborough Fort complex also has well-priced art and craft.

Duty-free goods are sold at Stetchers in the airport departure lounge, whilst local jams and honey are best bought from supermarkets. Zoom Caribbean on Pigeon Point beach sell a good selection of quality T-shirts and Carib memorabilia, and calypso, soca and reggae records, tapes or CD's are available from One World Music Shop on Airport New Road, opposite *Dillon's* restaurant.

Motorbikes are catching on fast and there are several outlets offering dirt bikes for about $25 per day. Some – such as Island – offer discounts for extended rental (take a bike for six days and you get a seventh free), and most also offer accompanied tours along off-road trails (see p.215). Check your bike and helmet before you ride away, as some are less than perfect. With a car or bike, it's imperative that you take note of every bump and scratch as well as checking the tyres (especially the spare and the jack etc), headlamps and indicators. If the car is damaged, let the company know immediately, and on no account let anyone unauthorized drive the car; as Tobago is so tiny, someone is bound to catch you at it, and you are liable for any damage. For details of other reputable operators, see Listings, p.279.

Lowlands: Crown Point
to Plymouth

Tobago's flattest, most accessible portion is clustered around a crowded five-kilometre stretch of **Milford Road** from the airport and Store Bay Beach – a tiny area known as **Crown Point** – through **Bon Accord**, **Canaan** and **Mount Pleasant**, and 10km north along **Shirvan Road** to **Buccoo**, **Mount Irvine** and **Plymouth**. Usually lumped together as "**lowlands**", the low-lying western tip is the island's most heavily developed region, home to most of its residents as well as the vast majority of hotels, restaurants, night-clubs and the most popular beaches. A highly commercialized hotchpotch of concrete and neon around Milford Road (bar the remote **bird-watching** paradise of Bon Accord Lagoon wetlands) combined with the less frenetic beaches and smart hotels that shoot off Shirvan Road, the area is hardly the "real Tobago", but its animation and sense of industry more than make up for an occasional lack of aesthetic charm and, whether you like it or not, the concentration of facilities and activities mean that you'll inevitably spend a lot of time here.

Tobago's most popular **beaches** are within shouting distance of the airport – **Store Bay** is a couple of minutes on foot, and **Pigeon Point** is about ten minutes further. The terrain between the two is jampacked with all the familiar tourist trappings – craft stalls, restaurants and bars advertising specials or happy hours, and the hoardings of endless resort hotels – and many people (especially the notoriously unadventurous Trinidadian holidaymakers) never make it any further. East of the beaches, Milford Road continues in the same vein, cutting through Tobago's tourist heartland to quieter stretches of sand; you'll rarely have to share **Canoe Bay**, and past here, the vacation ethic slackens a little; **Lambeau** and **Signal Hill** communities are the almost exclusive preserve of locals. Set atop the foothills of the island's modest mountains, both villages provide beautiful views of the unravelling flatlands to the west, and it's rare to see a foreign face bobbing in the waters of **Little Rockly Bay** below.

Another rash of tourism development lies along Shirvan Road, which cuts north from Milford along the coast. **Buccoo** harbours two main attractions: an abundant **reef**, trawled by fleets of glass bottom boats carrying snorkellers out to the coral and the **Nylon Pool**, a metre-deep bathing spot on a sandbar in the middle of the bay, as well as **Sunday School**, Tobago's biggest, brashest open-air party. Dominated by a palm-studded eighteen-hole **golf course, Mount Irvine** heralds the start of a series of glorious beaches, while historic **Plymouth**, with its cluster of forts and **mystery tombstone**, is also heavily visited. Potted attractions like the **Arnos Vale water wheel** complex and the Kimme **art exhibition** as well as plenty of restaurants and the fabulous prospect of watching a **turtle** lay eggs metres from your hotel room draw enthusiastic crowds of locals and tourists alike.

Accommodation

Though the sheer number of **hotels** and **guesthouses** crammed into Crown Point makes choosing accommodation mind-boggling, the tourist-friendly location keeps prices relatively high; you pay less for the same standard of room in more remote areas, and there are few bed-and-breakfasts or host homes here; most are located around Scarborough (see pp.248–258). Space is at a premium and many establishments are built back-to-back with little individuality and scant regard for aesthetics. You'll miss out on solitude; discos blare soca into the night air and road traffic is pretty constant, scaring away bird and animal life and making the place feel like the Costa Del Sol rather than an unspoilt Caribbean paradise. However, there are definite advantages to staying in the area; you'll be within walking

---

Villas

Though **villas** are conventionally seen as luxury accommodation, they can work out to be quite cost effective if you're travelling in a large group. There are hundreds scattered around the island – some are mentioned individually in the relevant chapter accounts and the majority are set around the Mount Irvine golf course – but a useful go-between is the Tobago Villas Agency office on Shirvan Road (PO Box 301, Scarborough, ☎ & fax 639 8737), which represents properties throughout the island. Their villas rent from around US$110 per week for a very basic one-bedroom unit to palatial residences with up to four bedrooms and every conceivable luxury at US$4200. Also on Shirvan Road, Island Investments (☎639 0929, fax 639 9050, email *islreal@tstt.net.tt*) are agents for a number of nearby villas. In the UK, The Owners Syndicate, 6 Port House, Plantation Wharf, Battersea, London SW11 3TY (☎0171/801 9801, fax 0171/801 9800, email *ownerssyndicate@compuserve.com*) represent several luxury villas in the Mount Irvine area. Prices per week are considerably cheaper in the low season (15 April–15 Dec); a unit sleeping up to six costs £750–1102 in the low season, or £1072–1800 in the high season. Units sleeping 8–10 cost £1033–1323 low season or £1555–2280 in the high season.

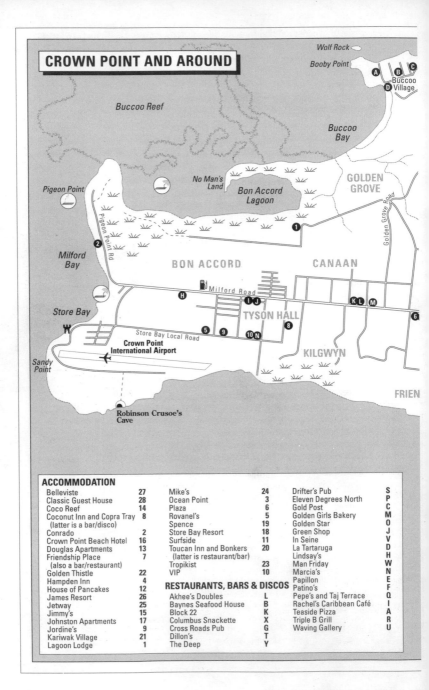

CROWN POINT AND AROUND

Wolf Rock
Booby Point
Ⓐ Ⓑ Ⓒ
Ⓓ Buccoo
Village

Buccoo Reef

Buccoo Bay

No Man's Land
Bon Accord Lagoon

GOLDEN GROVE

Pigeon Point

Golden Grove Road

❷

Milford Bay

BON ACCORD ❶

CANAAN

❷

Ⓗ Milford Road

Ⓘ Ⓙ

Ⓚ Ⓛ Ⓜ

Store Bay

TYSON HALL

❻

❺ ❾

Store Bay Local Road

❽

❿ Ⓝ

Crown Point International Airport

KILGWYN

Sandy Point

FRIEN

Robinson Crusoe's Cave

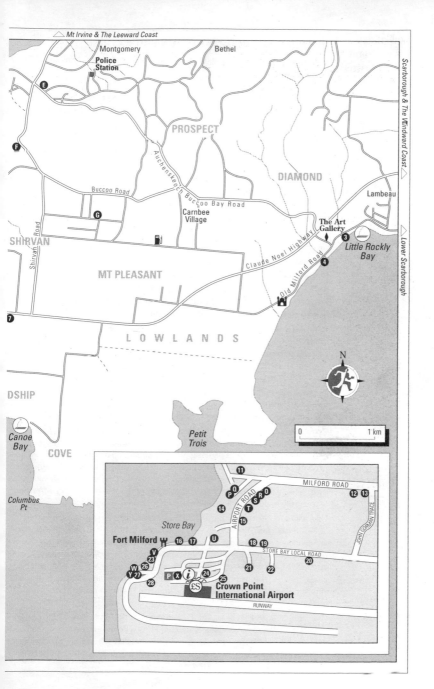

Mt Irvine & The Leeward Coast

Montgomery   Bethel

**Police
Station**

E

PROSPECT

F

DIAMOND

Buccoo Road

Carnbee
Village

SHIRVAN

G

Auchenskeoch Buccoo Bay Road

Lambeau

**The Art
Gallery**

*Little Rockly
Bay*

3

Shirvan Road

MT PLEASANT

Claude Noel Highway

Old Milford Road

4

7

L O W L A N D S

N

DSHIP

*Canoe
Bay*

COVE

*Petit
Trois*

0   1 km

*Columbus
Pt*

11

MILFORD ROAD

Q
P

S R O
T

12 13

Store Bay

14

15

Fort Milford

16 17

U

18 19

STORE BAY LOCAL ROAD

20

JOHN GORMAN TRACE

V
23

21   22

W 26
Y 27

P X

i

24

28

£S

25 **Crown Point
International Airport**

RUNWAY

Scarborough & The Windward Coast

Lower Scarborough

ACCOMMODATION PRICE CODES

All accommodation listed in this guide has been graded according to the following **price categories**:

① under US$10	② US$10–20	③ US$20–35
④ US$35–50	⑤ US$50–70	⑥ US$70–100
⑦ US$100–150	⑧ US$150–200	⑨ US$200 and above

Rates are for the cheapest double or twin rooms during the high season, normally mid December–mid April. During low season (mid April–mid December) rates are liable to fall by up to 25 percent (though this is rare at the cheap hotels), and proprietors may be more amenable to bargaining. Many hotels give rates in US dollars – we have followed suit. Payment can be made in either US or TT currency.

distance of the busiest beaches, restaurants and bars, and among the uniform, you'll find some of Tobago's most appealing hotels. The proximity of the airport (jet noise isn't a problem) also means that you can often walk straight from the tarmac to your room, though many hotels offer free transport from the airport or Scarborough sea port; call ahead and check at the tourism office or from one of the airport phone booths; phonecards are available from the small newsagents shop opposite the arrivals lounge.

Belleviste, Sandy Point, PO Box 69, Scarborough, ☎ & fax 639 9351, email *almondoz@tstt.net.tt*. Unattractive block-like exterior masking spacious, well-designed apartments. All have wooden fittings, a-c, satellite TV and full kitchen. Outside is a garden with barbecue pits, pool, children's play apparatus, gazebo overlooking the sea and a path to the beach. ⑤

Classic Guesthouse, NP Rd, Crown Point, ☎693 0742. Tiny place with small, basic rooms with fan and shared bathroom and kitchen facilities; there's also a self-contained two-bedroom cottage. Good for Tobagonian ambience. ④

Coco Reef, Airport New Rd, PO Box 434, Scarborough, ☎639 8571, fax 639 8574; US and Canada 800/221 1294, fax 305/639 2717; email *cocoreef -tobago@trinidad.net*. Spanking new peach-painted enclave of contrived luxury with perimeter walls, hastily manufactured private beach and the ambience of a hermetically sealed ghost town. Two restaurants, two bars, health spa, gym, pool, watersports and rooms with every associated frippery offer opulence at the expense of atmosphere. ⑨

Coconut Inn, Store Bay Local Rd, Bon Accord (PO Box 329, Scarborough), ☎639 8493, fax 639 0512, email *coconut@tstt.net.tt*. Distinctly Teutonic ambience – clean lines, spotless rooms, well-mown lawns and no-hassle atmosphere – nestled incongruously behind the *Copra Tray* bar. Apartments have kitchenette, a-c and verandah, and there's a pool on site. The seriously spacious "budget" rooms are set in another block; all have fans, mosquito nets and sink and shared access to the line of glimmering showers, large kitchen and TV lounge. ⑤

Conrado, Milford Extension Rd, Pigeon Point, ☎639 0145, fax 639 0755. The closest you can stay to the much-vaunted Pigeon Point; modestly proportioned garden or sea view rooms with carpet, a-c, satellite TV, phone and balcony. Friendly and busy with its own stretch of beach à la Pigeon Point, and a restaurant, bar and entertainment area. ⑥

Crown Point Beach, Store Bay Rd, PO Box 223, Crown Point, ☎639 8781, fax 639 8731, email *crownpoint@trinidad.net*. The largest hotel at the westerly side of Store Bay beach, with unsightly concrete room blocks uplifted by cabana-filled sprawling gardens overlooking the sea; staying in one of these is the better option. Rooms and cabanas have kitchen, a-c, phone, TV and small patio, and there's a pool, restaurant and tennis courts on site. Usually busy with a Trinidadian/European crowd. ⑥

Douglas Apartments, John Gorman Trace, Milford Rd, ☎ & fax 639 7723. Sparkling clean, spacious and varied Tobagonian-owned apartments at the Bon Accord end of Milford Road with 1–2 bedrooms – each with a couple of double beds for large groups – as well as lounge, full kitchen, patio, a-c, TV and priceless family atmosphere. ⑥

Golden Thistle, Store Bay Local Rd, ☎ & fax 639 8521. Tucked away behind Store Bay Local Rd, and good for those in a group who want relative seclusion with middle-bracket luxury. Rooms are standardized with a-c, TV, phone, kitchenette and a patio; there's a pool, bar and infrequently functioning restaurant on site. ⑥

Hampden Inn, Old Milford Rd, Lowlands, ☎639 7522, fax 639 7008, email *high@trinidad.net*. Efficient, friendly and German-run (popular with German clientele as well) but stuck in the backwoods. Large rooms scattered around a landscaped garden, all with a-c, huge bathroom and patio with hammocks; some have cable TV. Good restaurant on site. ⑤

House of Pancakes, cor. Milford Rd and John Gorman Trace, ☎639 9866. Three rooms at the back of this Milford Road restaurant, all very home-style with varied decor, double, single or bunk beds, a-c or fan and shared or private bathroom. Clean and comfy but not the prettiest of places, and there's nowhere to sit in the sun. ③

James Resort, Sandy Point, ☎ & fax 639 8084. The units are about as varied as you can get within walls of concrete but the Tobagonian owners are friendly and you're close to the action without being right in it. Rooms are cramped but neat and serviceable with a-c, TV and balcony while apartments (1–3 bedrooms) have a kitchen and more space. ⑤

Jetway, Crown Point, ☎ & fax 639 8504. Directly opposite the airport (1min walk), this is a good place to get your bearings. Clean and functional rooms with a-c and kitchenette; friendly but expect some airport noise. ④

Jimmy's, Airport New Rd, PO Box 109, Scarborough, ☎639 8292, fax 639 3100. One- or two-bedroom self-contained apartments right on the road in between Store Bay and Pigeon Point. Functional, clean and drably decorated with sitting room, kitchenette, a-c, TV and phone; a pool is under construction. ⑥

Johnston Apartments, Store Bay Rd, ☎ 639 8915, fax 627 1927. Set right above Store Bay and sharing the pool and restaurant of its larger neighbour, *Crown Point Beach*, these studios or one- and two-bedroom apartments are huge (some sleep eight) with ably equipped full kitchen, living room, a-c and instant access to the sand and sea. ⑤

Jordine's House, Store Bay Local Rd, ☎ & fax 639 1032. Good value, spacious self-contained apartments set in a residential section of Store Bay Local Road. Fan, a-c, kitchenette and a 5min walk to the supermarket. ④

Kariwak Village, Store Bay Local Rd, PO Box 27, Scarborough, ☎639 8442, fax 639 8441, email *kariwak@tstt.net.tt*. A jewel in the middle of Crown Point, though you'd hardly know it as the lush gardens, thatch-roofed cabanas and general sense of peace give a real feeling of retreat. Cabanas are split in two and furnished using local wood crafted on the premises; each has a-c and phone, or there's the option of larger and more luxurious garden rooms. Pool, jacuzzi and fabulous restaurant/bar on site, excellent and personal service. ⑦

Lagoon Lodge, Bon Accord Lagoon (PO Box 1054, Bon Accord, ☎639 8555, fax 639 0957, email *lagoon@trinidad.net*. Upmarket and completely unique private nature reserve on the edge of the lagoon – a boardwalk traverses the mangrove. Peacocks, parrots and an ostrich stroll the grounds, iguanas scurry and you get complete luxury and privacy in one of two creatively decorated self-contained houses with all mod cons (and a cook during the week), as well as use of kayaks, sailboat, pool, jacuzzi and mountain bikes. Rates include a car or jeep, no children allowed. Bliss for well-heeled seclusion-seekers. ⑧

Mike's, Store Bay Rd, ☎639 8050. Excellent value and two minutes from the airport, this busy Tobagonian-owned place has small but clean and inviting one- and two-bedroom apartments with a-c, TV and kitchenette. There's a mini-mart on site and the atmosphere is friendly and relaxed. ④

Ocean Point, Old Milford Rd, Hampden Lowlands, ☎ & fax 639 0973, email *oceanpoint@Caribisle.com*. Self-contained, spotless and semi-plush studios and suites on quiet Old Milford Road with a-c, cable TV, full kitchen and wood fittings. Small pool, sun deck, and restaurant on site. ⑦

Plaza Guesthouse, Friendship Estate, Milford Rd, Canaan. Very basic rooms in a down-at-heel but friendly Tobagonian-run guesthouse right on the road. You pay for what you get; a bed, fan and maybe an en-suite bathroom. ②

Rovanel's, Store Bay Local Rd, Bon Accord, ☎639 9666, fax 639 7908. Recently built to palatial splendour by its Tobagonian owner, this is one of the prettiest hotels in the area with brightly flowered landscaped gardens and grassy lawns, a large pool, restaurant and bar. Rooms are spanking new with phone, TV, a-c, hairdryer and patio; some have kitchenette. Staff are genuinely friendly and the place shines; try and catch it before the rates are hiked to a level justified by the quality. ⑦

Spence, Store Bay Local Rd, ☎ & fax 639 8082. Rather scruffy rooms, but inexpensive and close to the airport with a pool and restaurant on site. Eclectic design: some are split level, some have bunk beds, others doubles; all have a-c, TV and kitchenette. Popular with German clientele. ③

Store Bay Resort, Store Bay Local Rd, ☎ & fax 639 8810. A great bargain offered by the genial owners and five minutes from the airport and beaches to boot. Clean and well-maintained a-c apartments with kitchen and living room or a deluxe version with a TV. ⑤

Surfside, Milford Rd, ☎639 2418, fax 639 0614, email *surfside@ trinidad.net*. Set on the road to Pigeon Point beach, this has wall murals and truly Trinbagonian decor in roomy units with kitchenette, a-c, fan, TV and patio area. Vibrant, popular with Trinidadian holidaymakers and an excellent location on the road to the beach; discounts for long stays. ⑤

Toucan Inn, *Bonkers*, Store Bay Local Rd, PO Box 452, Crown Point, ☎639 7173, fax 639 8933, email *bonkers@trinidad.net*. Poolside octagonal wood cabanas chopped in half to make a cramped but comfy double room; all have a-c and fittings are made from local teak and pine. ⑤

Tropikist, Store Bay Rd, Crown Point, ☎639 8512, fax 628 1110. Popular with British tour groups and a real holidaymaker kind of a place with volleyball nets, pool and large grassy tanning area overlooking the beach. White tiles, a-c, phone, radio, fridge and glass patio doors give rooms a handsome degree of luxury, and there's a restaurant and bar on site. ⑧

VIP, Store Bay Local Rd, c/o PR Contracting, 119 Cacandee Rd, Chaguanas, ☎639 9096, fax 639 0581. Slightly out-of-the-way apartment block offering peace and competitive rates for the self-contained units; studios and one–two bedroom apartments have full kitchen, TV, phone, a-c and balcony. There's a mini-mart on site. ⑥

Woods Castle, Airport New Rd, Crown Point, ☎639 0803. Right in the centre of the action, this is good value with a-c, TV and two double beds in all rooms; some have kitchenette. There's a restaurant and bar on site. ④

The Runway to Store Bay

A two-minute walk from the airport brings you to the best place to swim in Crown Point, **Store Bay beach** (no set opening hours; free). Named after early Dutch settler Jan Stoer, this is some of the most popular sand in Tobago, and deservedly so; glass-bottom boat touts prowl, soca thuds through the air, Trinidadian holidaymakers consume vast quantities of curry crab and dumplin' and the fishermen still pull in the odd seine net to the accompaniment of clicking cameras.

Though fairly small and hemmed in by *Coco Reef* hotel and the rocks, the beach is excellent; tides govern the extent of the fine, off-white sand, and lifeguards patrol the areas flagged off for safe bathing. With a gentle shelve and crystal-clear, mirror-calm water, Store Bay is a good choice if you're travelling with children; occasionally, though, you'll see big breakers crashing against the mini-cave riddled volcanic rocks which overhang the sand. The bars opposite are a popular liming spot, particularly at sunset and beyond. The whole area was recently given a facelift; opposite the beach is a spanking new car park, pristine shower/changing facilities (daily

Store Bay is the finishing point for the annual Great Race power-boat contest each August (see Calendar of Events, pp.39–42) as well as a venue for open-air parties around Easter week-end.

Store Bay dining

An essential part of any visit to Tobago is a plate of **crab and dumplin'**, **macaroni pie with callaloo**, or **curry goat and vegetable rice** from one of the row of shacks facing Store Bay beach. This strip of eateries (from right to left there's *Miss Jean, Miss Trim, Joicy's, Alma's, Silvia's* and *Miss Esmee*) are *the* place for a tasty local-style meal; in fact, you'll probably find yourself heading to Store Bay come lunchtime even if you aren't planning to grace the beach. The rewards of eating here are simple; it's inexpensive, convenient and almost always tasty, though the use of a microwave to heat up your selection from an over-ambitiously large menu is a bit of a disappointment, and many bemoan that the cooking has suffered in the move from the original lean-to beach-side location. The fare of bake with fish or eggs, buljol and smoked herring for breakfast and goat, beef, chicken or veg roti, stewed beef or chicken, conch or crab and dumplin', pelau, vegetable rice, stewed lentils, macaroni pie, callaloo and ground provisions varies little from stall to stall, and neither does the cooking, but most plump for the eponymous *Miss Jean*, whose popularity at least ensures freshness. *Miss Esmee* is another favourite, but don't be discouraged from trying the others; *Miss Trim* is well worth a visit. All are open daily from around 8.30am to 8.30pm, but the flow of custom usually dictates.

10am–6pm; TT$1 per entry) with lockers for rent (TT$10 per day) as well as a couple of bars blasting out reggae and soca for the drinkers, an ice cream kiosk and the row of shacks housing the infamous cookshops – *Miss Jean*'s and *Miss Esmee*'s are local institutions – from which most purchase their lunch (see box overleaf). If you don't fancy local staples, try the Tobago Taxi Co-Op café for generous portions of chicken or fish with fries, sandwiches and hot dogs. The purpose built **craft shops** by the car park are one of the best places to buy souvenirs; Rasta-oriented jewellery, calabashes and carvings from "Father" are particularly well-made.

Fort Milford to Crusoe's Cave

Though it linked the airport with Store Bay and Pigeon Point before the *Coco Reef Hotel* was built, the road that shoots off toward the airport behind the Store Bay craft shacks is now the main route from the beach to hotel-filled Sandy Point and the **Fort Milford** stockade. Marked by a wall daubed with "It's nice to be nice", the fort was preceded by a Latvian settlement and a Dutch redoubt named Belleviste. Today's crumbling mass of gun-slitted coral stone was built by the British in 1777, and briefly appropriated by the French during their 1781–93 occupation of Tobago; five of the six cannons still pointing out to sea are British-built while the French contributed the other. Surrounded by bench-studded lawns that make a quiet chill-out spot for Tobagonians, the fort gives a panoramic perspective over Store Bay beach and Milford Bay right up to Pigeon Point.

Past the fort, the road swings left, skirting hotels and restaurants before meeting the fences of the airport runway. A right turn at this junction takes you onto what's known as NP Road, so called because there's a National Petroleum garage at its far reaches. As it circles the runway, the road passes the pretty and often deserted Sandy Point **beach**. Obscured by trees and shrubs, the beach is easy to miss; take the first dirt road into the bush (right opposite where the tarmac ends) and you'll emerge on to a picturesque strip of fine white sand and translucent sea bordered by sea grapes and palms. Swimming is safe if you stick to the left of the beach; currents get strong around the headland to the right which divides this stretch of sand from the more popular strip at Store Bay.

On the other side of the runway, NP Road takes you past a hand-painted sign marking the right turn to the ambitiously named **Crusoe's Cave**. A five-minute drive through cow pasture interspersed with the odd rambling home takes you to a clearing; ask for Mrs Crooks at the last house; her family own the land which leads to the cave, and she'll collect the entry fee (TT$5) and direct you down. The concrete steps and rocky pathway constructed for easy access do little for aesthetics, and the cave itself is small, with craggy limestone walls stained green by mineral drips and a visible depth of about 4.5m. Successive earthquakes have reduced the cavern; it

Robinson Crusoe's isle

"The Life and Strange Surprising Adventures of Robinson Crusoe of York,
Mariner; Who lived eight and twenty Years all alone, on an uninhabited
Island on the coast of America, near the mouth of the Great River of
Oroonoque; Having been Cast on Shore by shipwreck, wherein all the Men
perished but himself." Thus reads the introductory blurb to the first edition
of Daniel Defoe's *Robinson Crusoe*, dated April 25, 1719, cited as the
principal rationale of the claim that Tobago was the setting for Defoe's
epic: the fabled island was situated, like Tobago, off the coast of (South)
America near the mouth of the Orinoco River.

In the late seventeenth century, the then-sovereign Duke of Courland
commissioned an Englishman, John Poyntz, to develop the island. Poyntz
wrote a pamphlet praising Tobago's beauty and natural riches as well as
giving a physical description of the island. Believers argue that Defoe got
hold of the document and used it as the factual basis for his novel.

However, this clashes with the accepted notion that Defoe based the
book on the experience of Alexander Selkirk, a crew member on the ship
of English explorer and pirate William Dampier. During a voyage in the
Pacific Ocean, Selkirk quarrelled with another crew member and, rather
than continue in his company, he volunteered to be put ashore at the tiny
island of Juan Fernandez, off the coast of Chile. He spent four years alone
there before Dampier rescued him. After his return to England in 1711, his
story became well known through various pamphlets, on which Defoe's
novel was almost certainly based.

once stretched right back to Store Bay. The Crusoe connection came
about via the fertile imagination of the late Mr Crooks; having read
Defoe's novel, he sided with the local rumour that Tobago was
Crusoe's isle and concluded that this was as legitimate a base as any
other on the island for the fabled castaway. Whatever the reality, it's
a pretty spot with smashing views down to the white sand at Canoe
Bay, but don't expect the spectacular.

Pigeon Point

Running north from the airport past the entrance to Store Bay,
Airport New Road becomes Milford Road as it swings to the right
some 50m from the complex. Here, a left-hand turn (marked by the
neon constellation of the *Golden Star* bar and restaurant) leads to
Pigeon Point Road (also known as Milford Extension Road), taking
you past the spot where the Atlantic Ocean meets the Caribbean Sea.
The shoreline here – unlike the majority of Tobago's rugged beaches
– is definitively Caribbean; powdery white sand with turquoise sea on
one side and the ubiquitous swaying palms on the other, the latter an
attractive remnant of the time when the area was part of a coconut
plantation. Not surprisingly, you're advancing upon what most see as
the island's best **beach** – and its only private, fee-paying sand to
boot. The commercial trappings are ever-present; watersports outlets line the approach and cooing vacationers stop to photograph a
monkey who sits chained to a light-post by the entrance.

Watersports in the west

Buzzing jet-skis have not yet become a regular feature amid the surf (though you can rent them from Lazy Dayz watersports on Pigeon Point (US$30 for 15min), non-motorized watersports are freely available at the main Crown Point beaches and from the all-purpose outlet Mount Irvine Watersports (☎639 9379) at Mount Irvine beach complex (see p.242). You can rent snorkelling gear from itinerant touts or scuba concessions for US$5–10 per day, while windsurfing costs about US$30 for a half day at Pigeon Point and Mount Irvine beaches. Mini sailboats and kayaks (1hr; US$10)are also rented from these beaches. Exhilarating and not to be attempted after a rum punch session, hobie cats are mini-catamarans built for speed and balanced by the bodies of the passengers; hooked on to a trapeze, you swing out over the water when the craft reaches its highest speed. Trips are available from Cool Runnings at Turtle Beach and Pigeon Point (☎639 8363; 5hr for US$20, 1hr US$35); they also offer all-day trips aboard the hobies; see p.215. Wild Turtle (☎639 7936) at Pigeon Point offer kayaks, hobie cats, water-skiing and tube riding (US$20 for the first 20min, US$10 for a further 10min; water-ski lessons US$30), as well as banana boat rides; being dragged along on a large inflatable banana (US$20). Chartering a sport fishing boat is exhilarating but expensive; rich pickings of marlin, sailfish, tuna and dolphin are found all year round. A nippy boat accommodating up to six and equipped with rods, tackle and bait will cost around US$250 per half day, US$400 for a full day; try Dillon's Deep Sea Charters (☎639 8765), or local character Captain Frothy's boat *Hardplay* (☎639 7108). Ask around at Store Bay, Mount Irvine or Pigeon Point beaches if you're interested in joining a local fisherman aboard a pirogue; however, you'll get a better deal if you try one of the less developed fishing beaches, such as Castara or Parlatuvier (see pp.275–77).

Set at the end of its very own road, **Pigeon Point** (daily 8am–6.30pm; TT$10) is an immensely popular strip of glaring sand backed by almond and palm trees, shady picnic spots, volleyball courts and a flotilla of yachts moored around what must be Tobago's most photographed pier, a weathered wooden boardwalk with a thatch-roofed hut at the end. White sand on the sea floor lends the water that impossibly bright blue which typifies a postcard-style Caribbean beach, while gently shelving waters and tame currents make swimming benign, and there's ample space to stake out your niche without feeling cramped; you can take quite a long walk around the headland to another, less pretty, stretch of sand that borders the Bon Accord Lagoon. The busy central bar becomes a liming spot at sundown, when steel pans play away the last rays; cameras click, rum punch is downed and camcorders capture the best sunset view on the island. Behind the bar is a shoddy, down-at-heel shower block, while a complex of souvenir shops and braiding booths are on the other side. A cafe sells hot dogs, sandwiches, fries and surprisingly good daily specials; chicken, fish, vegetables, macaroni pie and provisions etc for around TT$20–30.

During the rainy season, mosquitoes from the nearby marsh have a field day – insect repellent is essential.

One of the most popular ways to explore the brine is a pleasure boat **cruise**. Several operators work the waters – their prices for a full day trip vary little (US$60–65 per person for a 6–8hr cruise and around US$35 for a 2hr sunset trip) and usually include lunch, snorkelling at Bon Accord Lagoon, Englishman's Bay or another similarly deserted cove and an open bar; private charters or sunset and moonlight dinner trips are also on the roster of most. Atmospheres vary from racy booze cruise to sedate sightseeing. Kalina Cats (☎639 6304 or 6306; Mon, Wed & Fri, 9am–5.30pm; US$65) offer touristic but fun catamaran cruises in a similar vein to those offered by the *Loafer* (☎639 7312; 7hrs: US$60), a catamaran converted for partying. Best of the bunch is newcomer *Natural Mystic* (☎639 7888), a 12-metre trimaran that unfurls the sails when the wind allows and serves up a sumptuous lunch. **Glass bottom boat** tours of Buccoo Reef (US$10) leave from Store Bay, Pigeon Point and Buccoo; see pp.228–29 for details.

Scuba remains popular, and there's some excellent diving to be had in the west, particularly around Buccoo, Mount Irvine, Arnos Vale and Culloden. Prices are consistent between the operators; one to three dives cost US$30 each, one-day resort courses from US$45, five day open water certification courses from US$300, advanced open water from US$200 and skin diving at around US$35. Reliable operators include SubLime (☎639 9386 or 9642, email *sublime@tstt.net.tt*), based at one of the west's best dive sites, sheltered Arnos Vale Bay, R&C Divers' Den (☎639 9006 or 680 8120), a locally-run operation based at Spence Apartments on Store Bay Local Road; Tobago Dive Experience (☎639 7034); Dive Tobago at Pigeon Point – catchphrase is "go down with a local" – (☎639 0202 or 2150); while Proscuba (☎639 7424 or 7517), a new outfit based at *Rovanel's* resort on Store Bay Local Road offer "scuba phones" for easy communication underwater, as well as Dutch, German and French speaking dive masters.

While Pigeon Point certainly has enough natural attributes to live up to its reputation, this is one of the few places in the island to suffer from development. The groynes constructed to curtail beach erosion have reduced the water circulation, and this – along with general pollution and poor management – has allowed algae to flourish on the sea floor, making local people question the sagacity of swimming in what on a bad day resembles a rather milky soup. Though water quality is monitored by local environmental groups, and the chance of getting sick is pretty scant, try to shower off as soon as you leave the water and avoid immersing your head; there's little to see in any case.

If you're driving into Pigeon Point, avoid parking under a coconut-laden palm – a single nut can cause a lot of damage if it lands on your vehicle.

East along Milford Road

Bisecting Tobago's low-lying southwest tip, ruler-straight Milford Road is the artery of the area, a busy main road traversing the Bon Accord, Tyson Hall, Canaan and Friendship communities. Trucks, cars and route taxis fly past, limers congregate on every corner – even the supermarket forecourt becomes a choice drinking spot of a Friday evening – and the whole stretch is the busiest you'll find away from Scarborough. One community melts seamlessly into another (boundaries seem to be a law unto themselves which only local residents can grasp), but as this is probably the most well-travelled thoroughfare on the island, the strip rapidly becomes familiar.

Bon Accord

Following the right-hand curve of the Airport New Road/Milford Road takes you into **BON ACCORD** district, though it's an area as loosely demarcated as any of the mini-villages skirting this central thoroughfare. North of the road is **Bon Accord Lagoon**, a sweeping oval of mangrove swamp and reef-sheltered, shallow water which forms one of the most important fish nurseries on the island. Though the marine life has been adversely affected by run-off from a nearby sewage treatment plant (out of action for the last twelve years but now being repaired), the lagoon remains a sanctuary for conch, snails, shrimp, oysters, crab, urchins and sponges – if you can see them amongst the thick sea grass – as well as fish which spawn amidst the protective roots of the mangrove trees and provide rich pickings for the bird life.

As most of the land skirting the swamp is privately owned – Britain's Princess Margaret stayed at one of the beach houses during a 1950s sojourn – access is problematic. You can get pretty close by turning down Golden Grove road from Milford and taking the first dirt track you come to – passing the crumbling remains of a windmill and cocoa drying house, once part of the Bon Accord sugar estate. At present, the best way to see it is during a Buccoo Reef boat tour (see p.242) that includes a barbecue at a deserted sandy spit on the lagoon's north side known as **No Man's Land**, an idyllic place to swim. You'll have to move fast to catch the area in its current unspoilt state, though, as it's slated as the site for a 600-room hotel. Planning permission has been granted and a road constructed, but though developers stress that not a single mangrove will be cut, it's inevitable that the character of the vicinity will change forever.

Canaan to Canoe Bay

Tyre shops, dusty rum bars and the obligatory coconut palms prevail as Milford Road continues eastward into **CANAAN**, an unremarkable district dominated by a row of shops in front of sprawling Milford Court, the south-west's largest housing scheme. The low-lying landscape made this part of the island a favourite amongst **sugar** planters; the entire area was once carved up into individual plantations; some – like Friendship Estate – have not yet shed their colonial names, while Canaan and Bon Accord received their unusual titles from Moravian missionaries who arrived in Tobago in 1789 to convert the populace. You can still pick out the odd bit of period architecture, such as the old windmills housing the *Peacock Mill* restaurant (signposted right turn at Friendship district). These days, though, this stretch of Milford Road with its peppering of rum bars is a nice place

Taxis travelling along Milford Road are usually plying the Scarborough–Crown Point route, but some turn off at Shirvan Road to Buccoo, Mount Irvine, Black Rock and Plymouth.

Adolphus James (☎ 639 2231) or Peter Cox (☎ 639 3093) are excellent guides for bird-watching around the lagoon.

to stop off for a drink and a spot of "ol' talk", the inconsequential rum-fuelled banter which goes hand-in-hand with the liquor. Due to the presence of a roti stall and the renowned *Block 22* fried chicken outlet, it also stays comfortably busy during the evenings.

Just after the turn-off for Buccoo (see p.237), a right-hand dirt track signposted for **Canoe Bay** leads to a pretty and seldom-visited **beach** (daily, daylight hours; TT$10), once the site of a large Amerindian settlement; the English named it Canoe Bay after the Indian pirogue fleets moored here. Today, the 56 acres around the bay are an appealing place to spend the day if you desire some peace; the entry fee covers use of the showers and bathrooms and you're free to explore – you may even discover the odd artefact poking up from the sand. The main area boasts lawns, thatched gazebos, picnic tables and a supremely private beach of clean yellow sand and calm waters – the view stretches right down to Crown Point and there's some good snorkelling to be had.

If you have your own tent you can camp at Canoe Bay for US$5; security, lighting and bathrooms are included.

Old Milford Road

Back on Milford Road, the tarmac widens as you approach Claude Noel Highway, named after a local boxer and built in the late 1980s as a swifter route into Scarborough than the narrow and weather-beaten Milford, which swings off right from the highway half a mile or so beyond the Shirvan Road turn-off. From this point, **Old Milford Road** is little more than a country lane; cattle graze, paint peels and signs of life are few and far between; look out for Tobago's only **mosque**, its glaring white walls and nippled turret somewhat incongruous among the surrounding degeneration. To the right of the road is a two-mile stretch of firm, grey, palm-backed sand named **Petit Trou** at its western end and **Little Rockly Bay** as far as the eastern Red Point outcrop where the Scarborough suburbs meet the ocean.

Petit Trou **beach** was used for horse racing before the Shirvan race track was constructed. The constant sea breezes make this a popular lunch spot, as the piles of fluttering take-away wrappers reveal – signs proclaiming "Thank-you for not littering" stand amid piles of trash. And though the white-tipped waves look picturesque, it's not the best place for a swim; the close proximity of Scarborough ensures that the murky brine is seasoned with a little sewage and the undercurrent can be dangerous. If you still want to take a dip, there are government-built facilities (daily, daylight hours; TT$1 per entry) in which to shower or change. Allfields Crown Trace, a turn-off from Old Milford Road toward the highway, houses the best place to buy (and view) local **art** in the island. The Art Gallery (Mon–Fri 9am–5pm; free) has an ever-changing collection of Tobagonian art, including pieces by local luminaries Jackie Hinkson and Sundiata. Works range from rather tacky, fluorescent sunset-and-palm-tree scenes to intense abstracts and gorgeous watercolours of gingerbread homes and local life.

Along the highway

Just past the Old Milford Road turning, the highway scoots past a forest-like plantation of coconut palms to the left. From here, the road begins to climb; once you've passed the Auchenskeoch Road (a convenient short-cut to Buccoo and Mount Irvine), you come to a set of traffic lights marking a crossroads; right leads to the hilly residential community of **LAMBEAU**, a tight-knit and completely un-touristic village, while turning left is the steep route up to **Signal Hill**, a great vantage point to take in the panoramic view of Crown Point and Lowlands beyond the forest-like coconut plantations. Throughout Tobago's chequered history, Signal Hill has been used as a lookout point, notably by signalmen communicating news of activities out to sea to nearby forts. Today, the area is home to the local comprehensive school where Tobagonian footballer **Dwight Yorke** was educated, as well as a base for the Trinidad and Tobago Regiment; listen out for strains of their marching band at practice.

The next right-hand turn-off from the highway is the route to **Shaw Park football ground**, a sprawling facility which occasionally doubles up as a concert venue. Sport is the main focus of the place, though, with football taking precedence. Advertised on the radio, in *Tobago News* or by word of mouth, games are great fun to attend, and as most take place in the cool of the night, the floodlights are the best way to tell if a match is on.

Turning left at the highway's next set of traffic lights brings you on to quiescent **Orange Hill Road**, a rambling route to the leeward coast at Mount Irvine. Past the attractive Spring Garden Moravian church, the road splits as if in disgust at the vicious potholes; left takes you into **PATIENCE HILL**, an attractively quiet rural community that makes a pleasant drive and a great way to get completely lost along the winding country roads; if you can find it, there's a fantastic view of Lowlands from the top of what locals call "Patience Hill Back Bottom Road". The right fork takes you into sparsely populated but pretty **ORANGE HILL** itself, its bougainvillea hedges and overgrown empty lots sliding loosely into Bethel and down to the coast (see p.242).

In high season, beach barbecues at Pigeon Point or Store Bay are advertised on fliers. Flambeaux and a steelband provide atmosphere; US$25–35 covers drinks and all the freshly-cooked seafood you can eat.

Eating

While the highlights of Tobagonian food – crab and dumplin' or pacro water – are sublime, the available variety isn't particularly wide, particularly in Lowlands, where it can be difficult to escape the expensive and bland tourist-oriented offerings; pasta or steak often take pride of place over *coocoo* or conch. It's not impossible to find good Tobagonian cooking, though, and even some of the smartest restaurants allow their callaloo to remain unadulterated by cream or a blender. If you're here in the slow season (April 15–Dec 15), bear in mind that many kitchens close at around 9pm.

Tobago street food

Trinidad-style **street food** is yet to make an impact in Tobago – even in Scarborough, it's impossible to find a good corn soup, but one notable exception is *Block 22*, a hulk of concrete at the Canaan end of Milford Road that makes the best fried chicken in Tobago; spicy batter and rum shop ambience keeps the cars double parked until 1–2am on the weekends. Next door, *Akhee's Doubles* (Mon–Sat 8am–8pm) serve passable roti (chicken, beef, channa or goat), doubles, aloo pies and pholouri. Also in this section of Milford Road, *Golden Girls Bakery* make excellent buljol or smoked mackerel and hops as well as sandwiches, pastries and a cracking carrot juice or peanut punch. You'll inevitably be drawn in by the local staples – "roti, conch and all kind ah ting" – served up by Miss Jean and co at Store Bay (see box, p.225), while a few hundred yards up Airport New Road, try *Triple B Burger Grill* for fish, beef or chicken burgers and fried potato wedges – usually open until 11pm. You'll find food stalls springing up wherever there is nightlife – *Golden Star* is a favourite place to pitch – where you can get chicken, souse, boiled corn and fish tea. For more familiar fast food, *KFC* and local burger joint *Royal Castle* are both in Scarborough.

Bonkers, Store Bay Local Rd, Crown Point, ☎639 7173. Still-tasty Tobagonian food with the corners smoothed away, served under the shady pavilion or at poolside tables – customers can take a dip. Breakfast is local and European, lunchtime sandwiches, soup (usually callaloo) with home-made bread, or pelau and salad, chicken, fish, chilli-con-carne and salads. Dinner highlights are roast chicken with rosemary, pork in pimento sauce and veg gumbo with coconut sauce.

Columbus Snackette, Crown Point. Popular drinking spot opposite the airport, that also serves great Tobagonian staples: flying fish, buljol or smoked mackerel breakfasts; roti, fried chicken and rice or stew pork for lunch and dinner. The Friday night barbecue is popular, offering a good lime as you eat.

Copra Tray, Store Bay Local Rd. Businesslike international menu, good for a light lunch – shrimp wonton, chicken wings, beef or fish salad, burgers and filled croissants – or a pre-drinking dinner of meatloaf, vegetable quiche, lasagne, calamari or pizza, served in a pleasant garden setting set back from the road.

Dillon's, Airport New Rd, ☎639 8765. Busy seafood restaurant midway between the turn-offs for Pigeon Point and Store Bay beaches, with an air-conditioned dining room and outdoor tables. Simple seafood lunches and snacks, and sumptuous dinners. Fish, lobster and shrimp are carefully prepared with a Creole flavour; steak or chicken are alternatives. Live music most nights and a seafood buffet every Wednesday. Closed Mon.

Eleven Degrees North, Store Bay Rd, off Pigeon Point Rd, ☎639 0996. Busy, upmarket and heavily stylized verandah setting with creative decor, hand-painted tables and regular art exhibitions (the menu reminds that all of it is for sale). Food combines local, Mexican and Cajun slants; jalapeno peppers, lobster crepes or samosas to start, carrot and spinach pasta with lobster, seafood enchiladas, pork burritos, steak fajitas and caramel bananas or guava cheesecake for dessert. Excellent service, closed Sun & Mon.

Friendship Place, Milford Rd, Canaan. Familial home cooking served up in a supremely genial rum bar-cum-restaurant. Food is fresh, tasty, inexpensive

Check whether menu prices include tax (up to 15 percent) and service charge (usually 10 percent). If a service charge is included, you don't have to leave a tip.

and available as long as there are customers. Menu staples include chicken or fish nuggets, pork chops, burgers, pizza and fajitas, all served with fries and salad.

Golden Star, cor. Milford and Pigeon Point roads. Chiefly recommendable for its easy-access location, food is mediocre – the fish, chicken, steaks, lobster and club sandwiches hold no surprises (or nasty shocks), but it's open late and service is cheerful and good.

Hampden Inn, Old Milford Rd, Lowlands. Good in-hotel restaurant serving medium-priced European fare; American or continental breakfast, sandwiches, salads, burgers and soups for lunch and pizza, spaghetti, curried or stewed fish, chicken and shrimp for dinner, accompanied by an African drumming show each Sunday.

House of Pancakes, Milford Rd, Bon Accord. Medium-priced breakfasts of cinnamon and nutmeg-laced pancakes with fresh bananas and walnuts; omelettes, bacon and eggs are also on offer. Dinner is Cajun-style: blackened fish or shrimp, shrimp jambalaya or seafood and okra gumbo. The roadside setting is noisy, but central and good for watching the world go by.

In Seine, Sandy Point Rd, Crown Point. Set on a covered wooden patio adjacent to the *Tropikist* hotel, the speciality here – as the name suggests – is seafood as fresh as it comes: fish, shrimp and lobster cooked to perfection, friendly service and plenty of sea breezes.

Kariwak Hotel, Store Bay Local Rd, ☎639 8442. Fresh herbs and spices, inventive slants on local staples and genuine love in the kitchen make this the best place to eat in Crown Point. Breakfast and dinner menus are set – usually with a meat, fish or vegetarian option – so everything is supremely fresh, succulently cooked and completely delicious. Accompanied by live music, the Saturday night buffet is particularly good. Great service and vegan food available.

Man Friday, *Sandy Point Beach Club*, Crown Point. In-hotel beachside diner serving Thai and international food; fried fish and potato hash, omelette or stuffed pitta bread for breakfast, sandwiches, salads or burgers for lunch, and satay platter, paella, pasta, "strong back" soup and lots of seafood for dinner.

Marcia's, Store Bay Local Rd, ☎639 0359. Completely Tobagonian, the fake flowers and genial owners make this one of the most welcoming small restaurants in the area. Open for dinner (call the day before for lunch) and offering great local food; red snapper Creole, lobster in coconut garlic sauce, stewed or curried conch and Sunday-style stewed chicken with macaroni pie and callaloo, all served with rice and ground provisions. Gorgeous cassava pudding for dessert.

Pepe's, Store Bay Rd, off Pigeon Point Rd. Copious menu served up in the open-sided downstairs section of this two-restaurant building. Usually full of foreign visitors gorging on sesame chicken wings or stuffed crab back appetizers and a huge range of chicken preparations; red wine and mushroom sauce, curry and coconut. Pepper shrimp is excellent, and a soup, salad and rum punch are included with every evening meal.

Rachel's Caribbean Cafe, Milford Rd, Bon Accord. Bright, cheerful, inexpensive and right at the roadside (there are a few tables inside); good for roti – chicken, fish, goat and ital veg – as well as heavily sweetened natural fruit juices, US-style breakfasts and potato or fish pies.

Ru-B-Lou's, Crown Point. Set on the corner of Airport New Rd and Store Bay Local Rd by the police station, this incredibly genial place offers hearty, inexpensive and flavoursome US-style breakfasts (daily 7–11am).

Sunday School

A Tobago institution, **Sunday School** is most definitely not for the pious. A massive beach party that the whole island seems to attend, Sunday School is the highlight of the week's nightlife, completely taking over Buccoo village with swarms of people, food stalls and cars squeezed sardine-style into available space. The action begins at around 8pm, when the Buccooneers Steel Orchestra play pan for a couple of hours. The crowd begins to thicken at around 10–11pm, when the sound system at the covered beach facilities begins to play, competing for the highest decibels with the music pumping out of *Hendrix Bar* across the road; this is also a nice place to sit and watch the human traffic. Music policy at the beach is inevitably Jamaican dancehall with the most popular soca tunes thrown in alongside hip hop and R&B, while you'll hear oldies (disco, Michael Jackson), soca, calypso and a little Jamaican reggae at *Hendrix*. Either dancefloor is jumping, as experienced winers display their skills, foreigners let loose or take a wining lesson and the gigolos (and tourists) scout for a partner – Sunday School is well-known as a kind of pick-up joint, so it's the ideal place to watch the intricate mating dance of thrill-seeking foreigners and those hard-working beach bums. Though Buccoo is busy every Sunday night, the largest Sunday School of the year takes place each Easter Monday, when several more sound systems add to the cacophony and parked cars back up all the way to the golf course.

Taj Terrace, Store Bay Rd, off Pigeon Point Rd. Right above *Pepe's*, this is the only Indian restaurant in Crown Point. All the regulars are here – tandoori and korma style lamb or chicken and the inescapable roti with chicken, beef, shrimp, lobster or vegetables. Conveniently located for a take-away lunch.

Waving Gallery, Store Bay beach facilities. Upstairs dining spot in the newly built beach facilities; no-frills food – fish sandwiches, hamburgers, hot dogs and salads and an extremely inexpensive buffet on a Friday night, eaten to the strains of an in-house sound system.

For more restaurants, see Scarborough (pp.257–258) and Plymouth (p.246).

Drinking and nightlife

Tobagonians tend to display less of the frantic party enthusiasm that characterizes Trini "feting", and much of the local nightlife revolves around the **bar** scene, a mix of rum shops and more tourist-oriented dives like *Copra Tray*. Tobago isn't smothered with heaving dancefloors, and even the bright lights of Crown Point offer limited options after dark, but you can find some excitement most nights of the week – consult roadside posters or ask around to find the current and ever-changing hotspots; Monday and Tuesday are often quiet as everyone recovers from Sunday School excesses. If you're looking for a place to **dance**, *Golden Star* is almost always lively – Thursday night parties and Scouting for Talent are the busiest nights – while *The Deep* is best at weekends. Other than the weekly bacchanal of **Sunday School** at Buccoo (see above), Friday (pay day for locals) is the biggest party night – Lowlands echoes with bass notes and many locals head for Scarborough to the *Great White* disco, the John Dial roadside dance at *Fairy Queen* bar or market square sound systems (see p.258). Aside from a flirtation during Carnival time, Tobagonian music policy is primarily dancehall reggae – Buju Banton and Sizzla are guaranteed floor-fillers – while only *The Deep* offers a more "international" playlist.

Larger hotels provide nightly **entertainment** for guests and non-guests alike, most of which manages to avoid the rather tacky limbo and fire-eating ilk of other islands. Some, such as the *Arnos Vale* cabarets (Weds and Fri) or anything featuring the Les Coteaux cultural dancers – are exceptionally good. Occasional **stageshows** are held at Shaw Park football ground or *Golden Star*; you'll see promotional billboards all around the island – this is also the method of choice for advertising the marvellous round of summer fishermen's **fetes**. Your only other options are a visit to the **casino** or **cinema** in Scarborough (see pp.248–258).

Bars and clubs

Bird's Nest, Crown Point (opposite the airport). Small rum shop that's good for liming with the usual crew of taxi drivers.

Bonkers, Store Bay Local Rd. Pleasant wooden bar area by the pool with nightly entertainment; calypso singers (Tues & Sat), steel band on Wednesday, a performance from the Les Coteaux dancers on Thursday and a "Native Spirit" floor show every Friday.

Columbus Snackette, Store Bay Rd (opposite the airport). Known as Uncle C's, this is an enduringly busy place to sink a few beers, with loud music over the weekends.

Copra Tray, Store Bay Local Rd. You'll inevitably grace these doors whilst in Tobago as this roomy, thatch-roofed bar with a dancefloor is one of the most popular liming spots for locals and tourists alike. Pool tables (TT$10 for half an hour), an outdoor patio to catch the breeze, a resident DJ and African drumming every Saturday night. Watch out for the prowling men-folk. Closed Sun.

Cross Rds Pub, Buccoo Rd, Carnbee. Expansive bar which comes to life each Saturday night for a "Back in Time" dance where an older set groove to 60s, 70s and 80s music.

The Deep, *Sandy Point Village* hotel, Crown Point. Air-conditioned subterranean disco popular with upwardly mobile locals and tourist crowds, good for a hassle-free dance. Moderate cover charge; women usually get in for free. Closed Sun–Tues.

Drifter's Pub, Milford Rd, Crown Point. Adjacent to *Dillon's* restaurant, this air-conditioned drinking hole is popular with tourists though locals make up a strong contingent as well.

Friendship Place, Milford Rd, Canaan. Excellent for meeting locals and visitors over a rum or a beer, busy most nights of the week.

Green Shop, Canaan, Milford Rd (opposite Milford Court). Well-patronized rum shop, good for a game of dominoes or a quiet lime.

Gold Post, Buccoo Village. Set just off Buccoo's main road, this is a quiet and intimate place to have a drink, with a pool table and meals available.

Golden Star Restaurant and Bar, Crown Point, ☎ 639 0873. One of Tobago's busy night-spots with an outdoor stage and a darkened indoor disco that remains enduringly popular with a young crowd of tourists, locals and those on the lookout for company. The entertainment varies every evening; movies on the big screen TV (6.30–9pm), karaoke, "Latin" night (Tues), and the marvellous "Scouting for Talent", an annual competition for Tobagonians with stars in their eyes. The nightly wining frenzy of JG's disco follows on from the entertainment. TT$15 cover charge on some nights.

Lindsay's Bar, Milford Rd, Bon Accord. Another Milford rum bar, friendly and inexpensive.

Waving Gallery, Store Bay. Cool and breezy upstairs spot for a drink (cocktails as well as Carib) and a lime as the beach traffic passes below. Sound system on Friday nights and a laid-back feel.

North to Buccoo

A kilometre or so before Milford Road widens into Claude Noel Highway, **Shirvan Road** strikes off to the left. Bristling with signs tacked up by enterprising restaurateurs and hoteliers, this is the route to Buccoo Bay and its famous **reef** (see box, p.240) as well as several generous yellow-sand **beaches** and the neat coastal town of Plymouth. The first stretch is bordered to the left by a plantation of towering coconut palms and to the right by thick hedges masking what was once Shirvan Park **horse racing track**. A fire in 1985 put a permanent stop to horse racing in Tobago, and the site then had a brief incarnation as Tobago's most popular nightspot, *Starting Gate*. Though it closed in 1996, a recent change of management means that it may once again be an evening hot spot; it's named after a rusting metal contraption in the back garden which originally started the races.

Studded with swanky restaurants, fruit stalls and simple board shacks, Shirvan Road continues north, passing turn-offs to quietly residential Mount Pleasant and Carnbee Village – the latter has a supermarket and petrol station. There's another cluster of tourist-oriented signposts at the next crossroads, known as **Buccoo Junction**. Here, route taxis running between Scarborough and the north coast pick up and drop passengers, so you'll often see beckoning hands if you're driving. The right turn at the crossroads is Auchenskeoch (pronounced or-kins-styor)/Buccoo Bay Road – take any left from here and you'll climb into the midst of one of Tobago's smartest residential areas; opulent villas sporting swimming pools, towering satellite dishes and sharing the same fantastic view of the Mount Irvine golf course (see p.242) and Buccoo Reef/Pigeon Point that can be seen from the road.

A little further up the road and you're at the outskirts of tiny **BETHEL**, a precipitously situated and completely charming rural village once home to infamously eccentric German artist Luise Kimme and her fisherman partner Albert Reynolds (see p.243); there are several wonderful views of Lowlands and the Buccoo coast from the village. From Bethel, Orange Hill Road eventually meets Claude Noel Highway.

Accommodation

Tobago's most **upmarket** hotels are clustered along the beaches between Buccoo and Plymouth, and the plush **villas** (see p.219) around the Mount Irvine golf course offer some of the plushest private accommodation you'll find, but not all the accommodation is the exclusive preserve of the well-heeled. There are plenty of middle bracket hotels and guesthouses, and the area makes one of the most appealing bases on the island; you're close to the action of Crown Point without being stuck right in it, transport is easy (taxis run along Shirvan Road from early mornings to late at night), and the beaches are marvellous.

Arnos Vale, Arnos Vale Estate, PO Box 208, Scarborough, ☎639 2881, fax 639 4629. Classy colonial-style hotel in 400 acres of beautiful bird-and-flower-filled private land and a protected cove of white sand and reef-filled sea. Popular with Italians, rooms are chintzy with rattan furniture, phone, TV, a-c and balcony. There's a pool, tennis courts, dive shop and excellent food. ⑧

Blue Horizon, Jacamar Drive, Mount Irvine, ☎639 0433, fax 665 5006; in US ☎305/592 1434, fax 305/592 4935. Commanding great views over the golf course and the sea from a hilly setting (you'll need a car), these spacious, cool rooms have a-c, cable TV, phone, living room, patio and full kitchen; some can sleep up to six. Nice atmosphere; laid back but efficient and a pool on site. ⑥

Cocorico Inn, PO Box 287, North and Commissioner sts, Plymouth, ☎639 2961, fax 639 6565, email *cocrico@tstt.net.tt*. Comfortable, family-run and very friendly with a restaurant, pool and quiet location in residential backstreets. Eclectic accommodation ranges from clean, simple rooms with fan to larger units with a-c, fridge, TV and kitchen. They also rent basic or luxurious self-contained one-two-or-three bedroom houses in Plymouth. ③

Footprints, Culloden Bay Rd, ☎660 0118, fax 660 0027, email *footprints@ trinidad.net*. Overlooking Culloden Bay, this remote, self-styled "eco resort" has its own nature trails, saltwater pools, excellent snorkelling metres from the rooms and oceans of peace and quiet. The accommodations are diversely built, ranging from standard suites to self-contained villas with jacuzzi, and the "lovers' retreat". There's an excellent restaurant on site. ⑨

Golf View, Buccoo Junction, Mount Irvine, PO Box 354, Scarborough; ☎639 9551, fax 639 0979. Good value for these clean, spacious and well-laid out rooms with a-c, TV, phone and optional kitchenette. There's a large pool in a pretty garden out front, though it's a bit close to the road. ⑤

Grafton, Black Rock, PO Box 25, Scarborough; ☎639 0191, fax 639 0030, email *grafton@trinidad.net*. Almost all-inclusive – most guests arrive on package tours – resort hotel dominating Stone Haven Bay. Comprehensive amenities; pool, tennis and squash courts, games room, two restaurants and a beach bar, nightly entertainment, watersports and scuba centre. Rooms are pleasant with balcony, a-c, fan, TV and phone, but don't justify the high walk-in rates; all include breakfast. ⑨

Hillcrest, Buccoo Rd, c/o Max Baden-Semper; in UK ☎0181/741 9264 or 563 0425, fax 748 6511. Set on a hilltop off Shirvan Road near Morshead's deli, the verandah of this luxurious five-bedroom villa commands a panoramic sea view of Buccoo Reef and the southwest coast all the way to the airport. Living room, dining room, full kitchen, a pool and spacious grounds complete the perfection. Rates cover ten people. ⑨

Jemma's, c/o Stacey Thomas, Black Rock PO, ☎639 7724. Tucked behind Turtle Beach, this three bedroom Tobagonian/German run outfit is beautifully decorated with rattan furniture and a nice verandah outside. Rooms are simple with mosquito nets and fans; the kitchen and bathroom are shared and breakfast is available. ③

KP's, Shirvan Rd, Buccoo, ☎ and fax 639 9481, email *kpatino@tstt.net.tt*. Brand-new room block adjacent to *Patino's* restaurant, these luxurious rooms are a bargain; all have a-c, cable TV, phone and an open-air kitchenette on the balcony. Convenient for Mount Irvine beach and route taxis. ⑥

Mount Irvine Hotel and Golf Club, Mount Irvine, PO Box 222, Scarborough, ☎639 8871, fax 639 8800. Built around a coral stone sugar mill and other plantation remnants, this grand old lady of Tobago hotels maintains a sophisticated elegance. Landscaped grounds with tennis courts, sauna, huge pool, three restaurants, five bars plus its own private stretch of beach and 18-hole golf course; guests get a 30 percent discount on green fees. Rooms are a bit dated but still luxurious with a-c, phone, satellite TV and patio; there are self-contained two bedroom bungalows as well. ⑨

Old Grange Inn, Buccoo Junction, Mount Irvine, PO Box 297, Scarborough; ☎ & fax 639 9395, email *grangeinn@trinidad.net*. Appealing rooms oozing 1980s ambience with wooden floors, a-c, phone and fridge or rather gloomy self-contained units with kitchenette, phone, a-c, TV and small patio. Large pool, good restaurant and near to the golf course. ⑥

Plantation Villas, Stone Haven Bay Rd, Black Rock, PO Box 435, Scarborough, ☎639 9377, fax 639 0455, email *villas@wow.net*. Gorgeous colonial-style three-bedroom villas with gingerbread fretwork, wraparound verandahs overlooking the sea and beautiful fittings; four-poster beds, rocking chairs and all mod cons; washing machine and drier, dishwasher, well-equipped kitchen, spacious living room, lots of extras and luxurious atmosphere. Pool and bar are on site and the sea is a minute away. Rates are for four persons. ⑨

Rolita, Jacamar Drive, Mount Irvine, ☎639 7970. Incredibly friendly and accommodating atmosphere with great views down to Pigeon Point. Rooms are plain, clean and breezy with fan and double bed, and there's a pool and inexpensive restaurant on site. Brilliant value and lots of fun. ③

Top O' Tobago, Arnos Vale Estate, c/o Tickets, PO Box 1687, Bath BA1 7YB, UK; ☎639 3166; in UK ☎01225/859530, fax 859916. Perched high above Arnos Vale Bay with pretty gardens, distant sea view and plenty of bird-life. Comfortably opulent main two-bedroom house sleeps up to seven and has large sitting room, cable TV, stereo, two bathrooms, fully equipped kitchen, patio and washer/drier. Smaller cabanas are stylish with kitchenette; all have use of the pool. Remote enough to merit a car but excellent value. ⑥

Turtle Beach, PO Box 201, Scarborough, ☎639 2851, fax 639 1495; in UK ☎0181/741 5333, fax 741 9030; in US ☎800/255 5859, fax 305/471 9547. A member of the Rex chain, this 1970s-style concrete edifice is right on the beach. Popular with tour groups, the sea-view rooms are suitably well-equipped with a-c, phone, kingsize or twin bed and balcony. Tennis courts, pool and restaurant are on site, and watersports are available. Children under 12 stay free. ⑧

Two Seasons, Pleasant Prospect, Shirvan Rd, ☎639 9461. Budget accommodation set back from the road between Mount Irvine and Stone Haven beaches. Rooms are plain with wood floors, fan and a bed, but the atmosphere is friendly and this is an excellent budget choice. Meals available from the pizza restaurant downstairs. ③

Sanctuary Villas, Black Rock, PO Box 424, Scarborough, ☎639 9556, fax 639 0019, email *sanctuary@tstt.net.tt*. Attractive, well designed and brand new, these two or three bedroom villas have all mod-cons; private pool, TV, a-c, phone, verandah, full kitchen and beautifully decorated living room. You're opposite Grafton beach and there's plenty of peace and quiet. Rates are for four people. ⑨

*For informa-
tion on villa
rentals in the
area, see
p.219.*

Seahorse Inn, Stone Haven Bay Rd, Black Rock, PO Box 488, Scarborough, ☎639 0686, fax 639 0057. Small, attractive and right on the beach; spartan but attractive rooms have appealing quirks like arched windows, teak floors and. All three have a patio with sea view, a-c and fan. Good restaurant on site (rates include huge breakfast) and evening entertainment during the high season. ⑥

Buccoo

The left turn at Buccoo Junction takes you into the small settlement of BUCCOO, haphazardly built around a calm and beautiful bay. Fishing remains a major industry here – the day's catch is sold by the beach facilities when the boats return in the late afternoon – but since the nearby reef has become a premier attraction, this close-knit community has begun to embrace tourism. Shopfronts are daubed with "Welcome to Buccoo", and the green space in front of the bay is the venue for the annual **goat races** – the scoreboard remains all year round as testament to the bitterly fought contests which take place each Easter (see box opposite). Buccoo gets a weekly energy injection when the masses descend for the **Sunday School** debauchery (see box, p.235) and the village is completely overtaken. The rest of the week sees a quieter scene, with the community (and its posse of skinny dogs) tidying up the revellers' rubbish and enjoying their peace and quiet while they can; families chat over garden walls and small boys take pleasure in diving off the fishing pier, despite the scummy waves that lap against the coarse grey sand. The combined effect of a Sunday job as a urinal and a muddy sea bed make Buccoo a terrible place to swim, though the palm-lined western fringe of the bay is more appealing with cleaner water and plenty of shells and coral fragments to collect. There are run-down government-built beach facilities, but hardly anyone uses them these days. Several roads shoot off right from Buccoo's main street, all of them dead ends; the last – Battery Street – terminates at a grassy bluff that was the original venue for the goat races, but close proximity to the cliffs that give sweeping views over Mount Irvine Bay prompted a shift to safer ground.

Buccoo Reef and Nylon Pool

Covering around twelve square kilometres of Caribbean seabed between Pigeon Point and Buccoo Bay, **Buccoo Reef** is the largest and most heavily visited in Tobago. Home to forty-odd species of hard and soft coral, the reef has taken around 10,000 years to grow into today's magnificent labyrinth. The predominant corals are hard stag and elkhorn, though you'll see waving purple sea fans and peach coloured fire coral as well, all of which make good feeding for the

brilliantly coloured trigger, butterfly, surgeon and parrot fish. To the
south of the reef is **Nylon Pool**, a gleaming coralline sandbar forming an appealing metre-deep swimming pool smack in the middle of
the sea. It's said to have been named by Princess Margaret during a
stay in the 1950s; she remarked that the water was as clear as her
nylon stockings.

Goat and crab races

Easter weekend in Tobago is what Carnival is to Trinidad; an unofficial
national holiday when the hotels are filled to the brim with Trinidadians on
a weekend break and the island erupts with festivities. A succession of
huge open-air parties and well-attended harvest feasts culminate at the
Buccoo goat races on Easter Tuesday, introduced by Barbadian national
Samuel Callender in 1925. Though attempting to race one of the most
intractable and belligerent animals in the world may seem a little ridiculous to the uninitiated, these tournaments are taken very seriously by
aficionados, who study the form (and character) of the sleekly groomed
animals and place bets on their favourites. Kept separately from the run-
of-the-mill roadside grazer and given fanciful names like Dance Hall King,
Nobody Wants Me, Nasty Man or Ben Johnson, racing goats never end up
in the pot, undergo a rigorous training routine, and return to the tracks
year after year. Prize specimens live out their days as stud goats to breed
more potential champions.

The preliminary round at the Mount Pleasant Family Fun Day on Easter
Monday gives everyone a chance to see which goat is running best, and by
Tuesday, Buccoo – still reeling from the two largest Sunday Schools of the
year – is transformed; the track is clipped and fenced in, the scoreboard is
resplendent with a new coat of paint and the starting gates are in place.
Food vendors and craft stalls line the streets and a carnival atmosphere
builds as fast as the crowds, who are kept entertained by dancing and
drumming in between stakes. Suitably attired in white shorts and a
coloured vest, the jockeys limber up by the side of the tracks; a necessary
exercise, as their ability to keep up with their goat (and keep hold of it) has
more influence on their success or failure than the capabilities of the goat
itself; animals are raced at the end of a rope, and guided or encouraged
with the help of a long stick. Sponsored by local businesses and given
grand titles like White Oak Classic or Penta Paints Stake A, the actual
races are a joy to watch once the jockeys manage to manoeuvre their
malignant charges into starting position. With wild-eyed stares, the goats
tear haphazardly down the track, often taking a diagonal course that trips
up other goats and runners alike to the delight of the spectators. The best
of the bunch battle for supremacy in the final "Champ of Champs" race,
while "Champion Jockey", "Champion Trainer" and "Most Outstanding
Goat" prizes are also presented.

The equally improbable **crab races** are taken a little less seriously.
Plucked from the ocean a couple of weeks before, the crustaceans are
encouraged to run both by tugs on a piece of string and by temporary withdrawal of food; choice morsels placed at the end of the wooden alleys
which keep the crabs on course are the incentive for the sideways dash to
the finishing line. Once all the races are over, the final all-night party
swings into action, and the dancing continues until dawn.

Sadly, however, human interaction is taking a devastating toll. Carelessly placed anchors and thoughtless removal of coral souvenirs – not to mention the inevitable pollution – mean that many parts bear more resemblance to a coral graveyard than a living reef. Large sections have died off completely, leaving white skeletons in their wake, while over-fishing has reduced fish and crustacean populations and misplaced spear guns have ripped chunks from the coral. The situation became so bad that Buccoo was declared a protected national park in 1973, but with scant resources to enforce the law, the legal status meant little and the damage continued practically unabated. Today, glass bottom boat operators are more conscientious, anchoring only on dead reef and warning visitors that touching or removing reef matter and shells is illegal, but they still hand out the plastic shoes which enable a single footstep to damage or kill hundreds of years' growth. You can do your bit by standing on seabed only and refusing to buy any coral trinkets, and a donation to Environment Tobago is a good way to help preserve Tobago's reefs.

If you want to see the reef, you'll have no difficulty in finding a **glass bottom boat** to take you; they leave from Store Bay, Pigeon Point and Buccoo – though if you choose the former, snorkelling time may be reduced as it's a longer journey to the reef. Basic tours include a trip across the unscathed deep-water coral garden as well as snorkelling and a dip in Nylon Pool; a 2–3 hour trip costs around TT$60 (US$10). Some operators make a day of it by including a beach barbecue at No Man's Land for around US$40. Some of the most reliable operators are Buccoo-based Johnson and Sons (☎639 8519), Mr Power who makes daily trips on his boat *POWER1* from Pigeon Point, or Hew's (☎639 9058) – just ask around on the beaches. These operators time their trips with the low tide, when snorkelling is at its best, while others will go anytime you want.

Though it lacks atmosphere, the semi-private section of beach maintained by Mount Irvine *hotel is a little superior to the public area; non-guests are welcome to swim, and you can use the showers if you're drinking from the bar.*

Mount Irvine

The swaying palms and shaven greens of Tobago's only **golf course** herald the outskirts of **MOUNT IRVINE**, the next coastal village past Buccoo. Straddled across Shirvan Road, the course is rated among the top fifty in the world, and was opened in 1968 as the main attraction of *Mount Irvine* hotel, which still owns and maintains the greens. At some 600 metres, with several onerous water holes and some wicked undulations, it offers a challenging game and plays host to the Tobago Pro-Am tournament every January. Green fees are US$25 for nine holes, US$40 for eighteen – there's also a weekly rate of US$220. Cart rental costs US$18 for nine holes, US$30 for eighteen; caddies charge US$7 for nine holes, US$10 for eighteen, and renting clubs costs US$10 for nine holes, US$15 for eighteen; all are subject to 15 percent VAT except caddie rates.

Past the golf course, the hitherto hidden coast swings spectacularly back into view; yachts bob on the waves and craggy volcanic

Old house at Grande Riviere

The Pitch Lake at La Brea

IAN CUMMING

Rasta Hats, Scarborough

A.D. TRILLO

Argyll Waterfall, Tobago

A.D. TRILLO

Scarlet ibis

DOMINIQUE DE-LIGHT

Pepper stall in southern Trinidad

DOMINIQUE DE-LIGHT

Back Bay, Tobago

Turtle beach, Tobago

A Tobago rum shop

Englishman's Bay, Tobago

Rainforest on Little Tobago

Liming on the pier, Charlotteville, Tobago

rock formations bordering Buccoo Point make an arresting back-drop to the west. There's a lovely section of yellow sand beach behind a low concrete bulwark just past the golf course; known as Mount Irvine Wall, the wide, wavy beach is popular with local devotees of a restorative "sea bath" who sit chatting in the emerald-green. Around the next bend is **Mount Irvine Bay Beach**, a regularly busy slip of fine yellow sand with just enough room for beach tennis and volleyball, surrounded by cutesy covered gazebos and the ubiquitous palms and sea grape trees. The facilities (daylight hours; TT$1) are adequate if a bit run-down, and there's a bar/restaurant on site doling out mountains of fried shark and bake. During the summer months, the water is calm enough to make exploration of the ornate offshore **reef** a joy, but Mount Irvine becomes one of the island's best **surfing** beaches between December and March, when huge breakers crash against the sand and plain swimming becomes a bit redundant. Boards can be rented from Mt. Irvine Watersports (☎639 9379) right next to the beach complex; they also rent out windsurfing and snorkelling equipment as well as Sailfish boats.

Lowlands: Crown Point to Plymouth

For more information on surfing in the islands, contact the Trinidad-based Surfing Association of Trinidad and Tobago (☎637 0763).

Kimme museum

Nestled in the hills behind the beach along Orange Hill Road (follow the signposts), the **Kimme Museum** is the private gallery of German sculptress Luise Kimme, who settled in Tobago in 1979, and set up a studio with local sculptor and fisherman Albert Prince. Her eerily beguiling wood sculptures look rather incongruous on display at Fort King George and the botanical gardens in Scarborough, but dotted around the surrounds of her quirky fretworked home, the collection is arresting; three-metre high figures carved from whole trunks of oak depict the subtlest nuances of Tobagonian dancing; and her interpretations of local folklore characters Mama L'Eau, La Diablesse and the Soucouyant are powerful. The museum is open only on Sundays (11am–2pm; free), though you can call and make an appointment on other days (☎639 0257). Meeting Luise Kimme – ever the eccentric artist – is an experience in itself, and she's always on hand to provide further insight into her work. You can buy copies of her evocative Tobago diary, *Chachalaca* (see Books, p.319), as well as photograph booklets of her pieces.

Marie's Mini Mart in Pleasant Prospect (right on the road between Mount Irvine and Stone Haven bays) is a convenient place to pick up basic supplies (Mon–Sat 8am–8pm, Sun 8am–7pm).

Black Rock and around

Past Mount Irvine, a newly-laid section of Shirvan Road swings away from the coast – the coast road is usually called Grafton Road from this point on. Its narrower forefather ran close to the sea, and though potholed and semi-private looking, you can still drive or walk along the old Stone Haven Road to access an excellent **beach** – often referred to as "Grafton Beach" after the resort hotel which dominates the sand from above. A glorious, wide swathe with coarse sand and year-round crashing waves that attract turtles to lay eggs (see p.305),

Stone Haven (as it's officially called) makes for marvellous swimming, and you can get refreshments, including hot lunches as well as rotis and sandwiches from *Dukes* beach bar, below the *Grafton* hotel; they also do a beach barbecue every Friday evening, accompanied by African drummers. The location of the hotel makes this a rather commercial beach in some ways, though; washing lines display pretty batik sarongs and you'll be periodically approached by roving craft vendors. Opposite the hotel's entrance on the main road is a sunbleached sign marking the entrance to the **Grafton Caledonia Bird Sanctuary** (daylight hours; free), founded by the late owner of the surrounding estate, Eleanor Alefounder, who began feeding hungry local birds following the devastation wreaked by Hurricane Flora in 1963 (see p.278). Since then, 4pm is the regular feeding time for the flocks of mot-mot, cocorico, banana quit and practically every other feathered specimen found on the island, many of which will peck right out of your hand. There's a café as well as extensive trails through the property which make excellent, easy and scenic hiking.

Less than a kilometre beyond Grafton Beach is another, far less developed strip of sand, and a ravishing one to boot. Masked by a thick belt of bush between Grafton Road and the sea, **Back Bay** manages an uncanny remoteness despite its central location, and it's one of the few places on the island where you can discard your bathing suit without offending locals and risking prosecution; however, this solitary nature demands caution as rumours of robberies are rife. To find the beach, continue along the coast past Mount Irvine; after rounding a bend in the road, look for an expansive house on the inland side, where a dirt track leads into the foliage, forking after a few metres – either path will take you to the shore.

The beach is wide and wild, with one main curve bordered by two smaller bays and a backdrop of trees which include a **manchineel**, a nasty specimen with poisonous green fruits and sap that's a severe irritant to the skin; look out for the warning sign. At the western corner of the bay, smooth yellow sand that's seldom disturbed by a footprint surrounds magnificent craggy outcrops divided by tracts of rough water boiling against the rock; swimming is dangerous all along the beach, so stick to paddling.

Continuing northeast, the road narrows as it enters **BLACK ROCK**, a busy, friendly village with a couple of nice rum shops, a small supermarket and a large electricity substation. On the western outskirts of town is a signpost for **Fort Bennet**, a still-intact stockade first established by English mercenary Lieutenant Robert Bennet in 1680. During the plantation era, the fort was expanded by British troops, who built a red-brick oven to heat up the metal used to make cannonballs and placed two cannons to defend the bay against US warships during the American War of Independence. The THA have added a gazebo, and the view over Mount Irvine Bay and the Pigeon Point headland is spectacular, particularly at sunset.

The Tobago hustle

Though tourist harassment in Tobago is far less of a problem than in many other destinations where the industry is a major earner, aggressive and unsettling attitudes are becoming increasingly common among a small number of people who seem bent on stressing you out, either through sexual harassment at the bars and clubs or over-insistent hustling of over-priced crafts on the more touristy beaches. It can be irritating and frustrating, especially if you're not in the best of moods, but it's important not to lose perspective. Many women do come to the island with a holiday romance in mind, so you can't blame people for trying it on just because it's not on your personal agenda; most hustlers are simply struggling to make ends meet in an island where unemployment stands at 25 percent (10 percent more than the national average for T&T) and career opportunities are severely limited. As Tobagonians on the whole are hugely generous hosts, warming to visitors with genuine respect and taking pride in showing you their island, it's not a surprise that the frustration of constantly having to pander to another's needs occasionally boils over in rudeness and even aggression.

If you do feel harassed, maintain your sense of humour, say no if someone's selling something you don't want, and make your intentions clear if someone offers themselves as your ideal Tobagonian partner; local women are not expected to dance with anyone but their lovers or friends, so you needn't feel pressured to accept an invitation. Should you be unlucky enough to need to report an incident to the police, do so at Old Grange police station (☎639 8888), off the Auchenskeoch/Buccoo Road.

Turtle Beach

Beyond a grating section of potholes marking the end of Black Rock, the road swings round a blind bend before entering a straight stretch. Trees mask the lovely **Turtle Beach**, a good kilometre of picturesque coarse yellow sand flecked with the occasional swathe of volcanic grey; there are several dirt tracks from which to enter the bay. The water shelves steeply from the beach and the waves are large, making exhilarating swimming, while a river at the western end has possibilities for a fresh water dip, but it's often dammed up and stagnant in the dry season. Jealously guarding pole position in the centre of the bay (only guests are allowed to use the purpose built sun shelters), the two-storey *Turtle Beach* hotel dominates the sand, and the constant presence of well-heeled guests has generated an ideal captive market for itinerant vendors. Like Grafton next door, the sand is patrolled by craft and aloe-purveyors who offer their inflatedly-priced wares with varying degrees of insistence, and the strip in front of the hotel is one of the few places in Tobago where you might feel hustled (see box above). If you do, head for a spot further away from the hotel; however the centre of the beach is the only place where you can buy drinks and snacks; *Celia and Sam's* also put on a sumptuous nightly beach barbecue with good local dishes – you sign up in the afternoon.

Though the beach is officially called **Great Courland Bay**, it acquired its colloquial title on account of the **turtles** that still lay eggs here in the dark of night (see box, p.305). The main laying season runs between March and August, and six weeks after the eggs are laid, hatchlings make a dash for the sea; an equally moving sight. All of the hotels along this stretch organize a turtle watch during the laying and hatching seasons, but if you're not staying in the area, contact Nick Hardwicke at *Seahorse Inn* (☎639 0686), or local turtle enthusiast and guide Harris McMillan (☎639 6575).

Plymouth

A mile or so beyond Turtle Beach, Grafton Road meets a junction – straight on is the Plymouth Road, which leads scenically to Scarborough via Whim, a quiet interior village, while to the left, a narrow bridge over the Courland River signifies the outskirts of **PLYMOUTH**, Tobago's first European community, settled first by a group of roving Latvians usually referred to as Courlanders, then by the Dutch and finally by the British (see History, pp.209–213). Today, it's an attractive little town, with neat board houses and an over-quota of rum shops lining the grid-patterned streets. Most visitors head straight for the main attractions of the so-called **mystery tombstone** and **Fort James**; rightly so, as there's little else of interest. Well signposted and sitting alone on a concreted platform close to the sea, the tombstone is an enigmatic if rather depressing reminder of Tobago's history of slavery. The double grave of a child and her 23 year old mother Betty Stiven, wife of one Alex Stiven, the "mystery" is the inscription; "What was remarkable of her; she was a mother without knowing it, and a wife without letting her husband know it, except by her kind indulgences to him". "Betty" is said to have been the African maid (and lover) of Alex Stiven, a wealthy Dutch planter. No-one knows the age of the child buried with her, and the general hypothesis has two strands; that she gave birth to Stiven's "mulatto" child, and he took charge of it, raising it as his but not acknowledging Betty as the mother, hence giving her "freedom" to carry on as his lover and making her a "mother without knowing it". The other theory is that the affair between Alex and Betty was illicit and scandalous but passionate, carried out in secret to save the face of white man who couldn't be seen to be falling for a slave. When she died giving birth to his child, he was so overcome with grief that he left this cryptic message as a commemoration of their love.

If you're driving up the coast, it's wise to fill your tank at Plymouth's petrol station, as it's the only one for miles (Mon–Sat 6am–8pm, Sun 6am–noon).

Opposite the tombstone, a road leads down toward the sea; turn right and you'll see the stark concrete blocks of the **Great Courland Bay Monument**, standing testament to the "bold, enterprising and industrious" Latvians – who colonised the area and lent their name to the bay. Carrying straight on past the tombstone brings you to Fort James, the oldest stockade in Tobago. The solid, roofed coral stone structure and four cannons that remain today are a British legacy, built in 1811, and there's an excellent view of Turtle Beach from the mown lawns behind.

Arnos Vale

From the centre of Plymouth, a well-signposted but narrow road meanders through luxuriant foliage toward **Arnos Vale**, one of the few sugar estates to keep its land, and parts of the plantation have been opened up to the public, while a resort hotel straddles the beachfront section of the property. The main point of access is at the old estate **water wheel**, now slickly packaged into a tourist attraction (daily 8am–11pm; TT$10). The wheel, pump and stream train that once transported sugar around the plantation have been restored, and you view them from a wooden walkway. The modest **museum** is disappointing, displaying a small selection of Amerindian pottery and colonial artefacts – horseshoes, pipes etc – found on the estate, and there are several trails leading off into the hinterland; guides are available. It's a pretty spot, lavish with flowering plants and lush foliage and nice for a relaxing drink after you've toured the estate. Past Arnos Vale, the road worsens into a shingle-littered dirt track passing the tiny but attractive villages of Golden Lane and Les Coteaux; the latter is known as a centre for obeah, and rumours of witchery and potions abound – the community hosts spooky story sessions during the Heritage Festival celebrations. Though road improvements may soon link Arnos Vale with the rest of the leeward coast, you'll have to go via the Northside Road from Scarborough until they're completed (see p.273).

Eating and drinking

Most of the **restaurants** built along Shirvan/Grafton Road are dedicated to the tourist palate, and many are quite flashy with prices to match, but you can get inexpensive local lunches from hole-in-the-wall eateries in Black Rock and Plymouth. All of the restaurants listed below are good for a **drink**, but the best place to sink a few beers in the area is the beautifully located *Ocean Edge* rum shop, perched on a cliff top overlooking Stone Haven Bay; a great place to while away the sunset hours. There are plenty of friendly, low-key rum shops in Buccoo, Black Rock and Plymouth; a good bet is *Michael's* in Black Rock.

Arnos Vale Waterwheel, Franklyn Rd, Arnos Vale Estate, ☎639 2881. Set in the grounds of the water wheel park, this classy, romantic and expensive restaurant has an eclectic and delicious menu; highlights are snapper, prawns, squid and mussels in a lemon grass and curry sauce or the chicken salad starter with peppers, gherkins, sultanas, almonds and basil in a balsamic vinegar dressing. There's a themed buffet each Wednesday and Friday with cultural shows in the theatre below.

Baynes Seafood House, Buccoo Bay. Good for medium-priced local cooking, especially pre-Sunday School, when there's a buffet and a performance from the Les Coteaux dancers. Grilled, poached or broiled fish, shrimp and lobster served in curry, coconut or Creole-style sauce are all adequate; stuffed snapper in a lemon butter sauce is recommended.

Black Rock Cafe, Black Rock, ☎639 7625. Friendly, popular open-air restaurant on the town's outskirts serving medium-priced local and continental breakfasts, soups, salads and fish dishes for lunch and daily dinner specials; steak, chicken and fish.

La Tartaruga, Buccoo Bay, ☎639 0940. Tobago's best – and most expensive – Italian restaurant, an open-air patio near the sea owned and run by a mercurial Italian émigré. For a set price of TT$165, you get a minimum five courses of authentic Italian fare; pesto a la Genovese, bruschetta, calamari and homemade pasta with a huge range of sauces. Puddings include a delicious creme caramel. Closed Sun and Mon.

Papillon, *Old Grange Inn*, Buccoo, ☎639 0275. Classy – and expensive – dining in a leafy patio or an air-conditioned room. Huge menu adding pastelles, conch in coconut milk, lamb kebabs and shark in rum and lime to the usual fish and chicken selections. Deeply satisfying pone with ice cream for dessert.

Patino's, Shirvan Rd. A contrary combination of Trinidadian and Canadian owners serving Polynesian-style food which works extremely well. The menu – ginger beef with Chinese mushrooms, hot and sour shrimp, sizzling Thai platter or lobster Polynesian – is well executed and supremely fresh, the garden patio setting is pleasant, and daily specials are good value.

The Emerald, Pleasant Prospect, ☎639 8272. Just off the road between Mount Irvine and Stone Haven bays, this is a breezy upstairs setting, good for moderately priced seafood, steaks and Creole-style oven-baked chicken.

Seahorse Inn, Stone Haven Bay Rd, ☎639 0686. Imaginative menu based around international staples; sandwiches, fish, shrimp and a good tuna pasta salad for lunch, and more sophisticated offerings for dinner: stuffed peppers, chef's paté, lobster bisque or fish chowder to start and excellent seafood, steaks, pork chops and chicken for the main. The chocolate gateau is delicious.

Shirvan Watermill, Shirvan Rd, ☎639 0000. Upmarket restaurant with tables beautifully set under the cut stone roof of an abandoned water mill. The "international" fare (steak, lobster etc) is beautifully cooked and the prices match the decor; cocktails are served at 5pm, dinner from 6pm.

Teaside, Battery St, Buccoo Point, ☎639 8437. Unpretentious, friendly and tucked away behind Buccoo Bay; main dish is pizza, good and reasonably priced with seven standard toppings. Wholewheat bases are available, as are natural juices –fig (banana) is recommended. Toasted sandwiches and homemade cookies are good too; they'll deliver to hotels and guesthouses in the west.

The Waterfront, *Mount Irvine Bay Beach Complex*, ☎639 9613. Home of award winning bake and shark, this is also good for local food in the evening; stew chicken or fish, curry goat, pepper shrimp, crab and dumplin' and roti. they also put on the occasional beach barbecue.

Two Seasons, Pleasant Prospect, ☎639 9461. Next door to *The Emerald*, the freshly-made pizza comes with white or wholewheat base and plenty of toppings. Brown rice and veg is a good option for non meat-eaters, and the stewed chicken in coconut milk or fish and fries are pretty tasty too.

Scarborough

Tobago's raucous, hot and dusty capital, precipitous **SCARBOROUGH** (population 18,000) is an immensely appealing place. Poking through the treetops, houses, roads and the canary-yellow facade of a furniture

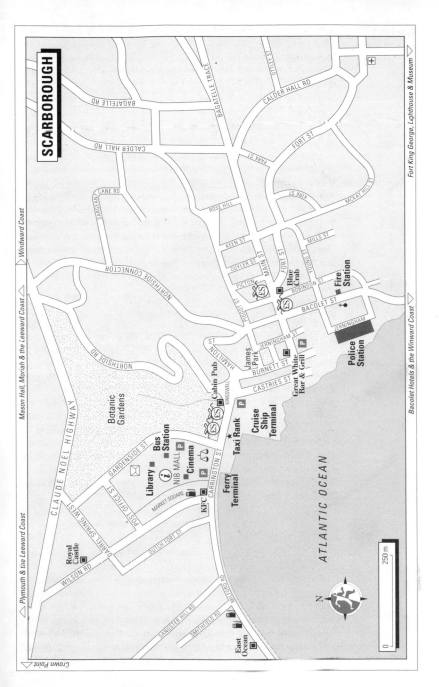

SCARBOROUGH

Windward Coast

Mason Hall, Moriah & the Leeward Coast

Plymouth & the Leeward Coast

Crown Point

Fort King George, Lighthouse & Museum

Bacolet Hotels & the Winward Coast

BAGATELLE RD
CALDER HALL RD
BAGATELLE TRACE
OTTLEY ST
CALDER HALL RD
FORT ST
PARK ST
CANE RD
SARGEANT
ROSE HILL
KIRK ST
MCKAY HILL ST
KEEN ST
MILLS ST
NORTHSIDE CONNECTOR
CUYLER ST
MAIN ST
FORT ST
YOUNG ST
PICTON
PIGOT ST
ROBINSON ST
Blue Crab
Fire Station
NORTHSIDE RD
BACOLET ST
JERNINGHAM
ST
James Park
JERNINGHAM ST
Police Station
CLAUDE NOEL HIGHWAY
HAMILTON
BURNETT ST
Great White Bar & Grill
Cabin Pub
CASTRIES ST
KINGSWELL
Botanic Gardens
Cruise Ship Terminal
Bus Station
GARDENSIDE ST
Library
NIB MALL
Cinema
Taxi Rank
ATLANTIC OCEAN
MARKET SQUARE
CARRINGTON ST
POST OFFICE ST
KFC
Ferry Terminal
DARREL SPRING WEST
DUTCH FORT ST
Royal Castle
WILSON RD
SANGSTER HILL RD
SMITHFIELD RD
MILFORD RD
East Ocean

N

250 m
0

Scarborough chain spill higgledy-piggledy down the hillside while the Atlantic provides a magnificent backdrop for the silhouettes of the **lighthouse** and **Fort King George**, perched at the top of the hill. The island's administrative centre and its main **port**, Scarborough is a flourishing town, brimming with a brisk vibrancy. Devoid of touristic pretensions, the town throbs with activity; street corners swarm with liming locals, stalls draped with clothes are perused by the shoppers, while the **market**, with its artistically arranged displays of intensely-coloured fruit and veg and constant sales banter of the stallholders, is irresistible.

Though it's the island's largest conglomeration of concrete, Scarborough is pretty tiny; the docking of the **ferry** from Trinidad is spectacle enough to draw crowds of onlookers – prospective passengers scurry by clutching parcels, cars and lorries inch along as they wait to board, bars spill over onto the pavement and food vendors fill the air with barbecue smoke. Away from the commercial clamour, the peaceful **botanical gardens** or the cool breezes and views from the port offer respite from the traffic and steep climbs that can make Scarborough a bit of an ordeal; visiting on an overcast day makes sightseeing more comfortable.

Some history

The **Dutch** were the first Europeans to settle in what became one of Tobago's most hotly contested pieces of land. They navigated the treacherous harbour rocks in 1654, constructed a fort and a few buildings, and named it **Lampsinsburgh**. Around the same time, a group of Courlanders (Latvians) were building up their stronghold on the opposite coast at Plymouth (see pp.209–213). In 1658, the Dutch captured it – an act that was to lead to the destruction of their own settlement a few years later when, in 1666, a fleet of English ships came to the aid of the Latvians and blew Lampsinsburgh to smithereens.

The English officially won the island in 1672, but didn't maintain a presence, allowing the Dutch to return and build Lampsinsburgh into a more substantial settlement, with houses, a single street and a church as well as warehouses and wharves at the harbour and a new fort armed with cannons. However, during the French assault of 1677, the newly improved fortifications proved to be the undoing of the Dutch; a French cannonball hit the ammunition dump, and the resulting fireball completely destroyed the structure and killed the 250 occupants. Though it's still commemorated in the current name Dutch Fort Road, there's nothing left of the settlement nowadays.

The British bestowed the name **Scarborough** when they regained control of Tobago in 1762, establishing the House of Assembly and constructing Fort King George. After a twenty-year lull, the struggle began anew; following a prolonged and bloody effort, during which they constructed the "French Fort" in nearby Calder Hall (see p.274), the **French** took control in 1781. Scarborough was renamed Port Louis, while Fort King George – with finishing touches added by

French soldiers – became **Fort Castries**. The town ricocheted between the British and French until Tobago was finally ceded to the British in 1814. Though Scarborough was a thriving commercial centre during the plantation era, it was the first place to suffer when the sugar industry collapsed in the 1870s; the House of Assembly was disbanded, and not reconvened until 1980.

Arrival, getting around and information

Most people enter Scarborough by **road** along the Wilson Road turn-off from Claude Noel Highway, following the one-way system toward the wharves bordering Carrington Street, the docking point for **ferries** to and from Trinidad, which moor up at the central terminal (for departures and prices, see Listings, p.279). There are two **taxi** stands on Carrington Street, a one-minute walk from the terminal (it should cost around TT\$45 to Crown Point), while the **bus station** is located on Greenside Street behind the NIB Mall, walkable in five minutes. Buses to all corners of the island run daily between 5am and 8pm; for details see p.216. Remember to pre-purchase your tickets before boarding. As Scarborough is so small, there are no bus services within the town, and as you can easily see all the sights by foot, a vehicle is unnecessary. For **information**, head to the offices of the Tobago House of Assembly, Division of Tourism on the third floor of NIB Mall (office hours; ☎639 2125 or 4636).

Accommodation

Though Scarborough and the Bacolet suburbs were popular in the 1960s and 70s during the early years of Tobagonian tourism, the area has now been overtaken by Lowlands. Some excellent options remain, though, particularly in suburban Bacolet. Prices are lower, and public transport is good. Staying in a host home or bed and breakfast (see Basics. pp.21–22) can be great if you're on a budget or fancy a little more intimacy with local lifestyles than a hotel can provide. The tourist board recommends a number of **host homes** in their standard accommodation listings booklet (available from offices worldwide) – most rent at around US\$20–35 per person, but you can often get a room for less than this, particularly if you're visiting in the off-season. The best way to find a good **B&B** is through Ms Miriam Edwards of the Tobago Bed and Breakfast Association (☎639 3926; c/o *Federal Villa*, 1–3 Crooks River, Scarborough).

Bacolet Bay Apartments, Bacolet St, ☎ & fax 639 2955, email *cross@ Cariblink.ne*t. Past its heyday but very friendly, great value and just a step away from Bacolet beach. Studios have kitchen, TV, a-c and a patio, suites are much larger with a living room; all rooms are a bit down-at-heel but clean and serviceable, and there's a pool on site. ④

Cyrus, c/o Mr Cyrus, St Cecilia Rd, Concordia, ☎ and fax 639 5172. Out of town in the Concordia heights, this expansive private home is built entirely from Guyanese greenheart wood. The owner's paintings cover the walls, and

Free car parking is available at the wharf lot on the corner of Carrington and Castries streets, in the NIB Mall car park off Greenside Street (strictly speaking for shoppers only), the lot behind the cinema and KFC, or the lot opposite the Great White bar on Main Street.

the gorgeous gardens are rich with bird life, easily viewed from the verandah. Fan-cooled rooms are spacious and spotless with private bath and shower; meals are available, excellent value. ③

Della Mira, 36 Bacolet St, ☎639 2531, fax 639 4018. Set in a pretty colonial-style house overlooking the sea with a pool, bar and restaurant on site, the basic rooms with bathroom and fan have seen better days, but the rates are reasonable. ④

Federal Villa, 1–3 Crooks River, Scarborough, ☎639 3926. Home of the B&B Association, rooms are set in a private house in the Scarborough suburbs. All are basic with fan and shared bathroom; nice friendly atmosphere. ②

Hope Cottage, Calder Hall Rd, ☎639 2179. Set in a 100-year-old colonial building just before the hospital, this is one of the oldest guesthouses in Tobago and a great bargain. Rooms are plain with private bathroom and a kitchenette, and there's a self-contained 3-bedroom cottage in the two-acre grounds. ②

Montpelier Cottage, Montpelier, Scarborough, c/o Mark and Zena Puddy, PO Box 14, Scarborough; ☎639 4931. Unique and utterly fabulous, as long you don't mind sharing a room with the occasional chicken, lizard or snake. This airy room in a private home built into jungle-like hillside has lattice windows, creative decor and a private bathroom. Rates include excellent home-cooked breakfast and huge evening meal. ④

Old Donkey Cart, 73 Bacolet St, ☎639 3551, fax 639 6124. Spacious, quirky garden or superior rooms with fridge, TV, phone, fans, unusual decor and great views of Bacolet Bay; the airy, open-plan penthouse suite is fabulous. Unusual overflow pool and restaurant on site; rates include breakfast and airport transfers. ⑦

Sandy's, cor. Fort and Main streets, ☎639 2737. Run by the friendly and hospitable owners of the *Blue Crab* restaurant, this homely place has two pretty and spotless rooms with fan and private bathroom. ④

Seaview Guesthouse, Bacolet St, ☎639 5613. Overlooking the sea 50 metres down the road from the *Old Donkey Cart*, this offers superb value and a friendly atmosphere. Brand new and spankingly clean apartments with full kitchen, fan, hot water and beautiful views; all share a communal liming patio. Meals are available. ③

Stella B Apartments, 79 Bacolet St, ☎639 5603. Two stylish, cool, self contained rooms in a friendly private home with fans, kitchen and all mod cons; Bacolet Beach is a short walk away. ④

Lower Scarborough: the mall and the market

Most vehicles enter town from the highway along car-choked Wilson Road, following the one-way system along Greenside Street, which takes you past the bus station and the back of **NIB Mall** to the right, and the botanical gardens to the left. The largest shopping centre in Scarborough, **NIB Mall** houses Christian bookshops, fast-food outlets and pharmacies, seating for shoppers as well as the **library**, a cool and pleasant place to pore over the collection of Caribbean-oriented titles. Also in this road-surrounded island is a car park that doubles as a venue for Carnival celebrations and sound system dances as well as the main **post office** (Mon–Sat 8am–4pm) and the food **market**. Main trading days are Friday and Saturday, but throughout the week, vendors vocally hawk every tropical fruit and vegetable you could imagine. The indoor meat section is an odoriferous melange of goat, beef, lamb, mutton and of course chicken, while fish on ice gleam at the back of the market, where stallholders attract custom by blowing on a **conch shell**. Trading reaches a peak on Friday, when the heavily-scented fruits and earth-encrusted ground provisions jostle for space with leather sandals, incense, mounds of soap powder, clothing and dry goods while carts selling snow cones, doubles and boiled corn do a roaring trade. It's a friendly and absorbing scene, great for bargains and interaction with Tobagonians away from the resorts. If you're after souvenirs, check out the **vendors mall**, a ramshackle collection of tarpaulin-covered stalls just south of the NIB Mall, where you'll find knitted Rasta hats, sandals, wood carvings and carved calabashes.

The Botanical Gardens
Opposite the bus station on Greenside Street is the back entrance to the **Botanical Gardens** (daily, daylight hours; free), a soothing oasis after the heat-retaining concrete and constant traffic fumes. Covering eighteen acres of ex-sugar estate, part of the Dal Fair and Rockly Vale plantations, the land was requisitioned by the British in the late nineteenth century with the intention of creating a public botanical garden, and the broad sweeps of lawn interspersed with planted beds and shade trees could pass for an English park were it not for the garish crimson of towering African tulips or flamboyant trees or the yellow and pink cascades of the poui trees, all bearing labels for easy identification. Near the botanical station is an **orchid house** displaying most of T&T's indigenous orchids as well as a few imported species, and below is a tiny fish pond graced by a Luise Kimme **sculpture**. It's an enchanting spot, often deserted save for the odd office worker taking lunch under a shade tree. At its highest point a covered gazebo affords a nice view over town and the sea. There are no guided tours as such, but the team of gardeners are usually available on site to answer questions.

You can also enter the Botanical Gardens from the highway – pull in at the signpost cunningly marked "Botanical Gardens Layby".

Upper Scarborough: the wharf to James Park
Though some older buildings remain in Scarborough's precipitous heights, most of the waterfront has been overtaken by a glut of concrete. Souped up in 1990 by the addition of a deep-water cruise ship pier, the harbour is soon to be given another new lease of life when the construction of a **promenade** along Milford Road reaches its long-awaited completion, giving the thronging crowds around *KFC* and Market Square somewhere to hang out. Proceeding east from *KFC* along the bank and bar-lined Carrington Street, you reach a junction known as **King's Well**, originally the site of the town's main watercourse but now a rum shop and restaurant of the same name; a sharp left takes you out of town along the Northside Road/Northside

Connector, while the sharp right is Castries Street and ultimately Main Street. Between the two, steeply inclining **Burnett Street** is one of Scarborough's best for knick-knack **shopping**, its tarmac decorated by a local shopkeeper with white-painted palm trees and hibiscus flowers. As the road reaches a plateau, you enter **James Park**, once the town's main marketplace but now a diminutive scrap of grass decorated with a bronze of A.P.T James, a former Minister of Tobago Affairs.

The park is bordered to the north by the Georgian facade of the old **courthouse**, which has housed the administrative offices of the Tobago House of Assembly since the judiciary were shifted to their current Bacolet Street base in the late 1980s. Built between 1816 and 1825, the cut-stone structure – as a tourist board plaque outside proudly proclaims – was considered one of the finest examples of Georgian architecture in the Caribbean on completion. Subsequent alterations have, unfortunately, smothered the brickwork with white paint and removed the pillars, leaving it a shadow of its former glory. A small monument outside, dating from the reign of King Edward VII, bears the inscription "One flag, one king, one empire". On the opposite side of the park to the Burnett Street edge, **Jerningham Street** houses a paved mini-park with benches, a fountain and a relief map of Tobago which gives a good perspective of the topography of the island.

Uphill to the Fort
Carrying straight on past James Park along Burnett Street brings you directly on to the sheering heights of bustling shop-and-office-lined **Main Street**. One hundred yards or so uphill are traffic lights marking the right turn on to **Bacolet Street**, the route to the fire station, the main police station (and only jail) as well as **Gun Bridge**. In commemoration of the town's historical discord, its stone walls are embellished with four cannons taken from Fort George, while musket barrels form the guard rails. A little further along is **St Andrew's Anglican Church**, originally built in 1819 but razed by Hurricane Flora in 1963 and reconstructed a year later. Further down Bacolet Street, the buildings thin out as you enter the quiet and attractive Bacolet suburbs (see p.256).

Fort King George
If you drive yourself to the fort, you can almost always find a parking space in the lot adjacent to the museum and main fort.

Back on Main Street and a few metres higher, well-signposted **Fort Street** forks off to the right, twisting its way up to the fort past the imposing Methodist Church and some attractive but dishevelled colonial architecture. Near to the top of the hill, a vine-wreathed red-brick building to the right is all that remains of an old **prison**, once part of the fort complex above; time and the elements have opened its tiny, dingy cells to shafts of sunlight. Round the next bend is Scarborough **hospital** and the start of the **Fort King George** complex. The first building on the left is the dome-shaped cover of an old **well**, built in

1926 to service the hospital. Opposite is the red brick **Fine Arts Centre** (Mon–Fri 9am–5pm, Sat & Sun 2–5pm; free), probably built as barracks or a military hospital and now extensively refurbished and graced with a new roof. The collection of paintings and sculpture by local and international artists changes every quarter.

A grassy path next to the Fine Arts Centre leads below the main fort to a landscaped **park**, lush with poui trees and colourful planted beds. Benches are perfectly placed for soaking up marvellous views back to lower Scarborough and the Orange Hill district. In the shade of a massive buttressed silk cotton tree is the decrepit **powder magazine**, its inner walls blackened by fires. The main fortification above is the largest in Tobago, built by the British and initially comprised of some thirty buildings but reduced to around ten by an 1847 hurricane. The fort was occupied by French troops between 1781 and 1793, who built the solid stone perimeter walls. Inspired by the French Revolution, the soldiers **mutinied** in 1790, imprisoning their officers and razing the town below.

Today, this peaceful spot 140 metres above sea level is favoured for its constant sea breezes and spectacular views of Bacolet Bay, Minister Point and the rugged interior to the west and Rockly Bay and the north coast of Trinidad to the east. By night it's a suitably deserted destination for a bit of in-car canoodling. Despite the profusion of cannons that still point out to sea, the tranquil atmosphere of the place makes it hard to imagine its military history. Behind the old officers' mess is the **lighthouse**, a squat structure transferred from Galera Point in Trinidad in 1958; the Fresnel lens beams 50 kilometres out to sea and sweeps spectacularly over the Scarborough suburbs.

Tobago Museum

The rest of the fort's buildings are ranged around the tidy lawns of Barrack Square, in the centre of which stand the long-limbed figures of Luise Kimme's "Tobago Jig". The buildings house the Culture Division of the Tobago House of Assembly, as well as the unmissable **Tobago Museum** (Mon–Fri 9am–5pm; adults TT$5, 13–15 year olds TT$2, children TT$1). Collated by the Tobago Trust, the small but fascinating collection of idiosyncratically labelled artefacts includes Amerindian plates, cooking wares, tools and talismans (one shaped like a penis, presumably for fertility) dating back to 2500 BC as well as pre-Columbian nostril bowls, used to inhale the intoxicating tobacco water favoured by the Indians. One unnerving exhibit unearthed during construction work at Mount Irvine beach in the 1970s is part of the skeleton of a young Indian; teeth, skull and ribcage are all clearly visible. Satirical colonial prints depicting the exploits of "Johnny Newcome in the West Indies" are well worth a look, as are the shells, fish fossils and military paraphernalia. Upstairs, there's a gallery of ancient maps, imported African drums, sculptures and some fascinating logs of the colonial era including notes on the sale of plantation slaves.

You can buy refreshments at a kiosk opposite the hospital, but as it's often closed, it's a good idea to bring your own, particularly if you're walking up.

Bacolet

As Bacolet Street eases out of town along the coast past Sandy Hall and Fairfield Complex, the main administrative base of the Tobago House of Assembly as well as the Tobago Hall of Justice court and the island's main cemetery, the roadside homes become noticeably upmarket. Though the area suffered a lull when Bacolet Street was replaced by Claude Noel Highway as the main route to the windward coast – Bacolet Street is also known as Old Windward Road – this is still a suburb of choice for Tobago's elite; the grand structures built along Bacolet Point stand testament to the wealth of their owners. The area enjoyed a heady prestige during the late 1960s and early 70s, when the **Beatles** frolicked on Bacolet Bay beach and the area boasted a couple of flashy hotels, the *Bacolet* and *Blue Horizon*. When they tried to cordon off the sand as the exclusive preserve of their foreign guests, Dr Eric Williams – the premier who once declared that he had no intention of ruling "a nation of waiters and bellhops" – intervened to keep the beaches public. The decision effectively sealed the fate of both properties; neither has recovered as yet, and you can still see what's left of *Blue Horizon* at the roadside.

Though you can stop off at the Cotton House Studio to view expensive batik work, the best reason to linger here is the deserted charm of crescent-shaped **Bacolet Bay Beach**, brought to the silver screen during the filming of Walt Disney's *Swiss Family Robinson*. It's a lovely spot, the black sand lapped by the vigorous green Atlantic (be aware of the occasional dangerous undercurrents) and shaded by palms and Indian almond trees; rough seas in winter also make it popular with surfers. Concrete steps down the cliff side lead to the sand from the road, and apart from the odd fisherman or Tobagonian family taking a salty bathe, you'll usually have it to yourself. Past the beach, the houses thin out as the road swings left to meet with the highway and the traffic on its way along the windward coast (see p.258–273).

The main Scarborough PO is the best place to post mail, being far quicker than the small regional postal agencies.

Practicalities

For **currency exchange**, you'll find the Bank of Commerce and Scotiabank on Carrington Street opposite the wharf, Royal and Republic banks on Main Street and First Citizens Bank on Lower Milford Road, of which Royal is the most efficient. All are subject to local opening hours (see Basics, p.12). There are several late-opening **petrol stations** around town – see Listings (p.280) for details. Scarborough is the departure point for **route taxis** serving the whole of the island, though finding where to catch your ride can be confusing. For Crown Point (TT$4–6) head to the NIB Mall car park; for Carnbee, Mount Pleasant, Buccoo and Plymouth (TT$4), go to the phone booth opposite *KFC* on Carrington Street. Taxis running the Northside Road to Castara (TT$6) and Parlatuvier (TT$10) leave from Carrington Street opposite the port, while cars going to L'Anse

For bus services to Scoarborough, see p.216

Fourmi (TT$12) leave from the NIB Mall car park on Greenside Street. **Maxis** to Charlotteville leave two or three times a day from outside the Royal Bank on Main Street (TT$10).

Eating and drinking

Scarborough is the best place in Tobago to sample **local food**. There are plenty of diners around town serving solid lunches for working men and women. *Glendale's Local Cuisine* on Glen Road, just outside town on the other side of the highway, is particularly good for lunches, but the food stalls in the market's indoor section are the best option for an inexpensive and memorable meal; try Harriet at stall five. Her renowned breakfasts – fried or roast bake, smoked herring, saltfish or fried fish – are ready to eat from 6am and are usually finished by 10am. Lunch is different every day; chicken, veg and ground provisions, lamb or goat with dumplings or pelau. Saturdays mean soup, and on Sunday it's traditional chicken, macaroni pie and callaloo. Go before 1.30pm or it's all eaten up.

The favourite **roti** outlet in town is at the coastal end of Dutch Fort Road in the small plaza, and you can get vegetable pies, pastries and pizza from *MJ's* at the corner of Bacolet and Main streets, but many still opt for the foreign allure of *KFC* on Wilson and Carrington streets or stick with what they know best at *Royal Castle* on Wilson Road – the spicy fried chicken, fish or veggie burgers and fries are available till 1am Thurs–Sat. **Vegetarians** should head for *E&F Health Foods* or *Mr D's* in NIB Mall; both serve weekday lunch specials; roti or buss up shut and veg. The best **Chinese** food in Tobago is cooked at *East Ocean*, a little way down Milford Road overlooking the sea (☎639 4535); the inexpensive menu has all the familiar dishes. You can order take-away or eat in the air-conditioned restaurant section, and they deliver large orders.

For a **sit-down meal**, try the enduringly popular *Blue Crab* (☎639 2737), a cool, open-air weekday lunch spot on the corner of Robinson and Main streets (dinner is by reservation only). The excellent Creole food is popular with an officey crowd; highlights are green fig salad, any style of fish and unsweetened natural juices. Stylish *Rouselle's Dining and Liming Spot* (☎639 4738) just out of town on the Old Windward Road in Bacolet, is great for dinner; the hardwood decor, breezy verandah setting and relaxed sophistication are reminiscent of a Port of Spain hang-out. Food is chic and tasty; lobster in lemon, white wine and garlic sauce, fish or chicken in Creole sauce or charcoal flamed pork chops with garlic and mustard; you'll usually need to make a reservation for dinner. Also in Bacolet, the Italian restaurant at the *Old Donkey Cart* hotel (73 Bacolet St; ☎639 3551) have good but expensive pasta as well as local and US-style breakfast and light lunches. Though the *Great White* on Main Street is best known as a liming spot, they serve a good lunch special – pelau, chicken, curry goat etc, eaten in the air-conditioned dining

Scarborough room next to the popular bar area, which has pool tables, satellite TV and loud music. Another good **drinking** spot is the eternally cheerful *Cabin Pub* on Carrington Street, where you can get fresh natural juices alongside the rum, Carib and continual banter. There are plenty more **rum bars** along Carrington Street that are well worth checking out; try the *King's Well Inn* at the junction with Crook's River.

Entertainment and nightlife
Until recently, Tobagonians had to make do with hard chairs, a poor quality screen and billows of cigarette smoke each time they went to the movies, but following a recent refurbishment the new *Gate* **cinema** (☎639 2066) is luxurious if less atmospheric, a state which the owners are eager to maintain by confiscating cigarettes and chewing gum at the door (customers can retrieve them after the show). Programmes are usually double bills (daily; midday, 4pm and 9pm with a late weekend show at 11pm; TT$10), and the box office closes one hour into the programme. Scarborough also boasts Tobago's only **casino**, the *Crystal Palace* (Tues–Sun; 6pm–2am), by the sea on the corner of Milford and Mount Marie roads. The blackjack and poker tables are usually busy, but most locals opt for a bout of easy to learn "all fours".

Dancing is best at the weekend; *Great White* on Main Street have a busy **club night** every Friday with reggae and soca spun for a predominantly local crowd by the talented DJ Neil (small cover charge), while there's sometimes a sound system jam in Market Square on Friday and Saturday; late night, plenty of reggae and best experienced in the company of locals. Another excellent Friday option is the dance at *Fairy Queen Bar* in John Dial, a five-minute drive east of town along the highway. Cars line the road and the good-natured drinking and dancing spills out on to the tarmac.

The windward coast

Rugged and continually breathtaking, Tobago's southern shoreline is usually referred to as the **windward coast**. Narrow and peppered with blind corners and potholes, the Windward Road spans its length and sticks close to the sea, providing fantastic views of choppy Atlantic waters and tiny spray-shrouded islands. The parade of languid coastal villages are a complete contrast to the developed west; groups of limers congregate outside rum bars, ladies in curlers sit chatting on the tarmac and football games on salt-seasoned grassy pitches are the height of an afternoon's activity.

Though rip tides and strong undercurrents make some of the most attractive-looking beaches unsafe for swimming, there are plenty of sheltered bays to take a dip in the cool Atlantic. Some – such as **Kings Bay** – have showers and changing rooms, but at most, you'll share the sand only with fishermen. Tour buses make regular rounds, stopping off at stock attractions like period plantation home **Richmond Great**

House, **Argyll Waterfall** or the famous *Jemma's* restaurant, perched among the branches of an almond tree, but most of the windward traffic is heading for the tiny village of **Speyside** and its smattering of guesthouses and small hotels. Nature is the main attraction here; Speyside's **reefs** rank among Tobago's best, while the **Little Tobago** island bird sanctuary has long been a magnet for serious ornithologists and amateur bird-watchers alike. Fifteen minutes drive from Speyside and directly opposite on the Caribbean coast, picturesque **Charlotteville** with its attractive hillside houses and perfect twin beaches is the last point of call on the windward route – the tarmac ends here, replaced by a treacherous and often impassable stretch of coastal track which divides the town from the rest of the leeward coast. Away from the firmly beaten track, there's also plenty to see. You can **hike** to many of the infrequently visited waterfalls scattered throughout the hilly southern interior, passing the crumbling remains of water wheels and sugar boilers along the way, while the wetlands and rivers surrounding the central **Hillsborough Dam** are great for bird and reptile watching; Tobagonian cayman frequent the waters.

Mount St George and around

East of Scarborough, the first stretch of highway ends abruptly a couple of kilometres past the town; the last fast and straight section of road sweeps past glorious **Hillsborough Bay** – sometimes called Hope by locals. Though the long stretch of windswept sand looks inviting, stick to paddling – the rip tides are dangerous. Past the beach and over a narrow bridge, the road swings round a sharp corner and into tiny **MOUNT ST GEORGE**. Though the flowered gardens of roadside houses are attractive, there's no discernible sign that this was once **Georgetown**, the island's first British **capital**, named in honour of King George III. The British began to develop Georgetown after they captured the island in 1762, building houses and a now-destroyed base for the House of Assembly, which held its inaugural meeting here in April 1768. British occupation was short-lived, however; by 1769, they shifted the capital to Scarborough. There's still one tenuous connection to sovereignty in the town, though; set at the top of a breezy hillock overlooking the village below is the official residence of the prime minister, a seldom-used, whitewashed structure that's closed to the public. A little further into the interior is Mount St George Youth Camp, where budding bad boys are forcibly sent to learn a trade.

If you're in the mood to linger, stop at the genial *Sparrow's Rest* right on the roadside for inexpensive and tasty lunchtime roti or a cool beer. You can also **stay** at *Vicky's Guesthouse* (☎660 2087 or 2089; ②), an expansive building west of the village that's often used for local weddings. The basic but clean rooms are of varying standard; you choose between a-c or fan, shared or private bathroom; some have a kitchen, but meals are available.

Granby Point and around

Past the main body of Mount St George, the road is littered with the small white stones that fall from trucks travelling from the Studley Park Quarry, a busy commercial enterprise that's steadily eating into the surrounding hillsides. A fanfare of brightly painted wooden walls and blooming flowers just outside the next village of **STUD-LEY PARK**, the *First Historical Café* makes an interesting stop even if you don't need refreshment. The pet project of charming retiree Kenneth Washington, the café is a shrine to the history of the island. Every inch of wall space is covered with handwritten accounts of Tobago's turbulent past alongside local anecdotes: "Tobago's first shipment of sugar left the island from Studley Park aboard a ship named Dolly". Aside from soaking up the written word, this is a comfortable place to sit and watch pelicans taking rich pickings from the shoals of small fish which inhabit the bay; seine nets are sometimes pulled in at the small **beach** below, which you can reach from the bar.

Beyond the café, turn right along the track signposted for the *Dry Dock Pub* and you come to an open lot beside the sea with a small children's **playground**. Head up the flight of concrete steps and through some rather fly-infested bush and you've arrived at **Fort Granby**, built by the British to protect Georgetown and briefly occupied by the French between 1781 and 1787. Nothing remains of the original fortification; the cannons have long gone, replaced by pretty gazebos, mown lawns and picnic tables. The views of the sea and nearby **Smith's Island** are fantastic, and there is excellent swimming to be had on either of the **beaches** which flank the point. Barbados Bay to the left is the more populated; the fisherman's shacks on the sand make it a friendly spot to hang out, while the more deserted **Pinfold Bay** on the other side is a better bet if you fancy a spot of sunbathing; neither has any facilities, however.

Practicalities

If you're in search of a **meal**, the *First Historical Café* is a good, if often painfully slow, choice; they serve egg and bacon breakfasts from 9am, inexpensive salads, burgers and sandwiches for lunch, and put on an open-air cook-out a couple of nights a week. The roti shop around the next bend is also excellent. For a bout of serious **drinking** or a lime with the fishermen, head for the *Dry Dock Pub* next to Fort Granby; tiny but with a great sea view and the chance to sink a Carib inside the converted hull of an old fishing boat. Accommodation is available at the expansive *Bougainvillaea Hotel* (☎660 2075, fax 660 2133, email *hylton@trinidad.net*; ⑤), a pretty but quiet property on an elevated bluff overlooking the sea. Rooms vary greatly from slightly dingy to tackily luxurious; all have fan or a-c and private bathroom but are overpriced; you should be able to get a discount if things are quiet. There's a pool and restaurant on site.

Inland to Hillsborough Dam

The inland roads from Mount St George or Studley Park are routes to the bird-watchers paradise of **Hillsborough Dam**, a forty-five minute drive from the coast depending upon the condition of the often muddy and rutted Castara Road, which doesn't actually go to Castara, tailing off into an undriveable and often impassable dirt track miles from the coast. A man-made reservoir built to hold half of Tobago's drinking water, you are officially supposed to get a pass from the local water authority WASA (☎ 639 8093) in order to enter Hillsborough, but hardly anyone bothers, clearing entrance with the security personnel on the gates instead. Though the concrete banks are pretty unattractive, they're overhung by the thick forest which provides an ideal habitat for the herons and other waterfowl which frequent the area. A more arresting sight are the cayman which heave themselves on to the banks to bask in the sun; obviously, this is not a great place to swim. There's usually somebody around to take you out onto the water aboard the dam's small rowing boat, a relaxing way to get close to the bird life. There are good possibilities for **river hikes** along the gentle streams which feed the dam, though it's best to go with a local guide as you can easily lose your way. Beyond Hillsborough, the road swings west, passing small-scale farms and homes. From Mason Hall, you can head north for the leeward coast (see p.273–279), or west for Scarborough and Lowlands.

Visiting the dam with expert ornithologist Harris McMillan (☎ 639 6575) is the best way to see the place; full day outings including lunch start at US$45.

Goodwood to Pembroke

As the Windward Road swings into the tiny village of **GOODWOOD**, with its appealing gingerbread houses, primary school and neat playing field, the coastal views begin in earnest; beginning with a spectacular panorama of the unravelling coast and distant **Richmond Island**. There's a track down to the beach from the centre of Goodwood; the greyish sand and ever-present palm trees are nothing to shout about, but it's a pleasant place for a swim, and popular with locals. Around the next bend in **GOLDSBOROUGH** is the signposted left turn to **Rainbow Falls**, a series of privately managed cascades along the Goldsborough River.

As the houses of Goodwood recede, the road climbs into yet another Lilliputian village, **PEMBROKE**, a serene fishing community spreading down to the sea from the road. It's a friendly place with a smattering of rum bars and a pretty clapboard Anglican church, St Mary's, set on cliffs overlooking the Atlantic. As the road dips down again, you can turn right to the **beach**, mostly dedicated to fishing as the fleet of pirogues and spread-out nets affirm, but nice enough for a swim. Pembroke is the venue for the annual **Salaka Feast** celebrations, now an important part of the July/August Heritage Festival. A kind of African thanksgiving to ancestors, the feast commemorates the efforts of the first slaves brought to the area, and honours the spirits through dancing, singing, storytelling, drumming and offerings of fruit and other foods, followed by plenty of eating and drinking. It's a lovely place to absorb unadorned Tobagonian life, and if you want to stay, two self-contained apartments are offered for rent at the *Paradise Villa* (☎660 4933; ③), signposted and set just off the road. Newly built, neither is the height of luxury but both are scrupulously clean with two small bedrooms, fans and a kitchen; the upstairs unit is nicer and airier with TV and phone. Inclusive of a huge breakfast, this is a real bargain.

Richmond Great House and Argyll Waterfall

A narrow bridge marks your entry to **Glamorgan**, a little bigger than neighbouring Pembroke and beautifully located atop its own hillock. Stop for a snack at *Gee Bee's* bakery or scout around for the remains of an **old water wheel** behind the school, run by the adjacent Seventh Day Adventist church. Just out of town, the road widens, dipping down and up again through a small valley – this is *the* place to overtake if you're stuck behind a slow-moving truck. Before the road begins its descent, you can turn in to a little **park** to the left; benches and planted beds make it a nice place to take in the fantastic views over the rolling hills of the Main Ridge approaches.

On the other side of the valley is the signposted left turn for **Richmond Great House** (☎ & fax 660 4467; ⑦), a hotel, restaurant and essential point of call for almost all of the tour buses that travel the Windward Road. Built of solid brick and whitewashed board in the eighteenth century, the house itself was the great house of the old Richmond sugar estate, and offers fantastic views over the rolling, jungle-smothered interior hills. It's now owned by Professor Hollis Lynch, a Tobagonian who lectures at Colombia University, and his extensive collection of African art and textiles is on display; tours (daily 9am–5pm; TT$10) are available. You can also visit for lunch, but you'll need to call ahead for dinner. Colonial style rooms are gorgeous, cool with varnished wood floors and a private bathroom, and there's a pool and tennis courts on site.

Past Richmond, the Windward Road returns to the coast at **Belle Garden**. Beyond the village, you'll usually see a cache of guides standing at the entrance road to **Argyll Waterfall** (daily 7.30am–5pm) and waving frantically for you to stop; most work with the Roxborough Visitor Service Co-Operative Society, set up in 1992 to co-ordinate guides and manage the area. To access the falls, turn off the road and follow a muddy but easily passable cocoa tree-lined path to a grassy parking lot where you'll see the clapboard booth of the Co-Op offices, the place to pay the entrance fee (TT$20) and hire a guide if you want one (TT$15); doing so will greatly improve your impression of the area, as they point out birds and flowers and show the way to less easily accessible cascades.

The falls are a pleasant 15-minute walk away, and you can hear the water long before you reach it. Argyll is the island's highest waterfall, tumbling 54 metres out of the greenery into a deep pool. It is also one of its most accessible, but to see the best parts you'll have to exert yourself a little and climb up the right hand side along steep and sometimes bushy paths. There are three main cascades; the second is particularly strong – increased flow during the rainy season creates a constant fine mist that soon soaks you to the skin. The second tier is great for a natural jacuzzi, as there are plenty of rocky seats on which to perch and get a pounding shoulder massage. If you're feeling energetic, you can climb up even further to the deepest swimming pool – and the smallest section of waterfall – where you can dive or swing in Tarzan-style on a vine. If the climb doesn't appeal, you can drive right up to the highest swimming spot.

Roxborough

The **ROXBOROUGH** environs are **cocoa** country; just before you enter town on the main road, a left fork cuts straight through one of Tobago's largest plantations. Beneath deep green or rusty brown leaves, the cocoa's distinctive, gnarled limbs are smothered with lime green or off-white lichen. The oval cocoa pods turn from bright green to brown, orange and sometimes purple as they ripen, at which point you can pick one, crack it open and suck sweet white pulp from the small black seeds. Sadly, cocoa is a declining industry these days, as local youth turn away from agriculture in favour of the quicker bucks to be had in tourism. The cocoa estate road swings back to the Windward at the outskirts of town, adjacent to the expansive fire station and community centre and the inland Roxborough/Parlatuvier Road, the route to the forest reserve and Caribbean coast (see p.273–279).

Roxborough is the largest town along this section of the coast. The main drag runs parallel to the sea, although – unlike almost everywhere else on the windward parade – there are even a few residential streets stretching inland. Despite the profusion of small shops, and the presence of a post office, police station and even a petrol station (Mon–Fri 9am–6pm), it's a peaceful place, though it hasn't always been so tranquil. In the hard times that followed emancipation, Roxborough was the scene of the infamous and bloody **Belmanna Riots** (see box overleaf). Today, though, it's attractive, friendly and unused to a tourist presence. Apart from filling up your gas tank, there's no real reason to stay here; though it's fine for swimming, the **beach** is nothing special and beyond the low-key rum bars there's little to do. If you want to linger, you should be able to find someone who's willing to put you up. There are a couple of good places to eat along the main street; for snacks, try *Pat's Vegetarian Treats*; inexpensive and tasty seafood or chicken sit-down meals are available from the *Sun Rising* or *Pelican View Atlantic Beach* restaurants. Delicious blended fruit drinks are sold from a roadside kiosk at the town end of the cocoa estate road.

Well-made, inexpensive craft – necklaces, calabashes, Rasta hats, leather goods and bamboo – are sold at Shumba's stall on the way to the falls.

If you're driving, check your petrol gauge as you pass through Roxborough, as the nearest petrol stations are in Charlotteville and Scarborough.

You can get a good overview of local blooms and fruit trees at Louis D'Or Nursery, just outside Delaford (open daily, daylight hours; free).

The Belmanna uprising

Disgusted with the low pay and abysmal working conditions which dogged the ailing sugar industry after emancipation, African plantation workers from the Roxborough Estate **revolted** in 1876, burning down the home of the estate manager and rioting in the streets with such vigour that one of their comrades was killed in the struggle with police. Enraged, the workers surrounded the police station and demanded that the chief officer, Colonel Belmanna – whom they held responsible for the death – should come out and confront them. Unwisely, he did; the mob descended, gouging out his eyes, mutilating his body and beating him to death. As the ranks of the workers swelled with sympathizers from surrounding villages, the unrest continued. Hopelessly outnumbered, the police could do little but call for external assistance and retreat; it came a week later in the form of a British warship, which transported hundreds of the dissenters to Scarborough, where they were slammed into jail and put on trial, most receiving a life sentence or banishment from the island.

The riot left self-governed Tobago in turmoil. Feeling they had completely lost control of the island and its predominantly black population, and fearing total anarchy, the Legislative Council swiftly washed their hands of the whole affair and handed the running of Tobago back to the British. On January 1, 1877, Tobago became a Crown Colony, but the Belmanna repercussions were not to be quelled so easily. Continual unrest throughout the island contributed to the final collapse of the sugar industry and the overall economic decline which led to the official coupling of Trinidad and Tobago in 1879.

King's Bay

Turning inland past Roxborough, the Windward Road swings through the hilltop village of **Delaford**, making one almighty bend at the outskirts to reveal a breathtaking view of the spiky coconut plantation surrounding beautiful, deep blue **KING'S BAY** below. In the midst of a cool green arbour of cocoa trees at the bottom of the hill is the spacious parking lot for **King's Bay Waterfall** (daily, no set hours; free). The most heavily manicured of any on the island, it was presented as a gift to the nation in 1987 by Delaford philanthropists James and Dorothy Rosenwald. It's a five-minute walk to the falls along a neat pathway well-cropped by cattle. Sadly, the actual cascade is a disappointment; damming has drastically reduced the flow of King's Bay River, reducing the waterfall to a shadow of its former glory. The worn rocks bear witness to the fact that a torrent once crashed down on them, but nowadays you're unlikely to see more than a trickle, even at the height of the rainy season. The once-deep pool at the base is murky and stagnant, and the only fun to be had is climbing the 30 metres to the top.

A far more satisfying time is to be had at **King's Bay beach** (daylight hours; free), one of the few along the windward coast to provide changing facilities (TT$1 to enter). With gentle waters, reefs and fine dark sand, King's Bay is one of the best beaches in the area, but apart from a handful of bathers, it's mostly favoured by fishermen, and is a great place to watch – and participate in –the pulling in of a seine net. The profusion of Carib Indian artefacts found here (on display at the Tobago Museum – see p.255) prove that King's Bay was the site of a large settlement; some suggest that the bay is named after Carib cacique (chief) King Peter, though it's more likely that that honour goes to King Peter's Bay on the north coast.

If you want to **stay** in the area, there are a couple of basic places nearby. Just before the King's Bay cocoa plantation, a road branches off to the sea, identifiable by the signs promoting the larger option, *Crab Inn* – "Carib is our speciality". Follow the rocky road for a couple of minutes until you reach a junction opposite a bar; turn right for the *Crab Inn* (c/o Mr James Edwards, ☎660 4285; ①). Rooms in this smart little concrete house adorned with religious texts are basic, with double bed, bathroom and – in a few cases – a kitchen, but the atmosphere is supremely friendly, aided and abetted by the net-mending shack and popular liming spot opposite. The sea is a five-minute walk away. The right turn from the bar junction leads to the *Restrite Sea Gardens Guest House* (c/o Mrs Joslyn Orr, ☎660 4220; ②). Set on a rather raggle-taggle section of the otherwise beautiful Delaford Bay, the two rooms are a bit down-at-heel but clean and appealing if your budget is tight. Both have patio space, two tiny bedrooms, shower and rudimentary kitchenette. If you don't want to feel isolated staying here, you'll need your own car – the nearest shops and restaurants are in Speyside or Delaford, at the latter, try *King's Bay Cafe*, beautifully situated with a sweeping view over the bay from the open back verandah, where hot meals, snacks, pastries, espresso and cappuccino are served.

Speyside

Past King's Bay, the coast swings out of view as the road turns inland through lush hills and green valleys broken only by the odd roti shack. Constant hairpin bends and a steep incline make the going pretty treacherous, so if you're driving, don't let your surroundings become too much of a distraction. However, it's hard not to get side-tracked by the amazing view which opens up as you round the last corner before the descent into **SPEYSIDE**. From the bench-dotted **lookout** point, you get a marvellous panorama of the town, **Tyrrel's Bay** with its turquoise waters and the stunning sight of **Little Tobago** and **Goat Island**. There's good forest hiking to be had along Murchiston Trace, a tiny road that strikes off right from the main just before the Speyside lookout; ask in the village for a local guide.

Accommodation

With so few **accommodation** choices and plenty of demand for rooms with such marvellous views and a background music of the sea, you'll need to book well in advance if visiting during the high season. If you get stuck without a roof over your head, you should be able to find someone who's willing to put you up in their home.

Blue Waters Inn, Bateaux Bay, ☎660 4341 or 4077, fax 660 5195, email *bwitobago@trinidad.net*. Speyside's largest and grandest hotel set around the semi-private and totally stunning Bateaux Bay. All rooms are spacious, with rattan furniture, fan, porch and a sea view; the choice is a standard unit or one or two bedroom self-catering rooms and bungalows; a-c (US$6 per day) is on request in all. There's a restaurant, bar, dive shop and tennis court on site as well as 200,000 square metres of land sprinkled with nature trails. Popular with divers but shut off from the village. ⑨

Davis Atlantic View, Main Rd, c/o *Jemma's* restaurant ☎639 4066. Right opposite *Jemma's* and a good budget option with two new, basic and clean rooms sharing a bathroom, kitchen and lounge and another with its own facilities. ③

Islanders Inn, Main Rd, c/o Harris McMillan, PO Box 385, Scarborough, ☎ & fax 639 6575, email *cattours@trinidad.net*. Perfect bay views, lively and popular with a young crowd, this is the best guesthouse in Speyside. Three of the four rooms overlook the sea; all have fan, bathroom and hot water. The bar below can mean late-night noise; breakfast is included in rates. ⑤

Manta Lodge, Main Rd, PO Box 443, Scarborough, ☎660 5268, fax 660 5030; in USA ☎800/544 7631. Colonial-style luxury dedicated to scuba enthusiasts. Standard rooms are small but stylish with ceiling fan and balcony; "superior" add more space and a-c, while the quirky attics have the lot plus a private sun deck on the roof. There's a good restaurant (breakfast is included in the rates), pool and dive shop on site, and you can access the nature trails which network the grounds. ⑨

*For details of
the accommo-
dation price
codes used in
these listings,
see p.222.*

Speyside Inn, Main Rd , ☎ & fax 660 4852. Simple and beautifully styled with priceless bay views, rooms vary from a circular tower to octagonal corner rooms; all have bathroom, balcony and fan. There's an excellent restaurant on site (rates include breakfast) and good swimming a step away. ⑤–⑦

The village

The last sizeable village on the windward coast, Speyside feels as remote as it is; just ten years ago the road was little more than a dirt track, and the pace of life remains so slow that it's nearly at a standstill. Though the town is slowly adjusting to its new role as a **scuba** paradise – and taking on some of the more negative aspects of such development – it still retains its fishing village atmosphere and small-town attitude. Everyone says hello on the street, and your face will be known to most of the locals after a day or two, as will your choice of hotel, what you had for dinner last night and who you ate it with. You'll find that forging genuine friendships here is not only inevitable but a lot easier than in the more commercialized west of the island. Interaction between local people and tourists is far more relaxed, but don't let go of all your common sense and assume that every smiling face means a friend.

As you descend into the village, a cluster of candy-floss coloured grocery shops and snack bars surround a large playing field to the right. This is a focal point for the community; regular football games draw crowds of spectators and it's a good place to get to know local people. A dirt track running between the playing field and the sea takes you to the **beach** facilities (daylight hours; TT$1 to enter). The sand here is slightly wider than in the central part of the bay, and the famous **reefs** are within swimming distance. It's also a good place to organize a **fishing** trip aboard a local pirogue; the fishermen will also be happy to take you to Little Tobago for around TT$50–70, though if you're interested in bird-watching, it's probably better to go in more expert company (see p.269). Carrying on along the main road brings you into the main village, a minimal parade of small shops, the post office and a couple of bars. Past the next corner is what could loosely be termed the tourist strip, though it's a far cry from the conventional concrete and neon. In Speyside, tourism means diving, so the strip consists of several dive shops, a couple of restaurants, including the ubiquitous *Jemma's*, built into a tree over looking the sea, and a couple of hotels.

Just past *Manta Lodge* hotel, the road forks; left takes you across the interior and into Charlotteville (see p.270), while the right turn is the route to the astonishingly blue waters and rich reefs of **Bateaux Bay**, site of the luxurious *Blue Waters Inn*. The rutted road takes you past the Speyside **water wheel**, seemingly a remnant of the plantation era; however, this now-rusting iron contraption is a relatively recent addition, thought to have been built in the late nineteenth century, but since 1900 it's been allowed to slide into its current state of disrepair. Beyond *Blue Waters*, the coast is almost completely uninhabited. The road to picturesque Belmont and Starwood bays is often impassable; if so, ask a local fisherman to take you aboard a pirogue. Both bays offer great snorkelling and diving.

Little Tobago and Goat Island

Of the two misshapen islets sitting three miles or so out of Tyrrel's Bay, **Goat Island** is the closer. You'll see one white house nestled in the centre, built as the Tobagonian holiday home of Caribbean devotee Ian Fleming, author of the James Bond novels. The house and the island are now privately owned and closed to the public. However, bird-watchers and hikers flock to the larger island, **Little Tobago**, a kilometre further out to sea. The most easterly point of the T&T republic, the 2-square kilometre outcrop has been known as "Bird of Paradise Island" since the beginning of this century, when it was bought by keen ornithologist Sir William Ingram. In 1909 he transported 24 Greater **Birds of Paradise** (*Paradisaea apoda*) from Aru island in New Guinea. Over the years, however, the birds were slowly extinguished by hurricanes and hunters. When Sir William died in 1924, his heirs gave Little Tobago back to the government on condition that it receive protected status. It has remained a bird sanctuary ever since, uninhabited except for one of the largest seabird colonies in the Caribbean, which includes impressive flocks of frigate birds, boobies, terns and the spectacular red-billed tropic bird, the latter

*More good
bird- watching
is to be had at
St Giles
Islands, a few
miles to the
north. It's a
major breed-
ing ground for
pelicans, terns
and frigate
birds, but cur-
rents make
access difficult.*

especially prevalent between October and June. You'll also hear the crows and clucks of feral cocks and chickens brought here by the now-departed resident caretaker, who was unable to catch his flock when he left the island.

Several trails cut during the island's brief spell as a cotton planta-tion mean there are good possibilities for **hiking**, though as Little Tobago is only 1.5km (1 mile) long at its widest point, these are hardly marathon treks. All the boats dock at a small beach facing the mainland, from where you get beautiful views of the town and Pigeon Hill above, one of Tobago's highest points. Here, there's a wooden shelter with toilets, benches, tables and a long list of do's and dont's for visitors; no smoking, squatting or fires etc. Concrete steps lead up the hillside, passing the ramshackle caretakers house, long-deserted but still displaying framed posters of Little Tobago's most common bird species. Well-signposted trails lead off from here through the dry and scrubby landscape; head for the cliffside nesting grounds of the red-billed tropic bird, where a lookout point provides

---

Speyside watersports

Speyside's main attraction are the amazingly rich coral **reefs** which net-work the bay. Generally pristine with little sign of bleaching or human dam-age, the reefs flourish on a rich diet of nutrients flowing in from Venezuela's mighty Orinoco River along the Guyana Current, ensuring a huge variety of marine life and some dazzling hues among the coral. Speyside also boasts one of the world's largest **brain corals**, an awesome 3.6 metres high and 5 metres feet across. Apart from the regular shoals of small fish – butterfly, grunt, angel, parrot and damselfish – the currents also attract a number of deep-water dwellers, including **nurse sharks**, **dolphins** and, most notably, manta rays. These regular visitors are usually around 7 metres long, and are so accustomed to the divers' touch that it's now common practice to hitch a ride by grabbing on to the body just beside the horns – known as taking a "Tobago Taxi". Though this seems rather questionable sport, local opera-tors claim that as the mantas make the first approach, they actually enjoy contact with humans, particularly a scratch on the back.

The most popular Speyside dive sites include Japanese Gardens, Angel Reef, Bookends and Blackjack hole, and most dives are of the drift variety. Operators to trust are Tobago Dive Experience at *Manta Lodge* (☎660 5268), the first operator to set up in the area, Aquamarine Dive at *Blue Waters Inn* (☎660 4341), and Tobagonian-owned Tobago Dive Masters next to *Jemma's* (☎639 4697). For sample prices see box, p.228–229. All of these operators rent **snorkel** equipment for around US$10 per day, and Aquamarine offer snorkelling trips for a rather inflated US$11 per person.

Glass bottom boats are a good way to see the reefs if you don't want to get wet, though you can always jump overboard for a spot of snorkelling as well. Frank's (☎660 5438), based at *Blue Waters Inn*, offers a basic tour with snorkelling at Angel Reef for US$10, drift snorkelling in front of Little Tobago ($15), as well as a boat tour around St Giles Island for $30. Fear Not (☎660 4654), based at *Jemma's* also do inexpensive Angel Reef tours (1.5hrs; US$10)

sweeping views and an opportunity to see birds in flight up close. Make sure you have enough drinking water with you, however, as no refreshments are available. To get the best from the island, hire an experienced guide such as Harris McMillan (☎639 6575) or David Rooks (☎639 4276), the man who persuaded David Attenborough that Little Tobago was sufficiently unique to be included in his famous BBC *Trials of Life* documentary. Based at *Blue Waters Inn*, Frank's Glass Bottom Boat (☎660 5498) offer a well-informed trip including snorkelling at Angel Reef for US$15 per person. Fear Not at *Jemma's* is cheaper; a two-hour trip costs around US$10.

Eating and drinking

Even during the high season, Speyside isn't exactly a metropolis; in the summer, you'll find the town pretty much deserted as some of the cafe's and dive operators shut up shop. **Restaurant** pickings are pretty slim; most head to *Jemma's Treehouse* (☎660 4066), where you're sure to get fresh food throughout the year. The setting is a novelty; the place lurches crazily in the boughs of a tree, limbs and leaves blend in with the tables, and the sea view is fantastic. The moderately priced Creole-style food is wonderful; breakfast (8.30–10am) is eggs, bacon or local fish dishes. Lunch (available until 4pm) consists of fish, shrimp or lobster, with imaginative veg: breadfruit or eggplant casserole, tannia fritters, fried plantain and salad. Dinner – fish, lobster, shrimp, lamb chops, steak or chicken with veg – is excellent, as are the puddings; pumpkin or orange chiffon pie, bread pudding and the delicious guava fluff, a mix of fruit pulp and beaten egg white. As Jemma is a Seventh Day Adventist, the restaurant doesn't serve alcohol and is closed from 6pm on Friday until Sunday morning. Next door, *Redman's Kitchen* serves inexpensive local breakfast, lunch and dinner, as do *Liz's Cafe and Bar*, the *Birdwatcher's Rest and Bar*, and *Islanders Inn* (☎660 4852) in the village; the last three are good drinking spots. Otherwise, you'll have to stick to the hotel restaurants; the chalked-up set dinner menu at *Speyside Inn* is particularly good and changes daily, featuring lots of imaginatively cooked local ingredients; tuna in mustard papaya sauce, sweet potato and tomato or christophene soup as well as a mean chocolate cake and key lime pie. Of the other large hotel restaurants, the *Green Moray* at *Manta Lodge* (☎660 5268) has lots of fairly expensive but well-executed seafood and international standards, while the *Fish Pot* at *Blue Waters Inn* (☎660 4341) serves average and expensive seafood. Snacks and lunches are available from the take-away which doubles up as a grocery store opposite *Islanders*, as well as the shacks around the playing field. **Entertainment** is thin on the ground and generally centred on dinner and a few drinks at any of the hotels. Most locals prefer the cheaper beers and lively atmosphere of the *Boatsman Bar* at *Islanders Inn*; they have a pool table and play music most nights of the week.

You should make dinner reservations for most Speyside restaurants, as space is limited during the winter; in the slow summer months, some places won't cook unless guests are assured.

Charlotteville

From Speyside, the Windward Road strikes inland on its way from
the Atlantic to the Caribbean coast, climbing steeply upward through
jungle-like mountain foliage before plummeting down to the opposite shoreline. Just before the descent, there's a stunning perspective
of Charlotteville and the sea from **Flagstaff Hill**; take the signposted
right turn from the main. Tobago's most easterly portion of tarmac
marks the last "civilization"; north of here, the countryside is completely undeveloped, with no electricity or piped water for the hardy
handful of small-scale farmers, bush hunters and fishermen. At the
peak of the hill, the road opens up to reveal a battered coastguard's
hut and tall pylon topped with a navigational beacon, a swathe of
grass with a covered gazebo and a fantastic view of Man of War Bay,
Booby Island and Cambleton Battery with the Sister's Rocks deep
out to sea. If you peek through the trees or risk climbing the pylon,
you can make out the hills of St Giles Island. This excellent vantage
point was utilized by British and French soldiers, who used mirrors
to signal the approach of a ship to their colleagues stationed at
Cambleton Battery below.

As the Windward Road begins its seaward plunge, the absurdly
pretty fishing village of **CHARLOTTEVILLE** swings into view; houses tumble willy-nilly down a hillside met by calm Caribbean waters,
while frigate birds swoop overhead and hissing cicadas keep up a constant refrain. Snugly situated under the protective cover of 2 kilome-
tre-wide **Man of War Bay**, Charlotteville is one of Tobago's foremost
fishing communities – more than 60 percent of the island's total catch
is brought in by local fishermen. Bordered on each side by steep
forested hills, the town has an isolated feel, as though time has been
suspended and commercial concerns put aside. Though the tourist
dollar is steadily encroaching upon this self-contained, tight-knit community, the atmosphere is so friendly that it's hard not to relax.

Despite the small-town atmosphere, Charlotteville is actually one
of Tobago's oldest communities, first settled by Caribs and then by
the Dutch in 1633 – for many years the bay was known as Jan De
Moor Bay after an early Frisian occupant. During the plantation era,
the surrounding area was divided into two successful estates, Pirate's
Bay and Charlotteville; sugar shipments made regular departures
from the bay, and the town prospered. In 1865, both estates were
purchased by the Turpin family, who still own much of the surrounding land.

Accommodation

If you're here between December and April, it's wise to book ahead,
as the town is fast becoming Tobago's most popular retreat. To cope
with demand during the high season, many local residents open up a
couple of rooms to visitors; ask around for possibilities, or call any
of the numbers listed opposite.

Charlotteville accommodation numbers

Mrs Alleyne: ☎660 4423	Mrs McKenna: ☎660 4446
Almondoz: ☎639 2631	Nicholson's: ☎639 8553
Cambleton House: ☎660 2217	Sharon or Sister Joe: ☎660 5717
Mrs Budd: ☎660 5607	Mr James: ☎660 5605

Belle Air Cottage, ☎660 4443. Self-contained house 100 metres up the road from the Pirate's Bay track. Various rooms with fan and double bed. ③

Cholson Chalets, Man of War Bay, c/o Hewitt Nicholson, 22 Calder Hall Trace, Northside Road, ☎639 8553. Completely charming green and white houses overlooking the beach at the Pirates Bay end of town. The deliciously anti-quated feel of the six simple rooms makes the basic romantic; muslin curtains and wooden floors, fans, private bathroom, optional maid service and a few kitchenettes; the upstairs flat is most appealing. Book early. ④

Irisville, c/o Rebecca Moore, ☎660 5340. Two self-contained units with two bedrooms, kitchen and bathroom. ③

Man-O-War Bay Cottages, Man of War Bay, c/o Pat Turpin, Charlotteville Estate, ☎660 4327, fax 660 4328. Situated right on the bay in pretty land-scaped gardens, the cottages are different shapes and sizes, with one, two, three or four bedrooms. All have fan, bathroom, hot water and kitchen, simple but attractive decor, books on the shelves, driftwood ornaments and an over-whelming feeling of peace. There's a small commissary on site, hiking tours are available and the maid/cook service is optional and costs extra. ⑦

The village

If you're seeking peace, quiet and great beaches, it's hard not to become utterly besotted with Charlotteville. The "town centre" with its hole-in-the-wall shops, gas station, post office and sprinkling of restaurants sticks close to the sand; the streets that stretch uphill form the residential section. There's little to do but enjoy the sea; arrange a **fishing** trip aboard the many pirogues which moor up in the bay, or just while away the hours on the white sand of **Man of War Bay beach.** It's clean, calm and inviting, with good snorkelling and changing/shower facilities (daylight hours; TT$1) as well as a lively beach bar and snack shop. Just past the main swimming area is the busy Charlotteville **Fisherman's Co-Operative** building, with its blackboard displaying the day's catch alongside messages to its mem-bers. Benches along the sea wall, the fishing pier and a covered pavil-ion are popular liming spots, great for soaking up the village scene.

In July, Man of War Bay is the venue for Tobago's most popular fisher-man's fete, held to cele-brate St Peter's Day.

Beyond the square, the coastal street turns inland, but a dirt track continues along the shoreline to the town's – and Tobago's – most attractive beach, **Pirate's Bay.** At the bottom of a flight of 150-plus concrete steps, you're rewarded with a stunning horseshoe of calm emerald green water and fine yellow sand, with a backdrop of trees, ferns and foliage. A tumbledown fisherman's hut and a smart pair of pit toilets are the only buildings in sight, and a freshwater rinse comes courtesy of a stream trickling down from the hills. There is fantastic **snorkelling** to be had in the translucent waters of the bay, but the pickings are particularly rich toward the left-hand side. The seventeenth-century buccaneers after whom the bay was named may have gone, but the bay still has its freebooters, a large colony of **frigate birds**, which feed by snatching recently caught fish from the beaks of smaller seabirds.

Cambleton Battery

Reached via a steep and potholed lane striking off from the main road on the western outskirts of town, **Cambleton Battery** (no set hours; free) was formally established by the British in 1777, who placed two cannons to defend against attack from marauding American warships sailing the Caribbean during the War of Independence; the sweeping views of Charlotteville, Booby Island and Pirate's Bay explain why they chose this site. It's a popular cooling-out spot for locals, who lime away a few hours under the shade of the gazebo. Past the battery, the track continues upward, but if you're driving, it's wise to go no further than the sign that warns "treacherous road – proceed at your own risk". If you have a dirt bike or four-wheel drive vehicle, you can proceed as far as the next bay, **Hermitage**, without too much trouble, but bear in mind that almost all of the island's rental companies will hold you fully responsible for any damage incurred along this stretch, and though it's attractively deserted with a shingle beach and plenty of washed up flotsam, the bay isn't really worth the trouble; rip tides also make swimming precarious. If you do decide to attempt the full stretch, it will take about an hour to cover the two miles to **L'Anse Fourmi**, where the tarmac begins again.

Eating and drinking

Though most of the available accommodations are self-catering, Charlotteville offers only limited **food shopping**; basic needs are covered by the small shops along Man of War Bay, and you can buy

The
leeward
coast and
Tobago
Forest
Reserve

fresh fish daily from the Fisherman's Co-Operative. **Restaurant** pickings are also quite slim, though a couple of the grocery stores offer take-away lunches and you can get good blended fruit drinks from the last rum bar before the Pirate's Bay track. *Eastman's* by the town square have catch of the day with chips, burgers and sandwiches, served up on a verandah overlooking the fishing pier.

On the other side of town, *Sharon and Pheeb's* is set on a balcony overlooking the main street and open daily for breakfast, lunch and dinner. Prices are moderate and the cooking excellent; saltfish, smoked mackerel or US-style breakfast, and lunches or dinners of fish, chicken, shrimp or lobster cooked Creole-style or with lemon butter or curry sauce. The bar is also a popular **drinking** spot. Fries, fish or chicken meals, drinks and good company are on offer at the beach bar, which also puts on a lively sound system party on Friday and Saturday nights. On the road behind *Man-O-War Bay Cottages* is the *Golden Dove* restaurant, another option for good local dishes.

Watersports

If you want to visit the excellent **scuba diving** sights in the area, the only reputable local operator is Man Friday (☎660 4676) near Man of War Bay beach. They offer resort and certification courses, single dives and packages, and rent out single and double **kayaks** (US$30/45 per day) and **snorkelling equipment** (US$8 per day).

The leeward coast and Tobago Forest Reserve

Beyond Plymouth, the leeward coast feels more remote than any other part of the island; curious eyes follow passing cars and tourist development is minimal, leaving the ravishing beaches at **Castara**, **Englishman's Bay**, **Parlatuvier** and **Bloody Bay** much the same as they were twenty years ago. These communities have made only minimal efforts to cater to visitors; clusters of bobbing pirogues in every bay or seine nets drying in the sun hint at the centrality of **fishing** to this area, and you'll often see machete-wielding fellows trudging the route to small-scale plantations or meandering along with a pack of hunting dogs. Inland of Castara, the protected **forest reserve** is traversed by the Roxborough–Parlatuvier Road, and thick vegetation rises sharply from the tarmac. Though the rainforest canopy looks thick and impenetrable, even the most confirmed city-dweller should find the managed trails.

From the look of most maps, you'd assume the most direct route to the leeward coast would be the coast road from Plymouth; however, this is actually the slowest route, and until a new surface is laid, you're best bet is to head for the leeward coast along the Northside Road from Claude Noel Highway at Calder Hall.

The
leeward
coast and
Tobago
Forest
Reserve

The Northside Road

Less than a kilometre east of Scarborough, the well-signposted **Northside Road** strikes into the interior, meandering straight across the middle of Tobago and connecting the windward with the leeward coast. A downhill right turn 50m or so from the highway (bear right at the bridge) takes you up a narrow, near-perpendicular road to **French Fort**, named after a Gallic invasion in 1781 and the site of a French garrison until 1787. It's now the home to several towering radio transmitters and satellite pylons, and the only hint of its history is a plaque nestled in the trees, but the panoramic **views** of Scarborough, Fort King George, Rockly Bay and Lowlands, the northern coast around Plymouth and Arnos Vale and the southeast as far as Granby Point make the journey up worthwhile.

Past the fort turn-off, the Northside Road swings past the armed guards and clipped hedges flanking the **President's House** (closed to the public), and continues its snaking climb, passing through the quiet residential communities of **Concordia** and **Cinnamon Hill**. Right in the centre of the island, close-knit **Mason Hall** is the most sizeable village, home of the island's first government school – built in 1938 – as well as a massive football pitch, clusters of snug gingerbread homes and a marvellous **waterfall** on the outskirts. To find it, look for the Craig Hall water intake, marked by a WASA sign. Half an hour's walking along the Sandy River is **Mason Hall Falls**, one of the island's tallest at about 50m. Taking the Craig Hall route takes you to the top of the main cascade, where there's another, smaller waterfall with pool deep enough to jump into without touching the bottom.

Mark Puddy leads excellent guided tours to Mason Hall Falls, while Ricarda Solomon's dirt-bike tours visit the base; see p.215 for details of both.

Moriah

Continuing north, the road begins its serpentine ascent of the lumpy, upturned-egg-box-like undulations that surround **MORIAH**, a roadside village teetering at the top of a particularly steep precipice; sheer drops plummet straight into a valley from the road, and the roofs of houses sit precariously parallel to the tarmac. Terraces on the surrounding hills support crops of pigeon peas and ground provisions, Baptist prayer flags flutter in the thermals and the views are superlative. A precipitous police station, clapboard parlours and a Moravian church – one of Tobago's earliest missions was located here – form the main body of the village. There are a couple of **rum shops** well worth a visit; the *Hardest Hard Rec Club*, on the road before you enter town, has a shady outdoor section, while *Man John's* bar, right on the other side of Moriah, is a popular, Rasta owned drinking spot with interesting wall murals.

A potholed downhill turn-off to the left as you leave the village leads to **King Peter's Bay**, a seldom-visited but beautiful yellow-sand beach named after a Carib cacique. Striking west into the bush over the next bluff takes you to an even more beautiful strip, with a good reef to boot. Beyond King Peter's Bay road, Northside Road heads for the coast, providing breathtaking views as you enter the tiny communities of **Des Vignes** and **Runnemede**; look out for a truly monumental **silk cotton** tree at the roadside; its buttressed roots are said to be haunted by jumbies (ghosts). For an even better vista, ask local directions to find the correct right turn for **Mount Dillon**, where benches are set up to admire the unravelling coastline.

Castara

After yet another downhill plunge, Northside Road slides into **CASTARA**, an attractive, easygoing fishing village that's slowly developing a nonchalant tourist-friendliness; low-key guesthouses are scattered on a hillside, while visitors dribble in to swim at the marvellous **beach** or splash in the nearby **waterfall**. Castara seems unlikely to be eaten up by resort hotels and beach bars; to ensure that development is in tune with the residents and actually benefits them, one German guesthouse owner has given locals a 30 percent share in his property. Fishing remains the main earner at present, and the beach is one of the best places to participate in the pulling of a **seine net**; still in constant use by the supremely friendly posse of Rasta fishermen. The village abandons its languid air each August, when the beach is packed with revellers attending the **Castara Fishermen's Fete**, one of Tobago's biggest; the drinking, dancing, eating and swimming start at about midday and continue until well after dark.

A layby above Castara offers the chance to park up and admire the view of the bay below.

Accommodation

Castara is the only village along this section of coast where you'll find a choice of places to stay, though almost all of the guesthouses are small-scale and located on a bluff overlooking the eastern portion of the beach. The town is gradually becoming more popular amongst seekers of solace, so it's wise to reserve a room before turning up. If you're stuck, try *McKnights*, a bar on the eastern outskirts that has a couple of rooms, but finding someone to put you up in their home shouldn't be a problem.

Blue Mango, Second Bay Rd, ☎ 639 2060. More upmarket than the competition, these simply furnished, stylish one- or two-bedroom self-contained cottages have great bay views, cool breezes, kitchens mosquito nets and plenty of privacy. ⑤

Naturalist, Castara Village, ☎ 639 5901 or 2642, email *natural@ trinidad.net*. Right at the edge of the beach, this is the best option in Castara; rooms are small but well-equipped and very clean; all have TV, radio, private bathroom and a kitchenette. The staff are extremely genial and will cook for you on request. The name refers to nature-lovers rather than potential strippers; "no nudity" was added to the roadside advertisements after guests got the wrong idea. ③

Sea Level, Second Bay Rd (no phone). Just up the hill from the *Naturalist*, this joint German/Tobagonian owned guesthouse is the largest (and newest) in the village. All rooms have a balcony, spacious bathroom, mosquito nets and fan; some have bunk beds for the backpackers while others have doubles and twins. Excellent value. ③

The
leeward
coast and
Tobago
Forest
Reserve

The village

Straddling the Northside Road, the main body of the village consists of weather-beaten rum shops and parlours interspersed with simple board homes. A bridge at the eastern edge of town crosses the **Castara River**; a ten-minute walk along the riverbed brings you to a small **waterfall** with a fairly deep swimming pool below. Crossing the playing field behind the bridge cuts the walking time, and the pool is popular among local lads cooling off after a game of football; these frenetic, foul-filled tournaments take place in the late afternoon, and often attract a small crowd of spectators. There's another waterfall on the river, about an hour's walk from the road; to find it, you'll need to hire a local guide in the village.

The main focus of the town, though, is its **beach**, a generous swathe of coarse, shell and pebble-strewn sand divided in two by the fast-flowing Castara River, which turns the water a murky brown during the rainy season and disappears completely during the parched dry months. If there hasn't been rain, the water is a joy, crystal-clear and relatively calm due to the protection of the surrounding forested headlands. Flotillas of seagull-infested pirogues bob out to sea, and there's always activity around the Fishermen's Co-Op building, where the day's catch is weighed, scaled and sold; impromptu gutting usually draws a posse of mangy pot-hounds that clear up the entrails with gusto. The changing facilities (daylight hours; TT$1) are opposite the Co-Op. If you want to follow the local example and take to the brine, ask around for Hilly Williams (☎639 6485), who arranges all-day fishing, snorkelling and waterfall-finding trips aboard a pirogue; food and drink are included (TT$150 per person). He can also take you to **Sorry Bay**, a beautiful remote cove to the west of the main bay, so-called because it's only reachable by boat.

Eating and drinking

There's a brace of places to **eat** on the beach; of the two, inexpensive *L&H Sunset*, set on a lofty patio next to the **Fishermen's** Co-Op, is more popular amongst locals. The classic Tobagonian cooking is excellent; usually revolving around fish, main dishes change daily – the traditional Sunday dinner of chicken, callaloo and macaroni pie is a gastronomic triumph, as is the cow heel soup. Right on the beach, *Cascreole* is more tourist-oriented, but the fish or chicken lunches and dinners are tasty nonetheless. The adjacent bar makes a good all-day **drinking** spot, and stays open as long as custom demands. There are a couple of general stores in the village, but the small bar-cum-parlour under *L&H* restaurant is convenient, opening daily 6am till very late; the religious/inspirational sayings painted on the walls make good reading, too. Blended fruit drinks (and a rudimentary selection of fresh veg) are available from a stall at the hilly eastern edge of the village.

Englishman's Bay to Bloody Bay

Past Castara, houses and shops melt away, and the Northside Road is flanked by enormous tufts of whispering, creaking bamboo, broken occasionally to reveal marvellous jungle-clad hilly prospects. The next worthy beach, **Englishman's Bay**, is easily missed as it's hidden from the road by a thick cover of bush; look out for the battered sign. Utterly ravishing and completely undeveloped, the bay offers a perfect crescent of pure white sand, deep blue water, offshore reef and nothing else – from the sea, the forested hillside appears completely untouched, as the bush drips right down to the sand. This looks set to change, though, as planning permission for a hotel development right on the beach has been granted, but at present, the bay remains deliciously remote, the "deserted beach" destination of many a pleasure boat cruise. Hot meals (including roti on Sundays), soft drinks and bamboo craft are sold at *Eula's* stall near the entrance.

Past Englishman's, the coast road climbs upward and inland, passing through the diminutive community of **Parrot Hall** before descending to reveal one of the most arresting views on the island; **Parlatuvier Bay**, flanked by an absurdly pretty hillside scattered with palms, terraced provision grounds and the odd house. Another crescent of pearly sand, the pier in the middle of the bay is testament to the village's dedication to fishing, as are the gulls which roost on the rocks at either side of the bay, patiently awaiting the return of the boats. **Swimming** is a vigorous experience; waves are usually quite strong and the water deepens sharply from the sand.

Built around the bay, the village consists of a few houses, a school and a couple of shops; one sells tourist souvenirs, while the other, presided over by local character Duran Chance, sells everything from floor wax to bread and rum. Above the shop, *Parlatuvier Tourist Resort* (☎639 5629; ②) is the only place to **stay** in the village. The breezy apartments have fan or a-c, bathroom, and kitchen. Inexpensive and delicious **meals** are available from *Bryner and Gloria's Riverside Restaurant* on the Northside Road, where you get lavish portions of local style fresh fish, lobster or shrimp with provisions for about TT$40–70; a bargain. Further east along the road, *Apache Cottage* do a good roti when they manage to open.

The last accessible beach on the coast is **Bloody Bay**, named for a battle between English soldiers and African slaves that took place here in 1771 that was fierce enough to turn the sea crimson with blood; Dead Bay River, which runs across the sand and into the sea, is named for the same reason. Directly opposite the bay and clearly visible three miles out to sea, the **Sisters Rocks** form an attractive chain. Beyond Bloody Bay, the formerly smooth tarmac ends abruptly, its pits and ruts continuing all the way to the lofty village of **L'Anse Fourmi**, remote enough to make the sight of a tourist a talking point. From here on only the bravest of drivers and hardiest of four wheel drives or dirt bikes can manage the track to Charlotteville – and you'd be foolish to attempt it if you're here in the rainy season.

The
leeward
coast and
Tobago
Forest
Reserve

Tobago Forest Reserve

Swinging inland from the Northside Road at Bloody Bay, the Roxborough–Parlatuvier Road is the route to **Tobago Forest Reserve** and the central mountain range, so things get pretty steep. Construction of the road began in 1958, but the ravages of Hurricane Flora in 1963 (see box below) were not repaired until the mid-1990s, and it's now a pleasurably smooth drive.

The reserve acquired its status as the oldest protected rainforest in the western hemisphere during the plantation era, when British scientist Stephen Hales began researching the relationship between rainfall and trees and communicated his findings to one Soame Jenyns, a British MP responsible for the development of Tobago. At the time, the island was a flourishing plantation, with most of the estates concentrated in low-lying areas. Gradually, though, the planters began encroaching on the more precipitous forest areas, felling trees for fuel or clearing land to make way for yet more sugar cane. It took Jenyns ten years to convince Tobago's planters that if they continued to cut down the forest, the island would soon be incapable of supporting the smallest of shrubs, let alone a massive sugar plantation. Ultimately, he was successful, and on April 13, 1776, 14,000 acres of central Tobago were designated a protected Crown Reserve.

The best way to get a feel for the rainforest is to walk in it, and there are two main points of access. **Gilpin Trace** is marked by a huge slab of rock by the road in front of a forestry division hut, hous-

---

Hurricane Flora

On September 30, 1963, **Hurricane Flora** swept over Tobago and completely devastated the island. Most of the banana, coconut and cocoa plantations were wiped out, and large tracts of the forest reserve laid to waste, with 30-metre high trees toppling like matchsticks; many still block the trails to this day. For Tobagonians, the hurricane was a total catastrophe; thirty people died, and hundreds of others suffered injuries. Sixty out of every hundred fragile board houses were razed to the ground, Moriah, Concordia, Argyll and Richmond were completely demolished, roads were impassable and there was no water or electricity outside Scarborough for more than six weeks.

A relief fund helped to repair the worst of the damage, and the UN provided foodstuffs that fed the population for nearly a year, while other Caribbean islands donated items as various as fevergrass (a bush remedy for colds and fevers) and roasted breadfruits. Though there are few signs of the damage left today other than some toppled trunks in the forest reserve, the hurricane changed Tobago's future forever; a tentative agricultural economy was abandoned, and the island began to devote its energy to tourism. Tobagonians still remember Flora with a shudder, but thankfully her force has never since been repeated. However, in 1997, Tobago was shaken by another natural disaster of less catastrophic proportion; on April 22, an **earthquake** measuring 5.9 on the Richter scale shook the island, destroying four homes and causing structural damage to several more.

The
leeward
coast and
Tobago
Forest
Reserve

ing a toilet and a water tank; it's also a great lookout point over the Caribbean, with views stretching all the way down to the Sister's Rocks below. Snacks and drinks are available at the weekends. A trail strikes straight into the forest from here, but unless you only plan to go a few hundred yards, it's advisable to hire a **guide**; you'll understand a lot more about forest dynamics, and you won't get lost. Good bets include Renson Jack (☎660 5175), a forest ranger who moonlights as a tour guide, David Rooks (☎639 4276) or Harris McMillan (☎639 6575). The next point of access is marked by another forestry hut a couple of kilometres down the road toward the windward coast; here, local guides hang out touting for business; a regular visitor, known as "Parrot Man" (☎639 1305 or 1252 or 5627) hires out well-needed rubber boots from the back of his jeep, as well as acting as a guide. His brother Dexter James (no phone) is another knowledgeable licensed forest guide usually to be found here or at his home on the main road in Bloody Bay; there's a "forest guide" sign outside. The forestry hut trail is pretty easy – though often very muddy – taking you through some spectacular forest dotted with mini-waterfalls. Huge bachac ant nests punctuate the trail, while lianas and vines block out most of the light. If you're feeling hardy, ask to be shown the Atlantic trail, two hours of hard walking. Away from the trail access points, the forest is pretty impenetrable, and the road continues south into Roxborough (see p.263).

Tobago Listings

Car and bike rental The most reliable companies for cars and jeeps include Auto centre, adjacent to the airport (☎639 4400), Rollocks (☎639 0328), Rattan's (☎639 8271) and Thrifty (☎639 8507 or 8111). For motorbikes and bicycles try Island Bikes (☎639 8587) or Baird's, who are another good bet for cars (☎639 2528). Bicycles are available from First Class (pager ☎662 3377, ID1973), who ply on the Fort Milford approaches in Crown Point every day (7am–7pm), or Glorious Rides, at Pigeon Point junction (☎639 7124).

Courier service As the postal service in Tobago can be anything but speedy, you might want to try the local branch of DHL in Lowlands (☎639 9244) if you need to send something abroad in a hurry.

Ferries Subject to periodical breakdowns, delays and a stomach-churning route that demands strong sea legs, the infamous ferry to Trinidad leaves Tobago Mon–Sat at 11pm, arriving in Trinidad about five hours later. There are three fares; economy (TT$25), tourist (TT$30) and cabin (TT$80); the latter sleep two, and should be booked at least two days in advance. Cars cost TT$57.50; all return fares are double the listed single rates.

Laundry Machine washes are available at Barton's Laundry on Store Bay Local Road (Mon–Sat 7am–5pm; ☎639 8915), who will pick up and deliver. A full load costs TT$35 plus TT$3 for detergent. White and Bright on Milford Road (Mon–Fri 8am–4pm, Sat 8am–1pm; ☎639 0921) charge TT$30 if you load the wash yourself, or TT$35 for a wash and dry service; detergent is TT$3.

The
leeward
coast and
Tobago
Forest
Reserve

Medical Complete with an Accident and Emergency department, Tobago's only **hospital** is just below the fort complex in Scarborough (☎639 2551 or 2552). For an **ambulance**, call ☎639 2222. If you need a **doctor**, try any of the physicians practising at the Triangle Building, Crooks River, Scarborough (☎639 1115) or Dr Melville (☎639 1722 or 660 5203). The best local gynaecologist is Dr Francis Jacobs in Scarborough (☎639 5727). Late opening **pharmacies** in Scarborough include Scarborough Drugs, opposite KFC on the corner of Carrington Street and Wilson Road (Mon–Sat 8am–8pm, Sun 8am–noon), and Tobago Pharmacy on Carrington Street (Mon–Thurs 8am–7pm, Fri 8am–8pm, Sat 8am–2pm). In Crown Point try Dove Drugs (daily 9am–7pm; closes occasional Sundays at noon) in the Real Value Plaza, located on Buccoo Bay Road, which runs from Claude Noel Highway to Shirvan Road, signposted for Auchenskeoch.

Money As there are no official bureau de change in Tobago outside the hotels, all transactions must be made at the **banks**; there's one branch of Republic Bank at Crown Point airport, but all the others are in Scarborough (see p.256); all are subject to the same opening hours (Mon–Thurs 8am–2pm, Fri 8am–noon & 3–5pm). 24-hour ATM's are located at Crown Point airport and adjacent to the Scarborough banks; all provide cash advances on credit cards. **Wire transfers** can be collected at any of the banks.

Petrol stations In Crown Point, the Canaan garage on Milford Road is the only port of call (Mon–Sat 7.30am–1pm and 3–9pm; Sun 8am–2pm); you can also try the Carnbee petrol station – take the first right from Shirvan Road or the turn-off from the highway marked for Auchenskeoch. Roxborough petrol station is open Mon–Fri 9am–6pm, and Plymouth's Mon–Sat 6am–8pm, Sun 6am–noon. Scarborough has the latest opening gas outlets; the Taxi Co-Operative garage on Wilson Road, and the three stations on Milford Road stay open until midnight daily. As a last resort, head for Hillsborough (Hope) Bay on the windward coast just outside Scarborough; ask around for directions to the man who keeps a reserve of (expensive) gas to sell to the desperate; fishermen often keep a container to fuel their boats as well.

Photography Fotomart have a shop on Burnett Street for film and developing (1-hour service available) as well as two easy-access booths (Mon–Fri 8am–6pm, Sat 8am–3pm), located at Mount Irvine beach complex and Store Bay.

Police There are five police stations in Tobago; Scarborough (☎639 2512 or 4737), Old Grange (☎639 8888), Moriah (☎639 2646), Roxborough (☎660 4333) and Charlotteville (☎660 4388). The island-wide emergency police line is ☎639 1200; alternatively, dial ☎999 for police, ☎990 for fire and ambulance.

Supermarkets The best supermarket is Penny Savers on Milford Road at the Canaan end; it's competitively priced, well-stocked and has lots of imported foods (Mon–Sat 8am–8pm; Sun 8am–1pm). In Crown Point, try the small but convenient Francis mini-mart just before Fort Milford in Crown Point (Mon–Sat 8am–6pm), or the View Port Supermarket (Mon–Thurs 8am–8pm, Fri & Sat 8am–9pm), opposite the Tobago Taxi Co-Op in the Canaan section of Milford Road. The well-stocked All in 1 Tobago Supermarket at the corner of Glen and Darrell Spring roads is open late (daily 7am–11pm) – turn left from the highway just past Scarborough turn-off. Morshead Delicatessen, on Buccoo Road (turn off Shirvan Road) sell imported cold meats and cheeses.

The
leewood
coast and
Tobago
Forest
Reserve

Taxis You can hail a car on almost all of Tobago's roads – make sure that you settle the price before getting in. Most large hotels have registered drivers, but they can be expensive. If you want to call a cab, try Tobago Owner Drivers' Association (☎639 2692) or Tobago Taxi Co-Operative (☎639 2659). Both have set rates which are pretty reasonable; drivers work until midnight or thereabouts. If you'd prefer a woman taxi driver, contact Liz Lezama (☎639 2309).

Telephones There are pay phones all around the island, most using the pre-paid phonecards available from small stores and pharmacies. However, making a call in the remote eastern end of the island is difficult; the only call-boxes in Speyside and Charlotteville are often out of order, so you'll have to resort to a hotel, which usually means a hefty mark-up on local and international calls. Due to fraud, many phonecard booths will not place **international** calls, but you can always make them from the ferry terminal booths and a few in the tourist areas. The local phone company (TSTT) in the Caroline Building, Wilson Rd, Scarborough (Mon–Fri 8am–4pm) offers inexpensive international calls and a send-and-receive **fax** service.

Therapies and treatments Ayurvedic **massage** and **reflexology** are available from holistic practitioner Usha Innis (☎639 8964; US$40 per hour), while UK trained Simon Abbot offers **shiatsu** (TT$200 per hour), and **yoga** classes are taken by Jacqueline Quesnel (☎639 8442); all of these practice from *Kariwak Village* hotel in Crown Point. **Waxing, facials, manicures** etc are available from Designer's Touch above Penny Savers Supermarket in Crown Point (☎639 8874).

Part 3

The Contexts

A brief history of Trinidad

For a history of Tobago, see p.209.

Trinidad was the first inhabited island of the Caribbean, having been settled by Amerindians from South America as early as 5000 BC. The early settlers were **Arawaks** – peaceful farmers and fishers – though after 1000 AD they were joined by more warlike **Carib** tribes. The Amerindians called the island "Ieri", the land of the hummingbird.

The Amerindians and the Spanish

When **Christopher Columbus** "discovered" the island in 1498, the population numbered around 35,000, most of whom lived in the coastal areas. There was a structured society, with organized villages and chiefs, and a self-sufficient economy that efficiently exploited the abundant natural resources, and extensive trade with the South American mainland. Sighting the three peaks of the Trinity Hills, Columbus renamed the island **Trinidad**, landing at Moruga on the south coast. Despite an initial skirmish with Columbus's sailors, the local tribes were considered the most friendly of all the Caribbean islands. This didn't suit the Spanish **slave traders** who followed hot on Columbus's heels; despite protests from Spanish priests such as Bartolomeo de las Casas, they gleefully exaggerated the Caribs' occasional ritual **cannibalism** to justify their activities.

The first permanent **Spanish settlers** came to Trinidad in 1592, where they built the small town of San José – present day St Joseph in the north of the island – complete with governor's residence, *cabildo* (council chamber) and church. Although the fledgling capital was sacked by **Sir Walter Raleigh** in 1595 as he headed for South America in search of El Dorado, it was soon rebuilt, and the colony maintained its precarious existence, growing tobacco and cocoa for export to Europe. In 1687, Capuchin monks arrived from Spain, setting up several **missions** around the island. Alongside the proselytizing, the missions were also a means to control the Amerindians through the *encomienda* labour system, a kind of semi-slavery in which the Indians were forced to work on plantations and build more churches.

To evade this threat to their way of life, some Amerindians moved to the rainforested interior. Others rebelled: in 1699, a group of Amerindians killed three Capuchin friars at San Rafael. The reprisals were savage, as Spanish troops slaughtered hundreds of Amerindians in the ensuing **Arena Massacre**. In addition, the Amerindians had to contend with European diseases such as smallpox, to which they had no resistance. Three hundred years after Columbus's arrival, the indigenous population had been all but wiped out.

The arrival of the Africans and the French

The Spanish empire, however, had neither the desire nor the resources to develop the island, treating it as little more than a convenient watering-hole en route to the riches of South America. The governors of Trinidad did as they pleased; illegal trading of goods and slaves was commonplace; and the poorly defended island suffered repeated attacks from French, Dutch and English **pirates**. When Don Pedro de la Moneda arrived from Spain to take up the governorship of the island in 1757, he found his St Joseph residence practically in ruins, and decamped to Port of Spain.

After centuries of indifference, the Spanish government was finally waking up to the fact that if it didn't develop this neglected colony, somebody else would. In 1783 it issued the **Cedula of Population**, a decree designed to encourage **French Catholic planters** suffering from Protestant discrimination in British Grenada and Martinique to settle in Trinidad. The amount of land they were designated depended on the number of slaves they brought with them. Immigrants of mixed race (termed coloured by the Spanish) who brought slaves could also receive land (though only half as much as their white counterparts), thus ensuring the development of a property-owning coloured middle class.

To implement this policy, Spain despatched a new governor, **José Maria Chacon**, in 1784. Under his energetic administration, the economy flourished, and people of French and African descent came to dominate the population. The island's culture also became increasingly French: it was during this period that **Carnival** was introduced, the French language created a local patois, and a society based on aristocratic principles of birth and connections developed.

As the repercussions of the **French Revolution** gave rise to civil and international wars throughout the West Indies, many more French – both republicans and royalists – sought refuge in neutral Trinidad. To Chacon's alarm, they brought their ideological conflicts with them. Along with the French came more coloureds, many with republican sympathies. A worried Chacon reported to Madrid that their radical ideas were encouraging the slaves to "dream of liberty and equality".

The British take over

The British, who already controlled much of the Caribbean, seized on the pretext that the island had become a nest of republicans and "bad people of all descriptions", despatching an invasion fleet under **Sir Ralph Abercromby** in 1797. The island had few defences: five ships compared to the British force of eighteen; two thousand men – many of whom had deserted – against seven thousand. The Spanish surrendered with hardly a shot being fired, scuttling their own ships in Chaguaramas harbour, and Chacon was recalled to Spain in disgrace. It has been argued that, as a staunch royalist, he may have deliberately offered little resistance, preferring Spain's British enemies to her republican French allies.

The terms of defeat offered by Abercromby were lenient; residents could retain their property and Spanish law remained in force. His choice of governor, **Thomas Picton,** was less fortunate. Left in charge of the island with near absolute powers, this harsh military officer soon instituted a **reign of terror**, deporting and executing suspected subversives on the flimsiest evidence – frequently con-

fessions obtained under **torture**. Slaves and freed coloureds – whom he regarded as dangerous republicans – bore the brunt of this oppression. Followers of African religious traditions were especially harshly persecuted; those suspected of practising obeah were hauled before a tribunal, and if found guilty were whipped, hanged, mutilated or burned to death. By 1802, Picton's activities had become an embarrassment to the British government, then facing an influential anti-slavery lobby at home, and he was demoted.

Trinidad presented the British government with a unique administrative conundrum. Other Caribbean islands such as Barbados were governed by colonial assemblies, but that was scarcely an option in Trinidad. Any such assembly would inevitably be dominated by planters, who would never tolerate the free coloureds sitting on the assembly; but since many of the latter were substantial property owners, it would have been difficult to exclude them under British law. The island therefore remained a **crown colony**, governed by French and Spanish law, with directions issued straight from the colonial office in London.

Various policies were tested in an attempt to curb the abuses of slavery, but these did little apart from infuriate the planters. Slaves were treated harshly, and a third of them died clearing the rainforests to make way for plantations. The slaves resisted by organizing secret societies with their own militias, and attempted several rebellions. One such, led by a powerful obeah man known as **King Samson**, was discovered and crushed at Christmas in 1805.

The British abolished the slave trade in 1807, but the planters' need for labour meant that slave smuggling continued. Even after the **Act of Emancipation** in 1834, the freed slaves were required to serve as apprentices for a further six years, and remained tied to their owners since the latter provided their living quarters. When the apprenticeship system was abolished in 1838, many former slaves moved to urban areas. As few labourers could be found to work on the estates, field wages in Trinidad rose to become the highest in the Caribbean.

The Indians arrive

The increased wages were not sufficient to make up for the labour shortage, however, so the British government sanctioned the immigration of **indentured labourers from India**. In May 1845 the first 225 arrived from Calcutta aboard the *Fatel Rozack*.

By 1917, when the indenture system finally came to an end, some 145,000 Indians, mainly from Calcutta, had come to the island. Fleeing from poverty and the increasingly harsh British rule in India, the immigrants had to sign contracts to work on the plantations for five years in return for their passage home at the end of that period. In 1854 the period of indenture was extended to ten years, and after 1895 the Indian immigrants had to pay a proportion of the cost of their return passage.

Though the system of indentured labour was better regulated and monitored than slavery, for the labourers the working and living conditions were practically indistinguishable. They lived in single-room **barrack houses**; insanitary conditions meant that disease was rife, and the shortage of women immigrants resulted in a high rate of murder and domestic violence. The plantation owners failed to honour pledges on wages and working conditions, while breaches of contract by the labourers were treated as criminal offences punishable by imprisonment.

Many did not return to India, but accepted land in lieu of their passage home. Known as "East Indians" – the label is still used today – to differentiate them from the "West Indians", they formed the lowest rung of society, working in the agricultural sector scorned by the Afro-Caribbeans because of its link with slavery. They became a tight-knit community, maintaining many of their own traditions; this was (and still is) resented by many of the descendants of African slaves, who had been forbidden to practise their religion and culture. The white ruling class, on the other hand, saw the mainly Hindu immigrants as heathens and barbarians, worshipping false idols and eating with their hands. Their children were viewed as illegitimate as Muslim and Hindu marriages were not recognized until 1945. Many children remained uneducated – the schools were either Catholic or presbyterian, and parents feared that they would be converted.

Yet the Indian indentured labourers contributed greatly to Trinidad's developing national identity. Just as the Europeans had brought Carnival, which had been taken up and enriched by former slaves, Indians brought their own festivities and culture. The Muslims introduced **Hosay**; the Hindus brought **Divali**. Indian food, such as roti and curry became staple foods for all Trinidadians. After their contracts had expired, many Indians turned to market gardening, broadening the country's agricultural base and making it less reliant on imports.

Other immigrants

Several companies of **black American soldiers** who had supported Britain in its 1812 war against the US were given grants of land in southern Trinidad, where they founded the villages named after the companies in which they had served. Other immigrants, mainly freed slaves from other **Caribbean** islands, were attracted to Trinidad by the high wages. **Africans** liberated by the British Navy on anti-slave patrols settled in urban areas, becoming craftsmen and construction workers, establishing strong communities that maintained their own cultural institutions and heritage. In 1853, the government brought 2500 **Chinese** to Trinidad to meet the continuing labour shortage on the plantations. The plan failed on account of the high transport costs and appalling mortality rate among the immigrants; those who survived tended to become shopkeepers, and their descendants constitute a small but visible minority. A brief experiment in bringing **Portugese** labourers to the country was discontinued, as the employment of Europeans in manual work was seen as a threat to the established racial hierarchy.

Except for a handful of **Jews** who settled in Trinidad during World War II, the last group to be added to the island's melting pot was the **Syrians** who came in 1913, seeking refuge from religious persecution in the Lebanon. Though they only account for 0.1 percent of the country's population, their dominance of the cloth trade has given them a high profile. They form a tight-knit community, disapproving of intermarriage and often sending for spouses from their native land.

The people get organized

Trinidadian society remained deeply stratified on the basis of race and class, with the white planters at the top of the heap. In the 1880s and 1890s, however, the status quo began to be challenged by reform movements. An improved **national education system** and an enlarged franchise inspired the formation of political lobbying groups linked to the international labour movement. The **Trinidad Workingmen's Association** (TWA) – which had close links to the British Labour Party – and the **East Indian National Association** were both established in 1897; while the **Pan African Association** and the **Ratepayers' Association** were formed in 1901. Dominated by black, coloured and Indian professionals, these organizations lobbied the British Colonial Office for an elected governing body for the island.

In 1899, Britain made ailing **Tobago** a ward of Trinidad, though the larger island itself still had no effective form of self-government. Resentment came to a head over the introduction of new **water rates**, and in 1903 a protest meeting in Port of Spain's Woodford Square erupted into a **riot**, in which eighteen people were shot dead by the police and the Red House – seat of the colonial government – was burned to the ground. Eventually, in 1913, Joseph Chamberlain, the British Secretary of State for the Colonies, agreed to an **elected assembly** for Trinidad and Tobago, albeit one with very limited powers; it was more than ten years, however, before the first Legislative Council convened in the rebuilt Red House.

Trinidad's burgeoning **oil industry** and the effects of **World War I** politicized the populace. High inflation led to strikes, resulting in increased cooperation between Africans and Indians, while black **West Indian regiments** returned from the Great War with stories of discrimination at the hands of the British they had been fighting to defend. The **East Indian Destitute League**, established in 1916, fought to abolish indentureship, supported by the National Congress which was then fighting for independence in India. A 1919 **dockyard strike** erupted into violence, and the government, alarmed by the anger and unity of the population, called in British troops to restore order. The tide had turned, however. Socialism, national independence, and the concept of black consciousness then being promoted in Jamaica by Marcus Garvey, were now firmly on the agenda.

In 1925, the TWA president **Arthur Cipriani** was elected to the new legislative council. A white French Creole who had fought with the British West Indians in the war, Cipriani campaigned hard for workers' rights and secured some important concessions, including compensation for industrial injuries. His essentially reformist politics had little effect on the underlying balance of power, however; wages were actually falling in real terms, malnutrition was widespread, living conditions grim, and industrial accidents claimed an appalling toll. As the world economy nosedived into the **Great Depression** of the 1930s, Cipriani soon found himself outflanked by a new generation of radicals.

In 1932, after trade unions were made legal, strikes broke out across the country. The oil workers soon found a charismatic leader in **Uriah Butler**, who broke away from the TWA to found the **British Empire Workers** in 1935. Black nation-alism became popular after the failure of the west to defend Ethiopia from Mussolini in 1935, while Indian race consciousness heightened after the visit of cultural leaders from their homeland.

One of the most influential groups of Trinidadian black intellectuals formed around the **Beacon**. Stridently anti-colonial, anti-government and anti-Catholic, this literary and political magazine ran from 1931 to 1934, exploring issues of West Indian identity and attempting to instil a sense of pride among Afro-Trinidadians. In its regular "India section" , Indo-Trinidadians wrote of their situation and the struggle for independence in India. Many of its contributors – who included Albert Gomes, C.L.R. James, Alfred Mendes and R.A.C. de Boisseiere – went on to become leading politicians.

Enter the Americans

World War II had a huge socio-economic impact on the island. Chaguaramas, the Bocas islands and Waller Field were leased to the **US military** in 1941 to provide a base for their Caribbean fleet. The Americans improved Trinidad's infrastructure and exposed the population to high-level technology for the first time. The **high wages** they were prepared to pay for the construction of buildings and roads, lured workers from the agricultural sector and ensured the decline of many estates. The influx of so many young American soldiers also had a profound effect. Their racial attitudes, cruder than the more subtle racism of the British, and the aura of easy money that attracted many Trinidadian women, soon caused the majority of the population to resent their presence.

The transition to Independence

In 1945 **universal suffrage** was granted to all those over the age of 21, though property and income restrictions were maintained for candidates to the legislature. Both the 1946 and 1950 elections were won by political parties linked to the trade unions. Britain, meanwhile, was not prepared to hand over total control while radical labour politics dominated the political arena.

In January 1956, a group of black intellectuals formed the **People's National Movement** (PNM) under the leadership of the Oxford-educated historian of Trinidad, **Dr Eric Williams**. The party's black nationalist policies, and the charismatic leadership and immense intellectual authority of "the Doctor", soon gained widespread support among a population tired of colonial government and the divisions within the labour movement. The PNM's only serious opposition was from the **People's Democratic Party** (PDP), with its base among the rural Hindus.

A **new constitution** opened up the possibility of party government, and made it easy for the winner to maintain one-party rule. After a controversial campaign that raised racial tension by portraying the PDP as reactionary Hindus, the PNM won the most seats in the **September 1956 election**. Though they lacked an outright majority the Colonial Office allowed them to form a government. The PNM were to remain in power for the next thirty years, with Eric Williams as prime minister until his death in 1981.

Many Caribbean leaders saw a **federation of West Indian islands** as the way forward for the region, and at first Williams was an enthusiastic proponent of the idea. With British support, it was decided that Trinidad should be the capital, and in 1958 a federal government was elected, with the Barbadian premier Grantley Adams as prime minister. But political rivalries and the reluctance of the larger islands to subsidize the smaller ones resulted in a watered-down federation with no tax-raising powers. When Jamaica voted to leave the federation in September 1961, Williams announced that "one from ten leaves nought" and followed suit. In May 1962 the federation was officially dissolved.

Though the PNM adopted a radical stance during the early 1960s under the influence of veteran Marxist C.L.R. James, persuading the US military to leave the country in 1961 and campaigning vigorously for independence, the party's essentially corporatist nationalism attempted to unite capital and labour, despite their conflicting economic interests. With the labour movement in disarray, politics was split on race lines, with government the preserve of Afro-Caribbeans, opposition that of East Indians.

Independence was granted in 1962 as Britain eagerly rid itself of its colonies. After the PNM created a new constitution without consulting the opposition PDP, the country seemed to be heading towards civil war; only a last-minute compromise by the PNM pulled it back from the brink. As the 1960s progessed, disillusionment began to seep through Trinidadian society. Independence, it seemed, had done little to change the colonial structure of society.

Protest, wealth and disillusionment

The late 1960s were marked by repeated industrial unrest. The **Black Power** movement, which had already made a profound impact on the political life of the United States, caught the imagination of many disaffected Trinidadians. In 1970 its supporters launched a wave of marches, protests and wildcat **strikes** that shook Trinidad to the core. Businesses and banks were bombed, and when the police shot dead a young Black Power member called **Basil Davis**, 60,000 people took to the streets for his funeral. The government declared a state of emergency; an **army mutiny** in Chaguaramas was only quashed when coastguard vessels prevented the soldiers from marching on Port of Spain by shelling the main road; and rumours abounded that a bloody coup had been averted and that plans had been discovered for mass executions of "enemies of the people".

The crisis proved cathartic. Many whites had fled the country; those who remained could no longer expect the deference to which they had been accustomed, while the government encouraged locals to be trained for jobs previously occupied by expatriates. The PNM owed its survival in office less to any strength of its own, however, than to the divisions in the opposition. "We are winning by default," PNM minister Hector McLean observed drily.

By the start of the 1970s, the country was practically bankrupt – but God was smiling on Trinidad. Vast reserves of **oil** were discovered off the east coast just as the world was sliding into the oil crisis of 1974, and Trinidad found itself swimming in money overnight. Ambitious public projects were undertaken and the country settled back to enjoy the boom years. But this sudden wealth had its down side. People got used to the easy life, productivity fell, agriculture dwindled, inefficiency, bribery (locally known as "bobol") and corruption clogged the system. Williams – who had hoped to to use the new wealth to improve the nation's economy and infrastructure – was criticized for "giving the people fish when he should have handed them a fishing rod."

When oil prices fell in the 1980s, the economy went into recession, unemployment rose sharply and inflation soared. Williams died in office in 1981, a disillusioned man with his policies in ruins; his former finance minister **George Chambers** took over the reigns. As the population became increasingly dissatisfied, the opposition parties started to unify. In 1986, PNM was ousted for the first time in Trinidad's post-Independence history, in favour of the **National Alliance for Reconstruction** (NAR), led by the Tobagonian **A.N.R. Robinson**, who had resigned from Williams's government in 1970.

This unlikely coalition between the parties representing trade unions, big business, the rural Indians and the Tobagonians tried to resolve some of the more pressing problems facing the country, but within a year the government was breaking up into factions. Harsh economic measures, including **devaluation** of the TT dollar and a stringent IMF-inspired recovery programme, were widely seen as undemocratic and beneficial only to the rich. In 1990, the **Jamaat-al-Muslimeen** – a revolutionary Muslim organization – attempted to overthrow the government, holding Robinson and several of his cabinet hostage. Though the coup was crushed and Robinson released after a six-day seige, the government's authority was irreparably undermined, and the following year the PNM returned to power under the leadership of **Patrick Manning**.

Over the next five years, the PNM stabilized the economy and paid off the IMF, helped by increased oil revenues as a result of the Gulf War. The 1995 election split the country down the middle, with the PNM and the Indo-Trinidadian **United National Congress** (UNC) both winning exactly seventeen seats. The two representatives of the the NAR held the balance of power; they used it to support the UNC, making **Basdeo Panday**, the leader of the sugar workers' union, the country's first Indo-Trinidadian prime minister.

Current issues

In recent years the UNC have concentrated on fighting **crime** and the growing **drug trade** in the country. Until the 1970s, T&T was virtually crime free, and by international standards, crime is still low; there were just 80 recorded murders in 1995, compared to 800 in Jamaica, a country with only twice the population. But for Trinbagonians – used to leaving their doors unlocked at night – the emergence of "bandits" has given rise to crime paranoia, with lurid accounts splashed across the newspapers daily.

Corruption also continues to be a cause for concern; in this small country, nepotism is commonplace, and as politics divides on race lines this often causes racial tension. Though Trinidad and Tobago is promoted as a rainbow nation – its national anthem includes the phrase "every creed and race finds an equal place" – **race** continues to be an underlying issue. It is certainly subtler than in Europe or America – there are no race riots or racially motivated killings in T&T – but big business is still dominated by the minority of white Trinis. In addition, the continuing rise of the Indo-Trinidadian population in economic, educational and numerical terms often arouses anxiety and resentment among the Afro-Caribbeans.

By international standards, however, Trinidad and Tobago is a model of racial harmony. It can also boast the most stable economy in the Caribbean; GDP has grown steadily since 1994, while unemployment and the level of external debt have declined. Oil continues to be an important source of revenue, but having learned from the heady days of the 1970s, the country is using the income it generates to develop other sectors, including manufacturing, finance, insurance and services. Serious inequalities remain: hi-tech malls coexist with board shacks whose inhabitants live without water and electricity; the social security system is minimal, and health care unaffordable for many. Life in Trinidad and Tobago is not easy for the majority, but compared with the rest of the Caribbean, the country is doing well, and its future looks bright.

A brief history of Carnival

T&T's most **popular export** and main **tourist attraction**, Carnival originated in southern Europe with the Roman feast of **Saturnalia**, a midwinter celebration of birth and renewal, and the inversion of the norm. It developed during the Middle Ages into the **Feast of Fools**, in which the pretensions of the medieval Catholic Church were scabrously mocked. The Church, unsurprisingly, did its best to suppress the festival, but in long run assimilation proved more effective, and Carnival was incorporated into the Catholic faith as a final binge (*carne vale* = "farewell to flesh") before the fasting period of Lent.

Carnival comes to Trinidad

Introduced into Trinidad by **French planters** in the late eighteenth century, Carnival was initially the preserve of the white Creole establishment. Celebrated in the three days prior to Ash Wednesday, it was a comparatively decorous affair in which the gentry made house to house visits to attend masqued balls. The Carnival principle of inversion allowed the white ruling class a brief fictive escape from the "cares" of power and respectability: the men would dress as "negres jardins" (field labourers), the women as "mulatresses", representing their slaves or their husbands' mulatto mistresses.

The slaves also celebrated Carnival, in semi-secret, on the plantations, and after **emancipation** in 1834, the ex-slaves took their own Carnival procession onto the streets in bands, accompanied for protection by groups of *batonniers* or stick

men. The revellers' costumes often satirized the affectations and eccentricities of their former masters with characters such as **Dame Lorraine**. A number of characters drew on West African traditions and folklore: a little demon known as **jab jab**, the stilt-walking **moko jumby**, and the **bats**. The parade was enlivened by the use of **percussion instruments** and the introduction of **canboulay**, a procession of flambeaux carriers celebrating the former plantation workers' newfound freedom from the difficult and dangerous task of saving burning cane fields – the name is derived from the French *canes brulées*, burning cane.

Satire and civil disobedience

Disapproving of what they saw as the "desecration" of the Sabbath by the first day of Carnival, the British authorities decreed in 1843 that the festivities could not begin until Monday morning. Since no time was specified, the carnivalgoers began to celebrate on the stroke of midnight – the origin of the wild procession known as **Jouvert** that begins Carnival today. Many of the masquerades acted out in the street processions took the form of trenchant satires of the colonial government, and in 1846 the authorities attempted to ban masking. Carnival found defenders in unexpected quarters, however: the French planters, keen to defend their own traditions in the face of increasing Anglicization, and the coloured middle class, whose desire for respectability kept them aloof from Carnival but who saw attempts to control it as an assertion of white domination.

Carnival continued to provide an outlet for irreverence and satire. New characters impersonated underworld archetypes: **jamettes** (prostitutes) and **jamets** ("sweetmen", or kept lovers), and the transvestite **pissenlets** (literally "wet-the-bed"). Masqueraders also outrageously parodied the British **sailors** stationed in the island by their colonial rulers. Bands organized **drumming** and **kalenda** (stickfighting), which is thought to have originated in the use of bamboo sticks to fight fires in the cane fields. None of this went down too well with the colonial administrators from Victorian Britain, and in 1877 **Captain Baker**, the island's police chief, began a campaign to tame Carnival. When British soldiers attempted to intercept a group of masqueraders in 1881, a **riot** broke out. Undeterred, the authorities went on to prohibit the jamets and pissenlets on the grounds of their lewdness. African-style drumming was banned in 1884, while canboulay and stickfighting – seen as a fire hazard and an incitement to violence respectively – were outlawed a year later under the **Peace Preservation Act**.

Carnival becomes respectable

Carnival was not so easily quashed, however, and a more sedate masquerade took to the streets in the following years. Social protest was chanelled into the emerging labour movement (see p.287), and Carnival became an officially-tolerated safety valve for social pressures, with the coloured middle class now becoming increasingly involved. The "cleaning up" of Carnival was furthered in the 1890s by the introduction of a **competition** for best band by a Port of Spain merchant and city councillor called Ignatius Bodu – fondly remembered by today's masquers as Papa Bodi.

In the course of the twentieth century, practically every aspect of Carnival became the subject of a competition. In 1921, the calypsonian Chieftain Douglas opened the first organized calypso tent to preview the songs that would be heard in the forthcoming Carnival; the tents proliferated, and as they became an established institution, the canvas gave way to permanent structures (though the name remains – see p.300).

During **World War II**, Carnival was suspended by the colonial government as a possible threat to public order, and when it returned on VE Day, 1945, it marched to the sound of a different drum – the **steel pan** fashioned from oil drums brought to the island by the US military. As the national independence movement gained momentum,

For more information on Carnival and a calendar of events, see pp.94–95, on mas camps see p.81, and on the work of Peter Minshall see p.108.

Carnival, with its music, masquerades, bands and competitions, flourished. Recognizing its importance to Trinidad's cultural identity and sense of nationhood, Eric Williams's newly-elected nationalist party established the **National Carnival Commission** in 1957 to organize and promote the festivities, and set up the Calypso King competition.

Since then, Carnival has continued to reflect the state of Trinidadian society and politics. In 1970, as the Black Power movement gained widespread support, many of the masquerades explicitly addressed the topics of racism and white control of the economy. And as women have come to take a more prominent role in public life, they have become increasingly involved in Carnival, to the point where they now make up the majority of the masqueraders. And while Carnival has become a celebration of Trinidadian identity and nationhood, its world-famous mas makers don't shy away from tackling ambitious or controversial themes such as the environment.

Though the actual **construction** of the costumes is becoming increasingly specialized and skilled, financial constraints have, sadly, led to the loss of many traditional Carnival characters as more and more mas camps turn to **bikini mas**, reducing their costumes to sequins, glitter and feathers attached to a basic bikini. A handful of designers are making a determined effort to preserve the link to Carnival's historic roots. Jason Griffith and his Sailor band ensure that **sailors** are still seen in the Carnival procession, while Peter Minshall has ensured the survival of characters such as **moko jumbies** in the performance section of his band.

Religion

Trinis sometimes joke that God must be from T&T, and it's easy to see why; deep faith and a laid-back attitude mean that while outsiders fret and panic, locals sit back calmly and wait with a belief that "Jah will solve all problems." Inconvenience is part of God's plan: if a taxi driver forgets to drop you at your requested destination, it's just as well – "nothing happens without a reason", and your driver's absent mindedness may well have saved you from a "spranger" waiting to relieve you of your wallet.

In this deeply spiritual republic, most people appear to hold some kind of religious conviction. Schoolchildren receive routine religious instruction and grow up making weekly visits to the church, temple or mosque. Adults are equally devout, with most people affiliated to one faith or another. Trinbagonian religion represents a polyglot of faiths as cosmopolitan as the population. Spain's long period of rule in Trinidad gave the **Catholic Church** a head start over other religions, and it retains the largest number of believers at 29.5 percent of the population. Most Indians remain **Hindu**, and devotees of that faith make up 23.8 percent of Trinidad's population, while **Muslims** number 5.8 percent. **Anglicans** account for 10.9 percent, 3.4 percent are **presbyterian** and the remaining 25.7 percent are a mix of Pentecostals, Seventh Day Adventists, Church of God, Moravians, Spiritual Baptists and followers of the Yoruba **Orisa** faith.

Indian religions

Brought to Trinidad by indentured Indian workers in the nineteenth century, **Hinduism** represents T&T's largest religious denomination after Catholicism. Though you'd hardly believe it judging by the proliferation of grandiose mosques, **Islam** has a smaller worship base, and much of the Muslim religious practice has changed little, save for the festival of **Hosay**, which has grown from a rather sombre affair to a carnivalesque party in which people of all denominations take part. All Muslims must adhere to the **pillars of faith**: pray five times a day, make a pilgrimage to Mecca if circumstances allow, keep the Ramadan fast in the ninth month of the Islamic calendar, participate in the giving of alms, and – most importantly – declare their faith openly,

accepting that "There is none worthy of worship except God (Allah), and that Muhammad is His servant and His messenger."

Hinduism in Trinidad

Centred upon the worship of multiple deities rather than a single god (see box, p.294), the central tenets of Hinduism include **dharma**, the laws of duty and order in the universe and society, while one's position in life is determined by the eternal cause-and-effect repercussions of **karma**. Though the indentured workers all worshipped under the banner of Hinduism, their wide ranging geographical and social origins reflected the huge **differences** in religious practice and status in India, and as they settled into their new life in Trinidad, they created a hybrid Hinduism that's unique to the island.

One of the main differences between Hinduism in Trinidad and in India is the lack of a **caste system** in T&T. The strong friendships forged during the passage, which gave rise to the term *jihaji bhai* ("ship brother") – transcended differences in social status, and many new-found friends chose to settle together and work the same plantations. Slowly, the caste system was eroded; only the priestly Brahman caste, whose **pundits** officiate at religious rites, has survived in Trinidad.

Rituals have also been modified. Whereas in India, prayers for blessing – called **pujas** – are lengthy processes, each with a specific meaning and directed toward a particular deity, in Trinidad several *pujas* are often combined. The list of articles necessary for a *puja* is long: oils, herbs, spices, ghee, incense, flowers, pictures (*murtis*) of the deity to be honoured, a bamboo flag pole and a **jhandi** (prayer flag) of the deity's assigned colour. Once the pundit arrives, he arranges the items and utters mantras that invoke the deity. The pole is then anointed and the flag raised, and all those present are considered blessed.

Daily rites include lighting **deyas**, reciting **mantras** and throwing **jal** (water); the latter is done by a designated child, who rises before the rest of the household and pours petal-laden water from a brass **lotah** near to a tulsi bush, a strain of basil that's planted in most Hindu gardens. Other

Some Hindu deities

Shiva The God of creation and destruction, all-powerful Shiva (alongside Vishnu) rides his faithful bull Nandi, and is often depicted with several faces, each with a third eye in the middle of the forehead, and his hair wreathed with snakes.

Vishnu Blue-skinned, four-armed Vishnu holds a conch, discus, lotus and mace, and is often depicted in the coils of a large snake. He has manifested on earth nine times; his tenth visit as Kalki will bring deliverance to the pure and destruction to the wicked.

Durga This fierce female goddess is Shiva's consort. She wears a garland of skulls about her neck, blood drips from her mouth, and in her ten arms she holds various weapons and the head of a demon.

Ganesh Red-skinned Ganesh, the elephant God, sits chubby and benign astride a lotus or throne, holding a water lily, conch, discus and a club or bowl of sweets. The deity of learning and literature, he is the author of the 100,000-stanza philosophical poem, the *Mahabharata*.

Lakshmi The goddess of light and prosperity, Lakshmi is associated with Diwali festivities. She sits on a lotus flower and embodies beauty, grace and charm. Her form varies depending on the incarnation of her consort Vishnu.

Saraswati Taking her name from a sacred Indian river, the goddess of purification, fertility, music and eloquence sits on a water lily or peacock and plays a sitar or lute. She is also the inventor of writing.

Hanuman Depicted as a large monkey bearing a mace, Hanuman is a demon-fighter, the God of acrobats and wrestlers, and the inventor of Sanskrit grammar.

Indian traditions that have acquired a Trini slant are the celebrations that now accompany the Phagwa and Diwali festivities (see pp.163 and 41).

During times of trouble, Hindus use two forms of healing magic. A **tabij** is a paper talisman inscribed with geometric designs of Sanskrit or Hindi lettering, which is folded and worn around the neck in a locket, while **totkas** are traditional ritual acts; sprinkling the first drops of a bottle of rum on the ground for the spirits (known to Hindus as **dih** rather than jumbies) or driving out evil by throwing five stones in different directions on the arrival of a groom at a wedding or a mother and new baby to the home.

African religions

Brought to T&T by enslaved blacks and further popularized by free Africans who arrived in their thousands during the nineteenth century, **African religions** centre upon the acceptance of a synthesis between the spiritual and temporal worlds. This belief in mystical powers – spirits or gods – which organize and animate the material universe is categorized in Western terms as "**animist**". The two main sects – **Spiritual Baptists** and the more secretive **Shango** or **Orisha** – are widespread, with a particular concentration in Tobago. In both creeds, spirits are seen to have a distinct influence upon the living and must therefore be respected, pacified, praised and wor-shipped through ritual dances, chants, drumbeats, offerings and prayer.

Spiritual Baptists

More overtly Christian than Orisha, the **Spiritual Baptist** faith first surfaced during the late nineteenth century, brought to the island by black Americans. Known as **Shouter Baptists** because of their propensity for loud and demonstrative worship, the sect was frowned upon by the British, who banned membership through the **Shouters Prohibition Ordinance** of 1917. **Shouter Baptist Liberation Day**, March 30, commemorates the abolition of this law in 1951 after years of campaigning.

Spiritual Baptists ground their beliefs in the Bible and worship the **Holy Trinity** of the Father, the Son and the Holy Ghost as three separate entities. They are well organized, and have their own specially designed churches with pews for the congregation, an altar from which the leader or priest preaches, and a **centre pole** decorated with flowers, jugs of water and candles to harness and attract the spirits. The characteristic white robes and colourful headwraps worn by followers (which signify their dedication to a particular saint or spirit) are a notable part of the Trinbago Sunday scenery, when you'll occasionally see bands of Baptists ringing their bells and chanting hymns in public. **Baptism**, where white-clad converts are ritually dipped into a body of moving water (usually the sea), is also commonly seen.

Lasting between three and six hours, **services** usually involve purification rituals designed to cast out **jumbies** (evil spirits) that might be lurking in the church; lighted candles are placed in front of doors and windows, incense is lit, brass bells are rung and perfumed water strewn about. Bible readings precede the chants and handclapping that intensify as **spirit manifestations** are brought about by a kind of hyperventilation known as **adoption**. Spirit possession – **catching the power** – is accompanied by bell-ringing and chanting called **trumpeting the spirit**, the origin of the "shouter" tag. Those who catch the power may grunt, gesticulate, speak in tongues or relay the counsel of the spirits in plain English, usually sharing their power by touching each of the assembled members.

Orisha

A Yoruba religion driven underground during British rule, **Orisha** (also Orisa or Shango) remains a clandestine cult. The faith centres upon worship of several deities called orishas, which are honoured through drumming, dancing, chanting and animal sacrifices. Each orisha's personality is described in stories that reveal their activities on earth, and each is assigned an individual drum-

beat, colour, day of the week, favourite food and liquor, sacrificial animal (usually a chicken or goat) and an association with a Christian saint, a tradition which allowed Orisha worship to be syncretized with Christian festivals when the faith was outlawed. The patron orisha of Trinidad and Tobago, **Shango**, is one of the most powerful deities. The god of thunder, fire, war and drumming, Shango carries an axe, his colours are red and white, his patron St Barbara, and his favoured day Saturday (sometimes Friday). Equally respected is **Ogun**, Shango's brother and another war orisha, who represents blacksmiths and iron, but there are hosts of others, and each member of the faith is aligned with an individual god through a spirit possession when they first enter the cult.

Orisha worship takes place in a **palais**, an open space sheltered from the elements by a galvanized roof and decorated with the symbols of individual orishas – daggers, cutlasses, hammers, jugs of water and ritual items such as olive oil for anointing and offerings of flowers, fruit and foods. Known as **feasts**, most ceremonies take place over several days, and begin with the specialized drum patterns that summon Ogun. Drumming, dancing, chanting and hyperventilation encourage possession of devotees by various orishas, while sacrifices may be performed to honour the spirits that descend.

Traditional herbal medicine

One of the most widely practised aspects of the traditional African belief system known as obeah is herbal medicine. From boiling up bois cano leaves for a cold or bois bande bark and ruction root to revive a flagging libido, many Trinbagonians make use of **herbal medicine**, and most know the uses of the common plants, herbs, roots and barks that make up the materia medica of what's called **bush**. Concoctions are usually brewed into a **tea** and drunk or infused into the skin through a **bush bath**, and the curative power of the remedies can take care of spiritual as well as physical health, getting rid of "blight" or maljo, the evil eye. Herbs must be picked during certain phases of the moon to ensure their effectiveness.

During the plantation era, every slave community had its **herbalist**, who doled out concoctions for every kind of ailment and presided

over births long before Western midwifery was available, prescribing remedies to ease the pain of childbirth and seeing the mother through the week-long "lying in" period, when special tonics were administered.

Elements of these traditions remain strong in Trinbagonian attitudes to health, particularly in the customs of **cooling** and **purging**, which clean the blood and purify the system. After a dose of cooling herbs such as wild senna, caraili, mauby or pawpaw bark, comes a purge of aloes or castor oil, a monthly ritual that has whole families queuing up outside the bathroom door as the medicine takes effect. Other popular remedies include lemon grass, black sage, shandelay and Christmas bush for **colds**, zebapik, chadon beni and fever or carpenter grass for **temperatures**, lime or St John's bush for **itching**, and soursop and ti Marie leaves for **insomnia**.

Folklore: obeah and jumbies

A retention of African animist traditions, **obeah** (from the Ashante term *obayfoi*, meaning witchcraft or magic) is the belief in a spiritual power that can influence events in the temporal world, curing disease, providing good fortune or wreaking revenge. Though sneered at by many, obeah still has its followers, particularly in Tobago and in rural areas of Trinidad, where **blue bottles** (the locally available brand of milk of magnesia is commonly used) are placed over front doors or in gardens to ward off the evil spirits known as **jumbies** (see box below).

Other superstitions include scrubbing the home with pumpkin leaves to drive out evil forces, avoiding sweeping the home after 6pm as doing so brushes away good luck, and entering the house backwards if you come home at midnight to avoid bringing in evil spirits. The **evil eye**, usually called **maljo** (*mal yeux*), is a widely believed concept; bad luck is commonly blamed on someone having "set maljo" on the recipient, and people wear red and black jumbie beads to fend it off.

Believers occasionally resort to hiring the services of an **obeah man** (or woman), also known as a bush doctor or herbalist, and an **ojhaman** or **seer-man** in the Indian community. Usually, the practitioner's extensive knowledge of natural medicines is the main reason for a consultation, and a variety of ailments are still successfully treated

---

Jumbies in Trini folklore

Douens The malevolent spirits of unbaptized children, these genderless waifs have backward-facing feet and hide their featureless faces beneath a wide-brimmed straw hat. They lurk in places where real children play; superstitious parents never call their child's name in the open, lest the douens may remember it and lure the child away.

Jackalantern A mysterious light that misleads night-time travellers, luring them deep into the bush before vanishing.

La Gahou Also known as lugarhoo, this spirit feeds on fresh blood. Iron chains slung about its body rattle and drag along the ground, and its sheaf of sticks function as a whip; it can alter its form (usually becoming a jackass or dog) as well as changing size from minute to monstrous. A pair of scissors opened to resemble a cross and a Bible placed at the head of the bed will force the hungry beast to revert to its human form.

La Diablesse An attractive female devil, La Diablesse (pronounced "jablesse") wears the floppy hat and flowing gown of French colonial times, and lures men (particularly unfaithful husbands) deep into the forest, never to return. At fetes, her frenzied dancing outshines the other women and attracts the men. The only way to distinguish her is by her feet; one is normal, the other a cloven hoof. She can only be avoided by wearing one's clothes inside out.

Mama D'Leau Spirit and protector of rivers and lakes, Mama D'Leau (pronounced "mama glow") sits naked at the edge of running water, incessantly combing her long hair. Beneath the water, she has the lower body of a snake, which she uses to pull any man who comes along to a watery death. To escape Mama D'Leau, you must remove your left shoe and walk home backwards.

Papa Bois Tall and strong, his hair entwined with leaves, Papa Bois is the guardian of the trees, birds and animals that live in the forests. He imitates animal calls, leading hunters deep into the bush to become hopelessly lost. Papa Bois is assisted by douens, who lead him to animal traps so that he can release the captives.

Phantom The keeper of the roads, this impossibly tall jumbie is visible only from the waist down, as his torso and head are hidden in the trees. He uses his long legs to straddle roads, stopping travellers and crushing them to death if they attempt to pass.

Soucouyant This female vampire lives in villages as a reclusive old woman. At night, she sheds her skin to travel the country in the form of a ball of fire searching for victims, her skin kept in an overturned mortar bowl until her return at daybreak. She can only be stopped by dousing the skin in salt, which prevents her from re-entering it, or dropping piles of rice in homes and at crossroads; she is compelled to pick them up one by one until sunrise brings about her discovery.

with bush baths, teas and decoctions of herbs, barks, leaves and roots (see box, p.295). Spiritual and physical problems are often viewed as part of the same thing, arthritis, for example, indicating that a curse has been placed on the sufferer.

In special circumstances, such as unrequited love, loss of an object or a string of bad luck, the obeah man may be paid to invoke or dispel a curse, doling powders comprised of roots and herbs, ashes, earth, blood, feathers, sulphur, cobweb, pitch oil, rusty nails, burnt toast or an ammonia-reeking plant gum called asafoetida, which are sprinkled, burnt, consumed or used in a ritual to bring on the desired effect – called **"working obeah"** – that is reversible only by a more powerful obeah man. But most obeah men and women today are hardly sinister characters cooking up bubbling potions under a full moon, but respected figures dispensing herbal medicines to rural communities.

Rastafari

Developed in Jamaica, **Rastafari** – particularly the well-organized, egalitarian **Twelve Tribes of Israel** sect, who have branches in both islands – has become increasingly popular in recent years, attracting a very visible local congregation. Believers and non-believers flock to reggae parties known here as **nyabinghis**, "Jah" has become

interchangeable with "God" in popular vocabulary, particularly among the youth, and the red, gold and green colours of the faith are everywhere.

With a mission of spreading love and unity, Rastafarians believe that Ethiopia's **Haile Selassie** is God or **Jah**, the 225th incarnation of King Solomon and a latter-day Christ. A second tenet is **repatriation** of all believers to the spiritual home of Africa and away from **Babylon**, the oppressive, corrupt society of the Western world and all that it represents.

Rastafarians live according to their interpretations of biblical readings; proverb 15:17 "Better is a dinner of herbs where love is, than a stalled ox and hatred therewith" directs their **ital** (natural and unprocessed) diet; no salt in cooking, no meat and few dairy products. Alcohol, cigarettes and chemical stimulants are also prohibited, though many Rastas see no problem with the odd drink or cigarette. **Ganja** (marijuana) is taken to aid meditations or used at prayer meetings: "He causeth the grass to grow for the cattle, and the herb for the service of man" (Psalm 104:14). **Reasoning** is central to the Rastafarian faith, designed to reveal truth and elucidate the wickedness of Babylon. **Dreadlocks** are directed by Leviticus 21:5; "They shall not make baldness upon their head, neither shall they shave off the corner of their beard".

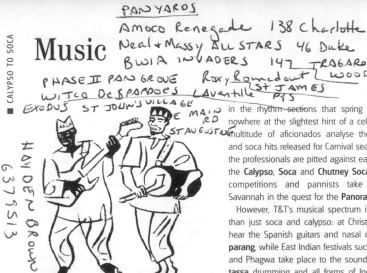

Handwritten annotations:
PAN YARDS
Amoco Renegade 138 Charlotte P.O.S.
Neal + Massy ALL STARS 46 Duke P.S
BWIA INVADERS 147 TRAGAROTE
PHASE II PAN GROVE Roxy Romedout WOODBROOK
WITCO DeSPADOES LAventille St JAMES
EXODUS ST JOHN'S VILLAGE E MAIN RD PTS
ST AUGUSTINE

HAYDEN BROWNE 6379513

Music

in the rhythm sections that spring up out of nowhere at the slightest hint of a celebration. A multitude of aficionados analyse the calypsos and soca hits released for Carnival season, when the professionals are pitted against each other in the **Calypso**, **Soca** and **Chutney Soca Monarch** competitions and pannists take over the Savannah in the quest for the **Panorama** title.

However, T&T's musical spectrum is far wider than just soca and calypso: at Christmas, you'll hear the Spanish guitars and nasal crooning of **parang**, while East Indian festivals such as Hosay and Phagwa take place to the sound of frenetic **tassa** drumming and all forms of Indian music are put on show at the Mastana Bahar talent contest. Jamaican dancehall reggae – called **dub** – is popular among the youth, and has been fused with calypso-style lyrics and hip-hop beats to create **rapso**, the republic's newest and most exciting genre.

Trinbagonian **music** is some of the most exciting, entertaining and thought-provoking in the Caribbean. Most Trinbagonians display a healthy dedication to their national musics: down-tempo, lyrically-based **calypso** (also called **kaiso**); the faster, more contemporary sounding, dance-oriented **soca**; and **steel pan**, that lilting tinkle that's synonymous with the region.

Most people have some direct connection with the industry as well, whether by entering the annual round of amateur calypso competitions to be crowned National Flour Mills or *Trinidad Guardian* **Calypso King** or **Queen**, or **beating iron**

Calypso to soca

The heart of T&T's music scene, **calypso** represents far more than catchy melodies and witty lyrics for the average Trinbagonian. Nearly everyone here is an expert scholar of the genre, capable of using the most obscure quote to illustrate an argument or make a moral point as well as

---

Parang

Trinidad's answer to carol singing, **parang** is one of the last living vestiges of Spanish occupation. A traditional Christmas music, parang is performed during the festive season, when groups of roving players – called **parranderos** – descend on private households to perform **aguinaldos**, sentimental Spanish songs accompanied by rapid, Mediterranean-style strums on four-stringed instruments, usually **mandolins** and **cuatros**.

The Spanish **lyrics** can be romantic or humorous, though many are devoted to **religious** themes such as the exploits of saints and the birth of Jesus. Whatever the lyric, the

music is always infused with a sense of joyous celebration, and the festivities are enhanced by the consumption of Spanish-derived dishes such as pastelles, arepas, pelau and strong draughts of rum or poncha crema, a spirit-laced eggnog.

Though the parang tradition has waned a little in recent years, it still remains strong in communities, such as Santa Cruz, San Raphael or St Joseph, dominated by people of Spanish and Amerindian ancestry. At Lopinot (see p.143), site caretaker and master parrandero Martin Gomez is usually willing to give a demonstration at any time of the year.

---

singing along to classic compositions without skipping a single nuance. Trinbagonians analyse calypsos endlessly until the messages in each year's crop become ingrained in the national consciousness. The poor people's newspaper, calypso has addressed every phase of T&T's development, commenting on shifts in society and attitudes to love, sex, marriage, masculinity, race and religion.

While many non-Trinidadians equate the genre with the glib Caribbean clichés of Harry Belafonte's "Banana Boat Song" or *Island in the Sun*, to its home audience, calypso has always been their most accessible form of **social commentary**. Calypsonians use double entendre and allegory to make points that would get a politician arrested for libel, and it's widely believed that Eric Williams's PNM government would not have enjoyed thirty years in power without the support of the beloved calypsonian Mighty Sparrow. Recognizing the revolutionary potential of the "people's music", one of the first actions of 1990 coup leader Abu Bakr was to establish a television station given over exclusively to replays of political calypsos critical of the government.

Calypso developed from the songs of praise and derision performed in Africa by a travelling troubadour known as a **griot**. First known as **cariso** or **kaiso**, calypso as we know it first emerged on the plantations during the 1700s, where slaves used song as a means of covert communication as well as a rhythmic accompaniment to their back-breaking work. Cariso was also a form of entertainment for the planters; notorious Diego Martin estate owner Pierre Begorrat could be tempered only by the sweet verses of **Gros Jean**, his personal **chantuelle**, as these nascent calypsonians were known.

After emancipation, when the chantuelles were able to express themselves as free men for the first time, they entertained Carnival revellers with insurgent and satirical quips. However, the British found these uninhibited displays unsettling and associated calypso with vulgarity, barbarity and **civil disobedience**, a stigma that remained for many years. Clashes between revellers and colonial officers, as well as objections to "obscenity" in lyrics from the upper classes, led to the prohibition of African drumming in 1884. In the absence of drums, musicians were forced to be inventive, and created the **tamboo bamboo** – tuned sticks of bamboo beaten on the ground to give a variety of percussive notes – to provide a legal rhythm for their mas and calypso.

Calypso's golden era

By the turn of the century, **calypso** had entered a period of rapid evolution: English replaced French patios and brass and string instruments took over from the basic rhythms of the tamboo bamboo. Armed with suitably boastful sobriquets, calypsonians such as **Atilla the Hun**, **Growling Tiger**, **Lord Invader**, **Lord Melody** and **Chieftain Douglas** refined their art and turned professional, performing for paying audiences at makeshift venues in downtown Port of Spain. Known as **tents**, these are still the best places to hear calypso at its most authentic (see overleaf). Though veiled in metaphor and double entendre, much of the early material was as risqué and **controversial** as it is today; sex, religion, race and satirical portrayals of public figures were the meat of calypsos that usually included the patois disclaimer **"sans humanité"** – "without mercy".

During the 1930s, calypso also found an overseas audience, largely through the efforts of white appropriators such as Paul Whiteman, whose "Sly Mongoose" had been a huge US hit in the 1920s. However, local singers – including Atilla and Roaring Lion – took trips to the US to record, and the genre gradually gained a level of social acceptance. Nevertheless, the colonial government still had a vested interest in controlling what they perceived to be subversive lyrics, and the 1934 Theatre and Dance Halls Ordinance enabled the **censorship** of so-called offensive compositions and the outright **prohibition** of pieces deemed particularly seditious. Any calypso seen to undermine British rule (or champion black culture) was unceremoniously banned. Calypsonians were required to submit their compositions for government inspection before public performance, and officers stationed in the tents ensured that songs met with British approval.

During World War II, calypso got another boost through the support of **American troops** stationed at Chaguaramas. Entertainment-hungry soldiers responded enthusiastically to calypso-based nightclub floor shows and the tents were packed to the rafters, the lyrics now accompanied by sophisticated **"brass bands"** named for the emphasis given to the horn sections. Foreign approval undermined British suppression, and calypso flourished, though the soldiers' preference for comedy and lighthearted frivolity rather than politics or picong (private jokes that went over the head of a foreign audience) led to a trivialization of the lyrics. However, the brawling, fornicating habits of the soldiers did not go unnoticed, and calypsonians documented the morally bereft Port of Spain society during American occupation. Lord Invader's infamously cynical smash hit "Rum and Coca Cola" (see Chapter 1, p.105) gave calypso international acclaim, ironically through an Andrews Sisters cover which sold five million copies in the US. Denied a share of the profit, Invader successfully sued.

Dominated by the inimitable **Lord Kitchener** and **Mighty Sparrow**, calypso continued to advance throughout the 1950s and 1960s. Tourists descended to experience this latest craze first-hand and the tents went from strength to strength, with new venues springing up each year. In 1956, Dr Eric Williams's newly elected PNM government created the **Calypso King** competition, and Sparrow swept to victory with the classic "Jean and Dinah", which gloried in the fact that local women would have to fall back on Trini men now that US soldiers had departed. Crowned monarch so many times that he was eventually barred from competition and given the special title of "Calypso King of the World", Sparrow continued to overshadow his competitors, and calypso lyrics settled into two strands: praise or picong for the "Doctor" and his administration, and salacious references to love and sex.

Though Independence in 1962 saw calypsonians infusing their lyrics with optimism, by the late 1960s, a new radical politics shook Trinidad, and militant lyricists such as **Valentino**, **Black Stalin** and **Mighty Chalkdust** delivered incisive commentaries on post-colonial society. But despite some innovations – **Calypso Rose** became the first female "king" in 1978, and the competition was renamed **Calypso Monarch** – the 1970s turned out to be a decade of stagnation for calypso. As the anti-establishment, pro-black themes of Jamaican roots reggae held sway over Caribbean musical tastes and sensibilities, calypso sank to an all-time low of banality.

People wanted something lively to jump up to on the road and in the fetes, and from the early 1980s **soca** (see opposite) began to overshadow its parent during Carnival season. While soca took care of the nation's need to "wine and grind and have a good time", calypso was allowed the breathing space to return to its roots. The genre received a massive creative boost in the middle of the decade through the sensitive, thoughtful work of a single artist, **David Rudder**. An unknown accountant and session singer who worked with brass band Charlie's Roots, Rudder burst on to the scene in 1986, securing an unheard of triple victory in the Young King, Calypso Monarch and Road March competitions with his beautiful, down-tempo "Bahia Girl"; his other entry, "The Hammer" (a celebration of the life of recently deceased Laventille pan legend Rudolph Charles) was received equally rapturously, and became an instant classic.

Rudder's victory sent shock waves through the calypso community. Previously, a budding calypsonian would only have dared to compete after a rigorous apprenticeship as a solo artist in the tents, earning the tacit blessing of the handful of established artists who had dominated the monarch competition since its inception. Rudder had no such patronage, and hadn't bothered to acquire a fanciful sobriquet or a wardrobe of sequinned stage clothes either. Though he entered Calypso Monarch the following year and was placed second with "Calypso Music" (acknowledged as one of the finest calypsos ever written), Rudder subsequently decided not to compete again, on the grounds that he preferred making music to winning prizes. It was a revolutionary and contentious gesture in a genre that tends to concentrate all its energy in capturing the attention of the Savannah judges, sticking to well-known formulas rather than attempting to evolve or develop. David Rudder has continued to release some of T&T's most original and thought-provoking compositions. Trinidad's answer to Bob Marley, he is also one of the few Trini singers to be embraced internationally while maintaining the support of his home audience.

Competitions and tents

In the 1990s, **kaiso** (the older term is now preferred by purists) continues to underpin the soca scene. In the **tents** that provide a practice run for the Monarch competition, an older crowd of enthusiasts disentangle the metaphors and squeal at the jokes hinged on local references that are often unintelligible without a good knowledge of Trinbago affairs and gossip. Most artists concentrate on two numbers during the season, usually one with a political slant and another with a more lighthearted theme, be it picong or sex. Whether they get to perform them both is up to the audience; after the first few verses, kaisonians leave the stage, returning only if the claps and catcalls are deemed loud enough to bring them back on.

These days, the most established tents have a fixed venue and a roster of regular artists supplemented by the year's crop of promising newcomers. Traditional kaiso is best heard at Kitchener's **Calypso Revue**, where the corrosive ML Sprangalang marshals a stalwart line-up that usually includes Cro Cro, Crazy, Pink Panther and Sugar Aloes, who caused controversy with his 1998 composition "Ah Ready" which contained a reference to the PM's wife Oma Panday. **Kaiso House** is equally good, with Black Stalin and Shadow topping a bill of Ella Andel, Singing Sandra and the United Sisters, Brother Resistance and GB. A mix of kaiso and soca makes **Spektakula Forum** one of the best attended tents, showcasing Trinidad Rio, Funny, Chalkdust and Gypsy with the year's most popular soca artists; in 1997, Andy Stephenson introduced an element of theatre with his Trini Michael Jackson act, demonstrating the "moon walk and wine" to great approval. Spektakula occasionally moves to the Savannah to accommodate its ever-growing audience, and most of the tents also participate in **clashes**, where kaisonians attempt to outwit each other with improvised material. (For addresses and practical information on the tents, see Carnival Calendar of Events, p.94–95.)

Soca

Most attribute the birth of soca to calypsonian **Lord Shorty** (now Ras Shorty I). Distressed at the moribund state of his art in the 1970s, he made a conscious decision to breathe new life into the genre. His souped-up rhythmic structure created an infinitely more danceable form that fitted in with the contemporary popularity of disco and took T&T by storm. Shorty wanted what he called **sokah** to reflect the soul of calypso, to deal with love and romance as well as the joys of feting, but his contemporary legacy is a party music, best heard during Carnival.

From January 1, soca artists release their new material in massive outdoor launch parties; one of the biggest is Crosby's launch, held outside the record shop in St James. Once released, the material does the rounds of the Carnival **fetes**, which whip the loyal listeners into a frenzy and provide a swift induction into soca culture; soon, everyone knows what to do when commanded to "follow the leader", "wave yuh rag" or show that they know which dance step accompanies each song. Alongside piped soca from the DJs, fetes usually have a live show which will consist of **brass bands** such as Blue Ventures, Question or Charlie's Roots backing the year's most successful soca artists, who all perform **covers** of everyone else's hits as well as their own numbers.

Since Blue Boy's "Soca Baptist" became the Road March of 1980, soca has dominated Carnival and become the music of choice among a nation of professional feters, sustained by more than 400 new releases per year. In 1994, the soca/calypso dichotomy was officially recognized when a separate **Soca Monarch** competition was set up. The climax of the soca madness that envelops pre-Carnival Trinidad, Soca Monarch has surpassed its parent event in terms of crowd numbers; it has been won for several years running by **Super Blue**, the new name adopted by Blue Boy after conquering drug addiction. The **Road March** title has now become more or less a soca domain, and is usually taken by **Xtatik**, a loose collective headed by elastic-waisted heartthrob **Machel Montano**.

Alongside a multitude of home-grown acts such as KMC, Iwer George, Tony Prescott, Anslem Douglas, and Chinese Laundry (the radio station-owning DJ stable whose Carnival truck is a favourite amongst "rude boy" teenagers), soca's main names also include a strong contingent from **Barbados**; outfits such as Krosfyah or Alison Hinds' Square One travel over for the season to headline at fetes. Successful soca (and calypso) artists are fostered in most eastern Caribbean islands, while Arrow, the man behind the world's most overplayed soca hit "Hot, Hot, Hot", actually hails from Montserrat.

Chutney soca

East Indians have given soca their own slant through **chutney**, which mixes sparse, fast soca beats with sitars and thumping dholak drums. Sung in a mixture of Hindi and English, lyrics tend toward the lighthearted, and chutney fetes – attended predominantly by young East Indians – have become a showcase for sensual dance steps that combine athletic wining with the delicate arm and hand movements of classical Indian dance. However, many older Hindus dislike chutney, finding the overtly sexual dancing and sometimes risqué lyrics distasteful.

Established in 1996, the **National Chutney Soca Monarch** competition is the annual focus for chutney artists, and the finals (usually held at Skinner Park in San Fernando) now attract up to 20,000 enthusiastic chutney converts. Chutney vocalists to look out for include the smooth **Rikki Jai** (1998 Chutney Monarch), Sundar Popo, Heeralal Rampartap, Sonny Mann and Drupatee Ramgoonai. Chutney has also influenced the conventional soca industry; white calypsonian Denise Plummer continues to flirt with the form and in 1998, mainstream soca artists Iwer George ("Bottom In De Road") and Machel Montano ("Harry Krishna") made forays into chutney.

Steel pan

Said to be the only new acoustic instrument of the twentieth century, the **steel pan** emerged naturally from the Trinbagonian propensity for using available materials as percussion instruments. During the Carnivals of the 1930s, **tamboo bamboo**-led kalinda music was supplied by bands of young men from deprived areas such as Port of Spain's Laventille and Belmont, who were unanimously viewed as "**bad johns**" or thugs by the more fortunate. With names such as Desperadoes and Invaders, these loosely-organized bands supplemented the tamboo with "**rhythm sections**", beating steel rods against anything from brake drums and buckets to dustbin lids to satisfy the urge for rhythm.

It was only a matter of time before someone realized that discarded saucepans or biscuit tins – and later the **oil drums** brought over by US troops – could be hammered into concave sections that produced rough notes; these early raw materials explain why steel drums are known as **pans**. Depending upon who you believe, the first pan was played at some point in the late 1930s, either by **Winston Spree Simon** of the John John band (now Carib Tokyo), who tapped out "Mary Had a Little Lamb", or **Neville Jules** of Hell Yard (now Neal and Massey All Stars) who managed the basic chords of a calypso called "Whoopsin, Whoopsin".

By the end of the war, experimentation with basic pans had produced up to fourteen notes, and the 1946 victory Carnival was dominated by the ringing of steel bands. However, the associations of **violence** lingered, and the **panyards** that sprang up throughout the East–West Corridor were widely viewed – probably quite correctly – as seething dens of iniquity. Feuds were common, and in 1950 a bloody **pitched battle** between Invaders and Tokyo had Carnival rev-

ellers running for cover. Calypsonian Blakie documented the clash: "It was bacchanal/Fifty carnival/Fight for so, with Invaders and Tokyo/When the two bands clash/Mamayoe, if yuh see cutlass/Never me again/To jump in a steelband in Port of Spain."

However, the violence tailed off after this and the movement gained respectability (and respect) as the music became more polished and complex. Soon, bands of up to 200 pannists played a sophisticated repertoire of classical pieces as well as calypso, and the nation's dedication to pan began in earnest. In 1950, the **T&T Steelband Association** (now Pan Trinbago) was established to promote and coordinate the movement, setting up a round of competitions that eventually led to the first annual **Panorama** tournament in 1963; twenty-odd years later, the steel pan was officially declared the national instrument by then-PM Patrick Manning.

These days, the panyard calendar revolves around Panorama, a hugely popular affair that involves almost all of T&T's steel bands and attracts around 25,000 people to Port of Spain's Savannah stage, renamed in local vernacular as the "**Big Yard**" during the event. To qualify for the event, bands from the **regional zones** compete at regional venues; the Port of Spain Savannah for the north, the Orange Grove Savannah in Tacarigua for the east, Skinner Park in San Fernando for central and south, and Shaw Park, Scarborough for Tobago. The bands that get the highest number of points qualify for the **preliminaries**, which are held a couple of weeks before Carnival (for more on Panorama and panyards, see pp.88 & 94). Other pan events include the October **World Steel Band Festival**, where bands from all over the world beat classical and calypso music pieces, while pan does sweet justice to jazz at **Pan Ramajay** in May, and at the **Pan Jazz Festival** in November (for details of these events, see Basics p.95).

The steel band

Transforming a dirty old oil drum to a shiny playable **steel pan** demands skill and experience, and the **craftsmen's** job is further complicated by the poor quality steel used to make most drums. The high proportion of impurities can result in an effect called **damping**, producing short, dull notes rather than sustained, clear tones. Surprisingly, empty steel drums are not that easy to come by, and shortages are common; in 1997, Pan Trinbago resorted to importing from Venezuela.

Once the raw material is secured, the drum begins its metamorphosis. All pans other than the bass must first be **cut** to size, and a five-pound sledgehammer is used to beat the unopened end into a convex shape. The pan is then **heated** over a wood fire; oil is used to **temper** the metal, and a coating of **chrome** gives a better surface and a shiny finish. The **tuner** than takes over, marking the notes and beating them out with a hammer and chisel, an extremely specialized process that's usually achieved with the help of some kind of keyboard. A finished pan will sell for around **TT$2500**.

In contemporary bands, different types of pan produce a variation of tones. The main melody is held by the **tenor** or **soprano** pan, which has the largest range of notes and the smallest skirt. **Guitar** and **cello pans** provide the background harmonies, and the booming **bass pan** underpins it all. However, no steel band would be complete without its rhythm section or **engine room**, as the percussion is known. In addition to a conventional drum kit, cow bells, shakers and scrapers, there is the **iron**, assorted bits of metal beaten with iron rods – an old brake drum produces just the right metallic clank. Known as **iron men**, the percussionists have to be pretty burly in order to keep up the repetitive beat for hours on end.

Each band is led by an **arranger**, who will adapt music from a variety of sources for the steel band. Though some arrangers work with more than one band, there are several long-standing relationships: Jit Samaroo and Renegades, Len "Boogsie" Sharp and Phase II Pan Groove, Pelham Goddard and Exodus, and Robbie Greenidge and Desperadoes. Though most bands used to play it safe and enter Panorama with calypsos familiar to audience and judges alike, original compositions have become popular since 1987, when Phase II won with a Boogsie Sharp original, "Dis Feeling Nice"; five bands entered with new material in 1998.

Most contemporary steel bands are comprised of between 50 and 200 volunteer pannists, who play one or two harmonic pans; with up to six instruments, bass pannists have to be pretty dexterous, twisting around to reach the right notes. A steel band is based at a **panyard**, usually a semi-open practice space where instruments are stored. As the band needs to be mobile, pans are housed in welded metal structures with wheels, plank floors and a galvanized canopy which can be pushed along by supporters; some bands also use flat-bed trucks to move through the streets. **Pan round the neck** bands are usually smaller, comprising 50 or so players who carry their instruments with a strap around the neck.

Reggae

After the bacchanal of Carnival, the nation gives up soca and calypso for Lent, and you'll find it difficult to pick up anything other than **reggae** or religious music on the radio. **Dub** to Trinbagonians, **reggae** has made massive inroads among the youth, who favour the "conscious" music of Rasta-oriented artists such as Capleton, Sizzla and Buju Banton as well as more upfront and lewd material from Jamaica. DJ families such as **Matsimela** and **Black Stone** play out at large indoor parties while **Chinese Laundry** rule the radio roost with their reggae-dominated playlist. Reggae has also lent its influence to soca, with many artists employing the vocal style (and the language and accent) or experimenting with **ragga soca**, an offshoot exemplified by Denise Belfon and Ghetto Flex's 1998 hit "Rock Yuh Body".

Rapso

Trinbagonian artists have also created their own musical forms, and the biggest newcomer is **rapso**, a politically conscious fusion of African-style drum beats, soca melodies and spoken calypso-esque vocals infused with the militancy of US rap. The movement was originated by **Lancelot "Kebu" Layne** and **Brother Resistance**, the "father of rapso" and the genre's main figurehead. Popularized by **3 Canal's** 1997 and 1998 Carnival shots "Blue" and "Mud Madness", rapso represents the freshest section of Trinbago music. Artists such as Resistance, Karega Mandela and Rubadiri Victor and the Chantwell collective write poetic, haunting lyrics that centre upon black empowerment and resistance to oppression; as Brother Resistance states, "rapso is the power of the word in the rhythm of the word." The proselytizing is always backed up by the stinging, drum-dominated rhythms that have earned a huge following among the youth; reggae-influenced, dance-oriented tracks like Ataklan's "Put It Up" or Kindred's "Hotter than Fire" were essential plays at 1998 Carnival fetes. **Rapso month**, held at venues across Port of Spain in April or May, is a great opportunity to hear the rising stars of this newest expression of T&T's seemingly endless musical fertility.

Flora and fauna

Joined to the **South American mainland** during the Ice Age when sea levels were lower, Trinidad and Tobago only became separate entities when movements of the Caribbean tectonic plates submerged the Orinoco Delta some 10,000 years ago. The islands owe their immense environmental diversity to this period of attachment, which has left them with many South American plants, animals and birds, as well as the **flora and fauna** found elsewhere in the Caribbean. Few places of relative size harbour such variety.

A wide range of **habitat** supports the wildlife; **Tobago** boasts the oldest **protected rainforest** in the western hemisphere along its main ridge of mountains, as well as **marshes** and **lagoons** in the western tip, a network of ornate offshore **reefs** and the **bird sanctuaries** of Little Tobago and the St Giles islands. In **Trinidad**, the rich **wetlands** at Nariva Swamp support several plant and animal species found nowhere else in T&T, while Caroni Swamp offers easy access to **mangroves** and their inhabitants. The dry, treeless prairie at Aripo – the island's only remaining true **savannah** plain – sustains unusual plants and orchids as well as bird life. The islands' hills are afforded some government protection, and contain three state reserves; the **Northern Range Sanctuary**, the **Valencia Wildlife Sanctuary** in the northeast and the **Trinity Hills Wildlife Sanctuary** in the southeast. However, with only ten game wardens and six forest rangers to defend the forests and the industrial wasteland of the west coast, the island's wildlife is under constant threat.

Animals

With more than 100 species of **mammal** roaming the forests and flats (not including T&T's 52,000 goats), hunting remains a popular pastime and wild meat is consumed with gusto when available. Most hunters go after the most common varieties; aside from the burgeoning populations of **red squirrel**, the smallest quarry is the herbivorous **agouti**, a brown, rabbit-sized rodent that looks like a long-legged guinea pig and feeds on fruits and leaves, and its larger relative the **lappe** or **paca**, which has longer legs and a pattern of stripes and spots on its fur. Equally desirable for the pot is the **manicou** or opossum, an unattractive cat-sized marsupial with a rat-like tail and a long snout that forages for scraps and carrion. The nine-banded **tatoo** or armadillo is increasingly rare, as is the brown-coloured **red brocket deer** (extinct in Tobago) and the **quenk**, an aggressive wild hog with small sharp tusks that eats roots, bulbs and occasionally snakes; some say they are immune to the bushmaster's venom. Another threatened species, the metre-long **ocelot** wildcat has been extensively hunted for its beautiful, leopard-like pelt.

Otters live in and around the Madamas and Paria rivers in Trinidad, but shy away from humans. Trinidad's cutest water-dwelling mammal, the herbivorous **West Indian manatee** or sea cow grows up to four metres long and can live for 50 years, but the destruction of its swampland habitat has decimated local populations; mature manatees need to eat as much as 400kg of weeds a day, and less than a hundred still live in the protected Nariva Swamp.

The islands' largest **monkey** colonies also live in Nariva; with red-furred, hulking frames and a bulbous, bearded larynx, troops of up to fifteen **red howlers** defend their territory with the deafening roars that prompted their name. Smaller but extremely intelligent, **weeping capuchin** monkeys live in chattering tree-top troops of up to twenty, and are able to use basic tools to crack open nuts as well as displaying their irritation at human intrusions by raining down a volley of sticks on curious heads. Around 60 species of **bat** inhabit T&T's forests and caves, most living on a diet of insects, fruit, nectar and pollen; however, the common **vampire bat** prefers a more gruesome food source, creeping up to sleeping livestock and drinking their blood; anti-coagulants in the saliva keep the blood from clotting.

Reptiles and amphibians

The largest of the 70 species of **reptile** is an endemic sub-species of the **spectacled cayman**, a 3-metre alligator with an elongated snout that inhabits swamps, rivers and dams feeding on fish and birds. Among the 47 different **snakes**, only four are venomous. With the girth of a man's arm and a length of up to 3 metres, the **fer-de-lance** is particularly aggressive, and is identifiable by its pointed head, yellow underside and chin and orange/brown triangular markings. The **bushmaster** is slightly longer (up to 4 metres) with a

burnt orange skin distinctly patterned by dark brown diamonds with smaller diamonds of orange within. Its venom can kill in a few hours (see Health, p.18); both snakes are known as mapepire (pronounced "mah-pee-pee") and inhabit forest areas. The two varieties of **coral snake** are smaller, rarer and less aggressive, they're easy to spot, with black skin and red and white rings around the body.

Known as macajuel (pronounced makka-well), **boa constrictors** – including **anacondas** – are T&T's largest snakes, and can grow anything up to a fearsome 10 metres in length. Most are patterned with indistinct brown diamonds that provide camouflage. They are not venomous, but can easily crush a large mammal in their powerful coils.

Among more than twenty species of **lizard** are **geckos**, usually referred to as zandolie or ground

---

Leatherback turtles

Weighing in at up to 700kg and measuring three to four metres across, **leatherback turtles** have undergone few evolutionary alterations in their 150-million-year history. Named for the soft, leathery texture of their ridged, blue-grey **carapace** (which is more like a skin than a shell, and bleeds if cut), leatherbacks spend most of the year in cool temperate waters gorging on jellyfish, often eating twice their body weight per day. However, during the **egg laying season** (March–July), females swim thousands of miles, returning to the beach of their birth to lay their own eggs in the sand, a fascinating, moving two-hour process that takes place under the cover of night.

Choosing a spot above the water line, the turtle excavates a metre-deep **egg chamber** with her muscular back flippers, her body heaving with the effort and her eyes dripping mucous tears to protect against grains of sand. A trance-like state takes over during the laying of around 100 soft-skinned white eggs, about the same size as a chicken's. After filling in the nest and compacting the sand, leatherbacks may make several decoy nests with their powerful front flippers to confuse predators. The process over, the leatherback drags herself back to the water.

Leatherbacks often return to the same beach up to ten times per season – a necessary repetition, as only 60 percent of all eggs laid

will mature into hatchlings – many are dug up by dogs or poachers – and only one or two of these will become fully-grown turtles. **Hatchlings** usually emerge from the sand about sixty days later, and make a moon-guided dash for the sea. Many are eaten by dogs, birds and fish; these days, any that manage to emerge during the day are herded into groups by wardens until darkness provides a little more safety.

You can see leatherback egg laying at Grande Riviere, Matura and Fishing Pond in Trinidad or Parlatuvier, Stone Haven Bay, Bloody Bay and Turtle Bay in Tobago. Trinidad's turtle laying beaches are **protected areas** during the laying season, and you need a **permit** to enter after dark; these cost TT$10 and are available from the Forestry Division at Long Circular Road in Port of Spain (☎ 622 7476, 3217 or 5214), or from the District Revenue Offices in San Fernando (☎ 652 2556 or 2317) and Sangre Grande (☎ 668 2518). In Tobago, most of the hotels along the Mount Irvine coast organize turtle-watching trips, and you can also contact Nick Hardwicke at the Seahorse Inn (☎ 639 0686). If you do go, keep quiet, stay 15 metres away and refrain from shining bright lights or taking flash photos until turtles have started laying; before this point, turtles are easily distracted and may return to the sea.

---

lizards. The **twenty-four hours lizard** gets its name from a local myth that, if you disturb one, it will attach itself to your body and remain there for 24 hours – at the end of which you die. The bright green, spiky-backed, herbivorous **iguana** is a favourite delicacy, especially if it's carrying eggs; unsurprisingly, it spends most of its time hiding from human captors in leafy treetops. The metre-long, dark brown **matte lizard** relies on speed to stay out of the cooking pot, raising itself onto its hind legs to accelerate to 11kph in two seconds.

T&T's commonest **amphibian** is the **crapaud** (pronounced "crappo"), a warty, hand-sized frog with a loud booming croak. Another frog, the **colostethus**, provides a night-time chorus reminiscent of a demented guinea pig. Trinidad's only endemic amphibian, the **golden tree frog**, lives on the epiphytic plants that cling to the rainforest trees. In addition to the land turtle, or **morocoy**, five species of **sea turtle** lay their eggs on local beaches; the green turtle, the olive ridley, the hawksbill (illegally poached for its tortoiseshell), the loggerhead and – rarest and largest of them all – the giant leatherback (see box overleaf).

Birds

With more than 430 recorded **birds** (250 of which breed on the islands), Trinidad and Tobago rank among the world's top ten in terms of species, and offer the best **bird-watching** in the Caribbean (see Basics, p.42). Adorning the republic's coat of arms, the **national birds** are the **scarlet ibis** (Trinidad) and the **cocorico** (Tobago); the latter is paradoxically classified as vermin. A native of Venezuela and best seen at the Caroni Swamp, the bright crimson ibis typifies the eye-catching colours of local species, while the golden-brown, pheasant-like cocorico has a fleshy, bright red turkey-style wattle at its throat and a loud, raucous call.

The sugar-water feeders at most hotels are a great way to see smaller birds at close quarters. Before Trinidad got its European name, the Amerindians called it **leri**, the land of the hummingbird. There are fifteen different species of these brightly coloured miniatures in T&T, of which the most frequently seen are the **copper-rumped hummingbird** and the **white-necked jacobin**, both with fabulous iridescent feathers, but the most unusual hummer is the 6cm **tufted coquette**, Trinidad's smallest bird and the third smallest in the world, with a red and yellow body, dark wings and a pretty red crest.

Both jet black, the blunt-beaked **smooth-billed ani** and the shiny **cowbird** with a sharper beak and beady yellow eyes are the local equivalent of pigeons. The audacious 10cm black and yellow **bananaquit** is supposed to subsist on nectar, but has become a frequent visitor to hotel breakfast tables, dipping its sharp little beak into fruits and sweet preserves. Seen wherever there are cattle, **white egrets** roost on ruminating rumps in a mutually rewarding relationship that provides the egret with a constant supply of insects and the cow some relief from bloodsuckers.

In the forests and flats, frequently sighted birds include **white-bearded manakins**, which perform intricate courtship displays in designated areas known as **leks** (several other species also use leks), several intensely coloured **woodpeckers**, **antbirds**, **trogons** and **tanagers** – the palm tanager is a cool olive with black flecks on its wings, while the bay-headed variety is a brilliant emerald with a russet head. Various **honeycreepers** display dazzling hues of turquoise and black; the purple variety's near-black feathers only show purple in the sunshine.

Of larger birds, common varieties include multicoloured **toucans**, **parrots**, **yellow orioles** and **giant cowbirds** as well as the crow-like **crested oropendola**, black with a yellow tail, cream beak, beady blue eyes and a marvellous way of building nests; metre-long, teardrop-shaped constructions of dry grass that hang in groups from tree boughs. Though it can be hard to spot the **bearded bellbird**, you'll certainly hear its penetrating "bok, bok" call in the forests. Birds of prey include the **peregrine falcon**, as well as several **kites** and **hawks**, including the **ornate hawk-eagle**, the largest of the lot. The ubiquitous **vultures** – called corbeaux – perform a necessary if unsavoury function by devouring dead animals.

Tobago sustains a few species not seen regularly in Trinidad, such as the **red-crowned woodpecker**, **rufous-tailed jacamar** and the **white-tailed sabrewing**. The smaller island is also the best place to see **blue crowned mot-mots** (locally called king of the woods), with deep orange breasts, green-blue heads and long flowing tail feathers, as well as seabirds such as the red-billed tropic bird. Offshore of both islands, **boobies** and **brown pelicans** trawl for fish, the latter being the only pelican to dive from great heights into the sea, scooping up its quarry in its large pouched bill. However, if a **frigate bird** is around,

Oilbirds

Squat, mottled brown and whiskered, oilbirds have the honour of being the world's only nocturnal fruit eating birds, and Trinidad supports eight breeding colonies. Spending the daylight hours inside their caves, oilbirds are unusually gregarious; up to forty birds will huddle on a single ledge, squawking and picking through each others' feathers for parasites. Mature birds venture into the open only at night, using sonar to assist their manoeuvres through the forests in search of palm, laurel and camphor fruits, often travelling as far as 120km from the colony in each foray. Fruits are swallowed whole and the seeds regurgitated, and in-flight consumption is an important agent of reforestation.

Oilbirds rear one brood of young each year, laying between two and four eggs over several days in nests constructed from regurgitated, cement-like matter that rapidly turns the snowy white clutch a dirty brown. Both parents share the 32-day incubation, after which the blind, featherless fledglings emerge, remaining immobile for up to three weeks and feeding on partially digested fruit pulp. Development is slow; a patchy cover of downy feathers grows after 21 days, and young birds do not fledge until they are 100 to 120 days old.

A young oilbird weighs twice as much as a mature one, due to the high fat content that gave rise to the name. The Amerindians and Capuchin monks used to boil the fledglings down for their oil, which they then used to fuel cooking fires and make flambeaux. The Amerindians also called the oilbird guacharo, "the one who wails and mourns", on account of the rasps, screams, squawks and snarls that make up its call; an eerie sound that also inspired the bird's French patois sobriquet, diablotin – devil bird.

smaller sea birds often lose their catch, as the frigate feeds on stolen goods snatched from the beak of more efficient fishermen.

Insects and spiders

With 92 varieties of **mosquito** in T&T, and far too many kinds of **cockroach** (ranging from 7cm dark brown pests to the rare albino variety), you could be forgiven for doing your best to disregard the rest of the country's invertebrate life, but many species are vital to the local ecosystems. More than 600 varieties of **butterfly** flit between local flowers, ranging from the 2cm crimson and black red devil to the bright blue 7cm emperor and the cocoa mort bleu, brown and mauve with eye-like spots on the wings.

Armies of black, brown or red bachac or **leaf-cutting ants,** with almost triangular heads and sharp, sizeable pincers, are divided into ranks. Large workers trim entire shrubs into coin-sized pieces and carry them on their backs to the nest, while smaller workers fend off any potential predators. The leaf-pieces are then shredded and chewed into compost for the cultivation of the fungus that feeds the colony. A single nest may discard as much as 20 cubic metres of waste material in five years, banking it up over the subterranean colony, which houses up to 2.5 million ants. Living in equally complex societies of up to one billion, **termites** attach their large, irregular earthen nests to the sides of trees; when crushed, termites give off the unmistakable odour of fresh carrots.

Aside from the spindly-limbed specimens that inhabit interior corners, the largest common **spiders** are black and red orb web spinners, about 8cm long including the legs, which spin the classic hexagonal trap. More unusual is the **trapdoor spider**, which conceals its forest-floor burrow with a hinged doorway, springing out to drag passing prey into the hole. Ten species of **tarantula** range from a delicately-hued violet and brown to hairy and black, and can measure anything between 8 and 15cm including the legs. Apart from a bird-eating variety, most are nocturnal insect hunters that construct their basic, messy-looking web tunnels on grassy banks or in dead wood.

Marine life

Sediment flows from the Orinoco River have prevented the build-up of extensive **reefs** around Trinidad, but off Tobago, where visibility ranges from 12 to 50m, are some of the Caribbean's richest and most pristine reefs. Among the sixty or so **coral** varieties are rotund brains, patterned with furrowed trenches, branching umber elkhorn and staghorn, stalagmite-like pillar coral and cool green star coral. Extremely striking are the gorgonian group of intricate soft coral sea plumes,

Coral reefs

A balanced and delicate ecosystem, **coral reefs** are colonies of **living polyps** growing over a hard limestone skeleton formed over thousands of years by deposits of calcium extracted from sea water. Each species develops in its own particular formation, and growth is incredibly slow; staghorn coral accumulates approximately 20cm per year, while the dominant reef-building boulder coral takes 20 years to reach similar proportions.

Resembling pea-sized anemones, the individual polyps feed on microscopic plankton, using stinging tentacles to impale, entangle or stun prey, causing a painful skin irritation if accidentally brushed up against. Reef-building corals have developed a symbiotic relationship with single cell algae – **zooxanthellae** – which live inside the polyps, extracting food and oxygen from sunlight through photosynthesis. The algae benefit polyps by processing nutrients and expelling waste such as carbon dioxide, and give corals their brilliant colours.

sea whips and purple sea fans while brilliant yellow anemones and red, brown, purple and green sponges provide a splash of colour, some growing up to three feet in diameter. **Caribbean spiny lobsters** and green or spotted **moray eels** lurk in the crevices between corals – if provoked, the eels can inflict a nasty bite.

Sand flats and seagrass fields between the reefs host spiny black **sea urchins**; the spines of round **white urchins** are too short to puncture skin. Long, thin and off-white, **sea cucumbers** sift through the sea floor to feed on deposited nutrients, while **starfish** and **queen conch** snails move slowly along the seagrass blades, hoovering up organisms that live there.

The reefs harbour a huge variety of multi-coloured tropical **fish**, including parrot fish, electric blue creole wrass, queen and French angel fish, striped grunts and spiny puffer fish – which balloon in size if threatened – as well as tarpon and trigger fish. Giant 7m **manta rays** are best seen around Speyside in Tobago (see pp.265–9); you'll also encounter smaller eagle, spotted and Atlantic torpedo rays, and southern stingrays. **Dolphins** and **porpoises** are common, while the docile 15m **whale sharks** are occasional visitors, feeding on plankton and small fish. Other **large fish** include reef, tiger and nurse **sharks**, grouper, dolphin (the fish not the mammal), kingfish (wahoo), tuna, blackjack, marlin, blue cavalli, sailfish, bonita, and barracuda.

Trees and shrubs

Although T&T's woodlands are disappearing at a rate of 2 percent a year, they still make up around 46 percent of the country's total land area. Several different forest types are found on the islands, including thick, warm and wet **evergreen** and **deciduous** woodlands. Higher elevations see **montane** forest, wet and cool with plenty of epiphytic growth, while the stubby two-metre canopy of **elfin** forest occupies only the highest mountain peaks.

About **350 species** of tree grow in T&T, including the exotically-named pink bark, gustacare, crapaud, saltfishwood, sardine, purpleheart, bloodwood, hairy cutlet and naked Indian. The main forest trees are **mora**, **teak**, **mahogany**, **cedar**, **cypre**, **Caribbean pine** and **balata**; the latter produces a milky latex used to coat golf balls. Immediately noticeable, the **bois cano** has large, deeply lobed leaves that dry into a distinctive claw shape while the mighty 40-metre **silk cotton** or kapok tree (its fruits contain the cotton-like kapok) boasts an impressive girth of buttressed roots spreading elegantly to meet the ground; Amerindians used entire trees for their dug-out pirogues. The spreading branches of the **samaan** are often employed to shade cocoa and coffee, while the **banyan** looks more like a collection of interweaved vines than a tree, as its boughs produce aerial roots that form secondary trunks when they reach the ground. The **tree fern's** diamond-patterned trunk and top-heavy crown of fern-like leaves lend a primeval aspect to high altitude forests.

Ornamental trees

A host of **ornamental** trees turn T&T's forests into a patchwork of colour in the dry months (Jan–April), when the intense orange-red flowers of the mountain **immortelle** compete with two varieties of **poui**, which shed their leaves to make way for cascades of dusky pink or bright yellow blossoms. The **cassia** also produces pro-lific cascades of deep yellow or pink flowers. Covering a flat, wide-spreading crown, the deep red **flamboyant** or poinciana flowers bloom in August as well as April; during the dry season, half-metre pods full of rattling seeds dangle from the leafless branches.

Flowering sporadically throughout the year, the 15-metre **African tulip** or "flame of the forest" pro-duces clusters of deep red blooms along outer branches; unopened buds in the centre of the flower are sometimes used as natural water pis-tols, as they contain a pouch of water which spurts out at speed when pressure is applied. Creating patches of mauve throughout Trinidad's forests, the crown of the **crepe myrtle** is usually smothered with blooms, while **bauhinia** or orchid tree and **jacaranda** add to the purple hues.

Fruit trees

Among the huge variety of **fruit trees**, the most easily recognizable is the **mango**, with its round-ed, dense crown of long, leathery leaves over a short trunk. Diminutive, twisty-branched **guava** trees grow wild throughout the islands; crack open one of its green-skinned, pink-fleshed fruit and you're sure to see a squirming contingent of small white worms. **Banana** plants are not trees in the strict botanical sense; their huge, tattered leaves grow from a central stem made up of over-lapping leaf bases. Covered by large purple bracts, the flowers hang from the main stem and even-tually develop into the fruit. **Plantain** trees are similar, with larger, less tattered leaves and bigger, more robust fruit. Equally easy to recognize, **paw-paw** (papaya) has a long hollow stem with large splayed leaves and fruit at the top. The fruit of **West Indian cherry** trees are bright red when ripe; they look similar to their temperate counterparts, but are much more sour. An excellent source of vitamin C, they are sweetened and juiced.

Still grown in groves for export, **cocoa** is easily identifiable by its lichen-smothered trunk, dark green shiny leaves and 20cm ridged oval pods that grow from the trunk and turn from light green to brown, yellow, orange or purple when ripe. Covered with a sweet white gloop, the beans inside are sucked when raw, but are usu-ally dried and roasted to make cocoa powder. **Cashew** trees, with their strongly-veined oval leaves, are common; the familiar nut pokes out of the bottom of a sweet-tasting, pear-shaped

red fruit. The oily liquid in the shell is a skin irri-tant, and deaths among susceptible cashew pickers are not unknown. With dark, evergreen leaves, **nutmeg** trees produce a peach-like fruit that encases the nut, itself covered with a bright red network of mace.

The lifeblood of many a craft vendor, the fruits of the **calabash** tree grow to more than 35cm in diameter and are traditionally halved and hol-lowed out to make bowls. Tall and compound-leaved, the **tamarind** tree bears a 10cm brown pod; when ripe, the inner seeds are surrounded by an acidic pulp that's used to make tamarind balls, drinks and as a seasoning. Used as a veg-etable but classified as a fruit, **breadfruit** was brought to the Caribbean by Captain Bligh aboard the *HMS Providence* as food for plantation slaves. With spreading branches decorated by large, messy-looking serrated leaves, the spherical fruits are lime green and pockmarked. Its close cousin is the chataigne or **breadnut**, a similar tree with smaller, spiky fruits that are eaten roasted.

Coastal trees and palms

Trinidad's swamps of red, black and white **man-grove** trees, with their dense tangle of aerial roots, protect coastal communities from hurricane surges, filter sediments that smother reefs, and provide a nursery for fish and crustaceans.

Among the most common seashore plants is the **Indian almond**, with its symmetrical branches; the nuts can be eaten once the outer pods turn brown, though they don't taste like conventional almonds. On exposed shores, the **sea grape** lies low and twisted, but in less windswept conditions it's wide and spreading, and can attain a height of 15 metres. The flat, round leaves are distinctively veined and turn a deep red as they mature. Once they've turned purple, the grapes are edible if a lit-tle sour. Definitely one to avoid, the **manchineel** also grows to about 15 metres with a wide spreading canopy dotted with indistinct green fruits and flowers, all of which are extremely **poi-sonous** – even standing below a manchineel dur-ing rain incurs blistering from washed-down sap.

Commercial plantations on both islands have made the **coconut** T&T's most prevalent palm. It's an incredibly versatile tree; the water and meat are consumed fresh at the jelly stage, while the flesh of older coconuts is grated and used in baking or immersed in water and strained to pro-duce the coconut milk that flavours a thousand local dishes. Coconut oil is used in soap, cosmetics and cooking, while the leaf fronds thatch roofs and make hats or floor mats, the husks are used to make floor buffers and pieces of hard shell are made into jewellery and cups.

There are many varieties of **ornamental palm**; often used to mark out driveways, the 30-metre **royal palm** is classically shaped with bushy fronds and a grey, ruler-straight trunk with a green section near to the top. Similar but even taller at an average of 40 metres, the **cabbage palm** has thicker, messier looking fronds. Squat and dominated by its spiky leaves, the **cocorite** is one of the commonest forest palms. The ultimate in tropical splendour, the **traveller's palm** is actually a member of the banana family – the name refers to mini-ponds at the base of the trunk that provide a convenient water source. Fronds fan out from the base in an enormous peacock's tail shape as high as 10 metres.

Plants and flowers

Of T&T's hugely various **wild plants**, some notable specimens include the **jumbie bead vine**, which produces shiny red and black poisonous seeds used in craft items and as good luck charms; they are said to ward off evil spirits and a bead kept in a purse will keep it filled with money. A variety of mimosa with scratchy stems, **Ti Marie** grows prolifically throughout the islands, and resembles a miniature bracken. It's also known as the sensitive plant for its ability to curl back its leaves at the slightest touch.

The largest of the epiphytes that grow along tree branches, electricity wires and any available surface is the **wild pine bromeliad**, a spiky-leafed relative of the pineapple that produces a battered-looking red flower. These "air plants" are not parasites – they draw their nutrients from the mineral-rich rainforest atmosphere – but host trees have been known to collapse under the weight of several of them. Ten-litre water reserves trapped between the leaves provide a habitat for insects and frogs. Other epiphytes include a 700-strong contingent of **orchids**, many of them so small that you'll need a magnifying glass to appreciate them. These chancers grow on living or dead plant or tree matter and in low-land savannahs such as Aripo in eastern Trinidad. In the lowland forests, both the **monkey throat** and the pendulous **jack spaniard** with its trailing wasp-like petals are particularly distinctive, while the common **lamb's tail** grows horizontally from large trees, and has attractive maroon-flecked green petals with a white and pink stamen.

T&T's most eye-catching flora, however, are the 2300 varieties of **flowering plant** which provide beds, borders and hedges with a splash of colour, and you'll often see several varieties of multicoloured **croton** leaves in between the blooms. The national flower is the **chaconia**, a wild poinsettia which grows throughout the local forests, but the ubiquitous **bougainvillea** is the most spectacular ornamental, its red, white, orange and pink papery bracts spilling out into intensely coloured clumps. Distinguishable by its protruding pollen-tipped stamen, **hibiscus** takes on an abundance of hues and shapes; the lacy **coral hibiscus** has clusters of tiny curling red petals and a red frill at the end of the stamen, while the popular **Mexican creeper** provides a clambering shower of delicate pink or white. A dark-leafed shrub with clusters of small red flowers, **ixora** is another popular ornamental that flowers throughout the year.

Flamboyant **tropical flowers** are grown commercially in T&T as well as flourishing in the wild. Brush-like **ginger lilies** are one of the commonest exotics; the deep pink or red bracts hide the insignificant true flower, and the shiny, banana-like leaves are used in flower arrangements. A close relative, the **torch ginger's** deep crimson cluster of thick waxy petals make an impressively showy head. However, the queen of local exotics – and the symbol of the PNM political party – are the 40 vividly coloured varieties of **balisier**, all members of the heliconia family, which include the aptly named **lobster claw** and the red, yellow and green **hanging heliconia**, which looks like a series of fish hanging from a rod. Equally prevalent are the artificial-looking **anthuriums**, a shiny, heart-shaped red, pink or white bract with a long penile stem or spadix protruding from the centre. The flashy **bird of paradise**, a blue and purple flower that resembles a bird's head graced by a deep orange crest, is rarer.

Language

T&T's rich and varied **vocabulary** stems both from the republic's tumultous history and from a local love of wordplay. Amerindians, Spanish and French have all left their mark in the names of towns and villages around the country such as Arima, Sangre Grande and Pierreville. In isolated villages such as Paramin in Trinidad, **French Creole** (or patois) is still a working means of communication for "older heads", **Spanish** resurfaces in parang lyrics, and **Hindi** is still spoken in Indian communities.

The diverse ethnic mix of the nation has also influenced **Creole English**; Trinis will say, "its making hot" as the French would say "Il fait chaud". Words such as *pomme cythere* (golden apple) and *dou dou* (sweetheart, from the French doux doux) are commonplace, and French patois phrases are still part of the vernacular; *tout bagai* and *toute monde* are catch-alls meaning "everything". Hindi words, such as *dougla* and *aloo* (potato), have also entered the language.

The language is often oblique and allusive. **Double entendres** – possibly a legacy of slavery, when people had to watch what they said – are common, especially in **calypsos** as a means of voicing political criticism while avoiding libel actions. Nicknames, such as Silver Fox for Basdeo Panday, the current prime minister, are used, and if you are not well versed in local slang you'll need a Trini interpreter to appreciate the subtleties of the songs.

Other idiosyncrasies include a habit of using the part to refer to the whole, calling an arm a hand, or a leg a foot – when someone breaks their arm, for example, they'll say "meh han break". People will also describe the afternoon as evening – it's common to be greeted with "good evening" at 3pm, while "goodnight" is used as a greeting. "Local" is used to refer to the country as a whole, everywhere else is "outside" or "in foreign".

Some Trini expressions

Cockroach have no right in fowl party Don't involve yourself in situations where you are unwelcome or out of place.

Crab in a barrel Futile backstabbing, from the way crabs will pull one another down in their attempts to escape from a barrel, so that none succeeds.

Crapaud smoke your pipe You are in big trouble.

De fruit doh fall far from de tree Children often turn out like their parents.

Every bread have it cheese Everyone, no matter how ugly, will find his or her matching partner.

Get cage before yuh ketch bird Before you can ensnare a woman, you need a house to put her in.

If you play with dog, you must get fleas Hanging out with lowlifes will eventually rub off on you.

Like yuh went to school in August and yuh best subject was recess A description of someone who is not too intelligent.

Man plans, God laughs It doesn't matter what you plan to do, it never turns out that way.

Now yuh cookin' with gas When you finally understand something; getting the picture.

When cock get teeth Pigs might fly.

Yuh cyar play sailor an' fraid power If you're going to be controversial you have to accept the consequences.

Zandolie fin' yuh hole Disparaging advice meaning know your place and stick to it.

Glossary

Abir Pink dye thrown around (and on each other) by participants of the Hindu Phagwa festival.

Ajoupa Amerindian building with a palm-thatch roof and walls of clay and cow manure.

All fours Popular card game, often played for money.

Babash An illegal, extremely potent bootleg white rum, also called bush rum and mountain dew.

Bachac Large, black-brown leaf cutting ant, which gives a nasty bite.

Bad John Man of violent or criminal reputation, now a bit outdated.

Bad head Being drunk or having a hangover.

Bamsie Bottom; backside.

Bandit A thief or mugger.

Bangarang Confusion, scandal, other people's business.

Bashment A big party or something very good, as in "de bashment fete for 98".

Bareback When a man is naked from the waist up. Also unprotected sex.

Bath suit Swim suit.

Beastly Used to describe an extremely cold beer.

Beat pan To play the steel pan.

Big truck Large bottom (usually owned by a woman).

Big up To promote yourself and give thanks to others.

Big yard Trinidad's largest panyard; the Savannah at Panorama time.

Bill it To roll a joint.

Block A specific area, as in "he cool, he's from my block"; also a liming spot for local youths, as in "mih see Harrison by de block las' night", and a place where weed is sold on the street.

Blue food Root vegetables such as dasheen or tannia.

Blues The TT$100 dollar bill.

Blunt A marijuana joint.

Bobo Cut, graze or scab.

Bobol Corruption, embezzlement.

Boldfaced Being pushy or demanding.

Boo No good, worthless, usually used in reference to low grade weed.

Bow To engage in oral sex.

Brands Name-brand clothing, usually sportswear.

Brass band The bands that back live acts at fetes; traditionally, soca and calypso songs hinge on a repeated brass refrain.

Break a lime To leave when a lime is in full swing, causing others to think about leaving, and often used to guilt-trip the person who wants to leave.

Brethren Friends.

Brush Sexual intercourse.

Brabadap Loud or uncouth person.

Buller Derogative term for a gay man.

Bump To get a light from someone else's cigarette.

Bumper Another word for backside, usually a woman's. Jamaican origin.

Bush Generic term for forests and undeveloped countryside, as in "me doh trust de bush, not at all". Also medicinal herbs; a "bush bath", "bush tea".

Buss To do something; eg to "buss a lime". Also bust, broken.

Cascadura Scaly black fish with a folklore; if you eat it, you're destined to end your days in Trinidad.

Charged Inebriated; drunk.

Chinee Person of Chinese descent.

Chip-chip Mollusc found on Trinidad's beaches; see **pacro**.

Chipping Slow shuffling walk with a rhythm dictated by the music from trucks and steel bands during Carnival.

Coolie Derogatory term for someone of Indian descent.

Creole A broad term describing a person of mixed European and African descent born in T&T. Also classic Caribbean food, such as callaloo and coo-coo.

Cut eye A nasty look, also a "bad eye".

Cutlass Machete.

Commesse Confusion, controversy.

Cook up/cook out Food prepared in one pot, usually outside.

Darkers Sunglasses.

Dougla Person of mixed Indian and African parentage.

Dotish Stupid, ridiculous looking. Sometimes "doltishness" as well.

Dou dou Sweetheart.

Ease up To slacken, as in "ease up you' mout'" (be quiet).

East Indian A person of Indian descent.

Ent Coined by Ronnie McIntosh's song of the same name, used at the end of a statement to mean "is that not so" or "that's true isn't it?".

Enviggle To persuade someone against their better judgement to do something.

Fatigue Witty repartee.

Fete A large, open-air party or concert; the biggest fetes are held around Carnival time.

Feting Attending fetes, partying.

Flambeaux A flaming torch made by filling a glass bottle with kerosene and lighting the cloth wick. Used by oyster salesmen to advertise their wares.

Flask A half bottle of rum.

Flex To let loose or party intensively, also a mode of behaviour, as in "I does flex positively".

Flim Film, movie.

Free up Relax, let go.

Fresh water yankee Mocking term for Trinbagonians who use foreign mannerisms picked up during short trips to the US.

Friending Having a sexual relationship with someone.

Frizzle-fowl Breed of chicken with rumpled feathers that make it look like it's been dragged through a hedge backwards.

Fronting Pretentious, false behaviour put on in order to impress others.

Funk The end of a weed joint, attached to a cigarette to make it last a little longer and give a subtle added high.

Gallery Verandah or porch where you can sit outside.

Get on bad To dance and jump up with abandon at a fete.

Goin' down Making a serious commitment in a relationship.

Ground provisions Root vegetable tubers (yam, dasheen etc), also just "provisions".

Gyal Girl, young woman.

Hard wuk Rough and passionate sex; **wuk** (work) is a general term for sex.

Hops Bread rolls, usually eaten as "hops an' ham".

Horrors Lots of problems, bad vibes caused by anger.

Horning Two-timing, being unfaithful to your partner.

Ignorant Quick to take offence, antagonistic.

Ital Rastafarian term meaning natural or pure, often used to refer to meatless food cooked with little salt.

Jammin' Working hard.

Jamette Woman of questionable morals; also a **jagabat**.

Jackspaniard Large, aggressive hornet-like wasp which delivers a vicious sting; also called a **jep**.

Jumbie Spirit or ghost, also a night person; "boy, you does favour a jumbie calling me at this time in de night."

Jump-up Frenetic partying or a frenetic party.

Kaiso Old-time word for calypso music, still frequently used in the calypso tents.

Ketch it To get high on marijuana.

Lackeray Gossiping.

Laginiappe Pronounced "lan-nyap", a little extra, a bonus.

Las' lap Final parade of revellers on Carnival Tuesday before the abstinence of Lent begins.

Licks To lash or hit someone.

Lickser Person who gets free things through sly methods, used with a tone of admiration.

Lime To socialize with friends on the street, in a bar, in a person's house, by a river, anywhere. T&T's favourite pastime.

Lock off Maintain a low profile for a while.

Lyrics Flirtatious sweet talk, usually from a man to a woman.

Macco A busybody prying into other people's business.

Macco man Derogatory term for an effeminate and gossipy man.

Continues over...

Maaga Skinny, slim.

Maljo Evil eye.

Malkadi Epilepsy, having a fit.

Mamaguy To fool someone with smart talk, making false promises.

Mampy Fat woman.

Mauvais langue Damaging gossip.

Melongene Aubergine, eggplant. Also called by its Indian name *baigan*.

Nannie Indian term for a woman's private parts.

Navel string Placenta, buried by the superstitious under a fruiting mango tree to ensure a prosperous life. Also used to denote someone's roots or a place they frequent, as in "yuh navel string eh buried in Carnival fete yuh know."

Ol' mas Raw and ready mas played on Jouvert morning.

Ol' talk Idle chatter.

One time Immediately, now.

Outside man/woman A person with whom you are committing adultery.

Pacro Sea barnacle cooked up into "pacro water", a thin fishy broth said to have aphrodisiac qualities.

Pan The steel drum as a musical instrument.

Pappy show From puppet show, meaning a nonsense, something inconsequential and ridiculous.

Parlour Small grocery store.

Pelt To throw.

Petit carem Dry spell in the middle of the rainy season, usually in September.

Picong The tradition of making fun of someone through an exchange of witty comments.

Piper Crack user.

Pitch oil Kerosene.

Plam plam Vagina.

Planasse To hit someone with the flat part of a machete.

Pot hound Skinny mongrel dog.

Pressure General term for stress or problems, as in "it real pressure, man."

Prim To be high on marijuana.

Provision ground Vegetable garden.

Puja Indian prayer or offering to the gods.

Pum pum Vagina. Pum pum shorts are tight hot pants.

Puncheon High proof rum.

Ras Dreadlocks or a person with them.

Raggamuffin Borrowed from Jamaican slang, in T&T this describes a young, streetwise person, as in Square One's 1997 soca hit of the same name; David Rudder sang "See de raggamuffin congregate" in 1998's "High Mas".

Real Plenty.

Reds Someone of African descent but with a light skin colour, also known as high brown.

Respect Used as a greeting especially between Rastafarians.

Safe A multi-faceted term mainly used as an affirmation meaning all will be OK.

Saga boy Flashy dresser.

Salt fish Salted cod, as well as a crude euphemism for a woman's vagina.

Scruntin' Penniless, broke.

Sea bath To go for a swim in the sea.

Semi demi An impromptu, informal performance.

Sensie Marijuana, short for sensimilla.

Sketel Usually a woman who sleeps around, but can also be used of a man.

Slackness Impolite, crude and low-down behaviour.

Spranger Crack user, petty thief or volatile person.

Sound system A crew of DJs operating the decks and providing the huge speaker boxes at fetes and parties.

Steups A sign of irritation, disapproval or derision also known as kissing or sucking the teeth. Dating back to the 1800s, this common sound in Trinidadian conversation came from the French planters who used it as a way of undermining the authority of the new British rulers.

Storm Getting into a fete without paying by climbing over the fence, sweet talking the doorman etc.

Stupidness The preferred term to describe ridiculous, slack, time-consuming actions or behaviour.

Sweetman A man who is financially supported by a woman.

Swizzle stick A whisk used for stirring callaloo or juicing fruits to make punch.

Tabanca The depression caused by the ending of a love affair. In extreme states, **"tabantruck"**.

Tan-ta-na Excitement, confusion.

Tanty Aunt or a person who is like an aunt.

Tapia Hut made with thatch and mud walls.

Ting A thing, woman or a euphemism for all kinds of eventualities – "tings a gwan".

Tobago love Disguising your feelings for a loved one, possibly due to finding it difficult to express your emotions.

Torshont (pronounced "torshore") A loofah.

Totie Penis; the title of Errol Fabian's 1998 calypso "Ato Tea Party" was a play on the word; all those named in the song were strenuous in their efforts to deny that they wanted to taste some of "Ato tea". (Ato Bolden is Trinbago's most celebrated athlete).

Trace A road or street that once was or still is a dirt track.

Travel Using public transport.

Vex Angry or annoyed.

Vex money Extra money to take out with you, in case you have an argument with your partner and have to pay your own way home.

Wapie A card game.

Wassi Lewd, uninhibited behaviour and dancing at fetes; wining down to the ground.

We is we You are among friends.

Wine To dance by rotating hips and bottom in an erotic manner. Your **wining bone** is what allows you to move with suitable sensuality.

Wrapping paper Cigarette paper used for rolling joints.

Wutless Worthless, no good.

Yampie Matter that collects at the corner of the eyes after sleep

Yard fowl Chickens raised in someone's backyard.

Zaboca Avocado.

Zig zag Altering your opinions to fit the circumstances.

Trini titbits

When opening a bottle of rum, a capful is thrown onto the ground "for the spirit".

In memory of the dead, on the day of their wake, the street where the deceased lived is lined with candles on the pavement.

Trinis avoid walking on concrete manhole covers, not out of superstition but from a well-founded fear that they will collapse.

On hearing T&T's national anthem, all Trinis come to a direct halt and stand silently to attention – you are expected to do the same.

Meals are rarely eaten together in families unless it is a special occasion; usually a pot with food is left on the stove for each individual to dip into when necessary.

Trinis go everywhere with their "rags" – a facecloth or bandanna to wipe sweat, wave in a fete or place over their head as night falls – to prevent dew causing a head cold.

Some Trinis – usually from poorer districts – cover their neck and chest with talcum powder as it reportedly keeps them feeling cool.

If it starts to rain, Trinis stop – waiting under shop awnings for the shower to pass. "It was raining" is a valid excuse for being late, even for a job interview.

All Trinis peel their oranges in the same way, using a knife in a circular motion from top to bottom, leaving the pith intact.

Expect a Trini goodbye to take half an hour from the point that they say they are leaving. If you're waiting for a lift, patience is essential while the goodbyes are done slowly and diplomatically to ensure no one is left out and a good vibe is kept.

Books

The following books should be readily available in the US, UK and/or T&T. Where a book is only published in one country we have specified which. It is also worth visiting the library in Port of Spain – many local authors whose work is unavailable abroad are well represented in its West Indian section. If you are staying for more than a couple of weeks, you can fill out a form, pay a TT$20 refundable deposit and borrow books. In Tobago they tend to be stricter – insisting that you are in the country at least three months before they lend you books.

Fiction and poetry

Michael Anthony *Cricket in the Road and Other Stories* (Heinemann, UK). An anthology of short stories evoking the atmosphere and lifestyle of Trinidad. Concise, thought-provoking pieces, rich in description. His novel *In the Heat of the Day* (Heinemann, UK) is centred on the period of industrial unrest that led to the 1903 water riots, while *The Year in San Fernando* (Heinemann, UK) is an acute portrayal of San Fernando in the 1940s, seen through the eyes of a teenage boy on a year's sojourn from his village home.

Kevin Baldeosingh *The Autobiography of Paras P* (Heinemann, UK). Biting satirical novel tracing the career of the entirely ludicrous Paras Parmanandansingh, with plenty of implicit references to society figures. Extremely funny.

Valerie Belgrave *Ti Marie* (Heinemann, UK). A romantic, passionate novel set in the late eighteenth century when Britain and Spain were fighting for control of Trinidad – a Caribbean *Gone with the Wind*, but far more intelligent and historically accurate.

Brother Resistance *Rapso Explosion* (Karia Press, UK). An excellent introduction to rapso poetry compiled by the father of the art form. These politically conscious poems describe the fears, hopes, dreams and lives of Trinidad's youth in contemporary Trini dialect.

Leroy Clarke *Douens* (Karaele, US). A book of unusual, intriguing drawings and poems that draw on Trinidadian folklore to explore issues of identity and conscience.

Marion Patrick Jones *J'Ouvert Morning* (Columbus Publishers, T&T). A novel spanning three generations of ordinary Trinidadians, detailing their lives and tribulations from the melodramatic to the mundane.

Earl Lovelace *While Gods are Falling* (Longman, UK). The author's first novel tells the story of a young man trapped by his family responsibilities and unfulfilled by his work as he struggles to survive in an impersonal city. *The Dragon Can't Dance* (Andre Deutsch, UK) is a powerful and passionate examination of the motivation behind Carnival – if you only read one book about Trinidad, make it this one. In *The Wine of Astonishment* (Heinemann, UK), Lovelace highlights the persecution of the Spiritual Baptists, while in *The Schoolmaster* (Heinemann, UK), a powerful and superbly handled allegory of colonialism, a repected schoolmaster abuses his position of power in an isolated and ill-informed country village.

Alfred Mendes *Black Fauns* (New Beacon, UK). An interesting and amusing book about the mainly female inhabitants of a barrack yard in the 1930s. As they attempt to cope with poverty, ambition and betrayal they reveal the sense of community that made barrack yard living bearable. The cleverly-plotted *Pitch Lake* (New Beacon, UK) highlights the snobbery, racism and insecurity of a young middle-class Portuguese man that eventually lead to his moral, spiritual and physical downfall.

Sharlow Mohammed *The Promise* (Sharlow, T&T). A powerful and evocative account of the experiences of the Indian indentured labourers. *When Gods were Slaves* (Sharlow, T&T) follows the fate of Anyika – the name means endurance – from his happy life in an African village through the trials of slavery in Trinidad.

Shani Mootoo *Cereus Blooms at Midnight* (Granta, UK). This Irish-Trinidadian-Canadian author's ambitious first novel deals with the relationship between an old woman dying in a Caribbean nursing home and her young gay nurse.

Pamela Mordecai and Betty Wilson (eds); *Her True True Name* (Heinemann, UK). Collection of short stories by women writers from the Caribbean. The T&T section includes work from Dionne Brand, Rosa Guy, Marion Patrick-Jones and Merle Hodge.

Shiva Naipaul *Beyond the Dragon's Mouth* (Hamish Hamilton, UK) blends journalistic and fictional anecdotes of the author's travels from Port of Spain to London, Liverpool, Hull, Iran and Surinam. *The Chip-Chip Gatherers* (Hamish Hamilton, UK) is a darkly funny tale of the machinations of the one rich man in a poor rural community. His novel *Fireflies* (Hamish Hamilton, UK) chronicles the moral, financial and spiritual decline of a rich and influential Indo-Trinidadian family with empathy and ironic humour.

V.S. Naipaul *A House for Mr Biswas* (Penguin, US/UK). Mr Biswas – a newspaper journalist trapped by poverty into living with his domineer-

Trinbagonian literature

It is scarcely surprising that with their diverse cultural heritage, opaque dialect and witty, imaginative, use of language, the people of Trinidad and Tobago have developed a **rich** literary heritage, producing a stable of world-class writers far out of proportion to the size of the country. This unique literary tradition emerged in the 1930s with the publication of the *Beacon*, a radical journal that ran from 1931 to 1934. Featuring poetry and short stories by young Trinidadian writers and intellectuals such as **C.L.R. James** and **Alfred Mendes**, the magazine fostered the development of "yard literature", social realist stories such as Mendes's *Black Fauns*, describing the experiences of poorer Trinidadians.

Trinbagonian literature flourished after World War II with the emergence of a new generation of novelists. **Samuel Selvon**'s wryly humorous novels chronicle both the experience of growing up in Trinidad and the trials and tribulations of an emigrant in London, while those of **Earl Lovelace** are a lyrical celebration of Trinidadian life and culture, its "shacks that leap out of the red dirt and stone, thin like smoke, fragile like kite paper balancing on their rickety pillars as broomsticks on the edge of a juggler's nose" (*The Dragon Can't Dance*).

The late 1950s saw the appearance of Trinidad's most internationally acclaimed novelist, **V.S. Naipaul**. The son of a journalist, Naipaul grew up in Chaguanas and Port of Spain, winning a scholarship in 1950 to study English at Oxford University. He wrote his first book, *The Mystic Masseur* (1957), at the age of

23 while working for the BBC Caribbean Service in London. It was his fourth, *A House for Mr Biswas*, that made his name in 1961. Drawing on the experiences of his father, the novel explores the frustration and claustrophobia of an ambitious intellectual in a colonial society. Naipaul's ironic treatment of the snobbery, corruption and small-mindedness of Trinidadian life has earned him an ambivalent reputation in his homeland. His brother **Shiva Naipaul** also garnered substantial literary acclaim with books such as *Fireflies* (1970) and *Beyond the Dragon's Mouth* (1984), before his sudden death of a heart attack at the age of forty in 1985.

Trinidad's best known poet, the Nobel prizewinner **Derek Walcott**, was actually born in St Lucia, but lived in Port of Spain for decades, establishing the Trinidad Theatre Workshop (see pp.73–74) there. An accomplished and prolific lyric poet, Walcott draws on the Elizabethan tradition, using both traditional rhyme and metre and free verse to explore issues of exile and identity and evoke the rich, heady atmosphere of the Caribbean.

Among **T&T poets** to look out for are Cecil Herbert, Errol Hill, Barnabos Romon-Fortune, E.M. Roach, H.M. Telemaque, Leroy Clarke, Krishna Samaroo, Wayne Brown and Kevin Baldeosingh. **Women poets** are numerous but hard to find published; perhaps the best anthology is *Washer Woman Hangs Her Poems in the Sun*, which includes a wide range of work dealing with subjects from the mundane to the supernatural, providing endless insights into the Trinbago mentality.

ing in-laws – struggles to establish his own identity. *In a Free State* (Penguin), a collection of five tales that won the Booker Prize in 1971, explores people's changing roles and attitudes when transplanted from their homelands, while the stories in *Miguel Street* (Andre Deutsch, UK) paint a picture of community life in Trinidad seen through the eyes of a small boy. *The Middle Passage* (Penguin) – the first of the travel books that have dominated Naipaul's later output – looks at the effects of colonialism on five societies in the Caribbean and South America.

Lawrence Scott *Ballad for the New World and other stories* (Heinemann, UK) . A clever collection of short stories evoking pre-Independence Trinidad and the experiences of a white boy growing up in the colony with ironic humour and sensitivity.

Samuel Selvon *A Brighter Sun* (Longman Drumbeat, UK). An evocative and amusing story of an Indo-Trinidadian young man learning the responsibilities of adult life during the upheavals of World War II. *The Lonely Londoners* (Longman, UK) is a witty account of a group of West Indian immigrants adjusting to the cold climate, racism and big city life of 1950s London. Its sequel, *Moses Ascending* (Heinemann, UK), is an ironic tale of an apathetic Trinidadian's experience of the Black Power movement and race relations in 1970s London.

Derek Walcott *Omeros* (Farrar, Straus, Giroux/Faber). An extraordinary tour de force that draws on Homer's *Odyssey* to produce a vast Caribbean epic of the dispossessed. Many of the works in Walcott's *Collected Poems 1948–1984* (Farrar, Straus, Giroux/Faber) evoke the sights and sounds of Trinidad, including the famous "Laventille", dedicated to V.S. Naipaul.

Margaret Watts (ed), *Washer Woman Hangs her Poems in the Sun* (Ferguson, T&T). An anthology of modern women poets from Trinidad and Tobago, full of marvellous poems tackling everything from Carnival to Caribbean men.

History and current affairs

Michael Anthony *First in Trinidad* (Paria, T&T) An over-detailed account of the first appearances in Trinidad of everything from the postal service to Carnival; his *The Making of Port of Spain* (Caribbean Publications, T&T) and *Towns and Villages* (Circle Press, T&T) will tell you everything you could ever want to know about the capital and many of the the villages respectively.

B. Bereton *A History of Modern Trinidad 1783–1962* (Heinemann, US/UK) The most comprehensive book on the island's history.

James Ferguson *Eastern Caribbean In Focus* (Latin America Bureau, UK). Overview of the history, culture, economics and societies of the eastern Caribbean.

P.E.T. O'Connor *Some Trinidad Yesterdays* (Inprint, T&T). Dry personal reminiscences of a son of a plantation owner and director of Texaco in Trinidad.

C.R. Ottley *Spanish Trinidad* (Longman, UK). An exhaustive account of Trinidad's history from 1498 to 1797. *The Story of Tobago* (Longman, UK) is an engaging account of Tobago's history from the Caribs to Hurricane Flora in 1965.

M.S. Ramesar *Survivors of another Crossing* (University of the West Indies Press, T&T). An excellent, informative book with photographs recording the experiences of the indentured Indians from 1845 to the 1930s.

Selwyn Ryan *Revolution and Reaction*, *The Disillusioned Electorate* and *The Muslimeen Grab for Power* (all University of the West Indies Press, T&T). Three excellent accounts of recent T&T history: the first covers the Black Power years, the slump of the 1970s, and the subsequent oil boom; the second deals with the economic downturn of the late 1980s, the disintegration of the PNM and the rise and rapid fall of the NAR; while the third analyses the causes and impact of the 1990 coup attempt.

E. Williams *History of the Peoples of Trinidad and Tobago* (A&B Distributors, US). Before becoming T&T's first prime minister, Williams was a respected academic and expert on Caribbean history; his book gives an excellent background to the development of the islands.

Trini life and culture

Gerard A. Besson (ed.) *Trinidad Carnival* (Paria, T&T). Reproduction of *Caribbean Quarterly's* 1956 Carnival edition, this collection of pieces from eminent Trinidadian academics and musicologists is sometimes a little heavy, but has fascinating accounts of the development of Carnival from the nineteenth century to the 1950s.

Adrian Bird *Trinidad Sweet* (Inprint, T&T). If you ignore the occasional sexist comment this book provides an excellent and detailed insight into Trinidadian culture, mentality and the island. Full of anecdotes, humorous observations and fascinating titbits.

Dave DeWitt and Mary Jane Willan *Callaloo, Calypso and Carnival* (Crossing Press, US). Lively and informative cookbook-cum-travel guide, with accounts of T&T as well as calypso, Carnival, culinary and wider history, as well as all the classic recipes from pelau to black cake.

Martin Haynes *Trinidad and Tobago Dialect (Plus)* (self published, T&T). Hard to get hold of out of Trinidad but well worth it; Trini patois divided up into themes; "jorts" (food) "t'reads" (clothes) and "fete-in" (partying) as well as some beautiful sayings, old wives' tales and proverbs.

C.L.R. James *Beyond a Boundary* (Duke University Press/Random House). Autobiographical book on cricket and life in Trinidad in the 1920s.

Paul Keens-Douglas *Lal Shop* (Keensdee, T&T). A collection of anecdotes written for the author's *Sunday Express* column "Is Town Say So", each piece is a random reproduction of classic "ol' talk", with titles such as "Yu ever stop to wonder how calypsonians get dey name?" or "Dat boil corn sufferin' from real malnutrition". Difficult to get hold of out of T&T, this engaging slice of rum shop banter written in patois gives a good picture of local sensibilities.

Peter van Koningsbruggen *Trinidad Carnival: Quest for a National Identity* (Macmillan, UK). An excellent examination of attitudes surrounding Carnival and its socio-economic impact on Trinidad.

Patrick Leigh Fermor *The Traveller's Tree* (Penguin, UK). Written in the late 1940s, this classic account of a Caribbean tour has an interesting section on Trinidad, describing Port of Spain with an eagle eye and analysing the island's history, as well as its music and the "saga boy" fashions of the time.

Amryl Johnson *Sequins for a Ragged Hem* (Virago, UK). Intense and personal portrayal of Trinidad, Tobago and other Caribbean islands as seen by a woman born in Trinidad but living in Britain.

Luise Kimme *Chachalaca* (self published, T&T). Evocative, intense snippets of Tobago life lovingly – and idiosyncratically – described in German and English by emigrant sculptor Kimme. Available from her studio in Tobago (see p.243).

John Newel Lewis *Ajoupa* (self-published, T&T, o/p). A marvellously idiosyncratic and enthusiastic account of the unique architecture of Trinidad and Tobago, illustrated by the author's own superb line drawings.

Zenga Longmore *Tap-Taps to Trinidad* (Hodder & Stoughton, UK). Caribbean travelogue with an excellent T&T account, during which the author is at the mercy of her tyrannical Trini aunt.

Peter Manuel *Caribbean Currents* (Latin America Bureau, UK). Excellent, well researched account of the Caribbean music scene with a strong T&T section that details the development of soca and calypso as well as Indian music and culture.

Peter Mason *Bacchanal! Carnival, Calypso and the Popular Culture of Trinidad* (Temple University Press/Latin America Bureau). Packed with interviews with calypsonians and costume designers, this is the most up-to-date and informative book on Trinidad's Carnival.

Olga Mavrogordato *Voices in the Street* (Inprint, T&T). Detailing the history of some of the many old buildings around Port of Spain.

John Mendes *Cote Ce, Cote La* (self published, T&T). The original dictionary of Trinbagonian words, with sections on Carnival and proverbs and drawings by Carnival designer Wayne Berkeley. Widely available on the islands.

Raymond Quevedo *Atilla's Kaiso* (University of the West Indies Press, T&T). Written by veteran kaisonian Atilla the Hun shortly before his death, this provides a true insider's view of the development of calypso as well as the lyrics of some of his best compositions.

Lystra St John *Remedies and Recipes of my Ancestry* (self published, T&T). A materia medica of Trinbago bush medicine with sections on supernatural illness, remedy and ailment lists, botanical and local names for herbs and a selection of African and Trinbagonian recipes.

Keith Warner *The Trinidad Calypso* (Heinemann, UK). Excellent history of calypso.

Steve Vertovec *Hindu Trinidad* (Macmillan, UK). Concise academic review of Hindu religion and culture in Trinidad, with an excess of facts and figures.

Natural history

Richard Ffrench *A Guide to the Birds of Trinidad and Tobago* (Macmillan, UK). Definitive guide to T&T's bird life with entries on all the species that include information on habitat, habits, appearance and calls as well as a description of the islands' natural history and environment. The pocket-sized version with pictures and descriptions of 83 common species is handy for travellers.

Julian Kenny *Native Orchids of the Eastern Caribbean* (Macmillan, UK). Beautifully illustrated orchid guide with special emphasis on Trinidad's orchids, written by a University of the West Indies professor.

G.W. Lennox & S.A. Seddon *Flowers of the Caribbean; Fruits and Vegetables of the Caribbean; Trees of the Caribbean* (all Macmillan, UK). Slim and handy reference volumes with glossy, sharp colour pictures and concise accounts.

Guidebooks

Comeau, Guy, Hesterman and Hill *T&T Field Naturalists' Club Trail Guide* (T&T Field Naturalists' Club, T&T). Definitive guide to hiking trails in Trinidad and Tobago with detailed descriptions, lengths and sketch maps. Useful sections on local geology and preparing for a hike but difficult to get hold of, though a new edition is in production.

Mike East *T&T; A Traveller's Guide* (Roger Lascelles, UK). Fairly detailed with a few colour pictures and good – if a little outdated – information.

Richard Ffrench and Peter Bacon *Nature Trails of Trinidad* (S.M Publications, T&T). Easy to use, up-to-date guide to hikes in Trinidad.

Kathleen O'Donnell and Harry Pefkaros *Adventure Guide to Trinidad and Tobago* (Hunter, US). Not very adventurous, and the hand-drawn maps are terrible, but the highly personal style makes for some interesting comments.

Elizabeth Saft (ed) *Insight Guide to Trinidad and Tobago* (APA, UK). Lavishly illustrated and full of good contextual information written by local experts, if a little thin on practicalities.

Jeremy Taylor *Trinidad and Tobago: An Introduction and Guide* (Macmillan, UK). Stronger on background than on practicalities, but a useful introduction to the culture of the islands.

Index

Stay in touch with us!

ROUGH*NEWS* **is Rough Guides' free newsletter. In three issues a year we give you news, travel issues, music reviews, readers' letters and the latest dispatches from authors on the road.**

I would like to receive ROUGH*NEWS*: please put me on your free mailing list.

NAME . . . .

ADDRESS . . . .

Please clip or photocopy and send to: Rough Guides, 62–70 Shorts Gardens, London WC2H 9AB, England or Rough Guides, 375 Hudson Street, New York, NY 10014, USA.

direct orders from

		UK	US	CAN
Amsterdam	1-85828-218-7	£8.99	$14.95	$19.99
Andalucia	1-85828-219-5	9.99	16.95	22.99
Antigua Mini Guide	1-85828-346-9	5.99	9.95	12.99
Australia	1-85828-220-9	13.99	21.95	29.99
Austria	1-85828-325-6	10.99	17.95	23.99
Bali & Lombok	1-85828-134-2	8.99	14.95	19.99
Bangkok Mini Guide	1-85828-345-0	5.99	9.95	12.99
Barcelona	1-85828-221-7	8.99	14.95	19.99
Belgium & Luxembourg	1-85828-222-5	10.99	17.95	23.99
Belize	1-85828-351-5	9.99	16.95	22.99
Berlin	1-85828-327-2	9.99	16.95	22.99
Boston Mini Guide	1-85828-321-3	5.99	9.95	12.99
Brazil	1-85828-223-3	13.99	21.95	29.99
Britain	1-85828-312-4	14.99	23.95	31.99
Brittany & Normandy	1-85828-224-1	9.99	16.95	22.99
Bulgaria	1-85828-183-0	9.99	16.95	22.99
California	1-85828-330-2	11.99	18.95	24.99
Canada	1-85828-311-6	12.99	19.95	25.99
Central America	1-85828-335-3	14.99	23.95	31.99
China	1-85828-225-X	15.99	24.95	32.99
Corfu & the Ionian Islands	1-85828-226-8	8.99	14.95	19.99
Corsica	1-85828-227-6	9.99	16.95	22.99
Costa Rica	1-85828-136-9	9.99	15.95	21.99
Crete	1-85828-316-7	9.99	16.95	22.99
Cyprus	1-85828-182-2	9.99	16.95	22.99
Czech & Slovak Republics	1-85828-317-5	11.99	18.95	24.99
Dublin Mini Guide	1-85828-294-2	5.99	9.95	12.99
Edinburgh Mini Guide	1-85828-295-0	5.99	9.95	12.99
Egypt	1-85828-188-1	10.99	17.95	23.99
Europe 1998	1-85828-289-6	14.99	19.95	25.99
England	1-85828-301-9	12.99	19.95	25.99
First Time Asia	1-85828-332-9	7.99	9.95	12.99
First Time Europe	1-85828-270-5	7.99	9.95	12.99
Florida	1-85828-184-4	10.99	16.95	22.99
France	1-85828-228-4	12.99	19.95	25.99
Germany	1-85828-309-4	14.99	23.95	31.99
Goa	1-85828-275-6	8.99	14.95	19.99
Greece	1-85828-300-0	12.99	19.95	25.99
Greek Islands	1-85828-310-8	10.99	17.95	23.99
Guatemala	1-85828-323-X	9.99	16.95	22.99
Hawaii: Big Island	1-85828-158-X	8.99	12.95	16.99
Hawaii	1-85828-206-3	10.99	16.95	22.99
Holland	1-85828-229-2	10.99	17.95	23.99
Hong Kong & Macau	1-85828-187-3	8.99	14.95	19.99
Hotels & Restos de France 1998	1-85828-306-X	12.99	19.95	25.99
Hungary	1-85828-123-7	8.99	14.95	19.99
India	1-85828-200-4	14.99	23.95	31.99
Ireland	1-85828-179-2	10.99	17.95	23.99
Israel & the Palestinian Territories	1-85828-248-9	12.99	19.95	25.99
Italy	1-85828-167-9	12.99	19.95	25.99
Jamaica	1-85828-230-6	9.99	16.95	22.99
Japan	1-85828-340-X	14.99	23.95	31.99
Jordan	1-85828-350-7	10.99	17.95	23.99
Kenya	1-85828-192-X	11.99	18.95	24.99
Lisbon Mini Guide	1-85828-297-7	5.99	9.95	12.99
London	1-85828-231-4	9.99	15.95	21.99
Madrid Mini Guide	1-85828-353-1	5.99	9.95	12.99
Mallorca & Menorca	1-85828-165-2	8.99	14.95	19.99
Malaysia, Singapore & Brunei	1-85828-232-2	11.99	18.95	24.99
Mexico	1-85828-044-3	10.99	16.95	22.99
Morocco	1-85828-169-5	11.99	18.95	24.99
Moscow	1-85828-322-1	9.99	16.95	22.99
Nepal	1-85828-190-3	10.99	17.95	23.99
New York	1-85828-296-9	9.99	15.95	21.99
New Zealand	1-85828-233-0	12.99	19.95	25.99
Norway	1-85828-234-9	10.99	17.95	23.99

UK orders: 0181 899 4036

around the world

		UK£	US$	CAN$
Pacific Northwest	1-85828-326-4	12.99	19.95	25.99
Paris	1-85828-235-7	8.99	14.95	19.99
Peru	1-85828-142-3	10.99	17.95	23.99
Poland	1-85828-168-7	10.99	17.95	23.99
Portugal	1-85828-313-2	10.99	17.95	23.99
Prague	1-85828-318-3	8.99	14.95	19.99
Provence & the Cote d'Azur	1-85828-127-X	9.99	16.95	22.99
The Pyrenees	1-85828-308-6	10.99	17.95	23.99
Rhodes & the Dodecanese	1-85828-120-2	8.99	14.95	19.99
Romania	1-85828-305-1	10.99	17.95	23.99
San Francisco	1-85828-299-3	8.99	14.95	19.99
Scandinavia	1-85828-236-5	12.99	20.95	27.99
Scotland	1-85828-302-7	9.99	16.95	22.99
Seattle Mini Guide	1-85828-324-8	5.99	9.95	12.99
Sicily	1-85828-178-4	9.99	16.95	22.99
Singapore	1-85828-237-3	8.99	14.95	19.99
South Africa	1-85828-238-1	12.99	19.95	25.99
Southwest USA	1-85828-239-X	10.99	16.95	22.99
Spain	1-85828-240-3	11.99	18.95	24.99
St Petersburg	1-85828-298-5	9.99	16.95	22.99
Sweden	1-85828-241-1	10.99	17.95	23.99
Syria	1-85828-331-0	11.99	18.95	24.99
Thailand	1-85828-140-7	10.99	17.95	24.99
Tunisia	1-85828-139-3	10.99	17.95	24.99
Turkey	1-85828-242-X	12.99	19.95	25.99
Tuscany & Umbria	1-85828-243-8	10.99	17.95	23.99
USA	1-85828-307-8	14.99	19.95	25.99
Venice	1-85828-170-9	8.99	14.95	19.99
Vienna	1-85828-244-6	8.99	14.95	19.99
Vietnam	1-85828-191-1	9.99	15.95	21.99
Wales	1-85828-245-4	10.99	17.95	23.99
Washington DC	1-85828-246-2	8.99	14.95	19.99
West Africa	1-85828-101-6	15.99	24.95	34.99
Zimbabwe & Botswana	1-85828-186-5	11.99	18.95	24.99

Phrasebooks

Czech	1-85828-148-2	3.50	5.00	7.00
Egyptian Arabic	1-85828-319-1	4.00	6.00	8.00
French	1-85828-144-X	3.50	5.00	7.00
German	1-85828-146-6	3.50	5.00	7.00
Greek	1-85828-145-8	3.50	5.00	7.00
Hindi & Urdu	1-85828-252-7	4.00	6.00	8.00
Hungarian	1-85828-304-3	4.00	6.00	8.00
Indonesian	1-85828-250-0	4.00	6.00	8.00
Italian	1-85828-143-1	3.50	5.00	7.00
Japanese	1-85828-303-5	4.00	6.00	8.00
Mandarin Chinese	1-85828-249-7	4.00	6.00	8.00
Mexican Spanish	1-85828-176-8	3.50	5.00	7.00
Portuguese	1-85828-175-X	3.50	5.00	7.00
Polish	1-85828-174-1	3.50	5.00	7.00
Russian	1-85828-251-9	4.00	6.00	8.00
Spanish	1-85828-147-4	3.50	5.00	7.00
Swahili	1-85828-320-5	4.00	6.00	8.00
Thai	1-85828-177-6	3.50	5.00	7.00
Turkish	1-85828-173-3	3.50	5.00	7.00
Vietnamese	1-85828-172-5	3.50	5.00	7.00

Reference

Classical Music	1-85828-113-X	12.99	19.95	25.99
European Football	1-85828-256-X	14.99	23.95	31.99
Internet	1-85828-288-8	5.00	8.00	10.00
Jazz	1-85828-137-7	16.99	24.95	34.99
Millennium	1-85828-314-0	5.00	8.95	11.99
More Women Travel	1-85828-098-2	10.99	16.95	22.99
Opera	1-85828-138-5	16.99	24.95	34.99
Reggae	1-85828-247-0	12.99	19.95	25.99
Rock	1-85828-201-2	17.99	26.95	35.00
World Music	1-85828-017-6	16.99	22.95	29.99

US/International orders: 1-800-253-6476

Tobago - Costara (West)
    Naturalist Beach Resort
    Blue Mango
    Sea Level Apartments

Green Mountain B & B Port of Spain (St. Ann's)
    Good trails & birding (809) 625-3773 $50/night

SHIANN'S - GOOD BREAKFAST (CHEAP

623-2500   Thur.- mon.   2pm - 11am   N5✔HØ   2 passengers
           Wed - Sun
           Fri - Tues   1HR

Food Maraval: Flags, China Palace ("Best" in Trini)
Gourmet Local food : La Fantasie in Normandie hotel

Pigeon Point - Tobago Beach

PAM = 473 443 6388
WORK = 473443 8182

• NOTES • St ANNES —
473440 2717
Carriacou — Grenade   Roydon's Guest House
M-F - 9 + 5³⁰   473 444 4416
   S = 9
   Sun = 8

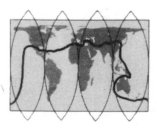

Our Holidays Their Homes

Exploring New Destinations?
Ever wondered what that means to the locals?
Ever seen things you're uncomfortable with?
Ever thought of joining Tourism Concern?

Tourism Concern is the only independent British organisation seeking ways to make tourism just, participatory and sustainable – world-wide.

For a membership fee of only £18 (£9 unwaged) UK, £25 overseas, you will support us in our work, receive our quarterly magazine, and learn about what is happening in tourism around the world.

We'll help find answers to the questions.

Tourism Concern, Stapleton House, 277-281 Holloway Road, London N7 8HN
Tel: 0171-753 3330 Fax: 0171-753 3331 e-mail: tourconcern@gn.apc.org